UNITED NATIONS CONFERENCE ON TRADE AND DEVELOPMENT
Geneva

# The least developed countries 1986 Report

*Prepared by the UNCTAD secretariat*

UNITED NATIONS
New York, 1987

## NOTE

Symbols of United Nations documents are composed of capital letters combined with figures. Mention of such a symbol indicates a reference to a United Nations document.

\*

\* \*

The designations employed and the presentation of the material in this publication do not imply the expression of any opinion whatsoever on the part of the Secretariat of the United Nations concerning the legal status of any country, territory, city or area, or of its authorities, or concerning the delimitation of its frontiers or boundaries.

\*

\* \*

Material in this publication may be freely quoted or reprinted, but acknowledgement is requested, together with a reference to the document number. A copy of the publication containing the quotation or reprint should be sent to the UNCTAD secretariat.

TD/B/1120

| UNITED NATIONS PUBLICATION |
| --- |
| *Sales No.* E.86.II.D.7 |
| ISBN 92-1-112225-2 ISSN 0257-7550 |

06000P

# Contents

|  | Paragraphs | Page |
|---|---|---|
| Abbreviations ............................................... |  | xii |
| Explanatory Notes ......................................... |  | xv |
| Foreword ................................................... | (i - iv) | xvi |
| Part One: REVIEW OF RECENT SOCIO-ECONOMIC DEVELOPMENTS IN THE LEAST DEVELOPED COUNTRIES ............. | 1 - 191 | 1 |

Chapter

| I. | Recent economic trends in the Least Developed Countries ........................... | 1 - 7 | 1 |
|---|---|---|---|
| II. | The savings-investment process in the Least Developed Countries ........................... | 8 - 26 | 6 |
|  | A. Investment ................................. | 8 - 9 | 6 |
|  | B. Mobilization of domestic savings ........ | 10 - 11 | 6 |
|  | C. Government budget ........................ | 12 | 9 |
|  | D. Taxes ...................................... | 13 - 15 | 9 |
|  | E. Non-tax revenues .......................... | 16 - 17 | 11 |
|  | F. Recurrent expenditures ................... | 18 | 11 |
|  | G. Institutions for mobilizing private savings ................................... | 19 - 25 | 11 |
|  | H. Conclusions ............................... | 26 | 13 |
| III. | Sectoral Developments ........................ | 27 - 143 | 15 |
|  | A. Food and agriculture .................... | 27 - 66 | 15 |
|  | 1. General trends .................... | 27 | 15 |
|  | 2. Agricultural production ........... | 28 - 42 | 15 |
|  | (a) Food production ............... | 28 - 32 | 15 |
|  | (b) Cash crops ................... | 33 - 36 | 18 |
|  | (c) Livestock ................... | 37 - 39 | 22 |
|  | (d) Fisheries ................... | 40 - 41 | 23 |
|  | (e) Forestry ................... | 42 | 23 |

GE.87-50019/6575E, 6579E, 6582E,
6584E, 6594E

|  |  | Paragraphs | Page |
|---|---|---|---|
| 3. | Elements inhibiting agricultural and food production in LDCs ............ | 43 - 47 | 23 |
| | (a) Exogenous factors ............ | 43 - 44 | 23 |
| | (b) Domestic policies ............ | 45 - 46 | 24 |
| | (c) Inadequate infrastructure ..... | 47 | 25 |
| 4. | Agricultural development policies .. | 48 - 60 | 25 |
| | (a) More effective use of market mechanism .................... | 50 - 51 | 26 |
| | (b) Mobilization of local population .................... | 52 | 26 |
| | (c) Diversification efforts ....... | 53 - 54 | 27 |
| | (d) Role of public sector ......... | 55 - 60 | 28 |
| 5. | International initiatives .......... | 61 - 66 | 29 |
| B. | Manufacturing .......................... | 67 - 99 | 30 |
| 1. | Industrial performance ............. | 67 - 68 | 30 |
| 2. | Industrial structure ............... | 69 | 32 |
| 3. | Factors influencing recent performance ........................ | 70 - 73 | 32 |
| 4. | Policy initiatives ................. | 74 - 98 | 33 |
| | (a) Divestment of public sector enterprises ................... | 75 - 85 | 33 |
| | (b) Improving the economic environment for private sector industrial activities .. | 86 - 91 | 36 |
| | (c) Policies in support of small-scale enterprises ............. | 92 - 96 | 37 |
| | (d) Programmes for African LDCs ... | 97 - 98 | 38 |
| 5. | Conclusions ........................ | 99 | 39 |
| C. | Energy ................................. | 100 - 110 | 39 |
| 1. | Current levels of energy consumption ........................ | 100 | 39 |
| 2. | Traditional sources of energy ...... | 101 - 102 | 39 |

|  |  | Paragraphs | Page |
|---|---|---|---|
| 3. | Oil production and exploration ..... | 103 | 41 |
| 4. | Alternative sources of energy ...... | 104 - 105 | 41 |
| 5. | Hydroelectric power ............... | 106 - 108 | 42 |
| 6. | Other electricity ................. | 109 | 44 |
| 7. | Implications of the fall in international oil prices .......... | 110 | 44 |
| D. | Transport and communication ............. | 111 - 124 | 44 |
| 1. | Transport .......................... | 114 | 45 |
| 2. | Roads ............................. | 115 - 116 | 45 |
| 3. | Railways .......................... | 117 - 118 | 47 |
| 4. | Air services ...................... | 119 | 47 |
| 5. | Communications .................... | 120 - 121 | 48 |
| 6. | Special problems of Land-Locked Least Developed Countries ......... | 122 - 123 | 50 |
| 7. | Special problems of Island Least Developed Countries ............... | 124 | 50 |
| E. | Environment and disaster ............... | 125 - 143 | 52 |
| 1. | Environmental problems and disasters affecting the Least Developed Countries ............... | 125 - 138 | 52 |
| | (a) Chronic environmental difficulties ................. | 125 | 52 |
| | (b) Desertification, deforestation and soil erosion ............. | 126 - 128 | 52 |
| | (c) Disasters ..................... | 129 | 54 |
| | (i) Drought ............... | 130 - 135 | 55 |
| | (ii) Grasshopper and locust infestations .... | 136 | 56 |
| | (iii) Other disasters ........ | 137 | 56 |
| | (d) Pollution .................... | 138 | 56 |

|  |  | Paragraphs | Page |
|---|---|---|---|
| 2. | Action taken in regard to environment and disasters .......... | 139 - 143 | 57 |
|  | (a) National policies ............. | 139 - 142 | 57 |
|  | (b) Recent institutional initiatives .................. | 143 | 59 |
| IV. | The external sector ......................... | 144 - 170 | 61 |
| A. | Recent trends in LDCs' trade ............. | 144 - 165 | 61 |
| 1. | General trends .................... | 144 | 61 |
| 2. | Overall exports .................... | 145 - 148 | 61 |
| 3. | Structure of LDCs' exports ......... | 149 - 152 | 63 |
| 4. | Commodity prices and export earnings .......................... | 153 - 156 | 67 |
| 5. | Imports ........................... | 157 - 159 | 68 |
| 6. | Direction of trade ................ | 160 - 163 | 71 |
| 7. | Conclusions ....................... | 164 - 165 | 72 |
| B. | Balance of payments .................... | 166 - 170 | 73 |
| V. | Women in the least developed countries ....... | 171 - 192 | 77 |
| A. | Demographic dimensions and social situation ................................ | 171 | 77 |
| B. | Economic participation .................. | 172 - 176 | 77 |
| 1. | Subsistence and domestic production ........................ | 173 - 174 | 77 |
| 2. | Self-employment .................... | 175 | 78 |
| 3. | Participation in the modern sector . | 176 | 78 |
| C. | Education ............................... | 177 - 178 | 78 |
| D. | Access and control over productive resources ............................... | 179 | 78 |

|  |  | Paragraphs | Page |
|---|---|---|---|
| E. | Projects for women, national measures and international support ............... | 180 - 189 | 79 |
| | 1. Projects for women in LDCs ......... | 180 - 183 | 79 |
| | 2. National measures ................... | 184 - 185 | 80 |
| | 3. Global strategies and international support .......................... | 186 - 189 | 80 |
| F. | Prospects ............................. | 190 - 192 | 81 |

|  |  | Paragraphs | Page |
|---|---|---|---|
| **Part Two:** | REVIEW OF INTERNATIONAL SUPPORT MEASURES IN FAVOUR OF THE LDCs .......... | 193 – 385 | 83 |
| **Chapter** |  |  |  |
| I. | Transfer of Financial Resources .............. | 193 – 227 | 83 |
|  | A. Recent Trends ........................... | 193 – 198 | 83 |
|  | B. Developments in individual countries .... | 199 – 201 | 85 |
|  | C. Donor's performance .................... | 202 – 212 | 85 |
|  | D. Aid targets and LDCs' capital requirements ........................... | 213 – 216 | 90 |
|  | E. New approaches, prospects and conclusions ........................... | 217 – 227 | 92 |
| II. | Aid modalities .............................. | 228 – 279 | 94 |
|  | A. Terms and conditions of aid ............ | 230 – 243 | 94 |
|  |    1. Grant element of concessional assistance ........................ | 230 – 236 | 94 |
|  |    2. Tying .............................. | 237 – 243 | 97 |
|  | B. Forms of aid ......................... | 244 | 98 |
|  |    1. Programme aid ..................... | 246 – 250 | 99 |
|  |    2. Food aid .......................... | 251 – 253 | 101 |
|  |    3. Local and recurrent cost financing . | 254 – 259 | 102 |
|  | C. Sector allocation ..................... | 260 – 279 | 103 |
|  |    1. Food and agriculture .............. | 261 – 264 | 103 |
|  |    2. Education and health .............. | 265 – 267 | 104 |
|  |    3. Other sectors .................... | 268 – 273 | 106 |
|  | D. Summary conclusions ................... | 274 – 279 | 107 |

|  |  |  | Paragraphs | Page |
|---|---|---|---|---|
| III. | Aid co-ordination and role of round tables and consultative groups ..................... | | 280 - 304 | 109 |
| | A. | The expansion since 1981 .............. | 280 - 282 | 109 |
| | B. | The role of country review meetings ..... | 283 - 289 | 118 |
| | C. | The evolution of country review meetings ................................ | 290 - 298 | 120 |
| | D. | Conclusions ........................... | 299 - 304 | 122 |
| IV. | The debt situation of least developed countries ................................. | | 305 - 350 | 124 |
| | A. | The evolution of LDCs debt problems ..... | 305 - 307 | 124 |
| | B. | Structure and recent trends in LDCs disbursed debt and debt service ........ | 308 - 319 | 124 |
| | | 1. Structure ......................... | 308 - 309 | 124 |
| | | 2. Recent trends ..................... | 310 - 312 | 125 |
| | | 3. Debt service ..................... | 313 - 319 | 125 |
| | C. | Debt relief increases and mechanisms .... | 320 - 341 | 128 |
| | | 1. Retroactive terms adjustment measures .......................... | 320 - 325 | 128 |
| | | 2. Coping with multilateral debt ...... | 326 - 331 | 134 |
| | | 3. Multilateral rescheduling .......... | 332 - 335 | 135 |
| | | 4. Debt management ................... | 336 - 337 | 137 |
| | | 5. Other measures .................... | 338 - 341 | 138 |
| | D. | New approaches to the debt crisis ....... | 342 - 344 | 138 |
| | E. | Conclusions ........................... | 345 - 350 | 139 |

|  |  |  | Paragraphs | Page |
|---|---|---|---|---|

V. Commercial policy measures .................... 351 - 368      141

   A.   Overall development .................... 351      141

   B.   Improved access to markets .............. 352 - 368      141

       1.   Recommendations in favour of LDCs .. 352      141

       2.   Tariff measures .................... 353 - 363      141

          (a)   Recent initiatives ............ 358 - 361      142

          (b)   Current situation of some LDCs ..................... 362 - 363      142

       3.   Non-tariff measures ................ 364 - 366      143

       4.   Restrictive business practices ..... 367      143

       5.   New round of multilateral trade negotiations ....................... 368      145

   C.   International co-operation in the field of commodities in favour of the LDCs ............................. 369      145

       1.   The Common Fund for Commodities .... 369      145

       2.   Programmes dealing with the compensation of export earnings shortfalls ......................... 370      145

          (a)   International Monetary Fund ... 371 - 372      146

          (b)   STABEX ........................ 373 - 378      146

          (c)   SYSMIN ........................ 379 - 382      149

   D.   Conclusions ............................. 383 - 385      152

|  |  | Paragraphs | Page |
|---|---|---|---|

Part Three: RECENT DEVELOPMENTS IN THE ECONOMIES
OF INDIVIDUAL LEAST DEVELOPED COUNTRIES   386 - 1013    153

| | | Paragraphs | Page |
|---|---|---|---|
| 1. | Afghanistan | 386 - 406 | 153 |
| 2. | Bangladesh | 407 - 423 | 156 |
| 3. | Benin | 424 - 442 | 160 |
| 4. | Bhutan | 443 - 464 | 163 |
| 5. | Botswana | 465 - 480 | 167 |
| 6. | Burkina Faso | 481 - 501 | 171 |
| 7. | Burundi | 502 - 514 | 175 |
| 8. | Cape Verde | 515 - 529 | 177 |
| 9. | Central African Republic | 530 - 546 | 181 |
| 10. | Chad | 547 - 562 | 185 |
| 11. | Comoros | 563 - 577 | 188 |
| 12. | Democratic Yemen | 578 - 589 | 192 |
| 13. | Djibouti | 590 - 601 | 195 |
| 14. | Equatorial Guinea | 602 - 627 | 198 |
| 15. | Ethiopia | 628 - 640 | 202 |
| 16. | Gambia | 641 - 657 | 206 |
| 17. | Guinea | 658 - 677 | 210 |
| 18. | Guinea-Bissau | 678 - 695 | 215 |
| 19. | Haiti | 696 - 708 | 218 |
| 20. | Lao P.D.R. | 709 - 730 | 221 |
| 21. | Lesotho | 731 - 748 | 225 |
| 22. | Malawi | 749 - 764 | 229 |
| 23. | Maldives | 765 - 780 | 232 |
| 24. | Mali | 781 - 798 | 237 |
| 25. | Nepal | 799 - 815 | 240 |
| 26. | Niger | 816 - 839 | 244 |
| 27. | Rwanda | 840 - 853 | 249 |
| 28. | Samoa | 854 - 875 | 252 |
| 29. | Sao Tome and Principe | 876 - 884 | 257 |
| 30. | Sierra Leone | 885 - 897 | 259 |
| 31. | Somalia | 898 - 911 | 263 |
| 32. | Sudan | 912 - 924 | 267 |
| 33. | Togo | 925 - 943 | 271 |
| 34. | Uganda | 944 - 963 | 275 |
| 35. | United Republic of Tanzania | 964 - 983 | 279 |
| 36. | Vanuatu | 984 - 1002 | 284 |
| 37. | Yemen | 1003 - 1013 | 288 |

Annex:   BASIC DATA ON THE LEAST DEVELOPED COUNTRIES

## Abbreviations*/

| | |
|---|---|
| AAAID | Arab Authority for Agricultural Investment and Development |
| ACP | African, Caribbean and Pacific |
| AfDB | African Development Bank |
| AfDF | African Development Fund |
| AFESD | Arab Fund for Economic and Social Development |
| AFTAAC | Arab Fund for Technical Assistance to African and Arab Countries |
| APEC | Action Programme for Economic Co-operation among Non-Aligned and other Developing Countries |
| BADEA | Arab Bank for Economic Development in Africa |
| CAEU | Council for Arab Economic Unity |
| CDCC | Caribbean Development and Co-operation Committee |
| CEAO | West African Economic Community |
| CEEAC | Communauté économique des Etats de l'Afrique centrale |
| CEPGL | Economic Community of the Great Lakes Countries |
| CFF | Compensatory financing facility |
| c.i.f. | Cost, insurance, freight |
| CILSS | Permanent Inter-State Committee on Drought Control in the Sahel |
| CMEA | Council for Mutual Economic Assistance |
| CRS | Creditor Reporting System (OECD) |
| D | Dalasis |
| DAC | Development Assistance Committee (of OECD) |
| DRS | Debtor Reporting System (World Bank) |
| ECOWAS | Economic Community of West African States |
| EDF | European Development Fund |
| EEC | European Economic Community |
| EIB | European Investment Bank |
| FAO | Food and Agriculture Organization of the United Nations |
| FBu | Burundi franc |
| f.o.b. | Free on board |
| FY | Financial year |

---

*/    Other than those explained in the text.

| | |
|---|---|
| GATT | General Agreement on Tariffs and Trade |
| GDP | Gross domestic product |
| GNP | Gross national product |
| GSP | Generalized system of preferences |
| IBRD | International Bank for Reconstruction and Development (World Bank) |
| ICA | International Commodity Agreement |
| ICARA | International Conference on Assistance to Refugees in Africa |
| IDA | International Development Association |
| IDB | Inter-American Development Bank |
| IFAD | International Fund for Agricultural Development |
| IFC | International Finance Corporation |
| IMF | International Monetary Fund |
| IPC | Integrated Programme for Commodities |
| kg | Kilograms |
| km | Kilometres |
| $km^2$ | Square kilometres |
| Kwh | Kilowatt/hours |
| LCBC | Lake Chad Basin Commission |
| LDCs | Least developed countries |
| M | Maloti |
| $m^3$ | Cubic metres |
| MFN | Most favoured nation |
| MRU | Mano River Union |
| mt | Metric tons |
| OAPEC | Organization of Arab Petroleum Exporting Countries |
| OAU | Organization of African Unity |
| OCAM | African and Mauritian Common Organization |
| ODA | Official development assistance |
| OECD | Organisation for Economic Co-operation and Development |
| OKB | Organization for the Planning and Development of the Kagera River Basin |
| OLADE | Latin American Energy Organization |
| OMVG | Gambia River Development Organization |

| | |
|---|---|
| OMVS | Organization for the Development of the Senegal River |
| OPEC | Organization of the Petroleum Exporting Countries |
| pop. | Population |
| PTA | Preferential Trade Area for Eastern and Southern African States |
| RF | Rwanda franc |
| SAAFA | Special Arab Aid Fund for Africa |
| SADCC | Southern African Development Co-ordination Conference |
| SDR | Special drawing right |
| SELA | Latin American Economic System |
| SITC | Standard International Trade Classification, Revision 1 |
| SNPA | Substantial New Programme of Action for the 1980s for the Least Developed Countries |
| UDEAC | Central African Customs and Economic Union |
| UN | United Nations |
| UNCTAD | United Nations Conference on Trade and Development |
| UNDP | United Nations Development Programme |
| UNDRO | Office of the United Nations Disaster Relief Co-ordinator |
| UNHCR | Office of the United Nations High Commissioner for Refugees |
| UNICEF | United Nations Children's Fund |
| UNIDO | United Nations Industrial Development Organization |
| UNTA | United Nations technical assistance |
| WFP | World Food Programme |
| WSTEC | Western Samoa Trust Estates Corporation |

## EXPLANATORY NOTES

The term "dollars" ($) refers to United States dollars unless otherwise stated. The term "billion" signifies 1,000 million.

Annual rates of growth and change refer to compound rates. Exports are valued f.o.b. and imports c.i.f. unless otherwise specified.

Use of a hyphen (-) between dates representing years, e.g., 1970-1979, signifies the full period involved, including the initial and final years.

An oblique stroke (/) between two years, e.g., 1980/81, signifies a fiscal or crop year.

The abbreviation LDC (or LDCs) refers, throughout this report, to a country (or countries) included in the United Nations list of least developed countries.

National currencies have been converted into United States dollars at the rates published by the IMF in International Financial Statistics. For flow figures (e.g. foreign trade, budgetary receipts and expenditures, debt service and aid statistics) the average exchange rates for the corresponding period was chosen. For stock figures (e.g. outstanding debt and exchange reserves) the exchange rate for the corresponding date was chosen.

In the tables:

Two dots (..) indicate that the data are not available, or are not separately reported.

A dash (-) indicates that the amount is nil or negligible.

A plus (+) before a figure indicates an increase; a minus sign (-) before a figure indicates a decrease. Details and percentages do not necessarily add up to totals, because of rounding.

## FOREWORD

(i)   The adoption of the Substantial New Programme of Action (SNPA) for the Least Developed Countries for the 1980s in 1981 by the United Nations Conference on the Least Developed Countries constituted a milestone in the efforts of the international community on behalf of the least developed countries.  The SNPA, whose objective is to provide at least an internationally accepted minimum standard of living, calls for substantially more international support to development plans and programmes of the least developed countries.  Although it is seen as crucial, increased external support is recognized as a complement to, not as a substitute for, domestic efforts by the least developed countries themselves.  The SNPA also contains provisions for specific follow-up action at the country, regional and global levels.

(ii)  UNCTAD continues to give a high priority to the work related to the least developed countries.  Its Intergovernmental Group on the Least Developed Countries met at a high level in 1985 to carry out the Mid-term Global Review of the SNPA and agreed on a set of conclusions and recommendations to speed up the implementation of the SNPA.  The problems of the least developed countries constitute one of the items on the agenda for the seventh session of the United Nations Conference on Trade and Development, which is scheduled for July 1987.  The session will provide a further opportunity for the international community to agree on concrete measures aimed at supporting the development efforts of the least developed countries.  A global review of the implementation of the SNPA will take place in 1990.

(iii) The SNPA entrusts UNCTAD with the focal role of monitoring its implementation at the global level.  As a contribution to the global monitoring exercise, the UNCTAD secretariat prepares annual reports on the least developed countries.  The present report, which is the third in the series, contains a review of recent socio-economic developments in the least developed countries and progress in the implementation of the support measures.  It also incorporates the Basic Data on the Least Developed Countries which the UNCTAD secretariat has prepared periodically for several years.

(iv)  The UNCTAD secretariat would like to take this opportunity to express its appreciation to the Governments members of UNCTAD and to international organizations which, by replying to its questionnaire on the implementation of the SNPA, provided useful inputs to this report.  It would also like to thank the organizations of the United Nations system for their co-operation, which has greatly facilitated the preparation of this volume.

PART ONE:   REVIEW OF RECENT SOCIO-ECONOMIC DEVELOPMENTS IN
THE LEAST DEVELOPED COUNTRIES

Chapter I

RECENT ECONOMIC TRENDS IN THE LEAST DEVELOPED COUNTRIES

1.    The economic situation of the LDCs 1/ deteriorated considerably since
1980.  In the 1970s, the average annual rate of GDP growth of about 4 per cent
had permitted a slight improvement in per capita GDP and living standards.
This rate, however, fell by one half between 1980 and 1984, leading to an
actual decline in the already low per capita output levels of LDCs to about
$206 (table 1). This level of per capita output is equivalent to one fourth of
the corresponding figure for the developing countries as a whole, a mere
4 per cent of that in the socialist countries of Eastern Europe, and as little
as 2 per cent of the average level registered in the developed market
economies.  However, according to preliminary estimates, economic performance
in 1985 improved, with a GDP growth rate of 2.6 per cent, mainly on account of
an improved agricultural performance in several African LDCs.  Yet, this rate
of growth merely matches the estimated population growth rate.  Therefore, the
relatively improved 1985 performance does no more than arrest the dangerous
slide of per capita incomes in LDCs at the depressed level reached in 1984.

2.    The poor recent performance of the LDCs as a group should not overshadow
the remarkable results achieved by a few individual LDCs.  Three among them –
Botswana, Cape Verde and Maldives – realized average annual growth rates
between 1980 and 1984 well in excess of the rate of 7.2 per cent established
by the SNPA, which is the rate required to double output in a decade 2/
(table 2).  Four others (Bhutan, Guinea-Bissau, Uganda and Yemen) were only
slightly below the target.  In some of these countries, however, high growth
rates merely reflect recoveries to former GDP levels following severe
setbacks.  Looking at the record in terms of per capita growth, 22 LDCs
registered absolute declines during the first four years of the 1980s.
Because of high population growth rates,  only a minimum annual growth of
3 per cent for the LDCs as a group could ensure a restoration of the 1981 GDP
level in these countries by the end of the decade.

3.    The record in the field of agriculture was a major factor determining
overall growth in the LDCs, as this sector still accounted for 42 per cent of
the GDP in 1983 for all LDCs combined and affected output indirectly through
downstream agro-industries.  Thus, five of the ten countries with improved
overall per capita growth performances also registered higher rates of
per capita agricultural production during the period 1980-1985, while only in
three countries did the two rates move in opposite directions:  in Djibouti
and Cape Verde, where the share of agricultural production in GDP is
relatively small (6 and 21 per cent respectively in 1983), and Somalia.
However, it should be noted that there were as many as 10 LDCs with improved
per capita agricultural performances whose overall economies did not achieve
higher per capita GDP growth rates between the two periods.

4.    The average share of manufacturing in LDCs' GDP is modest (7 per cent in
1983) as compared to agriculture.  Nevertheless, the number of countries in
which growth in that sector moved pari passu with the overall growth rate was

similar to that in agriculture. Thus, of the 10 countries that registered improved growth rates in their total output, 6 also recorded higher rates of growth of their manufacturing sectors, in three the directions were opposite and in one the growth rate of the manufacturing sector was unavailable.

5.    If overall per capita growth between the periods 1970–1980 and 1980–1984 is compared with the growth of export purchasing power 3/, it transpires that eight of the ten countries which registered improved overall growth also had improved the purchasing power of their exports. In six of these the export purchasing power experienced major turnarounds from negative annual rates ranging between −0.7 per cent to −16 per cent during the 1970s to positive rates ranging between 8.3 per cent to 13.3 per cent during the first half of the 1980s. Some LDCs, such as Botswana and Maldives, maintained their historically high performance levels thanks to the expansion of exports of diamonds in the former and increased earnings from tourism in the latter. From the viewpoint of their export concentration, it is apparent that the large number of LDCs with an agricultural export base (about one half) did less well during the 1980s than those with other export structures. Thus, the median GDP growth rate between 1980 and 1984 of the services-exporting LDCs (3 per cent) was twice as high as that of the agricultural-exporting LDCs, while the minerals and manufactures-exporting LDCs occupied an intermediate position.

6.    Of the 10 countries which have registered an improved per capita GDP performance between the periods 1970–1980 and 1980–1984, at least six showed declining or stable population growth rates between the two periods. Conversely, of the 21 LDCs which registered increased population growth rates between the two periods, only five were able to improve their overall growth rates.

7.    The high growth rates achieved by a few countries provide evidence that the target of the SNPA was attainable, given an appropriate domestic and external environment. The majority of LDCs have adopted austere fiscal policies during the 1980s, often coupled with currency devaluations. There is little evidence, however, that international support to these countries is adequate to enable them to recover their 1980 per capita output levels by the end of this decade, not to mention the achievement of the SNPA growth objective.

Table 1

Population, per capita GDP and growth of real product
in the least developed countries, 1970-1984

| | Population | | Per capita GDP ($) | Annual average growth rate of total real product (%) | | | | | | Annual average growth rate of per capita real product (%) | | | | | |
|---|---|---|---|---|---|---|---|---|---|---|---|---|---|---|---|
| | (millions) 1984 | annual average growth (%) 1970-1984 a/ | 1984 | 1970-1980a/ | 1980-1984 | 1980-1981 | 1981-1982 | 1982-1983 | 1983-1984 | 1970-1980a/ | 1980-1984 | 1980-1981 | 1981-1982 | 1982-1983 | 1983-1984 |
| Afghanistan b/ | 17.67 | 2.5 | 210 h/ | 3.7 | 2.7 | 1.8 | 2.0 | 4.8 | 2.1 | 1.2 | 0.1 | -0.8 | -0.5 | 2.1 | -0.5 |
| Bangladesh c/ | 96.73 | 2.5 | 145 | 3.7 | 3.8 | 6.8 | 0.8 | 3.6 | 4.2 | 1.0 | 1.6 | 4.7 | -1.5 | 1.4 | 2.0 |
| Benin | 3.92 | 2.8 | 241 | 3.4 | 3.6 | 10.9 | 4.0 | -1.9 | 1.6 | 0.7 | 0.4 | 7.5 | 0.9 | -4.9 | -1.5 |
| Bhutan d/ | 1.39 | 2.0 | 122 | .. | 7.0 | 9.0 | 10.8 | 6.1 | 2.6 | .. | 4.9 | 6.7 | 8.6 | 4.0 | 0.5 |
| Botswana c/ | 1.07 | 3.9 | 1041 | 9.0 | 11.8 | 8.6 | -2.5 | 23.6 | 19.4 | 4.9 | 7.5 | 4.3 | -6.4 | 19.0 | 15.0 |
| Burkina Faso | 6.78 | 2.1 | 133 | 4.0 | -1.4 | 3.5 | 0.0 | -4.8 | -3.9 | 2.0 | -3.7 | 0.9 | -2.4 | -7.0 | -6.1 |
| Burundi | 4.60 | 2.0 | 209 | 3.1 | 0.6 | 10.5 | -3.2 | -1.1 | -5.2 | 1.4 | -2.2 | 7.3 | -6.0 | -1.7 | -7.7 |
| Cape Verde | 0.32 | 1.1 | 296 | 0.3 | 7.6 | 7.3 | 4.8 | 0.7 | 18.4 | -0.6 | 5.5 | 5.1 | 2.7 | -1.2 | 16.2 |
| Cent.African Rep. | 2.52 | 2.1 | 236 | 2.2 | -0.2 | -2.3 | 0.4 | -2.3 | 3.6 | 0.0 | -2.4 | -4.6 | -1.9 | -4.5 | 1.3 |
| Chad | 4.91 | 2.1 | 118 | 1.8 | -7.0 | -9.0 | -7.3 | -7.0 | -4.6 | -0.2 | -9.1 | -11.1 | -9.4 | -9.1 | -6.7 |
| Comoros | 0.43 | 3.4 | 208 | -0.9 | 4.3 | 3.6 | 5.9 | 3.7 | 3.9 | -4.2 | 0.9 | 0.2 | 2.7 | 0.5 | 1.0 |
| Democratic Yemen | 2.08 | 2.4 | 449 | 2.6 | 1.9 | 6.6 | -4.6 | 4.0 | 2.0 | 0.3 | -0.9 | 3.5 | -7.3 | 1.2 | -0.7 |
| Djibouti | 0.35 | 6.3 | 574 i/ | 3.0 | 1.5 | -8.0 | 13.6 | 0.9 | 0.5 | -3.8 | -1.8 | -11.9 | 9.9 | -2.0 | -2.0 |
| Equatorial Guinea | 0.38 | 2.0 | 213 | .. | 1.3 | 2.3 | 3.8 | -3.0 | 2.3 | .. | -0.9 | 0.1 | 1.6 | -5.1 | 0.2 |
| Ethiopia e/ | 42.02 | 2.7 | 116 j/ | 2.6 | 1.5 | 2.5 | 1.4 | 4.7 | -2.4 | -0.1 | -1.2 | -0.3 | -1.3 | 1.9 | -5.0 |
| Gambia c/ | 0.71 | 3.4 | 288 | 4.1 | 1.6 | -8.2 | 9.5 | 14.7 | -7.5 | 0.6 | -0.6 | -10.3 | 7.1 | 12.2 | -9.5 |
| Guinea | 5.94 | 2.2 | 357 | 4.3 | 1.3 | 0.6 | 1.8 | 1.3 | 1.6 | 2.2 | -1.0 | -1.9 | -0.6 | -1.0 | -0.7 |
| Guinea-Bissau | 0.87 | 4.0 | 176 | 2.5 | 6.1 | 18.2 | 6.0 | -8.1 | 10.2 | -1.8 | 4.1 | 15.9 | 4.0 | -9.8 | 8.2 |
| Haiti f/ | 5.20 | 1.4 | 350 | 3.8 | -0.9 | -2.7 | -3.9 | 0.3 | 2.7 | 2.3 | -2.3 | -4.1 | -5.3 | -5.4 | 1.8 |
| Lao People's D.R. | 3.74 | 2.0 | 203 | -0.1 | 3.2 | 6.6 | 1.9 | -3.3 | 8.1 | -1.9 | 1.0 | 4.3 | -0.3 | -5.4 | 5.4 |
| Lesotho d/ | 1.48 | 2.4 | 195 | 9.6 | -0.5 | -0.4 | -3.6 | -1.4 | 3.7 | 7.1 | -3.0 | -3.0 | -6.1 | -3.8 | 1.2 |
| Malawi | 6.74 | 2.9 | 178 | 6.0 | -2.3 | -5.1 | 2.5 | 4.4 | 7.7 | 3.1 | -0.9 | -8.2 | -0.7 | 1.2 | 4.5 |
| Maldives | 0.18 | 3.1 | 432 | 13.6m/ | 9.0 | 7.9 | 9.6 | 5.9 | 12.9 | 10.2m/ | 5.8m/ | 4.7 | 6.4 | 2.8 | 9.5 |
| Mali | 7.87 | 2.3 | 137 | 3.8 | -0.1 | -1.8 | 5.9 | -4.1 | -0.1 | 1.6 | -2.9 | -4.6 | 2.9 | -6.8 | -2.8 |
| Nepal g/ | 16.12 | 2.4 | 155 | 2.7 | 4.5 | 8.3 | 3.8 | -1.4 | 7.4 | 0.2 | 2.0 | 5.7 | 1.4 | -3.6 | 5.0 |
| Niger | 5.95 | 2.6 | 279 | 5.0 | -2.0 | -5.3 | -2.7 | 7.2 | -6.7 | 2.4 | -4.8 | -8.0 | -5.5 | 4.2 | -9.2 |
| Rwanda | 5.86 | 3.3 | 282 | 8.0 | 2.3 | 8.1 | 1.1 | 3.0 | -2.8 | 4.5 | -1.0 | 4.7 | -2.2 | -0.3 | -6.0 |
| Samoa | 0.16 | 0.6 | 619 | .. | -1.9 | -9.0 | -1.0 | 0.4 | 2.1 | -0.3 | -2.5 | -9.6 | -1.6 | -0.2 | 1.5 |
| Sao tome & Princ. | 0.09 | 1.6 | 388 | 1.1 | -6.9 | -13.8 | 3.3 | -11.9 | -4.3 | -0.3 | -9.2 | -15.8 | 1.0 | -14.7 | -6.4 |
| Sierra Leone c/ | 3.54 | 1.6 | 283 | 1.8 | 0.3 | 1.3 | -0.2 | -0.3 | 0.5 | -0.3 | -1.5 | -0.5 | -2.0 | -2.1 | -1.3 |
| Somalia | 5.23 | 2.9 | 261 | 2.7 | 4.2 | 6.7 | 5.6 | 1.4 | 3.1 | -0.3 | 1.3 | 3.7 | 2.7 | -1.4 | 0.2 |
| Sudan c/ | 20.98 | 3.0 | 366 | 6.7 | 1.4 | 3.2 | -7.4 | -3.0 | -1.7 | 3.6 | -1.5 | 0.1 | 4.3 | -5.7 | -4.4 |
| Togo | 2.88 | 2.5 | 232 | 2.3 | -3.3 | -3.5 | -3.7 | -5.4 | -0.7 | 0.0 | -6.2 | -6.5 | -6.6 | -8.1 | -3.5 |
| Uganda | 14.96 | 3.1 | 220 k/ | -2.4 | 7.1 | 5.7 | 9.1 | 8.8 | 4.7 | -5.2 | 3.6 | 2.3 | 5.5 | 5.3 | 1.6 |
| U.Rep.of Tanzania | 21.49 | 3.4 | 250 | 4.5 | 1.4 | 2.1 | 1.3 | -0.4 | 2.5 | 1.1 | -2.0 | -1.3 | -2.1 | -3.7 | -0.9 |
| Vanuatu c/ | 0.13 | 2.9 | 683 l/ | .. | 3.0 | 2.0 | 2.0 | 3.0 | 5.0 | .. | 0.2 | -0.8 | -0.8 | 0.2 | 2.1 |
| Yemen c/ | 7.79 | 2.9 | 480 | 9.9 | 6.3 | 9.6 | 10.0 | 3.5 | 2.4 | 6.7 | 3.6 | 6.8 | 7.2 | 0.9 | -0.2 |
| All LDCS | 323.10 | 2.6 | 206 | 3.9 | 2.4 | 3.5 | 2.5 | 1.8 | 1.7 | 1.2 | -0.2 | 0.9 | -0.2 | -0.8 | -0.8 |
| All developing countries | 2471.7 | 2.4 | 870 j/ | 5.8 | 1.0 | 1.3 | 0.9 | -0.5 | 2.5 | 3.3 | -1.3 | -1.2 | -1.5 | -2.8 | 0.2 |

**Table 1** (continued)

Source: UNCTAD secretariat calculations based on data from the United Nations Statistical Office, the Economic Commission for Africa, the World Bank, and other international and national sources.

a/ Exponential trend function.
b/ Years beginning 21 March.
c/ Years ending 30 June.
d/ Years beginning 1 April.
e/ Years ending 7 July.
f/ Years ending 30 September.
g/ Years ending 15 July.
h/ 1981.
i/ Adjusted data, (i.e. excluding income accruing to non-national residents).
j/ 1983.
k/ GNP.
l/ 1982.
m/ 1974-1980.

## Table 2

### LDCs: frequency distribution of total and per capita GDP growth, 1970-1984

| (per cent per annum) | 1970-1980 | 1980-1984 | 1981 | 1982 | 1983 | 1984 |
|---|---|---|---|---|---|---|
| **A - Total GDP** | | | | | | |
| 7.2 or more | 5 | 3 | 10 | 7 | 4 | 7 |
| 5.0 to 7.1 | 3 | 4 | 5 | 4 | 2 | 1 |
| 3.0 to 4.9 | 11 | 7 | 3 | 5 | 9 | 6 |
| 1.0 to 2.9 | 10 | 11 | 6 | 8 | 3 | 10 |
| 0.0 to 0.9 | 1 | 2 | 1 | 3 | 4 | 2 |
| Sub-total | 30 | 27 | 25 | 27 | 22 | 26 |
| -0.9 to -0.1 | 2 | 4 | 1 | 1 | 2 | 2 |
| -2.9 to -1.0 | 1 | 3 | 3 | 3 | 4 | 3 |
| -4.9 to -3.0 | - | 1 | 1 | 5 | 5 | 3 |
| -5.0 or less | - | 2 | 7 | 1 | 4 | 3 |
| Sub-total | 3 | 10 | 12 | 10 | 15 | 11 |
| Total | 33 | 37 | 37 | 37 | 37 | 37 |
| **B - Per capita GDP** | | | | | | |
| 7.0 or more | 2 | 1 | 3 | 4 | 2 | 4 |
| 5.0 to 6.9 | 1 | 2 | 4 | 2 | 1 | 2 |
| 3.0 to 4.9 | 4 | 4 | 7 | 2 | 2 | 1 |
| 1.0 to 2.9 | 9 | 5 | 1 | 7 | 6 | 8 |
| 0.0 to 0.9 | 7 | 3 | 4 | 1 | 3 | 3 |
| Sub-total | 23 | 15 | 19 | 16 | 14 | 18 |
| -0.9 to -0.1 | 5 | 4 | 4 | 5 | 2 | 5 |
| -2.9 to -1.0 | 2 | 12 | 2 | 8 | 7 | 4 |
| -4.9 to -3.0 | 2 | 3 | 4 | - | 5 | 2 |
| -5.0 to -6.9 | 1 | 1 | 1 | 6 | 4 | 5 |
| -7.0 or less | - | 2 | 7 | 2 | 5 | 3 |
| Sub-total | 10 | 22 | 18 | 21 | 23 | 19 |
| Total | 33 | 37 | 37 | 37 | 37 | 37 |

Source: See table 1.

## Chapter II

### THE SAVINGS-INVESTMENT PROCESS IN THE LEAST DEVELOPED COUNTRIES

A.  <u>Investment</u>

8.  The statistical information on investment in the LDCs is, in general, scarce and of relatively poor quality.  For the year 1984 information is still very incomplete, while for 1985 virtually no data exist yet.  The available national accounts statistics indicate that there was a decline in the volume of investment over the period 1980-1984 of almost 10 per cent.  Given the modest growth in GDP, this would imply that investment as a share in GDP for the LDCs as a whole declined from 17.5 per cent in 1980 to 15.2 per cent in 1984.  For only eight out of the 21 LDCs for which this information is available, was an increase recorded in this share.  (see table 3)

9.  Data on exports of capital goods from developed market economies to LDCs are complete and updated until 1985.  Although these data represent only a part of total investments in LDCs, the decline over the period 1980-1984 indicates to what extent the decreasing availabilities of foreign exchange in the LDCs obliged them to cut back on their investment effort, thereby worsening their development prospects in the future.  (see table 4).  It should be considered that part of this decline in dollar terms is due to the revaluation of the dollar in this period.  In 1985 a recuperation of this kind of exports was recorded.

B.  <u>Mobilization of domestic savings</u>

10.  The major share of the investment finance is provided by external savings.  It is estimated that in the 1980s only about one sixth of investment was financed by gross domestic savings.  Owing to considerable savings from LDCs' nationals working abroad, who remitted these savings to their home countries, national savings represent about double this share.

11.  Economic growth of the least developed countries has been seriously constrained by the low rate of domestic savings, for it must be noted that not all investments can easily be financed with foreign savings and that the latter have not been forthcoming in the volume required to implement national development plans.  During the period 1980-1984 domestic savings were negative in almost one-third of the LDCs and exceeded 10 per cent of GDP only in five. (table 5).  The principal factors responsible for the very low and even negative savings rates are: (a) very low per capita income, which has been exacerbated by drought in most African LDCs, (b) the fact that savings rates are based on monetized savings and therefore leave out of account <u>ipso facto</u> savings occuring outside the monetized economy; , and (c) the lack of appropriate financial institutions and instruments suitable for tapping scattered small rural savings;  (d) inelastic tax structures and increasing recurrent expenditutes leading to persistent deficits in the current budgets, (e) interest rates which are frequently negative in real terms and (f) generally overvalued exchange rates which promote capital flight abroad.

Table 3

Gross capital formation as a share of GDP for the LDCs in 1980-1984
(Percentages based on values constant prices of 1980)

|  | 1980 | 1981 | 1982 | 1983 | 1984 |
|---|---|---|---|---|---|
| Afghanistan | -- | -- | -- | -- | -- |
| Bangladesh | 11.3 | 10.8 | 10.1 | 9.5 | 13.1 |
| Benin | 23.6 | 34.5 | 36.6 | 12.7 | 7.2 |
| Bhutan | -- | -- | -- | -- | -- |
| Botswana | 41.5 | 38.9 | 38.5 | 21.4 | 14.7 |
| Burkina Faso | 16.6 | 13.3 | 12.0 | 14.0 | 15.5 |
| Burundi | 13.3 | 16.5 | 12.8 | 22.3 | -- |
| Cape Verde | 25.5 | 25.4 | 25.2 | 22.2 | 24.5 |
| Cent. African Republic | 7.0 | 8.7 | 7.9 | 12.0 | 12.7 |
| Chad | 13.2 | 9.7 | 7.4 | 6.9 | 6.8 |
| Comoros | 34.4 | 27.8 | 26.7 | 28.7 | 43.8 |
| Democratic Yemen | -- | -- | -- | -- | -- |
| Djibouti | 18.5 | 25.6 | 24.9 | 25.1 | 23.4 |
| Equatorial Guinea | 19.4 | 20.0 | 19.9 | 19.1 | 19.3 |
| Ethiopia | 10.0 | 10.1 | 10.9 | 10.5 | -- |
| Gambia | 29.1 | 30.9 | 23.3 | 21.8 | 15.9 |
| Guinea | 15.8 | 14.3 | 13.8 | 14.0 | -- |
| Guinea-Bissau | 29.6 | 20.9 | 25.3 | 26.5 | -- |
| Haiti | 16.9 | 17.5 | 17.0 | 17.9 | 18.2 |
| Lao P.D.R. | -- | -- | -- | -- | -- |
| Lesotho | 39.8 | 40.9 | 41.5 | 43.9 | 46.4 |
| Malawi | 26.5 | 18.8 | 24.4 | 26.9 | 19.1 |
| Maldives | -- | -- | -- | -- | -- |
| Mali | -- | -- | -- | -- | -- |
| Nepal | 18.3 | 17.6 | 16.9 | 20.2 | 19.4 |
| Niger | 31.5 | 20.7 | 18.7 | 16.4 | 16.1 |
| Rwanda | 17.3 | 14.9 | 16.9 | 15.7 | 17.7 |
| Samoa | 33.1 | 38.3 | 25.6 | 24.0 | -- |
| Sao Tome & Principe | 33.8 | 24.8 | 41.6 | 20.1 | 27.1 |
| Sierra Leone | 16.2 | 13.5 | 11.6 | 11.6 | -- |
| Somalia | 5.9 | 20.1 | 18.7 | -- | -- |
| Sudan | 17.8 | 16.6 | 16.8 | 14.3 | 14.3 |
| Togo | -- | -- | -- | -- | -- |
| Uganda | 6.0 | 7.0 | 7.7 | -- | -- |
| United Rep. of Tanzania | 22.5 | 24.7 | 23.3 | 18.9 | 16.5 |
| Vanuatu | -- | -- | -- | -- | -- |
| Yemen | 40.7 | 32.0 | 27.1 | 18.7 | 16.7 |
| TOTAL ABOVE a/ | 17.5 | 16.8 | 16.3 | 14.6 | 15.2 |

Source: UNCTAD secretariat based on national and international sources.

a/ Excluding Afghanistan, Bhutan, Dem. Yemen, Lao P.D.R., Maldives, Mali, Togo and Vanuatu. Excluding also Somalia and Uganda in 1983. Excluding also Burundi, Ethiopia, Guinea, Guinea-Bissau, Samoa and Sierra Leone in 1984.

Table 4

Exports of capital goods from the developed market economies
to the LDCs a/

(Millions of dollars)

|  | 1980 | 1981 | 1982 | 1983 | 1984 | 1985 |
|---|---|---|---|---|---|---|
| Developed market economies b/ | 2 472 | 2 135 | 2 038 | 1 794 | 1 699 | 1 921 |
| North America | 279 | 286 | 245 | 206 | 252 | 247 |
| Western Europe, c/ of which: | 1 801 | 1 461 | 1 485 | 1 296 | 1 171 | 1 346 |
| EEC | 1 655 | 1 341 | 1 324 | 1 185 | 1 062 | 1 247 |
| Japan | 381 | 380 | 299 | 283 | 266 | 316 |

Source:  UNCTAD, based on UN-COMTRADE data base.

a/  Capital goods are defined according to the aggregation according to
the System of National Accounts of groups 41 (machinery and other capital
equipment) and 521 (industrial transport equipment) of the United Nations
classification, Broad Economic Categories, Series M, No. 53.

b/  Excluding Gibraltar, South Africa and Israel;  including Australia
and New Zealand.

c/  Excluding Gibraltar.

Table 5

Gross domestic savings as percentage of GDP:
average 1980-1984 (or latest available)

| Negative | 0-5 | 5-10 | 10-15 | Above 15 |
|---|---|---|---|---|
| Burkina Faso | Bangladesh | Benin | Comoros | Botswana |
| Cape Verde | Burundi a/ | Maldives | Malawi | Guinea |
| Central African Rep. | Equatorial Guinea | Mali | Togo | |
| Chad a/ | Ethiopia a/ | Nepal | | |
| Djibouti a/ | Gambia | Niger | | |
| Guinea-Bissau | Haiti | United Rep. | | |
| Lesotho | Rwanda |  of Tanzania a/ | | |
| Samoa | Sierra Leone | | | |
| Sao Tome and Principe | Sudan | | | |
| Somalia b/ | | | | |
| Yemen a/ | | | | |

Source:  World Bank, The Economic Commission for Africa, and other
international and national sources.

a/  1980-1983     b/  1980-1982

C.    Government budget

12.    Governments could play an important role in mobilizing domestic savings
for development either directly through surpluses in their recurrent budgets,
or indirectly by providing fiscal and monetary incentives to private savings.
However, in practice budgetary surpluses in most LDCs have been either
negligible or negative (see table 6).    Even in countries such as Bangladesh
and Nepal, which were able to generate substantial surpluses in their
recurrent budgets, the total annual revenues are growing at a lower pace than
recurrent expenditures.

D.    Taxes

13.    In almost all LDCs the tax structure has a narrow base and income
elasticities are low even compared to other developing countries.    Taxes on
imports, sales and excise taxes on a very limited range of consumer items,
such as tobacco, petroleum products and beverages provide the bulk of the
LDCs' tax revenues.    In fact in a great majority of LDCs these taxes account
for more than 80 per cent of tax revenues.    Receipts from import taxes depend
on the capacity of these countries to import, while taxes on exports have
tended to stagnate or decline along with the real value of recorded exports.
Since many LDCs have been forced to restrict imports in recent years on
account of unfavourable terms of trade and other factors affecting their
foreign exchange earnings, the base for import taxes has been correspondingly
narrowed.    Moreover, overvalued currencies in many LDCs might have further
reduced the value base on which such taxes were calculated.    Direct taxes,
such as income and payroll taxes, account for the bulk of the direct tax
revenue, since they are easier to collect than taxes on business and property
incomes.    Capital gains are not adequately taxed.

14.    Recognizing some of these weaknesses, many LDCs have made efforts to make
the tax system simpler and more broadly based and to improve tax
administration.    In Afghanistan, Ethiopia, the Central African Republic, Haiti
and Somalia the tax system has been simplified and better adapted to present
realities.    In Comoros, Rwanda and Somalia, the structure of taxes on
international transactions has been revised.    In its efforts to increase
revenues for development, Nepal has launched programmes for training tax
administrators, simplifying the tax system and improving the organization of
the tax administration.    Efforts have been made in many countries to reduce
tax leakages by streamlining the tax administration and reinforcing customs
departments.

15.    In spite of the efforts undertaken so far, the fiscal potential for
mobilizing developmental resources in LDCs has not yet been fully exploited.
According to an UNCTAD study, there is scope for increasing taxes on urban
property in some LDCs, such as Bangladesh, Nepal, and Sudan.    Assessed values
represent small fraction of current market values and where realized gains on
real estate transactions - often a multiple of the assessed values - are
entirely exempt.    The tax base can be further widened in many LDCs by covering
agricultural income effectively for tax purposes and introducing capital gains
taxes there as well.    Yields from existing taxes could also be increased by
strengthening fiscal administration - in part through tax-collector incentive
schemes - and closing loopholes in the existing tax laws.    This type of reform

Table 6: Government savings: 1981/82 to 1983/84

| Country | 1981/82 | | | 1982/83 | | | 1983/84 | | |
|---|---|---|---|---|---|---|---|---|---|
| | Revenue | Current exp | Savings | Revenue | Current exp | Savings | Revenue | Current exp | Savings |
| Bangladesh (Mil. Taka) | 24 826 | 17 893 | 6 933 | 26 249 | 19 472 | 6 777 | 30 330 | 25 031 | 5 299 |
| Bhutan (Mil. NU) | 124 | 169 | -45 | 138 | 209 | -71 | 225 | 216 | 9 |
| Botswana (Mil. Pula) | 282.8 | 205.8 | 77 | 370.0 | 233.6 | 136.4 | 511.4 | 297.9 | 213.5 |
| Lesotho (Mil. Maloti) | 111.1 | 116.6 | -5.5 | 134.8 | 121.7 | 13.1 | 169.9 | 141.5 | 28.4 |
| Malawi (K million) | 221.0 | 231.9 | -10.9 | 244.3 | 260.7 | -16.4 | 289.1 | 364.8 | -92.1 |
| Mali (CFF Billion) | 36 | 38 | -2 | 40 | 41 | -1 | 45 | 46 | -1 |
| Nepal (Mil. Rupee) | 2 668 | 1 522 | 1 146 | 2 842 | 1 997 | 845 | 3 404 | 2 263 | 1 141 |
| Sao Tome & Principe (DP mil.) | 537 | 590 | -53 | 518 | 764 | -246 | 655 | 421 | 266 |
| Sudan (Mil.S.) | 1 048 | 1 046 | 3 | 1 343 | 1 202 | 140 | 1 469 | 1 552 | -83 |
| Somalia (Mil.S. Sh.) | 2 558 | 3 634 | -1 076 | 3 911 | 5 188 | -1 277 | 3 780 | 6 663 | -2 883 |
| Djibouti (Mil. DJF) | 19 861 | 25 398 | -5 537 | 18 998 | 25 469 | -6 471 | 19 527 | 22 775 | -3 248 |
| Yemen A.R. (Mil. YRI) | 3 692 | 5 286 | -1 593 | 4 404 | 6 200 | -1 796 | 4 649 | 5 957 | -1 307 |
| Ethiopia (Mil. Birr) | 1 739 | 1 659 | 80 | 1 824 | 1 692 | 131 | 2 217 | 2 187 | 31 |

Source: National sources.

presupposes, however, that another - though hidden - form of taxation of the agricultural sector would be abolished, namely, the frequent use of administered producer prices well below international levels, no matter whether such price distortions appear directly or operate through overvalued exchange rates. While this form of "taxation" may be just as real as the more transparent types of taxation proposed here, it tends to be more arbitrary, because the proceeds thereof do not generally accrue in the form of budgetary revenue to be used for developmental expenditures, but rather serve to subsidize consumption by other sectors of the economy, either in the form of cheap locally-produced foodstuffs or by way of imports sold below their economic cost through the mechanism of an overvalued exchange rate.

E. Non-tax revenues

16. During the period 1981-1985, the share of non-tax revenues in total revenue, which consists mainly of dividends from public enterprises and revenue from services provided by the Government, has increased in Botswana, Burundi, Burkina Faso, Ethiopia, Lesotho, Malawi and Nepal. It has decreased in Bangladesh, the Central African Republic, Rwanda, Sierra Leone and the United Republic of Tanzania.

17. Public enterprises and utilities in many LDCs have not been able to earn reasonable returns on investments and have, in fact become a liability on the national economy. In recent years, several LDCs have initiated measures to improve the performance of these enterprises. For example, in some countries prices of goods and services provided by public enterprises were increased to bring them into line with market conditions. Several LDCs have implemented a privatization policy affecting public enterprises running at a loss (see section on manufacturing, paras. 75-85). While these measures are not aimed at increasing public revenues, they will nevertheless reduce the pressure on budgetary resources and make the latter available for higher-priority activities.

F. Recurrent expenditures

18. In several LDCs recurrent expenditures have been rising because of: (a) increasing expenditures on social services, general government administration, defence and security; (b) repair and maintenance services for completed development projects; (c) subsidies to public enterprises and utilities; and (d) debt service payments. In addition to the steps already taken to make public enterprises run on a self-financing basis, efforts have been undertaken to limit recurrent expenditures by streamlining administrative services; by introducing user participation in the cost of social services, particularly health services; and by rescheduling external debt. During the period 1981-1986 several LDCs (Bangladesh, Benin, Botswana, Bhutan, Burundi, Burkina Faso, Central African Republic, Haiti, Malawi, Lesotho, Nepal, Rwanda, Sierra Leone, United Republic of Tanzania) announced and implemented measures to restrain non-essential consumption and thus limit recurrent budget expenditures.

G. Institutions for mobilizing private savings

19. Some form of banking or other financial institutions has existed in almost all LDCs for a long time. But their activities were limited mainly to urban areas. In view of their inaccessibility to large parts of the rural

population, a substantial portion of savings and credit activities was
carried outside these financial institutions. In rural areas, savings were
kept in the form of physical assets such as land, livestock, housing, gold and
silver ornaments, while credit needs were met by money-lenders, land-owners
and traders, often at very high rates of interest. The need to mobilize more
private savings and channel them to productive investment, led to the
initiation of programmes for the development of credit institutions in several
LDCs.

20. These programmes include expansion of commercial banks and their
branches, improving depository functions of non-bank financial institutions,
issuing new financial instruments as well as the establishment of postal
savings banks, national insurance companies and employees' provident funds.
In Bangladesh, for example, six private banks were established in 1983/84,
including four joint ventures with foreign collaboration, in pursuance of the
policy of permitting the private sector to engage in banking. The number of
bank branches rose from 4,378 in June 1981 to 4,817 in June 1984, of which
3,225 were in rural areas. In Nepal two new commercial banks with foreign
collaboration were established in the first half of the 1980s. The total
number of branches in the country increased by 124 to 387 between 1980 and
1984. A Post Office Savings Bank was established in 1982. The Agricultural
Development Bank of Nepal and agricultural co-operatives (Sajahs) collect
rural savings. In Democratic Yemen, profits from the Bank of Yemen, the
National Bank of Yemen and the Insurance and Reinsurance Company accounted for
about 32 per cent of development expenditures in 1982.

21. In order to encourage the holding of financial assets the monetary
authorities in Bangladesh and Nepal have raised interest rates above the rate
of inflation, shifting real rates respectively to +5.5 per cent and +6.4 per
cent in 1984. In Yemen interest rates remained positive in real terms during
the period 1981-1984 as a part of the monetary authorities' policy of
discouraging capital outflows and minimizing the gap with the Eurodollar
rates. The policies of expanding bank branches and interest rate reform have
succeeded in increased monetization of the economy and in mobilization of
savings both in Bangladesh and Nepal. The ratio of long-maturity deposits,
such as savings and fixed-term deposits, as a proportion of GDP rose from
8.7 per cent and 11.4 per cent in 1980/81 to 13.9 per cent and 14.9 per cent
in 1983/84 respectively in Bangladesh and in Nepal. 4/

22. During the period 1981-1986, some African LDCs improved and diversified
the functioning of their financial institutions for mobilizing domestic
resources for development. In Burundi, a minimum compulsory savings scheme
was established in 1977, which provided for savings to be deducted from
salaries and the compulsory purchase of savings bonds. As a result of the
first measure, the receipts of the Caisse d'épargne du Burundi increased by
20 per cent between 1981 and 1983. 5/ In Mali an extra-budgetary account was
established with resources coming mainly from the difference between the
import and sales prices of petroleum products. The monetary authorities
increased the number of branches of the Banque de développement du Mali and
the Banque nationale pour le développement agricole. 6/ In order to gain the
confidence of the population, these banks organized special meetings with the
participation of representatives of local authorities and civic leaders. They
have also organized committees to reorient savings in cash and kind towards
the banking system. 7/

23. In Rwanda the system of popular banks (Banques Populaires) based on the principles of Raiffeisen has been reinforced. These banks function as co-operatives for savings and credit. During the period 1981-1984 their membership and the volume of their operations have doubled. 8/ In Burundi, a new network of savings and credit co-operatives, specializing in the rural activities is being set up. The first co-operatives of this type were established in 1985, and are expected to cover the whole country with at least one such "rural bank" in each commune within ten years. 9/ In the Sudan, the 1980 Investment Act updated the banking laws and enhanced the expansion of the country's financial infrastructure. There are at present nine joint-venture banks, six branches of foreign banks, three specialized banks, the Sudan Savings Bank and five commercial banks with branches in the main cities. In an attempt to provide incentives to savers and to facilitate mobilization of savings, interest rates on deposits were raised in the Gambia and Guinea-Bissau.

24. Several LDCs have organized or reinforced specialized financial institutions. For example, Mali established a full-fledged financial network to support village mutual aid associations. Moreover, a food security fund was established early in 1986 to support food production. A new rural development bank is being established in Nepal. Bangladesh Shilpa Bank and Bangladesh Shilpa Rin Sangstha cater to the credit requirement of the industrial sector. In the Sudan, the capital of the Industrial Bank was increased six-fold in 1985 to enable it to provide more credit to the private sector. The role of the Agricultural Bank has also been strengthened and the Bank played an important role in supporting farmers in the main food production areas and has helped to stabilize prices.

25. In addition to strengthening official banking institutions popular initiatives have led to the establishment of savings and credit institutions peculiar to the tradition of several LDCs, e.g. the "tontine" in Mali and Burkina Faso: credit unions in Lesotho; and the Muvandimwe and Umuganda in Rwanda could be cited as examples of such forms of non-official banking institutions. 10/

H.  Conclusions

26. With their low per capita income, the LDCs face severe difficulties in generating domestic savings. Nevertheless, several LDCs were able to achieve savings rates exceeding 10 per cent during the period 1980-1984. These experiences indicate that, despite low per capita income, the LDCs should, with appropriate policies and programmes, be able to mobilise substantial amounts of domestic savings for development. Such policies and programmes should include:

(1)  Increasing tax revenues by (a) improving the assessment and collection of income and property taxes; (b) raising the elasticity of indirect taxes; and (c) levying users' charges on the use of roads and bridges as well as participation in the cost of special services.

(2)  Improving the efficiency of public sector enterprises.

(3) Introduction of measures for effective control of the growth of
recurrent expeditures and restraining non-essential expenditures.

(4) Expansion of the network of commercial banks and the establishment
of specialized institutions, such as rural development banks,
co-operative and postal banks and savings institutions and insurance
companies.

(5) Introduction of appropriate financial instruments such as
development bonds with small denominations.

(6) A flexible interest rate policy to maintain positive real rates of
interest.

(7) An exchange rate policy designed to discourage capital flight.

## Chapter III

### SECTORAL DEVELOPMENTS

### A.  Food and agriculture

1.  General trends

27.  Agriculture is the single most important sector in the least developed countries.  It contributes 42 per cent of total GDP and absorbs 80 per cent of the labour force, as compared to 17 per cent and 56 per cent in the developing countries as a whole (1984 figures).  It provides the bulk of the export earnings of the majority of LDCs.  Yet, average productivity is much lower than in other developing countries.  What is more alarming, the agricultural sector of the LDCs has not been growing at the same pace as their population. Agricultural production per capita declined at an average annual rate of 0.8 per cent in 1970-1980 and of 0.6 per cent in 1980-1985.  During the 1980s, per capita agricultural and food production has increased in only eight LDCs (see table 7).  A remarkable recovery, however, was registered in 1985 due mainly to rainfall improvement in Africa, and has led to a 3.2 per cent average increase in per capita agricultural production in the LDCs.  All these overall trends, however, conceal differences among LDCs as well as among subsectors.

2.  Agricultural production

    (a)  Food production

28.  From 1970 to 1980 only four of the 37 LDCs showed annual growth rates of food 11/ production per capita of over 1 per cent a year.  The trend has not been significantly reversed during the 1980s:  only Benin, Gambia, Guinea-Bissau, Lao People's Democratic Republic, Uganda and Vanuatu have recorded a good performance during this period (average annual rates above 1 per cent, as compared to an overall rate of minus 0.9 for the LDCs as a group).  With the recovery in 1985, however, food production per capita increased by 3.0 per cent (see table 7).

29.  Thirteen LDCs have attained a relatively high level of self-sufficiency in cereal production (90 per cent or more) in normal years:  Afghanistan, Bangladesh, Bhutan, Burundi, Chad, Ethiopia, Lao PDR, Malawi, Nepal, Niger, Rwanda, Uganda and the United Republic of Tanzania.  On the other hand, five LDCs have alarmingly low levels of self-sufficiency in cereals (less than 25 per cent of total requirements):  Botswana, Cape Verde, Djibouti, Equatorial Guinea and Sao Tome and Principe.  Cape Verde, which has an arid or semi-arid climate and very little land suitable for agriculture, hardly produces one third of its food requirements in the best climatic conditions (see table 8).

30.  The food deficit in African LDCs was serious during the marketing year 1984/85 as a result of the drought.  With the return of the rains in 1985, however, production in drought-stricken LDCs has improved markedly.  Five LDCs (Botswana 12/, Cape Verde 13/, Ethiopia, Lesotho and Sudan 14/) have continued to require emergency food assistance in 1986.  Even in the Sudan, cereal output

Table 7

Growth rates a/ of agricultural and food production per capita
in the least developed countries
( % )

| Country | Agricultural production | | | | Food production | | | |
|---|---|---|---|---|---|---|---|---|
| | 1970-1980 | 1980-1985 | 1983-1984 | 1984-1985 | 1970-1980 | 1980-1985 | 1983-1984 | 1984-1985 |
| Afghanistan | -0.1 | -1.6 | -2.7 | -2.3 | -0.3 | -1.7 | -3.0 | -2.3 |
| Bangladesh | -0.3 | -0.2 | -1.9 | 0.4 | -0.2 | -0.3 | -1.2 | -0.9 |
| Benin | -0.3 | 4.4 | 15.2 | 10.0 | -0.1 | 3.8 | 13.7 | 9.7 |
| Bhutan | 0.5 | 0.3 | 0.1 | 0.3 | 0.4 | 0.4 | 0.1 | 0.3 |
| Botswana | -6.0 | -2.7 | -5.5 | 1.5 | -6.0 | -2.7 | -5.5 | 1.5 |
| Burkina Faso | -0.7 | 0.0 | -3.9 | 16.8 | -0.8 | 0.0 | -4.1 | 17.7 |
| Burundi | 0.8 | -0.4 | -5.7 | 5.1 | 1.0 | -0.7 | -3.2 | 2.6 |
| Cape Verde | 3.1 b/ | -6.3 | 19.3 | -0.4 | 3.0 b/ | -6.4 | 19.7 | -0.3 |
| Central African Republic | 0.0 | -0.5 | 2.8 | 1.5 | 0.0 | -1.0 | 0.7 | 0.3 |
| Chad | -0.4 | -1.1 | -13.8 | 17.3 | -0.1 | -1.4 | -11.9 | 17.4 |
| Comoros | -1.2 b/ | -1.2 | -3.1 | 0.4 | -1.0 b/ | -1.3 | -3.1 | 0.3 |
| Democratic Yemen | 0.0 | -1.8 | -2.4 | -2.0 | 0.3 | -2.3 | -2.4 | -2.0 |
| Djibouti | .. | .. | .. | .. | .. | .. | .. | .. |
| Equatorial Guinea | .. | .. | .. | .. | .. | .. | .. | .. |
| Ethiopia | -1.1 | -2.6 | -7.2 | 2.7 | -1.2 | -3.2 | -8.8 | 3.0 |
| Gambia | -5.8 | 1.5 | 7.1 | 20.2 | -5.9 | 1.5 | 6.7 | 20.4 |
| Guinea | -1.5 | 0.0 | -0.7 | 2.1 | -1.5 | 0.0 | -0.7 | 2.3 |
| Guinea-Bissau | -2.5 | 4.7 | 16.2 | -0.0 | -2.4 | 4.7 | 16.2 | -0.0 |
| Haiti | 0.0 | -0.5 | 0.5 | -6.4 | 0.0 | -0.9 | 1.7 | -7.0 |
| Lao People's Dem. Rep. | 0.2 | 3.9 | 14.0 | 5.0 | 0.2 | 3.9 | 14.1 | 4.7 |
| Lesotho | -1.6 | -0.6 | -0.7 | 9.8 | -1.0 | -0.7 | -0.5 | 11.0 |
| Malawi | -0.7 | -0.4 | -1.3 | 0.9 | -0.1 | -1.2 | -2.6 | -0.1 |
| Maldives | -1.4 b/ | -0.2 | -2.4 | -0.7 | -1.4 b/ | -0.2 | -2.4 | -0.7 |
| Mali | -0.8 | -1.2 | -4.6 | 5.8 | -0.5 | -1.3 | -5.1 | 5.4 |
| Nepal | -1.5 | 0.7 | -2.9 | -0.5 | -1.5 | 0.7 | -2.6 | -0.6 |
| Niger | 1.2 | -3.8 | -21.1 | 24.1 | -1.2 | -3.8 | -21.2 | 24.1 |
| Rwanda | 1.1 | -2.4 | -18.9 | 3.4 | 0.8 | -2.8 | -21.2 | 4.0 |
| Samoa | -1.7 b/ | -0.7 | 3.0 | -1.8 | -1.7 b/ | -0.7 | 3.2 | -1.8 |
| Sao Tome & Principe | -5.5 b/ | -4.4 | -9.6 | 0.0 | -5.5 b/ | -4.4 | -9.7 | 0.0 |
| Sierra Leone | -0.1 | -1.0 | -12.9 | 5.8 | -0.2 | -0.9 | -15.2 | 6.2 |
| Somalia | -2.3 | -2.6 | -2.7 | -0.9 | -2.3 | -2.6 | -2.7 | -0.9 |
| Sudan | -0.9 | 0.0 | -8.6 | 23.8 | -0.2 | -0.8 | -10.1 | 28.3 |
| Togo | -1.2 | -2.0 | 2.4 | 0.7 | -1.2 | -2.2 | 3.8 | -2.6 |
| Uganda | -3.2 | 2.5 | -3.6 | 2.5 | -2.4 | 2.3 | -4.2 | 2.6 |
| United Rep. of Tanzania | 0.4 | -1.8 | 1.5 | -1.8 | 1.5 | -1.4 | 1.4 | -1.6 |
| Vanuatu | 0.8 | 1.1 | 10.3 | -1.8 | 0.9 | 1.3 | 10.7 | -1.9 |
| Yemen | 0.4 | -1.9 | 0.8 | 5.7 | 0.0 | -1.9 | 0.8 | 5.9 |
| All LDCs | -0.8 | -0.6 | -3.2 | 3.2 | -0.5 | -0.9 | -3.7 | 3.0 |
| All developing countries | 0.5 | 0.3 | -0.4 | 1.6 | 0.7 | 0.3 | -0.7 | 1.2 |

Source : UNCTAD secretariat calculations based on information provided by FAO.
a/ Annual average growth rates based on exponential trend function.
b/ 1973-1980.

Table 8

## The Cereal Situation in the least developed countries
### (as of mid-September 1986)

| Least Developed Countries | Cereal self-sufficiency ratio (%) (normal year a/ unless otherwise specified) | Cereal production in latest completed crop year | | | Total import requirements (1985/86 or 1986) (estimated or anticipated) ('000 tons) | | | |
|---|---|---|---|---|---|---|---|---|
| | | Market-commercial year | Production b/ '000 tons | Total cereal production index 1/ | Total import requirements | Commercial imports | Food aid required | Food aid pledged 2/ |
| Afghanistan | 97 | Jul./Jun. | 4 310.0 | 96 | 300.0 | - | - | 50.0 |
| Bangladesh | 91 c/ | Jul./Jun. | 23 983.0 5/ | 106 | 1 600.0 | 60.0 | 10.0 | 1 086.0 |
| Benin 3/ | 81 | Jan./Dec. | 570.0 | 149 | 70.0 | 12.0 | - | 1.0 |
| Bhutan | 94 c/ | Jul./Jun. | 167.0 | 104 | 12.0 | - | - | - |
| Botswana 4/ | 24 | Jul./Jun. | 20.0 | 72 | 180.0 | 139.0 | 41.0 | 61.0 |
| Burkina Faso 3/ | 88 | Nov./Oct. | 1 586.0 | 138 | 70.0 | 70.0 | - | 53.0 |
| Burundi | 93 | Jul./Jun. | 422.0 | 107 | 30.0 | 20.0 | 10.0 | 12.0 |
| Cape Verde 4/ | 5 6/ | Jan./Dec. | 1.3 | 23 | 77.0 | 5.0 | 72.0 | 54.0 |
| Central African Rep. | 67 | Sep./Aug. | 108.0 | 101 | 35.0 | 31.0 | 4.0 | - |
| Chad 3/ | 91 | Nov./Oct. | 697.0 | 160 | 19.0 | - | 19.0 | 47.0 |
| Comoros | 40 | Jan./Dec. | 21.0 | 102 | 30.0 | 25.0 | 5.0 | 6.0 |
| Democratic Yemen | 28 c/ | Jan./Dec. | 114.0 | 99 | 220.0 | 50.0 | - | 5.0 |
| Djibouti | - | Jan./Dec. | - | - | 50.0 | 40.0 | 10.0 | 16.0 |
| Equatorial Guinea | - | Jan./Dec. | - | - | 7.0 | 4.0 | 3.0 | 1.0 |
| Ethiopia 4/ | 92 | Jan./Dec. | 5 220.0 | 95 | 1 170.0 | 270.0 | 900.0 | 955.0 |
| Gambia | 57 | Oct./Sep. | 127.0 | 147 | 32.0 | 14.0 | 18.0 | 15.0 |
| Guinea | 74 | Jan./Dec. | 588.0 | 117 | 90.0 | 46.0 | 44.0 | 33.0 |
| Guinea-Bissau | 74 | Jan./Dec. | 180.0 | 136 | 24.0 | 18.0 10/ | 6.0 | 11.0 |
| Haiti | 85 | Jul./Jun. | 390.0 7/ | 102 | 200.0 | 9.6 | - | 105.7 |
| Lao PDR | 100 d/ | Jan./Dec. | 1 507.0 8/ | 128 | 0.0 | - | - | - |
| Lesotho 4/ | 49 | Jul./Jun. | 167.0 | 112 | 160.0 | 120.0 | 40.0 | 56.0 |
| Malawi 3/ | 98 | Apr./Mar. | 1 523.0 | 98 | 25.0 | 24.0 | 1.0 | - |
| Maldives | n.a. | Jan./Dec. | - | - | 18.0 | 10.0 | - | 8.0 |
| Mali 3/ | 81 | Nov./Oct. | 1 378.0 | 121 | 275.0 | 170.0 | 105.0 | 107.0 |
| Nepal | 101 d/ | Jul./Jun. | 4 296.0 | 110 | 0.0 | - | - | 4.2 |
| Niger 3/ | 97 | Oct./Sep. | 1 821.0 | 114 | 18.0 | 10.0 | 8.0 | 98.0 |
| Rwanda | 91 | Jul./Jun. | 318.0 | 106 | 30.0 | 14.0 | 16.0 | 32.0 |
| Samoa | n.a. | Jan./Dec. | 1.0 | - | 13.0 | - | - | - |
| Sao Tome & Principe | 9 | Jul./Jun. | 1.0 | - | 10.0 | 5.0 | 5.0 | 3.0 |
| Sierra Leone | 83 | Jan./Dec. | 561.0 | 97 | 100.0 | 55.0 | 45.0 | 66.0 |
| Somalia | 58 | Jan./Dec. | 614.0 | 160 | 175.0 | 35.0 | 140.0 | 181.0 |
| Sudan 3/ 4/ | 89 | Nov./Oct. | 4 288.0 | 163 | 400.0 9/ | 100.0 | 300.0 | 683.0 11/ |
| Togo 3/ | 75 | Jan./Dec. | 465.0 | 113 | 35.0 | 25.0 | 10.0 | 2.1 |
| Uganda | 98 | Jan./Dec. | 1 837.0 | 163 | 20.0 | 5.0 | 15.0 | 5.0 |
| U.Rep. of Tanzania | 90 | Jun./May | 3 573.0 | 119 | 225.0 | 100.0 | 125.0 | 98.0 |
| Yemen | 52 c/ | Jan./Dec. | 397.0 | 64 | 700.0 | 534.4 | - | 81.0 |

Source: FAO and UNCTAD secretariat calculations based on FAO information.

a/ Calculated on the basis of FAO estimations of normal levels of cereal production and imports. Normal levels are estimated by FAO on the basis of average or trend values. b/ Including rice in paddy equivalent. c/ 1984. d/ 1985/86 or 1986.

1/ Estimated as a percentage of the five-year moving average.
2/ FAO has included all pledges reported to the Global Information and Early Warning System (GIEWS), whether for free distribution or market sale. However, there may be some cases where governments count some food aid received for market sale against commercial import requirements. Figures include pledges carried over from last year, and may exceed food aid requirements.
3/ LDCs with cereal surpluses which could - with donors' support - be exchanged for other foodstuffs which these countries need and/or redistributed internally in food deficit areas.
4/ LDCs requiring exceptional food aid in addition to structural food aid.
5/ Rice and wheat.
6/ Maize.
7/ Estimate for 1986.
8/ Paddy rice.
9/ In addition, emergency food requirements of 520,000 tons are estimated for 5.1 million people affected by the previous drought. This emergency relief could be provided from local surpluses of sorghum (cf. footnote 3/), for which purpose external assistance will be required.
10/ The Government has indicated that it will not be able to import this amount in full, owing to a shortage of foreign exchange.
11/ Including pledges for emergency food requirements.

in 1985 is estimated to have attained a record 4.3 million tons (as compared to a disastrous crop of 1.4 million tons in 1984), 63 per cent above the five-year average. Quantitative information on the current cereal situation in LDCs is contained in table 8.

31. After good to record harvests in 1985, exceptional surpluses of coarse grains have been available in 1986 in Benin, Burkina Faso, Chad, Malawi, Mali, Niger, Sudan and Togo. However, special programmes of international assistance are required to provide financial and logistic support to these LDCs for the internal distribution of the surpluses or for their export to neighbouring countries through triangular transactions and swap arrangements. Transactions of this type are already planned by several donors or are under way.

32. Despite the progress reported, improvements in food production arising from rainfall increases have not been immune from important setbacks. The rains in 1985 lasted in many cases for a shorter time than the growth cycle of foodcrops. Farming methods had been adapted to drought conditions and could not be adjusted, over a single crop season, to a situation of higher rainfall. For instance, farmers became accustomed to plant seeds at low altitudes and many plants were flooded with the return of the rains in 1985. The rains provided exceptionally favourable breeding conditions for grasshoppers, which have become a threat to 1986 crops, particularly in the Sahel. Locust infestations are particularly serious in eastern and southern Africa, where the 1987 crop could also be adversely affected. However, control programmes currently being implemented have had some success in reducing this threat. On the other hand, the bumper crop coupled with the supply of food aid has tended to lower prices and may thus discourage food production and investment: in early 1986, local market prices for foodstuffs were reported falling back to pre-drought levels in Chad, Gambia, Mali, Niger and Sudan. (To counter this tendency, a duty on imported rice was introduced in Niger in March 1986, and the purchase of 200,000 tons of grain by the national grain marketing agency was authorized.)

    (b)  Cash crops

33. The need to generate foreign exchange has led LDCs to promote export crops in which they have competitive advantage in spite of falling prices in world commodity markets. Cash crops have thus been made more productive and crop levels have been maintained or raised in a number of least developed countries (see table 9).

34. Available information for 1984-1985 points to significant increases in cotton production in Benin, Togo (where cotton production has outstripped processing capacity), the Central African Republic and Uganda (where production is, however, still well below the record 86,000 tons reached in 1970). Record cotton crops were registered in Sudan in 1984 and Burkina Faso and Mali in 1985. Cotton is in general carefully managed as a lucrative export crop, is given priority in allocation of foreign exchange and attracts a wide range of government support measures, ranging from annually adjusted producer prices to extension services and effective collection and marketing structures. The sharp decline in the international prices for cotton, however, has led to major losses in the cotton industry inasmuch as such prices are now below operating costs in a number of the LDCs concerned.

## Table 9

### Production of main cash crops in LDCs
('000 metric tons)

| | 1979-81 | 1983 | 1984 | 1985 |
|---|---|---|---|---|
| **Coffee** | | | | |
| Burundi | 30 | 36 | 26 | 36 e/ |
| Central African Republic | 17 | 10 e/ | 15 e/ | 18 e/ |
| Equatorial Guinea | 6 | 7 d/ | 7 d/ | 7 d/ |
| Ethiopia | 192 | 220 e/ | 240 e/ | 250 d/ |
| Haiti | 33 | 40 e/ | 38 e/ | 39 e/ |
| Lao PDR | 5.0 a/ | 5.3 | 5.7 | 5.9 |
| Malawi | 1 | 1 d/ | 1 d/ | 2 d/ |
| Rwanda | 25 | 27 | 32 e/ | 32 e/ |
| Sierra Leone | 11 | 5 | 10 e/ | 10 e/ |
| Togo | 8 | 6 | 3 | 10 |
| Uganda | 112 | 172 | 204 e/ | 210 e/ |
| United Republic of Tanzania | 56 | 51 e/ | 56 e/ | 56 e/ |
| **Tea** | | | | |
| Bangladesh | 38 | 45 | 38 | 43 |
| Burundi | 2.3 | 2.3 | 3.4 | 4 d/ |
| Malawi | 31 | 32 | 38 | 40 e/ |
| Rwanda | 6 | 7 | 9 | 8 d/ |
| United Republic of Tanzania | 17 | 16 | 16 | 17 e/ |
| **Cocoa** | | | | |
| Benin | | | | |
| Equatorial Guinea | 7 | 10 e/ | 7 e/ | 7 d/ |
| Haiti | 3 | 3 e/ | 3 e/ | 3 d/ |
| Samoa b/ | 1.3 | 1.8 | 0.7 | n.a. |
| Sao Tome and Principe | 7 | 5 e/ | 4 e/ | 5 e/ |
| Sierra Leone | 8 | 9 | 9 e/ | 9 d/ |
| Togo | 14 | 16 | 10 | 16 d/ |
| **Cotton lint** | | | | |
| Afghanistan | 27 | 22 e/ | 25 e/ | 25 e/ |
| Benin | 6 | 13 d/ | 26 d/ | 32 d/ |
| Burkina Faso c/ | 22 a/ | 30 | 34 | 44 f/ |
| Central African Republic | 9 | 12 e/ | 18 e/ | 22 e/ |
| Chad | 30 | 51 e/ | 34 e/ | 40 e/ |
| Ethiopia | 26 | 20 e/ | 22 e/ | 23 d/ |
| Haiti | 2 | 2 d/ | 2 d/ | 2 d/ |
| Lao PDR | 5.0 a/ | 5.0 | 5.1 | 4.7 |
| Mali | 48 | 50 e/ | 54 e/ | 63 e/ |
| Sudan | 116 | 201 | 219 e/ | 196 e/ |
| Togo c/ | 9 a/ | 10 | 23 | 27 f/ |

Table 9 (continued)

| | 1979-81 | 1983 | 1984 | 1985 |
|---|---|---|---|---|
| **Cotton lint** (continued) | | | | |
| Uganda | 6 | 10 | 19 | 17 d/ |
| United Republic of Tanzania | 58 | 44 | 48 | 46 e/ |
| **Jute and jute-like fibres** | | | | |
| Bangladesh | 1 018 | 954 | 837 | 1 158 d/ |
| Bhutan | 3 | 4 d/ | 4 d/ | 4 d/ |
| Nepal | 64 | 39 | 25 | 33 |
| **Sisal** | | | | |
| Ethiopia | 1 | 1 d/ | 1 d/ | 1 d/ |
| Haiti | 12 | 11 e/ | 10 e/ | 9 e/ |
| United Republic of Tanzania | 80 | 46 | 40 e/ | 40 d/ |
| **Groundnuts** | | | | |
| Bangladesh | 23 | 22 | 22 | 23 |
| Benin | 35 | 34 | 58 | 70 |
| Burkina Faso | 71 | 82 | 83 | 77 d/ |
| Burundi | 79 | 80 d/ | 80 d/ | 80 d/ |
| Central African Republic | 127 | 130 d/ | 130 d/ | 140 d/ |
| Chad | 100 d/ | 80 d/ | 90 d/ | 90 d/ |
| Ethiopia | 33 d/ | 31 d/ | 28 d/ | 28 d/ |
| Gambia | 151 | 106 | 114 | 120 d/ |
| Guinea | 85 d/ | 75 d/ | 75 d/ | 75 d/ |
| Mali | 94 | 70 d/ | 100 d/ | 120 d/ |
| Niger | 88 | 74 | 30 d/ | 40 d/ |
| Sierra Leone | 15 | 14 | 14 d/ | 14 d/ |
| Sudan | 497 | 413 | 386 | 344 e/ |
| Uganda | 90 | 100 d/ | 100 d/ | 100 d/ |
| United Republic of Tanzania | 58 d/ | 58 d/ | 59 d/ | 59 d/ |
| **Copra** | | | | |
| Samoa | 19 d/ | 24 e/ | 23 d/ | 23 d/ |
| Sao Tome and Principe | 4 d/ | 5 d/ | 4 d/ | 4 d/ |
| **Palm oil** | | | | |
| Benin | 30 | 33 | 34 | 37 |
| Guinea | 45 d/ | 45 d/ | 45 d/ | 45 d/ |
| Guinea-Bissau | 3 d/ | 3 d/ | 3 d/ | 3 d/ |

Table 9 (continued)

|  | 1979-81 | 1983 | 1984 | 1985 |
|---|---|---|---|---|
| **Palm kernels** |  |  |  |  |
| Benin | 75 d/ | 75 d/ | 75 d/ | 75 d/ |
| Guinea | 35 d/ | 35 d/ | 35 d/ | 35 d/ |
| Guinea-Bissau | 10 e/ | 6 e/ | 11 e/ | 11 d/ |
| **Tobacco** |  |  |  |  |
| Bangladesh | 44 | 50 | 48 | 47 e/ |
| Lao PDR | 19.1 a/ | 15.5 | 16.5 | 22.0 |
| Malawi | 53 | 72 | 70 e/ | 75 d/ |
| Nepal | 5 | 7 | 7 | 6 |
| United Republic of Tanzania | 16 | 14 | 16 | 17 d/ |
| **Bananas** |  |  |  |  |
| Bangladesh | 4 | 6 | 7 | 7 d/ |
| Cape Verde | 6 | 3 | 3 | 5 |
| Central African Republic | 3 | 3 d/ | 3 d/ | 3 d/ |
| Somalia | 8 | 8 d/ | 8 d/ | 9 d/ |

**Source:** FAO monthly Bulletins of Statistics; Bulletin de l'Afrique noire (17/7/86); and national sources available at the UNCTAD secretariat.

a/ 1981.

b/ Export volume.

c/ Figures correspond to harvest originating in specified calendar year.

d/ FAO estimate.

e/ Unofficial figure.

f/ Provisional estimate.

35. Similar incentives are given to other cash crops. Producers of cash crops generally tend to have better access to credit and other facilities, and the internal terms of trade in a number of cases have favoured the production of cash crops relative to foodgrains. Thus, tea production in Bangladesh reached 43,000 tons in 1985, as compared to 38,000 tons the preceding year. Export earnings from this commodity are thus expected to rise to $70 million in 1985/86 as compared to $57.5 million in 1984/85. Cash crop production in Nepal increased at an average annual rate of 6.8 per cent during 1981-1985 (compared to a target rate of 3.9 per cent) and by 7.4 per cent in 1984/85 alone. Tea production in Burundi increased by nearly 50 per cent in 1984 as compared to preceding years, and again in 1985. Cocoa production targets were reportedly exceeded in Equatorial Guinea in the 1984/85 season.

36. By contrast, some crops have been affected by drought and other environmental disasters. The most striking impact has been in the case of groundnuts, since overall production in the Sahelian region declined sharply over the past decade, with an acceleration in recent drought years. In addition to the decline in output arising from falling yields and fewer attractions for planters, plantation activities have been changed to satisfy local food consumption needs, further curtailing export availabilities. Other cash crops that declined markedly during the drought years of the 1980s are coffee in the Central African Republic, cocoa in Sao Tome and Principe, and bananas in Cape Verde. Banana production was also affected by diseases and storms in Samoa. Following heavy floods, cash crop losses were recorded in Bangladesh in 1984 in the following items: jute (nearly one million bales), cotton (9,000 bales), sugarcane (65,000 tons) and tobacco.

## (c) Livestock

37. Another traditional export item, cattle, responds perversely to the drought. Strong ecological pressure is exerted by cattle feeding in terms of use of pasture areas and water. Cattle need mobility and dispersion, while the pasture areas shrink because of the drought. As available pasture dries up and the cereal supply becomes limited and dearer, the opportunity cost of live animals increases considerably. Moreover, the weakened livestock is subject to epizootic diseases, particularly rinderpest. Cattle herds are naturally or forcibly depleted, and the leather supply increases. Therefore, while some of the sales of livestock and hides and skins may give a temporary boost to the volume of exports, this should not be regarded as a planned or regular export expansion.

38. The decline in the national herd during the drought years of the 1980s amounted to nearly 20 per cent in Cape Verde, 33 per cent in Botswana, 37 per cent in Niger and 55 per cent in Sudan. The livestock fecundity rate declined by 60 per cent in Mali. In Lesotho, the proportion of total mortality directly attributable to drought is estimated to have been as high as 50 to 60 per cent for cattle and 20 to 30 per cent for sheep and goats during the past five years of drought. Milk yields in this country dropped in 1982-1984 to 30 to 60 per cent of normal levels. In Burkina Faso, the Government had to pursue an active livestock de-stocking operation covering 16,000 head as a means of ensuring ecological relief, and most of these animals were sold to neighbouring countries. In Niger, the Government encouraged livestock owners to sell their cattle before they died from thirst or hunger.

39.  The livestock situation in drought-stricken LDCs reportedly improved with the rainfall increase in 1985 (cf. Burkina Faso, Chad, Mali and Niger). The conditions of the livestock population, however, have continued to deteriorate in several LDCs owing to poor pasture as a result of dry weather (Botswana, Djibouti, Somalia) and to plagues of insects (Sudan, United Republic of Tanzania). On the other hand, livestock has been increasing in the Central African Republic, where the bovine herd was estimated at 2.5 million head in 1984 as compared to 1.7 million in 1980.

### (d)  Fisheries

40.  Fisheries products are amongst the main export items of Cape Verde (accounting for around two-thirds of the export earnings), Democratic Yemen and Maldives (which has suffered from the decline in world tuna prices that began in 1982). The fisheries sector has been expanding in a number of LDCs, such as Sao Tome and Principe and Guinea Bissau (where shrimps and fish now represent nearly 40 per cent of total exports). Great fishing potential exists in Somalia, with 3,000 km of coast line, although this sector now contributes only one per cent of GDP. Exploitation of the fisheries potential in Cape Verde, the Comoros, Ethiopia, and Somalia is less than 20 per cent. Inadequate equipment and maintenance problems affect the ability to exploit the potential fish catch in many of these countries.

41.  Inland fishing has been developed in several land-locked LDCs. Fish is a major source of protein in land-locked Burundi and Malawi (and is around two-thirds of the total consumption of animal protein in the latter). Average annual production of inland fishing amounts to 10,000 tons in Niger, 30,000 tons in Lao PDR, 70,000 tons in Chad and 100,000 tons in Mali. This sector, however, seriously suffered from the drought in the Sudano-Sahelian region.

### (e)  Forestry

42.  The forestry sector is being developed in a number of least developed countries. In the Lao PDR, production increased from 77,000 $m^3$ in 1981 to an estimated 240,000 $m^3$ in 1985, and timber exports provided an estimated $8.6 million in foreign exchange earnings in 1985. Timber exports of Equatorial Guinea increased from 3,000 $m^3$ in 1978 to 103,000 $m^3$ in 1984 but are estimated to have declined by 15 per cent in 1985 (potential annual production is estimated at 300,000 $m^3$). Somalia and Ethiopia are two of the world's largest producers of incense, a forest product used for medicinal purposes and perfume. Forests cover over 60 per cent of the territories of Bhutan, Guinea-Bissau and Somalia.

### 3.  Elements inhibiting agricultural and food production in LDCs [15]/

### (a)  Exogenous factors

43.  The poor performance of least developed countries during the early 1980s in regard to agriculture and food production was made worse by the international economic setting and - especially in the African LDCs - by the unfavourable climatic conditions, exacerbated by civil disturbances and wars. The international economic setting has created severe import constraints, including restrictions on agricultural inputs such as seeds and fertilizers, and a generalized economic weakness to which agriculture has not been immune.

Depressed world markets and low international prices for agricultural commodities have limited the foreign exchange earnings of LDCs, whilst protectionism against agricultural commodities and processed agricultural goods inhibits these countries from diversifying their export base. Other factors related to the international economic environment have also had an adverse effect on the agricultural production of LDCs; these factors include the difficulty of access to international financial markets and the debt burden.

44. As regards environmental degradation, while it does have a man-made component related to the need to meet food requirements in a context of poverty (see the section on environment and disasters below), there is no doubt that adverse climatic conditions in many LDCs constitute a further burden that goes beyond their direct control. Climatic conditions, particularly the prolonged drought in Africa, have had a cumulative impact of successive failed harvests and have imposed a diversion of resources from development efforts towards emergency relief. It should be noted that 13 African LDCs were among the 20 worst-affected countries considered at the United Nations Conference on the Emergency Situation in Africa - which was held in Geneva in early 1985 - and among the 21 African countries which FAO identified as having abnormally high cereal import requirements in 1984/1985. Floods and droughts affected agricultural production in Bangladesh in four years during the first half of the 1980s, and total food loss arising therefrom was estimated at more than 2.5 million tons or more than 5 per cent of total GDP. Crop and pasture conditions in Afghanistan in early 1986 were rated below average for the second consecutive year, reflecting inadequate rainfall and displacement of the rural population. In contrast, given good weather, output increased remarkably well in several Asian LDCs: in the Lao PDR food production increased by 31 per cent in 1984; in Nepal agricultural output increased by 8.6 per cent in 1983/84; and in Samoa cocoa output increased by 11 per cent in 1983.

### (b) Domestic policies

45. As in other developing countries, the domestic policies of the least developed countries have tended to undermine local agricultural and food production. 16/ Prices for foodstuffs have been kept artificially low through price controls and/or procurement and sales policies of commodity-marketing boards. The main purpose has been to ensure adequate nutrition standards among low-income groups. Domestic prices have thus often been lower than the corresponding border prices: for example, the World Bank estimated that domestic (procurement) prices for wheat in the United Republic of Tanzania were only 45 per cent those of border prices, while, in Ethiopia, the ratio was 50 per cent for maize and less than 70 per cent for sorghum and wheat. 17/ The Economist Intelligence Unit reports that prevailing producers' prices for cash crops in Benin and Togo are well below the corresponding border prices. 18/ The low prices have tended to discourage production as well as investment in the agricultural sector. In certain cases, price controls on foodstuffs have been accompanied by producers' price increases and other incentives to export crops in a number of LDCs (cf. sub-section 2(b) above), yet production of export crops has been penalized in some LDCs by a public-revenue structure that is heavily dependent upon export taxes. 19/

46.  Overall macroeconomic policies, too, have entailed discrimination against agricultural and food production.  Import restrictions have been resorted to, through customs duties and/or quotas, in order to cope with external trade imbalances and to provide protection to the local manufacturing sector.  Such restrictions tend to keep exchange rates at overvalued levels.  The implications of currency overvaluation for agricultural and food production are twofold.  First, the local prices for exported commodities are kept high as compared to prevailing prices, thus undermining the competitiveness of domestic exporters as well as the financial position of national marketing boards.  Second, exchange rate overvaluation implies low prices for imported foodstuffs, which in turn tend to discourage local agricultural production. The depressing effects of exchange rate overvaluation also tend to nullify the incentives provided to agricultural production notably by means of farmers' subsidies and by the supply of agricultural inputs.

(c)  Inadequate infrastructure

47.  The fragmentation of plots under traditional land tenure systems, as well as inadequate transport, marketing, storage and processing facilities continue to discourage agricultural production in least developed countries. Post-harvest losses due to inadequate, traditional processing and storage practices are estimated to account for up to 18 per cent of agricultural production in the Lao PDR, 15 to 20 per cent in Lesotho, and for up to one third in many other LDCs.  Production, notably as regards foodgrains, has furthermore been constrained by lack of an adequate infrastructure aimed at facilitating the supply of seeds and other agricultural inputs as well as providing the financial resources which peasants need for operational and long-term investments.  A very small proportion of cultivated land has assured irrigation facilities (an average of 5 per cent of arable land is irrigated in 23 LDCs).  Fertilizer use is 5 kg/ha. as compared with 18 kg for the developing countries as a whole.  Lack of skilled manpower has also contributed to the poor performance of some export crop activities while farming techniques remain archaic.  According to FAO estimates, public expenditure in agriculture on a per capita basis has been lower in the LDCs than in the other developing countries, and the share of agriculture in total public investment in the former has been smaller than the contribution of this sector to GDP. 20/  Other factors identified by FAO as hampering agricultural production include poor administration of support services;  a shortage of suitable land in certain areas;  lack of suitable technology and associated inputs;  migration and increasing labour constraints, particularly in households headed by women;  structural constraints in existing farming systems;  increasing competition between crop farming and animal husbandry; and competition between cash and food crops in some regions. 21/

4.  Agricultural development policies

48.  A tendency towards the readjustment of agricultural strategies and policies in LDCs, however, can be clearly perceived.  The LDCs are now giving higher priority to agricultural development and are adapting their policies to the need to overcome insufficient food production and falling export earnings from the agricultural sector.  Increasing self-sufficiency in food forms part of the top priorities of the national development plans of virtually all of them.  Agricultural development has further been given serious attention in the context of regional and sub-regional organizations.

49. Policies regarding agricultural development naturally vary from one LDC to another according to their individual needs, priorities and economic systems. Nevertheless, four broad distinctive features can be identified in the current agricultural policies of most LDCs, and such features are discussed below.

### (a) More effective use of the market mechanisms

50. In the past, producers' price policies in LDCs were generally aimed at ensuring compatibility between foodstuffs prices and the income levels of urban populations. Prices thus tended to be kept artificially low, and this pattern had adverse effects on the domestic terms of trade of the agricultural sector, and therefore tended to discourage agricultural production and investment. Under the new policies, prices are now established which aim at being not only compatible with consumers' income levels but also remunerative enough to stimulate production. Producers' prices are therefore being raised or allowed to rise in many LDCs in response to the domestic supply-demand situation. Price controls on a score of commodities have recently been lifted in the United Republic of Tanzania. In Bangladesh and Nepal, procurement prices have been adjusted regularly and announcements of such price changes are made in advance of crop planting. In a number of cases, subsidies on agricultural goods are being gradually reduced or eliminated. The subsidy on rice in Sierra Leone was terminated in June 1986. The marketing and distribution of cereals and foodstuffs has been made more open to competition, and State monopolies in this field have been dismantled or limited in scope in some LDCs. In Gambia, commercial imports of rice in the 1985/86 marketing year (October/September) were, for the first time, left entirely to the private sector.

51. Other policy measures have contributed to increasing the efficiency of the export sector, even though the benefits derived therefrom by LDCs have been significantly reduced or nullified by the prevailing conditions in world commodity markets. Exchange rate depreciation has been undertaken during the 1980s in at least 20 LDCs (in 12 LDCs in 1985 alone) with a view to redressing persistent deficits in the balance of payments, and such depreciations have led to improvements in the competitive position of LDCs' export crops in world commodity markets. The removal of export taxes on tea in Bangladesh provided stronger producers' incentives and is thus likely to have contributed to the increase in the export sales of this commodity. In Nepal, an export levy on rice was reduced from 25 per cent to 10 per cent in 1984, and export restrictions on rice and oilseeds were lifted. A programme for the rehabilitation of the sisal sector in the United Republic of Tanzania (which had been nationalized in 1967) provides for the sale to the private sector in 1986 of 6 to 21 units operating in deficit. Some jute and cotton textile mills have been transferred to the private sector in Bangladesh.

### (b) Mobilization of the local population

52. The rural population is being increasingly mobilized with a view to boosting agricultural production and increasing productivity. Village associations have been promoted, inter alia, in Burkina Faso, Chad, Ethiopia, Lesotho, Mali and Niger. In Mali, a financial infrastructure is being created with a view to providing resources for initiatives by the village associations (tons villageois) and rural co-operatives. A network of savings and credit co-operatives specializing in the rural milieu has been promoted in Lesotho

and more recently in Burundi.  Co-operatives among ranch owners are being
promoted in Botswana, and the marketing of livestock is increasingly
undertaken by such co-operatives (from 7.4 per cent of total cattle marketed
in 1979 to nearly 20 per cent in 1984).  Farmers' clubs have been actively
engaged in rural development in Malawi and Sierra Leone.  In both Afghanistan
and the Lao PDR, the number of agricultural co-operatives has been increased
so as to ensure better organization of production and economies of scale.  In
Afghanistan, under the land reform programme, 32,700 hectares were distributed
to 6,200 families in 1984 and there were plans to distribute 52,000 hectares
to 10,000 families in 1985.  In the Lao PDR, co-operatives cover 45 per cent
of the agricultural land.  In Sao Tome and Principe, parcels of land have been
allotted to agricultural workers for their own use as a means of providing
incentives for food production.  Measures have been taken in Gambia to
facilitate women's involvement in agricultural production;  these include the
supply of land, financial credit and ox-carts as well as the establishment of
child care centres.

### (c)  Diversification efforts

53.  Dry-season crops have been promoted by means of the mobilization of the
rural population, the establishment of an appropriate financial
infrastructure, the development of seeds adapted to local conditions and the
improvement of irrigation systems.  Dry season crops have expanded
considerably in Burkina Faso, Mali and Niger.  A drought-tolerant variety of
sorghum has been introduced in Sudan.  Several crops (e.g. potatoes and
millet) and vegetables, pulses and fruit have been introduced recently in
Lesotho.  In Gambia, diversification is pursued through the promotion of food
crops with short cycles such as coarse grains, swamp rice, maize, millet and
sorghum.  Niger has successfully introduced manioc and is encouraging poultry
farming as a means of improving the nutritional intake of the population.  The
poultry sector is being transformed from a subsistence to a commercial
activity in Botswana and Sudan, and imports of chicken meat and eggs have been
reduced to approximately 5 per cent of total requirements in the former.  The
development of drought-resistant small stock (sheep, goats) is being promoted
in Botswana and the number of goats is estimated to have increased by
40 per cent during 1982-1984 (in contrast with the fall in the overall
national herd – cf. sub-section 2 (c) above).  In the Central African
Republic, the Government is encouraging cotton growers to develop food
production together with cotton, and sugar and palm oil are being promoted for
import substitution purposes.  In Bhutan, the area under cultivation of
oranges, potatoes, cardamon, ginger and vegetables has increased
considerably;  in the Lao PDR, production of tobacco, coffee, sugar and cotton
has been encouraged;  and in Nepal production of potatoes, tobacco and sugar
has increased.  A crop diversification programme is underway in Bangladesh and
gives emphasis to the promotion of potato, pulses, oilseeds and spices.

54.  Diversification is further enhanced by the development of the fisheries
sector including inland fishing.  In the Central African Republic, the number
of fish farms doubled to 8,000 ponds between 1979 and 1982.  Producers' price
support is envisaged to be given to the local fisheries sector in Guinea
through control of the volume of fish discharged by foreign vessels in the
local market.  Guinea is taking further measures to facilitate fishing
activities, including liberalization of this sector, support to small-scale
handicraft fishing and improvement of port facilities.  A number of measures
aimed at increasing the benefits derived from the fisheries sector are being

taken in Sierra Leone.  They include encouraging the operation of local companies, protecting territorial waters from poachers, boat building, establishing landing facilities and granting fishing licences on a more stringent basis.  Measures have been taken in Gambia in early 1986 with a view to promoting fisheries development, and these include the establishment of a fish processing and marketing company, duty exemptions and improved credit facilities.  The fisheries sector has been liberalized in Somalia since 1983. A shipyard is under construction in Ethiopia with the capacity to turn out 50 fishing boats per year.  In Bangladesh, the fisheries programme includes freshwater fish culture;  shrimp farming;  management, conservation and utilization of open-water fisheries;  creation of sanctuaries;  and research and training.  In the Lao PDR, the fisheries programme includes rehabilitation of fish seed farms and fish culture development.  The development of fisheries and rabbit farming is being promoted in Lesotho as a means of securing low-cost protein.  Training centres for fishermen have been opened in the Comoros and in Samoa.  In Djibouti, nomad tribesmen and women who lost their livestock during the drought are being recycled into the fisheries sector under a new IFAD-supported project.

### (d)  Role of the public sector

55.  The increased utilization of market mechanisms has been coupled with high priority for the agricultural sector in government policies and expenditure.  Areas where State involvement may be appropriate relate to those identified by FAO as priority areas for the rehabilitation of the agricultural sector, i.e. manpower training, improving the variety of crops, promoting appropriate technologies, establishing better links between research and extension activities, reforestation, small-scale irrigation programmes, livestock disease control, pest eradication, prevention of food losses, and improvement of distribution and transport facilities.

56.  Many LDCs have formulated national stock policies or practices to strengthen their food security, in line with the FAO Plan of Action on World Food Security.  Cereal banks at the village level are being established in Burkina Faso and Niger, as well as in mountain areas and in Maseru in Lesotho.  Buffer food stocks have been created in Bangladesh and Bhutan as part of the national food security programmes.  Participation of the public sector in regard to livestock has related principally to livestock marketing (Lesotho, Sudan), the construction of abattoirs (Botswana, Lesotho) and the control and prevention of animal diseases (Afghanistan, Bangladesh, Botswana, Lesotho, Mali, Sudan).  Ministries of livestock were created in Niger in 1985 and in Sudan in May 1986.

57.  Irrigation is an area in which the public sector of LDCs has been particularly active, and action in this regard relates to the construction both of small dams and of major irrigation projects.  In Gambia, the recently completed Jahally Pachaar irrigation project has yielded two rice crops a year, totalling nearly 10,000 tons or about one third of rice imports.  Other multipurpose water development projects are mentioned in section E.  On Environment and Disasters below.

58.  In general, policies in the LDCs have aimed at providing larger volumes of inputs to agriculture (seeds, fertilizers).  The ratio of foodgrain to fertilizer prices has normally been relatively high, and has thus encouraged

the offtake of fertilizers. Shortages of fertilizers have thus emerged in a number of cases. With the gradual phasing out of input subsidies in some LDCs output prices will need to be raised or allowed to rise so as to encourage food production.

59. The governments of LDCs have been actively involved in mobilizing financial resources for agricultural development. Agricultural lending increased significantly in Bangladesh during the past three years (short-term agricultural credit reportedly rose by 77 per cent in FY 1983 and by 66 per cent in FY 1984). A food security fund (fonds national d'autosuffisance alimentaire), amounting to more than CFA 2 billion, was established in Mali in February 1986. A rural development bank is being established in Nepal.

60. Research on drought-resistant seed varieties is being undertaken by Niger's National Institute for Agronomic Research (Institut national de recherches agronomiques) (INRAN) and in Somalia. Seed research and genetic improvement of cattle and poultry are being promoted in Bangladesh. In Afghanistan, 379 laboratory tests of various crops were carried out in 1984/85; and a programme of crop trials was initiated in Botswana in 1985. Livestock and range research is also being undertaken in this country. In Samoa, coconut output is expected to increase after the introduction of a hybrid plant. A National Agricultural Research Co-ordinating Council has been created in Sierra Leone with a view to establishing research priorities and developing a national research plan. The Government of Yemen plans to establish technical agricultural institutes and develop agricultural research. In Gambia, farmers are being trained in techniques designed to reduce post-harvest losses. Programmes to train peasants have been instituted in Ethiopia. In Bhutan, small-scale farmers are being trained to make use of the results of applied research and new technology in agricultural production, and a Centre for Agricultural Research has been established. A stronger public sector involvement in agricultural research in LDCs, however, will require a greater allocation of budgetary funds to the agricultural sector.

5. International initiatives

61. Some recent institutional initiatives at the regional or subregional levels involving LDCs deserve to be mentioned. In March 1985, a fisheries committee (Commission sous-regionale des pêches) was established by Cape Verde, Gambia, Guinea Bissau, Mauritania and Senegal with a view to strengthening co-operation and developing the fisheries sector in that zone. A fisheries association (Société communautaire de pêche) is to be established within the framework of the Economic Community of West Africa by Benin, Burkina Faso, Côte d'Ivoire, Mali, Mauritania, Niger and Senegal, and a ministerial meeting was held in this connection in November 1985.

62. The Twenty-first Summit of Heads of State or Government of the Organization of African Unity, held in July 1985 at Addis Ababa, adopted Africa's Priority Programme for Economic Recovery, 1986-1990 (APPER), whose main objectives include, inter alia, the improvement of the food situation and revitalization of agriculture, the easing of the external debt burden and the formulation of a common platform for action.

63. In January 1986, an appeal known as the Appel de Dakar was launched by the Heads of State or Government of member countries of the Permanent Inter-State Committee on Drought Control in the Sahel (CILSS) requesting donor countries and institutions to provide more support to the efforts being made by the Sahelian governments in agricultural development (CILSS comprises Burkina Faso, Cape Verde, Chad, Gambia, Guinea-Bissau, Mali, Mauritania, Niger and Senegal).

64. In early 1985, FAO, with the support of the governments of the affected countries, prepared and presented to two donors' meetings an Agricultural Rehabilitation Programme for Africa (ARPA), with a total implementation cost of $311 million. The main objective of the Programme is to help to arrest the present trend of declining food production and to lay the foundation for a resumption of the development of the agricultural sector. ARPA covers 25 drought-affected countries, of which 17 are LDCs.

65. A three-year Special Programme for Africa (amounting to $300 million) was approved by IFAD in early 1986 with a view to providing technical assistance for the long-term rehabilitation of agriculture in sub-Saharan Africa. The programme covers 22 countries of which 14 are LDCs.

66. FAO's study on African Agriculture - the next 25 Years was presented to the Regional Conference for Africa at its fourteenth session in September 1986. The study sketched out ways in which the African region could halt the decline in its per capita food production and start to move towards self-sufficiency. The Conference endorsed the study and approved the Director-General's Programme of Action for African Agriculture in which a four-point strategy is outlined including an input aid-in-kind programme on a sustained basis, improvements in producer incentives, institutions and rural infrastructure. Actions are also proposed to accord the highest priority to agriculture, to adopt conservation strategies and to improve the international economic environment.

## B.  Manufacturing

### 1.  Industrial performance

67. A moderate growth of the manufacturing activities in the LDCs was recorded during the period 1980-1984. In that period, the average growth rate of real GDP arising in the manufacturing sector was 2.6 per cent per annum. However, this figure masks wide variations in performance among the individual countries (see table 10).

68. With the exception of Benin, Yemen, Maldives and Gambia, no other country met the SNPA target of a 9 per cent overall annual growth rate for manufacturing output during 1980-1984 (see annex table 5). Countries

Table 10

Real GDP arising in the manufacturing sector in the LDCs

| | Level in dollars per capita 1984 | Share in total GDP 1984 | Annual average growth a/ 1980-1984 |
|---|---|---|---|
| Afghanistan b/ | (59) | (28) | 4.5 |
| Bangladesh | 13 | 9 | 2.2 |
| Benin | 24 | 10 | 24.2 |
| Bhutan | 5 | 4 | .. |
| Botswana | 73 | 7 | 8.2 |
| Burkina Faso | 20 | 15 | 2.8 |
| Burundi | (19) | 9 c/ | 5.7 f/ |
| Cape Verde | 15 | 5 | 4.7 |
| Central African Republic | 19 | 8 | -3.2 |
| Chad | 11 | 9 | -8.1 |
| Comoros | 12 | 6 | 5.0 |
| Democratic Yemen | 49 | 11 | 4.4 g/ |
| Djibouti | 57 | 10 | 0.6 |
| Equatorial Guinea | 11 | 5 | 1.7 |
| Ethiopia | 13 c/ | 11 c/ | 4.1 f/ |
| Gambia | 29 | 10 | 11.2 b/ |
| Guinea | 7 | 2 | 0.6 f/ |
| Guinea-Bissau | (7) | 4 c/ | |
| Haiti | (60) | (17) | -3.1 |
| Lao People's Dem. Rep. b/ | (14) | (7) | 2.2 |
| Lesotho | 14 | 7 | 3.7 |
| Malawi | 21 | 12 | 3.3 |
| Maldives | 22 | 5 | 14.6 |
| Mali | 10 | 7 | .. |
| Nepal | (6) | 4 c/ | .. |
| Niger | 11 | 4 | -1.6 |
| Rwanda | 51 | 18 | 5.5 |
| Samoa | (37) | 6 c/ | 9.4 f/ |
| Sao Tome & Principe | 39 | 10 | -3.3 |
| Sierra Leone | 17 | 6 | -3.1 |
| Somalia | (16) | 6 d/ | -0.8 g/ |
| Sudan | 33 | 9 | 3.3 |
| Togo | 16 | 7 | -5.2 |
| Uganda | (9) | 4 e/ | 3.6 f/ |
| United Rep. of Tanzania | 18 | 7 | -4.7 |
| Vanuatu | .. | .. | .. |
| Yemen | 43 | 9 | 18.2 |
| All LDCs | 18 | 9 | (2.6) h/ |

Source: UNCTAD secretariat calculations based on data from the United Nations Statistical Office, the Economic Commission for Europe, the World Bank and other international and national sources.

a/ Value added at constant prices.
b/ Total industry.
c/ 1983.
d/ 1982.
e/ 1981.
f/ 1980-1983.
g/ 1980-1982.
h/ Excluding Afghanistan, Bhutan, Burundi, Democratic Yemen, Ethiopia, Gambia, Guinea, Guinea-Bissau, Haiti, Lao People's Dem. Rep., Mali, Nepal, Samoa, Somalia, Uganda and Vanuatu.

recording growth rates of 5 per cent and more (besides those mentioned above) were Botswana, Comoros and Rwanda. Negative growth rates were registered for 10 countries, namely, Central African Republic, Chad, Guinea-Bissau, Haiti, Niger, Sao Tome and Principe, Sierra Leone, Somalia, Togo and United Republic of Tanzania. It must of course be borne in mind that industrial statistics of the LDCs do not always convey the full reality as they usually do not cover the small scale, cottage and artisanal sector, which seems to have grown in recent years and often contributes signficantly to supplying the population with manufactured goods.

## 2. Industrial structure

69. The industrial output of the LDCs consists mainly of consumer goods, with light industries playing a dominant role while the share of heavy industry is low. For 15 least-developed countries for which data are available, light industry accounted for an average of 77 per cent of Manufacturing Value Added (MVA) in 1980. 22/ This relationship does not seem to have changed to the advantage of heavy industry, which, being particularly import-dependent, has tended to operate considerably below capacity in recent years. The structure of the LDCs' manufacturing sector is marked by industries based on the processing of their own raw materials and import substitution industries. This is reflected in the high share of food processing and textile production, which together account for 56 per cent of the LDCs total manufacturing output (24 per cent and 32 per cent respectively). Other important consumer goods are beverages and tobacco products, which account for 14 per cent of total manufacturing. Basic industry does not contribute significantly to total output, the production of chemicals accounting for 9 per cent while metal-based engineering and wood products contribute only 6 per cent. Non-ferrous metallic minerals (4 per cent) and others (5 per cent) make up the remainder of the sector.

## 3. Factors influencing recent performance

70. The generally poor performance of manufacturing in the period 1980 to 1984 has both internal and external causes. On the external side, the persistent balance-of-payments deficits of most LDCs in recent years have harmed industrial output, causing severe cuts in imports of essential raw materials and spare parts and preventing the timely replacement of machinery. Apart from their direct impact on industrial operations, the foreign currency shortages have forced many countries to cut back on fuel imports, which has been seriously affecting the operation of their vehicle fleet, the maintenance of which has also been inadequate for lack of spare parts. As a result, raw materials for industrial processing could not be picked up in time in the countryside and the distribution of industrial goods to rural areas was impaired.

71. The severe impact which the scarcity of foreign reserves has had on industrial output reveals the high import dependence of many modern-sector enterprises. For the African countries, including the African LDCs, import contents in the manufacture of a broad range of industrial commodities approach 100 per cent for products of heavy industry. Even in the production of traditional goods like cheese, vegetable oil, flour, refined sugar, footwear and cement the average ratio of imports lies generally above 25 per cent. 23/

72. Prominent among the _internal_ factors that have restricted the growth of the manufacturing sector in 1983 and 1984 was the generally weak performance of agriculture. The lack of rural purchasing power has depressed demand for consumer goods and agricultural inputs particularly in the drought-stricken African countries, while the rural sector has been unable to provide the necessary supplies of raw materials on which agro-based industries depend. That the crisis in agriculture has so strongly affected industrial output suggests that the links between agriculture and manufacturing are particularly important in the LDCs.

73. The pressure of both external and internal factors has aggravated the long-standing problems of the manufacturing sector, problems which are mainly of a structural nature. Together they have resulted in a decline of industrial capacity utilization that has been particularly marked in African LDCs, where it is estimated to lie between 20 per cent and 60 per cent. 24/ With agricultural production picking up, many LDCs are again turning their attention to manufacturing, undertaking a thorough assessment of its deep-seated deficiencies and adopting drastic restructuring policies.

4. Policy initiatives

74. While each country is of course using a different range of instruments and different policy mix in rationalizing industry, several trends are clearly discernible:

- an emphasis on the rehabilitation of existing enterprises rather than on new projects;

- the tendency to divest unprofitable public enterprises, transferring them where possible into private entities or proceeding to liquidation, keeping in the public domain only enterprises of strategic importance or judged less suited to private management;

- measures in the field of fiscal and tax incentives as well as measures to protect domestic industries so as to create more favourable conditions for private business;

- new efforts to attract foreign investments;

- a new thrust on small-scale industry and its spatial distribution.

(a) Divestment of public sector enterprises (PSEs)

75. The generally poor performance of their public and parastatal enterprises has been a growing concern for many LDC Governments in recent years. As such enterprises have traditionally constituted the majority of modern sector

production units in many LDCs, their ineffectiveness weighs heavily on overall industrial performance. One of their more fundamental weaknesses lies in the often less than clear-cut overall objectives for their activities. Unlike private companies whose overriding goal is to make a profit which alone allows them to stay in the market and expand, public sector enterprises operate under guidelines which are more ambivalent. They often have to sell or deliver the goods they produce, for social and/or political reasons, at prices below production costs, to use inputs which are not the most economical and cost-efficient, and to maintain production lines for political or social rather than economic reasons. As a result many of them have been operating with losses that have been a substantial drain on government budgets.

76. To remedy this situation, many Governments have recently introduced programmes for the rationalization of public enterprises, including, where appropriate, selling them partly or wholly to the private sector. Among the LDCs that have initiated such programmes are Bangladesh, Burundi, the Central African Republic, Gambia, Guinea, Nepal, Niger, Sudan, Togo, Uganda, and United Republic of Tanzania.

77. The reorganization of the public sector of industry is a major aspect of Bangladesh's New Industrial Policy (NIP), adopted in June 1982, which constitutes a comprehensive framework of policies endorsing a greater role for the private sector of the economy. Its key objective is to limit the public sector to some very few basic and strategic industries such as telecommunications, air travel, forestry and power generation. In implementing this policy, 110 major public sector units were divested in fiscal year 1983 and 40 in 1985. In addition, 49 per cent of the share capital of some profitable public enterprises, whose control is to be retained in the public sector, is to be offered to the private sector.

78. Burundi's Fourth Development Plan (1983-1987) stipulates, inter alia, the transfer of viable parastatals to the private sector, while those that are unlikely to become profitable in the long run should be liquidated.

79. The Central African Republic has begun since 1980 to rehabilitate its public or mixed enterprises, restricting Government intervention to enterprises considered to be strategic, such as postal and telecommunication services, mining, energy and water resources; to large industrial and agricultural projects, and to areas where private initiative is lacking or insufficient. Several public and mixed enterprises which have been inoperative for some years have been closed or are in the process of being liquidated. The State forestry company, which has not been in operation since 1982, has been sold to a private entrepreneur and the oil and soap-producing company, the textile company and a palm oil company are now being managed by private companies with only minor state participation. Other enterprises such as the transport company (ACCF) and the company in charge of importing and distributing petroleum products (TOGAGES) have signed management contracts with private partners.

80. In the context of its Economic Recovery Programme, the Government of Gambia has announced measures for the privatization and rationalization of some state-owned enterprises and the sale of Government shares of a number of companies. Action has already been initiated for the sale of Government shares in Standard Chartered Bank (Gambia Ltd.), CFAO Gambia Ltd. and Banjul Breweries Ltd. Besides the need to stop the drain on the budget, the Government's decision has been motivated by the desire to provide more

opportunities for entrepreneurial talent. It is also hoped that Gambians who so far have placed their savings in fixed deposits or property, owing to the lack of other areas for investment will now place their funds in company shares.

81. The Government of <u>Guinea</u> has embarked since mid-1985 on a comprehensive restructuring of the industrial sector, consisting essentially of the State's withdrawal from productive sectors and activities which could be performed by private interests and the liquidation of non-performing companies. Also, it has decided that in principle all monopolies should be abolished. In this process, 10 enterprises are being liquidated and a further 17 have had their staffs reduced while a systematic search is under way for private partners, Guinean or foreign. If no partners are found they too will be liquidated. Private partners are also actively being sought for 11 firms which seem to offer good immediate prospects for privatization. As a result of these far-reaching reforms, it is to be expected that by the end of 1987 only a handful of enterprises - mainly public utilities - will remain in the Government portfolio.

82. <u>Niger</u> is envisaging "radical reforms" in its industrial structure. In this context, the Government is contemplating giving more weight to the private sector of the economy, to privatize many PSEs, and to leave to the State only the concern for the infrastructure. In July 1985, the Government initiated action on public and para-public enterprises which will either undergo a rehabilitation, be privatized or, if no buyers can be found, liquidated. For those enterprises remaining in the public domain, the management will be strengthened and a programme of technical assistance instituted.

83. Between 1983 and 1985, the Government of <u>Togo</u> has been undertaking an industrial restructuring programme whose key objectives include the selective withdrawal of the State from the industrial sector. The Government has leased the steel mill and oil refinery to foreign interests and undertaken the privatization of about 10 State enterprises already closed or working at reduced capacity, offering them either as associations, or for lease to domestic or foreign private interests. At a second stage, a further 10 enterprises are being selected for sale or for restructuring before being offered for sale. Those enterprises which will remain in the public sector are the electricity and water companies, the Port Autonome de Lomé, the Office Togolais des Phosphates and the agricultural marketing board.

84. In the framework of the Revised Recovery Programme published in October 1983, the Government of <u>Uganda</u> started to reduce its participation in industry by closing a number of industrial parastatal enterprises or transferring them to the private sector. The process of returning enterprises which had been nationalized in the Amin era to private hands had begun, but problems of ownership restoration have slowed down its effective implementation. The new Government will continue the above policies.

85. Several other LDCs, including <u>Nepal</u>, <u>Somalia</u>, <u>Sudan</u> and <u>United Republic of Tanzania</u>, have also taken concrete steps to streamline their public sector enterprises, including privatization.

(b) <u>Improving the economic environment for private sector industrial
activities</u>

86. Governments of the LDCs have been aware that the transformation of public
into private enterprises is no remedy in itself for industrial inefficiency.
In addition to rehabilitation measures at the enterprise level, a number of
LDCs have adopted new policies with the purpose of making industrial activity
more profitable, and of attracting private domestic and foreign investment and
entrepreneurial talent to manufacturing. The measures taken are numerous:
they range from tax incentives and more liberal depreciation allowances for
new enterprises to export promotion policies and import liberalization in the
form of reduced import duties on raw materials, machinery, spare parts and
tools. Enterprises producing essential goods have also received foreign
currency allowances on a priority basis. Some countries have resorted to
protectionist measures for their domestic industries, raising import tariffs
or introducing quantitative import restrictions. In addition, some countries
have provided advantages to foreign investors, particularly in the form of
guarantees for the repatriation of profits, dividends, interest payments etc.

87. The new industrial policy of <u>Bangladesh</u> includes investment and export
incentives, import liberalization measures and tax reductions for industrial
inputs and machinery, as well as improvements in industrial finance. Foreign
investment is encouraged by the Five-Year Plan 1981-85. Already in 1981,
investment protection and double taxation prevention agreements had been
concluded with EEC countries.

88. The new Investment Code adopted in 1984 by <u>Burkina Faso</u> provides a number
of benefits to industrial enterprises such as customs exonerations and tax
advantages. The Investment Code of <u>Guinea</u>, introduced in the same year,
guarantees equal conditions for all investors, regardless of nationality,
including property rights and access to the public market, protection against
nationalization or expropriation, and repatriation of earnings. Also since
that year, <u>Ethiopia</u> has removed all restrictions on profit repatriation and
allows majority foreign participation in industrial enterprises.

89. Under the new Industrial Policy of <u>Nepal</u> that was introduced in 1981, all
industries, except those connected with defense, were opened to private
ownership and investment. A variety of fiscal concessions and incentives has
been offered to attract private investment. Virtually every sector of the
economy open to private is also open to foreign investment, with the exception
of cottage and small-scale enterprises. Foreign investors receive advantages
regarding the repatriation of profits, dividends, interest payments, fees and
royalties.

90. In the context of reforming the country's industrial structure, the
Government of <u>Niger</u> has, <u>inter alia</u>, been envisaging the promotion of new laws
for the protection of private investments.

91. The Government of <u>Togo</u> has made a detailed study of appropriate policy
instruments for improving conditions for private investment such as customs,
taxes, trade and transport measures, price, credit and labour policies,
improvements in infrastructure and services and the provision of direct
incentive measures. Since April 1986 the industrial sector benefits from a

special tax system consisting of the abolition of all exit duties and taxes on industrial products and a reduction of fiscal entry duties by 75 per cent on unprocessed and semi-processed commodities, and by 50 per cent on processed goods.

(c)  Policies in support of small-scale enterprises

92.  An important issue in many recent Government programmes is support for small-scale enterprises (SSEs) which is often connected with policies aimed at greater industrial decentralization.

93.  The renewed emphasis on SSEs comes, inter alia, from the realization that they are less import-dependent than the larger enterprises of the modern sector.  This has given them a greater resilience to the foreign currency shortages of recent years which have severely affected operations of many large-scale enterprises.  By using domestic agricultural inputs for their production, the SSEs are also strengthening the country's self-reliance and self-sufficiency, a declared overall goal of many LDCs.  Their capital requirements are modest and by using more labour-intensive production methods employment creation per unit of capital invested is substantially higher than in large-scale enterprises.  Being less dependent than very large companies on a sophisticated infrastructure, SSEs are usually better equipped to operate in rural areas, thus enforcing links between agriculture and industry, contributing to the development of rural areas and helping to stem rural exodus.

94.  But while the great potential contribution of SSEs to a more self-reliant development has long been recognized, explicit policies to support them have often been lacking or weak.  In many LDCs, SSEs have developed without special assistance or preferential treatment, and often despite Government policies which have put them at a disadvantage relative to modern sector industrial enterprises.  The failure of many Governments "to mobilize fully the latent capacity of their small-scale producers" has recently been identified by the UNIDO Director-General as the single most important problem in industrial policies of developing countries. 25/  The reassessment of the manufacturing sector which is taking place in many LDCs has placed the benefits to be gained from a prospering SSE sector into proper perspective, as a result of which many LDCs have included improved support measures for SSEs into their industrial policy packages.

95.  In Bangladesh existing promotional activities for SSEs are being strengthened and credit facilities extended to meet the shortage of working capital of these firms.  In Burkina Faso's 1984 Investment Code new enterprises engaged in priority fields receive additional benefits when they are decentralized, i.e. being established at least 50 kilometres away from the four most important urban agglomerations of Ougadougou, Bobo-Dioulasso, Koudougou and Banfora.  Within the Ethiopian industrial strategy laid down in the ten-year Perspective Plan (1984/85-1993/94), the development of small-scale industries has an important place.  The promotion of cottage and small-scale industries also plays a key role in Nepal's medium-term adjustment programme, in the context of which the Government has facilitated the obtainment of licenses and registration of enterprises at the district level. Several other LDCs, including Bhutan, Rwanda and Togo, have either taken steps for the promotion of SSEs or are in the process of doing so.

96. It is particularly in African LDCs, where concern over declining rates of industrial capacity utilization has been mounting, that a new evaluation of SSEs is beginning to take place. This is reflected in the first African symposium on SSEs which took place in June 1986 in Morocco, organized jointly by the Association of African Development Finance Institutions (AADFI) and the World Assembly of Small and Medium-scale Enterprises (WASME). It brought together representatives of public and governmental agencies responsible for the promotion of SSEs from many African countries as well as representatives of a number of United Nations agencies and development banks. One of its results, the list of recommendations referred to as the Rabat Action Programme, calls for a number of policy measures to support and strengthen SSEs, including improved access to domestic savings, public contracts and appropriate technology, encouragement of entrepreneurial initiative and subcontracting activities, and elimination of legal and administrative obstacles in the economic environment hampering the activities of SSEs.

(d) Programmes for African LDCs

97. It is indeed in African LDCs that the need for industrial initiatives has been felt most acutely. In an effort to restore its industrial growth potential the Industrial Development Decade for Africa, covering 1980-1990, was launched by the General Assembly with the aim of speeding up the industrialization of the continent within the framework of the Lagos Plan of Action. The basic goal of the decade's strategy is to encourage an industrialization that sets in motion a process of internally-generated, self-sustained growth through an integrated development strategy which links industry with other vital sectors of the economy. The Programme reinforces the concepts of a self-reliant development and self-sustained industrialization that are presented in the Lagos Plan of Action. As the Director-General of UNIDO has pointed out, "implicit in the Decade Programme is a new approach to industrial planning which advocates a shift from excessive preoccupation with foreign exchange scarcity to the development of the capacity to assess and utilize each country's natural resources and its raw material endowment for the benefit of its people." 26/ The implementation of this Plan will greatly enhance the development prospects of African LDCs.

98. Another major initiative for African regional development comes from the Southern African Development Co-ordination Conference (SADCC) which announced, during the first half of 1985, an action programme with the aim of enhancing self-sufficiency for its eight member States, among which figure Botswana, Lesotho, Malawi and United Republic of Tanzania. The programme outlines 50 principal projects which together would require total investments of $US 860 million, placing major emphasis on such core industries as iron and steel, metallurgical and engineering, and petrochemical and natural gas. A formal joint five-year industrial development plan for the entire subregion will be launched in 1986. Besides efforts to raise external funding to establish new enterprises in core sectors, the SADCC action programme proposes to rehabilitate existing industries, upgrade investment policies and mechanisms and develop small-scale industry utilizing appropriate technology.

5. Conclusions

99. The unsatisfactory performance of manufacturing since the end of the 1970s has halted and in some cases even reversed the progress in industrial development achieved by a number of LDCs in the 1960s and early 1970s. A veritable de-industrialization process has in fact been taking place in many LDCs, so that for them the issue has been less that of expanding industrial capacity than of trying to maintain what has already been achieved. To put manufacturing back on a sound basis, many LDCs are today engaged in a fundamental restructuring process which often challenges the basic concepts on which their early industrialization was based. In this process, countries are de-emphasizing the establishment of ambitious large-scale industrial projects in favour of "medium and light industries to meet the growing needs of their population for essential consumer goods", as is stipulated by the relevant provisions of the SNPA. At the same time many LDCs are making efforts to implement the Programme's recommendations of encouraging and improving productivity in small-scale and cottage industries. Although the results of these far-reaching reforms will manifest themselves in the long term rather than the short term, it can be expected that they will contribute decisively to restoring the growth potential of this vital sector of the LDCs' economy.

C. Energy

1. Current levels of energy consumption

100. Per capita consumption of energy is low in the majority of the least developed countries. It varies from 78 kg of coal equivalent per year in Burundi to 883 kg in Sierra Leone, with an average for the LDCs of 313 kg as compared to 669 kg in the developing countries as a whole (1981).

2. Traditional sources of energy

101. Fuelwood, charcoal and bagasse provide the bulk of energy consumption in LDCs: around 80 per cent as compared to 26 per cent in the developing countries as a whole (see Table 11). Other traditional sources of energy (which are not included in the above figures) relate to animal power and crop residues.

102. The foreign exchange constraints faced by the LDCs, coupled with the rise in oil prices which took place since 1973 and continued until late 1984, have prevented many LDCs from reducing significantly the use of fuelwood and charcoal, a phenomenon which has had three major consequences: a tendency towards the depletion of these resources, the degradation of the ecosystem, and the weakening of the agricultural potential. 27/ Virtually all LDCs are facing current fuelwood deficits or prospective deficits in relation to demand by the year 2000, while deforestation has been aggravated by increased use of wood for energy purposes. The annual consumption of fuelwood reportedly corresponds to more than twice the sustainable yield in United Republic of Tanzania and more than 130 per cent in the case of Malawi. 28/ In Cape Verde, where forestry resources are practically non-existent, wood shortages are compensated for by the extensive use of animal droppings as a source of fuel but this pattern inhibits the use of such droppings as a natural fertilizer. 29/

Table 11: Share of fuelwood, charcoal and bagasse
in total energy consumption in LDCs
(in percentages)

| LDC | 1981 | 1984 |
|-----|------|------|
| Afghanistan | 64.3 | 58.9 |
| Bangladesh | 67.5 | 63.7 |
| Benin | 87.3 | 88.7 |
| Bhutan | 98.5 | 98.4 |
| Botswana | .. | .. |
| Burkina Faso | 90.9 | 91.4 |
| Burundi | 93.3 | 93.8 |
| Cape Verde | .. | .. |
| Central African Republic | 90.7 | 90.3 |
| Chad | 90.3 | 90.8 |
| Comoros | .. | .. |
| Democratic Yemen | 6.9 | 4.9 |
| Djibouti | .. | .. |
| Equatorial Guinea | 82.7 | 81.0 |
| Ethiopia | 92.9 | 93.3 |
| Gambia | 80.1 | 75.7 |
| Guinea | 71.5 | 70.9 |
| Guinea-Bissau | 80.1 | 79.2 |
| Haiti | 83.9 | 84.7 |
| Lao PDR | 90.6 | 92.5 |
| Lesotho | .. | .. |
| Malawi | 86.1 | 88.2 |
| Maldives | .. | .. |
| Mali | 86.9 | 86.4 |
| Nepal | 94.9 | 94.9 |
| Niger | 78.7 | 78.0 |
| Rwanda | 89.9 | 89.7 |
| Samoa | 33.8 | 31.7 |
| Sao Tome & Principe | .. | .. |
| Sierra Leone | 88.1 | 91.4 |
| Somalia | 75.0 | 76.5 |
| Sudan | 76.8 | 78.8 |
| Togo | 51.2 | 48.5 |
| Uganda | 90.9 | 90.8 |
| United Republic of Tanzania | 87.7 | 88.5 |
| Vanuatu | 24.2 | 23.5 |
| Yemen | .. | .. |
| | | |
| All LDCs | 80.8 | 79.3 |
| | | |
| All developing countries | 26.5 | 26.2 |

Source: UNCTAD secretariat estimates based on information from
United Nations, Energy Statistics Yearbook, 1984.

## 3. Oil production and exploration

103. A number of LDCs have embarked upon or promoted oil exploration and/or energy diversification as a means of preserving ecological balance and reducing dependence on imported oil. Oil production has been underway in Afghanistan (where reserves are conservatively estimated at 100 million barrels), and started in Benin (November 1982) and in Yemen (April 1986). Oil exploration has been encouraged or is currently underway in a number of LDCs. 30/ In this connection, agreements for oil exploration have been entered into by many of these LDCs with foreign companies and/or States. The actual or likely existence of oil has already been identified in Chad, Guinea, Guinea Bissau, Mali, Nepal, Niger and Sudan (where production was scheduled to start in 1986/87 but had to be delayed for security reasons). Proved and probable reserves in Sudan amount to approximately 150 million and 66 million barrels respectively.

## 4. Alternative sources of energy

104. Action has likewise been taken to develop alternative sources of energy which include natural gas, coal, methane gas, ethanol, renewable energy sources and hydroelectric power. Natural gas is available in: Afghanistan (reserves are estimated at 150 billion $m^3$ and annual output in 1984/85 at 2.8 billion $m^3$); Bangladesh (reserves are estimated at 10 trillion cubic feet - (283 billion cubic meters); Equatorial Guinea (where an offshore gas find was announced in 1984); Somalia (where production is being considered with financial support from the World Bank); and United Republic of Tanzania (where a fertilizer plant using gas as a feedstock is being planned). Rwanda is known to possess methane gas jointly with Zaire. Natural gas contributes 50 per cent of export earnings of Afghanistan. The share of natural gas in the total consumption of electricity in Bangladesh is estimated at 63 per cent in 1985. Significant coal reserves have been identified in Botswana (total proven reserves estimated at 17 billion tons), Malawi (800 million tons) and the United Republic of Tanzania (360 million tons). Major progress has reportedly been made in Botswana in substituting coal for imported oil, and a new 90 MW coal-fired power station is due for completion in 1986. New coal mines are being opened in Malawi and United Republic of Tanzania. Reserves of coal have been discovered in Niger.

105. New and renewable energy sources relate to solar energy, wind, geothermal energy, utilization of biomass for producing gas, ethanol and methanol, and recycling of crop residues. The potential of solar energy in LDCs is great as many of these countries have high levels of solar radiation. Solar energy has been promoted in Botswana: 402 solar water heaters have been installed, and solar electricity was tested in a number of clinics, health posts and schools with a view to ascertaining the suitability for widespread use in public buildings in rural areas. Tests of solar power units have been made in Djibouti and Mali. Ethanol (which can be added to gasoline) is produced in Malawi. Two projects on solar energy and wind power are being implemented in the SADCC region. A programme for the utilization of renewable energy resources in West Africa has been proposed by the ECOWAS Centre régional de l'energie solaire. A four-year pilot project aims at the installation of wind turbines in Cape Verde, where a study has also begun on the feasibility

of making use of the energy of the ocean's waves.    Under consideration is the feasibility of building a factory in Mali for the production of solar energy equipment and materials, including solar pumps and cooking stoves. 31/ Similarly, a project has been developed in Bangladesh for the development of new and renewable sources of energy and concentrates on the production and distribution of bio-gas plants, solar cookers, and research on various new sources of energy such as sunlight, wind and mini-hydro.    Briquettes for cooking stoves are made from groundnut waste in Gambia.

## 5. Hydroelectric power

106. Action in LDCs has been intensified in regard to development of hydroelectric power, most of which remains under-exploited.   While unit costs of hydroelectric schemes may be initially higher than those of thermal power, such costs tend to decline in the medium and long term as hydroelectric schemes have a longer lifetime and smaller maintenance cost than thermal power units.    Countries with significant hydroelectric potential include Bhutan (potential estimated at 6,000-8,000 MW), Burkina Faso, Burundi, Ethiopia (where only 2 per cent of total capacity of 12,000 MW is tapped), Guinea, Lao PDR (potential estimated at 18,000-20,000 MW compared with current installed capacity of 150 MW), Lesotho, Malawi (1,000 MW), Mali, Nepal (potential estimated at 25,000-30,000 MW, of which less than 1 per cent is currently utilized), Rwanda, Samoa, Uganda (with a potential estimated at about 2,000 MW and installed capacity at 150 MW - which is sufficient to meet present needs and export 30 MW to Kenya), and United Republic of Tanzania.    The share of hydroelectric power in current total production of electricity is particularly high (more than 80 per cent) in Bhutan, Central African Republic, Lao PDR, Malawi, Rwanda and Uganda (see table 12).

107. Many of the hydroelectric power projects relate to complex, large-scale endeavours (of which hydro electric power development is one of the various components), and this is the case inter alia of dams being constructed at Kompienga, Grand-Bagré and Noumbiel (Burkina Faso), Rwegura (Burundi), Konkouré (Guinea), Manantali (Mali), Bumbuna (Sierra Leone), Badhera (Somalia), and the Lesotho Highlands Water Project.    In Samoa, the production of electricity from hydro-sources more than trebled between 1980 and 1984, owing in particular to the completion of two hydro electric projects. Another major hydro-project is being completed in that country.    In Bhutan, the Chukha hydro-project (336 MW) is due for completion in 1986 and will permit export of energy to neighbouring countries.    An integrated river development scheme involving electricity production has been proposed by the Liptako-Gourma Regional Authority (which comprises Burkina Faso, Mali and Niger).    A hydroelectric power plant is being established at Ruzizi under a project developed jointly by Burundi, Rwanda and Zaire within the framework of CEPGL.    A joint hydroelectric project (62 MW) on the Mono river is being implemented by Benin and Togo.

108. Growing interest is being shown in the promotion of small hydroelectric schemes.   The advantages of small-scale projects are related to short implementation periods, small investment requirements and exploitation costs, and the possibility of involving local enterprises and manpower.   Small hydropower stations can often be erected on existing dams also being used for

Table 12: Production, trade and consumption of electricity in LDCs
(1984)
(Quantities in millions of kilowatt hours and in kilowatt hours per capita)

| LDC | Production | Imports | Exports | Consumption | | Share in production (%) | |
|---|---|---|---|---|---|---|---|
| | | | | Total | Per cap | Thermal | Hydro |
| Afghanistan | 1 045 | .. | .. | 1 045 | 73 | 26.8 | 73.2 |
| Bangladesh | 4 292 | .. | .. | 4 292 | 44 | 79.1 | 20.9 |
| Benin | 5 | 185 | .. | 190 | 49 | 100.0 | .. |
| Bhutan | 30 | 6 | .. | 36 | 26 | 70.0 | 30.0 |
| Botswana | .. | .. | .. | .. | .. | .. | .. |
| Burkina Faso | 115 | 0 | .. | 115 | 17 | 100.0 | .. |
| Burundi | 2 | 145 | .. | 147 | 33 | 100.0 | .. |
| Cape Verde | 25 | .. | .. | 25 | 79 | 100.0 | .. |
| Central African Rep. | 68 | .. | .. | 68 | 27 | 4.4 | 95.6 |
| Chad | 65 | .. | .. | 65 | 13 | 100.0 | .. |
| Comoros | 10 | .. | .. | 10 | 23 | 100.0 | .. |
| Democratic Yemen | 280 | .. | .. | 280 | 136 | 100.0 | .. |
| Djibouti | 148 | .. | .. | 148 | 418 | 100.0 | .. |
| Equatorial Guinea | 15 | .. | .. | 15 | 39 | 86.7 | 13.3 |
| Ethiopia | 760 | .. | .. | 760 | 21 | 25.0 | 75.0 |
| Gambia | 42 | .. | .. | 42 | 67 | 100.0 | .. |
| Guinea | 499 | .. | .. | 499 | 94 | 84.0 | 16.0 |
| Guinea-Bissau | 14 | .. | .. | 14 | 16 | 100.0 | .. |
| Haiti | 375 | .. | .. | 375 | 58 | 30.7 | 69.3 |
| Lao PDR | 990 | 30 | 690 | 330 | 76 | 4.0 | 96.0 |
| Lesotho | .. | .. | .. | .. | .. | .. | .. |
| Malawi | 511 | .. | 1 | 510 | 75 | 5.3 | 94.7 |
| Maldives | 11 | .. | .. | 11 | 64 | 100.0 | .. |
| Mali | 153 | .. | .. | 153 | 20 | 21.6 | 78.4 |
| Nepal | 350 | 80 | 6 | 424 | 26 | 10.0 | 90.0 |
| Niger | 245 | 130 | .. | 375 | 63 | 100.0 | .. |
| Rwanda | 135 | 15 | 0 | 150 | 25 | .. | 100.0 |
| Samoa | 41 | .. | .. | 41 | 252 | 61.0 | 39.0 |
| Sao Tome & Principe | 15 | .. | .. | 15 | 160 | 46.7 | 53.3 |
| Sierra Leone | 280 | .. | .. | 280 | 79 | 100.0 | .. |
| Somalia | 75 | .. | .. | 75 | 14 | 100.0 | .. |
| Sudan | 1 032 | .. | .. | 1 032 | 49 | 50.4 | 49.6 |
| Togo | 234 | 149 | .. | 383 | 135 | 63.7 | 36.3 |
| Uganda | 655 | .. | 215 | 440 | 29 | 1.2 | 98.8 |
| United Republic of Tanzania | 870 | .. | .. | 870 | 40 | 29.3 | 70.7 |
| Vanuatu | 24 | .. | .. | 24 | 176 | 100.0 | .. |
| Yemen | 295 | .. | .. | 295 | 46 | 100.0 | .. |
| All LDCs | 13 706 | 740 | 912 | 13 534 | 43 | 52.3 | 47.7 |
| All developing countries | 1 219 946 | 11 108 | 11 060 | 1 219 994 | 491 | 56.2 | 38.9 |

Source: UNCTAD secretariat estimates based on information from
United Nations, Energy Statistics Yearbook, 1984.

other purposes such as irrigation and supply of drinking water. Countries
where small hydroelectric schemes are being implemented or under consideration
include Benin, Burkina Faso, Equatorial Guinea, Ethiopia, Guinea, Lesotho,
Mali, Rwanda, Sudan, Togo and the United Republic of Tanzania.

## 6. Other electricity

109. Electricity production remains mostly thermal in the majority of LDCs
(60 per cent or more in 22 out of 34 LDCs - cf. table 12). The economical use
of such energy is in some cases undermined by low, subsidized power tariffs.
A programme to reduce power loss in Bangladesh includes improvement in power
factor, improvement of distribution system, and introduction of computerized
billing system in Dakha and other major cities. In addition, industrial and
high tension meters are being checked, calibrated and replaced as required.
The Sudan, Uganda and the United Republic of Tanzania have embarked on
integrated electric development programmes which include the rehabilitation of
existing capacities. The rehabilitation of central power stations is also
being carried out in other LDCs.

## 7. Implications of the fall in international oil prices

110. The single most important development in regard to energy relates to the
sharp fall in the international prices for oil which has taken place since
late 1984. The fall in oil prices is certainly likely to bring about some
relief in the foreign exchange expenditure of these countries. This should
not lead, however, to the conclusion that the net effects for the LDCs of the
decline in oil prices will be unambiguously positive. In the first place, the
current sharp decline in oil prices is bound to render unattractive many oil
exploration as well as energy diversification projects which were initiated in
the LDCs at the time of high oil prices: the opportunity costs of such
projects will be considerably higher under the new oil prices. The tendency
towards stronger dependence on imported oil may therefore acquire momentum.
Secondly, the decline in the foreign exchange earnings of oil-producing
countries will probably have depressing effects upon imports from, and
migrants' remittances to, LDCs. Some LDCs are already facing the need to
reabsorb returning labourers. Thirdly, many LDCs have been among the major
beneficiaries of financial assistance provided by oil-producing countries, an
assistance whose magnitude is likely to be curtailed in view of the sharp
decline in the export revenue of the latter countries.

## D. Transport and Communications

111. The structural weaknesses in the least-developed countries are
exacerbated by the very weak and inefficient transport and communications
system existing in these countries. Inadequate internal transport and
communications services have also been a major factor in limiting the
establishment of vital contacts between administrative centres and the rural
areas. A large majority of the rural population thus continues to be isolated
from the economic activities in the modern sector. Furthermore, the
initiatives of the governments in the LDCs to promote rural social development
programmes through literacy and public health campaigns are seriously
inhibited by poor communication services.

112. Over the past 15 years several LDCs have, however, undertaken major steps towards planning, building and operating transport facilities in conformity with national, regional and sub-regional needs. The LDCs' governments have been giving very high priority and allocating substantial outlays in their plans for the development of these sectors. For example, Nepal spent 16 and 14 per cent of its public expenditures on the development of transportation in the fiscal years 1983/84 and 1984/85 respectively. During the period 1982/83-1984/85, Sudan allocated about 18 per cent of its development expenditures to the transport and communication sectors. Bhutan, Democratic Yemen and Uganda have allocated one fifth of plan outlays to this sector.

113. At the regional level the regional economic commissions have also attempted to make a useful contribution. These efforts have resulted in regional highway proposals (such as the Pan-American, Trans-Asian and Trans-African highways) and have led to the proclamation of a Transport and Communications Decade for Africa in 1977 and for Asia and the Pacific in 1984. 32/ These efforts will certainly be of benefit to the least-developed countries of Africa and of Asia and the Pacific in the long run. However, so far their impact has been marginal.

1. Transport

114. The LDCs have a very underdeveloped transport sector. Roads are very few and of very poor technical standard. The road interlinkages are inadequate to permit easy cross-country access. The railway network is also very underdeveloped. The air services, which are limited to the main commercial and administrative centres, are generally irregular and passenger/cargo traffic by air is on average quite insignificant.

2. Roads

115. The data available for 18 LDCs indicate that, about the beginning of the decade, most of these countries had in every case less than 3,000 km of paved roads on average (see table 13). The greater part of the road network consists of unpaved roads on which traffic is necessarily intermittent, and which become disrupted and unusable during the rainy season. Progress in the development of roads continues to be extremely slow. Only a few of the countries for which data are available made improvements of any significance in expanding the length of their paved roads. For example, between the end of the 1970s and the first four years of the current decade, the length of paved roads in Burundi increased by about 2.6 times. During this period the length of paved roads rose by about 2.5 times for Guinea; 2.0 times for Yemen; 1.8 times for Lesotho; 1.7 times for Democratic Yemen and 1.6 times for Rwanda. For all the other countries the increase of paved roads during the five-year period 1979-1983 was quite marginal. Another indicator of the inadequacy of the road network in the LDCs is the low road density. Towards the end of the 1970s only seven countries for which data are available had a road density above 0.1 km per km$^2$. By about 1983 12 countries had a road density above that figure, but Samoa was the only one to have a road density of about 0.7 km per km$^2$. This extremely low level of development in the road sector is all the more evident if it is compared with the road density in other countries. In the United States of America and Brazil, for example, the road density is about 0.7 and 0.2 km per km$^2$ respectively. The limited road

Table 13: The road network in selected LDCs

| Country | Total road network (km) 1979 | Total road network (km) 1983 | of which: paved road (km) 1979 | of which: paved road (km) 1983 | Area ('000 km²) | Density of road network (km per '000 km²) 1979 | Density of road network (km per '000 km²) 1983 |
|---|---|---|---|---|---|---|---|
| Afghanistan | 18,790 | 18,852g/ | 2,784 | 2,846g/ | 647.5 | 29.0 | 29.1g/ |
| Bangladesh | 4,831 | 7,556 | 4,197 | 4,788 | 144.0 | 33.5 | 52.5 |
| Botswana | 8,026 | 8,026 | 963 | 1,200b/ | 600.4 | 13.4 | 13.4 |
| Burkina Faso | .. | 11,211 | .. | 1,760 | 274.2 | .. | 40.9 |
| Burundi | 5,410 | 5,400a/ | 280 | 744a/ | 27.8 | 194.6 | 194.2a/ |
| Cape Verde | .. | 2,250c/ | .. | 660c/ | 4.0 | .. | 562.5c/ |
| Central African Rep. | 22,560 | 22,560 | 374 | 451 | 623.0 | 36.2 | 36.2 |
| Chad | .. | 31,000b/h/ | .. | 253b/ | 1,284.0 | .. | 24.1b/ |
| Democratic Yemen | .. | .. | 982f/ | 1,650 | 333.0 | .. | .. |
| Djibouti | 2,000d/ | 2,795e/ | 200d/ | 300e/ | 22.0 | 90.9d/ | 127.0e/ |
| Equatorial Guinea | .. | 1,175c/ | .. | .. | 28.1 | .. | 41.8c/ |
| Ethiopia | 37,291 | 37,506 | 10,441 | 12,377 | 1,221.9 | 30.5 | 30.7 |
| Gambia | 3,083c/ | 3,083 | 462c/ | 462 | 11.3 | 272.8c/ | 272.8 |
| Guinea | 28,400f/ | 28,400c/ | 520f/ | 1,300c/ | 245.9 | 115.5f/ | 115.5c/ |
| Guinea-Bissau | .. | 3,100b/ | .. | 560b/ | 36.1 | .. | 85.9b/ |
| Haiti | .. | 3,000i/ | .. | 600i/ | 27.8 | .. | 107.9i/ |
| Lesotho | 4,000 | 4,085 | 250 | 458 | 30.4 | 131.6 | 134.4 |
| Malawi | 10,557 | 11,469a/ | 1,795 | 2,166a/ | 118.5 | 89.1 | 96.8a/ |
| Mali | .. | 18,000c/ | .. | 1,500c/ | 1,240.0 | .. | 14.5c/ |
| Nepal | 4,595 | 5,122c/ | 1,890 | 2,151c/ | 140.8 | 32.6 | 36.4c/ |
| Niger | .. | 19,000 | .. | 3,230 | 1,267.0 | .. | 15.0 |
| Rwanda | 6,580 | 6,820 | 342 | 539 | 26.3 | 250.2 | 259.3 |
| Samoa | 2,042 | 2,085e/ | 208 | 299e/ | 2.8 | 729.3 | 744.6e/ |
| Sao Tome and Principe | .. | 380b/ | .. | 250b/ | 1.0 | .. | 380.0b/ |
| Somalia | 21,244g/ | 21,311a/ | 2,310g/ | 2,585a/ | 637.7 | 33.3g/ | 33.4a/ |
| Sudan | .. | 19,110c/ | .. | 1,020c/ | 2,505.8 | .. | 7.6c/ |
| Togo | 6,999 | 7,000 | 2,437 | 2,415 | 56.8 | 123.2 | 123.2 |
| Uganda | .. | 27,000b/ | .. | 1,800b/ | 236.0 | .. | 114.4b/ |
| United Rep. of Tanzania | 45,351 | 53,613e/ | 3,220 | 3,379g/ | 945.1 | 48.0 | 56.7e/ |
| Yemen | 1,943 | 3,248a/ | 1,147 | 2,241a/ | 195.0 | 10.0 | 16.7a/ |

Source: ESCAP, Statistical Yearbook for Asia and the Pacific 1984; IRF, World Transport Data 1985; IRU, World Road Statistics 1979-1983; IRF, World Road Statistics 1979-1983; EIU, Annual Supplement 1984 and 1985; ECA, Review of Economic and Social Conditions in African Least Developed Countries 1984-1985 and National sources.

a/ 1984.  b/ Year between 1980 and 1985.  c/ 1981.  d/ 1977.  e/ 1982.  f/ 1978.  g/ 1980.
h/ There are 7,000 km of laterite roads and 24,000 km of dirt tracks.  i/ 1985.

network has been accompanied by the slow growth in the number of motor vehicles in virtually all the LDCs.  On average, the ratio of commercial vehicles in use in 23 LDCs was about 1.2 per 1,000 inhabitants in 1981 as compared to 6.2 for all developing countries.

116. Although many LDCs have been giving very high priority to road building and maintenance, several of them have, as a matter of policy, opted to build roads and bridges with low to medium axle and wheel weight limits in the interest of spreading available funds over more kilometres of road.  The lack of clear-cut rules and regulations for the circulation of vehicles, including all their technical features, such as weight, wheel and axle spacing, turning radius and braking capacity, has led to a situation in which the vehicles in use are not technically adapted to the road conditions.  The result is often rapid physical deterioration of the vehicles and bridge collapses.  It is of crucial importance that these rules and regulations should be established and strictly implemented at both national and sub-regional levels.

3.  Railways

117. The rail network in the LDCs is very rudimentary and in many cases it is linked to the hinterland through road services only.  This necessitates transshipment en route, which leads to delays and damage to cargo.  The data available for 14 LDCs indicate that, during the early 1980s, 11 of these countries had less than 1,000 km of rail.  Only Sudan, Uganda and the United Republic of Tanzania had rail routes of 4,800 km, 1,100 km and 2,500 km respectively.  In 1983 Bangladesh also had only about 2,900 km of rail.  The development of the rail network in recent years has been very marginal in virtually all the LDCs.

118. The scarcity of appropriate skills compounded by unsatisfactory maintenance of the railway infrastructure and equipment, sub-optimal wagon turnaround cycle times, the inadequacy of locomotive power and rolling stock and poor marshalling facilities have reduced the efficiency of rail transport considerably.  Seasonal imbalances in traffic have also led to a rise in operating costs.  Moreover, some of the railways are utilized for social purposes without regard for the economic consequences, and do not offer direct services to the small farmer or businessman located along their routes.  The cost of railway transport, which essentially provides services for long-haul operations, is, however, normally lower than on the existing roads given adequate concentrated traffic volume.  The LDCs should therefore make efforts to ensure that railways become commercially viable and, where feasible, further develop this mode of transport.  Efforts to improve railway operations should include working out more effective bilateral and subregional arrangements for linking railways with the neighbouring countries.  Such arrangements could make railways more efficient and economically viable.

4.  Air services

119. Although most of the LDCs have invested in the development of air transport infrastructure, not all of them have fully equipped international airports.  In most airports, the loading or unloading of aircraft and the movement of freight between aircraft and cargo sheds are not mechanized.  This leads to high operating costs.  Most of the airlines operating in the LDCs

also incur high operational costs because of the management inefficiency and the limited cargo and passenger traffic. Efforts to upgrade airport physical facilities to internationally accepted standards have recently been made in such countries as Botswana, Lesotho, Malawi, Rwanda, Burkina Faso, Chad and Sao Tome and Principe. The data for 18 LDCs indicate that the number of passengers carried on international scheduled services increased from 2 million in 1975 to 2.1 million in 1982 as compared to 28.9 million in 1975 and 57.7 million in 1982 for all developing countries. The highest increases during this period were recorded for Yemen (5 times), Guinea (4 times) and Somalia (4 times). For 10 of the LDCs the increase was only 1 to 2.5 times. In fact, the United Republic of Tanzania, Uganda, Afghanistan and Malawi recorded declines in international passenger traffic. Greater efforts are needed to streamline national air transport operations and ultimately to reduce the rates for services rendered. This could not only stimulate greater passenger traffic but also promote the development of crops and products which can be exported by air and thus enhance the profitability of air operations.

## 5. Communications

120. The communication services in the LDCs are very inadequate. In 1983, there were on average about 3 telephones per 1,000 inhabitants there as opposed to about 26 telephones in all other developing countries. Within this average wide differences exist, however. In 1983 Samoa had 26 telephones for every 1,000 inhabitants while Rwanda had only one telephone for the same number (see table 14). In the same year, there were 56 radio receivers per 1,000 inhabitants in the LDCs as against 137 for developing countries as a whole. There were also wide country variations in this respect. In 1983 there were between 200 and 243 radio receivers in eight LDCs and fewer than 80 radio receivers in 21 of them. The total number of post offices open to the public in 14 LDCs was about 1,533 as compared to 121,194 for 65 developing countries. The number of post offices per 100,000 inhabitants in the 14 LDCs was three as compared to 14 for 65 developing countries. Communication facilities are mainly concentrated in the main commercial centres and have hardly extended to the rural areas. Most of the LDCs are, however, well linked with traditional metropolitan centres in developed countries by modern telephone and postal systems.

121. The development of communication facilities in recent years has also been modest. The number of telephones per 1,000 inhabitants in the second half of the 1970s and beginning of the 1980s increased marginally for most of the countries, except in a few cases like Botswana (from 9.4 to 17.4), Maldives (from 2.5 to 13) and Sao Tome and Principe (from 8.8 to 23.8). It was with respect to radio receivers that there appears to have been a significant improvement in most of the countries. The number of radio receivers per 1,000 inhabitants increased from 30 to 56 in the same period for all the LDCs. For all the developing countries the number increased from 85 to 137. Substantial increases were recorded for Sudan (72 to 245), the Lao PDR (49 to 109) and Sierra Leone (92 to 201). Further efforts are also under way to improve the communication network in several LDCs, notably by the installation of microwave systems as in the case of Burkina Faso, the Central African Republic, Sudan and Uganda and the establishment of earth satellite stations in Ethiopia and Sudan.

Table 14: Communications facilities in the LDCs

| Country | Telephones Per 1,000 inhabitants | | Radio receivers Per 1,000 inhabitants | | Total number of post offices open to the public (number) |
|---|---|---|---|---|---|
| | 1975 | 1983 | 1975 | 1983 | 1983 |
| Afghanistan | 1.5 | 1.6b/ | 75a/ | 78 | .. |
| Bangladesh | 0.8c/ | 1.8b/ | 6f/ | 8f/ | .. |
| Benin | 3.4 | 4.0b/ | 50 | 76 | .. |
| Bhutan | .. | 1.5b/ | 5a/f/ | 9f/ | .. |
| Botswana | 9.4 | 17.4 | 75 | 117 | .. |
| Burkina Faso | 1.1 | 2.1 | 18 | 18 | .. |
| Burundi | 1.2 | 1.3 | 27 | 40 | 38 |
| Cape Verde | 5.5 | 5.6d/ | 110 | 150 | .. |
| Central African Rep. | .. | 1.7b/ | 34 | 57 | 76 |
| Chad | .. | 0.5b/ | 124 | 219 | 24 |
| Comoros | 4.8c/ | 4.8b/ | 112 | 129 | .. |
| Democratic Yemen | .. | 11.2d/ | 58 | 65 | 109 |
| Djibouti | 17.0 | 20.9 | 61 | 67 | 5 |
| Equatorial Guinea | .. | 3.0b/ | 245 | 306 | 19 |
| Ethiopia | 2.0 | 3.3 | 30 | 81 | .. |
| Gambia | 4.7 | 6.2b/ | 114 | 129 | .. |
| Guinea | 1.9e/ | 3.2b/ | 23 | 28 | .. |
| Guinea-Bissau | .. | 3.8b/ | 16 | 33 | .. |
| Haiti | .. | 4.0b/ | 20 | 23 | .. |
| Lao P.D.R. | 2.0 | 2.2b/ | 49 | 109 | .. |
| Lesotho | 3.2c/ | 4.3b/ | 19f/ | 28f/ | 130 |
| Malawi | 3.8 | 5.7 | 33 | 47 | 245 |
| Maldives | 2.5 | 13.0b/ | 22 | 88 | 23 |
| Mali | .. | 1.2b/ | 13 | 16 | 119 |
| Nepal | 0.8 | 1.2 | 9 | 25 | .. |
| Niger | 1.2 | 1.7d/ | 47a/ | 48 | 159 |
| Rwanda | 0.8 | 0.9b/ | 15 | 53 | .. |
| Samoa | 19.2 | 25.6b/ | 331 | 443 | .. |
| Sao Tome and Principe | 8.8 | 23.8 | 271a/ | 272 | 57 |
| Sierra Leone | 3.3c/ | 4.7b/ | 92 | 201 | .. |
| Somalia | .. | 1.6b/ | 17 | 30 | .. |
| Sudan | 3.7 | 3.4b/ | 72 | 245 | .. |
| Togo | 3.8c/ | 4.2 | 155 | 211 | 388 |
| Uganda | 4.1 | 3.7 | 22 | 22 | .. |
| United Rep. of Tanzania | 3.9 | 5.0 | 15 | 28 | .. |
| Vanuatu | 16.7 | 19.2 | 116 | 242 | .. |
| Yemen | .. | 8.1i/ | 14 | 16 | 141 |
| All LDCs | 1.9 | 2.8 | 30 | 56 | 1,533g/ |
| All developing countries | 14.3 | 25.8 | 85 | 137 | 121,194h/ |

Source: UN, Statistical Yearbook 1982; UNESCO, Statistical Yearbook 1985; ESCAP, Statistical Yearbook for Asia and the Pacific 1984; UPU, Statistique des services postaux 1983; ITU, Yearbook of Common Carrier Telecommunications Statistics (12th edition) and ITU, "Telecommunication for all" Nov. 1983.

a/ 1980.   b/ 1981.   c/ 1974   d/ 1982   e/ 1976.   f/ The number of licenses issued or set declared.
g/ Total of LDCs for which data are shown.   h/ Total of 65 countries.   i/ 1984.

6. Special problems of land-locked least developed countries

122. Sixteen out of 37 LDCs are land-locked and face additional transport bottlenecks in their international trade. The distances from the principal towns in LDCs to the main ports vary from 670 km to 2,690 km (see table 15). The international trade of these countries is dependent on the transit-transport infrastructures and services along the transit routes. The land-locked countries have little control, however, over the development and operations of such facilities within their transit neighbours. Furthermore, the latters' ability to improve, from their own resources, the transit-transport infrastructures and services in the ports and along the transit corridors is very limited because many of them are themselves developing countries. This underscores the need for international support in the development of the transit-transport systems in developing countries.

123. UNCTAD studies have indicated that transport costs (which include storage costs along the transit routes, insurance costs, costs due to extra documentation, etc.) in the international trade of land-locked countries are in many cases very significant because of the inadequacy of the facilities available. In 1982, freight costs as a percentage of the value of imports for land-locked countries constituted about 15.7 per cent as compared to 10.7 per cent for all developing countries. These high transportation costs reduce export earnings and increase import costs. In order to lessen these additional transport costs, land-locked countries will have to further promote co-operative arrangements with their transit neighbours with the aim of establishing a more efficient transit-transport system by, among other means, joint transit-transport planning, streamlining customs and trade procedures, improving management practices in the movement of transit cargo along the transit corridors and in the ports, and harmonizing procedures and technical standards for the smooth inter-state movement of commercial road transport vehicles and trains.

7. Special problems of island least developed countries

124. Island LDCs also face particular problems because of the lack of a well-organized and co-ordinated transport system. Most of these countries are small, remote and archipelagic, and their capacity to provide cargo volumes that would render services by ocean vessels commercially viable is limited. Even when these islands are located along the main shipping routes their infrastructure facilities are often technically unable to accommodate large vessels. These island LDCs will therefore generally have to depend heavily on improved inter-island feeder transport services. This will require expanded financial and technical assistance to develop appropriate types of vessels and aircraft equipped to provide the special service needed. Greater attention will also have to be given to the development of modern telecommunications systems that could be easily tailored to the particular requirements of these countries.

Table 15

Main access to the sea for land-locked developing countries

| Country | Distance to the sea a/ (km) | Means |
|---|---|---|
| Afghanistan | 2 000 - 10 600 | Road and rail |
| Bhutan | 800 | Road and rail |
| Botswana | 1 100 - 1 400 | Rail |
| Burundi | 1 455 - 1 850 | Rail and water |
| Central African Republic | 1 400 - 1 815 | Rail and water |
| Chad | 1 715 - 2 015 | Rail and road |
| Lao, People's Democratic Republic | 670 | Road, water and rail |
| Lesotho | 740 - 800 | Rail |
| Malawi | 560 - 700 | Rail |
| Mali | 1 170 - 1 289 | Rail and road |
| Nepal | 890 | Road and rail |
| Niger | 1 100 - 2 690 | Road and rail |
| Rwanda | 1 750 | Road, water and rail |
| Uganda | 1 450 | Road and rail |
| Upper Volta | 900 - 1 210 | Road |

Source: A transport strategy for land-locked developing countries. Report of the Expert Group on the Transport Infrastructure for Land-locked Developing Countries, TD/B/453/Add.1/Rev.1, United Nations publications, Sales No. E.74-11.D5. Updated by the UNCTAD secretariat.

a/ Distance from principal towns to main ports. The figures are the shortest and longest routes used.

E. Environment and disasters

1. Environmental problems and disasters affecting the least developed countries

(a) Chronic environmental difficulties

125. The majority of LDCs face one or both of two physical handicaps: aridity and mountainous terrain. Aridity is an obstacle to development inasmuch as it limits agricultural productivity and hampers development by imposing a low density of population and/or raising the spectre of famine. The broken terrain of mountainous LDCs increases communication and transport costs.

(b) Desertification, deforestation and soil erosion

126. Closely related to aridity are the interacting phenomena of desertification, deforestation and soil erosion, which can be defined as processes of degradation of fragile ecosystems arising from misuse or overuse of arid or semi-arid land by human beings and, in pastoral economies, by their livestock. The resulting ecological disequilibrium is manifested in the degradation of rain-fed agricultural lands, rangeland deterioration, and degradation and salination of irrigated land; declining availability of groundwater and surface water; loss of hydroelectric potential; and sand dune encroachment.

127. These phenomena affect the large majority of LDCs 33/: these countries are often arid, and misuse or overuse in such cases is the inevitable response of a very poor rural population trying to cope with its immediate need for subsistence. Deforestation and soil erosion in LDCs are thus exacerbated by the expansion of agriculture into woodlands and forests, growing population density, and great dependence on woodfuel. In the case of mountainous terrain (as in Burundi, Nepal and Rwanda), the choice of new land for cultivation is very limited, and farmers have to cultivate even on the steep slopes, thus provoking deforestation. In Haiti, erosion has been caused by over-exploitation of the hillsides and is exacerbated by the irregular but heavy rainfall. Declining soil fertility and erosion further result from increasing cropping pressure in traditional areas, overgrazing on diminishing pasture lands, and expansion of cropping into areas of marginal potential and more fragile ecology. In Ethiopia, some 22 million subsistence farmers (more than 70 per cent of the total population) live on the eroded slopes of the Central Highland Plateau, both ploughing and grazing deforested lands. A vicious circle operates accordingly in many LDCs: declining fertility and soil erosion lead to lower agricultural productivity, which forces a growing population to clear forests and to extend cultivation into marginal lands as a means of meeting food needs, which in turn reduces agricultural productivity, and so forth. Fuelwood scarcity arising from heavy dependence on firewood and from increasing demand has become an acute problem in many LDCs. Eighteen LDCs are thus among the 31 countries affected by acute scarcity of fuelwood or deficits, which were identified by a study commissioned jointly by UNDP, the World Bank and the World Resources Institute (see table 17). 34/

128. Forest area diminishes annually by 3.5 per cent of gross area in Malawi and by 5 per cent in Haiti. In the latter country, remaining wild forests

**Table 16: Least developed countries stricken by drought and desertification**

| REGION | LEAST DEVELOPED COUNTRY |
|--------|------------------------|
| Sub-Saharan Africa | Benin |
| | Botswana |
| | Burkina Faso |
| | Burundi |
| | Cape Verde |
| | Chad |
| | Djibouti |
| | Ethiopia |
| | Gambia |
| | Guinea a/ |
| | Guinea-Bissau a/ |
| | Lesotho |
| | Malawi |
| | Mali |
| | Niger |
| | Rwanda |
| | Somalia |
| | Sudan |
| | Togo |
| | Uganda |
| | United Republic of Tanzania |
| West Asia | Democratic Yemen |
| | Yemen |
| Central Asia | Afghanistan |

Source: Countries stricken by desertification and drought - Preliminary report of the Secretary General (A/40/392, E/1985/117, 24 June 1985), table 1.

a/ Stricken by drought but not currently affected by desertification.

Table 17: LDCs with fuelwood shortages

| LDCs affected by acute scarcity of fuelwood or deficits | Other LDCs with areas of fuelwood deficits |
|---|---|
| Afghanistan | Bangladesh |
| Botswana | Benin |
| Burkina Faso | Gambia |
| Burundi | Guinea |
| Cape Verde | Togo |
| Chad | Uganda |
| Comoros | United Republic of Tanzania |
| Djibouti | |
| Ethiopia | |
| Haiti | |
| Lesotho | |
| Malawi | |
| Mali | |
| Nepal | |
| Niger | |
| Rwanda | |
| Somalia | |
| Sudan | |

Source: World Resources Institute, Tropical Forests: A Call for Action, Report of an International Task Force convened by the World Resources Institute, the World Bank, and the UNDP, p.20.

reportedly amounted to 227 hectares by early 1986, as compared to 6,280 hectares in 1956. 35/ In 75 years Ethiopia's forest cover has fallen from 40 per cent to less than 3 per cent of the country's surface. Approximately one fourth of Nepal's forests have disappeared during the past 25 years; and it is estimated that there will be no accessible forests in the hills in 15 years' time and none in the Terai in 23 years' time. The loss of the forest cover in the United Republic of Tanzania reportedly amounts to 4,000 ha. per year. An evaluation report indicates that the 1.6 million ha. of forests in Somalia could be completely destroyed within 10 to 20 years. 36/

(c) Disasters

129. Least developed countries have been affected by the five main categories of disasters: drought, flood, cyclones, earthquakes, and armed conflict. On the basis of long-term information (1960-1981), 13 LDCs have been identified by UNDRO among the vulnerable and disaster-prone countries. Among them, Bangladesh is by far the most disaster-prone of the LDCs, and suffered 80 per cent of all the disaster deaths recorded for LDCs in the period 1960-1981. 37/ Disasters are particularly deadly in LDCs as disaster mortality per event tends to be higher the lower the income of the country affected, because of inadequate early warning and relief infrastructures.

### (i) Drought

130. Intertwined with desertification, drought is a natural phenomenon due to various climatic and meteorological factors, although there is some evidence that it may be induced by man-made devegetation. Specialists on the subject have pointed to three kinds of drought: meteorological, hydrological and agricultural. Meteorological drought is defined roughly as extended periods (i.e. two years or more) of below-average precipitation. Hydrological drought is reflected in the lowering of water tables, reduced river flows, depletion of groundwater aquifers, etc. Agricultural drought is reflected in damage to tree and field crops, reduced agricultural production, severe plant stress and crop failures. 38/

131. Drought has been an environmental phenomenon of particular concern to many LDCs in recent years. It reportedly affects 19 LDCs in Africa, and 3 in Asia (see table 16). Such LDCs are located in arid regions and thus are drought-prone. One characteristic of arid climates is not only low rainfall but also variable rainfall. The coefficient of variation in the Sudano-Sahelian zone, for example, is 30 to 50 per cent, as compared to 15 per cent or less in the wetter Guinean zone and the tropical rainforests of Central Africa. Man-made deforestation, soil erosion and erratic utilization of water resources have also contributed to creating the conditions for drought. And drought in turn speeds up the process of desertification.

132. Drought has been particularly acute in the African region. West Africa has experienced three prolonged drought periods in this century: around the years 1913 and 1940, and the current drought which has persisted with certain variations during the past 18 years. Droughts are characterized by short-lived respites and by intensifications with disastrous consequences. The present drought extended to normally forested regions of Africa, which include two LDCs, i.e. Guinea and Guinea-Bissau. 39/ It lowered water tables in rivers, lakes 40/, aquifers and dams, with adverse implications for countries that are developing their hydroelectrical potential. In Cape Verde many underground water sources have either dried up or have become saline. There has been an overall gradual erosion of productive land in many countries which were already heavily dependent on imported foodstuffs.

133. In 1983 and 1984, the drought persisted in the Sudano-Sahelian belt and spread through Eastern and Southern Africa. By late 1985 rains had returned in many of the drought-stricken countries, even though they came in some cases in the form of severe storms (Cape Verde), heavy floods (Burkina Faso) and torrential rain (Chad), thereby causing considerable damage in terms of crop losses, destruction of physical infrastructure, and transport difficulties. Insect pests have further arisen from sudden, heavy rainfall (Chad, Burkina Faso, Gambia, Guinea, Mali, Sudan, United Republic of Tanzania); and a lack of vegetation cover has increased erosion. Moreover, rains did not last long enough and were not sufficient to restore normal levels of water table and of soil water resources.

134. Despite the arrival of ample rains during the 1985/86 rainy season in various parts of Africa, drought conditions persist particularly in Cape Verde, Botswana (where rainfall remains 35 per cent below average), as well as in parts of Ethiopia and Sudan.

135. It is by no means certain that the once-traditional higher rainfall pattern is now returning to the area. The recent precedent of the years 1974-1975, when rainfall in the region increased only momentarily, should weaken hopes that the current improvement of rainfall is to be a long-standing phenomenon. On the basis of available information, a preliminary report of the Secretary-General of the United Nations stated that the "logical, if disturbing, conclusion that must be drawn is that drought is a recurrent phenomenon that the drought-stricken countries, especially of Africa, must learn to live with". 41/ In any event, the problems which have arisen from the present drought will not be eliminated automatically by the mere return of rains. The drought-stricken countries have indeed been subjected to severe economic disruption as a result of prolonged drought, and their medium-term and long-term development prospects have thereby been seriously jeopardized. 42/

### (ii) Grasshopper and locust infestations

136. Following the return of rainfall, grasshopper infestations are reported in Burkina Faso, Chad, Mali, and Niger; while locusts are threatening in particular Botswana, Ethiopia and Sudan. Other LDCs which may be hit by such plagues include Benin, Cape Verde, Guinea-Bissau, Rwanda, Uganda, and the United Republic of Tanzania. Crickets have caused serious damage to crops in Gambia.

### (iii) Other disasters

137. Table 18 provides information on least developed countries affected by natural disasters other than drought during the period 1984-1985. Of particular severity was the cyclone which ripped through the offshore islands of Bangladesh on 24 May 1985, inflicting a human toll of 11,000 people. During the 15 years of its existence as an independent nation, at least 32 tropical storms have swept across Bangladesh. Floods in Bangladesh in 1984 were the worst since 1974, with total damage estimated at $375 million. In addition, torrential rains affected Cape Verde, Chad and Sao Tome and Principe in 1985.

### (d) Pollution

138. Air and water pollution arising from rapid urbanization and/or uncontrolled industrialization is now becoming an environmental problem in several LDCs, as it has been in more advanced developing countries for many years. In Nepal, governmental concern exists over growing water pollution caused by both organic and chemical means and by dumping solid wastes along the river sides. In Botswana, a quality survey undertaken in 1982 found that water from traditional water sources (15 per cent of the sample) was highly contaminated. Some experts think that fish stock and production in Togo are adversely affected by pollution of the sea arising from phosphate wastes which are poured into the sea, either killing the fish or chasing them away from Togolese waters.

Table 18:  Least developed countries affected by natural disasters
other than drought during 1984-1985

---

Cyclones

    Bangladesh (1985)
    Comoros (1985)
    Vanuatu (1985) a/


Floods

    Burkina Faso (1984)
    Cape Verde (1984)
    Benin (1985)
    Nepal (1985) b/


Earthquakes

    Afghanistan (1984)
    Guinea (1984)

---

Source:  Office of the United Nations Disaster Relief Co-ordinator:
Report of the Secretary-General (A/41/295;  E/1986/65), 1 May 1986, annex IV.

a/  Cyclonic storms
b/  Floods and landslides

2.  Action taken in regard to environment and disasters

(a)  National policies

139. Action taken at the national level by LDCs has concentrated to a large
extent on afforestation and reforestation, soil conservation and land use,
establishment of institutional mechanisms, and irrigation;  whilst other
problems relating to environment and disasters are dealt with principally
through international initiatives (see sub-section (b) below).  Of relevance
in this context are the five main areas requiring major investments aimed at
reforestation which were identified by the aforementioned joint report
prepared by UNDP, the World Bank and the World Resources Institute:
agro-forestry, especially fuelwood capacity;  land-use practices, particularly
on upland watersheds;  establishment of industrial plantations;  ecosystem
protection and institutional strengthening.

140. Forestry policies have involved the promotion of tree planting (Bangladesh, Benin, Botswana, Burkina Faso, Burundi, Chad, Guinea-Bissau, Lao PDR, Malawi, Niger, Rwanda and United Republic of Tanzania); control over the cutting, transport and/or consumption of wood (Afghanistan, Bhutan, Burkina Faso); and ban on log exports. Soil conservation, erosion control and land use programmes have been undertaken in Burundi, Lesotho, Malawi, Rwanda and United Republic of Tanzania. Nepal formulated a National Forestry Policy in 1976 which, inter alia, promotes people's participation in forest management and reforestation at the community level and provides for training and advice to the population. A draft National Environment Protection Act has been prepared in that country providing for pollution control and for the opening of national parks and wildlife reserves (Nepal is a member of UNEP's Governing Council for 1984-1986). High level committees have been set up in Botswana, Ethiopia and Mali to deal with environment problems and related relief. In Bhutan, a Department of Forests was established in 1979 with responsibility for commercial logging so as to reduce ecological damage and promote forest management practices. Somalia has established a National Range Agency (NRA) whose tasks include the formulation of forestry development projects, the establishment of grazing and drought reserves, stockwater development, and the control of the use of disappearing plant species. Environmental research is in turn being carried out at the Institute of Environmental Studies of the University of Khartoum (Sudan). Land and soil surveys are an important component of Ethiopia's Ten-Year Perspective Plan.

141. Irrigation projects are carried out by most LDCs and are usually part of multiple water use activities. It is an expensive process that often does not provide a full return on capital costs on the basis of market prices; and yet it is important for the production of food and for other purposes including energy development. It is on these grounds that Burkina Faso has pressed ahead with four major irrigation projects, i.e. the dams of Douna, Kompienga, Grand Bagre and Sourou. The Gambia intends to construct a major bridge-barrage on the Gambia river which, inter alia, will permit irrigation of about 30,000 ha. of land. The greater role of the private sector is a salient feature of Bangladesh's irrigation programme for 1985/86.

142. In many cases, water development projects need to be undertaken jointly among neighbouring countries so as to ensure an equitable distribution of the costs and benefits which accrue therefrom. There are some specifically-focused inter-State institutions which co-ordinate river basin or lake development, a key feature of anti-drought and desertification strategy. These institutions include the Lake Chad Basin Commission, the Niger Basin Authority, the Gambia River Development Organization, and the Organization for the Development of the Senegal River (OMVS). Major dams being built at Manantali (Mali) and Diama (Senegal) are the outcome of regional co-operation between Mali, Mauritania and Senegal within the framework of the OMVS. The lakes behind the dams will cover a total of 400,000 ha, and will inter alia generate electricity and open the Senegal river for navigation.

(b)  Recent institutional initiatives

143. Many environmental problems can best be tackled by co-ordination and joint action by countries concerned, notably at the regional and subregional levels.  This approach has fructified in the case of policies to combat the drought in Africa.  Several common initiatives have been taken in the recent past with a view to coping with the effects of the drought particularly on the mid-term and long-term development of the affected countries.  Such initiatives include the following:

(i)  The Permanent Inter-State Committee on Drought Control in the Sahel (CILSS) 43/ launched in 1985 a new strategy which puts great stress on: measures to ensure widespread popular involvement in agricultural production; broadening and diversifying the productive basis of the economy;  and achieving a new ecological balance by the enrichment of the natural environment, the conservation of resources (especially wood energy resources), and the creation of appropriate legal frameworks. 44/

(ii)  An extraordinary ministerial meeting of CILSS (Niamey, 1985) decided to streamline the co-ordination of national policies of member countries in respect of rural development and the struggle against desertification.  A follow-up ministerial meeting was held at Dakar in January 1986.

(iii)  Two ministerial conferences were held in Dakar with a view to carrying out a joint policy to combat desertification in the CILSS, ECOWAS and Mahghreb countries, and in Egypt and the Sudan (July 1984 and November 1985). Agreement was reached, inter alia, on action aimed at ensuring regional co-operation and at the re-organization and revitalization of the relevant infrastructure in the region.

(iv)  A centre which provides agro-hydro-meteorological information to farmers and herdsmen (Aghrymet) has been established by CILSS in Niger.

(v)  An Intergovernmental Authority for Drought and Development in East Africa (IGADD) has been established by six countries (of which five are LDCs):  Djibouti, Ethiopia, Kenya, Somalia, Sudan and Uganda.  A meeting of Heads of State of these countries was held at Djibouti in January 1986.

(vi)  An African Ministerial Conference on the Environment was held in Cairo in December 1985 under the auspices of UNEP, ECA and OAU.  The Conference agreed on a five-year programme of action which is aimed at ensuring the preservation of the environment and self-sufficiency in food and energy.

(vii)  An international conference on forestry resources (SILVA) was held in Paris in February 1986 with the participation of several Heads of State, and dealt, inter alia, with deforestation problems of third world countries.

(viii) Crash programmes of assistance to establish national early warning projects in countries vulnerable to drought have been formulated by FAO in the countries members of CILSS, of SADCC, and in Ethiopia and Sudan.

(ix) UNSO has been providing technical assistance to, _inter alia_, 16 least developed countries of Africa. Projects include the promotion of fuelwood-saving stoves, the construction of small earthen dams and other irrigation and water harvesting systems, planting and development of drought resistant export crops, afforestation and reforestation, and assistance in range and livestock management.

(x) Institutional mechanisms to strengthen donor-recipient co-operation in regard to desertification and/or drought are being established particularly in Botswana, Lesotho and Mali. A Rehabilitation and Revival Plan to combat desertification has been presented by the European Commission to assist drought-stricken countries in rehabilitating their agriculture and in coping more effectively with any further drought.

(xi) An Emergency Centre for Locust Operation (ECLO) was established by FAO in mid-1986 and was entrusted with the implementation of an emergency plan of action for locust and grasshopper control in Africa.

(xii) In 1985, stringent measures to control international trade in ivory, and thereby protect the elephant herd, were adopted within the framework of the Convention on International Trade in Endangered Species of Wild Fauna and Flora (CITES) by a number of countries (whether exporters or importers). These include 13 LDCs: Afghanistan, Bangladesh, Botswana, Burundi, Central African Republic, Ethiopia, Malawi, Nepal, Niger, Samoa, Somalia, Sudan and the United Republic of Tanzania.

Chapter IV

THE EXTERNAL SECTOR

A.  Recent trends in LDCs' trade

1.  General trends

144. The external trade of the LDCs continues to show a negative balance with a record deficit of $US 8.9 billion in 1981.  Mainly thanks to a contraction of imports in 1982-1983 and an improved export performance in 1984, the deficit diminished slightly during 1982-1984.  However, the fall in export earnings in 1985 resulted again in a widening of the trade deficit of the LDCs.  The major factors, most of them still at work, behind this adverse development are an imbalance at the global level between supply and demand of the principal products of export interest to the LDCs - i.e. primary commodities - and a sluggish economic growth in the developed market economies, resulting in a downward trend in commodity prices.  In addition, a number of developed countries have maintained their export support schemes and subsidies to local production of commodities of export interest to LDCs such as oilseeds, sugar, and livestock.  Therefore, the efforts of the LDCs to boost their exports face severe constraints at a time when they need a buoyant external trade to yield the foreign exchange not only for coping with a mounting debt burden but also for carrying out the structural transformation of their economies in line with the provisions of the SNPA.

2.  Overall exports

145. The upward trend in the dollar value of exports from LDCs during the 1970s was reversed in the first half of the 1980s. 45/  During 1981-1983 the value of exports was virtually stagnating at about 90 per cent of the 1980 level.  In 1984, the total value of LDCs' exports almost recovered to the 1980 level.  However, this momentum could not be maintained in 1985, when the value of LDCs' exports declined by 7.2 per cent and was again below the 1980 level. (see figure 1).

146. In 1985, the total value of merchandise exports of the LDCs decreased by 4 per cent.  Twenty-three LDCs registered no increase in their export value, of which 18 recorded declines.  Five countries - namely Sudan, United Republic of Tanzania, Malawi, Ethiopia and Chad - experienced the severest setbacks in the export performance among the LDCs.  Their combined export loss in 1985 was as large as one and a half times the net export loss of the LDCs as a whole. Other LDCs, such as Sao Tome and Principe, Lesotho and Niger, have experienced a continuous decline in their exports over a longer period, resulting in reductions of the export value of 75, 64 and 60 per cent respectively since 1980.  On the other hand, a few countries managed to expand their exports despite the prevailing circumstances.  Somalia, whose exports had fallen by more than three quarters between 1982 and 1984, was able to recoup a small fraction of the loss suffered.  Nepal managed to increase its exports by 23 per cent, following on year-by-year increases since 1983 that brought that country's level beyond its 1981 record.  The best performance in absolute terms was achieved by Bangladesh and Botswana:  the former, however, was not able to confirm and improve upon its remarkable jump achieved in 1984, while Botswana was able to pursue its upward trend begun in 1978, that was only broken in 1981.

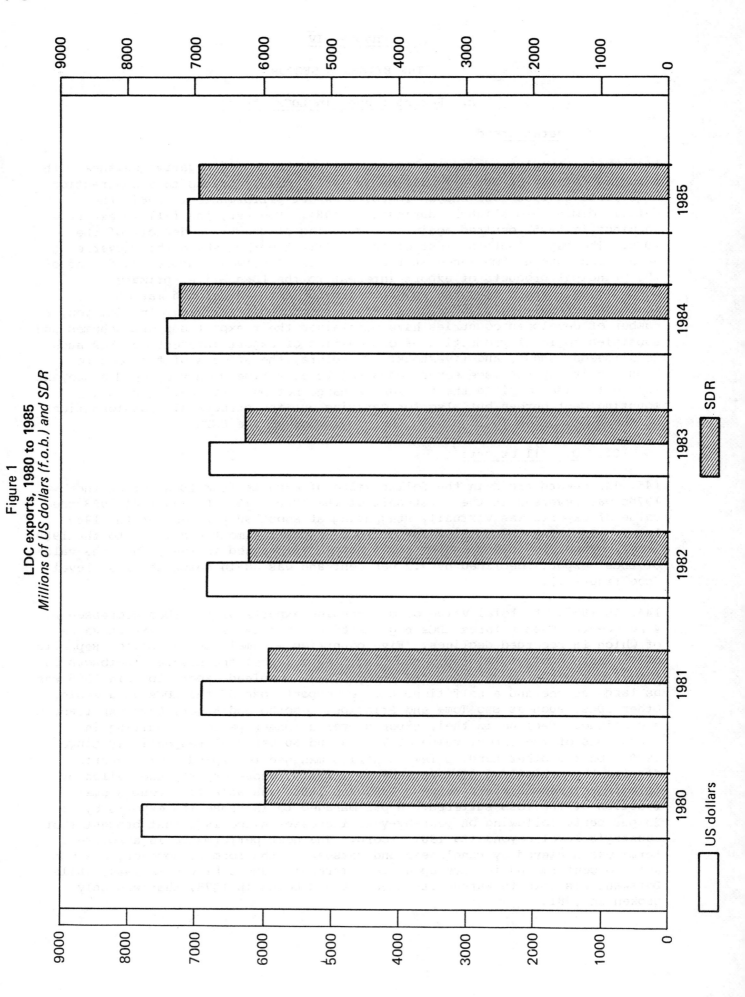

Figure 1
LDC exports, 1980 to 1985
Millions of US dollars (f.o.b.) and SDR

147. The exports of LDCs are heavily concentrated in only a few countries. Ten countries (Afghanistan, Bangladesh, Botswana, Democratic Yemen, Ethiopia, Guinea, Malawi, Sudan, Uganda, and United Republic of Tanzania) accounted for more than 70 per cent of all LDCs' exports in 1985. On the other hand, 18 LDCs together accounted for no more than 10 per cent of total exports of this country group in the same year.

148. Adjustment of overvalued currencies has been widely viewed as an appropriate policy for increasing exports. At least 20 LDCs, some of them repeatedly, depreciated their currency between 1980 and 1985. In a number of countries, the devaluation was quite substantial. In Somalia and Bangladesh, for example, the devaluation amounted to 92 and 47 per cent respectively from 1980 to 1985. Although a devaluation should make exports more competitive, in the case of the LDCs the devaluation alone may not result in the desired effects of sustained increases in exports because of the depressed general situation in the world commodity markets and the rigidities in the supply capacity.

### 3. Structure of LDCs' exports

149. The bulk of LDCs' exports still consists of either agricultural or mineral primary commodities, or a combination of both. In 1984, primary products accounted for about 86 per cent. The percentage of agricultural products, minerals and metals as well as petroleum products and natural gas in total exports amounted to 52, 20 and approximately 14 per cent respectively. Manufactured goods accounted for 14 per cent of total LDCs' exports in 1984 (see table 20). Most of the LDCs have so far achieved only marginal success in diversifying their exports.

150. The heavy dependence of LDCs on primary commodities is indicated by the share of the 18 primary commodities in the IPC 46/ in total LDCs' exports (see table 21). In Sao Tome and Principe, Uganda, Equatorial Guinea and Burundi, these primary commodities accounted for more than 90 per cent of total exports, in 14 other LDCs IPC commodities represented more than 50 per cent of total exports. Therefore, these countries should have a strong interest in a rapid implementation of the IPC (see also part two, chapter V, on commercial policy measures). But also the export performance of LDCs such as Niger, Democratic Yemen, Comoros, Maldives and Afghanistan, where IPC commodities are almost negligible in total exports, depends heavily on only a few primary commodities. The dependence on only a limited number of export products is one of the main factors that make those countries extremely vulnerable to price fluctuations.

151. Coffee, cotton, live animals (cattle, sheep, goats) as well as jute and tobacco are among the leading agricultural export products. However, primary commodities from the agricultural sector are among those export products which are most seriously affected by sluggish demand in the industrialized countries.

152. In a few LDCs such as Botswana, Guinea, Niger and Sierra Leone, the export of mineral commodities plays a significant role in their external trade. However, bauxite, natural phosphates, copper, diamonds and other traditional mineral products of export interest to LDCs have had increasingly to compete with substitutes in world markets. The technological change which is taking place in the developed countries is associated with a rapid

Table 19

LDC exports, 1978 to 1985
(Millions of $US (f.o.b.))

| Country | 1978 | 1979 | 1980 | 1981 | 1982 | 1983 | 1984 | 1985 |
|---|---|---|---|---|---|---|---|---|
| Afghanistan ............... | 322 | 494 | 705 | 694 | 708 | 730 | 735 | 710 |
| Bangladesh ................ | 552 | 641 | 738 | 662 | 667 | 690 | 934 | 927 |
| Benin ..................... | 27 | 46 | 63 | 34 | 24 | 32 | 33 | 40 |
| Bhutan .................... | .. | .. | .. | .. | .. | .. | .. | .. |
| Botswana .................. | 222 | 436 | 503 | 378 | 457 | 636 | 674 | 727 |
| Burkina Faso .............. | 43 | 77 | 90 | 75 | 56 | 57 | 80 | 66 |
| Burundi ................... | 69 | 104 | 65 | 71 | 88 | 80 | 98 | 110 |
| Cape Verde ................ | 2 | 2 | 4 | 3 | 4 | 5 | 5 | 5 |
| Central African Republic .. | 72 | 79 | 115 | 79 | 109 | 75 | 86 | 115 |
| Chad ...................... | 99 | 88 | 71 | 83 | 58 | 74 | 111 | 80 |
| Comoros ................... | 9 | 17 | 20 | 16 | 20 | 20 | 21 | 25 |
| Democratic Yemen .......... | 193 | 467 | 779 | 430 | 795 | 674 | 645 | 690 |
| Djibouti .................. | 18 | 11 | 19 | 21 | 20 | 25 | 26 | 26 |
| Equatorial Guinea ......... | 17 | 29 | 14 | 16 | 17 | 20 | 20 | 20 |
| Ethiopia .................. | 310 | 418 | 425 | 389 | 404 | 402 | 417 | 370 |
| Gambia .................... | 39 | 58 | 31 | 27 | 44 | 48 | 47 | 45 |
| Guinea .................... | 294 | 317 | 390 | 490 | 410 | 400 | 430 | 430 |
| Guinea-Bissau ............. | 10 | 14 | 11 | 14 | 12 | 23 | 18 | 14 |
| Haiti ..................... | 159 | 148 | 226 | 151 | 163 | 154 | 179 | 180 |
| Lao People's Dem. Republic | 12 | 35 | 31 | 33 | 40 | 40 | 20 | 29 |
| Lesotho ................... | 32 | 45 | 58 | 50 | 35 | 19 | 21 | 21 |
| Malawi .................... | 185 | 223 | 285 | 270 | 246 | 229 | 313 | 252 |
| Maldives .................. | 4 | 6 | 10 | 11 | 14 | 19 | 25 | 32 |
| Mali ...................... | 112 | 147 | 205 | 154 | 146 | 165 | 181 | 175 |
| Nepal ..................... | 88 | 109 | 80 | 140 | 88 | 94 | 128 | 161 |
| Niger ..................... | 283 | 448 | 566 | 455 | 333 | 288 | 228 | 223 |
| Rwanda .................... | 70 | 114 | 112 | 110 | 103 | 121 | 145 | 110 |
| Samoa ..................... | 11 | 18 | 17 | 11 | 13 | 19 | 19 | 15 |
| Sao Tome & Principe ....... | 21 | 22 | 20 | 14 | 9 | 6 | 7 | 5 |
| Sierra Leone .............. | 161 | 206 | 204 | 153 | 89 | 92 | 148 | 152 |
| Somalia ................... | 107 | 112 | 133 | 152 | 199 | 100 | 45 | 90 |
| Sudan ..................... | 533 | 535 | 543 | 658 | 499 | 624 | 629 | 374 |
| Togo ...................... | 241 | 218 | 335 | 212 | 177 | 162 | 191 | 190 |
| Uganda .................... | 350 | 436 | 345 | 242 | 347 | 372 | 399 | 380 |
| United Republic of Tanzania | 477 | 511 | 508 | 613 | 455 | 366 | 377 | 284 |
| Vanuatu ................... | 42 | 47 | 35 | 32 | 23 | 29 | 44 | 30 |
| Yemen ..................... | 7 | 14 | 23 | 47 | 39 | 27 | 65 | 106 |
| All LDCs ................. | 5 193 | 6 696 | 7 779 | 6 990 | 6 911 | 6 917 | 7 544 | 7 215 |
| All LDCs (millions of SDR) | 4 148 | 5 182 | 5 977 | 5 928 | 6 259 | 6 470 | 7 359 | 7 105 |

Source: UNCTAD secretariat calculations based on national and
international sources.

Table 20
Merchandise exports by principal products of the LDCs
in the period 1980-1984 a /b/

| Product | Absolute values in millions of dollars | | | | | Percentage share |
|---|---|---|---|---|---|---|
| | 1980 | 1981 | 1982 | 1983 | 1984 | 1984 |
| Agricultural products ......... | 3 840 | 3 485 | 3 381 | 3 682 | 3 882 | 49 |
| Coffee ...................... | 1 059 | 840 | 1 011 | 1 035 | 1 045 | 14 |
| Cotton lint ................. | 569 | 396 | 333 | 576 | 572 | 7 |
| Bovine cattle .............. | 234 | 253 | 232 | 229 | 229 | 3 |
| Sheep and goats ............. | 154 | 192 | 200 | 232 | 185 | 2 |
| Jute ........................ | 149 | 123 | 105 | 113 | 113 | 1 |
| Tobacco ..................... | 147 | 138 | 163 | 136 | 177 | 2 |
| Raisins ..................... | 131 | 124 | 90 | 122 | 90 | 1 |
| Cocoa ....................... | 126 | 88 | 64 | 73 | 100 | 1 |
| Groundnuts c/ ............... | 114 | 162 | 83 | 64 | 89 | 1 |
| Hides and skins d/ .......... | 109 | 102 | 99 | 110 | 73 | 0.9 |
| Tea ......................... | 107 | 112 | 117 | 132 | 194 | 2 |
| Other agricultural products ... | 941 | 955 | 884 | 860 | 1 015 | 13 |
| Forestry products ............ | 65 | 67 | 55 | 56 | 57 | 0.7 |
| Fishery products ............. | 87 | 67 | 75 | 96 | 136 | 2 |
| Fuels ....................... | 1 152 | 1 041 | 1 117 | 1 162 | .. | .. |
| Petroleum products ........... | 936 | 768 | 833 | 862 | 950 | 12 |
| Natural gas ................. | 216 | 273 | 284 | 300 | .. | .. |
| Mineral products ............. | 1 784 | 1 421 | 1 293 | 1 462 | 1 531 | 20 |
| Diamonds .................... | 533 | 331 | 394 | 559 | 600 | 8 |
| Uranium ore ................. | 464 | 337 | 268 | 290 | 224 | 3 |
| Bauxite ..................... | 250 | 276 | 253 | 263 | 361 | 5 |
| Alumina ..................... | 138 | 143 | 123 | 121 | 99 | 1 |
| Natural phosphates ........... | 135 | 104 | 78 | 67 | 105 | 1 |
| Copper-nickel matte .......... | 104 | 97 | 63 | 54 | 82 | 1 |
| Other mineral products e/ ..... | 160 | 133 | 114 | 108 | 60 | 0.7 |
| Manufactured products f/ ...... | 838 | 1 031 | 1 008 | 727 | 1 115 | 14 |
| Jute products ................ | 383 | 339 | 282 | 322 | 300 | 4 |
| Carpets ..................... | 111 | 82 | 90 | 54 | .. | .. |
| Other manufactured products f/. | 344 | 610 | 636 | 351 | .. | .. |
| Total of goods .............. | 7 766 | 7 112 | 6 929 | 7 185 | 7 807 | 100 |

Source:  UNCTAD secretariat calculations and estimates based on FAO,
United Nations Statistical Office and other international and national sources.

a/  Products with an export value of more than $100 million in 1980 are
ranked according to order of importance, within major categories, excluding
Bhutan.

b/  Figures may not add exactly owing to rounding.

c/  Including oil and cake.

d/  Excluding furskins.

e/  Provisional estimates.

f/  Residual item, which may have a wide margin of error.

Table 21

Share of commodities covered by the IPC in the total
LDCs' exports, 1970-1984
(Percentages)

| Country | 1970 | 1975 | 1980 | 1984 |
|---|---|---|---|---|
| Afghanistan ................... | 10.7 | 16.0 | 5.7 | 1.5 |
| Bangladesh .................... | 74.6 | 87.1 | 72.5 | 58.1 |
| Benin ......................... | 76.9 | 60.3 | 78.0 | 65.4 a/ |
| Bhutan ........................ | .. | .. | .. | .. |
| Botswana ...................... | 30.4 | 37.5 | 13.4 | 10.0 |
| Burkina Faso .................. | 40.4 | 42.0 | 51.0 | 86.0 |
| Burundi ....................... | 95.4 | 92.8 | 93.2 | 92.8 |
| Cape Verde .................... | 20.0 | 0.0 | 10.0 | 12.3 |
| Central African Republic ...... | 56.8 | 69.4 | 63.7 | 50.4 |
| Chad .......................... | 79.0 | 69.0 | 57.1 | 37.5 a/ |
| Comoros ....................... | 16.0 | 5.0 | 2.0 | 1.9 |
| Democratic Yemen .............. | 5.1 | 2.0 | 2.1 | 0.2 |
| Djibouti ...................... | .. | .. | .. | .. |
| Equatorial Guinea ............. | .. | .. | .. | 90.4 a/ |
| Ethiopia ...................... | 71.6 | 53.5 | 69.4 | 65.6 |
| Gambia ........................ | 90.0 | 99.6 | 90.6 | 54.7 |
| Guinea ........................ | 45.7 | 80.0 | 63.5 | 84.5 |
| Guinea-Bissau ................. | 72.5 | 72.8 | 52.0 | 65.0 |
| Haiti ......................... | 77.8 | 59.6 | 60.0 | 32.3 |
| Lao People's Dem. Republic .... | 65.7 | 47.3 | 31.4 | 26.6 |
| Lesotho ....................... | .. | .. | .. | .. |
| Malawi ........................ | 38.5 | 21.3 | 31.3 | 36.1 |
| Maldives ...................... | 6.6 | 37.5 | 30.8 | 0.4 |
| Mali .......................... | 41.8 | 54.8 | 52.7 | 38.1 |
| Nepal ......................... | 20.8 | 16.9 | 40.8 | 27.2 |
| Niger ......................... | 69.7 | 9.8 | 0.1 | 0.3 |
| Rwanda ........................ | 78.8 | 84.0 | 80.8 | 75.7 |
| Samoa ......................... | 82.0 | 90.0 | 76.4 | 85.8 |
| Sao Tome & Principe ........... | 100.0 | 100.0 | 74.0 | 98.7 |
| Sierra Leone .................. | 31.7 | 39.3 | 34.4 | 37.4 |
| Somalia ....................... | 28.1 | 14.4 | 5.5 | 5.0 |
| Sudan ......................... | 82.1 | 80.4 | 63.2 | 49.3 |
| Togo .......................... | 92.2 | 90.4 | 62.2 | 81.0 |
| Uganda ........................ | 85.4 | 98.5 | 95.0 | 93.7 |
| United Republic of Tanzania ... | 50.0 | 50.8 | 57.4 | 69.5 |
| Vanuatu ....................... | 50.0 | 60.1 | 33.3 | 66.9 |
| Yemen ......................... | 60.0 | 84.6 | 0.8 | 3.5 |

Source: Calculated on the basis of TD/B/IPC/STAT/1 (Vol. 1),
pp. 144-154; UNCTAD, Yearbook of International Commodity Statistics, 1985,
TD/B/C.1/STAT.2. UNCTAD secretariat calculations.

a/ Figures for 1983.

expansion of a variety of new types of synthetic materials. The increasing substitution of synthetic fibers, plastics and ceramics for natural products is likely to erode the LDCs' exports of primary commodities.

### 4. Commodity prices and export earnings

153. The overriding feature in the international markets for major LDCs' export commodities was the dramatic decline in prices during the first half of the 1980s. The prices of almost all primary commodities of export interest to LDCs dropped precipitously, bringing dollar prices of a large basket of commodities exported by developing countries to less than three quarters of the 1980 level as of mid-1986, despite the drastic fall of the dollar that had occurred by that time.

154. Table 22 provides information on the price trend for some commodities of importance for LDCs' exports. Groundnuts, of which Gambia is a major exporter, fetched in the first half of 1986 about 40 per cent less than the 1979-1981 average. The price of cotton, which is a major cash crop for Chad, Mali, Sudan and other LDCs, plummeted by 42 per cent over the same period. Wide fluctuations in world prices have prevailed in regard to other agricultural commodities of export interest to LDCs such as tea, cocoa and fresh tuna (exported by Maldives). Mineral commodities, which figure high in the export list of Botswana, Niger, Guinea and Sierra Leone, have lost more than a quarter of their value.

155. On the other hand, mainly owing to adverse weather conditions in the main producing areas, world prices for jute increased markedly in 1984 and early 1985. But Bangladesh as a prominent supplier of this product to the world market was unable to take full advantage from this development, because heavy floods had lowered jute production. As regards commodities, which have recorded nominal price increases in the 1980s, it should be kept in mind that these increases have been neither substantial enough to make up for losses experienced in other commodities during the same period, nor are there any indications that they will be longer-lasting than previous booms. In fact, tea prices in the first half of 1986 were below one half of their 1984 averages, while the zenith of coffee prices was reached early in 1986. Moreover, the decline of the dollar reduces the purchasing power of export products expressed in that currency for imports purchased in Western Europe and Japan, which supply about 40 per cent of LDC imports.

156. The fall in commodity prices since 1980 has adversely affected the foreign-exchange earnings of the LDCs. 47/ During the period 1978-1983, for which detailed information on a country-by-country basis is available, 48/ the average annual shortfall in export earnings for important commodities exported by LDCs was about $770 million (calculated on the basis indicated in the footnote b/ to table 23). This amount represented 11 per cent of the average annual exports of LDCs during the same period. Such a loss in export earnings over the period of six years covered is equivalent to more than two thirds of the total concessional assistance rendered to the LDCs in 1983. This represents a substantial loss of financial resources indispensable for restructuring the LDCs' economies and advancing their socio-economic development.

Table 22

Indices of dollar prices of primary commodities of export interest to LDCs
(1979-1981 = 100)

| Commodity | 1981 | 1982 | 1983 | 1984 | 1985 | 1986 a/ |
|---|---|---|---|---|---|---|
| Coffee ..................... | 76 | 82 | 84 | 92 | 87 | 121 |
| Cocoa ..................... | 78 | 66 | 80 | 90 | 85 | 78 |
| Tea ........................ | 100 | 112 | 155 | 261 | 159 | 129 |
| Sugar ..................... | 92 | 46 | 46 | 28 | 22 | 36 |
| Groundnuts ................ | 112 | 68 | 69 | 80 | 64 | 60 |
| Cotton .................... | 99 | 85 | 99 | 95 | 70 | 58 |
| Sisal ..................... | 91 | 84 | 81 | 83 | 74 | 72 |
| Jute ...................... | 97 | 104 | 126 | 282 | 360 | 163 |
| Hides ..................... | 71 | 86 | 108 | 148 | 130 | 100 |
| Minerals, ores and metals ... | 94 | 82 | 85 | 79 | 76 | 73 |

Source:   UNCTAD: Monthly commodity price bulletin, 1960-1984 supplement,
Geneva 1985.
UNCTAD: Monthly commodity price bulletin, vol. VI, No. 7,
Geneva 1986.

a/   January to June 1986.

5.   Imports

157. With regard to the imports of LDCs, it is noteworthy, that their nominal value decreased by 6 per cent between 1980 and 1985.  After a short-lived upswing in 1981, when the import value of all merchandise surpassed the 1980 level, it declined steadily from 1982 to 1985 (see table 24). 49/

158. During the period 1981-1986, a number of LDCs embarked either independently or in conjunction with their efforts to obtain fresh external financial resources on economic adjustment measures.  As of 30 June 1986, 8 out of 21 stand-by arrangements of the IMF had been signed with LDCs.  These arrangements, normally conditioned upon prior acceptance by borrowing-LDCs of an economic adjustment programme, were available to Bangladesh, Central African Republic, Guinea, Mali, Nepal, Niger, Somalia and Togo.

159. A major objective of the economic adjustment programmes of LDCs is to address imbalances in their external trade.  However, since a major thrust is directed at the reduction of imports, these programmes imperil the countries' long-term development objectives, if they are unable to arrest the short-term deceleration of economic activity.  In line with this policy, Sierra Leone reduced its imports by 66.2 per cent, Sao Tome and Principe by 47.4 per cent and Togo by 38.2 per cent from 1980 to 1985.  The effects of such drastic import reductions, which will inevitably have adverse consequences for investment in productive capacity, infrastructure and social services, "call into question the future ability of many countries to respond to the needs of their populations and to bring about the changes in the structure of production necessary to restore growth and development." 50/

## TABLE 23

### Commodities and export earnings shortfalls of 33 LDCs in 1978-1983

| Country | Commodity dependence a/ 1983 | Commodities involved | Total estimated export b/ earnings shortfalls ($ millions) |
|---|---|---|---|
| Afghanistan | 34.9 | Fruits, hides and skins, cotton | 246.0 |
| Bangladesh | 33.7 | Fish, jute, tea, non-bovine meat | 222.6 |
| Benin | 77.3 | Cocoa, coffee, cotton, fish, vegetable oils and oil seeds | 11.4 |
| Botswana | 15.2 | Copper, bovine meat, hides and skins, non-bovine meat | 82.8 |
| Burkina Faso | 83.3 | Cotton, bovine meat, hides and skins, vegetable oils and oil seeds | 49.2 |
| Burundi | 95.0 | Coffee, cotton, tea | 109.8 |
| Cape Verde | 80.6 | Fish, bananas | 1.2 |
| Central African Republic | 77.7 | Coffee, timber, tobacco, cotton, non-bovine meat | 55.8 |
| Chad | 63.6 | Cotton, fish | 33.0 |
| Comoros | 82.9 | Spices, vegetable oils and oil seeds | 3.0 |
| Democratic Yemen | 3.0 | Fish, cotton | 13.8 |
| Equatorial Guinea | ~0.4 | Cocoa, coffee, timber, fish, bananas | 11.4 |
| Ethiopia | 94.6 | Cotton, coffee, hides and skins, vegetable oils and oil seeds | 357.6 |
| Guinea | 97.5 | Bauxite, coffee, vegetable oils and oil seeds | 697.8 |
| Gambia | 57.2 | Vegetable oils and oil seeds, fish | 56.4 |
| Guinea-Bissau | 67.8 | Timber, vegetable oils and oil seeds | 11.4 |
| Haiti | 38.5 | Bauxite, cocoa, coffee, hard fibres | 108.0 |
| Lao Peoples Democratic Rep. | 51.5 | Coffee, timber | 25.8 |
| Malawi | 95.6 | Tobacco, tea, sugar, cereals, vegetable oils and oil seeds | 323.4 |
| Maldives | 66.1 | Fish | 3.6 |
| Mali | 78.0 | Cotton, vegetable oils and oil seeds | 153.6 |
| Nepal | 49.6 | Cereals, jute, milk and butter, roots, timber | 54.0 |
| Rwanda | 93.1 | Coffee, tea, tin | 145.2 |
| Samoa | 76.8 | Bananas, cocoa, roots, timber, vegetable oils and oil seeds | 12.0 |
| Sao Tome and Principe | 47.9 | Cocoa, vegetable oils and oil seeds | 22.8 |
| Sierra Leone | 68.9 | Bauxite, cocoa, coffee, fish, vegetable oils and oil seeds | 80.4 |
| Somalia | 95.1 | Bananas, fish | 1.8 |
| Sudan | 28.1 | Cotton, hides and skins, vegetable oils and oil seeds, roots, cereals | 526.8 |
| Tanzania (United Rep.) | 92.1 | Coffee, cotton, hard fibres, tea, tobacco, vegetable oils and oil seeds | 424.8 |
| Togo | 69.6 | Cocoa, coffee, cotton, phosphates, vegetable oils and oil seeds | 261.0 |
| Uganda | 94.6 | Coffee, cotton | 435.0 |
| Vanuatu | 83.4 | Cocoa, fish, vegetable oils and oil seeds, bovine meat | 22.2 |
| Yemen | 3.5 | Coffee, cotton | 37.2 |

Source : UNCTAD: "Commodities earnings shortfalls and an additional compensatory financing facility" (TD/B/AC.43/2), table 1.

a/ Exports of primary commodities (SITC section 0,1,2 (less groups 233,244,267), 4, division 68 and item 522.261 as percentage of all merchandise exports (SITC sections 0 to 9).

b/ Calculated as the difference between actual value of exports of commodities involved in each of the years 1978 to 1983 vis-à-vis the value for each of those years of the exponential trend calculated on the basis of a moving 10 year period ending in the specific year in question. Fluctuation and dependency thresholds set at 1.5 per cent.

## Table 24

### LDC imports, 1978 to 1985
### (Millions of US dollars (c.i.f.))

| Country | 1978 | 1979 | 1980 | 1981 | 1982 | 1983 | 1984 | 1985 |
|---|---|---|---|---|---|---|---|---|
| Afghanistan ............... | 591 | 686 | 552 | 622 | 695 | 780 | 800 | 770 |
| Bangladesh ................ | 1 350 | 1 531 | 1 973 | 1 813 | 1 737 | 1 587 | 2 042 | 2 170 |
| Benin ..................... | 312 | 320 | 331 | 542 | 464 | 320 | 310 | 400 |
| Bhutan .................... | .. | .. | .. | .. | .. | .. | .. | .. |
| Botswana .................. | 353 | 521 | 691 | 799 | 686 | 736 | 679 | 596 |
| Burkina Faso .............. | 224 | 301 | 358 | 338 | 346 | 288 | 211 | 225 |
| Burundi ................... | 98 | 152 | 168 | 161 | 214 | 183 | 186 | 186 |
| Cape Verde ................ | 43 | 41 | 68 | 70 | 70 | 80 | 84 | 113 |
| Central African Republic ... | 55 | 70 | 81 | 95 | 127 | 52 | 87 | 120 |
| Chad ...................... | 217 | 85 | 74 | 108 | 109 | 157 | 171 | 190 |
| Comoros ................... | 19 | 28 | 33 | 34 | 32 | 32 | 30 | 30 |
| Democratic Yemen .......... | 575 | 393 | 652 | 673 | 1 599 | 1 483 | 1 543 | 1 290 |
| Djibouti .................. | 94 | 104 | 125 | 120 | 115 | 115 | 110 | 110 |
| Equatorial Guinea ......... | 9 | 19 | 26 | 31 | 42 | 30 | 30 | 30 |
| Ethiopia .................. | 522 | 567 | 722 | 739 | 787 | 876 | 942 | 935 |
| Gambia .................... | 100 | 141 | 163 | 122 | 97 | 115 | 98 | 94 |
| Guinea .................... | 234 | 253 | 270 | 320 | 310 | 300 | 360 | 420 |
| Guinea-Bissau ............. | 42 | 61 | 55 | 50 | 50 | 65 | 48 | 60 |
| Haiti ..................... | 221 | 266 | 354 | 448 | 387 | 440 | 472 | 470 |
| Lao People's Dem. Rep...... | 76 | 94 | 131 | 125 | 130 | 140 | 145 | 160 |
| Lesotho ................... | 273 | 360 | 464 | 528 | 527 | 587 | 312 | 250 |
| Malawi .................... | 338 | 398 | 440 | 350 | 311 | 311 | 269 | 284 |
| Maldives .................. | 12 | 20 | 29 | 31 | 43 | 57 | 53 | 53 |
| Mali ...................... | 285 | 359 | 440 | 385 | 332 | 345 | 368 | 421 |
| Nepal ..................... | 221 | 254 | 342 | 369 | 395 | 464 | 416 | 460 |
| Niger ..................... | 306 | 462 | 594 | 510 | 442 | 350 | 330 | 400 |
| Rwanda .................... | 179 | 192 | 243 | 256 | 276 | 269 | 295 | 220 |
| Samoa ..................... | 53 | 73 | 63 | 67 | 50 | 56 | 50 | 51 |
| Sao Tome and Principe ...... | 22 | 20 | 19 | 17 | 15 | 10 | 12 | 13 |
| Sierra Leone .............. | 260 | 297 | 414 | 312 | 240 | 166 | 166 | 151 |
| Somalia ................... | 241 | 246 | 348 | 512 | 330 | 179 | 109 | 112 |
| Sudan ..................... | 1 198 | 1 110 | 1 576 | 1 578 | 1 285 | 1 354 | 1 147 | 771 |
| Togo ...................... | 450 | 518 | 550 | 435 | 391 | 284 | 271 | 264 |
| Uganda .................... | 255 | 197 | 293 | 388 | 427 | 428 | 371 | 375 |
| United Republic of Tanzania | 1 143 | 1 077 | 1 226 | 1 212 | 1 131 | 822 | 847 | 1 028 |
| Vanuatu ................... | 62 | 73 | 71 | 58 | 59 | 63 | 67 | 71 |
| Yemen ..................... | 1 283 | 1 492 | 1 853 | 1 758 | 1 521 | 1 593 | 1 655 | 1 598 |
| All LDCs .................. | 11716 | 12781 | 15772 | 15976 | 15772 | 15117 | 15086 | 14891 |
| All LDCs (in million of SDR) | 9358 | 9892 | 12131 | 13548 | 14286 | 14141 | 14718 | 14666 |

Source: UNCTAD secretariat calculations based on national and international sources.

6.  Direction of trade

160. The analysis of the direction of LDCs' exports indicates, that the trade
flow still follows the historical pattern:  the bulk of the LDC's exports
continues to be consigned for developed market-economy countries, whereas
exports to other developing countries have ranged between 25 and 30 per cent
of total exports.  The share of the socialist countries in LDCs exports has
been stagnating at approximately 11 per cent (see table 25).

Table 25

Direction of LDCs' exports, 1970-1985
(in percentages)

| Principal markets | 1970 | 1980 | 1981 | 1982 | 1983 | 1984 | 1985 a/ |
|---|---|---|---|---|---|---|---|
| Developed market-economy countries .. | 65.7 | 62.3 | 58.0 | 61.8 | 62.4 | 58.7 | 60.9 |
| Of which : | | | | | | | |
| EEC ............................ | 42.8 | 36.4 | 37.6 | 35.9 | 37.2 | 40.1 | .. |
| Japan .......................... | 4.6 | 4.6 | 2.9 | 3.4 | 2.3 | .. | .. |
| United States ................. | 13.0 | 12.2 | 14.9 | 15.2 | 14.2 | 11.5 | .. |
| Developing countries ............... | 25.1 | 27.2 | 30.0 | 28.0 | 26.6 | 30.2 | 28.3 |
| Socialist countries ................ | 9.2 | 10.4 | 11.9 | 10.1 | 11.0 | 10.7 | 10.7 |

Sources:  UNCTAD, "The least developed countries, 1985 report",
TD/B/AC.17/25/Add.1 (B).
IMF, Direction of Trade Statistics Yearbook 1986.
UNCTAD secretariat calculations.

a/  Preliminary figures.


The exports of all LDCs to developed market-economy countries accounted
for about 61 per cent of total LDCs' exports in 1985.  Twenty-three LDCs
directed more than 50 per cent of their exports to developed market-economy
countries, while for 13 LDCs this share was even higher than three quarters.
The major markets for LDCs exports among the developed market-economy
countries continued to be the EEC and the United States.

161. Developing country markets accounted for 28 per cent of LDCs exports in
1985.  However, the distribution of LDC exports to other developing countries,
including LDCs, varies widely.  Djibouti, Maldives and Somalia consigned 96,
77 and 74 per cent respectively of their exports to other developing
countries, compared to Haiti, Afghanistan and Sierra Leone with shares of 3, 4
and 5 per cent respectively.  Other developing countries were of minor
importance as destinations for their exports.  For many LDCs there is still
scope to increase further the volume and the value of their exports to other
developing countries within the framework of South-South co-operation.

162. The value of the LDCs' exports to socialist countries amounted to approximately $790 million in 1985. Among the socialist countries, the USSR absorbed about 70 per cent of all LDCs' exports to this group of countries. However, only Afghanistan and, to a lesser extent, Ethiopia, Democratic Yemen, and Lao People's Democratic Republic have significant export links with socialist countries, thus indicating an area for potential expansion of LDCs' trade.

163. In 1985, the value of total LDCs' imports amounted to $14.8 billion. About 60 per cent of these imports originated from developed market-economy countries, with EEC and the United States as main suppliers. About 30 per cent of the LDCs' imports had their origin in other developing countries. The socialist countries accounted for approximately 10 per cent of LDCs' imports, having increased their share by a quarter since 1980 (see table 26).

Table 26

Geographical distribution of LDCs' imports, 1970-1985
(in percentages)

| Imports from | 1970 | 1980 | 1981 | 1982 | 1983 | 1984 a/ | 1985 b/ |
|---|---|---|---|---|---|---|---|
| Developed market-economy countries | 62.3 | 55.5 | 53.2 | 55.6 | 55.2 | 55.8 | 59 |
| Of which: | | | | | | | |
| EEC ......................... | 31.8 | 31.4 | 29.1 | 29.9 | 29.6 | 29.5 | 31 |
| United States .............. | 10.8 | 6.6 | 6.4 | 7.0 | 7.8 | 7.5 | 8 |
| Japan ...................... | 7.7 | 7.4 | 7.7 | 7.5 | 7.0 | 8.8 | 9 |
| Developing countries ............. | 30.7 | 34.4 | 31.4 | 28.9 | 29.6 | 31.5 | 30 |
| Socialist countries ............. | 5.5 | 7.5 | 9.4 | 12.9 | 11.9 | 9.7 | 10 |

Source:   UNCTAD, "The least developed countries, 1985 report", TD/B/AC.17/25/Add.1(B).
IMF, Directions of Trade Statistics Yearbook, 1986.
UNCTAD secretariat calculations.

a/   Provisional figures.

b/   Estimates.

7.   Conclusions

164. The LDCs' percentage of world exports has been declining over the past decades and fell to a mere 0.37 per cent in 1985 (as compared to 0.8 per cent in 1970). Because of the adverse effects of a host of current developments - such as moderate economic activity in the developed market economies as their main trading partners, changes in the demand pattern for LDCs' export products, increased competition in international markets and the emergence of substitutes for traditional products - the LDCs as a group are less and less in a position to defend, let alone to expand, their marginal share in

international trade.  The resulting sharp limitation on the import capacity of these countries undermines all efforts to bring about a rapid change in their economic situation.  If left to itself, this situation is unlikely to right itself in the short run, but will definitely worsen in the years to come.  Therefore, a basic objective in internal economic adjustment programmes should be a reallocation of human, capital and financial resources earmarked for the export sector so as to use the comparative advantages of these countries to the maximum extent.

165. Internationally, on the other hand, special efforts are required to ensure and provide adequate markets for expanded LDCs' exports, including semi-processed and processed goods.  The main trading partners of the LDCs should refrain from imposing tariff or non-tariff barriers that could run counter the LDCs' efforts to improve their export performance.  Moreover, the special needs of the LDCs should find adequate reflection in multilateral and bilateral trade negotiations and agreements.  A renewed effort and an unconventional approach by both the LDCs and the industrialized countries appear to be necessary to invigorate and strengthen the LDCs' external trade so as to give a strong impetus to their economic development.

## B.  Balance of payments

166. The balance of payments for the LDCs shows an average annual current-account deficit of about $6 billion for 1983-1984, compared to an average of $8 billion during the period 1980-1981 (see table 27).  This reduction of the current-account deficit was due mainly to a decrease of the trade deficit and, to a lesser extent, to increased net private transfers, including migrants' transfers, workers' remittances and other transfers.  The reduction in the trade deficit was exclusively due to a slash of annual imports from $15.8 billion in 1980-1981 to $13.7 billion in 1983-1984.  Exports did not contribute to the decline of the trade deficit, inasmuch as they also fell, namely from $8 billion in 1980-1981 to $6.8 billion in 1983 and recovered only partially to $7.4 billion in 1984.  Since in most LDCs the level of imports is closely associated with overall economic activity, the dominant strategy of reducing the current-account deficit by means of import reductions bears the risk of deteriorating these countries' economic performance, if perpetuated over a longer period.

167. The sharp decline in oil prices in 1986 is expected to reduce the fuel import bill of the LDCs by almost $1 billion, i.e. one half of its 1983 level.  However, these savings should be seen against the decline in financial flows to the LDCs from OPEC countries and decreased workers' remittances. (For further discussion, see part two, chapter I on transfer of resources.)

168. Gross payments of interest by the LDCs, which had increased markedly between 1980 and 1982, remained close to the $0.9 billion level during the period 1982-1984.  Since the bulk of the LDCs' debt is owed to official lenders and therefore bears fixed interest rates, the sharp decline in international lending rates, which began in 1982, is likely to have but a moderate effect on the LDCs' interest payments and, hence, on their current-account balance.  However, the decline in interest rates may become meaningful in new borrowings, even though interest rates charged by official lenders declined to a lesser extent than those of private lenders.  (For further discussion of this point, see part two, chapter IV, on the debt situation of the LDCs.)

Table 27

Balance of payments of the LDCs a/
(Billions of dollars)

|  | 1980 | 1981 | 1982 | 1983 | 1984 | 1985 b/ |
|---|---|---|---|---|---|---|
| Current-account balance c/ ... | -7.9 | -8.0 | -7.8 | -6.2 | -6.0 | -6.2 |
| Exports of goods f.o.b. d/ ... | 8.0 | 7.7 | 6.6 | 6.8 | 7.4 | 6.8 |
| Imports of goods f.o.b. d/ ... | -15.7 | -15.9 | -14.6 | -13.5 | -13.8 | -13.5 |
| Non-factor service receipts .. | 2.4 | 2.7 | 2.6 | 2.4 | 2.3 | .. |
| Non-factor service payments .. | -4.8 | -4.6 | -4.3 | -4.2 | -4.2 | .. |
| Income from labour .......... | 0.4 | 0.4 | 0.4 | 0.5 | 0.4 | .. |
| Receipts of interest ......... | 0.5 | 0.5 | 0.5 | 0.3 | 0.3 | .. |
| Payments of interest ........ | -0.6 | -0.8 | -0.9 | -0.9 | -0.9 | .. |
| Net direct investment income . | -0.2 | -0.1 | -0.2 | -0.2 | -0.2 | .. |
| Net private transfers e/ ..... | 2.2 | 2.3 | 2.1 | 2.8 | 2.8 | .. |
| Capital-account balance f/ .... | 7.3 | 7.3 | 7.0 | 6.1 | 6.1 | 6.5 |
| Overall balance g/ ........... | -0.6 | -0.7 | -0.8 | -0.9 | -0.1 | 0.3 |

Source: UNCTAD secretariat calculations based on data from IMF and other international and national sources.

a/  Figures may not add exactly owing to rounding.

b/  Provisional estimate.

c/  Excluding net Government transfers.

d/  The trade figures differ from those reported in the trade returns because of adjustments for coverage, evaluation, timing, inland freight, etc.

e/  Including migrants' transfers, workers' remittances and other transfers.

f/  Including official transfers and errors and omissions.

g/  Financed by monetary authorities' reserve holdings and IMF drawings.

169. While virtually all LDCs regularly run current-account deficits at a level close to their joint trade deficits - implying a virtual equilibrium in their combined service transactions and private transfers - the relative importance of the trade deficit within the current account deficits varies widely from one country to another. Among the sample of 19 LDCs shown in table 28, Botswana actually runs a substantial trade surplus, which is more than offset by outflows on account of dividends and interest. Democratic Yemen and Yemen, on the other hand, are the largest importers of the sample after Bangladesh, but have virtually no merchandise exports with which to finance them. Both rely heavily on private transfers from emigrant workers, but even then require strong inflows of official transfers to finance their huge trade deficits. Lesotho has a similarly one-sided trade balance, but finances most of it by workers' remittances, leaving only a modest current-account deficit.

170. Despite the unquestionable and growing debt burden faced by LDCs, of which only the interest portion is identified in these tables - amortization is merged with other capital movements and with official transfers - it is noteworthy that the net deficit on non-factor services, such as freight, insurance, tourism and banking services is three to four times as heavy as that on net interest payments. Among the 19 countries included in the sample, all but three, which have important tourist incomes, showed deficits on the non-factor service account.

Table 28

Balance-of-payments for selected LDCs in 1984

(Millions of dollars)

| Country | Exports of goods f.o.b. | Imports of goods f.o.b. | Trade balance | Non-factor services balance | Labour income | Receipts of interest | Payments of interest | Direct investment income | Net private transfers | Current account balance a/ | Capital account balance b/ | Overall balance |
|---|---|---|---|---|---|---|---|---|---|---|---|---|
| Bangladesh | 932 | -2338 | -1406 | -270 | 0 | 73 | -122 | 0 | 472 | -1253 | 1212 | -42 |
| Botswana | 674 | -555 | +119 | -73 | 20 | 50 | -29 | -125 | 6 | -43 | 167 | 124 |
| Central African Republic | 115 | -140 | -25 | -51 | 0 | 3 | -12 | -0 | -11 | -97 | 104 | 6 |
| Chad | 111 | -129 | -18 | -56 | 0 | 1 | -2 | 0 | -2 | -77 | 96 | 19 |
| Comoros | 7 | -30 | -23 | -38 | 0 | 1 | -2 | 0 | -3 | -64 | 58 | -6 |
| Democratic Yemen | 31 | -825 | -794 | -100 | 0 | 34 | -16 | 0 | 479 | -397 | 392 | -5 |
| Ethiopia | 414 | -787 | -373 | -66 | 0 | 12 | -38 | 0 | 146 | -307 | 247 | -60 |
| Haiti | 204 | -333 | -129 | -84 | 11 | 0 | -16 | -2 | 44 | -187 | 158 | -29 |
| Lesotho | 28 | -423 | -395 | -21 | 344 | 0 | -7 | -3 | 2 | -58 | 68 | 10 |
| Maldives | 23 | -61 | -38 | 27 | 0 | 22 | -9 | -4 | -1 | -24 | 24 | -0 |
| Mali | 177 | -255 | -78 | -130 | 0 | 0 | -28 | 0 | 21 | -215 | 215 | 0 |
| Nepal | 133 | -424 | -291 | 62 | 0 | 5 | -5 | 0 | 35 | -195 | 179 | -16 |
| Rwanda | 143 | -198 | -55 | -81 | -2 | 8 | -5 | -8 | 2 | -141 | 154 | 14 |
| Samoa | 20 | -46 | -26 | -3 | 0 | 0 | -2 | -0 | 20 | -10 | 13 | 3 |
| Sierra Leone | 133 | -150 | -17 | -6 | 0 | 0 | -14 | -18 | 8 | -48 | 27 | -21 |
| Somalia | 41 | -466 | -425 | -73 | 0 | 1 | -7 | 0 | 163 | -340 | 322 | -18 |
| Sudan | 520 | -601 | -81 | -27 | 0 | 10 | -174 | 0 | 276 | 5 | -18 | -14 |
| Vanuatu | 32 | -51 | -19 | 7 | 0 | 8 | -3 | -13 | 7 | -13 | 11 | -2 |
| Yemen | 9 | -1402 | -1393 | -59 | 0 | 35 | -21 | 0 | 992 | -446 | 366 | -80 |
| Total c/ | 3745 | -9212 | -5467 | -1042 | 374 | 264 | -509 | -175 | 2644 | -3911 | 3796 | -114 |

Source : UNCTAD secretariat calculations based on IMF balance-of-payments tapes.

a/ Excluding official unrequited transfers.
b/ Including official unrequited transfers and errors and omissions.
c/ Total of selected LDCs.

## Chapter V

## WOMEN IN THE LEAST DEVELOPED COUNTRIES

### A.  Demographic dimension and social situation

171. Women form an important pool of human resources in the LDCs, accounting
for about 50 per cent of their total population.  Many still live out in the
country in small villages where sanitation is poor, easy access to potable
water supply is lacking and medical facilities are inadequate or hard to
reach.  Consequently, their average life expectancy at birth is substantially
lower than that of their female counterparts in the developed world - 47 years
as against 77 years respectively during 1980 to 1985.  Furthermore, women in
the LDCs tend to be afflicted by high morbidity and mortality associated with
repeated child-bearing.  More women than men die in the reproductive age of 14
to 45 years, and maternal mortality is among the leading causes in this age
range.  Some economic and social indicators for women in the LDCs are
presented in table 29.

### B.  Economic participation

172. Women's involvement in productive and economic activities is extensive
but their contribution tends to be under-estimated in production and labour
statistics.  This is because women's work takes place in the family setting
(as unpaid family workers) or because they are more active in the urban
informal sector and as secondary part-time or seasonal workers where such work
is difficult to measure.  Women's official activity rate in LDCs (27 per cent
in 1983) is thus shown to be half that of men.  The lack of recognition of
women's full contribution has often resulted in inadequate policies in
development plans which could enhance women's role in development.

#### 1.  Subsistence and domestic production

173. Over 80 per cent of women in the LDCs live in the rural areas.  Most of
them are engaged in subsistence production and in supplying food to their
families.  They contribute 60 to 80 per cent of agricultural labour on their
small-scale farms.  Men help initially with clearing the bush and cutting down
the trees, but the remaining agricultural work - such as hoeing, weeding,
tilling the soil and harvesting - is the women's responsibility.  In cash crop
production, women often participate as unremunerated family labour and
seasonal workers on plantations, and they do not have control over the income
from the production.  In addition to this, women spend much of their time on
housework.  The preparation of meals includes the arduous tasks of fetching
water and firewood, which often have to be carried long distances and over
difficult terrain.  Access to safe water is still available to only a small
section of the population.  In 1983, 34 per cent of the rural population had
access to safe water (figure based on the average of 25 LDCs for which
information is available).  Women, therefore, have to fetch water from the
public wells and it is common for them to carry 10 to 15 litres on each trip.

174. Women in some LDCs - e.g., Botswana, Lesotho and Yemen - where
large-scale migration of males occurs have the additional responsibility of
looking after the household in the absence of their menfolk, either

permanently or temporarily. In Botswana, 10 per cent and in Lesotho 60 per cent of the rural households are headed by women. Although they assume the responsibilities of heads of households they do not acquire the actual status which would give them access to credit and other resources. 51/

### 2. Self-employment

175. Women predominate in marketing and trading, especially in Benin, Haiti, Sierra Leone and Togo. Despite their central role in the distributive trade, studies attest to women's meagre income (usually below the minimum wage), most of which goes to meet the immediate needs of the family. Women tend to predominate only in the retail trade, while wholesale trade is almost wholly in the hands of men. The wholesale trade is a central subsector in the economy from which women are being excluded for lack of capital. Few women obtain credit on the strength of their own standing and most of the women traders have perforce to rely on indigenous credit associations for capital.

### 3. Participation in the modern sector

176. Women's share of non-agricultural occupations is small, which indicates their low participation in the modern sector. According to data available for six LDCs, paid female employees constitute an insignificant proportion of less than 20 per cent. Generally, when women are in salaried employment they are much more likely to be concentrated in low-level and middle-level jobs. Their share of managerial category is insignificant while their relatively larger share in the professional category is found in the traditionally female dominated fields such as teaching, clerical, nursing and administrative positions. In effect, women's employment status is a reflection of their education standards and the social problems and obstacles they face.

### C. Education

177. Women in LDCs generally lag behind men in education. Except for Botswana and Lesotho, where the literacy rate for women equals or surpasses that of men, the disparity in the LDCs is very wide. For example, in Yemen, 3 per cent of women were literate in 1985 as compared to 27 per cent for males; in Burkina Faso the corresponding figures are 6 per cent for females and 21 per cent for males, and in Afghanistan it is 8 per cent as against 39 per cent.

178. In line with the literacy trend, the percentage of females attending schools is smaller than that for males at all levels - primary, secondary and university. The gap gets wider the higher the level. The average enrolment of females in the LDCs in primary school was 50 per cent in 1985, which trails behind a male enrolment of 70 per cent. Of the 37 LDCs, female enrolment in primary schools has reached 90 per cent in the case of four countries, Botswana, Cape Verde, Lesotho and United Republic of Tanzania, while this mark for male enrolment was attained by 11 LDCs.

### D. Access and control over productive resources

179. Land is the most important asset in an agrarian economy. Yet women in LDCs have little control over land. In many cases they do not have a legal

right to own land and their situation has been made worse by the modernization process whereby the disappearance of communal land tenure has caused them to be dispossessed of their land and men have been recognized as the new owners, thereby decreasing women's control over productive resources. However, even in situations where women have a legal right of tenure, customary law, family traditions, inheritance systems and their acceptance of subordination often prevent women from exercising that right. As the recognized landowners, men have ultimate authority over land and its use as collateral for credit. It follows that services such as marketing, input delivery systems and extension information are directed to him. The predicament of women farmers is highlighted in the case of Botswana and Lesotho, where widespread male migration has led women to become heads of households and yet these women do not have control over the productive resources. The practice is that they have to wait for the men to apply for credit, hire tractors etc.

## E.  Projects for women, national measures and international support

### 1.  Projects for women in LDCs

180. Over the past decade, the implementation of projects for women has gathered momentum. However, while these projects have led to positive changes, many of them have failed to integrate women in mainstream development. One of the main deficiencies lies in the project approach, which often assumes a reformist character and does not contribute to structural changes. For example, the creation of income-generating projects for women, which concentrated on handicrafts production, were very often designed as part-time activities to give women supplementary income, but they ignored women's main economic activities and their critical need for full-time employment and income to sustain themselves and their families.

181. Moreover, development assistance appears to have largely by-passed women farmers. Indeed the allocation of choice land, favourable price policies, training, and available credit to purchase seeds, fertilizers and tools have in general been diverted to cash crop production, thereby hampering the attainment of the goal of self-sufficiency in food production and women's ability to earn an independent income.

182. On the other hand, several small-scale grass-root projects have shown that women can be effectively integrated in development through appropriate project design and delivery. 52/ These projects, with emphasis on participatory development, are organized by women on their own initiative or through interaction with supporters from outside to gain access to the factors of production. They are considered to have achieved some measure of success as they have contributed to the improvement of women's living conditions and have increased their self-reliance and income-earning opportunities.

183. Essentially such schemes have succeeded in transforming the status of poor women because for the first time it gave them access to development resources, ownership of major assets of production and a sense of collective strength. 53/ A notable feature of these schemes is that they all support women in their main economic activities.

## 2. National measures

184. National Governments have undertaken measures to promote the
effectiveness of women's participation. For example, in order to promote
women's access to education, Nepal has embodied in its Seventh Development
Plan (1985-1990) such measures as fixing quotas for increasing the admission
of girls in the formal educational institutions as well as in various training
programmes in technical and non-technical subjects such as health, education,
agriculture and engineering. Girls have been given free education and
preference in the distribution of free text books. Consideration has also
been given to making education programmes more relevant to women's role, for
example by aiming at increasing women's participation in the conservation,
development and growth of forests.

185. An important development which has enhanced women's effective
participation is the establishment of national machinery for women. These
organizations are now established in more than half of the LDCs and they play
a catalytic role in influencing mainstream development policies and
programmes. 54/ While this type of machinery has contributed to creating an
awareness of women's issues, in a number of cases it has been marginalized in
the power structures, and in some others it has not effectively mobilized
women's issues and interests, particularly at the grass-root level.

## 3. Global strategies and international support

186. Since the beginning of the United Nations Decade for Women in 1975,
several global strategies aiming, inter alia, at improving the status of women
have been launched. Of special relevance to women's needs in the LDCs are the
United Nations International Drinking Water and Sanitation Decade, Health for
all by the Year 2000, the Lagos Plan of Action (which accords priority to
enhancing the skills and training of rural women and to reducing their
household chores in order to make them more productive), and the World
Conference on Agrarian Reforms and Rural Development (which adopted an
important programme of action for the integration of women in rural
development, including equitable access to land, water, other natural
resources, inputs and services and equal opportunity to develop and employ
their skills). To give teeth to the implementation of measures after the
United Nations Decade for Women ended in 1985, the Nairobi Forward Looking
Strategies for the Advancement of Women (FLS), which was adopted at the
Nairobi Conference to review and appraise the achievements of the
United Nations Decade for Women in July 1985, identified specific areas for
action. 55/

187. A System-Wide Medium-Term Plan on Women and Development for the period
1990-1995, translating the objectives of the FLS into specific tasks for the
different organizations, will be presented to the second regular session of
the Economic and Social Council in 1987. The international organizations have
already intensified their programmes in this direction. The Food and
Agriculture Organization of the United Nations (FAO) is directing efforts at
improving support services for women in recognition of women's role in food
security, especially at the household level. The International Labour Office
(ILO) has implemented specific projects on women and assisted at the national
level. For instance, it has helped to develop women's textile establishments

in Lao People's Democratic Republic and a poultry farming school in Bangladesh for rural youths (particularly girls); and it has provided commercial training for women in Botswana. During 1984 to 1985, 14 LDCs have benefited from a UNESCO programme aimed at improving the enrolment of girls in primary schools and their access to technical and vocational education.

188. Several bilateral and multilateral donors to the LDCs indicated 56/ that they have made women's role and needs an integral part of their aid policies. The Federal Republic of Germany, for example, is inclined to support those sectors - i.e., agriculture, water supply, energy - where women could benefit directly. The African Development Bank, the Asian Development Bank, the Inter-American Development Bank (IDB), the International Fund for Agricultural Development (IFAD), the World Bank 57/ and the Organisation for Economic Co-operation and Development 58/ have also incorporated in their work programmes projects which will enhance women's productive capacity and economic role. IFAD, for example, is undertaking projects which aim at reducing the drudgery of women's domestic chores as well as specific activities like the provision of special credit, organization of productive activities for women, and addressing agricultural extension services and training specifically to women.

189. Finally, at the thirty-third session of the UNDP Governing Council in June 1986, it was decided to take into account women's roles and needs in the preparation and conduct of round-table meetings of the least developed countries.

F. Prospects for the future and conclusions

190. Special increased efforts are needed to improve effectively women's economic and social conditions in the LDCs, not only because, under general conditions of poverty, women tend to bear the greatest burden of disadvantages, but also because development hinges to such a great extent on women's status. 59/

191. Discernible trends show that, unless appropriate measures are taken, women will face increasing competition for scarce resources in the formal wage sector in the light of worsening climatic and socio-economic conditions in the rural sector. Tehnological transfer will continue to displace women from their traditional activities while favouring men in newly-created employment opportunities, thereby forcing women more into the informal sector. Also, increased urban migration poses problems for the landless poor, among them the poor rural women, who, with no training whatsoever, will invariably land up in low-level service jobs or be exploited for their labour. Women who are in trade and marketing activities will have little chance of being integrated into the formal sector because of their lack of access to capital, technology and training.

192. Real and sustainable progress can only be achieved if global development strategies for women are translated into specific action programmes at the national and local levels, as an integral part of the regular activities of ministries, and if women's economic and productive contribution are given due recognition by development planners, lawmakers and lawenforcers, project managers, agricultural specialists, educators, community leaders and other key groups.

Table 29

Status of women in the least developed countries

Column definitions:

- (1) Labour force participation rate (female/male)
- (2) Growth of female labour force – (1960/1980)/(1980/2000)
- (3) Female life expectancy – (1975–1980)
- (4) Per cent of adults literate, 1985 (women/men)
- (5) Enrolment in primary schools, 1985 (female/male), per cent
- (6) Enrolment in secondary schools, 1985 (female/male), per cent
- (7) Per cent of women employees in professional and technical positions (maj. group 0/1)
- (8) Per cent of women employees in admin. and managerial positions (maj. group 0/2)
- (9) Per cent of women employees in the service sector (maj. group 0/5)
- (10) Per cent of women attended during childbirth by trained personnel
- (11) Females practising family planning (% of eligible couples)
- (12) National machinery responsible for the advancement of women, G-Governmental; NG- Non Governmental, SG - Semi-Governmental

| Country | (1) | (2) | (3) | (4) | (5) | (6) | (7) | (8) | (9) | (10) | (11) | (12) |
|---|---|---|---|---|---|---|---|---|---|---|---|---|
| Afghanistan | 5/54 | 2.5/3.4 | 37 | 8/39 | 12/23 | 6/16 | 7 | 1 | 25 | 5 | 1 | National Women's Association, 1976 |
| Bangladesh | 6/54 | 3.0/3.4 | 54 | 22/43 | 56/71 | 11/27 |  |  |  |  | 19 |  |
| Benin | 23/44 | 1.9/2.2 | 42 | 16/37 | 49/96 | 15/36 |  |  |  |  | 17 | Organisation of the Revolutionary Women of Benin, G – 1983 |
| Bhutan | 39/59 | 1.8/2.3 | 43 | 17/29 | 17/29 | 2/7 |  |  |  |  | 1 | National Women's Association, NG – 1981 |
| Botswana | 26/43 | 1.7/2.1 | 54 | 69/73 | 105/92 | 28/22 | 57 | 7 | 61 | 52 | 5 |  |
| Burkina Faso | 2/48 | 1.6/2.0 | 31 | 6/21 | 21/36 | 3/6 |  |  |  | 5 |  | Ministry of Social Affairs, G – 1974 |
| Burundi | 62/59 | 1.3/2.0 | 56 | 26/43 | 40/59 | 3/5 |  |  |  | 15 |  | Ministry of Women's Affairs, G – 1982 |
| Cape Verde | 5/54 | 3.0/2.6 | 56 | 39/61 | 205/206 | 10/13 |  |  |  | 53 |  |  |
| Central African Rep. | 52/58 | 1.5/1.8 | 36 | 29/53 | 57/108 | 11/26 |  |  |  | 45 |  | Ministry of Labour, Special Women's Unit, G – 1982 |
| Chad | 16/58 | 1.5/2.3 | 35 | 11/40 | 24/57 | 2/10 |  |  |  | 35 |  |  |
| Comoros | 20/67 | 1.4/2.0 | 50 | 40/56 | ../.. | ../.. |  |  |  |  |  |  |
| Democratic Yemen | 3/50 | 3.7/4.2 | 45 | 25/59 | 54/131 | 8/16 |  |  |  |  |  |  |
| Djibouti | ../.. | .. | 44 | ../.. | ../.. | ../.. |  |  |  |  |  | UNFD, SG – 1977 |
| Equatorial Guinea | 3/58 | 2.6/2.4 | 44 | ../.. | 41/66 | 14/23 |  |  |  | 12 |  | Ministry of Labour, Special Women's Unit, G – 1980 |
| Ethiopia | 34/54 | 1.9/2.1 | 43 | ../.. | 54/85 | 15/33 |  |  |  | 25 |  | Revolutionary Ethiopia Women's Association, NG – 1980 |
| Gambia | 44/56 | 1.3/1.6 | 35 | 15/36 | 54/85 | 15/33 |  |  |  | 90 |  |  |
| Guinea | 37/56 | 1.7/2.0 | 40 | 17/40 | 23/47 | 10/26 | 26 | 8 | 8 |  |  |  |
| Guinea-Bissau | 3/78 | 0.8/2.3 | 43 | 35/40 | 47/92 | 3/14 | 40 | 33 |  | 15 | 19 |  |
| Haiti | 34/51 | 0.9/1.3 | 52 | 68/77 | 13/13 | 40 |  |  | 66 |  |  |  |
| Lao P.D.R. | 44/54 | 1.2/1.7 | 49 | 76/92 | 83/93 | 15/25 |  |  |  | 75 |  |  |
| Lesotho | 25/53 | 1.2/1.8 | .. | 84/62 | 126/95 | 28/19 | 25 | 6 | 18 | 45 | 5 | Bureau of Women's Affairs, Prime Minister's Office, G |
| Malawi | 37/46 | 1.7/2.1 | 44 | 31/52 | 57/78 | 3/6 |  |  |  |  |  |  |
| Maldives | 37/57 | .. | .. | ../.. | ../.. | ../.. |  |  |  |  |  |  |
| Mali | 12/60 | 1.8/2.3 | 50 | 11/23 | 18/31 | 5/12 | 20 | 7 |  | 14 | 41 | National Union of Malian Women, (1974) |
| Nepal | 39/58 | 1.9/2.2 | 43 | 12/39 | 49/104 | 17/41 | 11 | 5 | 12 | 4 |  | Women Services Co-ordination Committee, NG – 1977 |
| Niger | 51/50 | 3.0/3.3 | 42 | 9/19 | 24/40 | 5/11 |  |  | 25 | 25 |  | Women's Association, NG – 1975 |
| Rwanda | 56/55 | 2.5/2.7 | 64 | 33/61 | 63/66 | 2/4 | 28 | 2 | 17 | 20 |  |  |
| Samoa | 8/44 | .. | 64 | ../.. | ../.. | ../.. | 47 | 19 | 42 | 60 |  |  |
| Sao Tome and Principe | 20/43 | .. | .. | 21/38 | 43/62 | 12/24 | 52 | 9 |  | 88 |  | Women's Advisory Committee, Prime Minister's Department, G – 1979 |
| Sierra Leone | 27/51 | 1.5/2.1 | 34 | 6/18 | 21/38 | 12/25 | 34 |  |  | 30 |  | Ministry of Social Welfare and Rural Development, G – 1957 |
| Somalia | 23/56 | 2.0/2.2 | 43 | ../.. | 21/38 | 12/25 |  |  |  | 2 |  | Somali Women's Democratic Organization, 1977 |
| Sudan | 12/47 | 3.4/3.8 | 46 | ../.. | 46/61 | 17/22 |  |  |  | 5 | 27 | Executive Bureau of the Sudan Feminist Union, SG – 1971 |
| Togo | 35/48 | 2.4/2.2 | 39 | 28/54 | 88/133 | 18/48 |  |  |  | 50 |  | Directeur Général de la Condition Féminine, G – 1977 |
| Uganda | 28/56 | 2.2/2.5 | 51 | 49/66 | 49/66 | 6/12 |  |  |  |  | 50 | National Council of Women, SG – 1978 |
| Utd. Rep. of Tanzania | 45/54 | 2.2/2.5 | 51 | 45/70 | 90/97 | 3/5 |  |  |  | 50 |  | Union of Women of Tanganyika (UWT) |
| Vanuatu | 43/49 | .. | .. | ../.. | ../.. | ../.. | 32 | 8 | 62 |  | 1 |  |
| Yemen | 6/46 | 3.3/3.8 | 42 | 3/27 | 25/107 | 3/20 |  |  |  | 20 |  | Women's Association, NG – 1958 |
| All LDCs | 48/64 |  | 42 | 25/107 | 50/70 | 34/47 |  |  |  | 20 |  |  |

Column (1) Source: ILO, Yearbook of Labour Statistics, 1978 to 1985, table 1. For Bangladesh, Benin, Botswana, Burundi, Chad, Comoros, Ethiopia, Haiti, Samoa, Sao Tome and Principe and Togo data are for period between 1980 and 1984. For the remaining countries, data are for period between 1975 and 1979.

Column (2) Source: ILO, Labour force estimates 1950–1970, projections 1975–2000 vols. I to III.

Column (3) Source: United Nations Demographic Yearbook, 1983.

Columns (4), (5) and (6) Source: UNCTAD, Basic Data on The Least Developed Countries, 1986.

Columns (7), (8) and (9) Source: ILO, Yearbook of Labour Statistics 1977 to 1985, table 2B.

Column (10) Source: UNCTAD, Basic Data on The Least Developed Countries, 1986 (op.cit.).

Column (11) Source: World Bank, World Development Report, 1984.

Column (12) Source: Replies to questionnaires sent to Governments by the World Conference to Review and Appraise the Achievements of the United Nations Decade for Women, August 1983.

PART TWO

REVIEW OF INTERNATIONAL SUPPORT MEASURES IN FAVOUR
OF THE LEAST DEVELOPED COUNTRIES

Chapter I

TRANSFER OF FINANCIAL RESOURCES

A. Recent trends

193. After increasing seven and a half times in nominal terms between 1970 and 1980, net ODA receipts of LDCs stagnated at around $7 billion during the years 1980 to 1984 (except in 1981 when ODA dropped to $6.6 billion). Non-concessional flows, which had increased more than eleven-fold during the 1970s and reached a peak of $1.1 billion in 1980, dropped during the 1980s, to $457 million in 1984. Total external resource flows available to LDCs thus declined during the 1980s, from $8.2 billion in 1980 down to $7.5 billion in 1984.

194. Expressed in terms of their command over imports, i.e., deflated by LDCs' import unit price index, LDCs' total external resource receipts in constant dollars grew at an average annual growth rate of 7.8 per cent during the 1970s. During the 1980s, because of the continuous decline in import prices since 1981, external flows to LDCs in the years 1982 to 1984 were at higher levels than in earlier years. Yet the total level of ODA in 1984 was only 44 per cent above the average level in 1976-1980, and thus far from the doubling envisaged in the SNPA. Moreover, the modest growth registered in the 1980s did not match population growth and, in constant per capita dollars, the level of external flows available to LDCs in 1984 was more than 5 per cent lower than in 1980 ($26.5 as compared to $28.0).

195. Discernible trends show, especially in more recent years, an increase in multilateral aid from agencies mainly financed by DAC countries, and declines in OPEC aid as well as in net guaranteed private export credits, direct investment and other private flows (see table 30).

196. Available information on financial resources for developing countries in 1985 points to an increase in DAC bilateral aid (which for the LDCs may well have exceeded $4 billion in that year while it had fluctuated in earlier years between $3.2 billion and $3.5 billion) owing to substantial increases in aid to Africa, both for emergencies and structural adjustment. On the other hand, this increase may have been at least partly offset by continued declines in OPEC aid as well as in export credits and bank lending during 1985. 60/

197. The world economic crisis which imposed severe stringency on aid allocations in donors' budgets, the general tightening in conditionality not only by multilateral financial institutions but also by many bilateral donors, and the appreciation of the United States dollar against other donors' currencies which further lowered dollar-denominated aid flows have all contributed to the sluggish flow of ODA.

198. On the part of the LDCs severe adjustment programmes were undertaken, which implied cuts in imports and in new projects and less recourse to external finance. Moreover, during that period, LDCs saw their GDP growth grinding to a halt, their debt obligations and problems escalating and their

Table 30

Total net resource receipts of LDCs

| | Commitments a/ ($ million) | | | | | | Disbursements ($ million) | | | | | | Percentage of total | | | | | |
|---|---|---|---|---|---|---|---|---|---|---|---|---|---|---|---|---|---|---|
| | Average 1976-1980 | 1980 | 1981 | 1982 | 1983 | 1984 | Average 1976-1980 | 1980 | 1981 | 1982 | 1983 | 1984 | Average 1976-1980 | 1980 | 1981 | 1982 | 1983 | 1984 |
| **Concessional flows** of which: | 7112 | 10333 | 8710 | 8665 | 8958 | 9565 | 4866 | 6970 | 6587 | 7051 | 7049 | 6996 | 88.1 | 85.4 | 91.9 | 90.1 | 93.7 | 93.9 |
| DAC | 5353 | 7830 | 6926 | 6646 | 6918 | 7614 | 3726 | 5392 | 5224 | 5437 | 5295 | 5800 | 67.4 | 66.1 | 72.9 | 69.4 | 70.3 | 77.8 |
| Bilateral | 3367 | 4993 | 3993 | 3643 | 3717 | 4266 | 2339 | 3409 | 3242 | 3472 | 3192 | 3386 | 42.3 | 41.8 | 45.2 | 44.3 | 42.4 | 45.4 |
| Multilateral b/ | 1986 | 2837 | 2934 | 3004 | 3202 | 3348 | 1387 | 1983 | 1982 | 1965 | 2102 | 2414 | 25.1 | 24.3 | 27.7 | 25.1 | 27.9 | 32.4 |
| OPEC | 1260 | 1406 | 1106 | 1539 | 1490 | 939 | 854 | 1021 | 873 | 1073 | 956 | 600 | 15.4 | 12.5 | 12.2 | 13.7 | 12.7 | 8.1 |
| Bilateral | 1074 | 1194 | 834 | 1236 | 1253 | 667 | 752 | 887 | 674 | 909 | 813 | 519 | 13.6 | 10.9 | 9.4 | 11.6 | 10.8 | 7.0 |
| Multilateral c/ | 185 | 211 | 273 | 303 | 236 | 272 | 102 | 134 | 199 | 164 | 143 | 81 | 1.8 | 1.6 | 2.8 | 2.1 | 1.9 | 1.1 |
| **Non-concessional flows** of which: | | | | | | | 658 | 1192 | 581 | 779 | 477 | 457 | 11.9 | 14.6 | 8.1 | 9.9 | 6.3 | 6.1 |
| DAC guaranteed private export credits | | | | | | | 414 | 873 | 201 | 178 | 93 | 81 | 7.5 | 10.7 | 2.8 | 2.3 | 1.2 | 1.1 |
| DAC direct investment | | | | | | | 68 | 55 | 107 | 169 | 30 | 32 | 1.2 | 0.7 | 1.5 | 2.2 | 0.4 | 0.4 |
| **Total external flows** | | | | | | | 5524 | 8162 | 7169 | 7830 | 7526 | 7453 | 100.0 | 100.0 | 100.0 | 100.0 | 100.0 | 100.0 |
| **Memo items (in 1980 $) d/** | | | | | | | | | | | | | | | | | | |
| Total ODA ($ million) | 9559 | 10333 | 8975 | 9320 | 10067 | 10981 | 6537 | 6970 | 6788 | 7584 | 7922 | 8031 | | | | | | |
| Per capita ODA ($) | 34.5 | 35.4 | 30.0 | 30.4 | 32.0 | 34.0 | 23.6 | 23.9 | 22.7 | 24.7 | 25.2 | 24.9 | | | | | | |
| Total external flows ($ million) | | | | | | | 7392 | 8162 | 7386 | 8421 | 8459 | 8556 | | | | | | |
| Per capita external flows ($) | | | | | | | 26.7 | 28.0 | 24.7 | 27.4 | 26.9 | 26.5 | | | | | | |

Source: UNCTAD secretariat calculations based on data from the OECD secretariat, the World Bank and the UNCTAD secretariat.

a/ ODA commitments only

b/ From multilateral agencies mainly financed by DAC member countries.

c/ From multilateral agencies mainly financed by OPEC member countries.

d/ External flows in real terms are expressed in terms of LDCs' command over imports in 1980.

creditworthiness strongly impaired, causing a slump not only in export credits but also in bank lending and direct investment (which, however, had never been important for these countries). 61/

## B. Developments in individual countries

199. In two-thirds of the LDCs, external per capita receipts (both concessional and total) were lower in 1984 than in 1980. In the majority of these countries non-concessional flows declined at a faster rate so that the share of concessional receipts increased and was higher in 1983-1984 than in 1980-1981 (see table 31). Yet important differences in levels exist among countries. Small countries tend to receive much larger amounts in per capita terms (in general above $80 and up to and over $300 on the average during the years 1980 to 1984), whereas most of the larger LDCs receive relatively small amounts (in most cases below $16 per capita). Apart from a few exceptions, average external receipts in medium-size LDCs range between $20 and $70 per capita, which constitutes a considerable span (see table 32).

200. Data for the 1980s show that, while high levels of external receipts (in per capita terms, and in terms of recipients' GDP) are generally associated with relatively high investment ratios, they are only in a few cases associated with positive economic growth rates. Apart from some small countries, examples of large aid recipients which succeeded in increasing income levels during that period are Somalia, Yemen, Benin and Botswana. The two latter also engaged in considerable non-concessional borrowing (see table 32).

201. The main recipients of DAC bilateral and multilateral ODA in 1984 are shown in table 25C of the annex. The major ODA donors to individual LDCs are listed in table 27 of the annex.

## C. Donors' performance

202. With a view to providing substantially increased flows to LDCs, and possibly a doubling of ODA flows by 1985, two alternative aid targets were established in the SNPA. Under these targets which, following Conference resolution 142 (VI), were to be "achieved by 1985 or as soon as possible thereafter", and which were reaffirmed in the mid-term review of the implementation of the SNPA, all bilateral donors should provide 0.15 per cent of their GNP as ODA to LDCs or double their ODA to LDCs (compared to average flows in the period 1976-1980).

203. Moreover, in order for an increasing volume of concessional assistance to be directed to LDCs, it was also recommended that donors should channel their multilateral aid particularly to those multilateral development institutions that address the needs of the LDCs. Multilateral institutions should consider ways and means of increasing the share of their total flows to LDCs.

204. When the SNPA was adopted, and in the course of subsequent meetings, as well as in the replies to the UNCTAD questionnaire on the implementation of the SNPA, 62/ donors have made known their interpretation of the SNPA aid targets.

Table 31

## Per capita net resource receipts of individual least developed countries

| | Total ($ per capita) | | | | | Concessional ($ per capita) | | | | | Share of concessional flows in total financial flows (per cent) | | | | |
|---|---|---|---|---|---|---|---|---|---|---|---|---|---|---|---|
| | 1980 | 1981 | 1982 | 1983 | 1984 | 1980 | 1981 | 1982 | 1983 | 1984 | 1980 | 1981 | 1982 | 1983 | 1984 |
| AFGHANISTAN | 21.0 | 16.8 | 10.1 | 20.0 | 11.8 | 20.3 | 16.9 | 10.0 | 20.0 | 11.9 | 96.7 | 100.1 | 98.2 | 100.1 | 100.5 |
| BANGLADESH | 14.0 | 12.1 | 15.1 | 12.8 | 13.1 | 14.4 | 12.2 | 14.9 | 12.0 | 12.7 | 102.8 | 101.0 | 98.8 | 93.8 | 97.3 |
| BENIN | 113.4 | 33.2 | 52.5 | 29.4 | 43.6 | 26.4 | 22.9 | 22.0 | 28.1 | 20.3 | 23.3 | 69.1 | 41.8 | 95.3 | 46.7 |
| BHUTAN | 6.5 | 7.5 | 8.5 | 9.5 | 12.9 | 6.5 | 7.5 | 8.5 | 9.5 | 12.9 | 100.0 | 100.0 | 100.0 | 100.0 | 100.0 |
| BOTSWANA | 58.1 | 116.1 | 119.2 | 126.1 | 169.2 | 116.5 | 101.7 | 102.2 | 100.4 | 95.8 | 99.6 | 87.6 | 85.6 | 79.6 | 56.6 |
| BURKINA FASO | 38.1 | 35.0 | 39.2 | 29.6 | 25.9 | 35.5 | 34.6 | 32.4 | 27.8 | 26.1 | 93.1 | 99.0 | 82.7 | 94.0 | 101.1 |
| BURUNDI | 32.3 | 32.4 | 37.1 | 41.7 | 33.0 | 31.2 | 28.9 | 30.1 | 33.8 | 29.7 | 96.7 | 89.2 | 81.2 | 81.0 | 90.1 |
| CAPE VERDE | 211.4 | 172.0 | 218.1 | 209.6 | 205.9 | 211.4 | 171.0 | 193.4 | 196.5 | 203.7 | 100.0 | 99.1 | 88.7 | 93.8 | 98.9 |
| CENT.AFRICAN REP. | 55.4 | 44.2 | 42.5 | 41.1 | 46.0 | 48.3 | 43.3 | 37.7 | 38.5 | 45.4 | 87.1 | 97.9 | 88.9 | 93.5 | 98.8 |
| CHAD | 7.6 | 11.8 | 12.7 | 19.6 | 23.0 | 7.9 | 13.2 | 13.1 | 19.9 | 23.4 | 104.0 | 112.1 | 102.8 | 101.7 | 101.8 |
| COMOROS | 112.3 | 127.3 | 91.0 | 104.3 | 97.8 | 109.7 | 115.1 | 90.0 | 101.0 | 93.6 | 97.7 | 90.4 | 98.9 | 96.8 | 95.7 |
| DEMOCRATIC YEMEN | 133.0 | 76.1 | 102.4 | 75.4 | 75.5 | 65.3 | 70.5 | 88.0 | 87.6 | 77.3 | 49.1 | 92.7 | 85.9 | 116.3 | 102.5 |
| DJIBOUTI | 229.4 | 202.8 | 175.2 | 198.3 | 407.1 | 229.7 | 195.4 | 174.3 | 193.9 | 326.3 | 100.1 | 96.3 | 99.5 | 97.8 | 80.2 |
| EQUATORIAL GUINEA | 28.4 | 30.8 | 33.5 | 55.7 | 69.3 | 26.4 | 27.2 | 46.6 | 53.1 | 62.0 | 93.0 | 88.3 | 130.9 | 95.2 | 89.5 |
| ETHIOPIA | 7.2 | 8.2 | 9.0 | 10.9 | 13.6 | 7.2 | 7.8 | 9.2 | 10.5 | 12.3 | 100.1 | 95.1 | 94.5 | 96.1 | 90.6 |
| GAMBIA | 132.4 | 128.1 | 67.3 | 54.5 | 88.2 | 90.1 | 99.5 | 74.4 | 60.7 | 77.5 | 68.0 | 77.6 | 110.5 | 111.3 | 87.9 |
| GUINEA | 28.1 | 21.7 | 13.7 | 13.4 | 23.0 | 18.2 | 17.4 | 11.3 | 13.0 | 22.1 | 64.9 | 80.1 | 82.7 | 96.7 | 96.0 |
| GUINEA-BISSAU | 88.5 | 89.2 | 77.6 | 79.0 | 73.2 | 74.7 | 82.4 | 76.2 | 76.7 | 65.4 | 84.4 | 92.4 | 98.8 | 97.0 | 92.4 |
| HAITI | 24.6 | 22.7 | 27.4 | 24.7 | 26.0 | 21.4 | 21.3 | 25.3 | 23.2 | 25.9 | 89.2 | 94.0 | 97.9 | 106.0 | 99.9 |
| LAO PEOPLE'S DEM.REP. | 25.6 | 26.3 | 27.4 | 23.3 | 21.2 | 25.9 | 26.1 | 27.5 | 23.2 | 20.9 | 101.1 | 100.2 | 100.2 | 99.6 | 98.6 |
| LESOTHO | 67.7 | 75.9 | 66.4 | 73.6 | 62.8 | 67.8 | 74.3 | 63.6 | 72.2 | 65.9 | 100.1 | 97.9 | 95.7 | 98.1 | 104.8 |
| MALAWI | 31.6 | 31.3 | 21.1 | 16.1 | 23.8 | 24.1 | 22.4 | 19.1 | 17.9 | 23.5 | 76.2 | 71.6 | 90.3 | 111.0 | 98.6 |
| MALDIVES | 145.9 | 106.8 | 12.7 | 55.5 | 42.6 | 146.5 | 76.4 | 33.1 | 66.6 | 43.1 | 100.4 | 71.5 | 261.9 | 120.0 | 101.3 |
| MALI | 38.3 | 33.9 | 27.4 | 28.8 | 40.2 | 38.4 | 33.3 | 26.2 | 28.7 | 41.0 | 100.2 | 98.2 | 95.7 | 99.8 | 102.0 |
| NEPAL | 11.0 | 12.2 | 13.1 | 12.6 | 12.5 | 11.1 | 12.2 | 13.2 | 12.8 | 12.3 | 101.0 | 100.0 | 100.6 | 101.7 | 98.4 |
| NIGER | 47.4 | 67.8 | 52.0 | 36.4 | 23.5 | 32.1 | 36.3 | 44.7 | 30.7 | 27.2 | 67.7 | 53.6 | 85.9 | 84.1 | 115.8 |
| RWANDA | 30.3 | 28.9 | 28.0 | 29.1 | 27.6 | 30.2 | 28.9 | 27.4 | 27.3 | 28.1 | 99.7 | 100.0 | 98.0 | 93.8 | 101.6 |
| SAMOA | 160.8 | 158.1 | 151.5 | 199.0 | 84.1 | 165.3 | 161.3 | 152.8 | 171.2 | 125.6 | 102.8 | 102.0 | 100.8 | 86.0 | 149.3 |
| SAO TOME & PRINCIPE | 45.9 | 70.1 | 111.2 | 131.5 | 130.9 | 45.9 | 70.1 | 111.2 | 131.5 | 130.9 | 100.0 | 100.0 | 100.0 | 100.0 | 100.0 |
| SIERRA LEONE | 28.1 | 19.9 | 27.0 | 19.4 | 20.5 | 28.1 | 18.5 | 26.6 | 19.4 | 17.2 | 99.9 | 92.8 | 98.6 | 100.0 | 83.9 |
| SOMALIA | 113.5 | 76.4 | 125.3 | 61.7 | 77.6 | 94.9 | 75.4 | 94.5 | 65.9 | 75.2 | 83.7 | 98.7 | 75.5 | 106.9 | 96.9 |
| SUDAN | 45.3 | 36.0 | 40.0 | 56.6 | 34.1 | 38.5 | 35.9 | 36.7 | 48.7 | 30.7 | 85.1 | 99.7 | 91.8 | 86.0 | 89.9 |
| TOGO | 69.5 | 19.1 | 35.3 | 39.3 | 40.2 | 34.2 | 23.7 | 26.0 | 39.4 | 38.1 | 49.3 | 124.5 | 79.3 | 101.5 | 94.6 |
| UGANDA | 10.4 | 11.3 | 12.3 | 10.4 | 11.2 | 8.6 | 10.0 | 9.7 | 9.4 | 11.0 | 82.6 | 88.5 | 78.0 | 90.3 | 98.0 |
| UN. REP. OF TANZANIA | 44.8 | 43.4 | 37.4 | 27.8 | 28.5 | 35.8 | 35.0 | 34.4 | 28.9 | 26.2 | 79.9 | 80.7 | 92.0 | 103.9 | 92.1 |
| VANUATU | 369.9 | 250.9 | 266.4 | 278.5 | 355.5 | 304.7 | 259.4 | 215.1 | 216.5 | 191.8 | 104.0 | 103.4 | 80.7 | 77.7 | 54.0 |
| YEMEN | 77.2 | 58.0 | 68.1 | 61.9 | 41.7 | 65.3 | 54.7 | 58.1 | 41.9 | 41.7 | 84.6 | 94.3 | 85.4 | 67.7 | 100.0 |
| ALL LDCS | 28.0 | 24.0 | 25.5 | 23.9 | 23.1 | 23.9 | 22.0 | 23.0 | 22.4 | 21.7 | 85.4 | 91.9 | 90.1 | 93.7 | 93.9 |
| ALL DEVELOPING | 38.3 | 43.0 | 37.2 | 44.2 | 33.1 | 15.9 | 15.0 | 13.6 | 12.9 | 12.6 | 41.5 | 35.0 | 36.6 | 29.3 | 37.9 |

Source: UNCTAD secretariat calculations based on data from the OECD secretariat, the World Bank, the UNCTAD secretariat, the United Nations Population Division and the United Nations Statistical Office.

Table 32

GDP growth, financial flows, savings and investments in individual LDCs

| | Annual average growth rates of real GDP (1980-1984) | | Percentage share in GDP (average 1980-84) | | | Population in millions (1984) | GDP per capita $ (1984) | Total financial flows per capita $ Average 1980-1984 | ODA |
|---|---|---|---|---|---|---|---|---|---|
| | Total | Per capita | Total Financial flows | Savings | Investment | | | | |
| **Large LDCs** | | | | | | | | | |
| Uganda | 7.1 | 3.6 | 5.2 | ... | 7.8 a/ | 15.0 | 220 | 11.1 | 9.8 |
| Nepal | 4.5 | 2.0 | 8.2 | 10.1 | 18.6 | 16.1 | 155 | 12.3 | 12.3 |
| Bangladesh | 3.8 | 1.6 | 9.4 | 2.1 | 11.2 | 96.7 | 145 | 13.4 | 13.2 |
| Afghanistan | 2.7 | 0.1 | 8.8 b/ | ... | ... | 17.7 | 210 g/ | 15.9 | 15.7 |
| Ethiopia | 1.5 | -1.2 | 8.1 a/ | 3.4 a/ | 10.4 a/ | 42.0 | 116 f/ | 10.0 | 9.5 |
| Sudan | 1.4 | -1.5 | 9.7 | 1.1 | 15.4 | 21.0 | 366 | 42.4 | 38.1 |
| United Rep.of Tanzania | 1.4 | -2.0 | 12.7 | 9.1 | 18.4 | 21.5 | 250 | 36.0 | 31.9 |
| **Middle size LDCs** | | | | | | | | | |
| Botswana | 11.8 | 7.5 | 12.4 | 18.9 | 34.1 | 1.1 | 1041 | 119.6 | 103.0 |
| Bhutan | 7.0 | 4.9 | 7.7 | ... | ... | 1.4 | 122 | 9.0 | 9.0 |
| Yemen | 6.3 | 3.6 | 13.7 | -24.2 | 30.7 | 7.8 | 480 | 61.0 | 52.1 |
| Somalia | 4.2 | 1.3 | 25.7 | -0.8 c/ | 16.7 c/ | 5.2 | 261 | 90.4 | 80.9 |
| Benin | 3.6 | 0.4 | 19.2 | 9.7 | 20.0 | 3.9 | 241 | 53.6 | 23.9 |
| Lao People's Dem.Rep. | 3.2 | 1.0 | 16.2 | ... | ... | 3.7 | 203 | 24.7 | 24.7 |
| Malawi | 2.3 | -0.9 | 13.4 | 15.1 | 21.3 | 6.7 | 178 | 24.6 | 21.3 |
| Rwanda | 2.3 | -1.0 | 11.2 | 3.0 | 13.6 | 5.9 | 282 | 28.7 | 28.3 |
| Democratic Yemen | 1.9 | -0.9 | 23.3 | ... | ... | 2.1 | 449 | 91.8 | 78.0 |
| Guinea | 1.3 | -1.0 | 6.1 | 16.4 | 13.1 | 5.9 | 357 | 19.9 | 16.4 |
| Burundi | 0.6 | -2.2 | 15.3 | 2.8 a/ | 16.6 a/ | 4.6 | 209 | 35.4 | 30.8 |
| Sierra Leone | 0.3 | -1.5 | 6.3 | 2.4 | 11.0 | 3.5 | 283 | 22.9 | 21.9 |
| Mali | -0.1 | -2.9 | 20.1 | 10.1 d/ | 28.2 d/ | 7.9 | 137 | 33.7 | 33.5 |
| Central African Rep. | -0.2 | -2.4 | 16.5 | -6.4 | 9.9 | 2.5 | 236 | 45.7 | 42.6 |
| Lesotho | -0.5 | -3.0 | 27.1 | -88.5 | 37.8 | 1.5 | 195 | 69.2 | 68.7 |
| Haiti | -0.9 | -2.3 | 7.9 | 2.8 | 16.5 | 5.2 | 350 | 24.6 | 24.1 |
| Burkina Faso | -1.4 | -3.7 | 19.5 | -12.1 | 14.6 | 6.8 | 133 | 33.4 | 31.2 |
| Niger | -2.0 | -4.8 | 12.5 | 9.7 | 19.4 | 6.0 | 279 | 45.0 | 34.1 |
| Togo | -3.3 | -6.2 | 12.8 | 15.1 | 27.4 | 2.9 | 232 | 40.5 | 32.9 |
| Chad | -7.0 | -9.1 | 9.5 | -3.4 | 8.4 | 4.9 | 118 | 15.1 | 15.7 |
| **Small LDCs** | | | | | | | | | |
| Maldives | 9.0 | 5.8 | 20.0 | 10.3 d/ | 30.7 e/ | 0.2 | 432 | 71.1 | 71.9 |
| Cape Verde | 7.6 | 5.5 | 64.8 | -23.5 | 26.4 | 0.3 | 296 | 203.5 | 195.2 |
| Guinea-Bissau | 6.1 | 4.1 | 37.5 | -2.6 a/ | 27.8 | 0.9 | 176 | 81.4 | 75.1 |
| Comoros | 4.3 | 1.1 | 42.1 | 11.0 | 35.0 | 0.4 | 208 | 106.2 | 101.6 |
| Vanuatu | 3.0 | 0.2 | 39.9 c/ | ... | ... | 0.1 | 683 h/ | 304.3 | 251.2 |
| Gambia | 1.6 | -0.6 | 29.0 | 4.4 | 23.4 | 0.7 | 288 | 93.4 | 80.1 |
| Djibouti | 1.5 | -1.8 | 41.7 | -5.4 | 23.3 | 0.4 | 574 | 244.6 | 225.0 |
| Equatorial Guinea | 1.3 | -0.9 | 21.9 | 0.8 | 17.4 | 0.4 | 213 | 44.0 | 43.5 |
| Samoa | -1.9 | -2.5 | 22.6 | -6.6 | 29.6 | 0.2 | 619 | 150.6 | 155.1 |
| Sao Tome and Principe | -6.9 | -9.2 | 22.9 | -17.3 | 29.6 | 0.1 | 388 | 99.1 | 99.1 |

Source: UNCTAD secretariat, based on information from the World Bank, ECA, the OECD secretariat, the UN Population Division and other international and national sources.

| | | | |
|---|---|---|---|
| a/ 1980-1983. | c/ 1980-1982. | e/ 1984. | g/ 1981. |
| b/ 1980-1981. | d/ 1981-1984. | f/ 1983. | h/ 1982. |

205. Among DAC donors - DAC aid accounts for almost 80 per cent of LDCs' aid receipts - the 0.15 per cent target has been traditionally well exceeded by four donors (Denmark, the Netherlands, Norway and Sweden). Since the adoption of the SNPA, the target has been exceeded, in addition, by Belgium in 1981 to 1983 and France in 1984 (see table 33). Of the remaining DAC countries that have committed themselves to the target, none except Canada, accepted 1985 as a target date, and none except Finland, which plans to reach this target by 1987, accepted any other precise time frame. In replying to the UNCTAD questionnaire, the Federal Republic of Germany stated its intention of reaching the 0.15 per cent target "as soon as possible thereafter" (i.e., after 1985); the United Kingdom stated that it would reach it "in the context of efforts to reach 0.7 per cent target" and Austria that it aimed at "doubling ODA to LDCs as soon as possible after 1985 with the envisaged long-term approach to reach ultimately the 0.15 per cent target".

206. A few DAC countries have doubled their ODA to LDCs in current dollars as compared to average flows during the period 1976-1980: Australia (in 1982), Austria (in 1981), Finland (in 1983 and 1984), Italy (in 1982 to 1984), and Switzerland (in 1983). 63/ While aid from Australia and Austria is very small in terms of GNP, aid from Finland, Italy and Switzerland has reached 0.1 per cent or even more (see table 33).

207. The United States, Australia and New Zealand have not endorsed the SNPA aid targets. None the less, during the period 1982 to 1984, the United States ODA to LDCs was 70 to 78 per cent higher than during the period 1976-1980.

208. The socialist countries of Eastern Europe view the aid targets set up in the SNPA "as being directed towards the industrially developed States of the capitalist system" 64/ and their assistance to developing countries as having a different nature, purpose and character than that provided by other countries. 65/ Information on the volume, terms and distribution of their assistance is, however, not available on a systematic basis. The USSR reported during the mid-term global review that it provided 1.3 billion roubles (1.5 billion dollars) 66/ or 0.17 per cent of its GNP as net transfers to LDCs in 1984. Czechoslovakia, which may be the second major socialist donor country to LDCs, reported that the volume of its assistance to them in 1984 had reached 0.15 per cent of its national product. In its reply to the UNCTAD questionnaire, the German Democratic Republic reported that it had extended over M500 million to LDCs in 1983 amounting to 0.12 per cent of national income produced.

209. In the context of South-South co-operation, LDCs have been receiving aid from OPEC donors, China and other developing countries. OPEC concessional assistance, which constitutes the most important source of these flows, has continued to exceed, in terms of donors' GNP, the 0.15 per cent target on the average as in the past. Among OPEC countries, major donors to LDCs are Saudi Arabia and Kuwait. During the 1980s the 0.15 per cent target was also exceeded by the United Arab Emirates and Qatar, except in 1984, and it was exceeded in 1981 and 1983 by the Libyan Arab Jamahiriya (mainly because of contributions to multilateral agencies). OPEC's concessional assistance has fluctuated with the changing revenues of the oil exporters and their varying terms of trade. OPEC aid dropped considerably in 1984 and is likely to have continued to drop in 1985. The fall in oil prices in 1986, which constitutes a further financial squeeze on OPEC countries' earnings, is expected to be translated into further cuts in aid provisions in 1986 and possibly subsequent years. 67/

Table 33

ODA a/ to LDCs from DAC and OPEC member countries

| | % of GNP | | | | Current prices ($ million) | | | | |
|---|---|---|---|---|---|---|---|---|---|
| | 1981 | 1982 | 1983 | 1984 | Average 1976-1980 | 1981 | 1982 | 1983 | 1984 |
| Australia | 0.06 | 0.10 | 0.08 | 0.07 | 67.3 | 88.3 | 159.3 | 122.3 | 122.3 |
| Austria | 0.04 | 0.04 | 0.03 | 0.03 | 12.1 | 26.3 | 23.4 | 20.6 | 21.5 |
| Belgium | 0.16 | 0.15 | 0.15 | 0.14 | 126.6 | 158.1 | 126.8 | 119.0 | 106.0 |
| Canada | 0.11 | 0.11 | 0.13 | 0.13 | 266.7 | 309.8 | 328.6 | 413.3 | 413.6 |
| Denmark | 0.25 | 0.29 | 0.29 | 0.28 | 126.6 | 137.4 | 155.1 | 157.2 | 148.9 |
| Finland | 0.08 | 0.08 | 0.11 | 0.12 | 25.0 | 41.1 | 40.0 | 53.2 | 57.9 |
| France | 0.12 | 0.12 | 0.13 | 0.16 | 460.2 | 700.0 | 652.5 | 690.0 | 756.4 |
| Germany, Fed.Rep.of | 0.12 | 0.12 | 0.13 | 0.12 | 685.7 | 840.9 | 790.1 | 825.2 | 721.1 |
| Italy | 0.06 | 0.07 | 0.08 | 0.13 | 117.0 | 219.6 | 250.1 | 287.6 | 437.8 |
| Japan | 0.05 | 0.05 | 0.06 | 0.07 | 459.6 | 577.9 | 559.6 | 718.9 | 800.4 |
| Netherlands | 0.29 | 0.29 | 0.25 | 0.29 | 297.4 | 408.6 | 396.5 | 332.6 | 359.8 |
| New Zealand | 0.04 | 0.03 | 0.03 | 0.03 | 8.0 | 8.5 | 7.8 | 7.2 | 6.5 |
| Norway | 0.29 | 0.37 | 0.38 | 0.31 | 117.0 | 159.5 | 199.0 | 201.3 | 162.7 |
| Sweden | 0.26 | 0.31 | 0.26 | 0.21 | 241.6 | 286.0 | 298.4 | 229.4 | 196.8 |
| Switzerland | 0.08 | 0.08 | 0.11 | 0.10 | 51.1 | 83.1 | 77.1 | 106.7 | 92.2 |
| United Kingdom | 0.11 | 0.11 | 0.10 | 0.09 | 400.2 | 586.6 | 530.3 | 453.9 | 392.1 |
| United States | 0.03 | 0.04 | 0.04 | 0.04 | 795.8 | 939.2 | 1 397.1 | 1 411.0 | 1 353.8 |
| TOTAL DAC | 0.08 | 0.08 | 0.08 | 0.08 | 4 257.9 | 5 571.0 | 5 991.7 | 6 149.6 | 6 149.9 |
| Algeria | 0.08 | 0.08 | 0.04 | 0.06 | 22.4 | 34.3 | 31.4 | 20.8 | 27.7 |
| Iran(Islamic Rep.of) | 0.00 | 0.00 | 0.00 | - | 19.3 | 0.1 | 0.02 | 4.4 | - |
| Iraq | 0.06 | 0.06 | 0.01 | 0.00 | 51.8 | 15.4 | 16.3 | 1.2 | 0.8 |
| Kuwait | 0.71 | 0.84 | 0.98 | 0.92 | 181.4 | 226.9 | 214.5 | 254.0 | 244.6 |
| Libyan Arab Jamahirya | 0.21 | 0.08 | 0.15 | 0.02 | 36.4 | 58.4 | 25.0 | 43.0 | 6.3 |
| Nigeria | 0.12 | 0.03 | 0.02 | 0.05 | 25.8 | 89.1 | 21.1 | 16.0 | 28.2 |
| Qatar | 0.41 | 0.29 | 0.23 | 0.10 | 20.2 | 29.6 | 19.0 | 13.6 | 6.1 |
| Saudi Arabia | 0.31 | 0.59 | 0.71 | 0.51 | 534.2 | 499.0 | 904.5 | 785.9 | 509.5 |
| United Arab Emirates | 0.29 | 0.35 | 0.22 | 0.12 | 141.0 | 90.3 | 102.8 | 58.2 | 32.5 |
| Venezuela | 0.04 | 0.04 | 0.06 | 0.01 | 15.7 | 25.5 | 25.9 | 38.0 | 5.0 |
| TOTAL OPEC | 0.19 | 0.23 | 0.22 | 0.17 | 1 048.2 | 1 068.7 | 1 360.5 | 1 235.2 | 860.7 |

Source:  UNCTAD secretariat calculations, based on information provided by the OECD secretariat, the Government of France and information collected by the UNCTAD secretariat.

a/  Including imputed flows to LDCs through multilateral channels.

210. As regards multilateral aid, although clear trends are not easily discernible for individual donor countries, on the whole during the 1980s contributions to multilateral agencies mainly financed by DAC member countries have fluctuated around a rising trend. In 1985 they declined, but this reflected the accidental timing of contributions of a number of major donors to IDA. 68/

211. The share allocated to LDCs in these multilateral programmes (in particular IDA and UNDP) increased on the average during that period, exceeding 30 per cent in 1984 (see annex table 26). In general, multilateral financial institutions providing concessional assistance to LDCs have indicated 69/ that they do not plan to increase the share allocated to LDCs. However, there could be a continued increase in the overall average of this share. Firstly, the Special Facility for sub-Saharan Africa, established by the World Bank in 1985, will result in greater commitments and disbursements to LDCs in sub-Saharan Africa. Moreover, the prospects of IDA 8 at $12 billion could mean a further concentration on LDCs. The Commission of the European Communities also foresees a gradual growth over several years in its share of concessional assistance to LDCs, owing to general policy orientation including the extension of STABEX, 70/ despite minor variations due to project cycles and the new programme approach under the Third Lomé Convention.

212. OPEC countries' contributions to multilateral agencies mainly financed by them started declining in 1983. The share allocated to LDCs in these programmes fluctuated, exceeding 44 per cent during the 1980s and reaching 57 per cent in 1984.

### D. Aid targets and LDCs' capital requirements

213. On the assumption that the SNPA aid targets were met in 1985, the combination of 0.15 per cent of donors' GNP as ODA to LDCs and the doubling of ODA to them, (taking into account the known intentions of donors) would not have led to the overall doubling of flows to LDCs as envisaged in the SNPA. Immediately after the United Nations Conference on the Least Developed Countries in September 1981, the Secretary-General of UNCTAD, in his assessment of the prospects for ODA to LDCs, had already indicated this expected shortfall. 71/ According to present estimates, increased aid flows to LDCs through the fulfilment of aid targets could result by 1990, when the global review of the SNPA takes place, in a level of aid in real terms to LDCs that is only some 30 per cent higher than in 1984. 72/

214. LDCs' projected capital requirements in 1990 are presented in table 34. They are estimated according to three different scenarios: (a) a base-line scenario which assumes a rate of economic growth for the LDCs equivalent to their population growth of 2.6 per cent annually; (b) a scenario which assumes that GDP growth of the LDCs will gradually reach the SNPA target of 7.2 per cent in 1995; and (c) a scenario in which this target would be reached in the year 1990. It must be recalled that 7.2 per cent was the target growth rate set out to enable LDCs to double their total income over the decade.

215. The methodology is the same as that used in the projections prepared a year ago. 73/ However, since last year's assessment, the levels of various prices and their expectations, particularly those of oil, but also those of

other primary commodities and of manufactured products, have changed
drastically and international interest rates have dropped considerably.  It
was therefore considered important to make a tentative reassessment of the
projections in the light of these developments. 74/

Table 34

Balance of payments of the least developed countries, 1985 and 1990

(Billions of dollars at current prices) a/

| | 1985 estimate | 1990 projections | | |
| | | Base | Modified SNPA, postponed until: | |
| | | | 1995 | 1990 |
|---|---|---|---|---|
| Exports, f.o.b. | 6.9 | 9.3 | 10.9 | 11.2 |
| Imports, f.o.b. | 14.0 | 20.1 | 24.1 | 26.4 |
| Trade balance, goods | -7.1 | -10.8 | -13.3 | -15.2 |
| Non-factor services, net | -0.9 | -1.4 | -2.0 | -2.6 |
| Investment income payments, net | -1.1 | -2.1 | -1.2 | -1.2 |
| Private transfers, net | 2.9 | 2.8 | 3.2 | 3.2 |
| Current account balance | -6.1 | -11.5 | -13.2 | -15.8 |
| Change in reserves | -0.3 | -0.9 | -1.7 | -2.0 |
| Net capital requirements | 6.4 | 12.4 | 14.9 | 17.8 |

Source:   UNCTAD secretariat calculations.

a/   Details may not add up to totals owing to rounding.

216. The results accordingly show that estimates of LDCs' capital requirements
are lower than those presented earlier. 75/  None the less, according to the
revised estimates, in order just to maintain their total income at present
levels in real terms, LDCs would require capital flows to double (in nominal
terms) by 1990 (see table 35).  Since the attainment of the SNPA targets by
1990 by all donors committed to these targets would yield a real increase in
ODA of only 30 per cent (see para. 213 above), this may not even be sufficient
to enable LDCs to maintain present income levels.  To accelerate growth, LDCs
would need much larger capital flows and aid.

E. New approaches, prospects and conclusions

217. Poverty and low development standards of recipients continue to be a major criterion for aid eligibility and for determining the conditions and modalities of aid. However, this criterion is viewed in conjunction not only with the recipient's needs, development priorities and executing capability but also - and increasingly - with its overall policies and undertaking of economic reform and adjustment measures. In addition, traditional links and strategic and economic interests play their role.

218. In view of the stringency affecting aid programmes, aid effectiveness has become a major preoccupation of donors and recipients. In their replies to the UNCTAD questionnaire, donors from the group of DAC countries and also from among the socialist countries of Eastern Europe have stressed that aid would be effective only when provided in support of the LDCs' own efforts to carry out sound policy reforms and to reshape their social and economic structure. 76/ A number of DAC donors have in some cases subordinated the provision of assistance to an LDC to its conclusion of an adjustment programme with the IMF.

219. While donors thus appear to attach increasing importance to economic factors and structural conditions within recipient countries that impinge on the effectiveness of assistance - a number of them have also referred to cases of limited absorptive capacity in LDCs as a constraint to aid implementation - LDCs have stressed the need to enhance aid effectiveness through improved modalities on the part of donors, including the provision of more flexible forms of aid, increased aid in the form of grants, and, to the maximum possible extent, untied, through predictable flows and simplified procedures. 77/

220. A view expressed by the World Bank regarding the effectiveness of external assistance is that unless the recipient government has laid down as precisely as possible its own economic development priorities and targets, it is very difficult for donors to provide assistance and to support those policies and priority programmes efficiently. On the other hand, the success of reforms and adjustment depends very largely on the support of donors. 78/

221. Recent declines in interest rates and oil prices are favourable to prospects of higher economic growth in industrial countries and hence of increased ODA. 79/ However, the extent to which LDCs will be able to obtain additional resources in the coming years will largely depend on their ability to develop and implement macro-economic and structural adjustment programmes that are credible to donors. In this respect, allowance will have to be made for the fact that, even under the best of circumstances, and despite careful implementation of programmes, LDCs' economic progress is bound to be slow because of their structural constraints. Moreover, LDCs will continue to be extremely vulnerable to adverse developments in the external economic environment where many uncertainties remain. 80/

222. Likewise, although donors have expressed support for increased multilateral lending by the World Bank and multilateral development banks, as well as by IMF, and although the prospect of greater lending by IDA, the establishment of the Special Facility for sub-Saharan Africa of the World Bank and the newly created Structural Adjustment Facility of the IMF should increase concessional resources available for LDCs, the tightening of conditionality may impair access to these resources. For instance, up to now only eight African LDCs have been able to draw on the sub-Saharan Facility. 81/

223. Export credits and bank lending are expected to increase moderately in 1986, but this increase may not help LDCs, which have been strongly compressing imports, have traditionally had very limited access to bank lending, and have now to face debt ratios at very difficult levels. In most cases they cannot afford increases in commercial borrowing without severe consequences for their balances of payments. Moreover, shortages of external liquidity accompanied by erosion of creditworthiness in several of them, as well as more restrictive policies instituted by export credit agencies, may continue to hamper the extension of export credits.

224. LDCs will have to continue to rely mainly on ODA. Only ODA can appropriately finance development in the priority sectors identified in the SNPA, such as rural development, physical infrastructure and social services, where projects may have high social rates of return but in general do not generate the foreign exchange required to service loans at commercial rates.

225. The Task Force on Concessional Flows of the Development Committee of the World Bank considered ways and means of coping with the low-income countries' increasing need of resources, including: (a) increasing the effectiveness of official aid; (b) changing present country allocations of ODA; and (c) concentrating the expected increments in ODA on low-income countries. Other options considered were: (d) combining ODA with less concessional flows in ways which would result in a higher overall volume of external resources; and (e) supplementing ODA flows by encouraging increased flows of voluntary contributions (from private voluntary organizations/NGOs), contributions of ODA from new donors, earnings from trade, and foreign private investment.

226. The Task Force concluded, however, that each of the above options had only limited possibilities and stated that "no single one of the measures considered above, nor any combination of them, will cope adequately with the challenge of development in the low-income countries. Since there is no escaping the need for predominant reliance on traditional, appropriated concessional assistance, donor governments should exert redoubled efforts to increase the supply of ODA as a matter of urgency." 82/ It also stressed that while aid effectiveness should be improved such improvement could not substitute for increases in aid flows.

227. Clearly aid volumes have been inadequate in the 1980s and present commitments under the SNPA are not sufficient to restore import levels and allow resumed and sustained growth in the LDCs. Much stronger efforts than those presently envisaged are therefore required on the part of donors, including a better understanding of LDCs' requirements and problems.

## Chapter II

## AID MODALITIES

228. One main conclusion emerging from aid experiences in the last two decades is that most aid has played a productive development role. The need to improve aid's basic effectiveness, however, has been recognized as well. 83/ Already the SNPA itself and, more recently, the conclusions and recommendations adopted by the Intergovernmental Group on the Least Developed Countries at the mid-term global review of progress towards the implementation of the SNPA, 84/ include a number of provisions whereby not only donors' aid policies and practices are to be improved but also recipient actions and co-ordination of aid by donors and recipients are to be strengthened.

229. The following section is concerned with the first aspect in relation to aid modalities, and it covers issues regarding terms and conditions of aid as well as forms and sector allocation of aid. This is, however, an area that is often not amenable to quantitative assessment, in which practices may lag behind stated policies. Monitoring of progress is thus particularly difficult.

### A. Terms and conditions of aid

#### 1. Grant element of concessional assistance

230. The economic and financial situation of the LDCs and their limited debt servicing capacity require that financial and technical assistance be extended to them on highly concessional terms, preferably in the form of grants. 85/

231. The average grant element of concessional assistance 86/ received by the LDCs from all donors combined increased from 86 per cent in 1981 to 89 per cent in 1983, then dropped to around 85 per cent in 1984. These trends mainly reflect those of bilateral concessional aid extended by non-DAC donors. During this period, the overall grant element of concessional assistance from DAC countries remained stable at 93-94 per cent on the average. That of multilateral institutions mainly financed by them declined slightly, to 88 per cent in 1984.

232. DAC has adopted quantitative norms in its Recommendation on Terms and Conditions of Aid, which stipulate, inter alia, that ODA to the LDCs should be essentially in the form of grants and, as a minimum, that the average grant element of all commitments from a given donor should either be at least 86 per cent to each LDC over a period of three years or at least 90 per cent annually for the LDCs as a group. Since 1981, several DAC countries have shifted their aid programmes with LDCs to an all-grants basis, in addition to those which already provided all their ODA to LDCs on that basis. The great majority of DAC countries thus now extend their bilateral concessional assistance to LDCs mainly or entirely in grant form. In 1984, the aid programmes of 11 DAC members were on an all-grants basis, and, in practice two other members also extended aid to the LDCs in this form. However, three major DAC donors (France, Italy and Japan) continue to provide an important share of their aid to LDCs in the forms of loans, and the terms of their aid in 1984 still fell short of the norms concerning aid to LDCs set down in DAC's own Terms Recommendation. 87/

233. The concessionality of bilateral aid from OPEC countries improved over the period 1981-1984 as a whole. The average grant element of new concessional commitments from these countries rose from 66 per cent in 1981 to 90 per cent in 1983, then, with a declining volume of commitments, fell back to 79 per cent in 1984. The average grant element of concessional assistance (grants and loans combined) from the multilateral agencies mainly financed by OPEC countries over this period fluctuated between 55 per cent and 43 per cent (see table 35).

234. An important share of concessional assistance received by the LDCs (close to 40 per cent of commitments in 1981-1984) nevertheless continues to be in the form of loans. During the period 1981-1984, the terms of concessional loans extended to LDCs by the multilateral agencies mainly financed by DAC members remained very soft, carrying on average a grant element of over 80 per cent. Bilateral concessional loans accorded to the LDCs by DAC countries on average carried a grant element of 60 per cent or below, closely corresponding to the average loan terms of DAC bilateral aid lending to all developing countries. Bilateral concessional loans from OPEC countries on average carried a grant element of well over 50 per cent, while the grant element of concessional loans from multilateral agencies mainly financed by these countries remained at 50 per cent or below (see table 35). The socialist countries of Eastern Europe also provide loans to the LDCs.

235. Within concessional aid programmes, loans are still being extended to LDCs on terms corresponding to a grant element of less than 50 per cent. Moreover, both multilateral and bilateral donors to some extent provide development finance on non-concessional terms to the LDCs. 88/ Scope thus remains for further increasing grant financing for LDCs and softening the terms of loans extended to them.

236. As regards associated or mixed financing, under which ODA is linked to less concessional and/or essentially commercial transactions, its practice appears to have been more widely used in aid programmes in recent years. This type of financing has been extended to LDCs by a number of DAC donors, in particular for projects in the transport, communications and energy sectors. The concessionality of such transactions with LDCs is reported to be around 35 per cent and to have tended to increase. 89/ A proposal to raise the minimum grant element required in associated financing transactions with the poorest countries (currently 25 per cent) has been under discussion in the OECD. The Intergovernmental Group at the mid-term global review of the SNPA urged donors to take the necessary steps to ensure that transactions financed by any type of associated financing are generally avoided for LDCs because of their relatively hard terms; if contracted, it should be ensured that such transactions with LDCs contain a high component of official development assistance.

Table 35

Grant element of total concessional commitments and of
concessional loans to LDCs, 1981-1984
(Percentages)

| Donor or donor group | 1981 | 1982 | 1983 | 1984 |
|---|---|---|---|---|
| Australia | 100 | 100 | 100 | 100 |
| Austria | 94 | 95 | 99 | 100 |
| Belgium | 99 | 98 | 98 | 99 |
| Canada | 100 | 100 | 100 | 100 |
| Denmark | 95 | 97 | 99 | 100 |
| Finland | 95 | 99 | 100 | 100 |
| France | 89 | 82 | 80 | 78 |
| Germany, Federal Republic of | 99 | 99 | 96 | 99 |
| Italy | 55 | 71 | 90 | 80 |
| Japan | 85 | 82 | 88 | 89 |
| Netherlands | 98 | 100 | 99 | 100 |
| New Zealand | 100 | 100 | 100 | 100 |
| Norway | 100 | 100 | 100 | 100 |
| Sweden | 100 | 100 | 100 | 100 |
| Switzerland | 100 | 100 | 100 | 100 |
| United Kingdom | 100 | 100 | 100 | 100 |
| United States | 96 | 98 | 96 | 97 |
| DAC countries | 94 | 93 | 94 | 94 |
| of which:  loans | 58 | 60 | 57 | 59 |
| Multilateral agencies mainly financed by DAC | 91 | 89 | 88 | 88 |
| of which:  loans | 82 | 82 | 82 | 81 |
| OPEC countries | 66 | 77 | 90 | 79 |
| of which:  loans | 52 | 55 | 54 | 54 |
| Multilateral agencies mainly financed by OPEC | 53 | 55 | 43 | 53 |
| of which:  loans | 48 | 50 | 40 | 49 |
| Grant element of total concessional commitments to LDCs from all sources | 86 | 87 | 89 | 85 |

Source:  UNCTAD secretariat estimates mainly based on OECD/DAC and UNCTAD
data.

## 2. Tying

237. Aid tying continues to be an issue of major importance for LDCs. Such practices may not only entail higher costs and less efficient procurement, but also other disadvantages which may be especially harmful for these countries, characterized as they are by a weak economic structure and scarce planning and technological capacity. LDCs can least of all afford inefficient use of resources and dislocation of development effort. Moreover, varying tying and procurement rules may impose an administrative burden on them.

238. Under paragraph 70(b) of the SNPA, donor countries and institutions agreed to provide, to the maximum extent possible, ODA loans and grants to the LDCs on an untied basis. The Intergovernmental Group at the mid-term global review of the SNPA urged donors to take the necessary steps to ensure that aid to LDCs is untied to the maximum extent possible; when not possible, necessary steps should be taken to help offset the disadvantages of tying.

239. In 1984, slightly over one-fifth of bilateral DAC aid to the LDCs as a group was reported to be untied. Approximately two-thirds of bilateral commitments, of which technical co-operation and food aid accounted for an important part, were estimated to have been tied (see table 36). Tying provisions and practices of DAC countries vary widely among them. In general, tying policies with regard to LDCs seem not to differ from those applied to other developing countries. Some DAC members have, however, reported special tying rules for LDCs (or more liberal local cost financing provisions applied to them, for instance by Denmark).

240. Because of a change in reporting methods, 1984 data are not directly comparable with those of earlier years, 90/ and this makes it difficult to draw any general conclusions about trends in tying since the adoption of the SNPA. Variations in the figures are also due to debt relief extended to the LDCs following Board resolution 165(S-IX) adopted in 1978 on measures for the retroactive adjustment of aid terms. In 1981-1982, the share of untied aid in bilateral concessional commitments from DAC countries was estimated at less than 30 per cent, as compared to 37 per cent in 1979 and 42 per cent in 1980. 91/ The relatively high share of untied commitments, especially in the latter year, is explained by a large component of debt forgiveness, recorded as untied aid.

241. In their replies to the UNCTAD questionnaire, several DAC countries have reported increasingly covering local costs in the LDCs, or intending to raise the priority of this or other forms of untied assistance in their aid programmes with these countries. 92/

242. Concessional assistance by OPEC countries and multilateral agencies mainly financed by them is generally free of procurement restrictions. Procurement undertaken by other multilateral agencies normally takes place on the basis of competitive bidding in their member or subscribing countries, ensuring a wide range of prospective suppliers and effective competition. All aid from the socialist countries of Eastern Europe, including their multilateral contributions, is tied to procurement in the donor country.

Table 36

Tying status of concessional commitments to LDCs from DAC countries
and multilateral agencies, 1981-1982 and 1984
(Percentages)

|  | 1981 | 1982 | 1984 |
|---|---|---|---|
| 1. Concessional commitments from DAC countries and multilateral agencies | 100 | 100 | 100 |
| Multilateral and untied bilateral | 57 | 56 | 56 |
| Partially tied bilateral | 8 | 6 | 8 |
| Tied bilateral, including technical co-operation and food aid | 35 | 38 | 36 |
| 2. DAC bilateral concessional commitments | 100 | 100 | 100 |
| Untied | 29 | 24 | 22 |
| Partially tied | 12 | 12 | 14 |
| Tied, including technical co-operation and food aid | 59 | 64 | 64 |
| - of which: technical co-operation | 29 | 29 | 27 |
| - of which: food aid | 9 | 10 | 13 |

Source: UNCTAD secretariat estimates based on data provided by the OECD
secretariat.

243. Complete untying of aid would be an ideal situation. Where this is not
possible, constraints on LDCs imposed by tying rules could be eased by
simplifying procurement procedures, granting waivers when appropriate and
introducing margins of preference or other means to promote local industry in
the LDCs as well as regional trade opportunities, and appropriate selection
and design of projects and programmes, with sufficient provision for local
cost financing, training, etc.

B.   Forms of aid

244. The change in the economic situation of the LDCs since 1981 and the
budgetary and balance-of-payments constraints that they currently face have
brought about corresponding shifts in aid requirements. Many of these
countries have had to cut down on planned development expenditure, and the
scope for launching new investment projects has been reduced. There is more
emphasis than previously on rehabilitation and maintenance of existing
investments. The importance of sector aid has been brought out in this
context.

245. Moreover, the adjustment efforts of the LDCs 93/ also require support in the form of commodity and programme assistance to sustain import capacity and the balance of payments, as well as specific budget support and local and recurrent cost financing to ease their budgetary situation. The need for supporting these adjustment efforts through more flexible forms of aid was indeed one of the new elements brought out in the mid-term global review of the implementation of the SNPA. 94/ All these changes in aid requirements have clearly emerged in the country review meetings held for individual LDCs.

### 1. Programme aid

246. In response to the above needs, many donors have indicated giving, in their aid programmes with LDCs, less emphasis to project aid and more emphasis to programme aid, including sector assistance, general import financing and balance-of-payments support as well as commodity aid. The types of aid provided to LDCs by DAC donors are set out in table 37. Specific initiatives have been taken. For instance, the Federal Republic of Germany has launched a new instrument (called sector-related programmes) for the rapid provision of goods and services, primarily for rehabilitation and maintenance of existing capacities. Multilateral agencies have also instituted facilities to provide more flexible forms of aid, of which the quick-disbursing structural and sectoral adjustment programmes and rehabilitation projects of the World Bank and the sectoral import support programmes being prepared under the Third Lomé Convention are examples.

247. While some donors have indicated that they extend support to the LDCs' adjustment programmes mainly through reorientations within their bilateral aid programmes and through the World Bank and IMF facilities, others - such as France - have special financial instruments for giving budgetary and balance-of-payments assistance to specific adjustment efforts of the LDCs. Careful appraisal of new investment proposals, increasing emphasis on assistance to the continuation of existing projects rather than the initiation of new ones, and efforts to strengthen production-oriented projects also form part of DAC donors' response to the LDCs' aims of adapting their development and investment programmes to changing economic circumstances.

248. During the period under review (1981-1984), the reorientation towards increasing programme aid was not yet, however, fully reflected in commitments recorded as general economic support. 95/ Many LDCs, including countries that have undertaken adjustment efforts with or without the support of formally agreed external support programmes, continued to receive relatively little external aid in the form of general economic support for those efforts during this period. The recorded amount of general economic support, including food aid, to LDCs from DAC sources, bilateral and multilateral combined, decreased from $1.3 billion in 1981 to $1 billion in 1982 and 1983, then increased to $1.6 billion in 1984. In DAC member countries' bilateral aid programmes, the amount of general economic support appears to have risen relatively little over this period as a whole and an increasing share of bilateral aid recorded in this category up to 1984 took the form of food aid. This was offset by an increase in the share as well as in the amount of new aid in the form of general economic support extended to LDCs under the multilateral programmes mainly financed by the DAC countries (see table 38). In 1985, substantially increased aid for emergency relief and structural adjustment in Africa 96/ is likely to have further increased general economic support for many LDCs, although at the time of writing this report exact amounts and details were not yet known.

Table 37

DAC countries: Types of aid provided to LDCs in 1981-1985 and intentions

| Type of aid extended to LDCs | Australia [a] | Austria [a] | Belgium [b] | Canada [b] | Denmark | Finland | France | Germany, Federal Rep. of | Ireland | Italy [b] | Japan [a] | Netherlands | New Zealand [a] | Norway [b] | Sweden [a] | Switzerland | United Kingdom [a] | United States of America [a] |
|---|---|---|---|---|---|---|---|---|---|---|---|---|---|---|---|---|---|---|
| Budget and balance-of-payments support | no | | | yes | yes | yes | yes+ | no | no= | yes | yes= | yes= | no | yes | no | yes+ | no | yes= |
| Local cost financing | yes | yes= | yes= | yes | yes | yes | yes | yes | yes= | yes= | no= | yes= | yes | yes= | yes= | yes+ | yes= | yes= |
| Debt relief | no=[c] | | | no[c] | yes | yes= | yes | yes | no=[c] | yes+ | yes= | yes= | no[c] | no[c] | no[c] | no=[c] | yes= | yes= |
| Project aid | yes= | yes= | yes+ | yes | yes | yes | yes+ | yes=[a] | yes+ | yes+ | yes+ | yes- | yes | yes= | yes= | yes | yes- | yes= |
| Rehabilitation aid | yes= | | | | yes | yes+ | yes | yes+ | yes+ | | | yes= | | | | yes | | |
| Maintenance aid | no= | | | | yes | yes+ | yes | yes+ | no= | | | yes= | | | | yes | | |
| Recurrent cost financing | yes | | yes= | yes | yes | yes | yes | yes=[a] | | no | no= | yes= | yes | yes= | yes= | yes | yes= | yes= |
| Current import finance, including food aid | yes= | yes | yes | yes | yes | no | yes | yes | yes= | yes | yes | yes= | yes | yes | yes | yes= | yes | yes= |
| Emergency and disaster relief, including emergency food supplies | yes= | yes= | yes= | yes | yes | yes | yes | yes | yes= | yes= | yes+ | yes= | no | yes= | yes+ | yes | yes+ | yes= |

+ Priority increased.
= No change in priority.
– Priority decreased.

Source: Country replies to the UNCTAD questionnaire on the implementation of the SNPA received up to end September 1986.

a/ Types of aid extended in 1981 to 1983 (as reported in replies to the 1984 UNCTAD questionnaire).

b/ Types of aid extended in 1981 (as reported in replies to the 1982 UNCTAD questionnaire).

c/ Aid to the LDCs provided entirely in grant form.

249.  OPEC donors have always provided a major share of their bilateral aid in the form of balance-of-payments and budget support.  General economic support from OPEC sources to LDCs is estimated to have increased from some $0.7 billion in 1981 to close to $1 billion in 1983.  As total commitments from OPEC donors fell in 1984, the amount of general economic support they were able to provide the LDCs may have been reduced to about half the 1983 level.  Among OPEC multilateral agencies, the OPEC Fund, in particular, has provided significant amounts of programme assistance.

250.  In their replies to the UNCTAD questionnaire, socialist countries of Eastern Europe (e.g. Czechoslovakia, the German Democratic Republic) have also reported having provided commodity assistance to the LDCs.

## 2.  Food aid

251.  Many of the LDCs have structural food deficits, and food aid is a regular feature of the economies of some of these countries.  Additional food aid needs arose in particular from the recent drought and famine in sub-Saharan Africa.  The international donor community has responded to these requirements with substantial assistance.  In 1984, over $1 billion was disbursed as food aid to the LDCs through specific multilateral programmes and bilateral governmental channels in DAC countries.  The United States, Canada, Australia, Japan and the Federal Republic of Germany provided the bulk of DAC bilateral food aid deliveries.  Non-DAC donors and multilateral agencies have also provided assistance, including food aid, in response to the sub-Saharan drought emergency.

### Food aid disbursements to LDCs, 1981-1984
(million $US)

|  | 1981 | 1982 | 1983 | 1984 |
|---|---|---|---|---|
| WFP | 217.2 | 217.9 | 229.5 | 290.5 |
| EDF | 126.1 | 135.0 | 57.3 | 136.0 |
| DAC bilateral | 579.7 | 538.2 | 481.2 | 637.1 |
| Percentage of food aid in overall disbursements from DAC countries and multilateral agencies mainly financed by them | 18 | 16 | 15 | 18 |

252.  In emergency situations, food aid has to be provided according to needs.  However, it has been recognized that this is a form of aid which may tend to prolong aid dependence.  Food aid can discourage moves towards increasing food self-sufficiency by depressing prices and delaying urgent investments in the rural sector.  Food output and consumption patterns can be adversely affected, and dependence on food imports sustained.  Hence the importance of integrating food aid with other forms of aid within comprehensive development and assistance programmes, in particular as they relate to food security, and of finding ways to utilize food aid as a tool for

financing development projects notably in the agricultural sector. Emergency food aid requires careful management in order not to weaken efforts to deal with structural food deficits, 97/ and it is important for it to be complemented by support for reconstruction and rehabilitation.

253. In their replies to the UNCTAD questionnaire, several donors have made a distinction between food aid supplied as part of emergency relief efforts and food aid as development assistance, a more restrictive attitude prevailing with regard to the latter. Attempts are being made to reduce the possible adverse effects of food deliveries, and to link them to LDCs' longer-term programmes for increasing food output and food security, or to food-for-work projects in these countries. Co-ordinating machinery for emergency and food aid inputs has reportedly been strengthened, notably in France.

### 3. Local and recurrent cost financing

254. As indicated above, in recent years many LDCs were compelled to adopt austerity and adjustment programmes. These programmes in general encompass demand management measures, notably public expenditure restraint and, in many cases cutbacks in development expenditure and investment programmes. The scope for expanding local revenue in these countries is limited, even more so in periods of economic retrenchment. The budgetary constraints and the difficulties experienced by LDCs in this situation in providing counterpart funds for development projects, and meeting recurrent financing obligations have been brought out time and again in the country review meetings held since 1981.

255. The scarcity of local funds to meet counterpart requirements of aid projects has been identified as a factor delaying project and programme implementation. Such delays risk leading to a perception of weakening aid absorptive capacity and a vicious cycle of diminishing development funding. The obvious solution is for donors to provide appropriate budget support and to take on an increasing proportion of total project costs, including local costs. One of the recurrent themes in country review meetings has indeed been the appeal by LDCs to donors to contribute increasingly to financing the local costs of development projects.

256. While there are no quantitative data on the overall extent of local cost financing in LDCs, available information gives evidence of - in principle - a forthcoming attitude on the part of donors towards participating in this type of financing. Most donors undertake local cost financing in LDCs, and some of them are raising its priority or have instituted more liberal policies with regard to such financing in these countries.

257. Some donors have reported higher ceilings for participation in local costs in LDCs or agreement to finance project inputs which LDC governments are normally expected to provide from their own resources as well as flexibility in requirements for counterpart personnel and their financing. Another example of the type of special arrangements warranted by the LDCs' current financial situation is reported by the Asian Development Bank (AsDB) which has provided special assistance to LDC borrowers to help complete projects which had been delayed due to shortages in local funds. The modality of financing local (and recurrent) costs with counterpart funds generated by commodity import schemes should also be mentioned.

258. The same budgetary constraints that require a higher proportion of local cost financing by donors have also made it increasingly difficult for LDCs to fund recurrent financing needs.  Appeals to donors to participate increasingly in the financing of recurrent costs of projects have thus been repeatedly made by the LDCs at their country review meetings.  This issue takes on special importance with the new emphasis on sustaining operations and maintenance and on rehabilitation of existing investments that is evident in many LDCs.  Many donors do provide recurrent cost financing to LDCs, although there may be some fear that such financing if prolonged will create or sustain aid dependence.  However, it has generally been recognized that provision for donor participation in recurrent cost financing and meeting maintenance requirements should be accompanied by provisions for gradual take-over by the recipient.  A special case has been made for recurrent cost financing for essential service facilities and for projects that do not generate revenue directly in such sectors of the social and economic infrastructure as education, rural development, roads, etc. 98/

259. Project design should from the outset be such that there is no unnecessary burden on the LDCs, and, for all projects, recurrent and local costs should be assessed systematically and resources for financing them should be identified from the design stage. 99/  A new awareness of and concern about the long-term recurrent cost burden arising from development programmes and projects and about maintenance requirements is indeed apparent in many LDCs.  These issues are now being given increasing weight in LDCs' development planning, and some of these countries have commenced to screen new development projects carefully and to attempt to avoid taking on projects with heavy recurrent cost implications.  Donors can support these efforts in project selection and design and can help by agreeing to assist in the operation and maintenance of ongoing or completed projects, with arrangements for their gradual transfer and integration into the recipient country, necessary training, etc.  Such assistance already seems to be the practice of some donors.  Others have reported the extension of project periods or institution of special policies, allowing, for instance, for the financing of incremental recurrent costs during project implementation.  The general impression is that many donors are in effect currently taking steps to meet LDCs' needs both for local and recurrent cost financing and, with respect to the latter, the attitude of donors may now be more forthcoming than a few years previously.

C. Sector allocation

260. At the mid-term global review of the implementation of the SNPA, food, agriculture and rural development, as well as human resources and social development, were sectors which received special emphasis.

1. Food and agriculture

261. Food and agriculture has traditionally been the priority sector in DAC bilateral aid programmes with the LDCs, as well as in the multilateral programmes mainly financed by DAC member countries.  In 1981-1983 this sector was allocated on average around 15 per cent of new bilateral commitments from DAC donors, and 30 per cent of multilateral commitments.  In 1984 the amount

of aid going to agriculture appears to have fallen slightly, mainly due to the decline of new commitments to agriculture from the multilateral agencies, the share of this sector in multilateral commitments contracting to 17 per cent (see table 38). Over the period 1981-1984, more than $5.6 billion was allocated to aid agriculture in the LDCs from DAC sources alone.

262. OPEC countries in 1981-1984 allocated on average less than 4 per cent of their bilateral commitments to LDCs to food and agriculture. However, the multilateral OPEC agencies seem to have reoriented their lending programmes with LDCs to give more emphasis to agriculture, and in 1984 this sector accounted for one-third of the new commitments from these agencies.

263. A review of the development strategies of individual LDCs reveals the high priority assigned to agricultural development and improvement of the living conditions in rural areas, and the readjustment of LDCs' programmes and policies now taking place with a view to strengthening the agricultural sector and expanding the output of both food and export crops. 100/ This calls for correspondingly strengthening the support given by donors to LDCs' agricultural and rural development programmes and projects. In case the decline observed in 1984 in aid to agriculture is not merely temporary and due to the bunching of new commitments but is related to problems in absorptive capacity in this sector, determined efforts need to be made to overcome such constraints.

264. In their replies to the UNCTAD questionnaire as regards priority sectors of aid, the importance given to food, agriculture and rural development was confirmed by multilateral and bilateral donors alike. Among DAC members, the Commission of the European Communities, the Federal Republic of Germany, Finland and the Netherlands and, among multilateral financial institutions, the African Development Bank, the Arab Fund for Economic and Social Development (AFESD) and the World Bank reported intending to further raise this sector's priority. Food production and food security as well as broader aspects of rural development and infrastructure were brought out as areas of special interest by many donors. 101/

### 2. Education and health

265. In 1981-1984 the education sector was on average allocated some 3 per cent of ODA commitments from DAC countries and multilateral agencies mainly financed by them, and the health sector was allocated on average 6 per cent. Education was given somewhat more weight in the multilateral programmes (an average of 5 per cent of total commitments in 1981-1984), whereas on average no more than 2 per cent were allocated to this sector in bilateral DAC programmes. Australia, Denmark and Switzerland, and, among the socialist countries of Eastern Europe, Hungary, have stated education and health to be priority sectors in their assistance to LDCs; Australia and Finland intend to give increasing weight to health and nutrition, and the Netherlands to education and training, in their bilateral programmes.

## Table 38

### Concessional commitments to the LDCs by sector and purpose, 1981-1984

| Donor | Year | Agriculture | Industry, mining and construction | Energy | Transport and communications | Health | Education | Other services | General economic support c/ | Food aid | Emergency and distress relief | Other and unallocated, including technical co-operation | Total |
|---|---|---|---|---|---|---|---|---|---|---|---|---|---|
| | | *Percentage of total* | | | | | | | | *of which:* | | | *Millions of dollars* |
| DAC | 1981 | 21 | 3 | 5 | 9 | 5 | 3 | 1 | 18 | 7 | 1 | 35 | 6921 |
| | 1982 | 23 | 3 | 8 | 10 | 7 | 3 | 2 | 16 | 7 | 1 | 28 | 6640 |
| | 1983 | 22 | 2 | 9 | 10 | 6 | 4 | 2 | 15 | 7 | 1 | 30 | 6913 |
| | 1984 | 15 | 3 | 11 | 12 | 5 | 3 | 2 | 21 | 8 | 2 | 28 | 7612 |
| - Bilateral | 1981 | 16 | 3 | 4 | 9 | 5 | 2 | 1 | 27 | 9 | 1 | 33 | 3993 |
| | 1982 | 16 | 3 | 5 | 8 | 7 | 2 | 2 | 23 | 10 | 2 | 35 | 3643 |
| | 1983 | 14 | 2 | 9 | 8 | 7 | 2 | 1 | 23 | 11 | 1 | 33 | 3717 |
| | 1984 | 13 | 3 | 8 | 10 | 7 | 2 | 2 | 26 | 13 | 1 | 29 | 4266 |
| - Multilateral a/ | 1981 | 27 | 3 | 6 | 9 | 4 | 5 | 1 | 6 | 4 | 1 | 38 | 2928 |
| | 1982 | 32 | 5 | 11 | 12 | 6 | 4 | 2 | 6 | 3 | 1 | 22 | 2997 |
| | 1983 | 32 | 2 | 9 | 13 | 6 | 6 | 2 | 5 | 3 | 0 | 26 | 3196 |
| | 1984 | 17 | 3 | 14 | 14 | 5 | 5 | 3 | 14 | 3 | 3 | 26 | 3346 |
| OPEC | 1981 | 6 | -18- | | 13 | - | 0 - | [2] | 60 | .. | 0 | 3 | 1114 |
| | 1982 | 1 | -28- | | 13 | - | 0 - | 0 | 48 | .. | 4 | 10 | 1556 |
| | 1983 | 4 | -13- | | 14 | - | 1 - | 1 | 66 | .. | 2 | 2 | 1495 |
| | 1984 | 11 | -16- | | 12 | - | 1 - | - | 54 | .. | .. | 4 | 939 |
| - Bilateral | 1981 | 8 | -11- | | 11 | - | 0 - | - | 69 d/ | .. | 0 | - | 834 |
| | 1982 | 2 | -26- | | 8 | - | 0 - | 0 | 56 d/ | .. | 5 | 8 | 1236 |
| | 1983 | 2 | -6- | | 13 | - | 1 - | 1 | 77 d/ | .. | 2 | 2 | 1253 |
| | 1984 | 2 | -15- | | 7 | - | - | 1 | 73 | .. | .. | 2 | 667 |
| - Multilateral b/ | 1981 | - | -38- | | 18 | - | 1 - | 1 | 33 | .. | - | 11 | 280 |
| | 1982 | - | -36- | | 32 | - | 1 - | 2 | 12 | .. | 1 | 17 | 320 |
| | 1983 | 13 | -48- | | 22 | - | 1 - | 1 | 4 | .. | 1 | 13 | 242 |
| | 1984 | 33 | -19- | | 22 | - | 1 - | [8] | 9 | .. | .. | 9 | 272 |

Source: UNCTAD secretariat estimates mainly based on OECD/DAC and UNCTAD data.

a/ Commitments from multilateral agencies mainly financed by DAC member countries.

b/ Commitments from multilateral agencies mainly financed by OPEC member countries.

c/ Including current imports financing, emergency and disaster relief, budget support, balance-of-payments support and debt reorganization.

d/ Including technical co-operation.

266. Half of UNDP's resources for LDCs in 1985-86 were allocated to the education sector. Among other multilateral programmes, IDA and the African Development Bank were the most important donors in the areas of education and health. The World Bank plans to at least double its lending for population and health-related projects during the next few years. In OPEC aid programmes, the share of education and health has overall been limited. However, AFESD reports human resources development as a priority sector and intends to give more weight to education and training in its future assistance to LDCs. Furthermore, the share of education in the OPEC Fund's lending programme with LDCs was substantially expanded in 1985.

267. Training is one of the most important forms of co-operation with the LDCs on the part of the socialist countries of Eastern Europe, e.g. Czechoslovakia and Hungary, as well as of China. China has, for instance, provided extensive training in the field of health and reports having sent medical teams to 25 LDCs.

### 3. Other sectors

268. At the mid-term global review of the implementation of the SNPA, donors were requested to support measures to ensure energy supply and conservation in LDCs, their industrial development efforts, and the improvement of their physical and institutional structure. Strengthening transport and communications facilities, in particular, is vital for the development of the LDCs, not least for the land-locked and island countries among them.

269. An increasing share of aid commitments to LDCs has, since 1981, been allocated to energy development both in DAC bilateral aid and in multilateral programmes. By 1984, the share of this sector had risen to 11 per cent of new commitments to LDCs by DAC countries and multilateral agencies mainly financed by them. Commitments more than doubled in dollar terms from 1981 to 1984. Among multilateral agencies, energy held a particularly prominent place in the Asian Development Bank's lending programme (accounting for 38 per cent of loans to its least developed member countries in 1983-85), within which growing emphasis on indigenous energy development is expected.

270. On the other hand, the share of aid allocated from the DAC group to industrial development, including mining and construction, has been relatively small. On average, 2 to 3 per cent of total commitments from DAC countries and multilateral agencies mainly financed by them was allocated to this sector in 1981-1984, although in some bilateral aid programmes the sector was relatively important. Denmark has reported industry and construction as a priority sector in bilateral financial assistance. With growing agricultural development, the Asian Development Bank foresees likely increased financing for agro-industries.

271. Industrial and energy development, together with transport and communications, have been the major co-operation sectors in OPEC aid, accounting for the bulk of its project aid to the LDCs. An increasing share of resources (from 9 per cent in 1981 to 12 per cent in 1984) has also been devoted to transport and communications in DAC aid programmes, owing to increased financing of this sector from the multilateral agencies mainly

financed by DAC countries. For instance the African and Asian Development Banks are involved in this sector as part of their assistance to infrastructural development. Australia reports intending to raise the priority given to aid to transport and communications.

272. As regards the economic co-operation of the socialist countries of Eastern Europe with the LDCs, it has taken, _inter alia_, the form of participation by the socialist countries in a number of important industrial and infrastructural projects.

273. Some donors have reported attempting to strengthen the sectoral focus within their assistance programmes. Thus a sectoral studies section has been established within the Australian aid administration. In the Netherlands, three special sector programmes (for rural development, for industrial development and for education and research) became operational in 1985. Agriculture sector studies will increasingly provide the framework for the Asian Development Bank's continued involvement in this sector, and the World Bank is undertaking an expanded programme of sector work in support of ongoing adjustment programmes.

## D. Summary conclusions

274. Available evidence indicates little overall change in aid modalities during the first few years of the implementation of the SNPA, up to 1984, although readjustments and improvements were undertaken under some individual donor programmes. The terms of aid extended to the LDCs remained generally soft, but no relaxation in regard to aid-tying was apparent. Recorded programme aid, apart from food aid and emergency relief, increased relatively little between 1981 and 1984.

275. With respect to the terms of aid, continuing attention needs to be paid to extending appropriate financing terms to these countries and adapting the terms of aid programmes to their requirements and debt-servicing capacity. Scope still remains for further increasing grant financing for LDCs and softening the terms of loans extended to them, as well as of associated financing packages. Various means also exist for easing the constraints imposed on LDCs by current tying rules.

276. Donors are clearly making efforts to adapt some modalities of their aid programmes with LDCs to these countries' changing requirements, notably by new programmes for sector assistance and import support, a greater accent on rehabilitation and maintenance of existing capacities, and readiness to consider local and recurrent cost financing. Some multilateral initiatives have been particularly important in mobilizing resources in support of LDCs' structural adjustment programmes. It is to be expected that these reorientations will translate, _inter alia_, into increased programme aid for the LDCs in the second half of the decade.

277. The efforts undertaken by the LDCs since the adoption of the SNPA to elaborate and present new economic and development programmes and the concomitant strengthening of aid co-ordination mechanisms enable LDCs' needs as regards various forms of aid to be more precisely determined and better

known to donors. Country reviews held for individual LDCs have, among other
requirements, brought out these countries' urgent need of quick-disbursing
assistance in the years ahead. The situation requires careful monitoring to
ensure that these needs are met sufficiently rapidly and on an adequate scale.

278. With respect to the sectoral allocation of aid, as regards project and
sector assistance the bulk of the increase in commitments in 1984 from DAC
countries and multilateral agencies mainly financed by them seems to have been
directed to energy development and transport and communications projects. The
increase in commitments from OPEC donors in 1982-1983 was again directed
mainly to industrial and energy development and to general economic support,
although in 1983-1984 OPEC multilateral agencies did allocate an increasing
share of their resources to agriculture. The sectoral priorities and
reorientation of priorities reported by some donors in their responses to the
UNCTAD questionnaire seem, however, to indicate that resources may in the
future be shifted to such sectors as food and agriculture, rural and human
resources development, and health.

279. Multilateral agencies mainly financed by DAC members have been major
providers of funds to agricultural development programmes and projects in the
LDCs, as well as to health and education programmes. Safeguarding and
expanding the capacity of these agencies to commit new funds to the LDCs thus
takes on particular importance in the context of the SNPA.

## Chapter III

## AID CO-ORDINATION AND THE ROLE OF ROUND TABLES AND CONSULTATIVE GROUPS

### A.  The expansion since 1981

280. One of the most visible results of the United Nations Conference on the Least Developed Countries has been the institution of round table mechanisms for many LDCs which previously lacked such fora for discussions with their development partners, and the setting up of additional consultative groups, in pursuance of paragraph 111 of the SNPA.  Almost all LDCs are now covered by such arrangements, with UNDP and the World Bank acting as the main lead agencies.

281. At the time of the Paris Conference, only a few LDCs had organized round table meetings with UNDP support.  World Bank-sponsored consultative groups or aid groups were active for three LDCs, and Haiti had a mixed commission for the implementation of external co-operation programmes instituted under OAS auspices. 102/  Five years later, by mid-1986, 28 LDCs had arranged a country review as foreseen under the SNPA 103/ and five more LDCs were actively preparing their first review meeting (see table 39).  Only four LDCs, including Vanuatu which was placed in the LDC group by the General Assembly at its fortieth session, were not covered by any country review arrangements.

282. The SNPA stated that the first round of country reviews should take place as soon as possible and preferably by 1983.  The country review process has, however, proved demanding in terms of preparations and inputs, and the first round of these meetings has taken longer to implement than was originally envisaged.

Table 39

Tentative schedule of country review meetings as follow-up
to the Substantial New Programme of Action
(as of December 1986)

| Least developed country | Government focal point | Consultative mechanism/lead agency | Date of country review meeting |
|---|---|---|---|
| **AFRICA** | | | |
| - Benin | Ministry of Planning, Statistics and Economic Analysis | UNDP Round Table | Held 28 Feb.- 4 March 1983 in Cotonou. |
| | | Consultations Suvalau-Porga highway | Tentatively scheduled for end 1986. |
| | | Sectoral consultations for telecommunications and civil aviation | Tentatively planned in late 1986. |
| - Botswana | Ministry of Planning | Modalities for possible sectoral consultations under consideration | |
| - Burkina Faso | Ministry of Planning | UNDP Round Table | RT tentatively planned for late 1986 with In-country Review in 1987. |
| - Burundi | Ministry of Planning | UNDP Round Table | Held 8-11 Feb. 1984 in Bujumbura. |
| | | Sectoral consultations for rural development, energy and education under consideration | Planned for mid-1987. |

Table 39 (continued)

| Least developed country | Government focal point | Consultative mechanism/lead agency | Date of country review meeting |
|---|---|---|---|
| - Cape Verde | Secretary of State for Co-operation and Planning | UNDP Round Table | Held 21-23 Jan. 1982 in Praia and 22-23 Oct. 1986 in Geneva with In-Country Review meeting scheduled for 30 Nov.-4 Dec. 1986 in Praia. |
| - Central African Republic | Haut Commissariat au Plan, aux Statistiques et à la Coopération internationale, Présidence de la Republique | UNDP Round Table | Planned for early 1987. RT preliminary review meeting held 11-12 March 1986 in Bangui. |
| - Chad | Ministry of Planning (Commissaire au Plan) | UN/OAU meeting on Reconstruction of Chad | Held 29-30 Nov. 1982 in Geneva. |
| | | UNDP Round Table | Held 4-6 December 1985 in Geneva. |
| | | Sectoral consultations for cotton | Held 20-22 May 1986 in Washington. |
| | | Sectoral consultations for agro-sylvo-pastoral sector; | Planned for 10-14 Nov. 1986 in N'Djamena. |
| | | for transport | Planned for March 1987. |
| - Comoros | Ministry of Planning | UNDP Round Table | Held 2-4 July 1984 in Moroni; periodic review to be determined. |
| - Djibouti | Ministry of Planning | UNDP Round Table | Held 21-23 March 1983 in Djibouti. |
| | | Sectoral consultations for energy | Planned for end 1986/ beg. 1987. |

Table 39 (continued)

| Least developed country | Government focal point | Consultative mechanism/lead agency | Date of country review meeting |
|---|---|---|---|
| - Equatorial Guinea | Presidency | UNDP Round Table | Held 19-21 April 1982 in Geneva. a/ RT scheduled for March/April 1987. |
| - Ethiopia | Ministry of Planning | Undetermined | |
| - Gambia | Ministry of Planning | UNDP Round Table | Held 22-30 Nov. 1984 in Banjul. |
| | | Sectoral consultations for health; for fisheries | Held Dec. 1984 in Banjul; held in June 1985 in Banjul. |
| | | Special consultations for balance of payments | Held in Sept. 1985 in London. |
| | | Sectoral consultations for agriculture and water | Tentatively scheduled for Jan.-Feb. 1987. |
| -Guinea | Prime Minister's Office | World Bank Consultative Group | Preparatory meeting held on 11 April 1986; forthcoming CG scheduled for February 1987. |
| - Guinea-Bissau | Prime Minister's Office | UNDP Round Table | Held 21-23 May 1984 in Lisbon; periodic review held 16-18 April 1985 in Bissau. |
| | | Consultations with NGOs | Held 3-10 November 1985. |
| | | Sectoral consultations on health; and for agriculture and fisheries | Held 4-6 Feb. 1986 in Bissau; planned for Feb. 1987 in Bissau. |

Table 39 (continued)

| Least developed country | Government focal point | Consultative mechanism/lead agency | Date of country review meeting |
|---|---|---|---|
| - Lesotho | Ministry of Planning | UNDP Round Table | Held 14-17 May 1984 in Maseru. |
|  |  | Sectoral consultations for water and sanitation | Held 11-13 June 1985. |
|  |  | Special sectoral consultations for integrated rural development and for employment generation | Proposed. |
| - Malawi | Ministry of Planning | UNDP Round Table | Held 28-29 Feb. 1984 in Blantyre. |
|  |  | World Bank Consultative Group | Held 21-22 January 1986 in Paris. |
| - Mali | Ministry of Planning | UNDP Round Table | First RT held 13-16 Dec. 1982 in Bamako. RT held 21-23 Nov. 1985 in Geneva followed by a country review meeting held 2-5 Dec. 1985 in Bamako. |
|  |  | Sectoral consultations for food strategy, for drought and desertification, for employment, for liberalization, for institutional reforms, for primary health care and demography and for non-project aid, recurrent costs and structural adjustment | Dates to be determined. |
| - Niger | Ministry of Planning | UNDP Round Table | Tentatively planned for Feb. 1987 with In-country Review meeting in September 1987. |

Table 39 (continued)

| Least developed country | Government focal point | Consultative mechanism/lead agency | Date of country review meeting |
|---|---|---|---|
| - Rwanda | Ministère des Affaires étrangères et de la Coopération | UNDP Round Table<br><br>Consult.with NGOs<br><br><br>Sectoral consultations for water and sanitation, and for education | Held 1-4 Dec. 1982 in Kigali.<br>Held in June 1985.<br><br>Held in Jan. 1986 in Kigali,<br><br>under preparation. |
| - Sao Tome and Principe | Ministry of Co-operation | UNDP Round Table<br><br>Sectoral consultations for rural development, incl. food strategy, fisheries and cocoa, together with consultations for energy and water, transport and problems of land-locked countries<br><br>Meeting of NGOs | Held 9-11 Dec. 1985 in Brussels.<br><br>Held 17-22 May 1986 in Sao Tome.<br><br><br><br><br><br><br><br>Planned for end Nov. 1986 in Sao Tome. |
| - Sierra Leone | | UNDP Round Table | Planned for early 1987 in Geneva. |
| - Somalia | Ministry of National Planning | World Bank Consultative Group | Held 24-26 Oct. 1983 in Paris; special meeting held 23 Jan. 1985 and 5-6 Nov. 1985 Scheduled March 1987. |
| - Sudan | Ministry of Finance & Economic Planning | World Bank Consultative Group | Held 12-14 Jan. 1983 and 14-16 Feb. 1984. |

Table 39 (continued)

| Least developed country | Government focal point | Consultative mechanism/lead agency | Date of country review meeting |
|---|---|---|---|
| - Togo | Ministry of Planning | UNDP Round Table | Preliminary consult. for RT/country review held in Jan. 1985 in Paris; RT/country review held 26-28 June 1985 in Lomé. |
| | | Sectoral consultations for rural development; for infrastructure, social sector and human resources management; for non-project financing | Held 23-26 March in Kara; Planned for end 1986. Foreseen during first half of 1987 (All to be held in Lomé). |
| - Uganda | Not specified | World Bank Consultative Group | Held in May 1982, Jan. 1984 and on 24-25 Jan. 1985 in Paris. |
| - United Rep. of Tanzania | Ministry of Planning and Economic Affairs | World Bank Consultative Group | Held 11-12 June 1986 in Paris. |
| LATIN AMERICA | | | |
| - Haiti | Secretariat of State for Planning | Joint Commission for External Co-operation Programmes in Haiti | Held 1-2 Feb. 1984 in Port-au-Prince. |
| | | Caribbean Group for Co-oper. in Economic Development | Scheduled 21-22 Nov. 1986 in Washington. |

Table 39 (continued)

| Least developed country | Government focal point | Consultative mechanism/lead agency | Date of country review meeting |
|---|---|---|---|
| **ASIA** | | | |
| - Afghani- stan | Department of Foreign Economic Relations of the State Planning Committee | UNDP Round Table | RT held 9-18 May 1983 in Geneva. |
| - Bangla- b/ desh | Ministry of Finance, External Resources Division | World Bank Consultative Group | Held in April 1982, on 9-10 April 1984, 9-10 May 1985 and 14-15 April 1986 in Paris. Next scheduled for April 1987. |
| - Bhutan | Economic Division, Ministry of Foreign Affairs | UNDP Round Table | First RT held 9-18 May 1983 in Geneva; second RT held 24 April 1986 in Geneva. |
| - Lao P.D.R. | | UNDP Round Table | First RT held 9-18 May 1983 in Geneva; second RT held 24 April 1986 in Geneva. |
| - Maldives | External Resources Section, Ministry of Foreign Affairs | UNDP Round Table | First RT held from 9 to 18 May 1983 in Geneva; c/ second RT held on 25 April 1986 in Geneva. |
| - Nepal b/ | Ministry of Finance | World Bank Consultative Group | Held in Dec. 1981, 5-6 Dec. 1983 and on 16 Jan. 1986 in Tokyo. |
| - Samoa | Prime Minister's Office | UNDP Round Table | First RT held 9-18 May Geneva; second RT held 22 April 1986 in Geneva. |
| - Vanuatu | | Discussions for holding exploratory consultations with donors under way. | |

## Table 39 (concluded)

| Least developed country | Government focal point | Consultative mechanism/lead agency | Date of country review meeting |
|---|---|---|---|
| **WESTERN ASIA** | | | |
| - Democratic Yemen | Ministry of Planning | | To be determined. |
| - Yemen Arab Republic | Central Planning Organization | Second Yemen International Development Conference. | Held in April 1982. |

a/ A UNDP Round Table was held in April 1982 for Equatorial Guinea, but as the country was not added to the list of LDCs until the thirty-seventh session of the General Assembly at the end of 1982, this meeting did not take place within the framework of paragraph 113 of the SNPA.

b/ Also attended the joint session of the Asia/Pacific Round Table Meeting in 1983.

c/ A Special Meeting of Development Partners was convened by the World Bank on 16 July 1984.

### B. The role of country review meetings

283. The country review meetings were conceived as a mechanism for regular and periodic review and implementation of the SNPA at country level, and their agenda was set out in paragraph 113 of the Programme. Their main purpose can be summarized as securing assistance and contributing to the increase in (and improvement in the quality of) external resources available to LDCs; and the appropriate integration of these resources with the recipients' domestic resources to support their priority development objectives.

284. No clear evidence is obtainable, however, as to the impetus which the country review process may have given to increase aid flows to the LDCs concerned. As can be seen from table 40, for the group of LDCs as a whole average new aid commitments in 1982-1984 were only 0.8 per cent higher than in 1979-1981. Somewhat over half of the LDCs benefited from higher commitments after the Paris Conference. Countries with higher commitments can be found in all groups, as well as among countries which held no country review meetings during the period 1981-1984.

285. The agenda for the country review meetings as set out in paragraph 113 of the SNPA also foresaw a review of aid conditions, terms and modalities, and consideration of ways and means of assisting the LDCs in expanding their trade. Issues related to the former (aid practices and management) have had a prominent place in the deliberations at these meetings, with several of the early round tables devoting special sessions to aid modalities. Trade issues have more rarely been touched upon in the country reviews. 104/

286. The mid-term global review of the implementation of the SNPA was the occasion for the Intergovernmental Group on the Least Developed Countries to review the arrangements for follow-up and monitoring of the SNPA at the national level, and both LDCs and their development partners gave their views on country-specific experiences of round tables and consultative or aid group meetings. Information in this respect was also provided in the replies to the UNCTAD questionnaire on the implementation of the SNPA.

287. On the whole, the initial results of the country review process were deemed unsatisfactory in terms of encouraging increased resource flows and a candid discussion of specific development issues, but the meetings were considered by the Intergovernmental Group to have provided a good basis for future development co-operation. 105/

288. In the LDCs' view, the results of individual review meetings have in general been limited, and expectations have not been fulfilled. LDCs have indicated that since the Paris Conference their governments have made considerable efforts to improve their policies and have adopted and presented economic programmes as requested in the SNPA, but these efforts have been far from satisfactorily matched by donors. Except in a few cases no appreciable increase in commitments has resulted, pledges have not been transformed into firm commitments, and the aid inflow has been slower than expected. LDCs have also expressed disappointment that review meetings have not mobilized new donors. However, the utility of such meetings has been recognized, for instance as an occasion for dialogue with donors and in creating an awareness among them of LDCs' aid requirements.

Table 40

Concessional commitments to the LDCs, 1979–1981 and 1982–1984

| | Average concessional commitments in $ million | |
|---|---|---|
| | Average 1979–1981 | Average 1982–1984 |
| **First country review meeting held in 1982** | | |
| Cape Verde | 70.8 | 81.3 |
| Chad | 61.9 | 103.9 |
| Equatorial Guinea | 14.5 | 20.8 |
| Mali | 259.0 | 353.8 |
| Rwanda | 197.7 | 195.4 |
| Yemen | 506.7 | 478.9 |
| **First country review meeting held in 1983** | | |
| Afghanistan | 509.3 | 246.8 |
| Benin | 107.5 | 130.3 |
| Bhutan | 10.8 | 27.6 |
| Djibouti | 76.2 | 129.0 |
| Lao P.D.R. | 109.6 | 92.0 |
| Maldives | 20.4 | 15.3 |
| Samoa | 33.8 | 20.1 |
| **First country review meeting held in 1984** | | |
| Burundi | 189.2 | 139.5 |
| Comoros | 54.8 | 56.2 |
| Gambia | 80.1 | 65.6 |
| Guinea-Bissau | 65.9 | 87.5 |
| Lesotho | 125.5 | 97.6 |
| Malawi | 180.1 | 166.1 |
| **Consultative or aid groups having met in 1981–84** | | |
| Bangladesh | 1 802.5 | 1 747.6 |
| Nepal | 250.4 | 313.9 |
| Somalia | 428.1 | 422.2 |
| Sudan | 843.2 | 856.3 |
| Uganda | 165.5 | 277.1 |
| Haiti | 102.5 | 162.7 |
| **No country review meeting in 1981–84** | | |
| Botswana | 132.6 | 112.3 |
| Burkina Faso | 285.2 | 243.0 |
| Central African Republic | 102.8 | 133.6 |
| Democratic Yemen | 249.3 | 358.2 |
| Ethiopia | 335.7 | 522.7 |
| Guinea | 167.7 | 208.9 |
| Niger | 274.1 | 282.8 |
| Sao Tome & Principe | 5.6 | 11.1 |
| Sierra Leone | 105.6 | 75.3 |
| Togo | 107.3 | 135.7 |
| United Republic of Tanzania | 838.8 | 594.4 |
| Vanuatu | 47.8 | 28.6 |
| **TOTAL** | 8 919.6 | 8 995.3 |

Source: UNCTAD secretariat estimates mainly based on OECD/DAC and UNCTAD data.

289. Donor countries have stressed the important role that country review meetings are to play as part of a continuous process 106/ of exchange of information and consultations to arrive at a common understanding and possibly joint programming. They consider that the review process has served to assist LDCs in the elaboration of development plans and in focusing donors' attention on these countries' needs and that the meetings have contributed to better understanding and dialogue between LDCs and donors, and have facilitated a flow of more appropriate and better co-ordinated assistance. The role of country review meetings in improving the quality of assistance and enhancing aid effectiveness has been emphasized. Development banks and financial institutions are generally in favour of further strengthening aid co-ordination.

## C. The evolution of country review meetings

290. Since the launching of the SNPA, important changes have taken place with regard to the format, follow-up and attendance at country review meetings, in particular the round tables arranged with UNDP as lead agency. The UNDP in 1984-1985 undertook an evaluation of the early round tables convened under the SNPA, which revealed "the need for an intensive and systematic upgrading of the round table process". 107/ Weaknesses in preparation and lack of follow-through were identified, as well as the need for improved effectiveness of the support provided by UNDP and for strengthening the capabilities of the LDCs concerned. Consequently a so-called new format has been instituted for UNDP-sponsored round table meetings. The first country review meeting under this format was arranged by two African LDCs in late 1985 and by Asian LDCs in April 1986.

291. At the outset, the round table approach was somewhat divergent from that of the World Bank-sponsored consultative groups. The latter mechanism had been instituted long before the SNPA was adopted (and the majority of consultative groups in existence are still for non-LDC countries). 108/ Consultative groups were always more focused on an overall discussion of policies and resource requirements. Statements made in these groups of donors' intentions to provide assistance are related to aggregate financing requirements under policies and programmes under review, providing the recipient country with an overall assessment of external resource availability. In contrast, early round table. were often largely based on a sector-by-sector presentation of LDCs' development plans and programmes, eliciting pledges from donors against specific projects.

292. Membership in consultative and aid groups was always restricted and is still so, whereas governments of the LDCs that organized the early round table conferences tried to secure the broadest possible participation of donors including, in addition to traditional aid partners and potential donors, other developing countries from within and outside the region, most major international organizations, the United Nations agencies and other international and non-governmental organizations.

293. With the introduction of the new UNDP format for round tables, the two main types of review mechanisms have become closer to each other in approach. Agendas for the UNDP-sponsored round tables have become more selective and more policy-oriented, and co-operation between the two main lead agencies in preparations for the meetings has been reinforced.

294. A main feature of the new round table format 109/ is its multi-stage character. The round table conference proper is conceived as the main event in the process. It is intended to be the first step in the dialogue between the LDC Government and its main donors on macro-economic and sectoral development policies and on priority requirements, and to lead to policy commitments from the LDC as well as commitments by participating donors. As limited participation is seen as necessary for such policy discussions, attempts are being made to restrict attendance at these round table conferences to the principal development funding partners of the LDC concerned.

295. Other proposed changes concern venue (the intention is to hold the new-format round tables in Geneva, whereas earlier round table meetings were held in-country) and chairmanship; UNDP proposes, if the LDC government so agrees, to chair the round table conferences with the LDC government assuming the co-chairmanship.

296. Lastly, another major element of the round table process as envisaged under the new format are sectoral and special programme consultations, to follow up the main conferences. In-country review meetings with larger attendance may also be arranged for all interested aid partners. In many LDCs, follow-up to both early round tables and under the new format has already been instituted or envisaged at sectoral level. Some in-country meetings to discuss sectoral policies and programmes were arranged in 1985, and a number of others were under active preparation.

297. The World Bank has also undertaken evaluation of its co-ordination experiences, notably in the context of the Joint Programme of Action for sub-Saharan Africa. One reform to introduce under the relatively long-established and well-tried consultative group format, which is considered to be useful, is to harmonize decisions on aid and debt relief, bringing together the different representatives handling aid and debt within creditors and donor governments. 110/ The Bank reports having taken steps to strengthen the consultative and aid group process, in particular to support institutional arrangements for follow-up and monitoring at the country level, providing a useful opportunity for information-sharing and early attention to problems of project implementation and follow-up on agreed action. The Bank and UNDP have reached an agreement on guiding principles for aid co-ordination in sub-Saharan Africa. They will expand their collaboration and joint efforts to organize and make more effective both consultative groups and round tables.

298. At the mid-term global review of the implementation of the SNPA, the steps taken by the World Bank and UNDP to improve the consultative groups and round tables were welcomed. Scope for further improvement was noted as regards follow-up to country review meetings by co-ordination at the local and

sectoral levels, and as regards co-ordination of the activities of the
United Nations system at the country level. A number of important
recommendations were made as regards future co-ordination of aid to the LDCs
and the role of round tables and consultative groups in this respect. Donors
in a position to do so were urged to support development plans or programmes
of LDCs with multi-year, predictable and monitorable commitments and timely
disbursements. The international community and the multilateral agencies were
requested to ensure that review meetings result in facilitating an increased
flow of external assistance through, inter alia, better understanding and a
candid dialogue between LDCs and their development partners, and to harmonize
terms and procedures of donors to the extent possible in order to achieve a
co-ordinated approach conducive to the implementation of the development
programmes of the LDCs.

## D. Conclusions

299. Since the adoption of the SNPA, the scope for dialogue between the LDCs
and their development partners has been vastly expanded, offering new
possibilities for co-ordination between the partners and for providing more
effective support for the LDCs' development programmes as well as for their
policy adjustments. Round tables and consultative groups have come to be
increasingly regarded and planned as an ongoing process of consultation,
information and negotiation between development partners. The expansion of
various follow-up activities, including the institution of co-ordination
arrangements at the local level, is another prominent characteristic of the
country review process as it has evolved.

300. The mobilization of increased resources for the LDCs and their more
effective utilization remain the overriding objectives of the SNPA and should
be the main focus for co-ordination efforts during the second half of the SNPA
decade. The necessary co-ordination machinery has largely been put in place
during the first half of the 1980s but it would require further strengthening,
particularly at the field level. LDCs have shown their willingness to engage
in candid dialogue with their donors, which are increasingly consulted in the
LDCs' planning process. 111/ LDCs need to see tangible results, in terms of
increased donor support.

301. Extension of the use of multi-year commitments or medium-term aid
indications from donors, or other ways of enhancing the predictability of aid
flows, would greatly facilitate development planning in the LDCs. Moreover,
the complementarity of efforts would have to be ensured and extended to cover
debt relief as well as aid.

302. Apart from the establishment of a clearer link between LDCs' economic
reforms and development programmes and the timely provision of increasing aid
flows in appropriate forms, several other issues need continuing attention in
the context of the country review process. Thus, effective monitoring, not
only of the recipients' progress in the implementation of their programmes but
also of donors' support measures, should be instituted. As brought out at the
mid-term global review of the implementation of the SNPA, the harmonization of
terms and procedures could also be an important element in further improvement
of co-ordination.

303. Finally, means of enlisting new donors and assuring the possibilities of all potential development partners to contribute effectively to the development process of the LDCs, merit consideration. Many smaller countries and organizations including non-governmental bodies (NGOs) 112/ have indeed a potentially valuable contribution to make to the development of the LDCs. Several of the more advanced developing countries have technical assistance and training programmes from which LDCs could benefit. 113/ Moreover, active participation by United Nations organizations, which have also for their part expressed their interest in contributing to the LDCs' development efforts within their fields of competence, should be ensured; many of them have set up special programmes to assist the LDCs and have attempted to direct increasing resources to them.

304. It has been foreseen that round table conferences under the new format could be followed by in-country conferences in the form of review meetings of all interested aid partners, including United Nations agencies and NGOs, to report on the conclusions of the round table conferences and elicit support for agreed policy and programmes. By mid-1986 this type of follow-up has taken place in Mali and Togo. Such meetings with larger attendance could have a role to play, and should be given commensurate weight in order not only to maximize support from traditional major donors but also to mobilize additional support, through searching for and actively enlisting the participation of new and non-traditional donors and other countries and organizations in a position to contribute to the implementation of the SNPA.

Chapter IV

THE DEBT SITUATION OF THE LEAST DEVELOPED COUNTRIES

A.    The evolution of LDCs' debt problems

305. The LDCs experienced a very rapid growth of external indebtedness during the 1970s 114/ as a result of severe external imbalances.  As this was not matched by an improvement in their general economic situation, debt service obligations became increasingly burdensome.  The LDCs' debt situation worsened considerably in the 1980s when the world economic crisis added to the vulnerability of their debt servicing capacity already exacerbated by their structurally limited export base.  Global recession reduced demand for their exports, which consisted mainly of primary commodities.  Escalating debt service obligations from borrowings in earlier years, compounded by falling export earnings and rising import costs, exerted severe pressure on the LDCs' balances of payments. 115/

306. To cope with their balance-of-payments problems, many LDCs made efforts to bring about external stabilization, essentially in the form of cutbacks in imports and government expenditure.  These cuts affected not only current outlays but also investment, with the resultant slowing down of development activity.  In 1984, while the total overall balance-of-payments deficit of the LDCs had been considerably reduced, 116/ accumulated debt reached 50 per cent of their GDP on the average, and in some cases, even exceeded it.  Although on the average a modest economic recovery took place in 1985, 117/ LDCs' debt ratios are not estimated to have improved in that year.

307. In the 1980s debt servicing thus became unsustainable for several countries which fell into arrears in their payments.  A number of them had to seek debt relief and resort to multilateral debt reschedulings.  Reschedulings provide, however, only temporary relief and the added burden is felt in later years.  LDCs' debt service obligations for the years ahead are at levels considerably higher than during the first half of the 1980s.

B.    Structure and recent trends in LDCs' disbursed debt
      and debt service

1.  Structure

308. LDCs' total external debt, including short-term debt, is estimated to have reached $33.7 billion at the end of 1984 and to have climbed to a level of some $38 billion at the end of 1985.  The LDCs' debts are concentrated in 10 countries, namely, Afghanistan, Bangladesh, Democratic Yemen, Ethiopia, Guinea, Mali, Somalia, Sudan, the United Republic of Tanzania and Yemen, which accounted for 72.3 per cent of the LDCs' total debt at the end of 1984.  All these countries have accumulated debts of over $1 billion at least.  Among them, Bangladesh and Sudan are the biggest debtors, with, at that time, accumulated debts of about $5.3 billion and $6.0 billion respectively, corresponding together to a third of the total debt for all LDCs.

309. As can be seen from table 40, over 90 per cent of LDCs' external debt consists of medium-term and long-term debts, the major part being concessional debts (66 per cent), mainly to multilateral agencies (27 per cent) and non-OECD countries (26 per cent).  LDCs' short-term debt exceeds $2 billion

and accounts for 7 per cent of these countries' total external debt, according to estimates available for the years 1982 to 1984. LDCs' use of IMF credit doubled between 1980 and 1983, when it reached $2.2 billion. It fell to $2.0 billion in 1984 then rose again to $2.2 billion in 1985.

## 2. Recent trends

310. Recent trends indicate a steady deceleration in the rate of growth of LDCs' total external debt (see table 40). In 1984, it grew by only 3 per cent as compared to some 10 per cent in 1983 and 1982, 13 per cent in 1981 and 16 per cent in 1980. This deceleration can be explained for the most part by the stagnation and decline of financial flows (excluding grants) to LDCs, and debt relief. In 1985, however, the increase was some 13 per cent but the larger part of it was due to the impact of the United States dollar depreciation which entailed a significant upward revaluation of non-United States dollar denominated debt stocks. 118/ Stocks in non-United States dollars are relatively significant in the case of LDCs. 119/

311. During the 1980s LDCs' concessional debt grew at a faster rate than non-concessional debt which was influenced by a fall in private lending. The growth of the former has mainly been due to debts owed to multilateral agencies which have constituted an increasing share of LDCs' concessional debt - 44 per cent in 1984 as compared to 38 per cent in 1980 (see table 41).

312. The share in the LDCs' total debt of bilateral debt to non-OECD countries (mainly OPEC and socialist countries) has also increased to a minor extent but there has been a marked drop in the share of ODA debts to OECD member countries. This drop is the outcome of action taken under Board resolution 165 (S-IX) in which developed donor countries agreed to seek to adjust the terms of past bilateral ODA, 120/ or to adopt other equivalent measures to improve the net flows of ODA to poorer developing countries, particularly the LDCs. It is also due to the fact that the majority of DAC countries have been providing an increasing proportion of their aid to LDCs in the form of grants.

## 3. Debt service

313. The evolution of LDCs' debt service payments during the 1980s is in line with the changes in the structure of these countries' debt as described above, especially the relative increase in concessional debt, and also reflects the important reschedulings that took place under the aegis of the Paris Club and with commercial banks. A favourable development since 1981 is the softening of the average terms of lending which is reported to have continued in 1985. 121/ The effect of the continuous decline in interest rates was, however, relatively moderate because the LDCs' debt is owed mainly to official lenders. Interest rates to official lenders declined relatively little compared to the sharp decline in interest rates to private lenders.

314. Debt relief operations, in particular reschedulings, caused LDCs' debt service payments to stabilize around $1.5 billion during 1981 to 1983, after they had increased substantially in the preceding years. In 1984, these payments are estimated to have reached $1.9 billion, which is equivalent to one-fifth of LDCs' combined exports. In 1985, they were contained at some $2 billion. 122/ The 30 per cent increase of debt service in 1984 is accounted for mainly by export credits extended in earlier years and to

Table 40 (a)

LDCs' external debt (at year end) and debt service,
by source of lending, 1982 to 1985

| | External debt | | | | | | | | Debt service | | | | | | | |
|---|---|---|---|---|---|---|---|---|---|---|---|---|---|---|---|---|
| | $ million | | | | % of total | | | | $ million | | | | % of total | | | |
| | 1982 | 1983 | 1984 | 1985 | 1982 | 1983 | 1984 | 1985 | 1982 | 1983 | 1984 | 1985 | 1982 | 1983 | 1984 | 1985 |
| I. Long-term and medium-term | 27 718 | 30 413 | 31 371 | 36 000 | 93.0 | 93.1 | 93.2 | 94.7 | 1 304 | 1 252 | 1 663 | 1 800 | 84.9 | 85.3 | 87.2 | 90.0 |
| A. Concessional | 18 858 | 20 734 | 22 293 | .. | 63.3 | 63.4 | 66.2 | .. | 429 | 439 | 601 | .. | 27.9 | 29.9 | 31.5 | .. |
| (a) Bilateral | 11 786 | 12 635 | 13 171 | .. | 39.5 | 38.7 | 39.1 | .. | 308 | 302 | 402 | .. | 20.0 | 20.6 | 21.0 | .. |
| – OECD countries | 3 916 | 3 912 | 4 266 | 4 000 | 13.1 | 12.0 | 12.7 | 10.5 | 110 | 107 | 143 | 100 | 7.2 | 7.3 | 7.5 | 5.0 |
| – Other countries | 7 870 | 8 721 | 8 905 | .. | 26.4 | 26.7 | 26.4 | .. | 198 | 195 | 259 | .. | 12.9 | 13.3 | 13.6 | .. |
| (b) Multilateral | 7 072 | 8 102 | 9 125 | c/ | 23.7 | 24.8 | 27.1 | c/ | 122 | 138 | 199 | c/ | 7.9 | 9.4 | 10.4 | c/ |
| B. Non-concessional | 8 859 | 9 683 | 9 075 | .. | 29.7 | 29.6 | 27.0 | .. | 874 | 816 | 1 062 | .. | 56.9 | 55.6 | 55.7 | .. |
| (a) OECD countries | 5 999 | 6 503 | 6 064 | 7 000 | 20.1 | 19.9 | 18.0 | 18.4 | 602 | 573 | 793 | (800) | 39.2 | 39.0 | 41.6 | (40.0) |
| – Export credits | 4 049 | 4 920 | 4 384 | 5 000 | 13.6 | 15.1 | 13.0 | 13.2 | 393 | 441 | 602 | 600 | 25.6 | 30.0 | 31.6 | 30.0 |
| – Capital markets | 1 861 | 1 514 | 1 610 | 2 000 | 6.2 | 4.6 | 4.8 | 5.3 | 206 | 125 | 176 | 200 | 13.4 | 8.5 | 9.2 | 10.0 |
| – Other private | 90 | 70 | 73 | .. | 0.3 | 0.2 | 0.2 | .. | 4 | 7 | 14 | .. | 0.3 | 0.5 | 0.7 | .. |
| (b) Other countries | 1 677 | 1 947 | 1 837 | .. | 5.6 | 6.0 | 5.5 | .. | 145 | 101 | 94 | .. | 9.4 | 6.9 | 4.9 | .. |
| (c) Multilateral | 1 184 | 1 234 | 1 175 | c/ | 4.0 | 3.8 | 3.5 | c/ | 131 | 145 | 177 | c/ | 8.5 | 9.9 | 9.3 | c/ |
| II. Short-term | 2 071 | 2 260 | 2 303 | .. | 7.0 | 6.9 | 6.8 | .. | 231 a/ | 217 a/ | 244 a/ | 200 a/ | 15.0 a/ | 14.8 a/ | 12.8 a/ | 10.0 a/ |
| (a) Export credits | 430 | 481 | 477 | .. | 1.4 | 1.5 | 1.4 | .. | | | | | | | | |
| (b) Banks | 1 639 | 1 778 | 1 826 | 2 000 | 5.5 | 5.4 | 5.4 | 5.3 | | | | | | | | |
| III. Total external debt | 29 793 | 32 678 | 33 670 | 38 000 | 100.0 | 100.0 | 100.0 | 100.0 | 1 536 | 1 468 | 1 907 | 2 000 | 100.0 | 100.0 | 100.0 | 100.0 |
| IV. Memo item: Use of IMF credit | 1 853 | 2 203 | 2 040 | 2 200 | | | | | | | | | | | | |

Source: Information supplied by the OECD secretariat and OECD, Financing and external debt of developing countries, 1985 Survey.

a/ Interest payments.

b/ Figures rounded to the nearest million.

c/ Total multilateral (concessional and non-concessional) debt and debt service in 1985 are estimated at $12 billion and $0.4 billion respectively,
corresponding to shares of 31.6 per cent and 20 per cent respectively.

Table 41

Evolution of public and publicly guaranteed debt and debt service of LDCs,
1978, 1980 to 1984

| | Outstanding debt disbursed (at year end) | | | | | | | | | | Debt service | | | | | | | | | |
| | $ billion | | | | | | % of total | | | Average annual growth(%) | $ million | | | | | | % of total | | | Average annual growth(%) |
| | 1978 | 1980 | 1981 | 1982 | 1983 | 1984 | 1978 | 1980 | 1984 | 1980-84 | 1978 | 1980 | 1981 | 1982 | 1983 | 1984 | 1978 | 1980 | 1984 | 1980-84 |
|---|---|---|---|---|---|---|---|---|---|---|---|---|---|---|---|---|---|---|---|---|
| A. Concessional: | 9.5 | 13.4 | 15.4 | 17.4 | 19.4 | 20.5 | 73 | 70 | 73 | 11.1 | 229 | 283 | 368 | 367 | 381 | 527 | 41 | 37 | 43 | 16.8 |
| (a) Multilateral agencies | 3.0 | 5.1 | 6.0 | 7.0 | 8.0 | 9.1 | 23 | 26 | 32 | 15.8 | 48 | 80 | 103 | 122 | 137 | 202 | 9 | 10 | 17 | 25.5 |
| (b) DAC countries | 3.1 | 3.2 | 3.3 | 3.7 | 3.8 | 3.7 | 24 | 17 | 13 | 3.9 | 66 | 62 | 67 | 73 | 76 | 84 | 12 | 8 | 7 | 8.0 |
| (c) Socialist countries of Eastern Europe | 0.9 | 1.5 | 2.0 | 2.2 | 2.6 | 2.8 | 7 | 8 | 10 | 15.8 | 73 | 72 | 129 | 98 | 62 | 96 | 13 | 9 | 8 | 7.6 |
| (d) China | 1.1 | 1.4 | 1.2 | 1.2 | 1.3 | 1.0 | 9 | 7 | 4 | - 7.6 | 1 | 4 | 6 | 4 | 4 | 6 | 0 | 1 | 0 | 7.1 |
| (e) OPEC countries | 1.0 | 2.0 | 2.6 | 2.9 | 3.3 | 3.5 | 8 | 10 | 12 | 15.2 | 28 | 45 | 42 | 51 | 69 | 98 | 5 | 6 | 8 | 21.6 |
| (f) Others | 0.3 | 0.3 | 0.3 | 0.4 | 0.4 | 0.4 | 2 | 2 | 2 | 5.5 | 13 | 20 | 22 | 20 | 34 | 41 | 2 | 3 | 3 | 19.0 |
| B. Non-concessional: | 3.5 | 5.7 | 6.8 | 7.5 | 7.9 | 7.7 | 27 | 30 | 27 | 7.7 | 327 | 480 | 627 | 575 | 580 | 695 | 59 | 62 | 57 | 9.6 |
| (a) Multilateral agencies | 0.5 | 0.7 | 0.9 | 1.0 | 1.0 | 1.2 | 4 | 4 | 4 | 11.7 | 43 | 86 | 98 | 123 | 139 | 176 | 8 | 11 | 14 | 19.0 |
| (b) Bilateral creditors: | 0.7 | 2.0 | 2.1 | 2.7 | 3.5 | 3.4 | 5 | 11 | 12 | 14.0 | 73 | 117 | 159 | 167 | 155 | 164 | 13 | 15 | 13 | 8.7 |
| DAC countries | 0.3 | 1.1 | 1.2 | 1.4 | 2.0 | 1.9 | 2 | 6 | 7 | 14.5 | 31 | 88 | 99 | 57 | 85 | 106 | 6 | 11 | 9 | 4.6 |
| OPEC countries | 0.3 | 0.4 | 0.5 | 0.8 | 1.0 | 0.9 | 2 | 2 | 3 | 18.4 | 17 | 6 | 0 | 60 | 2 | 4 | 3 | 1 | 0 | -9.2 |
| Others | 0.1 | 0.5 | 0.5 | 0.4 | 0.5 | 0.6 | 1 | 2 | 2 | 8.0 | 24 | 23 | 60 | 51 | 68 | 54 | 4 | 3 | 4 | 25.3 |
| (c) Private creditors, of which: | 2.3 | 2.9 | 3.8 | 3.8 | 3.4 | 3.1 | 18 | 15 | 11 | 1.4 | 211 | 277 | 370 | 284 | 285 | 355 | 38 | 36 | 29 | 6.4 |
| (i) Suppliers' credits | 1.2 | 1.1 | 1.1 | 1.0 | 1.0 | 0.7 | 9 | 6 | 3 | 10.5 | 121 | 138 | 160 | 98 | 85 | 88 | 22 | 18 | 7 | -10.7 |
| (ii) Financial markets | 1.1 | 1.8 | 2.7 | 2.7 | 2.5 | 2.4 | 9 | 10 | 8 | 6.8 | 88 | 138 | 210 | 186 | 197 | 264 | 16 | 18 | 22 | 17.6 |
| TOTAL | 13.0 | 19.1 | 22.2 | 24.9 | 27.3 | 28.2 | 100 | 100 | 100 | 10.1 | 556 | 772 | 998 | 944 | 962 | 1 222 | 100 | 100 | 100 | 16.5 |

Source: World Bank Debtor Reporting System (DRS). Under the DRS, 33 least developed countries report to the World Bank on their external debt to all creditors, incurred or guaranteed by their public sector. Afghanistan, Bhutan, Lao People's Democratic Republic and Sao Tome and Principe are not covered by the DRS. The data are thus not comparable with the data in table 40.

multilateral lending. The marginal increase in 1985 was principally due to lending by multilateral institutions. Multilateral lending in principle is not subject to debt relief operations.

315. Since reschedulings have only a temporary effect in curbing debt service payments, it is necessary to look at projected debt service payments to appraise the real dimension of the LDCs' debt obligations. Projections for the second half of the 1980s point to annual levels of service due that are at least twice the level of debt service actually paid by LDCs in 1984.

316. In line with the changes in the structure of debt is the steady increase in the share of concessional debt service payments, of which a discernible feature is the increase in the share of debt service paid to multilateral agencies and the decrease in the share of concessional debt service paid to DAC countries (see tables 40 and 41). However, notwithstanding that the main part of the LDCs' debt is concessional and that its share has been increasing, LDCs' debt service payments arising from non-concessional debts have continued to form the greater part of LDCs' total debt service payments.

317. Almost two-thirds of LDCs' non-concessional debt service payments arise from export credits to OECD countries. Debt to multilateral agencies both concessional and non-concessional, and concessional debt to OPEC countries also form an important (and increasing) share of LDCs' debt servicing burden (see tables 40 and 41). None of these debts come under the purview of Board resolution 165 (S-IX).

318. At the country level, the same general trends in debt and debt service are discernible. In most LDCs' the burden of debt considerably worsened between 1980 and 1984. Both the ratios of debt to GDP and of debt service to exports increased appreciably. On the other hand, in the majority of cases, the non-concessional share of total debt and debt service decreased, while the multilateral share expanded (see table 42).

319. Somewhat over half LDCs' debt service in 1984 was paid by the 10 major debtors (see para. 308). Projections show that their share will increase in the second half of the decade. The situation of the remaining 26 LDCs is still precarious. They have debt ratios at d'fficult levels 123/ and many of them have a relatively high share of non-concessional debt. Moreover, it must be recalled that repurchases and service charges to the IMF add to the debt service burden of many LDCs. LDCs' repurchases to the IMF exceeded $250 million in 1984 and 1985 (as compared to $133 in 1982 and $157 in 1983).

## C. Debt relief measures and mechanisms

### 1. Retroactive terms adjustment (RTA) measures

320. The initiative launched in 1978 with the adoption of Board resolution 165 (S-IX) has proved to be one of the most successful and beneficial for the LDCs. Since then 31 LDCs have benefited from debt relief measures provided by 15 DAC countries (see table 43). The nominal value of all these measures is estimated at $4.1 billion, of which $3.0 billion was in the form of debt cancellation (see tables 44 and 45). Some donors from the group of socialist countries of Eastern Europe appear also to have taken debt relief measures benefiting major LDC recipients.

## Table 42

### Debt indicators for individual LDCs, 1980 and 1984

| COUNTRY | Debt disbursed ($ million) | | Debt service ($ million) | | % share of non-concessional in: | | | | Debt/GDP (%) | | Debt service/ exports (%) | | % share of short-term in total external: | |
|---|---|---|---|---|---|---|---|---|---|---|---|---|---|---|
| | | | | | total debt | | total debt service | | | | | | debt | debt service |
| | 1980 | 1984 | 1980 | 1984 | 1980 | 1984 | 1980 | 1984 | 1980 | 1984 | 1980 | 1984 | 1984 | 1984 |
| Afghanistan | 1 195 | 1 350 | 180 | 41 | 8 | 8 | 16 | 78 | 34 | .. | 26 | 5 | 0.5 | 2 |
| Bangladesh | 3 614 | 5 264 | 109 | 200 | 7 | 11 | 54 | 36 | 32 | 45 | 15 | 21 | 1 | 4 |
| Benin | 484 | 582 | 24 | 39 | 63 | 54 | 92 | 87 | 43 | 62 | 38 | 118 | 33 | 35 |
| Bhutan | - | 3 | - | 0 | .. | 33 | .. | - | - | 2 | 0 | - | 40 | 0 |
| Botswana | 283 | 371 | 40 | 48 | 66 | 69 | 100 | 90 | 32 | 33 | 8 | 7 | 3 | 6 |
| Burkina Faso | 295 | 425 | 17 | 26 | 25 | 27 | 59 | 65 | 22 | 47 | 19 | 43 | 6 | 10 |
| Burundi | 151 | 346 | 7 | 18 | 11 | 16 | 86 | 39 | 16 | 36 | 11 | 18 | 3 | 5 |
| Cape Verde | 20 | 73 | 0 | 6 | 2 | 47 | 83 | 83 | 19 | 93 a/ | 0 | 120 | 0 | 0 |
| Central African Rep. | 164 | 131 | 12 | 24 | 45 | 53 | 50 | 33 | 21 | 22 | 17 | 21 | 32 | 4 |
| Chad | 156 | 121 | 12 | 6 | 31 | 28 | (67) | 0 | 16 | 21 | 10 | 32 | 2 | 0 |
| Comoros | 50 | 106 | 2 | 3 | 4 | 8 | (50) | 33 | 42 | 110 a/ | 3 | 14 | 3 | 0 |
| Democratic Yemen | 549 | 1 222 | 23 | 56 | 6 | 5 | 35 | 38 | 86 | 131 | 3 | 7 | 4 | 10 |
| Djibouti | 28 | 123 | 6 | 18 | 29 | 49 | 50 | 89 | 9 | 33 a/ | 32 | 69 | 16 | 10 |
| Equatorial Guinea | 57 | 103 | 2 | 1 | 37 | 62 | 86 | 100 | 138 | .. | 14 | 5 | 6 | 50 |
| Ethiopia | 704 | 1 529 | 35 | 124 | 14 | 23 | 51 | 73 | 17 | 32 a/ | 8 | 30 | 4 | 4 |
| Gambia | 118 | 181 | 2 | 8 | 25 | 30 | 47 | 25 | 50 | 88 | 6 | 17 | 18 | 27 |
| Guinea | 1 111 | 1 197 | 128 | 107 | 39 | 29 | 58 | 38 | 63 | 59 | 33 | 25 | 4 | 6 |
| Guinea-Bissau | 104 | 152 | 4 | 4 | 31 | 24 | 96 | 50 | 67 | 99 | 36 | 40 | 8 | 20 |
| Haiti | 269 | 593 | 22 | 24 | 17 | 33 | 91 | 67 | 18 | 33 | 10 | 13 | 12 | 29 |
| Lao P.D.R. | 75 | 415 | 2 | 5 | 7 | 1 | 50 | 60 | 13 | 55 | 6 | 12 | 6 | 33 |
| Lesotho | 76 | 139 | 6 | 15 | 34 | 19 | 83 | 80 | 18 | 37 a/ | 10 | 54 | 1 | 0 |
| Malawi | 746 | 761 | 70 | 84 | 48 | 37 | 87 | 85 | 65 | 63 | 25 | 27 | 5 | 7 |
| Maldives | 28 | 52 | 0 | 11 | 0 | 29 | 0 | 55 | 65 | 68 | 0 | 61 | 20 | 8 |
| Mali | 692 | 1 039 | 17 | 18 | 9 | 6 | 71 | 28 | 49 | 97 | 8 | 10 | 5 | 22 |
| Nepal | 185 | 442 | 13 | 11 | 3 | 3 | 69 | 9 | 10 | 18 | 16 | 9 | 5 | 38 |
| Niger | 608 | 805 | 87 | 112 | 65 | 56 | 76 | 89 | 24 | 57 | 15 | 32 | 9 | 7 |
| Rwanda | 161 | 253 | 3 | 8 | 3 | 3 | (67) | 38 | 14 | 16 | 4 | 06 | 13 | 27 |
| Samoa | 57 | 61 | 5 | 4 | 39 | 16 | 86 | 75 | 51 | 62 | 29 | 21 | 0 | 0 |
| Sao Tome and Principe | - | 29 | - | 1 | .. | 31 | .. | 100 | - | 80 | - | 10 | 6 | 0 |
| Sierra Leone | 389 | 463 | 43 | 23 | 46 | 44 | 95 | 70 | 35 | 46 | 21 | 16 | 24 | 43 |
| Somalia | 749 | 1 462 | 20 | 46 | 5 | 27 | 80 | 37 | 47 | 80 | 15 | 102 | 3 | 10 |
| Sudan | 3 953 | 5 484 | 100 | 155 | 53 | 52 | 47 | 81 | 46 | 71 | 18 | 21 | 8 | 27 |
| Togo | 916 | 781 | 78 | 95 | 70 | 55 | 94 | 85 | 81 | 117 | 23 | 50 | 8 | 8 |
| Uganda | 609 | 710 | 15 | 108 | 56 | 38 | 73 | 71 | 24 b/ | 22 b/ | 4 | 27 | 4 | 2 |
| United Rep. of Tanzania | 1 734 | 2 713 | 115 | 85 | 38 | 38 | 87 | 61 | 35 | 54 a/ | 23 | 23 | 5 | 18 |
| Vanuatu | 10 | 65 | 3 | 12 | 20 | 94 | 33 | 100 | 10 b/ | 79 c/ | 9 | 27 | 35 | 25 |
| Yemen | 984 | 1 825 | 47 | 117 | 12 | 11 | 68 | 60 | 38 | 49 | 204 | 254 | 13 | 18 |
| Total LDCs | 21 324 | 31 371 | 1 239 | 1 663 | 31 | 29 | 63 | 64 | 35 | 50 | 16 | 21 | 7 | 13 |

Source: UNCTAD secretariat calculations based on information from the OECD secretariat, the World Bank and other international and national sources.

a/ As a percentage of GDP in 1983.
b/ As a percentage of GNP.
c/ As a percentage of GNP in 1982.

Table 43

Action taken under Section A of resolution 165(S-IX) by DAC creditor countries in favour of LDCs

| DAC creditor country / LDCs debtor country | AUSTRALIA | AUSTRIA | BELGIUM | CANADA | DENMARK | FINLAND | FRANCE | GERMANY, Fed. Rep. of | ITALY | JAPAN | NETHERLANDS | NEW ZEALAND | NORWAY a/ | SWEDEN | SWITZERLAND | UNITED KINGDOM | USA b/ |
|---|---|---|---|---|---|---|---|---|---|---|---|---|---|---|---|---|---|
| Afghanistan ............. | | | | X | | | | | | X | | | | | | X | |
| Bangladesh ............. | | | X | X | X | X | X | X | | X | X | | | X | X | X | X |
| Benin ................... | | | | X | X | | X | X | X | | | | | | | | |
| Bhutan .................. | | | | | | | | | | | | | | | | | |
| Botswana ................ | | | | X | X | | | X | | | | | | X | | X | |
| Burkina Faso ............ | | | | X | X | | X | X | | | X | | | | | | |
| Burundi ................. | | | | | | | X | X | | | | | | | | | |
| Cape Verde .............. | | | | | | | | | | | | | | | | | |
| Central African Republic . | | | | | | | X | X | | | | | | | | | |
| Chad .................... | | | | X | | | X | X | | | | | | | | | |
| Comoros ................. | | | | | | | X | | | | | | | | | | |
| Democratic Yemen ........ | | | | X | | | | | | | | | | | | | |
| Djibouti ................ | | | | | | | X | X | | | | | | | | | |
| Equatorial Guinea ....... | | | | | | | | | | | | | | | | | |
| Ethiopia ................ | | | | | X | | | | X | X | | | | X | | | |
| Gambia .................. | | | | | | | | X | | | | | | | | X | |
| Guinea .................. | | | | | | | X | X | X | | X | | | | | | X |
| Guinea-Bissau ........... | | | | | | | | | | | X | | | | | | |
| Haiti ................... | | | | | | | | X | | | | | | | | | X |
| Lao People's Dem. Republic | | | | X | | | | | | X | | | | | | | |
| Lesotho ................. | | | | | | | | X | | | | | | | | X | |
| Malawi .................. | | | | X | X | | | X | | X | X | | | | | X | X |
| Maldives ................ | | | | | | | | | | | | | | | | | |
| Mali .................... | | | | X | | | X | X | | | | | | | | | |
| Nepal ................... | | | | X | X | | | X | | | X | | | | X | X | |
| Niger ................... | | | | X | X | | X | X | | | | | | | | | |
| Rwanda .................. | | | | | | | | X | | X | | | | | | | |
| Samoa ................... | X | | | | | | | | | | | | | | X | X | |
| Sao Tome & Principe ...... | | | | | | | | | | | | | | | | | |
| Sierra Leone ............ | | | | | | | | X | | | X | | | | | X | X |
| Somalia ................. | | | | | | | | X | X | | | | | | | | X |
| Sudan .................. | | | | X | | | | X | X | X | X | | | X | | X | X |
| Togo ................... | | | | X | | | X | X | | | | | | | | | |
| Uganda ................. | | | | X | X | | | X | | X | X | X | | | | X | |
| United Rep. of Tanzania .. | | | X | X | X | X | | X | X | X | X | | | X | | X | X |
| Yemen .................. | | | | | | | | X | | X | X | | | | | | X |

Source : Information as of September 1986, based on replies to UNCTAD's Questionnaire and TD/B/866 and Corr.1 and TD/B/915 and Add.1 and 2.

a/ ODA to LDCs is being provided on a grant basis.  b/ See footnote 124.

NOTE : A cross (X) indicates that action has been taken, by the DAC creditor indicated, in favour of the corresponding least developed country. (C) refers to action under consideration.

Table 44

SUMMARY TABLE OF DEBT CANCELLATIONS

(Millions of US dollars)

| | Australia | Canada | Denmark | Finland | France | Germany Fed.Rep.of | Italy | Japan | Luxem-bourg | Nether-lands | Sweden | Switzer-land | U.K. | TOTAL |
|---|---|---|---|---|---|---|---|---|---|---|---|---|---|---|
| Afghanistan | | 1.2 | | | | | | X | | | | | 2.1 | 3.3 |
| Bangladesh | | 16.8 | 39.1 | 6.7 | 14.4 | 472.5 | | X | | 43.1 | 10.0 | 7.7 | 33.3 | 643.6 |
| Benin | | 14.1 | 6.2 | | 4.0 | 20.4 | 0.8 | | | | | | | 45.5 |
| Bhutan | | ⟨D⟩ | | | | | | | | | | | | - |
| Botswana | | 34.0 | 2.7 | | | 33.7 | | | | | 6.1 | | 42.9 | 119.4 |
| Burkina Faso | | 0.9 | 3.5 | | 17.8 | 92.7 | | | | 7.5 | | | | 122.4 |
| Burundi | | | | | 0.3 | 30.1 | | | | | | | | 30.4 |
| Cape Verde | | | | | | | | | | | | | | - |
| Central African Rep. | | | | | 1.6 | 13.3 | | | | | | | | 14.9 |
| Chad | | | 1.8 | | 15.2 | 6.1 | | | | | | | | 23.1 |
| Comoros | | | | | 5.0 | | | | | | | | | 5.0 |
| Democratic Yemen | | | 2.7 | | | | | | | | | | | 2.7 |
| Djibouti | | | | | 11.1 | 3.4 | | | | | | | | 14.5 |
| Equatorial Guinea | | | | | | | | | | | | | | - |
| Ethiopia | | | | 1.8 | | | 9.8 | X | | | 10.9 | | | 22.5 |
| Gambia | | | | | | 10.9 | | | | | | | 11.0 | 21.9 |
| Guinea | | | | | 2.8 | 23.6 | 6.4 | | | 1.0 | | | | 33.8 |
| Guinea-Bissau | | | | | | | | | | 9.8 | | | | 9.8 |
| Haiti | | | | | | 8.4 | | | | | | | | 8.4 |
| Lao P.D.R. | | 2.4 | | | | | | X | | | | | | 2.4 |
| Lesotho | | | | | | 12.0 | | | | | | | 0.6 | 12.6 |
| Malawi | | 36.8 | 15.8 | | | 49.1 | | X | | 7.2 | | | 64.3 | 173.2 |
| Maldives | | | | | | | | | | | | | | - |
| Mali | | 1.9 | | | 13.2 | 93.8 | 1.5 | | | | | | | 110.4 |
| Nepal | | 2.4 | 2.8 | | | 43.1 | | X | | | | 5.8 | 4.6 | 58.7 |
| Niger | | 37.7 | 7.6 | | 6.2 | 98.0 | | | | | | | | 149.5 |
| Rwanda | | | | | | 56.2 | | X | 0.3 | | | | | 56.5 |
| Samoa | X | | | | | | | | | | | | 0.4 | 0.4 |
| Sao Tome and Principe | | | | | | | | | | | | | | - |
| Sierra Leone | | | | | | 47.5 | | | | 5.5 | | | 18.2 | 71.2 |
| Somalia | | | | | | 56.8 | 28.7 | | | | | | | 85.5 |
| Sudan | | | 7.6 | | | 237.0 | 7.4 | X | | 16.9 | 10.2 | | 20.4 | 299.5 |
| Togo | | | 9.3 | | 3.7 | 101.0 | | | | | | | | 114.0 |
| Uganda | | 2.2 | 7.3 | | | 26.6 | | X | | 3.6 | | | 25.2 | 64.9 |
| U.R. of Tanzania | | 37.7 | 114.6 | 26.5 | | 188.5 | 12.2 | X | | 53.3 | 50.7 | | 5.3 | 488.8 |
| Yemen | | | | | | 107.0 | | X | | 17.2 | | | | 124.2 |
| Total | .. | 188.1 | 221.0 | 35.0 | 95.3 | 1831.7 | 66.8 a/ | 56.3 a/ | 0.3 | 165.1 | 87.9 | 13.5 | 228.3 | 2989.3 |

Source: Information supplied by creditor countries to the UNCTAD secretariat.

a/ Including interest payments.

Note: "X" indicates debt cancellations undertaken by the creditor country in favour of the individual debtor country but amounts are not allocable by debtor country.

Table 45

Nominal value of other measures taken with respect to ODA debt
(Millions of US dollars)

| | Belgium A | Belgium B | Canada A | France B | Germany, Fed.Rep.of A | Netherlands A | Sweden A | U.K. A | USA C | Total |
|---|---|---|---|---|---|---|---|---|---|---|
| Afghanistan | 1.9 | 0.05 | x | | | | | | | x |
| Bangladesh | | | x | 4.6 | x | 13.7 | 2.0 | | 317.3 | 339.6 |
| Benin | | | x | 2.0 | x | | | | | 2.0 |
| Bhutan | | | | | | | | | | – |
| Botswana | | | x | | x | | 1.2 | 1.1 | | 2.3 |
| Burkina Faso | | | x | 8.3 | x | 2.2 | | | | 10.5 |
| Burundi | | | | 0.2 | x | | | | | 0.2 |
| Cape Verde | | | | | | | | | | – |
| Central African Rep. | | | | 1.9 | 2.7 | | | | | 4.6 |
| Chad | | | | 8.4 | 0.9 | | | | | 9.3 |
| Comoros | | | | 3.0 | | | | | | 3.0 |
| Democratic Yemen | | | | | | | | | | – |
| Djibouti | | | | 3.1 | 0.3 | | | | | 3.4 |
| Equatorial Guinea | | | | | | | | | | – |
| Ethiopia | | | | | | | 2.0 | | | 2.0 |
| Gambia | | | | | x | | | | | x |
| Guinea | | | | 0.8 | x | 0.2 | | | 27.0 | 28.0 |
| Guinea-Bissau | | | | | | 0.7 | | | | 0.7 |
| Haiti | | | | | 1.6 | | | | 53.0 | 54.6 |
| Lao P.D.R. | | | x | | x | | | | | x |
| Lesotho | | | | | | | | 0.2 | | 0.2 |
| Malawi | | | x | | x | 1.4 | | 1.5 | 2.4 | 5.3 |
| Maldives | | | | | | | | | | – |
| Mali | | | x | 5.6 | x | | | | | 5.6 |
| Nepal | | | x | | x | | | | | x |
| Niger | | | x | 3.2 | x | | | | | 3.2 |
| Rwanda | | | | | x | | | | | x |
| Samoa | | | | | | | | | | – |
| Sao Tome and Principe | | | | | | | | | | – |
| Sierra Leone | | | | | 9.2 | | | 4.0 | 10.1 | 23.3 |
| Somalia | | | | | x | 5.9 | 1.8 | 0.8 | 78.2 | 78.2 |
| Sudan | | | | | 21.1 | | | | 175.0 | 183.5 |
| Togo | | | | 0.9 | 5.0 | | | | | 22.0 |
| Uganda | 0.2 | | x | | | 0.6 | | 3.7 | | 9.3 |
| U.R. of Tanzania | | | x | | x | 12.3 | 9.5 | 1.9 | 25.0 | 49.9 |
| Yemen | | | | | x | 0.6 | | | 3.0 | 3.6 |
| Total | 2.1 | 0.05 | 30.0 | 42.0 | 311.1 | 37.6 | 16.5 | 13.2 | 691.0 | 1143.6 |

Source: Information supplied by creditor countries to the UNCTAD secretariat.

A = Waiving of interest payments.
B = Refinancing of debt interest.
C = Agreement to allow payment of debt in local currency.

Note: "x" indicates action taken by the creditor country in favour of the individual debtor country but amounts are not allocable by debtor country. The totals for LDCs include unallocated amounts.

Table 46

LDCs bilateral concessional debt disbursed and concessional debt service
by main creditor country a/ and group of countries

| | ODA debt (outstanding at year end) (billions of dollars) | | | | | | ODA debt service payments (millions of dollars) | | | | | |
|---|---|---|---|---|---|---|---|---|---|---|---|---|
| | 1978 | 1980 | 1981 | 1982 | 1983 | 1984 | 1978 | 1980 | 1981 | 1982 | 1983 | 1984 |
| DAC countries | 3.14 | 3.18 | 3.26 | 3.65 | 3.82 | 3.71 | 65.9 | 62.0 | 66.8 | 72.7 | 75.8 | 84.4 |
| of which: | | | | | | | | | | | | |
| United States | 1.07 | 1.38 | 1.47 | 1.66 | 1.77 | 1.79 | 22.0 | 26.9 | 32.6 | 38.9 | 32.2 | 41.4 |
| Japan | 0.47 | 0.92 | 0.98 | 1.18 | 1.26 | 1.25 | 6.7 | 12.9 | 17.9 | 18.4 | 21.6 | 26.4 |
| France | 0.18 | 0.20 | 0.24 | 0.25 | 0.26 | 0.30 | 11.4 | 11.7 | 8.2 | 9.9 | 14.4 | 11.0 |
| Germany, Fed. Rep. of | 1.04 | 0.35 | 0.24 | 0.24 | 0.22 | 0.10 | 16.6 | 7.9 | 4.4 | 3.5 | 3.9 | 2.9 |
| Denmark | 0.17 | 0.15 | 0.15 | 0.15 | 0.14 | 0.13 | 1.4 | 0.0 | 0.0 | 0.0 | 0.0 | 0.2 |
| Socialist countries of Eastern Europe | 0.94 | 1.54 | 1.97 | 2.17 | 2.60 | 2.77 | 73.2 | 71.9 | 129.2 | 97.6 | 61.6 | 96.3 |
| of which: | | | | | | | | | | | | |
| USSR | 0.77 | 1.32 | 1.73 | 1.91 | 2.31 | 2.50 | 64.6 | 58.0 | 109.9 | 72.1 | 40.0 | 62.8 |
| German Dem. Rep. | 0.04 | 0.05 | 0.06 | 0.08 | 0.11 | 0.10 | 0.7 | 0.8 | 3.3 | 5.0 | 6.8 | 15.6 |
| Other developed countries | 0.17 | 0.20 | 0.19 | 0.19 | 0.20 | 0.19 | 5.2 | 9.7 | 12.1 | 6.2 | 8.3 | 11.3 |
| OPEC countries | 1.00 | 1.97 | 2.62 | 2.94 | 3.28 | 3.48 | 28.3 | 44.8 | 42.4 | 50.9 | 69.3 | 97.9 |
| of which: | | | | | | | | | | | | |
| Saudi Arabia | 0.32 | 0.91 | 1.16 | 1.31 | 1.51 | 1.64 | 16.1 | 23.2 | 16.7 | 13.0 | 19.8 | 31.7 |
| Kuwait | 0.23 | 0.38 | 0.46 | 0.53 | 0.60 | 0.64 | 7.8 | 7.3 | 9.0 | 15.4 | 18.7 | 21.0 |
| Iraq | 0.18 | 0.30 | 0.38 | 0.44 | 0.42 | 0.40 | 1.8 | 7.5 | 7.9 | 14.3 | 13.3 | 26.3 |
| United Arab Emirates | 0.17 | 0.23 | 0.31 | 0.35 | 0.38 | 0.41 | 1.5 | 4.6 | 6.0 | 5.9 | 12.8 | 10.6 |
| Libyan Arab Jamahiriya | 0.06 | 0.08 | 0.24 | 0.24 | 0.30 | 0.31 | 0.3 | 0.5 | 2.0 | 1.8 | 3.1 | 3.7 |
| Other developing countries | 0.12 | 0.12 | 0.10 | 0.18 | 0.15 | 0.12 | 8.0 | 10.8 | 9.5 | 14.2 | 25.6 | 29.8 |
| Total bilateral concessional b/ | 6.50 | 8.39 | 9.40 | 10.36 | 11.32 | 11.37 | 181.2 | 203.5 | 265.6 | 245.2 | 244.2 | 325.4 |

Source: World Bank Debtor Reporting System (DRS). Under the DRS, 33 least developed countries report to the World Bank on their external debt to all creditors, incurred or guaranteed by their public sector. Afghanistan, Bhutan, Lao People's Democratic Republic and Sao Tome and Principe are not covered by the DRS.

a/ Country with an ODA debt to LDCs exceeding $100 million in 1984.

b/ Including unknown lenders.

321. Developments continue to take place. At the mid-term global review of the implementation of the SNPA (in October 1985), the Netherlands announced the decision by its Government to cancel all remaining ODA debts of LDCs, amounting to 30 million guilders (about $10 million). At the United Nations special session on Africa, held in May 1986, Canada announced the decision to apply a moratorium on repayment of outstanding ODA loans for African countries (of which 26 are least developed) for an initial period of five years, which Canada is prepared to extend for further periods of five years until the year 2000. Denmark, also in connection with this special session, has cancelled all outstanding debt of the United Republic of Tanzania, and, in response to a request from Bangladesh, all outstanding ODA debt from that country to Denmark has also been cancelled in 1986.

322. The scope for further debt relief under Board resolution 165 (S-IX) now concerns only a limited number of developed creditor countries. On the basis of 1984 estimates at year end, the United States and Japan account for 82 per cent of LDCs' debt to DAC countries. 124/ In the case of the LDCs' debt to the socialist countries of Eastern Europe, 90 per cent is owed to the USSR. In view of the relatively small magnitudes involved (in particular in terms of donors' GNP), the potential should exist for obtaining further debt relief from these major creditors as well as from other creditors concerned.

323. The granting of retroactive terms adjustment measures by all bilateral donors would benefit all LDCs as they have all accumulated bilateral ODA debts. The majority of LDCs are indeed mainly ODA-reliant and, although the share of multilateral concessional debt has been expanding, the major part of their concessional debt is still bilateral.

324. It is estimated that the cancellation of ODA debt service payments currently due to DAC countries would yield a debt relief to LDCs of some $190 million per year during the remaining decade. In the case of a cancellation of the debt service payments due to the socialist countries of Eastern Europe and other developed donors, the annual debt relief to LDCs would be some $375 million.

325. If similar measures were undertaken by the other donors which are not covered at present under Board resolution 165 (S-IX), this would give LDCs an additional annual amount of debt relief of the order of $390 million.

2. Coping with multilateral debt

326. In its conclusions and recommendations at the mid-term global review of the SNPA, the Intergovernmental Group on the Least Developed Countries noted "that the repayment of debt to multilateral assistance institutions is one of the elements in the overall debt service burden of LDCs" and invited "those institutions to take this into account in their lending programmes for LDCs". 125/

327. Multilateral debt, which accounts for over one quarter of LDCs' total debt, is generally considered as non-negotiable because of the statutes and revolving character of multilateral financing agencies. In order to ease the considerable burden of the corresponding debt service on LDCs, at least temporarily, suitable arrangements such as refinancing schemes and interest-subsidy schemes could be set up, which would allow past loans to be converted to IDA terms. A first step would be the provision of new loans to

LDCs at IDA terms.  Concessional resources could be mobilized through the creation of special facilities to which LDCs have preferential access.

328. The IMF's newly created Structural Adjustment Facility (SAF) for poor countries constitutes an example of such facilities.  The LDCs will stand to benefit from renewed trust fund lending by the IMF, whereby SDR 2.7 billion ($3.1 billion) will be made available to low-income (i.e., IDA-eligible) countries with protracted balance-of-payments problems, which agree to undertake medium-term (three-year) structural adjustment programmes.  The framework of such programmes is to be developed jointly by the IMF and the World Bank.  The Fund's resources will be derived from the repayment of loans made from the sales of IMF gold in the mid-1970s.  The IMF will provide the money in 10-year loans at 0.5 per cent interest, with a five-year grace period, semi-annual payments to be made over the next five years.  Borrowing rights are based on IMF quotas.  At present, of the 58 eligible countries (excluding China and India which have indicated that they do not intend to use SAF resources), 36 are least developed (Botswana is not eligible).

329. Another new facility is the Special Facility for Sub-Saharan Africa of the World Bank which became effective on 1 July 1985 and which provides concessional assistance over a three-year period to support the policy reform efforts in eligible countries.  Up to now eight operations totalling $240.9 million have been approved for LDCs (Togo, Rwanda, Malawi, Somalia, Equatorial Guinea, Guinea-Bissau, Guinea and Niger).

330. The prospect of greater lending by the IDA, if agreement is reached on a $12 billion replenishment over the three years beginning in July 1987, should also help to improve the debt profile of the LDCs.  At present IDA credits are granted for 50 years including 10 years grace before repayment of principal. There is no interest charge, only a service charge of 0.5 per cent on undisbursed balances and of 0.75 per cent on disbursed balances.

331. The tightening of conditionality in multilateral lending by the World Bank and IMF may, however, limit LDCs' access to available resources. Moreover, some other major multilateral creditors of LDCs provide credit at less concessional terms than those mentioned above.  According to 1984 estimates, debt to IDA constitutes over 60 per cent of LDCs' multilateral concessional debt but debt service payments to IDA are less than 30 per cent of total concessional debt service paid to multilateral agencies (which exceeded $200 million in 1984).  Moreover the amount of debt service paid to multilateral agencies providing non-concessional loans to LDCs is of the same order of magnitude as that paid by LDCs in respect of their concessional multilateral loans (although multilateral concessional debt is almost eight times larger than multilateral non-concessional debt).  The need for additional measures (including softening of conditionality) to cope with LDCs' multilateral debt is thus both great and urgent.

### 3.  Multilateral reschedulings

332. In the past decade, nine African LDCs, namely the Central African Republic, Equatorial Guinea, Malawi, Niger, Sierra Leone, Somalia, Sudan, Togo and Uganda, have rescheduled their outstanding obligations, amounting altogether to $2.3 billion, through the Paris Club.  Five of them have also renegotiated their commercial debt (altogether $1.1 billion) at the London Club (see table 47).  All of these LDCs face relatively large

Table 47

LDCs multilateral debt renegotiations, 1977-1985

($ million)

| | 1977-1981 | 1982 | 1983 | 1984 | 1985 | 1977-1985 |
|---|---|---|---|---|---|---|
| **Paris Club a/** | | | | | | |
| Central African Republic | 55 (50) | – | 13[E] (19) | – | 14[E] (7) | 82 (76) |
| Equatorial Guinea | – | – | 30[E] (20) | – | 29[E] (26) | 29 (26) |
| Malawi | – | 24 (25) | 33 (30) | 39[E] (30) | 32[E] (20) | 54 (45) |
| Niger | – | – | – | – | – | 104 (80) |
| Sierra Leone | 68 (49) | – | – | 88 (12) | – | 156 (61) |
| Somalia | – | – | – | – | 142[E] (85) | 142 (85) |
| Sudan | 373 (475) | 174 (105) | 502 (540) | 179[E] (280) | – | 1 228 (1 400) |
| Togo | 262 (452) | – | 114 (150) | 51[E] (120) | 22[E] (31) | 449 (753) |
| Uganda | 56[E] (50) | 22[E] (20) | – | – | – | 78 (70) |
| Total above | 814 (1 076) | 220 (150) | 629 (759) | 357 (442) | 239 (169) | 2 322 (2 596) |
| **Commercial banks** | | | | | | |
| Malawi | – | – | 59 | – | – | 59 |
| Niger | – | – | – | 28 | – | 28 |
| Sierra Leone | – | – | – | – | 25[E] b/ | 25 |
| Sudan | 638 | – | – | – | 230[E] | 868 |
| Togo | 68 | – | 74 | – | – | 142 |
| Total above | 706 | – | 133 | 28 | 255 | 1 122 |

Source: World Bank, World Debt Tables, 1985 (1986 edition) and OECD, Financing and external debt of developing countries, 1985 survey.

Note: Figures indicate renegotiated amounts as reported by the countries or, when footnoted with "E", as estimated by the World Bank. Figures in parenthesis are estimates by OECD.

a/ No agreement for LDCs took place prior to 1977.

b/ Agreed in principle, but not completed in 1985.

non-concessional debt obligations. Most of them have an overall external debt exceeding 50 per cent of their GDP. All, except Somalia, have a share of non-concessional debt in total debt above the LDCs' average and five have a non-concessional debt which is larger than their concessional debt (see table 42).

333. Although these reschedulings have provided some relief and lowered the debt service ratio, 126/ they are only stop-gap measures which have relatively little effect in ameliorating the debt situation in the long run. For LDCs with debt problems of a structural nature, which in many cases are engaged in adjustment programmes, 127/ the long-term solution lies rather in a substantial increase in concessional aid flows. Only greater flows will enable these countries to raise savings for investment in order to generate the growth needed to service their debt obligations. However, so far multilateral reschedulings have precluded discussions concerning additional flows. Another shortcoming of multilateral reschedulings is that negotiations do not include multilateral creditors to which LDCs have such a high (and rising) level of obligations. Moreover, for some LDCs the principal bilateral creditors are OPEC members or socialist countries of Eastern Europe, which are not represented at the Paris Club.

334. It can be seen from table 46 that most of the countries repeated their debt reschedulings. A way of avoiding these repeated multilateral reschedulings is to introduce more flexibility, by granting LDCs reschedulings at concessional rates that provide for longer consolidation periods than those accorded in the past. Moreover, discussions concerning additional aid should be held concomitantly.

335. Since country review meetings should bring together all donors and result in facilitating an increased flow of external assistance to the LDCs, 128/ they could provide an adequate forum for discussing debt. A recommendation along these lines was made at the mid-term global review. 129/

## 4. Debt management

336. Debt management has become a major preoccupation for the LDCs and a central element in their efforts to contain their mounting debts. A few LDCs have already taken steps to establish debt management units to monitor external debt obligations or committees to review proposed new loans.

337. The LDCs, however, are countries where technical and managerial personnel are scarce and institutional infrastructure deficient. Hence the attention drawn at country review meetings to the need to strengthen their debt management capabilities in order to ensure better information on debt outstanding and enable the implications of additional borrowing to be analysed. In the conclusions and recommendations of the mid-term global review an invitation is addressed to donors and relevant international organizations to assist the LDCs in such strengthening. 130/ Technical assistance to implement effective debt management systems is to be viewed as an essential component of external support.

5.  Other measures

338. Many solutions to deal with debt difficulties have been proposed, ranging from schemes for new agencies to mechanisms such as interest capping and insurance. 131/ Most of them relate to commercial debt and therefore concern LDCs only to a relatively minor extent.

339. Examples of solutions 132/ to reduce LDCs' debt burden include:

-   calling for a multi-year (e.g. five-year) moratorium on all their public and private debt service;

-   limiting debt servicing to a fixed percentage, e.g., 10 per cent of export earnings, compatible with the country's economic and social development needs. (In 1984 debt service payments accounted for 20 per cent of exports of LDCs on the average.) Payments due in excess may be added to outstanding principal with an extended payment scheduled or financed by an interest compensatory facility, paid in local currency.

340. To increase concessionality of debt, existing financial institutions would buy LDCs' debts from commercial banks and stretch out LDCs' loans to long maturities with low interest rates. 133/

341. Finally, the encouragement of direct investment, which unlike bank lending, does not generate pre-determined servicing costs - its costs are linked to profitability, being paid in the form of profit remittances and royalty payments - is one solution to help LDCs meet their capital requirements without having to borrow at commercial rates. However, so far, despite the incentives provided, including insurance schemes to cover political risks, the number of LDCs able to attract foreign direct investment has been minimal. Although certain sectors like mining and manufacturing can offer good investment returns, LDCs with their limited market potential, poor infrastructure and scarce skills have little attraction for private investors.

### D.  New approaches to the debt crisis

342. Debt has been very much at the heart of the discussions in various multilateral fora and in particular in the last meetings of the IMF Interim Committee and the Development Committee of the World Bank. Attention has focused on the problems of the most heavily indebted countries, none of which are least developed, but the problems of the poorest debtors have also been recognized.

343. These discussions have led to the view that a lasting solution to debt problems requires adjustment and growth in indebted countries. All parties concerned (debtors, industrial countries, commercial banks and financial and development institutions) are to pool their efforts so that medium-term growth-oriented macro-economic and structural adjustment programming can be

designed and implemented as soon as possible (with enhanced participation in the design and monitoring of programmes by the World Bank and IMF). On the part of debtor countries a commitment to policy reforms has to be made. On the part of industrial countries, policies that will promote a further decline in real interest rates, expansion in international trade, improvements in commodity prices, greater stability in exchange markets and increased external capital flows are called for. For low-income countries (comprising the LDCs) the need for provision of concessional assistance in support of adjustment programmes is recognized. 134/

344. At the origin of this approach is the debt strategy initiative of the United States Treasury Secretary, presented at the IMF and World Bank meeting at Seoul in October 1985, which was aimed at major debtor countries and has received wide support. 135/ The emphasis placed on changing domestic policies and on conditionality, however, rather than on external variables (over which control and agreement is much more difficult to reach) has been widely criticized. The vulnerability of poor countries, including the LDCs, to external developments has been stressed. Greatly increased concessional flows, softer conditionality, and greater flexibility in reschedulings have been called for.

## E.  Conclusions

345. Despite the deceleration in the growth of LDCs' indebtedness, and an increase in the share of concessional debt in their total debt, LDCs' debt obligations for the years ahead are expected to reach - at least up to the end of the decade - much higher levels than in the first half of the 1980s, thus endangering prospects for resumed economic growth in these countries. Even with careful economic management, progress is expected to be slow because of the structural weaknesses of their economies. Export prospects are bleak and debt relief measures will thus continue to be needed for several years more.

346. A key strategy to cope with LDCs' debt is the gradual softening of average debt terms while the long-term solution requires sustained economic growth and lies in a substantial increase in concessional aid flows to these countries. As recognized in the SNPA, only with a substantial increase in aid flows will the LDCs be able to pursue and carry through growth-oriented policies and programmes.

347. Concessional flows to LDCs stagnated, however, during the years 1980 to 1984 (complete information for 1985 is not yet available). 136/ Major efforts are thus needed in bilateral assistance through additional flows and liberal debt relief. In order not to hamper prospects of increased availability of resources from major multilateral financial institutions, softer conditionality must be granted to LDCs.

348. An improvement in the world trading environment with better commodity prices and greater access to markets is also a necessary precondition to an expansion in the demand for LDCs exports so as to raise their foreign exchange availabilities and their debt servicing capacity. Although recent international developments such as falling interest rates should to a limited extent help to ease LDCs' debt situation, there are no signs of improvement in the world trading environment for the LDCs. In 1985, world trade remained sluggish and commodity prices fell considerably.

349. In the immediate future, conventional measures will continue to have to be taken, including in particular ODA bilateral debt forgiveness, and flexible renegotiation of other official and officially guaranteed debt at concessional terms.  Innovative measures will have to be devised to cope with multilateral debt servicing.

350. Unless the international community continues to address these problems, many LDCs will find themselves sooner or later unable to service their debt fully.

Chapter V

COMMERCIAL POLICY MEASURES

A. Overall development

351. The level of exports of the LDCs continues to be extremely low in absolute terms. These exports consist mainly of primary commodities and are concentrated on only a few products. This situation reflects not only the low level of economic development of these countries, but also the difficulties encountered by them in exporting their products. The SNPA contains a special section aimed at facilitating the LDCs' exports by promoting and supporting appropriate commercial policy measures at the international level. However, despite a period of sustained growth in the developed market economies, progress in the liberalization of world trade in favour of the LDCs' exports is limited. In fact, current protectionist tendencies, including tariff as well as non-tariff measures, are widely contemplated and pose a threat of further restrictions on exports from LDCs.

B. Improved access to markets

1. Recommendations in favour of LDCs

352. In view of the general situation outlined above, the SNPA 137/ has made specific recommendations for improved access to markets for LDC exports. These recommendations include the simplification and improvement of preferential schemes of various kinds in order to provide the fullest possible duty-free treatment. Extending the list of products, examination of the rules of origin issue and the extension of country coverage must all be given due consideration. Schemes of generalized preference should give special consideration to the problem of LDCs. Action in the appropriate forums is recommended with a view to reducing any tariff and non-tariff protection, which may hinder the least developed countries' exports of major processed goods.

2. Tariff measures

353. The generalized system of preferences (GSP) was a major policy initiative of the 1960s and proved to be a viable instrument for trade co-operation between developed and developing countries in the 1970s and 1980s. The system is a highly complex preferential arrangement. In general, manufactured and semi-manufactured products are covered by the GSP, some of which receive unlimited duty-free treatment, while others only up to the level of quotas and/or other limitations. The very few agricultural products eligible for GSP treatment are subject to various tariff cuts. Since the GSP covers mostly manufactured and semi-manufactured products and only selected agricultural products, beneficiaries with a wider industrial base and more diversified industrial exports stand to benefit more than those relying on exports of agricultural products and raw materials.

354. The trade performance of the LDCs under the GSP remained basically the same as that described in the 1985 report. As shown in table 48, only a small fraction of total imports from LDCs into EEC and six other OECD preference-giving countries for which recent data are available were MFN dutiable and would therefore fall within the purview of the GSP.

355. There is a wide variation in the rate of utilization of the GSP among the LDCs as well as in the schemes used. As shown in table 48, the utilization rate, defined as the ratio between the value of GSP-covered imports which actually received preferential treatment and the value of MFN dutiable imports, for the national GSP schemes cited ranged from 15 per cent for the scheme of Austria, 31 per cent for the United States, 66 per cent for Switzerland, 71 per cent for Japan, 77 per cent for Canada, 79 per cent for the EEC and 100 per cent for New Zealand.

356. These figures reflect the small size of LDCs' exports as well as a concentration of these exports on dutiable agricultural products. Only an insignificant share of total exports from LDCs receive preferential treatment under the GSP, mostly because of narrow product coverage of agricultural products under the schemes and other regulations (health and safety), or because officials in the LDCs do not have the necessary skills and experience in dealing with the complexities of various schemes and the rules of origin.

357. The information received from preference-giving socialist countries of Eastern Europe 138/ indicates that they extended and improved their autonomous systems of general preferences in favour of the LDCs. These schemes do not contain any restrictive rules such as built-in safeguard mechanisms, quotas or ceilings. Moreover, there are no exclusions from GSP treatment of particular categories of products. Unified rules of origin apply a single value-added criterion.

(a) Recent initiatives

358. As mentioned above, the SNPA calls for simplification and improvement of preferential schemes with a view to providing the fullest possible duty-free treatment to the exports of the LDCs. Recent initiatives in this area are outlined in the following paragraphs.

359. The Norwegian scheme has been improved and extended several times, the latest on 15 March 1985 when 34 groups of agricultural products and 13 groups of industrial products were added to the scheme, which grants special treatment to LDCs, regardless of the exceptions that applied to other beneficiaries.

360. The Finnish Government enacted legislation, with effect from 1 May 1985, to add Djibouti, Equatorial Guinea, Sao Tome and Principe, Sierra Leone and Togo to the list of LDCs enjoying special concessions. It added one product 139/ to its scheme for the benefit of the LDCs.

361. Japan increased by 100 per cent the ceiling on the value of imports for which certificates of origin or, in the case of lower priced goods, certificates of direct consignment are not required. LDCs have been exempted from the ceiling limitation on woven fabrics of jute or other textile bast fibres. 140/

(b) Current situation of some least-developed preference-receiving countries

362. In May 1986, during the fourteenth session of the UNCTAD Special Committee on Preferences, the representatives of LDCs stated that the measures

introduced since the thirteenth session had not lived up to their expectations. The small improvements in the schemes with respect to both product coverage and tariff treatment fell far short of the sense of urgency conveyed in the agreed conclusions, adopted by the Special Committee at its thirteenth session, in particular, the need to give special attention to products of interest to LDCs in the field of agriculture, textiles and footwear, not covered by the schemes in order to enhance the opportunities offered by the schemes.

363. The trade performance of the least developed countries under the GSP remained basically the same as that described in the 1985 report. Table 48 gives additional trade information regarding preferential imports by certain preference-giving countries. In essence preferential imports from these countries remain very small, mostly because of narrow product coverage of agricultural products.

### 3. Non-tariff measures (NTMs)

364. Non-tariff measures increasingly constitute an important obstacle for the expansion of LDC exports. These barriers against the LDCs' exports consist of para-tariff, price and volume control measures, health and safety standards, among others. Agricultural export products of the LDCs are mostly subjected to NTMs.

365. A related question to be addressed in respect of NTMs on products of export interest to the LDCs is that of the escalation in the incidence of NTMs at higher levels in the processing chains. The effect of such escalation is to inhibit further processing of such products in the LDCs and thus maintain them in their position as suppliers of raw materials. The removal of restrictions at the higher levels in the processing chains would greatly improve the prospects for increasing value-added in the LDCs.

366. In the conclusions, attached to the Protocol extending the Multifibre Agreement for a further period of five years from 1 August 1986 until 31 July 1991, the contracting parties referred to the specific problems of the LDCs. They agreed normally not to impose restraints on exports from LDCs. However, if circumstances oblige the importing country to introduce restraints on exports from the LDCs, the treatment accorded to these countries should be significantly more favourable than that accorded to the exports of other groups of countries.

### 4. Restrictive business practices

367. Restrictive business practices such as collusive tendering, tied purchases, price fixing, and cartel arrangements affect adversely prices, marketing and distribution of exports and imports of the LDCs. More often than not, restrictive business practices impede or negate the realization of benefits that should accrue to the LDCs from liberalization of tariff and non-tariff barriers. With a view to reducing the adverse effects of restrictive business practices on the trade and economic development of the LDCs, the Set of Multilaterally Agreed Equitable Principles and Rules for the Control of Restrictive Business Practices specifically states that the developed countries in particular should take into account in their control of non-governmental trade restrictions the development, financial, and trade needs of the LDCs. 141/

Table 48

Imports of selected preference-giving countries from LDC beneficiaries of their scheme
(Figures for the latest year available, in million of $US)

| Preference-giving country and year (1) | | Total imports (2) | MFN dutiable imports (3) | GSP imports | | Percentage (4)/(3) (6) | Shares (5)/(4) (7) |
|---|---|---|---|---|---|---|---|
| | | | | Covered a/ (4) | Preferential b/ (5) | | |
| Austria | 1984 | 23.7 | 11.3 | 10.1 | 1.5 | 89.0 | 14.8 |
| Canada | 1984 | 37.8 | 10.5 | 7.3 | 5.6 | 69.5 | 76.7 |
| EEC | 1983 | 640.7 | 517.8 | 328.4 | 260.0 | 63.4 | 79.2 |
| Japan | 1983/84 | 219.0 | 44.6 | 9.2 | 6.5 | 20.6 | 70.6 |
| New Zealand | 1983/84 | 11.7 | 3.1 | 2.9 | 2.9 | 93.0 | 100.0 |
| Switzerland | 1984 | 40.2 | 36.8 | 20.1 | 13.2 | 50.0 | 65.7 |
| United States of America | 1982 | 844.4 | 287.7 | 153.5 | 47.9 | 53.4 | 31.2 |
| Hungary | 1982 | 15.0 | 15.0 | 15.0 | 15.0 | 100.0 | 100.0 |

Source: UNCTAD, Tenth general report on the implementation of the generalized system of preferences (TD/B/C.5/105), Geneva 1986, annex II.

a/ Indicates the coverage of MFN dutiable imports by the respective national GSP schemes.

b/ Indicates the GSP-covered imports which actually received preferential treatment.

### 5. New round of multilateral trade negotiations

368. In the Ministerial Declaration, adopted at the special session of GATT at Punta del Este in September 1986, the contracting parties highlighted the particular situation and problems of the LDCs. They agreed that the new round of multilateral trade negotiations should result, inter alia, in positive measures to facilitate the expansion of the LDCs' trading opportunities. Furthermore, they reconfirmed, that appropriate attention should be given by member States to the expeditious implementation of the relevant provisions of the 1982 Ministerial Declaration concerning the LDCs.

### C. International co-operation in the field of commodities in favour of the LDCs

### 1. The Common Fund for Commodities

369. The Common Fund for Commodities 142/ was conceived as a major element of the Integrated Programme for Commodities, designed to strengthen the price stabilizing effect of international commodity agreements by ensuring the availability of funds for development, productivity improvement, marketing and distribution, market promotion, and the promotion of local processing before export. The Common Fund Agreement provides that, in determining its priorities for the use of the resources of the Second Account, the Fund shall give due emphasis to commodities of interest to the LDCs. As of 15 January 1986, 90 countries had ratified the Agreement establishing the Common Fund for Commodities, thereby fulfilling one requirement for its entry into force. The second requirement for the Agreement's entry into force is that the countries which have ratified should represent two thirds of the Fund's directly contributed capital. As of 31 October 1986, the countries, which had ratified the Common Fund Agreement, accounted for 58.51 per cent, i.e. 8.1 per cent short of the required percentage. Of those LDCs which took part in the negotiation of the Agreement, 34 LDCs are among the founding membership of this new institution. The Maldives and the Lao People's Democratic Republic have not taken action in favour of signing or ratifying the Agreement.

### 2. Programmes dealing with the compensation of export earnings shortfalls

370. There are two operational programmes dealing with this question – the Compensatory Financing Facility of the International Monetary Fund and the STABEX/SYSMIN scheme of the EEC. In view of the shortcomings of existing facilities for dealing with the problems in the commodity sector, attention has been given in UNCTAD, especially in recent years, to the question of the need for an additional commodity-specific scheme and its possible forms. An UNCTAD group of experts recommended the establishment of an additional facility which would compensate commodity export earnings shortfalls specifically and that the funds provided would focus on supply factors. 143/ The work on the rules and modalities of this additional complementary facility and the analysis of the need for such a facility are continuing.

### (a)  International Monetary Fund

371. The aim of the IMF Compensatory Financing Facility (CFF) is to provide financial assistance to IMF members experiencing balance-of-payments difficulties resulting from temporary export shortfalls or cereal import excesses that are temporary in nature and due largely to factors beyond the control of the respective IMF member. 144/

372. The number of LDCs using the IMF-CFF as well as the amount of foreign exchange purchased within this scheme has been rather limited. In 1981, this facility was used by 12 LDCs, totalling in net purchases SDR 133.6 million; in 1985, 3 LDCs with net purchases of SDR 3.2 million took advantage of the IMF-CFF. In 1983, 1984 and during the first half of 1986 as well, the repayments by the LDCs within this scheme outweighed their purchases, i.e. net IMF-CFF purchases by the LDCs as a group turned negative during these periods (see table 49).

### (b)  STABEX

373. STABEX is a commodity-specific compensatory financing system of a regional nature which aims at stabilizing the export earnings of ACP countries. The least developed among the ACP countries are given special treatment. Transfers are in the form of grants and in years of shortage of funds, preferential consideration is given to their request. In 1984, the financial resources transferred to LDCs within the STABEX scheme amounted to only $US 19.1 million as compared to $US 39.3 million in 1982 (see table 50).

374. The Third ACP-EEC Lomé Convention introduced changes into STABEX which expand country and product coverage, reduce dependence and fluctuation thresholds and add further conditions for the use of transfers.

375. As for the least developed ACP countries, the commodity dependence threshold has now been fixed at 1.5 per cent of total earnings from exports to all destinations during the year of application. The fluctuation threshold was also lowered to 1.5 per cent (as compared to 2 per cent originally) for this group of countries.

376. With regard to the use of transfers, new provisions stipulate that before the transfer agreement is signed, the recipient country has to communicate substantial information related to the programmes and operations for which the funds are to be allocated. Explanations have to be given if funds are to be used in a sector other than the one in which the shortfall occurred. A report on the actual use of the funds is required within specified deadlines. The Commission is empowered to suspend decisions on subsequent transfers should the required information not be presented.

Table 49

Finance made available to LDCs under the IMF Compensatory
Financing Facility, 1981 to June 1986
(In millions of SDR)

| Country | 1981 | 1982 | 1983 | 1984 | 1985 | 1986 */ |
|---|---|---|---|---|---|---|
| Afghanistan | - | - | - | - | - | - |
| Bangladesh | -10.4 | 108.1 | -19.3 | - | 34.6 | -22.0 |
| Benin | - | - | - | - | - | - |
| Burundi | - | - | -4.8 | -4.8 | - | - |
| Central African Republic | 7.6 | - | -0.2 | -3.3 | -4.4 | -1.1 |
| Chad | 2.2 | - | - | -2.7 | 3.5 | 0.9 |
| Comoros | - | - | - | - | - | - |
| Democratic Yemen | - | - | - | - | - | - |
| Djibouti | - | - | - | - | - | - |
| Equatorial Guinea | 4.1 | - | - | -4.8 | -4.5 | -1.2 |
| Ethiopia | 18.0 | -2.2 | -18.0 | -20.3 | -9.0 | 30.8 |
| Gambia | 9.0 | -2.2 | -2.2 | -1.1 | -2.3 | 1.3 |
| Guinea | - | - | - | - | - | - |
| Guinea-Bissau | 1.9 | -0.3 | -0.4 | -0.4 | -0.9 | 0.5 |
| Haiti | 17.0 | - | - | - | -6.4 | -4.3 |
| Lao People's Democratic Republic | -1.6 | - | - | - | - | - |
| Lesotho | - | - | - | - | - | - |
| Malawi | 12.0 | -11.7 | 2.7 | 5.3 | -0.7 | -1.9 |
| Maldives | - | - | - | - | - | - |
| Mali | - | - | -1.3 | -3.2 | -0.6 | 0.6 |
| Nepal | -0.2 | -4.8 | -4.9 | -5.2 | -3.9 | - |
| Niger | - | - | 24.0 | - | - | - |
| Samoa | 1.3 | -0.6 | 0.5 | -0.5 | -1.0 | -0.5 |
| Sao Tome and Principe | - | - | - | - | - | - |
| Sierra Leone | -4.5 | - | 20.7 | - | - | - |
| Somalia | - | - | - | - | 32.6 | - |
| Sudan | 36.8 | -24.8 | 10.5 | -14.5 | -4.5 | - |
| Togo | - | - | - | - | - | - |
| Uganda | 35.0 | -0.6 | -11.9 | -25.6 | -25.6 | -11.3 |
| United Republic of Tanzania | 5.4 | -7.1 | -24.0 | -12.6 | -3.7 | - |
| Yemen | - | - | - | - | - | - |
| Total | 133.6 | 53.8 | -28.1 | -93.7 | 3.2 | -8.4 |

Source: IMF reply to the UNCTAD questionnaire, and IMF, International Financial Statistics (various issues).

*/ January to June 1986.

## Table 50

### Transfer of financial resources to LDCs within the STABEX scheme, */
### 1982-1984
#### (In millions of US dollars)

| Country | 1982 | 1983 | 1984 |
|---|---|---|---|
| Afghanistan | - | - | 0.1 |
| Bangladesh | - | - | - |
| Benin | 2.6 | - | 0.4 |
| Bhutan | - | - | - |
| Botswana | - | - | - |
| Burkina Faso | 1.0 | - | - |
| Burundi | - | - | 0.4 |
| Cape Verde | - | - | 0.2 |
| Central African Republic | 1.6 | - | - |
| Chad | 3.5 | - | - |
| Comoros | 0.3 | - | 3.1 |
| Democratic Yemen | - | - | - |
| Djibouti | - | - | - |
| Equatorial Guinea | - | - | - |
| Ethiopia | - | 3.9 | 3.5 |
| Gambia | 1.9 | - | - |
| Guinea | - | - | - |
| Guinea-Bissau | 0.4 | 1.2 | - |
| Haiti | - | - | - |
| Lao People's Democratic Republic | - | - | - |
| Lesotho | 0.6 | - | - |
| Malawi | 2.6 | - | - |
| Maldives | - | - | - |
| Mali | 3.4 | 2.6 | - |
| Nepal | - | - | - |
| Niger | - | - | - |
| Rwanda | - | 0.4 | - |
| Samoa | 1.4 | - | 0.1 |
| Sao Tome and Principe | 2.6 | 2.8 | - |
| Sierra Leone | 6.1 | - | 3.7 |
| Somalia | - | - | - |
| Sudan | - | 6.5 | - |
| Togo | 6.9 | 11.4 | 5.7 |
| Uganda | - | - | - |
| United Republic of Tanzania | - | 4.5 | 4.9 |
| Vanuatu | 4.2 | - | - |
| Yemen | - | - | - |
| All LDCs | 39.3 | 33.4 | 19.1 |

Source:  UNCTAD secretariat calculations based on information from the EEC secretariat.

*/  Transfers to LDCs within the STABEX schemes are not repayable.

377. The new STABEX scheme is applicable to commodities whose values are about 73 per cent of agricultural exports of the least developed ACP countries and 42 per cent of their total exports (see table 51). However, the new STABEX does not cover a number of commodities - such as live animals, tobacco, fresh fish, meat and other agricultural products - which are of particular export interest to some least developed ACP countries (e.g. Somalia, Malawi, Cape Verde, Central African Republic).

378. Under the Third ACP-EEC Lomé Convention, 27 least developed countries are covered by STABEX. At the sixth session of the Intergovernmental Group on the Least Developed Countries, held in September-October 1985, 145/ the EEC announced its intention to introduce a STABEX-type arrangement to compensate export earnings shortfalls in agricultural commodities, including jute, for nine least developed countries not signatories of the Lomé Convention: Afghanistan, Bangladesh, Bhutan, Democratic Yemen, Haiti, the Maldives, Nepal, Lao People's Democratic Republic, and Yemen.

(c) SYSMIN

379. The prime objective of SYSMIN is to help restore the viability of the mining industry in the ACP countries concerned (rehabilitation, maintenance, rationalization). Where this aim is found to be unattainable, the system may give backing to diversification measures.

380. The application of the new SYSMIN scheme could be of some potential importance for the least developed ACP States. The share of ores and metals (excluding precious minerals) in the total exports of the least developed ACP States was approximately 26 per cent at the beginning of the 1980s equivalent to twice that of the other developing countries; but, as might be expected, it was not evenly distributed among all least developed ACP countries. The importance of ores and metals in exports (excluding precious minerals) differs from one least developed ACP State to another. In 1982, for example, the share of ores and metals was very important for Guinea (95 per cent), Niger (90 per cent) and Togo (52 per cent), as compared to 98 per cent, 80 per cent and 60 per cent respectively for 1981. 146/ For most of the rest of the least developed ACP States, this share was not significant.

381. It should be recalled that a least developed ACP country that has experienced a shortfall in its export earnings from mineral products (excluding precious minerals, oil and gas) of the magnitude of 12 per cent or more may apply for financial aid from the resources allocated to the special financing facility. As a result, .he SYSMIN theoretical coverage of least developed ACP countries' exports has been extended from 15 per cent under Lomé II to 26 per cent under Lomé III (see table 52).

382. All current facilities provide only limited amounts of compensation for the export earnings of the LDCs. In fact, for the period 1977-1982 these facilities covered only 33 per cent of total shortfalls. 147/ A programme for a compensatory financing scheme covering all major commodity exports of the LDCs and paying 100 per cent shortfalls would be a desirable instrument for tackling the LDCs' problem of export earnings shortfalls from commodity exports.

Table 51

Lomé III STABEX scheme coverage for LDCs' exports */

| Country | As % of country total exports | As % of country agricultural exports |
|---|---|---|
| Benin | 77.9 | 93.7 |
| Botswana | 4.2 | 8.4 |
| Burkina Faso | 64.0 | 75.3 |
| Burundi | 85.9 | 96.7 |
| Cape Verde | 8.4 | 13.3 |
| Central African Republic | 48.1 | 92.1 |
| Chad | 82.7 | 98.2 |
| Comoros | 78.0 | 99.4 |
| Djibouti | 12.5 | 36.6 |
| Ethiopia | 82.5 | 96.0 |
| Gambia | 47.2 | 50.0 |
| Guinea | 0.8 | 94.0 |
| Guinea-Bissau | 56.1 | 68.5 |
| Lesotho | 20.0 | 87.0 |
| Malawi | 19.3 | 21.5 |
| Mali | 76.5 | 84.6 |
| Niger | 1.6 | 12.1 |
| Rwanda | 89.2 | 100.0 |
| Samoa | 57.2 | 73.4 |
| Sao Tome and Principe | 99.6 | 100.0 |
| Sierra Leone | 20.1 | 79.8 |
| Somalia | 18.3 | 19.2 |
| Sudan | 65.5 | 70.8 |
| United Republic of Tanzania | 73.9 | 93.1 |
| Togo | 31.7 | 99.2 |
| Uganda | 96.7 | 99.5 |
| All least developed ACP States | 42.4 | 72.8 |

Source: Calculated on the basis of the Handbook of International Trade and Development Statistics, 1984 Supplement, and Official Journal of the European Communities, L 347, vol. 23, 22 December 1980, pages 17-22; ACP.CEE.e 141, pages 114-125.

*/ Conditional example: Lomé III rules of 1985 are interpreted with data for 1981.

Table 52

Evolution of SYSMIN coverage or LDCs' exports */

| Country | Lomé II | Lomé III |
|---------|---------|----------|
| Botswana | 18.8 | 24.5 |
| Burundi | 2.1 | 5.5 |
| Cape Verde | - | 21.9 |
| Central African Republic | - | 1.3 |
| Djibouti | - | 1.5 |
| Guinea | 98.3 | 98.3 |
| Guinea-Bissau | - | 1.0 |
| Malawi | - | 0.4 |
| Niger | - | 79.9 |
| Rwanda | 10.2 | 10.2 |
| Sierra Leone | 10.2 | 33.2 |
| Sudan | 0.2 | 0.2 |
| United Republic of Tanzania | - | 4.7 |
| Togo | 50.5 | 60.9 |
| Uganda | - | 0.2 |
| All least developed ACP States | 15.4 | 26.2 |

Source: Handbook of International Trade and Development Statistics, 1984
Supplement; Official Journal of the European Communities, L 347,
vol. 23, 22 December 1980, pages L 347/22; 23,53; ACP/CEE/e 141.

*/ Conditional example : Lomé II and Lomé III rules are interpreted
with data for 1981.

## D.  Conclusions

383. Although some improvements have been made, particularly in tariff
preference schemes and the STABEX and the SYSMIN system, there is still room
for further amelioriations.  High priority should be accorded to the removing
of non-tariff measures.  As regards the GSP, an improvement in its efficiency
could be accomplished by (a) extension of the list of products, (b) more
simple rules of origin, and (c) extension of the duration of schemes.

384. Developed countries should provide preferential treatment to imports of
goods produced by the LDCs and explore the possibilities of promoting
long-term arrangements for the sale of export products of LDCs, in line with
the conclusions and recommendations of the mid-term global review of the SNPA.

385. Concerning further promotion of international co-operation in commodities
of interest to the LDCs the following proposals made in the Least Developed
Countries 1985 Report deserve serious consideration:

(1)  Special attention should be given in the course of the future
operation of the Common Fund for Commodities to the provision of its
Agreement that, in determining priorities for the use of the Second
Account, the Fund should give due emphasis to commodities of interest to
the least developed countries.

(2)  In specific commodity agreements the small producers among the LDCs
should be exempted from quota restrictions and from the obligation to
share the financial costs.

(3)  Considering that the LDCs export only a very small proportion of
their export commodities in processed form and that their participation
in the marketing of their export commodities is limited, special
provisions might be envisaged for these countries in frameworks for
international co-operation on these issues.  Developed countries should
consider providing STABEX type facilities to all LDCs.

PART THREE

RECENT DEVELOPMENTS IN THE ECONOMIES OF INDIVIDUAL
LEAST DEVELOPED COUNTRIES

1.  AFGHANISTAN

Economic performance

386. Economic performance and development in Afghanistan must be examined against the background of its continuing political difficulties and the state of internal instability which has existed since the start of the 1980s.  This constraint has caused severe damage to the economic infrastructure which has been officially estimated at more than $700 million, equivalent to 22 per cent of GNP in fiscal 1979/80. 148/  Nevertheless, GDP in 1984/85 registered a growth rate of 3.7 per cent compared to 2.1 per cent in the preceding year.

387. Two-way foreign trade has been officially estimated at $1.6 billion in 1984/85, representing an increase of 9 per cent compared to the preceding fiscal year.  While exports have been estimated at $660 million, i.e. a decline of 1.6 per cent compared to 1983/84, imports rose by 17 per cent in the meanwhile.  Public, private and mixed enterprises are reported to have transacted 50 per cent, 46 per cent and 3 per cent respectively of total exports in 1984/85, of which exports to the USSR alone - all covered by bilateral agreements - accounted for 55 per cent.  This represented a 6 per cent decline in the Soviet share of exports compared to the preceding year.  Major exports consist of natural gas, production of which is almost entirely directed to the Soviet Union;  cotton;  karakul skins;  carpets; and fresh and dried fruits, sold largely in Western Europe, India and the Middle East.  Planned targets in the export of certain commodities were not fully achieved.  Imports, which amounted to $965 million in 1984/85, consist largely of machinery, consumer goods, petroleum and transport equipment.

388. The trade deficit measured on a CIF/FOB basis reached $305 million in 1984/85, reversing the recorded surplus of $72 million in 1981.  According to the IMF, foreign reserves excluding gold amounted to $295 million at the end of 1985, which was well above the levels recorded over the preceding four years.

389. The manufacturing sector is predominantly concerned with processing local agricultural raw materials and the production of cotton and woollen yarns, sugar, cement, chemical fertilizers based on natural gas, edible oils, soaps, spare parts for transport and engineering equipment and pharmaceutical products.  The output of manufactured products has risen in recent years and a 7 per cent growth rate was reported in 1984/85 compared to the previous year.

390. In a land-locked country such as Afghanistan, the improvement of the inland transportation system constitutes a major instrument for overcoming this geographical handicap.  With substantial foreign aid in the building of roads, airports and other transport facilities in the 1970s, the country now has a relatively well-developed road network connecting the major urban centres.  Revenues derived from the transport sector are officially reported to have risen in 1984 compared to the preceding year due to an increased volume of goods transported.  However, Ariana Airlines has performed relatively less successfully due to the suspension of certain international

traffic rights. Political and security difficulties affecting traditional transit routes have been compensated by an improvement and increased use of transit facilities through the USSR.

391. The communication sector between the provinces is reported to have been strengthened and revenues are reported to have increased by 10 per cent in 1984/85 compared to the preceding year. Similarly, radio broadcasting and television receiver sets have been provided to the provinces.

392. Afghanistan is endowed with rich mineral and other natural resources, most of which have not been tapped. Among the recently discovered minerals, uranium is reported to have been extracted. Moreover, the Government has conducted numerous geological surveys with the assistance of the USSR.

393. The country's main energy resource is natural gas, reserves of which are estimated at 150 billion cubic metres. Average annual output was 2.5 billion $m^3$ during first part of the 1980s, rising to 3 billion $m^3$ in 1984/85. Although oil reserves are officially estimated at a modest 100 million barrels, there are indications that the real figures are considerably higher. Thus, drilling and exploration for gas and oil, both on the ground and by satellite, as well as the building of refineries, have been recently intensified.

394. Although the country's electricity generating capacity from hydroelectric stations rose by more than 20 per cent between 1975 and 1982, yearly production targets were not achieved in 1984/85 due to the cutting of the transmission lines, which resulted in frequent stoppages of power in the capital city. A total power-generation target of 1.2 billion kw/h has been set for 1985/86, of which 58 per cent would be in the form of hydropower and the rest would come from diesel thermal plants.

Environment and disasters

395. There are considerable forested areas in the eastern part of Afghanistan, which have been affected by cutting and slashing. This situation has created alarm, so that the Government adopted policies to control deforestation by introducing substitutes for wood fuel consumption, but these efforts have not proved successful so far.

396. The country comprises rough terrain and is vulnerable to drought. Much of the country's agriculture relies on a delicate water management system of dams and irrigation channels. In late 1984 a drought occurred, the effects of which have been significant for the entire economy. Moreover, both Government and unofficial reports agree that the present political situation has affected internal security in the country. Recent reports by the United Nations High Commissioner for Refugees (UNHCR) estimate that approximately 2.4 and 1.3 million Afghans have sought shelter across the border in Pakistan and Iran respectively.

Human resources and social development

397. The overall literacy rate in Afghanistan is little more than 10 per cent and less than 5 per cent among women. Mortality is high, while life expectancy at birth is less than 45 years. As many as 80 per cent of the population live in rural areas at subsistence levels.

398. The Government is reported to have taken energetic measures to upgrade the level of social services and to eliminate illiteracy, giving particular emphasis to adult educational programmes. Official sources report that adult enrolment in educational institutions and other literacy courses has increased by 17 per cent from 1983 to 1984. Moreover, additional schools, new departments, faculties, technical and vocational schools have been established during the 1980s.

399. The health sector has also been given considerable importance by the authorities through the establishment of hospitals, mother and child health-care centres and expansion of other medical facilities. Increased vaccination against various diseases, particularly malaria, has been undertaken. The Government has reaffirmed its commitment to the WHO target of "Health For All by the Year 2000".

## Development planning and policies

400. The 1985/86 plan aims to continue the present trend towards the concurrent strengthening of the public, mixed and co-operative sectors with active participation of the private sector. However, due to internal instability, the Government has had only limited success in the achievement of its overall development objectives.

401. A new five-year plan, covering the period 1986-90, is now in the final stages of preparation. The main objectives are rehabilitation and reconstruction of institutions, increased exploration activities for mineral resources, particularly natural gas, implementation of programmes of land and water reforms, improvement of tax collection and educational systems and expansion of foreign trade.

## Mobilization of domestic resources for development

402. In view of the very low level of ODA to Afghanistan, the Government has recognized the fact that increased domestic resource mobilization is an important element in the country's rapid development. In 1984/85, $80 million, equivalent to 51 per cent of total development expenditures, was financed from domestic sources. In 1985/86, overall development expenditures are estimated at $170 million, of which $92 million (54 per cent) will be financed from domestic resources.

403. Official sources state that total Government revenue in 1984/85 showed an increase of 12 per cent compared with that of the preceding year. This has been achieved by measures aiming at increasing revenue from public enterprises through improved management, and reducing subsidies on items such as petroleum products. Moreover, the Government has widened the tax base and restrained expenditure.

## Transfer of external resources, debt, capital requirements

404. Aid flows from bilateral DAC and multilateral sources dropped to $13 million in 1983, compared with an average of $103 million during the period 1977-1979. Although the growth of assistance from CMEA countries has more than compensated the drop from DAC donors, it has not been enough to cover the external resources required to achieve the country's development

objectives.  Aid worth $150 million is anticipated for 1985/86, of which the
USSR and other CMEA countries are expected to provide $142 million
(95 per cent) while the remaining $8 million will come from the United Nations
system and other countries.

405. Afghanistan's external public debt is estimated to have increased to over
$1.7 billion by the end of 1983, much of which is owed to the USSR.  The
debt-service-to-exports ratio for 1985 has been estimated at 18 per cent but,
in fact, debt repayment has been rescheduled by the CMEA creditors due to the
present political difficulties.

## Mechanism for the follow-up and monitoring of the SNPA

406. The last Round Table Meeting for Afghanistan with its development
partners was held in Geneva in May 1983.  In his presentation, the head of the
Afghan delegation stated that the Government had carried out its national
commitments under the SNPA, in identifying short-, medium- and long-term plan
objectives, working out sectoral programmes and assessing resource
requirements, all of which were presented at the Round Table Meeting.  On the
same occasion, the Afghan delegation expressed concern over the postponement
of aid and restrictions placed on other capital flows to their country.

## 2.  BANGLADESH

## Economic performance

407. Development in Bangladesh, which had a per capita GDP of about $130 in
1984, continues to be constrained by poor natural resources, high population
growth (2.2 per cent p.a.) and low domestic savings.  Preliminary estimates
indicate that the GDP growth rate in FY 1984/85 149/ remained at about
3.5 per cent, compared to the target of 5.4 per cent, in spite of improved
development programmes and policies.  The failure to achieve the projected
growth rate target was due to unusually severe flooding, which seriously
damaged agricultural production and affected other parts of the economy in
1984, but it was in line with the average growth rate for the 1980s.

408. After lessened strain in 1983 and early 1984, the balance of payments
deteriorated considerably in 1985, partly due to high grain imports
necessitated by the 1984 floods.  In 1984/85 Bangladesh had to import almost
1.2 million tons of grain at a cost of $245 million.  The balance-of-payments
situation was further worsened by a decline of workers' remittances to
$370 million, which was 60 per cent less than in 1983/84.  As a result,
foreign exchange reserves fell by $140 million in 1984/85 to a level of
$395 million, which was equivalent to less than two months' imports.  Reserves
fell to less than $275 million later in 1985, but recovered early in 1986 to
their level one year earlier.  In 1985/86 the balance of payments was expected
to benefit from increased export earnings ($927 million in 1984/85) and an
upturn in remittances from abroad.  However, the situation will be aggravated
by substantial loan repayments due during 1986 and 1987 for recent food grain
imports on deferred terms.

409. A "New Industrial Policy" was instituted in 1983, in the pursuit of which
a National Committee for Industrial Development under the chairmanship of the
President was established in July 1985.  The "New Industrial Policy"

emphasizes the generation of industrial employment, a reduction of the role of the public sector in manufacturing through an alleviation of the regulatory constraints heretofore placed on the private sector and the development of non-traditional exports. The latter policy includes measures such as duty-free entry for imported inputs of exported products, preferential access to credit for exporters and the creation of bonded warehouses designed for ready-made garments, an initiative which has proved extremely successful. Bangladesh gross garment exports increased from $11 million in 1982/83 to $31 million in 1983/84 and reached $116 million in 1984/85. Within three years, the garment industry created about 70,000 jobs for low-income women.

410. At the end of 1985, the foundations were laid for one of Asia's biggest fertilizer factories, which is expected to cost $470 million. The plant's capacity is estimated at 560,000 tons per annum.

411. Improvement in overall management and efficiency of the transport network has been the major goal for the country's transport and communication programmes in 1984/85, a sector contributing an estimated 5.6 per cent to GDP. The Government has directed significant efforts to improving the railway system as well as extending, upgrading and rehabilitating the national and regional highways. One hundred and seventy-five upazila (districts) were connected by roads during the Second Five-Year Plan (SFYP) period (1980-1985). Moreover, in order to develop an efficient transportation network, an inter-modal study is now in its final stage. Work for the improvement of ports, shipping and inland waterways was carried out in 1984/85, while in the area of civil aviation all the airports of the country were equipped with improved communication facilities, navigational systems as well as safety services. The communications sector has seen considerable improvement, including the extension of nationwide direct-dialling facilities.

412. Natural resources in Bangladesh are limited. There is a proven gas reserve amounting to 12.4 trillion cubic feet. Production of natural gas in 1984/85 increased around 14 per cent in comparison with the previous year's output. Moreover, the increasing role of natural gas is reflected in the fact that it provided about 52 per cent of all commercial energy consumed in 1984/85 compared with 37 per cent in 1979/80.

413. While the use of natural gas continues to increase, the supply of traditional fuel has been declining sharply due to the rapid increase of population and the depletion of forest resources. In order to meet this situation, attention has turned towards development of new and renewable sources of energy. These efforts include the production and distribution of bio-gas plants, solar cookers and other energy sources.

Environment and disasters

414. Due to its geographical location, Bangladesh suffers from cyclones, floods and other natural disasters. Fifty-seven per cent of the total area is vulnerable to floods. The heavy floods in May 1984 were the worst in many years. Thousands of lives were lost, the cattle herd was decimated and large crop areas in the southern and eastern districts were damaged. These and earlier floods, coupled with drought in other areas of the country, depressed

cereal production to 15.5 million tons in 1984 compared to a target of
16.1 million tons.  At the Aid Group Meeting in May 1985, the donors commended
the Bangladesh authorities for the manner in which the effects of the
devastating floods of 1984 had been managed.  It was further noted by the
members of the Group that a famine disaster of high magnitude had been avoided
by the efficient operation of the public grain distribution system.  However,
another major flood hit the country in May 1985, the effects of which on the
economy have been severe.

## Human resources and social development

415. An extensive school reform during the early 1980s was quite successful in
increasing the number of schools and student enrolment, even as educational
levels were raised.  The focus of the educational programme in the mid-1980s
continue to be on decreasing illiteracy, on skill development through the
expansion of scientific, technical and vocational training to meet local and
overseas demands, as well as on the training of teachers and decentralization
of the educational administration.  Moreover, the mass education programme
which had been deferred from the last two years of the Second Five-Year Plan
(1980-1985), has now been revived.  This revival will affect about
2.4 million illiterates of the 10-to-30-year age group, to whom teaching
materials and other facilities have been provided.

416. The Government has strenghtened institutional arrangements designed to
encourage employment abroad.  A programme for the promotion of overseas
employment has been instituted, which analyses the declining trend in overseas
employment and proposes remedial measures, including the identification of
previously untapped countries offering opportunities for employment of labour
from Bangladesh.

417. In 1984/85, the health sector was allocated 2.9 per cent of the overall
national budget, which contrasts well as compared to earlier years of the
SFYP.  Primary health care for all is seen as the key approach, with emphasis
on rural areas.  Out of 81 major projects proposed for the health sector in
the Second Five-Year Plan, 48 had been successfully completed by 1985.  A
noteworthy feature explaining the successful implementation of the above
projects was the Government's deliberate effort to enlist the active
participation of local communities, self-governing public bodies, the private
sector and voluntary associations in supporting and maintaining the health
services established under the programme.

## Developing planning and policies

418. Fiscal year 1984/85 marked the completion of the Second Five-year Plan
and the twelfth year of the country's planned development.  The Plan was
launched with high expectations in terms of external resources and growth
targets, but it was soon upset due to changes in the international economic
environment in the early 1980s, which included a doubling of oil prices and
the subsequent recession.  Despite these difficulties, the Government's
planning efforts have had some impact on the average citizen, e.g. the
population policy of the Second Plan succeeded in depressing the annual
population growth rate from 2.7 per cent in 1974 to 2.2 per cent in 1984.

419. The Third Five-Year Plan released in December 1985, covering FY 1985/86 to FY 1989/90, maintains poverty alleviation and job creation as its central themes. Other basic objectives of the Plan are: (a) further cuts of the population growth rate from 2.2 per cent in 1984/85 to 1.8 per cent in 1989/90; (b) the expansion of educational facilities; (c) the development of the country's technological base to facilitate long-term structural changes in the economy; and (d) national self-sufficiency in foodstuffs, particularly through increased grain production.

Mobilization of domestic resources for development

420. Domestic resource mobilization has been accorded a very high priority in the country's development strategy. The Government's efforts in this area have been concentrated on raising the share of tax revenue in GDP, improvement in the financial performance of public sector enterprises, and reduction of public expenditure, particularly of various consumption and production subsidies.

421. During fiscal 1984/85 only modest measures to improve tax administration were introduced. However, actual revenues generated were greater than during the preceding year and amounted to $132 million against the budgeted $125 million. This gain was largely due to increased collection of customs duties resulting from the increase in rates. A special programme to improve collection of income taxes started to operate during 1984. In 1985/86 the Government instituted tighter monetary and credit polices designed to control price inflation and to improve the external balance. Moreover, the Government has been encouraging the mobilization of small savings in all sectors during the second and third Plan periods.

Transfer of external resources, debt and capital requirement

422. External financing plays a significant role in the country's development strategy and donors have been relatively generous within the framework of the World Bank consultative aid group arrangement. The revised estimate of disbursements of foreign economic assistance during fiscal 1984/85 stood at $1.43 billion, which was 16 per cent more than the previous year. The 1984/85 total included $303 million for food aid; $470 million for other programme aid, and $700 million for project aid. During 1984/85 net loan disbursements amounted to $467 million, raising outstanding total debt to about $4.9 billion in June 1985. This growing debt burden caused the debt service-to-exports ratio to increase from 10 per cent in 1979 to 19 per cent in 1985, a trend expected to continue.

Mechanism for monitoring and follow-up of the SNPA

423. At the Consultative Group meeting held in Paris in April 1986, 25 donor governments and institutions met under the chairmanship of the World Bank. While noting the significant progress made in several fields, they urged the Government to give particular attention to: domestic resource mobilization; project implementation; export diversification; action to improve the general efficiency of the public administration; and measures to alleviate poverty. Both the World Bank and IMF at that meeting underlined the debt problem confronting Bangladesh and the importance of maintaining at least the past real levels of medium-term aid commitments. The World Bank

representative indicated IDA commitments of about $1.2 billion during the
period FY 1985 to FY 1987. This aid was expected to continue to support the
Government's priorities of achieving foodgrain self-sufficiency, reducing
population growth, eliminating mass illiteracy, creating additional employment
opportunities for the increasing number of landless, and accelerating domestic
energy development. The Bangladesh delegation, while expressing some
satisfaction, noted that the Government had hoped for an increase in food and
programme aid, including assistance for operations and management
expenditures. Moreover, it had also expected specific pledges in support of
the private sector.

## 3. BENIN

### Recent economic performance

424. Benin had a minimal growth rate of 0.4 per cent and 1.6 per cent in 1983
and 1984 respectively. For 1985 real GDP is thought to have fallen by
5 per cent, after account has been taken of an inflation rate of around
10 per cent. These fluctuations have been heavily influenced by the
agricultural sector. Since 1984 the country has known good rainfall and a
return to normal agricultural production levels. As an open economy, however,
Benin depends to a great extent on the economic activity in the surrounding
area. The fact that Nigeria closed its borders with the neighbouring
countries from 1983 until March 1986, and that the economy of Niger is still
depressed, put a brake on the economy of Benin. Trade with Nigeria virtually
came to a standstill and transit trade with Niger was slowed down.

425. Agriculture is the economy's leading sector. In 1983 it accounted for
40 per cent of GDP, but employed about 70 per cent of the active population.
Agricultural production declined from 1980 to 1983, largely due to drought and
irregular rainfall. Other depressing factors included agricultural pricing
policies and low use of inputs, such as fertilizers and insecticides. But in
the crop year 1984/85 the harvests of the four main foodcrops (i.e. maize,
yams, manioc and sorghum/millet) recovered to, or exceeded the levels before
the 1982/83 drought period. Of the cash crops (palm oil, cotton and coffee),
cotton gave the most remarkable result: the harvest forecast for 1985/86
(107,000 tons) is more than three times as high as the one reaped in 1982/83
(32,000 tons). The production of palm oil is still low, however. After
two years of good rainfall, the plantations are beginning to recover, but the
1984/85 harvest still yielded less than the one of 1982/83. This also affects
the relevant downstream agro-industry.

426. Benin has a significant livestock herd, officially estimated in 1981 to
include 80,000 head of cattle, over 1 million sheep, 1 million goats, over
half a million pigs and 14 million poultry. The country lost about one third
of its total herd in the 1982/83 season because of shortages of fodder and
water.

427. On the basis of the trade figure estimates used to establish the balance
of payments, Benin's trade deficit in 1982 well exceeded the value of its
exports. In the subsequent two years imports were forced down by one third,
while exports in 1984 recovered to their 1982 levels, after a severe decline
in 1983. This recovery was achieved primarily through the growth of

agricultural production. As a result the trade deficit shrank by CFAF 20 billion between 1982 and 1984, to reach CFAF 50 billion in 1984 ($115 million). However, by 1985 this trend of falling imports and growing exports seems to have come to an end. On the basis of partner countries' trade data, Benin's trade deficit with the developed market-economy countries roughly doubled in 1985.

## Environment and disasters

428. The period of drought has come to an end. Both 1984 and 1985 have known good rainfall. This turnaround was so extreme that some crops were ruined by excessive rainfall and that areas in the Mono province were flooded. Nevertheless the country still needed food aid, e.g. a Japanese grant for the purchase of 2,700 tons of rice.

## Human resources and social development

429. Due to the Government's difficult budget situation, all expenditures, including social and educational programmes, had to be cut across the board by 10 per cent in 1985. However, with the help of UNESCO and the OPEC Fund, 70 schools were constructed in rural areas.

430. In pursuance of the priority accorded by the 1983-1987 development plan to rural development, investments in this sector were directed towards the management of water supplies and opening the interior by improving country roads. Benin received loans of CFAF 1,500 million ($3.3 million) and grants of CFAF 500 million ($1.1 million) for digging wells in 1986. Similarly a CFAF 2 billion ($4.5 million) loan was received in 1986 for paving and improving 1,000 km. of earth roads.

## Development planning and policies

431. Benin's 1983-1987 Development Plan aims at an annual growth of 5 to 6 per cent. The priority is put on rural development, which receives 23 per cent of the planned outlays, followed by infrastructure, which is allocated 21 per cent. The plan emphasizes the development of foodcrops and the commercialization of agricultural products. Five major projects in the fields of industry, infrastructure and exploitation of natural resources are discussed below in greater detail.

(a) Industry

432. Benin completed two major industrial projects in co-operation with Nigeria, with a 45 per cent equity share in each: a sugar mill in Save and a cement plant in Onigbolo. The bulk of these plants' output was to be sold on the Nigerian market, whose import needs exceed the two factories' production capacities. From the start, marketing problems in Nigeria have prevented full capacity utilization, as a result of which neither plant is profitable. Discussions at ministerial level were held early in 1986 but did not resolve the problem.

(b)  Infrastructure

433. By virtue of its transit role for the land-locked neighbouring countries Niger and Burkina Faso, Benin's transport sector is particularly important. In the period 1979 to 1983 it absorbed a quarter of public investment and accounted for around 20 per cent of employment.  Moreover, Benin earns 20 per cent of its GDP from transit trade to Niger and Nigeria.  As the focal point both of its domestic and transit system, 150/ the Port of Cotonou witnessed an expansion of its capacity in the years 1981-1983.

434. As the major form of transit transport to Niger, the railway linking the two countries is operated by the Organisation Commune Bénin-Niger des Chemins de Fer et des Transports (OCBN), a company jointly run by Niger and Benin. The OCBN received a FF 100 million ($11 million) credit in 1985 to maintain and upgrade the Benin/Niger connection, and a further credit of FF 124 million ($17.8 million) was granted in March 1986, of which 16.1 per cent was allocated to the Governments of Benin and Niger each and the remaining 67.7 per cent to the OCBN directly.

435. Benin has also secured finance for the paving of the Dassa-Save-Parakou road, which will ensure an all-year connection of the interior of the country with the Port of Cotonou by road.  The project is economically viable but will compete with the above-mentioned railway.  After completion of the road, Benin intends to improve the Parakou-Bétéron-Porga road to Burkina Faso.  This will also benefit the Port of Cotonou, whose expanded capacity remains largely unutilized so far.  The construction of these roads will strengthen Benin's role as a regional trade and transit centre.

(c)  Natural resources

436. Benin's per capita energy consumption is one of the lowest in the world: 65 kg coal equivalent, as compared to an average of 87 kg for other countries at the same income level.

437. Commercially exploitable energy resources are limited to the offshore Semé oilfield.  Savannah woodlands covering 60,000 km$^2$ account for two thirds of energy consumption.  This is followed by petroleum (24 per cent) and electricity.  The latter two sources must be largely imported, since petroleum consumption exceeds local production, and electricity is imported from the Akosombo hydroelectric plant in Ghana.

438. As from 1983 Benin licensed commercial oil production at the Semé oil field to a Norwegian oil company.  At the end of 1985 the concession was unexpectedly sold to another company.  In the course of the ensuing controversy, which was followed by a drop in world oil prices, both the Norwegian firm and the second company were reported to have stopped operations.  With the freezing of multilateral credits for further development, the future of the field remains in doubt.

439. Until 1982 electricity was principally imported from the Akosombo hydroelectric dam in Ghana.  After the 1982/83 drought, during which the dam's production went down, Benin started to produce electricity domestically.  In a joint project with Togo, Benin is constructing a hydro-electric dam on the Mono River, which will be a cost-effective solution for Benin's growing energy

needs, which rose by 14 per cent per year in the period 1970-1980.  The new
dam will have a capacity of 62 MW, half of which will be allocated to Benin,
which should make the country largely self-sufficient for its electricity
production.

## Mobilizations of domestic resources for development

440. Domestic savings have always been low in Benin.  The 1983-1987
development and investment plan was jeopardized because of insufficient local
financing.  In 1982 the Government issued a decree to encourage savings and
investments by nationals and foreigners.  The governing Revolutionary Party
took measures to reduce the Government deficit, mainly by cutting expenditures
other than salaries and wages.

## Transfer of external resources, debt, capital requirements

441. Since 1981, Benin's long-term debt has oscillated around $600 million.
Until 1982 debt was exclusively of a long-term character.  But from 1982
onwards Benin has taken up short-term credits, which led to a sharp increase
of debt-service payments.  The latter amounted to $60 million in 1984,
corresponding to 40 per cent of its export earnings.  Benin is eligible to
draw on the new Structural Adjustment Facility of the IMF, within the
framework of its quota of SDR 31.3 million.  A debt rescheduling of the Paris
Club is expected for 1987.

## Mechanisms for the follow-up and monitoring of the SNPA

442. Benin had drafted an investment plan for the 1983 Round Table Meeting,
many of whose objectives were similar to the SNPA recommendations.  The
country strives for self-sufficiency in food, import substitution and local
production in small- and medium-sized enterprises.  Two meetings have been
announced by UNDP for the course of 1986:  one on civil aviation and one on a
highway to Porga.

4.  BHUTAN

## Economic performance

443. By all available indications, economic performance during the 1980s,
particularly in fiscal years 1983/84 and 1984/85, 151/ has been favourable.
Preliminary results of the 1984 survey of agriculture, a sector which accounts
for 44 per cent of GDP, indicates that the growth of grain production averaged
6 per cent annually during the period 1981-1983.  This high rate of growth was
due to an exceptionally favourable monsoon in 1983 compared to earlier years.
According to the Planning Commission, GDP for 1984 was estimated at
$169 million on the basis of a population of 1.2 million and a per capita GDP
of $140.  It is estimated that real GDP grew by an average annual rate of
6.4 per cent between 1981 and 1984, but this masks a steady decline of these
growth rates, which fell to a mere 2.6 per cent between 1983 and 1984.

444. During the period 1982-1984, Bhutan continued to run overall
balance-of-payments surpluses, with respect to both India and other
countries.  According to official sources, total foreign-exchange reserves
increased from $22 million as of 31 March 1981 to $48 million on

31 March 1985, within which convertible-currency reserves rose from $5 million to $14 million, the remainder being in Indian rupees, the principal intervention currency, with which the ngultrum is freely convertible at parity.

445. India remains the predominant trade partner, taking approximately 95 per cent of Bhutan's exports, and providing almost 90 per cent of its imports. Indian rupee reserves on 31 March 1984 were equivalent to about four months' imports from India, while convertible-currency reserves at that date would cover about one year's imports from abroad. Such reserve-import ratios are high compared to other LDCs. Preliminary estimates for FY 1984/85 show that Bhutan had balance of trade deficits with both India ($45 million) and the rest of the world ($8 million), the latter of which was more than offset by inflows of tourism earnings ($1.8 million) and aid receipts ($10 million). Bhutan has no debt service problem, as borrowings from overseas began only recently and almost all loans are on concessional terms.

446. Agriculture is the dominant sector, contributing over 50 per cent of GDP. Over 90 per cent of the economically-active population is engaged in agriculture, including animal husbandry. Although crop production continues to rely on traditional farming practices, a 6 per cent annual increase in production was achieved during the first half of the Fifth Plan period (1980-1986). Despite these gains, the basic Fifth Plan target of self-sufficiency in the staple cereals (rice and maize) has not been achieved.

447. The manufacturing sector is in its early stages of development: in 1984 it accounted for only about 4 per cent of GDP and less than 3 per cent of the labour force. The industrial/mining sector is essentially composed of a cement factory, fruit processing plants, gypsum mining as well as forestry and agro-based plants.

448. While the domestic market is small, the export market has been of considerable interest. Most important manufacturing enterprises have been sponsored privately and are export-oriented. The Government is currently reassessing its policy of requiring 80 per cent local ownership in important industrial ventures and is considering selling to private investors its shares of successful projects, such as the Penden Cement Plant.

449. As a land-locked country, the transport sector plays a significant role in Bhutan's development. During the early 1980s, the Government emphasized road construction and upgrading of the present road network. Under the current Plan, large-scale projects, such as the East-West and North-South highways and suspension foot-bridges, are being implemented.

450. DrukAir, the national airline established in 1983, continues to operate flights to Calcutta successfully. A second international airport has been approved by the Government, for which preliminary surveys have already begun. In the area of communications, a microwave link-up with the Indian telephone network, a 50-kw shortwave radio station and double-circuit telex facilities have been established with the assistance of the Indian Government, the World Bank and the United States.

451. Bhutan's forests, which cover 50 per cent of its area, constitute the country's most valuable natural resource. The focus of forestry development programmes during the first half of the Fifth Plan period (1980/81-1986/87) was on wood-based industries. Accordingly, increased emphasis is being given to developing the logging infrastructure and reforestation.

452. In the energy sector, the focus of activity is the on-going work on the 336 MW Chukha hydro-electric project, the first phase of which was scheduled to be commissioned by mid-1986. This project has cost the Government Nu 1,367 million ($124.2 million), most of which is financed by India. At full operation, this project will provide a reliable source of power to Western Bhutan and the surplus will be exported to India, providing the country with substantial export earnings.

## Environment and disasters

453. The Government is fully conscious of the need to maintain the country's ecological balance and has identified reforestation as an instrument to preserve the fragile Himalayan environment. To this end, a Department of Forests has been established to protect the logging industry and to assure that the requirements of the existing downstream industries can be met without damaging the country's environment.

## Human resources and development

454. While school enrolment grew by almost 11 per cent in 1983/84 compared to 1982/83, this growth fell to 7 and 5 per cent in the two subsequent years. The strategy for educational development has been to consolidate and improve existing programmes and facilities rather than to rapidly expand the physical infrastructure, as had been the case in the past. Available information shows that the Government has met the targets set for the physical infrastructure in education. The Government's strategy in education reasons that, by virtue of its relatively small population, Bhutan's comparative advantage lies in developing a sophisticated labour force with a high-quality education.

455. Although considerable resources have been devoted to the public health sector, its standards have remained among the lowest in the world. The Government is determined to continue its efforts towards preventive measures, safe water supplies, the extension of the network of basic health units (BHUs) and the increase of the numbers of village health workers. As of 1985, three new hospitals had been built, a total of 22 BHUs established and 11 new dispensaries opened. Health services have suffered generally from a shortage of trained manpower and a difficulty in securing sufficient numbers of nationals qualified to undertake training programmes.

## Development planning and policies

456. Bhutan's development planning experience dates back to 1961, when the country's first Plan was drawn up. The underlying objectives of the Fifth Plan (1980-1986) were to increase the country's economic self-reliance by reducing Bhutan's heavy dependence on external technical and financial assistance in the preparation and implementation of development plans.

457. Preparations for the Sixth Plan (1987/88-1991/92) have already begun and financial issues were being resolved during 1986. To involve local-level participation in the planning process, the Sixth Plan is to be based on further decentralization, from the district level of the current Plan to the block level. These blocks already exist as administrative subdivisions of the districts.

458. At present, it appears that there will be little change in sectoral development strategies as compared to the Fifth Plan. This is due in part to the large number of carry-over projects, but also to the fact that the strategies and pace of development in most sectors are well conceived and suited to Bhutan's needs. However, two issues regarding the institutional structure of Government have arisen: (a) whether the existing institutions are sufficient in size and scope to manage Bhutan's increasingly complex development process; and (b) whether the existing institutional structure is itself conducive to efficient management of development.

459. Apart from the above issues, which are under serious governmental consideration, the rural population has proved responsive to the Government's development initiatives.

## Mobilizaton of domestic resources for development

460. One of the basic constraints in the process of economic and social transformation in Bhutan has been modest ability to mobilize domestic resources for development. During the first Five-Year Plan, the limited internal resources could only meet the needs of the administrative structure. The sources required for the process of development were beyond the capacity of the rural economy, and could therefore be initiated only with external assistance.

461. During the Fifth Plan period, the Government built up budget revenues from Nu 101.7 million ($12.9 million) in 1980/81 to Nu 278.7 million ($23.46 million) in 1984/85, a 82 per cent increase in dollar terms, largely from increased taxes on company profits and trading establishments gross turnover, and rising after-tax public enterprise earnings. At the same time, it held growth of maintenance (recurrent) expenditures to under 10 per cent annually, by vigorously restricting civil service growth and public property maintenance. As a result the Government has been able to meet its maintenance expenditures from current revenues and to build up a modest surplus that can be reallocated for development expenditure purposes (Nu 31 million, or $2.82 million in 1984/85).

## Transfer of external resources, debt and capital requirements

462. From 1980/81 to 1984/85 the share of development expenditures on this GDP almost doubled but most of this was financed by external assistance. India was the largest single donor, accounting for over 68 per cent of total budgetary aid flows. Annual assistance from overseas sources grew almost three times during the 1980s. This has reflected increased assistance from traditional sources, such as the United Nations system, but more importantly, the emergence of new donors, including IDA, the Asian Development Bank and the Kuwait Fund. All in all, Bhutan received a very high per capita level of aid in 1984/85: $37, excluding the Chukha project contribution, and $69 including it.

463. Development expenditures for the Sixth Plan are estimated at
Nu 8,811 million ($801 million), of which $304 million, or 38 per cent, will
be mobilized domestically, and $497 million, or 62 per cent, will be financed
from external contributions.  India will continue providing a major portion
under that country's ECDC/TCDC arrangements.  The recent debt
service-to-export ratio has been about 2 per cent, a very low figure compared
to other LDCs.

## Mechanism for monitoring and follow-up of the SNPA

464. The second Round Table Meeting for Bhutan, held in Geneva in April 1986,
was attended by representatives of 13 countries, as well as several
multilateral financial institutions and international organizations.  During
the discussions, the priorities set by the Government were generally supported
by the donors.  These include:  increased food production and agricultural
productivity;  the need to keep the investment strategy under review;  careful
implementation of the decentralization programme;  monitoring of
environmentally sound agricultural cultivating practices;  expansion of local
revenues;  and diversification of exports.  The need for strengthened aid
co-ordination was stressed, including further donor-Government consultation to
determine the appropriate form of follow-up to the Round Table Meeting.  There
was a positive response to Bhutan's requests for further external assistance
and both traditional and new development partners expressed their willingness
to contribute.

## 5.  BOTSWANA

## Economic performance

465. Botswana had one of the highest growth rates among the LDCs in the 1970s,
GDP increasing by close to 10 per cent annually in real terms.  However, the
decade of the 1980s started inauspiciously with the slump in the world
minerals market and with the onset of drought.  Real output contracted in
several sectors, and the budget and balance-of-payments position deteriorated,
compelling the Government to adopt a number of austerity measures in early
1982 and to devalue the pula.  These measures and the subsequent improvement
in the diamond market restored overall balance in the economy and real GDP
growth resumed.  Drought conditions, however, persisted into 1986.

466. Apart from the drought, the following major factors have affected
Botswana's economy since it overcame the recession at the beginning of the
decade:  a substantial increase in mining output, following the beginning of
operation of the new Jwaneng diamond mine in 1982;  diamond-led export
growth;  and changes in the external value of the pula boosting government
revenue and export proceeds in local currency terms.  After a decline in
1981/82, the volume of mining output in 1983/84 was more than double the
1980/81 level.  With diamond output reaching capacity, expansion in the mining
sector is now levelling out.  In 1984/85, growth in this sector is believed to
have been relatively modest.  Since mining accounts for around 30 per cent of
GDP, the rate of increase in total GDP in real terms slowed down considerably
in 1984/85.

467. Except for 1981, Botswana's overall balance of payments has shown a
surplus in the current decade. In 1983, the trade balance (adjusted to
exclude customs duty for imports) and the current account moved into surplus
as well. Estimates for 1985 indicate a further strengthening of the
balance-of-payments through substantially increased export proceeds from
diamonds, copper-nickel and beef. Government continues to follow a flexible
exchange rate policy. In August 1985, with inflation accelerating in the
subregion, a small revaluation of the pula (3 per cent) was implemented to
lessen inflationary pressure. 152/

468. Thanks to the favourable recent balance of payments and budgetary trends,
Botswana set out on its Sixth National Development Plan period from a
relatively comfortable position: foreign exchange reserves at end-1985
amounting to an import cover of 17 months, a substantial budget surplus
expected for 1986/87 (as in the two previous fiscal years) and a low debt
service ratio. Longer-term uncertainties, however, weigh on the country's
future and Botswana faces many difficult challenges in the current plan
period. Among them are diversification of the economy, employment generation
for a rapidly growing labour force, providing social and other public services
for a growing population, rural development, drought recovery and improved
food security. Botswana will have to cope with these challenges in a
situation which is expected to be very different from the rapid expansion
which the mining sector experienced during the early 1980s.

469. The factors which increased external and government revenue in 1984 and
1985 were largely exceptional in character. Thus, the very high diamond
revenues in the latter year were to a large extent due to the strength of
the United States dollar relative to the pula. The early 1980s have amply
demonstrated Botswana's vulnerability to external factors. The Government
continues to pursue a countercyclical policy, aiming to build up cash balances
and foreign exchange reserves during good years to allow a rundown when
needed, such as in 1981/82.

## Disasters

470. Botswana faced its fifth consecutive year of drought in 1986. Food
output was again expected to be far below requirements, resulting in
exceptionally high cereal import and food assistance needs for 1986/87. The
livestock situation also remained critical. The Government has appealed for
further assistance to its drought relief programme. So far supplementary
feeding programmes have been successful in staving off famine and the spread
of malnutrition.

## Human resources and social development

471. The number of Batswana employed in the formal sector rose from 65,500 in
1978 to just over 100,000 in 1983, from 15 to 19 per cent of the citizen
working age population. Employment projections for the Sixth Plan indicate
that domestic employment and self-employment opportunities may rise by 11,500
a year, while the labour force will increase by 21,000 a year. In addition,
decreasing employment opportunities abroad may add another 2,000 persons to
the work force annually. Increasing numbers of Batswana of working age will
have to depend on traditional agriculture for their living, or face
underemployment or unemployment - one of the central concerns underlying

current economic and development policy. A manpower planning exercise is carried out annually. Current efforts in the field of rural development centre on the provision of rural services, a strategy for development in communally owned areas, and strengthening of local institutions.

Development planning and policies

472. Botswana's Sixth National Development Plan, adopted in 1985, covers the fiscal years 1985/86 to 1990/91. Overall planning objectives have been retained from the previous Plan, including the two main themes: employment creation and rural development. The Sixth Plan reflects the change in the budgetary situation expected to mark the latter half of the 1980s. In the past, mineral development brought rapid and large returns. There is now no major new mineral development project in the pipe-line and government financial constraints are expected to grow tighter. The expected reduction in the rate of growth of government revenue will diminish the scope for offering increased government services. Consequently, the strategy for the Sixth Plan will lay more emphasis on encouraging the private and parastatal sectors - parastatals are financially autonomous - to generate growth and employment opportunities. The Plan stresses that most Batswana live in the rural areas and the particular need to expand rural work opportunities and increase the share of resources available to these areas. Increased attention is directed to food and agriculture, national water supply and water development, housing, and environmental concerns. In its general orientation and specific features, the Plan takes up many of the concerns brought out in the SNPA.

473. During the Sixth Plan, the general growth rate in the economy is expected to slow down considerably and provide for much less rapid increases in per capita income than hitherto. During the previous Plan period (1979/80 to 1984/85), total GDP is estimated to have increased on average some 10 per cent annually in real terms, with the mining sector expanding at a rate of 20 to 25 per cent. During the second half of the decade, mining is expected to grow at an annual rate of only 3.5 per cent and total GDP at a rate of 4.8 per cent in real terms (as compared with an estimated population growth rate of 3.3 per cent). Hopes for expansion are pinned on the manufacturing sector inter alia. The overall balance of payments is expected to show a declining surplus throughout the plan period, and the current account is expected to be in deficit. Projections build on a number of critical assumptions. One of them is that the drought would not continue. It is further assumed that world diamond prices keep pace with international inflation and that world demand expands so that by 1987 Botswana can sell all its current diamond output. The availability of foreign aid is another key variable. If developments should be less favorable than assumed in any of these three areas, revenue projections and the GDP growth rate would be significantly affected.

474. The Sixth Plan's budgetary targets are to restrain recurrent expenditure growth to 6.8 per cent per annum in real terms and development expenditure growth to 2 per cent (as compared to growth rates of over 11 per cent and close to 7 per cent respectively in the preceding plan period). Local skilled manpower will remain scarce, and the concern is not to pre-empt these skills to the detriment of the private and parastatal sectors. Therefore manpower considerations as well as recurrent cost considerations have influenced the budgetary targets. An annual ceiling has been set for projects involving long-term recurrent cost commitments. In addition, some drought-related

projects have been included in the development programme for the early years
of the Plan period and provision made for a greater share of projects without
significant long-term recurrent cost implications.

475. In the areas of employment and rural development, the Financial
Assistance Policy (FAP) and the Arable Lands Development Programme (ALDEP),
aimed at small-scale dryland farmers, are major programmes which will be
continued under the Sixth Plan.  The drought has brought a new emphasis on
agricultural rehabilitation needs and measures to encourage local food
production.  A comprehensive National Food Strategy was finalized in 1985 and
a white paper on the subject subsequently discussed in the National Assembly.
The strategy set out key areas for activity during the Sixth Plan, including a
strategy for arable agriculture, development of irrigated agriculture,
nutritional improvement, drought relief and contingency planning, a
post-drought recovery programme and maintenance of a strategic grain reserve
for national food security.  A new accelerated rainfed arable programme was
introduced in 1985 and livestock development projects are also underway.

476. Major infrastructural development projects in transport,
telecommunications, power and water are being pursued, some of them due for
completion in the early part of the Plan period.  Preparations have started
for drawing up a comprehensive national Water Master Plan.  A pilot plant has
proved the technical feasibility of exploiting the Sua Pan soda-ash deposits.
Investment partners are now being sought for the further development of this
resource.

477. As concerns the mobilization of domestic resources for development,
general economic policies are geared to encourage savings and investment, and
there are specific institutions and incentives in this area as well.  The FAP
scheme is a major vehicle for promoting industrial development through
financial and fiscal incentives for new income and employment-generating
activities.  New initiatives have been taken to further encourage Batswana
entrepreneurship and develop the financial sector.  The Ministry of Commerce
and Industry has been reorganized to enable it to service the private sector
more effectively, and in this connection the role of the Botswana Enterprise
Development Unit (BEDU) is being refocused towards providing training and
other services for small-scale enterprises.  The Botswana Development
Corporation has launched an investment trust to encourage share ownership by
Batswana.  Further measures to develop the financial sector are under
consideration, including instituting a general mortgage guarantee scheme.  In
view of the need to broaden the tax base, a review of the tax system is being
undertaken.

Transfer of resources, capital requirements, debt

478. External capital, both aid and private capital, has played an important
role in Botswana's development.  The net inflow of concessional aid reached a
peak of $107 million in 1980, whereafter it contracted in the following year
and then stabilized in nominal terms at a level of $101-103 million in
1982-1984.  At the same time, the net inflow of official capital on
non-concessional terms has expanded rapidly, increasing from $4 million in
1980 to $63 million in 1984.

479. Grants and loans under multilateral and bilateral aid programmes are expected to continue to finance a large part of development activities under the Sixth Plan. Total development expenditure foreseen during the six-year Plan period, excluding parastatal borrowing channelled through the government budget, amounts to pula 1,297 million (in 1985/86 prices) equivalent to about $680 million (at the average 1985 exchange rate). Plan projections assume an inflow of development grants as well as direct government borrowing remaining constant in real terms. Total external borrowing requirements are expected to increase well above historical levels, mainly on account of large parastatal investment programmes partly in progress. Government and parastatal debt service combined is expected to rise from some 5 per cent of merchandise export earnings in 1985/86 to some 10 per cent by the end of the plan period. A debt monitoring system is being instituted.

Mechanisms for monitoring and follow-up of the SNPA

480. Monitoring and follow-up of the SNPA in Botswana is the responsibility of the Ministry of Finance and Development Planning. Follow-up with donors is undertaken through bilateral contacts within the existing framework for consultations. It may be noted that Botswana provides an example of co-ordinated efforts in mounting emergency programmes very much in line with the recommendations concerning disaster relief which emerged from the mid-term global review of the SNPA, held in October 1985. Since the onset of the drought, the Government's Inter-Ministerial Drought Committee has mapped out comprehensive action programmes for drought relief. An Early Warning Technical Committee monitors rainfall and agricultural conditions as well as nutritional status and food supplies. A United Nations Inter-Agency Drought Committee was formed in early 1984 to develop co-ordinated support for the Government's relief and recovery efforts and has provided, inter alia, inputs to strengthen the Government's food distribution network.

6. BURKINA FASO

Economic performance

481. Real per capita GDP declined by 2.4, 7.0 and 6.1 per cent in 1982, 1983 and 1984 respectively, falling to $209 in the last year.

482. Exports consist mainly of cotton and sheabutter (65 and 15 per cent respectively in 1984). Livestock was the third main export item in 1984, but its recorded share in total exports fluctuates widely along a generally downward trend, but this leaves out of account significant unrecorded exports of this commodity. Export earnings fell from $57 million in 1983 and $60 million in 1984 to a mere $40 million in 1985, mostly as a result of a sharp decline in the international prices for cotton and of border barriers to livestock trade with certain neighbouring markets. Migrant labour (particularly to Côte d'Ivoire and Ghana) is a major source of foreign exchange. The trade deficit had shrunk in 1983 and 1984 due principally to lower imports, but was estimated to have grown again in 1985 ($280 million as compared to $210 million in 1984). The rate of coverage of imports (exports as percentage of imports) is around 20 per cent on the basis of customs data; but rises to 33-45 per cent on balance-of-payments information, reflecting the importance of unrecorded exports to neighbouring countries.

483. Per capita food production decreased at an average annual rate of
2 per cent during the period 1980-1984 as a consequence of the drought, soil
erosion and lack of agricultural inputs.   Cereal import requirements were
estimated at 300,000 mt during the crop year November 1984/October 1985, as
compared to domestic production of 1.12 million mt.   However, with the return
of rains and higher producer prices, the 1985/86 crop year was the best in
10 years, with total food production rising to an estimated 1.59 million mt.
As a result, cereal import requirements fell to 103,000 mt., most of which was
to be imported commercially.   In 1986, the Government appealed for special
external financial assistance for the purchase of local surpluses of grain in
the South and their distribution in the deficit areas, where there is a
shortfall of about 40,000 mt.   By mid-1986, donor assistance had been provided
for the purchase of some 37,000 mt.   The livestock situation has also
improved as a result of more favourable weather and of livestock vaccination
campaigns.

484. Deposits of a number of minerals, such as diamonds, nickel, copper, zinc
and silver, have been discovered, but their quantity and quality have not yet
been accurately assessed.   The country's development prospects could be
greatly enhanced by the exploitation of the gold deposits located in the Poura
region and the manganese deposits in Tambao.   The exploitation of the Poura
gold deposits stopped in 1966, but was resumed in 1984.   Gold production is
expected to amount to around 20 mt. over the next eleven years and to yield
$22 million per year at the average gold prices prevailing in 1985.   Other
gold deposits are known to exist.   The exploitation of the Tambao manganese
deposits (120 million mt.) is to start after completion of the 320-km railway
to Abidjan (Côte d'Ivoire).

485. The contribution of the manufacturing sector to GDP at current prices has
fluctuated between 11 and 15 per cent during the period 1975-1984.
Manufacturing is still largely limited to the processing of a few agricultural
goods (e.g. cotton, sugar).   A plastics company was established with both
public and private capital in early 1986.

486. An annual inflation rate averaging 16 per cent (as measured by the
consumer price index) from 1976 to 1980 led to a policy of public spending
cuts and promotion of farm production, which succeeded in reducing the
inflation rate to less than 8 per cent per year during the period 1980-1985.

Environment and disasters

487. The drought adversely affected the domestic economy with particular
strength during the early 1980s.   Improvement in rainfall has been observed
since late 1984 but has been accompanied by heavy floods which inter alia
devastated the northern town of Gorm-Gorm.   An infestation of grasshoppers and
borers affected 25,000 hectares of crops in 1985.   The danger of grasshopper
damage facing the main season cereal crop (planted from May 1986 onwards) was
effectively mitigated by governmental control programmes.   The water table is
still below normal in many areas and a lack of vegetation cover has increased
soil erosion.  The cutting, transport and consumption of wood are being
strictly controlled, and local tree planting is promoted by the Government so
as to avoid environmental degradation.

488. To counter the effects of the drought, the Government has decided to promote dry season market gardening. It is also undertaking agricultural and livestock recovery schemes to counteract population migration from deficit to surplus areas.

489. Major projects in the field of water-resource development are being implemented. These include the construction of major dams at Grand Bagré (involving a power capacity of 7.5 MW and irrigation of 5,000 ha), Douna, Kompienga and Souru. This last project by itself is expected to lead to the production of 290,000 mt. of cereals per year and to facilitate animal husbandry and fish farming.

## Human resources and social development

490. The nation-wide hospital capacity is about one bed per 1,600 persons with one doctor for every 10,000 persons. The Government views the health situation as an emergency and, in October 1985, decided to launch a "crash programme" to provide health facilities in villages. A programme of child immunization involving an estimated 2.5 million children was recently implemented with success. The Government has set itself the objective of ensuring a total supply of 10 litres of water per day per inhabitant. In addition to the above-mentioned major water-resource development projects, policies in this regard include the construction of small earth dams and the drilling of wells, of which 217 were actually dug in 1985.

491. According to official estimations, the literacy rate has been raised from 16 per cent in 1983 to 22 per cent in early 1986. A reform of the educational programme is being drafted in line with the priority status accorded to it by the National Development Plan for 1986-1990.

## Development planning and policies

492. The National Development Plan for 1982-1986 was reinforced by a far-reaching Programme populaire de développement (People's Development Programme) covering the period October 1984-December 1985, involving total investments of CFAF 160.7 billion (about $360 million), of which 23 per cent were earmarked for rural development. The National Development Plan for 1986-1990, which was launched in August 1986, involves a high degree of decentralization and the effective participation of the broad masses at all stages of implementation.

493. Agricultural development figures prominently among the country's key priorities. Producer prices for agricultural goods have been raised with a view to improving farmers' income and encouraging production. Support has been given to producers of counter-season crops (tomatoes, onions, cabbage, salads).

494. In February 1985, work began on the construction of a 345-km railway, which will connect the capital (Ouagadougou) with Tambao, where deposits of manganese and limestone are located. Dam construction is another national priority.

495. A project was approved in early 1986 by Côte d'Ivoire and Burkina Faso for the construction of a 225-km power line linking the two countries, whereby the former would supply electricity to South-Western Burkina. The project is due to be completed in 1989, subject to international support.

Mobilization of domestic resources for development

496. During the period 1980-1984, consumption remained regularly higher than GDP. The negative savings rate was around 10 to 11 per cent in 1980-1982 and reached a peak of 15 per cent in 1983. The investment rate declined steadily from 26 per cent of GDP in 1975 to 12 per cent in 1983, but rose slightly to 14 per cent in 1984. In view of the negative savings rate, the level of investments is a function of aid disbursements and debt accumulation.

497. Participation of the local population in rural development has been promoted. Many co-operative groups have been created and their work is co-ordinated by the Union des Coopératives Burkinabé des Agriculteurs Maraîchers (UCOBAM). The construction of the above-mentioned railway relies to a large extent on volunteer labour.

498. A new investment code enacted in August 1984 takes the following elements into account in considering requests for approval of investments (art. 15): compatibility with the national development plan, degree of integration in the national economy through balance-of-payments and linkage effects, establishment of the headquarters in the national territory, participation of the public sector, utilization and degree of processing of local raw materials and employment creation. Foreign investment in vital or priority sectors may not exceed 49 per cent of total equity.

Transfer of external resources, debt, capital requirements

499. Concessional assistance declined steadily from $219 million in both 1980 and 1981 to $177.4 million in 1984. Compensatory financing for export earnings shortfalls granted under the EEC's STABEX scheme amounted to ECU 8.3 million during the period 1975-1983.

500. External disbursed debt rose from $391 million in 1983 to $454 million in 1984. The ratio of debt service to (customs-recorded) merchandise exports has fluctuated around 45 per cent since 1982 (48 per cent in 1984). Until early 1985, the debt burden had been aggravated by the appreciation of the United States dollar, inasmuch as 40 per cent of total debt service is denominated in this currency. The more recent depreciation of the dollar *vis-à-vis* the CFA franc should thus provide some relief in this regard.

Mechanisms for monitoring and follow-up of the SNPA

501. The country's review meeting with donors was tentatively planned for late 1986, with an in-country review scheduled for 1987. A number of sectoral meetings have already been held with donors interested in financing specific projects of national interest.

7. BURUNDI

## Economic performance

502. Burundi's economy, heavily dependent on coffee earnings, entered a difficult period in the beginning of the 1980s. Terms of trade deteriorated sharply between 1979 and 1981, the Government's revenue base weakened, and large deficits built up in the budget and the balance of payments, leading to a running down of reserves and a mounting public debt burden. The Government attempted to redress the situation notably by cutting back imports and government spending. The Burundi franc was devalued by 22.3 per cent in November 1983, at which time its peg was switched from the United States dollar to the SDR. Some improvement in the balance of payments was observed after 1984, as coffee revenues increased, but the overall economic situation remained precarious.

503. The Government consequently launched a comprehensive new economic adjustment programme in 1986, as a sequel of which the currency was devalued again by 15 per cent in July 1986. This three-year programme aims to diversify the economy and restore financial equilibrium. It sets out a wide range of measures in various areas, such as public expenditure, public enterprises, agriculture, trade and industry, and credit allocation. The first phase of the programme, covering the years 1986-1987, will be supported by credits worth $31.2 million from the World Bank and its Special Facility for Sub-Saharan Africa for import financing, by special joint financing of close to $19 million from bilateral donors and by IMF assistance for related stabilization measures. The latter are composed of (a) a stand-by arrangement for SDR 21 million concluded with the Fund in August 1986; and (b) a simultaneous loan of SDR 20 million (of which SDR 8.54 million was drawn immediately) under the Fund's new Structural Assistance Facility, making Burundi the first country to draw on the resources of this facility.

504. The year 1981 was a good agricultural year, with a bumper coffee crop. Real GDP contracted in 1982, recovered slightly in 1983 mainly due to an expanded output of export crops, and contracted again in 1984. Overall, the three-year period 1982-1984 was characterized by stagnation and setbacks in subsistence agriculture and a falling per capita income level.

505. In 1984, agriculture suffered from drought conditions and there was a major fall in the output of both food and export crops. These developments were not compensated by the relatively good performance in several branches in the secondary and tertiary sectors. Inflation accelerated, partly due to the rise in food prices following the drought. Prospects for the 1985/86 coffee harvest were promising, however, and a recovery in real GDP with a growth rate of around 5 per cent was forecast for 1985. Coffee alone accounts for over 80 per cent of Burundi's exports.

506. The external position stabilized somewhat in 1983 and 1984. Coffee export prices and terms of trade partly recovered from their 1981/82 lows but, more importantly, coffee and tea export volumes expanded vigorously in both 1984 and 1985 while the dollar value of imports, which had jumped by almost one third in 1982, were stabilized at a lower though rising level in the

subsequent three years.  As a result, the trade deficit, which had risen to
$126 million in 1982, was brought back to its 1981 level of less than
$90 million both in 1984 and 1985.  However, rising interest payments on
external debt and a fall in grant aid caused foreign exchange reserves to
remain at the low level to which they had fallen in 1982.

507. On the budgetary side, the Government has attempted to improve tax
collection, raised tax rates and introduced new taxes.  At the same time,
attempts have been made to check growth in public expenditure, with
re-inforced austerity measures applied to the current budget since 1984 and
development spending restrained over the years 1982-1986.  The ordinary
(current) budget was brought back into balance in 1984, but the overall
Treasury deficit remained high, due in part to a shortfall in revenues
earmarked for the development budget.  Past accumulations of domestic payments
arrears and rising debt service continued to weigh on the budget.  Under the
1984 STABEX régime, Burundi was accorded compensation for a shortfall in
cotton exports in 1980-1983, which amount was allocated to the 1986
development budget.

## Disasters

508. Late and below-normal rains throughout the country in 1984 led to a
shortfall in crop production, exceptional food shortages and a need for
emergency food shipments to Burundi.  Following abundant rainfall in 1985, the
overall agricultural and food supply situation returned to normal.  However,
requirements for agricultural rehabilitation support remained.

## Human resources and social development

509. On-going programmes in this field aim, _inter alia_, at providing primary
schooling to all school-age children by 1987/88, establishing a comprehensive
health care system throughout the country, immunization of infants,
establishing an integrated programme for maternal and child health care
including population education, and promoting the integration of women in
national development.  Habitat in Burundi is scattered over the countryside,
and establishing villages is seen as an important means to provide better
social and other services to the rural population.

## Development planning and policies

510. Burundi's Fourth Five-Year Economic and Social Development Plan spans the
years 1983 to 1987.  The Plan proposed an investment programme of
FBu 107 billion (about $1,200 million) at 1981 prices.  During the Third Plan,
investment amounted to FBu 64 billion, less than half of the planned amount.
During the first two years of the Fourth Plan period, the estimated rate of
implementation of the planned investment programme was around 75 per cent. One
of the aims under the Fourth Plan is to invest more in the directly productive
sectors (agriculture, industry, mining and energy) as against the economic and
social infrastructure, which had previously been emphasized.  The share of the
directly productive sectors in public investment expenditure was reported to
have been raised to 45 per cent by 1984 as compared to less than 40 per cent
during the previous Plan period (1977-1982).  In the context of the new
economic adjustment programme, a revised public investment programme setting
out priority investment needs was prepared for the years 1986-1988.

511. Increasing agricultural output to ensure food self-sufficiency remains a priority aim in Burundi. Programmes and projects pursued to this end included extending the use of selected seeds and fertilizer, improving farming techniques and promoting agriculture at higher altitudes. In the area of cash crops, tea and cotton development programmes were underway. A number of regional development associations (Sociétés Régionales de Développement), set up under the aegis of the Ministry of Agriculture, have provided a framework for these efforts, as well as for various rural development programmes, emphasizing in particular housing, water supply and rural electrification. In other sectors, several mineral exploration and energy development projects were pursued and in the area of infrastructural development, road improvement and telecommunications development programmes continued.

Transfer of external resources, capital requirements, debt

512. The net inflow of concessional aid to Burundi showed a steadily increasing trend up to 1980. Net disbursements fell slightly in 1981, to $122 million, but increased to $151 million in 1983. In 1984 disbursements from several major donors stagnated or even declined, and the total net aid inflow fell to $137 million.

513. Total external financing requirements for the Fourth Plan (1983-1987) were estimated at FBu 84 billion, corresponding to an annual average of around $185 million. From 1981 to 1983, Burundi had increasing recourse to financing on non-concessional terms, both from official and private sources, to complement the aid inflow. Non-concessional financing amounted to an annual average of $33 million in 1982 and 1983, but in 1984, this inflow fell back to the 1981 level of $15 million. As loans have assumed an increased share in total external financing, including an important component of non-concessional borrowing, external debt obligations have built up. External debt service in 1984 pre-empted over 10 per cent of current budget receipts and 15 per cent of export earnings compared to 5 per cent and 7 per cent respectively in 1982.

Mechanisms for monitoring and follow-up of the SNPA

514. The Fourth Plan and associated financing requirements were presented to the Round Table meeting held in Bujumbura in February 1984. Sectoral consultations with donors on rural development were planned for mid-1987, and similar follow-up action for energy and education was also under consideration. The Planning Ministry, which is attached to the President's Office, is in charge of monitoring and follow-up of the SNPA.

8. CAPE VERDE

Economic performance

515. Gross domestic product in real terms is estimated to have increased every year during the period 1980-1984. The leading sectors have been construction - which includes public investment projects financed by foreign aid - and services, in particular those provided at Sal International Airport. However, gross national product has declined over the same period. This is due essentially to the slowing down of the remittances of Cape Verdians living abroad. These remittances represent an inflow of foreign exchange of the order of 10 times the value of domestic merchandise exports and are of critical importance to the economy of Cape Verde.

516. Agriculture accounts for less than 20 per cent of GDP. Its development
is constrained by the nature of the soil, which is mainly steep and rocky.
Of the basic food consumed by the population - maize, beans, rice and
wheat - only the first two are grown locally. Prolonged drought and erratic
rainfall have been responsible for the very poor food production of the 1980s
reflected in the table below.

### Production of basic foodstuffs, 1980-1985
(thousands of metric tons)

|        | 1980 | 1981 | 1982 | 1983 | 1984 | 1985 |
|--------|------|------|------|------|------|------|
| Maize  | 7.0  | 3.0  | 4.4  | 2.7  | 2.5  | 1.3  |
| Beans  | 4.0  | 0.5  | 3.0  | 2.2  | 5.4  | 2.2  |

Source: Ministry of Rural Development.

517. Even under normal weather conditions, domestic production covers only a
very small fraction of the food requirements. Thus, for the marketing year
1985/86 it is estimated that cereal imports (including food aid) amounting to
76,000 tons are needed compared to estimated consumption of 80,600 tons of the
four basic foodstuffs mentioned above. Owing to a shortage of fodder the
livestock population has decreased from 156,000 in 1981 to 129,000 in 1984.
In spite of the investments made in fishing, including mechanization of
traditional craft and the installation of cold-storage space, fish production
appears to be declining, particularly in the small-scale sector. Thus, it is
reported that as a result of maintenance problems, the number of small
mechanized fishing vessels has declined from 455 in 1983 to 388 in 1984.

518. Industry accounts for less than 5 per cent of GDP. A major project
completed in 1983 has been the construction of the CABNAVE Shipyard in
Mindelo, at a cost of some $40 million, in association with Dutch and
Portuguese partners. This facility can handle ships of up to 110 metres in
length, corresponding to about 7,000 dwt. However, this shipyard has been so
far severely under-utilized, partly due to the unforeseen dispersal of the
world fishing fleet from the Cape Verde region.

519. Domestic visible exports, mostly fisheries products, bananas and salt,
continue to be very low; in 1984, they covered less than 4 per cent of
imports. Re-exports, consisting of bunkering and stores to carriers at
Mindelo for ships and at Sal for aircraft are more significant. The
completion of the airport improvement at Sal in 1983 had led to increased
revenue from this source until 1986 (see para. 529 below).

## Environment and disasters

520. Cape Verde is one of the countries covered by the United Nations Office
for Emergency Operations in Africa. Since 1968, the country has been more or
less continuously affected by severe droughts. This has seriously disrupted
agricultural and livestock production, and many underground water sources have
either dried up or become saline. Some of this environmental damage is
believed to be irreversible. In both 1984 and 1985, rains came in the form of
severe storms which themselves caused direct damage to hydraulic
infrastructure, crops and terraced land through flooding.

## Human resources and social development

521. A major problem is the difficulty encountered in giving the population access to water. The cumulative effect of years of drought is creating serious water problems, and on certain islands the situation is at times critical. In spite of the on-going programme to increase the water supply, including the expensive process of desalinating sea water, which exists in Sao Vicente and Sal, and is being installed in Boa Vista, the situation appears to have worsened. It was estimated that only 20 per cent of the archipelago's population had access to running water in 1985, as compared to 27 per cent in 1982, while even in these cases strict rationing was in force. Malnutrition, although a lesser problem, is believed also to have been aggravated by the drought.

522. In education, 80 per cent of the 7-12 age group were receiving primary education in 1982, but the main emphasis is to attempt to improve the quality of education at the primary level and to develop technical education. The Government has reported that the lack of funding has seriously affected progress in this sector.

523. Unemployment is a major problem. In 1985, out of an active population of 107,000, only 32,000 were in permanent employment, with 48,000 in non-permanent employment, including those working on development projects financed by sales of food aid, and 27,000 unemployed. The extent of underemployment is also reflected by the fact that at least 340,000 Cape Verdians - more than the resident population - live and work abroad.

## Development planning and policies

524. The First National Development Plan covered the period 1982-1985. Inasmuch as food self-sufficiency was and is not a realistic prospect, the strategy proposed by the Plan was to arrest environmental degradation, and to develop industry, including fishing, as well as to promote activities designed to take advantage of the geo-economic position of the country. The Plan envisaged expenditures of CV Esc.22.1 billion at 1982 prices ($379 million), but, as a result of annual reviews, this was revised downwards to CV Esc.19.6 billion ($336 million). Implementation has been somewhat below expectations, given that actual expenditures for the period 1982-1984 are estimated at CV Esc.11.3 billion, compared to the revised estimates of CV Esc.14.3 billion. This is partly due to lack of funding as well as to Government caution in contracting external loans. A new Plan for 1986-1990 was issued late in 1986. This Plan provides for major reforms in public administration and education, as well as agrarian reform, so as to make the whole country more development-oriented.

## Mobilization of domestic resources for development

525. Although the narrowness of the resource base does not allow for budgetary savings, several efforts to mobilize domestic resources are worth highlighting. One is the positive contribution of public enterprises (other than water desalination, which is subsidized) to the national budget. Another

aspect is the mobilization of the unemployed to work in public works and infrastructure projects. Finally, the remuneration of savings has been increased: in January 1985, the interest rate on time deposits of more than a year was increased from 6.5 per cent to 10 per cent for residents and to 12 per cent for emigrants depositing in local currency.

## Transfer of external resources and debt

526. External aid disbursements (including food aid, capital aid and technical assistance) during the 1980s have been maintained at a per capita level more than eight times the average for all LDCs. Their magnitude has been of the order of 60 per cent of GDP.

527. The provision of food aid, both on an emergency basis and under long-term agreements (with France, Switzerland, the United States and the European Economic Community), combined with improved storage and distribution facilities has meant that the disastrous famines, which have occurred on several occasions in the country's history, have been avoided. This type of aid is also of particular importance, since proceeds from its sale have been used to finance labour-intensive development projects.

528. External public debt has increased from about $20 million in 1980 to more than $82 million at the end of 1984, which is almost equivalent to GDP. Debt servicing has correspondingly increased from 0.3 per cent of the combined proceeds from the exports of goods, services and remittances in 1980 to over 8 per cent in 1984. However, given the Government's caution in contracting new loans or drawing on agreed lines of credit, it is projected that this ratio will not increase in the future.

## Mechanism for monitoring and follow-up of the SNPA

529. Cape Verde was one of the first countries to organize a Round Table Meeting with its development partners after the 1981 Paris Conference. This took place in June 1982 in Praia, with UNDP acting as the lead agency. The Secretariat of State for Co-operation and Planning is the focal point responsible for continuing contacts with foreign-aid agencies. During the First Plan planning units were established and subsequently strengthened in the main ministries responsible for administrating aid projects. The next Round Table Conference occurred in October 1986 in Geneva, followed by an in-country review in Praia in December 1986. The donor community was generally supportive of the Government's policies, but only few were able to accede to Cape Verde's appeal for multi-annual commitments to match the country's medium-term policy and planning requirements. The urgent need to compensate for losses expected from the declining revenues of the country's International Airport were recognized.

9. CENTRAL AFRICAN REPUBLIC (CAR)

Economic performance

530. The economic and financial policy measures taken by the Government since assuming power in 1981 began to bear fruit in 1984, when a positive growth rate of 8.7 per cent (equivalent to 6.1 per cent on a per capita basis) first reversed the declining trend that had characterized the CAR's economy since the mid-1970s. Real GDP growth in that year was due in particular to increases in agricultural production, which included higher exports of cash crops as well as production increases in the sectors of forestry, mining and manufacturing. Although the growth rate in 1985 slowed down considerably (to 2.7 per cent), it was still above the average registered during the 1970s. In 1986 the growth rate of the previous year was expected to be maintained.

531. Accounting for 31 per cent of GDP, agriculture remains the mainstay of the economy, with food crops amounting to almost 40 per cent of value added in that sector. Over the past decade and up to the 1983/84 season, food production had stagnated or slightly declined, while the population had increased by 31 per cent. Between 1982/83 and 1983/84, for example, the production of cassava and paddy rice fell by 17.5 per cent and 6.6 per cent respectively, while production decreases also occurred in other foodstuffs. Large quantities of food aid had to be supplied after the 1983 drought. The unsatisfactory record of food production was due not only to climate, but also to the fact that mandatory official producer prices had been kept below free market prices. The new policy of treating official prices merely as indicative floor prices is expected to have a stimulating effect on production.

532. Although the CAR's major cash crops - coffee, cotton and tobacco - constitute only about 3 per cent of GDP and 5 to 6 per cent of agricultural value added, they account for about 40 per cent of merchandise export earnings, with coffee alone accounting for about 25 per cent. In the 1984/85 season, 153/ coffee output rose by 18 per cent to 14,601 tons as against 12,378 tons for the previous crop year. Coffee earnings for 1985 are estimated at $50 million as against $29.7 million in 1984. Cotton, while contributing only about 3 per cent to value-added in agriculture and 1 per cent to GDP, accounted for 12 to 13 per cent of exports in 1983 and 1984. In 1982, the Government introduced comprehensive reforms and raised official producer prices in the subsequent two crop years, as a result of which the cotton harvest grew to 34,400 tons and 46,300 tons in crop years 1983/84 and 1984/85 respectively. As a result, cotton export earnings were likely to rise to about CFA francs 11 billion ($24.5 million) both in 1985 and 1986, inasmuch as the increase in the export volume was expected to outweigh the effects of depressed world cotton prices.

533. The CAR has rich forestry reserves covering 3.4 million hectares, or 5.5 per cent of the country's surface, of which about 2.7 million hectares are exploitable. Timber exports, mostly sapele, contributed more than one fifth to the CAR's foreign-exchange receipts during the 1980s. However, production and exports have been marked by fluctuations, mainly as a result of inadequate domestic transport facilities and unreliable export routes. Both production and exports reached a low in 1983, but are thought to have recovered in 1984. As a consequence of the high transportation costs, the share of

timber processed domestically has risen from 67 per cent in 1981 to
74 per cent in 1984.   With world demand for tropical timber expected to grow,
long-term prospects of the sector seem promising, provided that transportation
bottlenecks are overcome and forestry administration is strengthened.

534. Mining resources comprise diamonds, gold, iron, uranium and petroleum.
Diamonds compete with coffee as the CAR's most important source of export
receipts, contributing between one quarter and one third of merchandise
exports during the 1980s.   In recent years, official receipts have stagnated,
however, owing to illegal exports trying to evade the high export taxes.   In
order to revive diamond production and raise budgetary revenues from mining,
the Government has started revising legislation on mining operations,
marketing, taxation, control and security, and has successively reduced the
diamond export tax from 20 to 14 per cent in 1984 and to 12 per cent
in 1985.   As a result, the local-currency value of official diamond
production increased by 33 per cent in 1984, about half of which was due to a
rise in volume, while the other half was attributable to the 15 per cent
appreciation of the CFA franc to the United States dollar.   Diamond exports
earned around $27 million per year in 1984 and 1985, accounting for
approximately one quarter of total export receipts.   In order to attract the
interest of prospective investors, the Government has started to reorganize
its system of collecting, compiling and disseminating information on the
diamond sector.

535. The role of manufacturing in the economy is both small and lacking in
dynamism:  in 1984 this sector contributed only 8 per cent to GDP and recorded
a growth rate of 1.4 per cent as against the previous year.   Most large
enterprises are in public hands, and many have been operating at a loss.   The
Government is undertaking a restructuring programme, in the process of which
it is re-privatizing, fully or partly, the enterprises whose activities could
be performed by private entrepreneurs, liquidating non-viable enterprises and
eliminating subsidies to those enterprises which are judged viable.   In the
future, Government intervention will be confined to strategic enterprises,
such as the post and telecommunications services, mining, energy and water
resources, to large industrial and agricultural projects and to areas where
private initiative is not forthcoming.   A rehabilitation programme comprising
debt consolidation, an improvement of the enterprises' liquidity situation and
the provision of working and investment capital has been devised for the
enterprises which are to remain in the public sector.

536. While the CAR's trade balance was positive throughout most of the 1970s,
as imports were kept below the slowly-increasing export earnings, consistent
deficits have been recorded since the late 1970s.   At $22.9 million, the
deficit in 1983 showed a marked improvement against 1982, when it had amounted
to $38.2 million, and in 1984 it rose only slightly to $25.4 million despite
the impact of the drought on export earnings.   With reduced import costs
thanks to the fall in oil prices and higher foreign-exchange earnings from
coffee, the trade deficit is expected to have narrowed in 1985.   The current
account deficit also improved substantially in 1983 and 1984 as against 1982,
from $54.2 million to $34.8 million and $31.5 million respectively.   It was
the CAR's weak export performance which significantly contributed to the high
trade deficits during the early 1980s, in particular the poor performance of
agriculture and unfavourable world market prices for cotton, timber and coffee

during that period.   The stagnation of merchandise imports since 1981 (at about $140-$150 million per year) was due mainly to the fact that a large share of them was tied to investment projects which have been implemented only slowly.

## Environment and disasters

537. The holding of the first International Conference on the Protection of Wildlife (fauna) in the Central African Republic shows the growing concern of the Government for environmental protection.   The Conference ended with the recommendation to protect effectively the country's elephants, which are threatened with extermination, since their population has fallen from 80,000 in the mid-1970s to 15,000 in 1985.   After the Conference, a Presidential order was issued forbidding the collection and marketing of ivory throughout the national territory.   For the ivory still held in stock, a special export permission will be required.   According to FAO estimates, CFA francs 6 billion ($17.4 million) are required to equip the special guards who are to prevent poaching.

## Human resources and social development

538. Enrolment in primary education is one of the highest in Africa (64 per cent), but teaching materials are scarce and buildings are in poor condition, contributing to declining attendance and growing illiteracy among the young.   In order to enable the educational system to prepare students more effectively for the tasks awaiting them in agriculture and in technical fields, an educational reform programme was adopted in 1984, the main elements of which include:

    (a)   the provision of pre-vocational training in the lower secondary cycle;

    (b)   the adoption of a practically-oriented curriculum, including subjects relevant to village life during the first ten years of schooling;

    (c)   limiting access to secondary and higher education to the best students;    and

    (d) making Sangho, the national language, the teaching language during the first two years of primary schooling.

539. In the public health field, the CAR has launched a five-year strategy, comprising a reorientation of the health services towards primary health care and a renewal of existing health care structures.

## Development planning and policies

540. The current development plan, presented as the National Action Programme, 1982-85, identifies the rehabilitation of agriculture, the reconstruction and maintenance of a network of roads classified of priority importance, education, and the elimination of the large fiscal deficit as the most pressing development tasks.

541. Of the total investments projected for 1985, rural development was to receive 35 per cent, infrastructure 31 per cent, industry 20 per cent, and social affairs (education, public health and public administration) 14 per cent.   Since 1983, investments in agriculture have in fact risen considerably in absolute as well as in relative terms;  in 1984 they accounted for 37 per cent of total investments, compared to less than 30 per cent from 1980 to 1983.   Moreover, a large part of the relatively high investments for infrastructure (40 and 31 per cent of total investments in 1984 and 1985 respectively) reflects the costs of road reconstruction, which has also benefited the rural sector.

## Mobilization of domestic resources for development

542. In 1985, projected revenues were equivalent to 14.6 per cent of GDP, deriving mainly from import duties, turnover taxes and payroll taxes, while income taxes on companies and individuals were of minor importance.   The share of budgetary expenditures in GDP during that year was marginally higher (14.8 per cent).   Following a reduction in the number of civil servants and a freezing of their salaries, wages and salaries were held down to 45 per cent of total outlays in the 1986 budget, compared to 62 per cent two years earlier.   Largely owing to this policy of public-sector austerity, the recurrent budget of 1986 is only 5.8 per cent higher than in 1985 in nominal terms (CFA francs 36.44 billion (equivalent to $105 million), which corresponds to a fall of about 6 per cent in real terms.   Expenditures of the development budget have increased only slightly to CFA francs 18.14 billion ($52.24 million).   As a result of the appreciation of the CFA franc against the United States dollar and some debt relief (see below), the burden of debt servicing will be eased, making it possible to envisage a reduced budget deficit (from 3.7 per cent to about 2.2 per cent of GDP) as compared to the 0.2 per cent of GDP agreed to under the terms of the IMF stand-by programme (see below).   As of 1984, gross domestic savings were still negative to the extent of - 4 per cent of GDP, partly covered by foreign subsidies to finance the fiscal deficit.

## Transfer of external resources, debt, capital requirements

543. Average annual per capita aid disbursements since 1980 ($74) have been low in comparison with other West African countries.   However, from 1983 to 1984 the CAR's ODA receipts increased from $93.5 million to $129 million. France remained the major donor, providing 70 per cent ($58.8 million) of bilateral aid.   ODA disbursements from the United States increased from $1 million in 1983 to $4.1 million in 1985, but are expected to drop to $3.9 million in 1986.   Multilateral assistance rose by 61 per cent - from $28 million to $45.2 million - between 1983 and 1984.   In July 1985 the EEC signed a new indicative programme under the Lomé III Agreement, 80 per cent of which will be directed to the agricultural sector.

544. The external debt has continued to outpace the country's debt-servicing capacity.   The public and publicity-guaranteed external debt outstanding and disbursed has risen from CFA francs 16.8 billion ($83.6 million) at the end of 1979 to CFA francs 98.1 billion ($204.5 million) at the end of 1984, representing 38 per cent of the CAR's GDP.   In efforts to monitor and service the debt effectively, the Autonomous Debt Amortization Fund in the Ministry

of Finance has been reorganized.    The debt has been regularly serviced with earmarked government revenues, notably taxes on beer consumption and diamond exports, supplemented by general budgetary revenues.

545. In November 1985, a debt rescheduling took place in the framework of the Paris Club.    A total of $10 million of public or publicly-guaranteed external debt was rescheduled over a period of ten years, plus a grace period of five years.    Moreover, the CAR negotiated a 18-month IMF stand-by agreement of SDR 15 million in September 1985 to support its programme of economic and fiscal reforms, including the reduction of the budgetary and the current account deficits.    By 31 August 1986 it had only drawn SDR 4.5 million thereof;  its overall use of IMF credit by that date had in fact fallen below the level used prior to the stand-by agreement.

## Monitoring and follow-up of the SNPA

546. A round-table meeting between the CAR and its bilateral and multilateral donors was scheduled for early 1987 following a two-day preparatory meeting in Bangui in March 1986.

## 10.  CHAD

## Recent economic performance

547. GDP at constant prices has declined every year from 1977 to 1984 due notably to civil strife and, more recently, to the drought in the Sahelian region.    As a result of this particularly unfortunate combination of natural and man-made disasters, per capita GDP fell from $225 in 1980 to $117 in 1984, which places Chad at or close to the bottom of the world list.

548. Exports consist mainly of cotton (78 per cent in 1983 and 80 per cent in 1984) and live animals.    Export earnings from cotton have been seriously affected both by the drought and by the sharp fall in international prices since early 1985.    Such earnings declined by 51 per cent in the crop year November 1984/October 1985 when the cotton harvest fell by around 40 per cent as compared to 1983/84.    As a result of increased producer prices for cotton and with the return of rainfall in 1985/86, the cotton harvest attained 1970s levels (115,000 - 120,000 mt as compared to 95,000 mt. in 1984/85).    Export prices for this commodity, measured in CFA francs, fell by nearly 60 per cent between 1983 and June 1986, thus becoming lower than local production costs. Losses of Cotontchad, the State-owned cotton marketing organization, were estimated at CFA francs 18.1 billion ($39 million) in 1984/85 as compared to net gains of CFA francs 1.3 billion ($3.5 million) in 1982/83.    Depressed world prices are expected to add a further loss of CFA francs 9 billion ($25 million) in 1985/86.

549. The primary sector (exclusive of mining) contributes around one half of GDP, of which inland fishing represents 4 to 5 per cent (70,000 mt. per year).    Per capita food production decreased at an average annual rate of 4.2 per cent during the period 1980-84.    But as a result of the improvement in rainfall, the cereal harvest for 1985/86 recovered remarkably and reached 696,000 mt, twice the previous harvest and 60 per cent above the average for the previous five years.    The cereal import requirements of 19,000 mt. for

1985/86 (as compared to 280,000 mt. the previous year) are covered by carried-over pledges of 43,000 mt. Nevertheless, external assistance is needed for the internal distribution of local surpluses in food-deficit areas. As a result of the good harvest, however, local market prices have fallen sharply in many areas, which may act as a disincentive for the 1986/87 cereal season. The livestock situation has improved as a result of ample fodder and water supplies.

550. Deposits of a number of minerals have been discovered (sodium, limestone, bauxite, iron ore, and tungsten), but the quantity and quality of such deposits have yet to be accurately ascertained. Surveys have furthermore indicated the existence of oil at Kanem, but security problems connected with the country's political conflicts have hindered oil-drilling activities.

551. The manufacturing sector contributed 7.1 per cent of GDP in 1983. Its average output declined at an annual average rate of 2.4 per cent during the period 1980-84. A textile industry is already in operation (Société textile du Tchad). Other industries relate to the production of beer, sugar and cigarettes. Plant underutilization has increased as a result of lack of foreign exchange necessary to import essential inputs and spare parts.

552. The problems arising from Chad's land-locked status are compounded by the poor road network (300 km of paved road). Normal speed on certain stretches attain only 20 to 30 km/hr during the dry season, while some segments are virtually impassable during much of the year. Transport bottlenecks have seriously hampered the distribution of food aid. However, a bridge across the Chari linking Cameroon and Chad, which was put into operation in 1985, should speed distribution of foodstuffs, fuels and other essential imports, of which 90 per cent come through the port of Douala in Cameroon. Another bridge over the Majo-Kebbi was opened in July 1986. Both bridges benefited from international assistance.

Environment and disasters

553. The 1984/85 drought was even more devastating than that of 1972/73. The surface of Lake Chad had shrunk to 3,000 km$^2$ at the end of 1984, whereas it normally varies between 13,000 and 28,000 km$^2$. As a result of the decline in water levels, fish production fell by 50 per cent. Livestock losses attributable to the drought were estimated at 10 per cent of the total herd, but were as high as 90 per cent in some areas, such as the Kanem prefecture.

554. Rainfall in 1985 was generally sufficient and well distributed, but in some cases torrential rains caused serious flooding, crop losses and transport difficulties. Moreover, the rainfall ceased abruptly in September 1985 and was not sufficient to restore normal levels of underground water reserves.

555. Pest attacks on dry-season crops and livestock have been reported. Furthermore, crickets and rats are threatening as much as 30 to 50 per cent of the 1986 cereal crop.

## Human resources and social development

556. Because of the impact of the drought on food production, per capita calorie supplies fell from 1,794 in 1977-1979 to 1,603 in 1981-1983, while average requirements are about 2,200 calories per day.   It is estimated that only one quarter of the population has access to safe drinking water.

557. The establishment of a medical surveillance network during 1984/85 helped to identify seriously affected geographic areas and to alleviate malnutrition and chronic diseases among vulnerable groups, particularly displaced persons.   A health/nutritional control programme and a nation-wide, UNICEF-supported vaccination programme are being carried out.   Village pharmacies are being established.

## Development planning and policies

558. A two-year interim development plan has been prepared for the period 1986-1988, to be followed by longer-term plans.   The main objectives of the interim plan are:  meeting food and sanitation needs;  redressing the effects of the drought;  increasing domestic production;  and ensuring an equitable distribution of income.

559. Action is being taken to establish a system of dual harvests by the development of a dry-season cereal crop and vegetable farming.

## Mobilization of domestic resources for development

560. The investment rate amounted to only 12 per cent of GDP in 1984, as compared to 23 per cent and 17 per cent estimated for 1973 and 1977 respectively.   Participation of the local population in rural development has been promoted.   Village groups, a novel form of organizaton of the rural population in Chad, are expected to play a significant role in rural development.

## Transfer of external resources, debt, capital requirements

561. Total external debt (disbursed) amounted to $123 million in 1984, or 21 per cent of GDP.   ODA disbursements increased from a trough of $35.3 million in 1980 to $114.9 million in 1984, as compared to the 1978 peak of $125.3 million.   Chad has been negotiating a stand-by arrangement with the IMF.   Compensation for export earnings shortfalls in cotton has been obtained from the EEC Stabex scheme (ECU 13.7 million during the period 1975-83) and from IMF's Compensatory Financing Facility for a total of SDR 20.6 million at three occasions between 1976 and 1985.

## Mechanisms for monitoring and implementation of the SNPA

562. An International Conference for the Economic Development of Chad was held in Geneva in December 1985 and aid pledges were reportedly made for a total amount of $450 million.   Sectoral meetings are being organized as a follow-up to this Conference, at which donors are expected to make specific pledges. Such consultations on transport and cotton were held in Washington in May 1986.

11.  COMOROS

Economic performance

563. The progress made by the Comoros in recent years can be regarded as
fairly satisfactory.  Real GDP is estimated to have increased by 4.1 per cent
per year on average over the period 1980-1984.  However, the population
increase, currently around 3 per cent per year, continues to be high, so that
per capita incomes have increased only very slightly.  The most dynamic
sectors in the economy have been services, as well as construction and public
works, which have increased their share in GDP.

564. The Comoros continue to be highly dependent on food imports; 42 per cent
of food consumption was imported in 1984, mostly in the form of rice, flour
and meat.  These food imports absorbed more than two-thirds of merchandise
export proceeds.  In spite of increases in particular items of domestic food
production, food dependency has increased in recent years, as the rate of
increase in consumption has outstripped the rate of increase in production.
Among the positive trends are the increase in maize production (26 per cent
between 1982 and 1984), which is supported by an EEC project, and that of
coconuts (where a World Bank/IDA project, involved in particular in rodent
control, has been implemented since 1981).  The poultry sector is also
developing well, in part due to the availability of more maize used as feed.
On the other hand, rice and fish production are stagnating.

565. Between 1980 and 1983, the total value of exports increased considerably,
but in 1984 there was a decline.  Some 98 per cent of all exports are
accounted for by three relatively uncommon products: vanilla, cloves and
ylang-ylang (Table 53).  Copra, a traditional export, is now of only minor
importance.  The prices obtained for vanilla have risen substantially since
1981, and Comoros is the second largest world supplier of this product, after
Madagascar.  For cloves, prices increased from 1981 to 1983 but have declined
sharply since.  This is believed to be a result of increased production in
Indonesia (a major consumer) and Brazil.  Exports of ylang-ylang essence
depend on the economic situation in the perfume industry in developed
countries.  Although the Comoros supply 90 per cent of world production, the
country is not in a position to set market prices because of strong
competition from synthetic products and from canaga, produced by Indonesia and
Malaysia.

566. One of the major problems of the Comoros is the high cost of freight and
insurance:  these items represented about 54 per cent of the value of f.o.b.
imports in 1984 - certainly one of the highest ratios by world standards.  In
order to alleviate this problem, which is partly due to the lack of a
deep-water port, the Government has decided to embark on a major
transformational investment by building a modern deep-water port at Mutsamudu
in the island of Anjouan.  At the time when this decision was taken (1982) the
cost of this project was estimated at nearly 10 billion Comoro francs (about
$30 million).  Construction was started in 1983, with financing from the
African Development Bank, BADEA, the Abu Dhabi Fund, the Kuwait Fund, the
Islamic Development Bank and the OPEC Fund.  The new port is expected to be
operational in 1986, and will allow the berthing of ships up to 15,000 tons.

567. Industry is mostly limited to the transformation of agricultural products for export.  Its share in GDP has decreased in recent years, from 4.8 per cent in 1981 to 3.9 per cent in 1984.

568. In spite of a good potential, tourism is not an important activity at present.  A new hotel was opened in 1984, and the number of visitors (1,500) was up 10 per cent on 1983.

Table 53.  Main export commodities by value and volume, 1980-1984
(Value in millions of Comorian francs, a/ volume in
metric tons and units prices in thousands of Comorian
francs per ton)

|  | 1980 | 1981 | 1982 | 1983 | 1984 b/ |
|---|---|---|---|---|---|
| Total export value (f.o.b.) | 2,364 | 4,461 | 6,434 | 7,419 | 7,053 |
| Vanilla |  |  |  |  |  |
| Value | 193 | 2,169 | 4,201 | 3,542 | 4,203 |
| Volume | 13 | 160 | 259 | 177 | 161 |
| Unit price | 14,846 | 13,556 | 16,220 | 20,011 | 26,106 |
| Cloves |  |  |  |  |  |
| Value | 1,247 | 1,728 | 1,473 | 3,181 | 1,995 |
| Volume | 816 | 929 | 585 | 1,134 | 907 |
| Unit price | 1,528 | 1,860 | 2,518 | 2,805 | 2,200 |
| Ylang-Ylang |  |  |  |  |  |
| Value | 403 | 453 | 715 | 558 | 735 |
| Volume | 33 | 40 | 63 | 49 | 64 |
| Unit price | 12,212 | 11,325 | 11,349 | 11,388 | 11,484 |
| Other products (including copra) |  |  |  |  |  |
| Value | 531 | 111 | 45 | 138 | 120 |

a/   The Comorian franc is pegged to the French franc at the rate of 50 to 1.

b/   Provisional.

569. Electricity consumption is increasing in part as replacement of wood and charcoal, resources which are being rapidly depleted.  Ninety per cent of the electricity is generated from imported oil.  The hydro potential is limited, e.g. on the main island (Grand Comoro) there are no permanent streams or rivers.  The price of electricity is high and is one of the constraints to the development of industry.

## Human resources and social development

570. Starting from a very low level, the Comoros have made some progress in education. Thus, the number of pupils enrolled in educational establishments rose from 17,400 in 1972/73 to 76,500 in 1981/82. The situation is, however, still far from satisfactory: in primary schools there is a drop-out and repetition rate of about 25 per cent because of curricula which are unsuited to the Comorian environment and because of poor quality instruction, which is, in turn, the result of the fact that the teaching staff have substandard qualifications (only 19 per cent of primary teachers have received proper training). Textbooks are in short supply; classrooms are in poor condition and in many cases are used on a three shift system. A college has been set up to improve primary education by providing basic teacher training.

571. The health situation continues to be very precarious. According to the latest available data (1983-1986 Interim Development Plan), life expectancy at birth is 41 for men and 44 for women; and 80 per cent of the population suffers from malaria. Health infrastructure and personnel are grossly inadequate and, because of budgetary constraints, the Government has to rely on external assistance for funding more than 60 per cent of health expenditure.

## Development planning and policies

572. The Comoros have little experience in development planning. A first Interim Plan for Economic and Social Development for the period 1983-1986 was published in mid-1984. At the same time, the Government prepared a development programme for the period 1983-1990, which was presented at the donors' conference held in July 1984. However, the authorities have indicated that the information and projections made in these documents are flawed by incomplete or unreliable data. The main objective is to move gradually towards food self-sufficiency, while improving the nutrition level of the population. Other objectives are the improvement of transport links ("désenclavement") - external as well as within the archipelago - water and energy development, health and training.

573. The responsibility for planning lies with the President's Office. One problem which makes plan implementation more complex in the Comoros than elsewhere is the allocation of responsibility between the Federal Government and the Governorates (one for each island). The main central institutional structure responsible for rural development is the CEFADER (Federal Support Centre for Rural Development), which supports and co-ordinates a number of CADERs, each responsible for rural development in a particular region, including the provision of rural credit.

## Mobilization of domestic resources for development

574. The Comoros continue to need external budget support to finance recurrent expenditure, whereas almost the whole of public investment is financed by external sources. In fact, over the period 1980-84, about two thirds of the consolidated budget (Federal, governorates and annexed budgets) were financed by external grants. Since 1982, when a central tax administration became operational, a number of measures have been taken to improve mobilization of domestic revenue: the turnover tax was extended to cover a wide range of

goods and transactions and its administration reinforced. This has yielded
positive results inasmuch as internal revenue increased by 37 per cent between
1982 and 1983. However, there was a decline in overall tax revenue in 1984,
due in part to the lower level of exports, which together with imports produce
more than 85 per cent of tax revenues.

575. The mobilization of domestic savings was formerly handicapped by the
inefficient functioning of the only commercial bank in the country. This bank
has closed down and was replaced by the Banque Internationale des Comores (a
subsidiary of a multinational bank) in 1982, and indications are that
deposits - including savings deposits - have increased rapidly. In order to
attempt to mobilize domestic savings, as well as to attract private foreign
investment, a new Investment Code was promulgated in May 1984.

## Transfer of external resources and external debt

576. Most of the increase in external financing in Comoros has been in the
form of loans (see Table 54). Some of these loans, in particular some of the
financing for the port of Mutsamudu, has been on near-commercial terms. This
trend has been accompanied by a sharp increase in debt service payments.
Until 1981, these payments were relatively small, i.e. less than 3 per cent of
exports of goods and non-factor services. However, the debt service ratio has
risen considerably since then, reaching 15 per cent in 1984, and a projected
34 per cent in 1986, when the first amortization payments for the Mutsamudu
project become due.

Table 54. External transfers in the balance of payments (1980-1984)
(billions of Comorian francs)

|  | 1980 | 1981 | 1982 | 1983 | 1984 a/ |
|---|---|---|---|---|---|
| Unrequited public transfers | 5.4 | 6.5 | 6.3 | 7.7 | 7.7 |
| Long-term capital, net | 3.4 | 3.0 | 6.4 | 7.2 | 10.2 |
| Total net external financing | 8.8 | 9.5 | 12.7 | 14.9 | 17.9 |

a/ Estimated.

## Mechanism for monitoring and follow-up of the SNPA

577. The Comoros held a meeting with its development partners, called the
First Conference of International Solidarity for the Development of Comoros,
in Moroni on 2-4 July 1984. On this occasion the Government presented its
programme for economic and social development for the period 1983-1990. The
Conference was attended by 17 countries and 11 financial institutions, as well
as organizations of the United Nations system, regional organizations and
non-governmental organizations. A follow-up conference on a smaller scale is
planned in principle for 1986.

## 12.  DEMOCRATIC YEMEN

Economic performance

578. A preliminary evaluation of the implementation of the Second Five-Year Development Plan, 1981-1985, which envisaged a 10.5 per cent annual growth rate in real GDP, points to a fluctuating economic performance:  a 6.6 per cent real growth rate of GDP in 1981 was followed by a decline of 4.6 per cent in 1982, owing to the sharp flood-induced decline in agricultural production, in the following two years the economy experienced a moderate but weakening recovery as real GDP increased by 4 per cent in 1983 but slowed down to 2 per cent in 1984.  Aside from the floods, progress was hampered by the decline in workers' remittances and the stagnation in the construction and transport sectors, which had supported growth in earlier periods.

579. The trade balance, as derived from either customs or balance-of-payments series, has remained persistently in deficit.  According to customs figures, exports and imports reached a peak of $795 million and $1,599 million respectively in 1982, reflecting high levels of re-exported petroleum products.  Thereafter, exports averaged $670 million while imports ranged between $1,290 million and $1,543 million between 1983 and 1985.  The balance-of-payments series (which includes only the value added of re-exported petroleum products, but excludes the huge crude oil component in both directions) gives a trade balance with a wide structural deficit.  According to this series, exports averaged no more than $42 million during the period 1981-83, and declined to $30.7 million in 1984.  Imports, which averaged $671 million during the period 1981-1983, reached a high of $824.6 million in 1984. This deterioration went a long way to explain the growing deficit on current account, which more than doubled in 1984 as compared to 1982, increasing from 18 per cent of GDP to 39 per cent in 1984. Although the vital private transfers (mainly workers' remittances) remained fairly constant at about $450 million annually in the period 1982-1984, official transfers declined from an average of $124 million in 1981-1982 to a mere $29.5 million in 1984.  Long-term capital, which had been rising steadily since 1979 to reach a record of $255 million in 1983, compounded the decline in official transfers, by falling to $136 million in the following year.  The "net errors and omissions" item, which had been negative during the period 1981-1983, registered a substantial reversal in 1984 reaching $159.9 million. This might possibly be due to leads and lags in the reporting of imports in 1984 and/or under-reporting of foreign aid inflows and of private remittances.  In addition, there was a large inflow of short-term capital which increased from $2.9 million in 1983 to $63.4 million in 1984.  In view of these two unexplained but mitigating developments net international reserves have remained relatively stable, declining by 11 per cent in 1984 to $248.7 million at the end of that year.  By September 1985, reserves had declined by a further 17 per cent.

580. The agricultural sector contributes about 10 per cent of GDP.  Democratic Yemen imports almost two thirds of its cereal needs, 70 per cent of its edible oil requirements and 100 per cent of its needs of sugar, rice, pulses and tea.  It approaches self-sufficiency only in vegetables and sorghum.  The main constraint to agricultural production is the scarcity of arable land, which only covers about 0.2 per cent of the country's total land area.  The country

has a vast potential in the fishery sector by virtue of a coastline extending for 1,500 km and a continental shelf covering an area of 22,000 sq. km. However, this potential has yet to be fully exploited for lack of finance and the necessary infrastructure.

581. The manufacturing sector, which is mainly based on import substitution and the Aden oil refinery, accounts for about 10 per cent of GDP. The refinery is the main industrial enterprise with a capacity of 8 million tons annually. Its production fluctuated widely in recent years and is estimated to have reached the break even point in 1982. As a result of the damage caused by the events of January 1986 (see following section) and the decline in supplies of crude oil, the refinery is operating at present at about 20 per cent of its capacity. Other manufacturing activities are essentially agro-based.

582. In view of the lack of energy resources, energy requirements are met by imported oil. Since exploration for oil has not been encouraging, the main emphasis in this sector is on the generation of more electricity. The Second Five-Year Development plan (SFYD), 1981-1985, projected investments of $197 million by the Public Corporation for Electric Power, which are designed to make power accessible to about 44 per cent of the population in 1985 as compared to 29 per cent in 1982. The extractive industry is confined to salt mining and quarrying.

## Environment and disasters

583. Democratic Yemen experienced an internal conflict in January 1986, which caused loss of life and material damage. These events occurred while the country was still recovering from the aftermath of the unprecedented rains and the subsequent floods of 1982, which caused damage to the irrigation system, topsoils, livestock, roads, bridges and housing. The burden of rehabilitation and reconstruction has proved to be beyond the capacity of the Government.

## Human resources and social development

584. One of the major constraints to Democratic Yemen's development effort is the scarcity of skilled manpower. This situation has been further aggravated in recent years by labour emigration to neighbouring Gulf countries, which absorbed almost 20 per cent of the total labour force. The SFYD Plan emphasizes the need to increase participation of women in the labour force, improve manpower productivity and expand vocational and technical education, which is free. The primary school enrolment ratio was envisaged to increase during the Plan period from 57 per cent to 97 per cent. However, the implementation of Plan in the educational sector was adversely affected by the serious financial difficulties faced by the country, which led to the postponment of several projects. Thus, the primary school enrolment ratio is estimated at present at about 67 per cent and the adult literacy rate at about 41 per cent as compared to 57 per cent and 27 per cent respectively in 1970. In order to improve the poor health conditions prevailing in the country, emphasis is given to primary health care (PHC) and the establishment of health facilities. It is estimated that over the past decade the number of hospitals increased by 93 per cent, health centres by 300 per cent and health units by 200 per cent. The access of the population to safe drinking water is being expanded. Housing conditions are also being improved; the private sector is encouraged to play an active role in this area.

## Development planning and policies

585. Since independence, the Government has pursued a socialist strategy of development relying primarily on a strong public sector and on co-operatives. The Government has substantially strengthened its planning capability through the Ministry of Planning and other technical ministries and departments.  A triennial plan and two successive five-year plans have been implemented since the early 1970s.  The major objectives of the development strategy are:
(a) to satisfy the basic needs of the population;  (b) to develop the productive capacity of the economy in agriculture, fishery, manufacturing, transport and power;  and (c) to raise the educational standards of the people, emphasizing primary and technical education.  The Second Five-Year Development Plan (SFYD) (1981-85), which envisaged a total investment outlay of $1,475 million, assumed that 30 per cent of this amount would be financed from domestic sources, as compared to about 28 per cent in the First Five-Year Plan (1976-1980).  This target was exceeded in the first two years of the Plan, as domestic financing accounted for about 41 per cent and 45.5 per cent respectively.  The effective implementation of the Plan was impeded by the severe unanticipated financial difficulties (see section on transfer of external resources below) and the 1982 floods, which caused the Government to reorient its efforts towards reconstruction and rehabilitation.

## Mobilization of domestic resources for development

586. The major domestic sources of development financing are the contributions of public sector enterprises, which are obliged to channel 85 per cent of their net profits to the development budget, and local bank credits.  As several of these enterprises have been operating at a loss, domestic bank financing - provided mainly by the Bank of Yemen (the central bank) and the National Bank of Yemen (a commercial bank) - has increased in recent years, accounting for 32 per cent of development expenditure in 1982.

## Transfer of external resources, debt, capital requirements

587. The total requirement for external resources during the SFYD Plan was estimated at $1,032 million (at 1981 prices and exchange rates), i.e. an average of about $206 million per annum.  Total financial inflows fell far short of this amount during the period 1981-1984, except in 1982.  Thus, in 1984 these inflows were estimated at only $157 million.  The socialist countries of Eastern Europe provided about 67 per cent of external assistance during this period, followed by Arab bilateral and multilateral donors, which accounted for another 21 per cent of the total.

588. Total external debt was estimated at about $1.3 billion at the end of 1984 as compared to about $1.0 billion at the end of 1982.  Due to the concessional terms of most loans, the debt service payments of $62 million in 1984 did not exceed the equivalent 9.7 per cent of exports of domestic goods and services, as compared to 7.4 per cent in 1982.

## Mechanism for the monitoring and follow-up of the SNPA

589. The Government of Democratic Yemen has deferred indefinitely the convening of the round table conference which had been tentatively scheduled for November 1985.  The Ministry of Planning is the focal point for the monitoring and follow-up of the SNPA.

## 13.  DJIBOUTI

Economic performance

590. Djibouti is very poor in natural resources and the economy is dominated by the tertiary sector, which accounts for over 70 per cent of GDP.  The growth in this sector is susceptible to fluctuations in regional and international demand for the services offered by Djibouti and is the main factor behind the fluctuations in economic performance.  Thus, real GDP, which grew by an average rate of 1.3 per cent between 1980 and 1985, has slowed down to a rate of less than 1 per cent over each of the last three years.  Given annual population growth rates ranging between 2.6 and 4.5 per cent during this period, this implies a decline of per capita income since 1980.

591. In view of the above-mentioned structure of the economy, commodity exports, mainly livestock and hides and skins, are insignificant and exports of non-factor services, i.e. earnings from the transportation and communications infrastructure and banking services, are the main exports of domestic origin.  Exports increased from $21 million in 1981 to $26 million in 1985.  A further increase was envisaged in 1986, due to increased port activity as a result of the evacuation of foreigners from Aden through Djibouti.  Recorded imports steadily declined to $110 million in 1985 compared to the 1981 level of $120 million.  The trade deficit declined from 46 per cent of GDP in 1981 to about 37 per cent in 1984.  The trade figures used in the calculation of balance-of-payments series are considerably higher in both directions:  the export side shows figures that are between 5 and 15 per cent higher, since they include re-exports of goods from Somalia, Ethiopia and other land-locked countries, as well as services provided to the French military base and its personnel.  However, the import figures are nearly three times as high as the recorded figures, probably due to unrecorded aid imports and transit trade.  Exports, thus defined, increased from $106 million in 1981 to $123 million in 1983, but stagnated at this level in 1984 and 1985 as a result of the depreciation of the French franc against the United States dollar, to which the Djibouti franc is pegged, and the financial policies adopted by the French Government, both of which affected purchases by the military and expatriate aid personnel.  But imports increased from $212 million in 1981 to $294.8 million in 1985;  their level depends in great part on the aid policies of France, which is both the largest trade partner and donor.  The balance on current account reversed from small surpluses in 1982 and 1983 to a deficit of $21.4 million in 1984 and $49 million in 1985.

592. The agricultural sector, dominated by livestock raising, contributes on average about 6 per cent of GDP.  The growth rate of agricultural production was estimated at an annual average of 3.5 per cent between 1981 and 1985, i.e. slightly ahead of the population increase.  The major constraints to agricultural development are the scarcity of arable land which represents only about 0.23 per cent of the land area, the hot arid climate and the scarcity of water resources.  As a result, the country imports at present all its cereal requirements, which have averaged about 43,000 tons over the past five years.  Livestock, estimated in 1978 at 40,000 head of cattle, 50,000 camels and 900,000 goats and sheep, has been adversely affected by the drought of 1983 and 1984.  The development of fishing is limited by the short coast line;  the fish catch averaged about 290 tons annually during the period 1981-1984.

593. The manufacturing sector is also of minor importance, contributing about 6.3 per cent of GDP. At present, production is mainly confined to soft drinks and mineral water. Manufacturing production, which had declined after 1980, increased by 2 per cent in 1984. Other industrial activities include extraction of limestone, gypsum and clay. The development of the manufacturing sector is constrained by the small size of the domestic market, the low purchasing power of neighbouring countries, all of which are LDCs, lack of energy resources and shortages of skilled manpower.

594. The main economic activity of the country is based on its transport and communication infrastructure, mainly composed of the Port of Djibouti, the airport and the telecommunications system. This sector contributed 31 per cent of the country's non-aid foreign exchange receipts in 1982. The Port of Djibouti, which became an autonomous entity in January 1982, employs about 2,500 persons (about 5.5 per cent of the labour force). It has an annual capacity of 640,000 tons, with 2,400 m of quays. The activity level in the Port, which stagnated during the period 1977-1983 has declined since then. The volume of merchandise traffic and the number of ships calling at Djibouti declined by 28 per cent and 13 per cent respectively in 1985 as compared to 1983, owing to competition from other ports in the area, mainly Assab (Ethiopia) and Jeddah (Saudi Arabia). However, in early 1986, it was reported that traffic in the Port had increased by 20 per cent and bunkering operations by 80 per ent, as a result of the events in Democratic Yemen. As part of the modernization of the Port and to enhance its role as a trans-shipment centre, a cold-storage entrepot and a container terminal with a capacity of 25 containers per hour were established in 1985. UNCTAD is implementing a UNDP-financed project to rationalize and improve operations in the Port through the provision of consultants and training. As an addition to the existing 500 km network of paved roads, two highway projects, connecting Djibouti to Tadjoura and Loyada, are under construction. Inasmuch as about 106 km of the 781 km railway line to Ethiopia is in Djibouti territory, the EEC is providing funds to improve the track and purchase new rolling stock. With its reliable telecommunications system Djibouti is becoming an important regional centre. It is linked by a radio telephonic network with Yemen and Saudi Arabia, and by microwave with Democratic Yemen and Somalia. Djibouti is also a member of the Medarabtel project to improve communications between the Mediterranean and the Arab countries.

## Disasters

595. The refugee population was estimated at about 42,000, or more than 10 per cent of the population, in 1980. A programme of repatriating Ethiopian refugees with the assistance of the UNHCR, was completed in November 1984. However, as a result of the drought and famine in Ethiopia, a new influx occurred in 1985 and the number of refugees was estimated at about 23,000 persons in mid-1986. The presence of this large number of refugees has placed further pressure on the ability of the Government to provide basic needs to its citizens.

Human resources and social development

596. The population of Djibouti was estimated at 364,000 in 1985, implying an annual growth rate of 2.8 per cent.  The development of human resources assumes a high priority in the 1982 Law on Economic and Social Orientation, which is the basis for economic and social development in Djibouti.  Education is free and enrolment in 1986 at the primary and secondary levels was 49 per cent and 30 per cent respectively above the 1981 level.  About 15 per cent of the population continues to be affected by tuberculosis and the sequels of malnutrition, despite governmental efforts to expand the availability of free care for the entire population.  As the city of Djibouti, where two thirds of the population lives, continues to expand, the urban infrastructure is facing continuous pressure and is unable to provide minimum services for almost one third of its inhabitants.

Development planning and policies

597. The overall objectives of the 1982 "Law on Economic and Social Orientation" are to strengthen the international role of Djibouti as a transit centre, to increase the income of the citizens and to improve its distribution.  To realize these objectives, high priority is given to human resources development, strengthening the transportation system, particularly through the development of the Port, increasing agricultural and industrial production and expansion of the social services.  The Public Investment Programme for 1983-1989, which was formulated within the overall context of the above-mentioned 1982 Law, included 72 projects at a total cost of $570 million.

Mobilization of domestic resources for development

598. Several measures have been initiated since 1978 to reduce the burdening of the budget deficit, such as an increase of the tax rates and a broadening of the tax base.  Thus, internal revenue increased by an annual average rate of 16.5 per cent between 1978 and 1982.  Receipts from direct taxes almost doubled during the same period.  However, budgetary receipts hardly increased in real terms between 1982 and 1985 as a result of the stagnation of receipts from the domestic excise and profits taxes.  This was partially offset by a decrease in subsidies and the strict control of other public expenditures, which declined by a cumulative rate of 11 per cent between 1982 and 1985.  With final consumption exceeding GDP by an average of 16 per cent in 1982 and 1983 and 25 per cent in 1984 and 1985 and an investment level equivalent to 20 per cent of GDP in 1985, Djibouti continues to rely on external support to finance not only public investments, but also recurrent expenditures.

Transfer of external resources, debt and capital requirements

599. Total financial flows to Djibouti, which had remained at an annual average of about $65 million during the period 1980-1983, increased to about $87 million in 1984, due to the increase in the non-concessional flows, particularly export credits.  The major part of concessional assistance is provided by France in the form of budget subsidies as well as civilian and military technical assistance.  The pledges made at the 1983 Donors' Conference in Djibouti have not been fulfilled, the fulfilment rate being less than 10 per cent during 1984.

600. The weak fiscal performance and the steady decline of external grant aid from 24 per cent of total revenue in 1978 to 6.7 per cent in 1985 have led to a threefold increase in total external debt from the end of 1982 to the end of 1984 and the drawing down of the reserves of the Caisse nationale de développement. Total external debt was estimated at about $146 million at the end of 1984, with debt service payments of $20 million, which is equivalent to about 16.2 per cent of total export earnings.

## Mechanism for the monitoring and follow-up of the SNPA

601. A Donors' Conference was held in Djibouti in November 1983, at which the Government presented its Investment Programme for the period 1983-1988. The Conference was attended by 36 donor countries and 33 national and multilateral institutions. The Conference marked the first occasion for co-ordination of external financial and technical assistance to Djibouti. The monitoring and follow-up of the SNPA and the pledges made at the Conference is the responsibility of the Ministry of Planning. Sectoral consultations for the energy sector were planned for end 1986/beginning 1987.

## 14. EQUATORIAL GUINEA

## Economic performance

602. Since 1979, when the previous régime was overthrown, the country has undertaken considerable efforts to stem the steady economic decay, experienced for about 10 years. However, these endeavours have resulted in only meagre results so far. The country has not yet succeeded in revitalizing its economy. For the period 1980-85, the growth rate of GDP (at constant prices) is estimated at about 1 per cent per annum. Given a population growth rate of about 2 per cent, the economy is in fact deteriorating. GDP per capita was estimated at $255 in 1983.

603. Following its entry into the CEEAC (Economic Community of Central African States) and UDEAC (Central African Customs and Economic Union), both in 1983, the country became a member of the BEAC (Banque des Etats de l'Afrique Centrale) on 2 January 1985. The country also became a member of the African Coffee Association, following an agreement signed on 24 July 1985.

604. By joining the BEAC, the CFA franc became the unit of currency. The substitution of this convertible currency for the previous inconvertible legal tender, the ekwele, implied a devaluation of the latter by 82 per cent. 154/ Both measures are expected to affect positively the export performance of the country and to reduce the smuggling of cash export products, in particular cocoa and coffee.

605. In 1984-85, France made more than FF 50 million (about $5.5 million) available to Equatorial Guinea to cover the costs related to the country's entry into the BEAC (share in the Bank's capital, exchange of previous money in circulation, reserve funds, etc.). Despite this financial assistance, the country underwent a period of severe illiquidity and high inflation during the first half of 1985. The former was caused mainly by a rapid outflow of the newly convertible currency for imported consumer goods, which were sold at subsidized prices to ease the effects of that transition with many being

re-exported to neighouring CFA countries, causing shortages and price
inflation.  The doubling of prices between the end of 1984 and June 1985 was
also abetted by the practice of some traders to equate the new CFA franc
prices with the old Ekwele prices on a parity basis, despite the 4:1 currency
conversion ratio.  The extreme shortage of both cash and fiduciary currency
caused prices to recede significantly from mid-1985 onwards to a level roughly
one third above those prevailing prior to the currency conversion.

606. The change in the currency, coupled with a marked devaluation, led to an
increase of the export volume by 34 per cent in 1985.  Export earnings,
however, increased only by 25 per cent.  This was mainly due to the
unfavourable price trends on the international markets for cocoa, the main
export item.  Although the import value remained constant ($29.6 million in
1985, as against $30.0 million in 1984), the trade balance remained negative,
with a deficit of $6.2 million in 1985.

607. Agriculture is the mainstay of the country's economy, on which the
performance of most other economic activities depends.  It provides the
livelihood to the majority of the population, accounts for almost all of the
country's foreign exchange earnings and thus influences the entire economic
spectrum and living conditions of the people.  The agricultural sector
therefore has a tremendous impact on socio-economic activities, apart from its
high development potential.

608. Within agriculture, the cocoa subsector is of paramount importance.
Cocoa accounted for more than two thirds of the country's total export
earnings in 1984.  The country, which had once a reputation for its
high-quality cocoa, experienced a drastic decline in production after
independence (1968), from about 38,000 tons in 1967 to an estimated level of
less than 9,000 tons in the season 1984-1985.  By 1984 cocoa acreage had
fallen to about 40 per cent of the 46,000 hectares once in production.

609. Equatorial Guinea has both the physical and economic potential to restore
production of cocoa to previous levels.  However, to that end it will be
necessary to address those very factors which have contributed to the
decline.  Among the most serious ones are the chronic shortage of trained
labour, uncertainty of land tenure rights, insufficient and erratic provision
of modern inputs to growers, and disorganized collection of cocoa from primary
producers.

610. In 1985, the country undertook remarkable steps to increase cocoa
production.  Producer prices have been raised, being now the highest in
BEAC member countries.  The largest rise occurred in the top grade, thus
providing a price incentive to grow the best quality cocoa.  Furthermore,
since in the past much of the crop was sold in neighbouring countries for
convertible currency, cocoa can now be sold in the country legally for
CFA francs.  Both trends gave way to a much more optimistic outlook for the
recovering process of the cocoa subsector.  For the season 1985-1986, a rise
of the cocoa production volume to 15,000 tons is projected.

611. The production and the export of timber is the second most important
economic activity, accounting for about 25 per cent of the export earnings
in 1984.  The Government has granted 13 concessions to foreign companies,

permitting them to exploit an area of 315,000 hectares.  Timber production
experienced a remarkable growth from 27,000 m$^3$ in 1980 to 103,029 m$^3$
in 1984.  Nevertheless, timber production still falls far short of the
pre-independence peak level of more than 310,000 m$^3$ in 1967.  With a proper
reforestation programme, timber production could well return to a ceiling of
300,000 m$^3$ per year.

612. Coffee production has become marginal since independence.  It fell from
9,000 tons per year in the late 1960s to less than 500 tons in 1984-1985.
However, the authorities expect a positive response by the coffee growers to
the establishment of a dual price system.  Two different price levels were set
up - one for coffee sold at or near where it was grown and one for coffee
actually delivered to the port of Bata.  The premium paid for hulled coffee
evacuated to Bata is more than 50 per cent over the price paid for the same
grade in the interior.  This measure was intended to increase coffee
production and to get the crop to the market.

613. Livestock production is virtually negligible and destined exclusively for
local consumption.  Cattle herds were destroyed in the 1970s and animal
diseases decimated the pig population.  Currently, the country is undertaking
efforts to expand chicken production.

614. The main food products for local consumption are cassava, sweet potatoes,
bananas, coconuts as well as palm oil and palm kernel.  Since these products
are almost exclusively grown in the subsistence economy, data on their
production values and volumes are difficult to obtain.  Equatorial Guinea has
abundant natural resources, allowing the country to be self-sufficient in
food.  Nevertheless, food imports, including wheat flour, rice and meat,
accounted for a quarter of all imports in 1984.

615. Except for limited exploitation of alluvial gold, mineral resources are
barely explored.  Presumed deposits of ores, such as copper, iron and uranium,
have not yet been tapped.  Oil exploration off the coast of Bioko has been
underway for several years, but so far with limited success.  In 1985, a
foreign company applied for an extension of its license to explore an on-shore
area of Southern Rio Muni.  No major finds have yet been announced.

616. The manufacturing sector contributes only 5 per cent of total output,
corresponding essentially to the elementary processing of timber and cocoa.
The inadequacy of electricity supply is a major constraint for the rapid
expansion of this sector.

617. A major obstacle for a comprehensive economic development of the country
is the weak infrastructure.  The road system is far below basic requirements,
impeding inter alia the prospecting for minerals and the transportation of
timber.  It needs both modernization and extension.  The ports on the island
as well as on the mainland are inadequately equipped and in poor repair.  The
national airline that linked the island with the mainland has ceased
operations.  Plans to set up a new joint-venture airline which was to take up
its service early in 1986, had to be postponed due to financial constraints.

Human resources and social development

618. The lack of trained staff, mainly due to a large exodus of skilled manpower in the 1970s, is keenly felt in almost all economic sectors. Efforts to supplement and to improve existing technical and managerial resources through the employment of expatriate staff in certain key positions, particularly in the cocoa subsector, proved to be less successful than expected.

619. Regular water and electricity supplies are not available even in the capital city. Health services are very limited: only five indigenous physicians are available for a population of about 360,000 inhabitants. Malaria affects 80 per cent of the population. Since 1980, 63 rural health centres have been established.

Development planning and policies

620. Central government budgeting resumed in 1980 and a Ministry of Planning and Economic Development was created late in 1982. Focal units for sectoral planning have been established in the ministries concerned. A programme for reconstruction and reorganization, containing emergency measures, was formulated for the period 1980-1981, and was followed by a programme for economic recovery for 1982-1984.

621. Agricultural policies aim at the increase of production both for export and local consumption. Producer prices of cocoa were raised and the massive currency devaluation removed a heavy burden on exports. Since 1985, abandoned plantations are being redistributed with a view to enhancing agricultural production. A number of programmes have been instituted to promote fishing, including the improvement of fish conservation and transport, support for small-craft fishing and establishment of a workshop for the construction of fishing boats.

Mobilization of domestic resources

622. The Government has recognized the fact that increased domestic resource mobilization is an important element for accelerating the country's development. In January 1984, the National Credit Board was created, its main objective being to design a sound credit policy for the country.

623. A major step to redress the weak banking system and to complete the country's integration into the Franc Zone was the signing of an agreement between the Government and the Banque internationale pour l'Afrique Occidentale (BIAO) on 15 April 1985. The agreement stipulates the establishment of a new branch of BIAO Afribank in Equatorial Guinea with facilities in the capital Malabo and in Bata on the mainland. Tne new branch has a capital stock of CFA 300 millions, of which 51 per cent are contributed by BIAO Afribank. The remaining 49 per cent are raised by public and private sources within the country.

## Transfer of external resources, debt, capital requirements

624. At the end of 1984, the gross external liabilities amounted to $129.2 million. Grace periods on suppliers' credits extended in the early 1980s had begun to expire, which resulted in a doubling of scheduled amortization payments between 1983 and 1984. Overall debt service payments due in 1984 would have reached a level of $10-12 million, absorbing more than 50 per cent of the country's export earnings. At the Paris Club Meeting on Equatorial Guinea in July 1985, an agreement was reached with the country's main creditors to reschedule all debt service payments falling due from 1 January 1985 to 30 June 1986 and 95 per cent of arrears on both principal and interest that fell due before 1985. Repayment of the amounts consolidated is to be over a period of ten and a half years, including a grace period of six years.

625. The decision to join UDEAC and BEAC, as well as the commitment by the economic authorities to give greater weight to the use of the market mechanism, seems to have positively affected the capital inflow from abroad. The country received an IMF stand-by credit of SDR 9.2 million in 1985 and IDA approved a $9.3 million agricultural credit to help the Government restore cocoa production and exports to their past levels. Co-financing of the $16.2 million project is anticipated from BADEA ($2.8 million), OPEC ($1 million), and the EEC ($0.9 million).

626. As a signatory to the Lomé III Convention, the country has been allocated ECU 12 million of EDF funds for 1986-90, from which the EEC will finance two road projects. The European Investment Bank (EIB) has announced a ECU 6 million credit line for hydroelectric projects, which are to be co-financed by the French Caisse centrale de coopération économique (CCCE).

## Mechanisms for the monitoring and follow-up of the SNPA

627. An International Donors' Conference was held in April 1982 with a view to securing the support of the international community for economic reactivation projects presented by the Government. A meeting to pursue discussion and action on foreign assistance to the country took place in 1983. Equatorial Guinea is currently preparing the next donors' conference which is scheduled to be held in March 1987.

## 15. ETHIOPIA

### Economic performance

628. The multifaceted detrimental effects of the severe drought on agriculture and livestock still prevail and have adversely affected the overall economic performance. In addition, the industrial sector has faced capacity constraints due to the lack of domestic investment resources and shortages of raw materials. Thus, real GDP, which is estimated to have increased by 4.7 per cent in FY 1982/83 155/ over the previous year's level, declined by 2.4 per cent and by 6.5 per cent in FY 1983/84 and 1984/85 respectively.

629. The poor performance of the agricultural sector, and the slow recovery in international coffee prices from their extremely low levels in 1981, have caused overall economic stagnation and, recently even a decline in export earnings. Thus, the dollar value of exports which declined by about 8 per cent between 1980 and 1981, fluctuated within a narrow range around $410 million during the period 1982-1984, but in FY 1984/85 they declined by 15.8 per cent. In February 1986, the IMF approved a drawing equivalent to SDR 35.3 million related to this export shortfall under its Compensatory Financing Facility (CFF). Imports, on the other hand, increased by about 5.6 per cent annually between 1980 and 1985, amounting to $935 million in 1985. Nevertheless, the current account deficit, which peaked in 1981 at a level estimated at $250 million (equivalent to 5.8 per cent of GDP), had declined to $127 million in 1984. This was brought about essentially by the increase in private and official transfers, which multiplied sixfold and fourfold respectively between 1981 and 1984, to reach $145 million and $186 million respectively, reflecting the large food relief operation launched in favour of Ethiopia in 1983-1984. Long-term capital inflows, amounting to $207 million and $192 million in 1983 and 1984 respectively, were well above the long-term average. But a major outflow of identified and unidentified short-term capital amounting to more than $200 million caused net international reserves to fall to a 20-year low of $44.3 million at the end of 1984, which was equivalent to no more than two and a half weeks' imports. But during 1985 and early 1986, the reserve situation had improved substantially: by end-May 1986 reserves had recovered to $250 million, a level not attained since 1981 and corresponding to three months' imports.

630. Besides the drought and the resulting population displacement, agricultural production has been adversely affected by lack of essential inputs and is estimated to have declined by 9.9 per cent in 1983/1984 and by a further 16 per cent in 1984/1985. Production of the major food crops had declined by a total of 45 per cent in those two years, while production of coffee, the main cash crop, suffered a net decline of almost 30 per cent over the same period. However, coffee production is thought to have returned to its long-term upward trend in 1985/1986. In 1985 total cereal import requirements were estimated at 1.2 million metric tons, corresponding to 18.3 per cent of the country's overall consumption needs. Although prospects for 1986 were deemed good due to the return of rains, import requirements were still estimated at about 1.6 million metric tons. With 27 million head of cattle, 42 million sheep and goats and 1 million camels, animal resources represent a major asset of the country, but in terms of output this sector contributed only about 0.3 per cent of GDP in 1984.

631. Manufacturing accounts for only about 10 per cent of GDP; within this sector food processing accounts for 30 per cent of manufacturing production, textiles 27 per cent, beverages 15 per cent, and other manufactures, such as tobacco, leather and footwear, wood, chemicals and construction material, the rest. Manufacturing output increased by 3.8 per cent and 1.6 per cent in FY 1983/84 and FY 1984/85 respectively, despite the overall recession of the economy in those two years.

632. Highways forward about two thirds of the country's seaborne trade and the greater part of the internal commerce. The length of all-weather roads has more than doubled since the mid-1970s to about 20,000 km in 1986, but this is still regarded as inadequate. It is estimated that about 75 per cent of the farms are situated more than half a day's walking distance from a road. The mountainous topography of the country and the poor links between its parts have been major constraints to relief efforts during 1984 and 1985. In some parts of the country food relief had to be dropped by plane to the starving population. Due to the deficiency of the road systems, air transport plays an important role: apart from its international routes, Ethiopian Airlines maintains regular operations among 30 domestic airports. In the telecommunications sector, the Government is planning to establish a second satellite station and 200 telephone exchanges with bilateral and multilateral assistance.

633. The mining sector is still underdeveloped, contributing about 0.3 per cent of GDP. Exploitation of gold and platinum is carried out on a limited scale, but exploration for coal, petroleum and other minerals is being undertaken. At present, Ethiopia is still entirely dependent on imported petroleum, which absorbed around 45 per cent of export earnings during the period 1981-83, declining to about 35 per cent in 1985. The hydroelectric potential is estimated at 60 billion kWh, of which only about 2 per cent is tapped. As a result, wood, charcoal, biomass and animal waste account for a substantial share of energy consumption.

## Environment and disasters

634. The share of the country's land area covered by forests has fallen from about 44 per cent at one time to only about 3.5 per cent. This depletion was caused by the expansion of cultivation and the use of wood for firewood and construction purposes. This deforestation has contributed to recurrent droughts causing widespread famine. The worst drought and resulting famines in the country's recent history occurred during the period 1983-1985. In 1984 over 9 million people were affected. Despite improved weather conditions in 1985/1986, about 6 million people still continue to need food aid. The Government is implementing a resettlement programme initiated in 1984 to move 300,000 families (1.5 million people) from the drought-affected highlands of the North to the Southwest and West of the country. By late 1985, about 600,000 people had already been moved.

## Human resources and social development

635. The 1983-85 drought and the resulting population displacement has adversely affected government programmes in the social sectors. Priority had to be given to feeding the starving population and preventing the spread of communicable diseases. Notable progress had been achieved previously in the field of education, such as crash literacy campaigns, training programmes and the expansion of the capacity of educational and training institutions. Thus, the adult literacy rate and the primary school enrolment ratio in 1984 were estimated at 55 per cent and 46 per cent respectively as compared to 15 per cent and 24 per cent in 1975. The government's objectives are to increase primary school enrolment to 66.5 per cent and wipe out illiteracy completely by 1994. The health situation continues to be a cause for

concern.  Starvation, malnutrition and ill health are widely prevalent,
especially in rural areas.  Only about 6 per cent of the population has access
to safe drinking water.  In the continuing famine situation, priority is given
to emergency maternal and child health services, control and treatment of
communicable diseases and environmental health.  The population covered by
health services is projected to increase to 80 per cent by 1994 and the infant
mortality rate is to be reduced from its present high level of
144 per thousand to less than 70 per thousand.

## Development planning and policies

636. Ethiopia's Ten-Year Perspective Plan covers the
period 1984/1985-1993/1994.  The cumulative gross investment required is
estimated at Br 32 billion ($15.4 billion) at 1980/1981 prices.  The
implementation of the Plan, which is to be phased into three successive
sub-plans of two, three and five years' duration respectively, has been
affected by the need to reorient efforts towards relief and rehabilitation of
the drought-affected population.  The Plan envisages a 6.5 per cent average
annual growth rate of GDP in real terms, as compared to the 2.6 per cent
growth rate achieved in the pre-drought period of 1975-1983.  Value added by
the agricultural sector is planned to increase at an average annual rate of
4.3 per cent and that of the industrial sector (including manufacturing,
mining, construction, electricity and water supplies) at 10.8 per cent.  As a
result, the share of agriculture in GDP is to decline from 48 per cent at
present to 39 per cent at the end of the Plan period, while that of the
industrial sector is to increase from 16 per cent to about 24 per cent.  The
main emphasis of the Plan is on industrial expansion, with almost 45 per cent
of planned investment outlay earmarked for this sector.  High priority is also
placed on the rehabilitation of the agricultural sector through reforestation
and afforestation, soil and water conservation and expansion of irrigated
farming and the development of livestock and fisheries.  Several agricultural
projects costing about $170 million, to be funded by the World Food Programme
(WFP) and IDA, were to be implemented in 1986.

## Mobilization of domestic resources for development

637. Gross domestic savings, which represented 4.5 per cent of GDP in 1980,
declined to 2.7 and 1.9 per cent in the following two years, but recovered to
3.4 per cent in 1984.  This share is expected to increase to 15 per cent of
GDP in 1994, the terminal year of the Ten-Year Plan.  In view of the increased
expenditure for relief and rehabilitation and the decline in government
revenue, the budget deficit as a proportion of GDP increased from 7.9 per cent
in FY 1983/1984 to 9.6 per cent in FY 1984/1985.  As in 1983/1984, about
57.4 per cent of the deficit in 1984/85 was financed from external sources and
42.6 per cent from domestic borrowing.  About 55.5 per cent of the total fixed
investment of the Ten-Year Plan is to be generated from domestic sources.

## Transfer of external resources, debt and capital requirements

638. Total financial inflows more than doubled between 1980 and 1984, reaching
$571 million, of which concessional loans and grants represented about
90.5 per cent.  However, even this relief inflated level falls considerably

short of the annual $700 million required on average over the course of the Ten-Year Plan. Moreover, even the recent increase of ODA received by Ethiopia is one of the lowest among the LDCs when measured on a per capita basis: about $9.9 compared to $22 for all LDCs.

639. Total external debt increased from $1.1 billion at the end of 1982 to $1.58 billion at the end of 1984, while debt service payments increased from $69 million in 1982 to $129 million in 1984, corresponding to 15 per cent and 23 per cent of exports of goods and services in those two years respectively.

## Mechanism for the monitoring and follow-up of the SNPA

640. Ethiopia is among the few LDCs which have not yet held a country review meeting as envisaged by the SNPA. However, several meetings with donors were organized by the Relief and Rehabilitation Commission to assess the overall emergency situation, including the consequential financial and food aid requirements. The Government is expected to present its investment Programme within the framework of the Ten-Year Plan to a donors' meeting, whose date and venue remain to be determined. The Central Planning Supreme Council is the focal point for the monitoring and follow-up of the SNPA.

## 16. GAMBIA

## Economic Performance

641. Agriculture forms the backbone of Gambia's economy and variations in agricultural output in recent years have led to unstable economic growth. The agricultural sector comprised 32.6 per cent of GDP in fiscal year (FY) 1984/1985 156/ and provided employment to 70 per cent of the population. A succession of droughts in recent years hit the production of the major export commodity - groundnuts - which accounts for about 85 to 90 per cent of Gambia's domestic exports. Owing to the severity of the foreign-exchange crisis, real GDP, which had risen by 14.7 per cent in 1983, fell by 7.5 per cent in 1984 and by 8.7 per cent in 1985. Positive growth was registered in some sectors of the economy, however, but this was not sufficient to reverse the overall downward trend. Sectors which had shown positive growth include livestock, manufacturing and tourism.

642. Owing to declining volumes, groundnuts exports took a significant downturn after 1979: from an average of $38 million during the period 1975-1979, their average value fell short of $20 million in the subsequent five-year period, and was well below that level in the first half of 1985. The government's efforts to reduce balance-of-payments and fiscal deficits resulted in the slowing of development activity. Adjustment measures by way of cutbacks in imports have helped to reduce the trade deficit from $133 million in 1980 to $49 million in 1985, but the chronic trade deficits have led to an increasing external debt requiring heavy servicing charges, thereby adding a strain on the balance of payments. Although the share of government expenditures in GDP rose from 38.5 per cent to 39.9 per cent between FY 1980/1981 and FY 1984/1985, the overall fiscal deficit fell from 19 per cent of GDP to 18.3 per cent during the same period and was expected to fall to 17.5 per cent in FY 1986/1987. This is the result of higher revenues achieved thanks to improved revenue collection methods introduced in 1985, the windfall effect of the currency devaluation resulting from its floating, and the increase of certain import duties.

643. The tourist industry, on the other hand, has grown spectacularly.
Tourist arrivals in 1984 had doubled as compared to 1982 owing to an enlarged
hotel capacity. Provisional estimates for FY 1985/1986 indicated an increase
of 6 per cent over the previous period. However, the net foreign-exchange
earnings of this sector are small because of its low value-added content. Its
direct contribution to GDP (value added of restaurants, hotels and local tour
operators, etc.) is estimated at about 2 per cent, while the inclusion of
indirect effects (expenditure by employees in the tourist sector) raises its
contribution to an estimated 5 to 7 per cent of GDP. Another important source
of foreign exchange for Gambia is the re-export trade which accounted for
31 per cent of total recorded exports in FY 1984/1985. Moreover, an
additional portion of this trade was not recorded. However, growing deficits
on other service and income payments (including debt service) led to an
erosion of the country's foreign-exchange reserves, which fell from
$8.4 million at the end of 1982 to $1.7 million three years later,
corresponding to barely one week's imports.

644. To arrest the economic deterioration, the Government embarked on a series
of adjustment measures. In February 1984, it devalued the national currency
by 25 per cent against the pound sterling, to which it was pegged until the
end of 1985, and in the first quarter of 1986 the currency was again devalued
by as much as 50 per cent against the United States dollar. In August 1985,
the Government adopted the Economic Recovery Programme discussed below.

## Environment and disasters

645. Gambia has been plagued by droughts recurring every two to three years.
This has become an environmental disaster giving rise to desertification which
affects its agriculture and livestock production.

646. Its geography also imposes limits on cultivation. The land bordering the
Gambia River, which divides the country in two, is swampy. During the dry
season the salt water which is washed upstream by the river tends to render
large areas of potentially irrigable and fertile land unexploitable. The
building of a bridge/barrage on the Gambia River could help overcome these
problems. However, a study which had been carried out for almost a decade
revealed that such a project would have ecological consequences causing
substantial economic losses, particularly of river fish resources and the
swamp-bred mangroves which currently provide the country with much of its
firewood.

## Food and agriculture

647. Traditionally, agricultural activity was concentrated on groundnuts.
Frequent droughts and declining world prices caused groundnut production to be
halved from an average level of 156,000 tons in FY 1974/1975 to 75,000 tons in
FY 1984/1985. Under the two Development Plans covering FY 1975/1976-1979/1980
and FY 1981/1982-1985/1986 respectively, top priority was given to developing
the food and agriculture sector, because it offered the potential for import
substitution and diversification for exports, thereby easing the pressure on
the balance of payments. There are signs of positive changes. Producer
prices for groundnuts, which were increased five times during January 1985 to
May 1986, has partly contributed to the increase in marketed groundnut output

from 45,000 tons in FY 1984/1985 to 54,000 tons in FY 1985/1986. On average, food accounted for about 32 per cent of total merchandise imports from 1981 to 1985. Development efforts for this sector are directed towards a rapid increase in food crops with short production cycles, such as coarse grains, swamp rice, maize, millet and sorghum, as well as greater diversification through increased output of meat, fish resources, horticultural products and cotton. The completion of the Jahally Pachaar irrigation project has yielded two rice crops a year, with a total output of 10,000 tons, thereby offsetting about a third of the Gambia's rice imports. It is estimated that food self-sufficiency could be attained by 1995 at the present rate of population growth.

648. Cotton grown in the uplands is a new cash crop which may reduce Gambia's dependence on a single export crop. There are indications that world cotton prices are likely to be more stable in real terms over the next decade than those of groundnuts. However, the potential for cotton farming is limited both by the area suitable for cultivation and the higher inputs and labour requirements than for other crops. Financial and fiscal incentives have also given a boost to the fisheries sector during 1986. It has attracted significant investments of both local and foreign capital.

## Human and social development

649. The expansion and improvement of social and welfare services constitute the key objectives of the Second Development Plan. Primary and secondary school enrolment has doubled from 1975 to 1985, but the ratio between female and male enrolment has remained unchanged at 1:2. Major efforts have been made to provide adequate and safe water supplies and low-cost housing. Family planning services have become an important component in the country's health care programme, because a clear-cut population policy was laid down for the first time in the Second Plan. A National Women's Council and a Women's Bureau have also been established, which are to help promote the integration of women in national development.

## Development planning and policies

650. Under the First Development Plan nearly one half of investments were allocated to the transport sector. Thus, the country's trunk road network tripled between 1975 and 1985. Under the Second Development Plan there was a major shift in priorities from the physical infrastructure (e.g., transport, communications and public utilities) to directly productive sectors, particularly agriculture. More than one third of the proposed development expenditures were allocated to agriculture and industry, with 27.6 per cent directed to agriculture alone.

651. During the implementation period, severe budgetary and balance-of-payments difficulties led the Government to adopt a series of economic stabilization measures within the framework of an Economic Recovery Programme launched in August 1985. The Programme contains measures directed not only towards the stabilization of the economy, but also towards recovery and long-term growth. It hopes to achieve these objectives by containing demand and expenditure on the one hand, and by encouraging output on the other, through appropriate fiscal incentives and pricing policies, particularly in the agricultural sector and other productive sectors such as fisheries, livestock and tourism. The strategies adopted encompass the following:

(a)  A flexible exchange rate was introduced in January 1986 to encourage the flow of foreign exchange.

(b)  A revised Public Investment Programme was adopted for the period FY 1984/1985 to FY 1987/1988, superceding the last two years of the Second Plan.  The revised programme aims to improve productivity in public investment, by focusing on quick-gestation projects producing tradeable goods and on sectoral rehabilitation projects;

(c)  The public sector is to be reformed through the curtailment and major reallocation of recurrent governmental expenditures, increased revenue mobilization and the improved performance of the parastatal enterprises;  and

(d)  Growth and employment in the productive sectors is to be stimulated through reforms in the pricing, fiscal and monetary policies.

## Mobilization of domestic resources for development

652. The greater part of Gambia's investment programme has always been met by external resources.  The scope for mobilizing domestic resources is limited by the country's low per capita income and its very narrow resource base.

653. The Government was required to intensify efforts in mobilizing domestic resources under two stand-by agreements with the IMF in 1982 and 1984.  In fact, it even had difficulty in meeting its planned contribution of 15 per cent of the total investment programme under the Second Plan.  Taxes contribute 75 to 85 per cent of the government's domestic revenue. Measures applied to raise additional revenue included higher rates of existing taxes, introduction of new taxes and improvements in tax collection;  progressive reduction of subsidies on sales of rice, fertilizers and petroleum;  and direct cost recovery, particularly from fees and charges in the health sector.  At the same time efforts were made to prune the government's recurrent expenditures.  Interest rates on bank deposits were increased in order to encourage increased domestic savings.  In addition, liberal fiscal incentives to private investors, technical assistance and low-interest loans to small entrepreneurs were provided in order to stimulate private investments.  Despite all these measures, the country's gross domestic savings rate fell from 7.6 per cent of GDP in 1980 to 0.3 per cent in 1985.

## Transfer of external resources, debt and capital requirements

654. A persistent current-account deficit and the very low and declining savings rate led Gambia to depend heavily on foreign aid for its development. Its total external debt registered a significant increase as from 1979, when fiscal deficits became acute, growing from $28.3 million at the end of 1978 to $118 million at the end of 1980 and $181 million at the end of 1984, corresponding to 50 per cent and 88 per cent of GDP in these last two years respectively.  Although most of this debt is on highly concessional terms, the structure of Gambia's debt has serious implications for the future balance of payments.  Thus, about 44 per cent of the outstanding debt is owed to multilateral organizations and cannot therefore be rescheduled.  Because of increased amortization, the debt-service-to-exports ratio rose from 6 per cent in 1980 to 23 per cent in 1984.  This rapid increase in debt servicing is due

principally to the substantial arrears owed to the IMF in connection with two stand-by credits of SDR 16.9 million and SDR 12.8 million granted in 1982 and 1985 respectively. Payments in the order of SDR 1 million per month were expected to fall due in FY 1985/1986 and FY 1986/1987. In addition, Gambia has a stock of approximately $12 million in commercial arrears as well as $23 million in arrears to the Western African Clearing House and other financial institutions. For the immediate future, the country's debt service obligations will most likely have to be met by further external assistance in the form of debt rescheduling or exceptional balance-of-payments support.

655. Under the revised Public Investment Programme (FY 1984/1985 – FY 1987/1988), capital requirements were estimated at $320 million, of which 18 per cent were allocated for project financing, 22 per cent for technical assistance, 20 per cent for food aid, 13 per cent for balance-of-payments support and 27 per cent for recurrent cost financing.

656. At a special consultation on balance of payments held on 25-26 September 1985 under the auspices of the World Bank, the Government received $25 million worth of pledges of balance-of-payments support.

## Mechanisms for monitoring and follow-up of the SNPA

657. As a follow-up to the Round Table Meeting held in Banjul in November 1984, a series of regular sectoral consultations have been organized. Consultations on the health and fisheries sectors took place in December 1984 and June 1985 respectively. Sectoral consultations for the agriculture and water sectors were tentatively scheduled for January-February 1987.

## 17. GUINEA

## Economic performance

658. Guinea's economic growth in terms of GDP has been disappointing, reaching only 2.3 per cent in 1985 as compared with 1984. In fact, per capita growth stagnated, as population continued to increase at 2.2 per cent per year. Thus, the fundamental restructuring undertaken by the Government since 1984, which has touched all sectors of the economy, has not yet had a decisive impact on economic performance. Given the long-term nature of the reform measures, however, the fact that most of them were introduced only in the course of 1985 and the state of disarray of the economy at that time, early results could not have been expected. Nevertheless, signs of improvement are clearly visible and there is reason to consider 1985 as the turning point in the country's economic history.

659. Agriculture remains the basis of the Guinean economy, accounting for 38 per cent of GDP in 1983 and employing some 80 per cent of the population. Low producer prices (including a tax on production), shortages of agricultural inputs and transport problems had caused output to stagnate during the past two decades, despite the favourable climatic and soil conditions. Thus, falling production of food grains has turned this former net exporter into a major importer of grain (120,000 tons in 1984/1985). These imports absorbed an estimated 30 per cent of total export revenues in

recent years; moreover they were over and above the 25,000 to 45,000 tons received in the form of food aid. Nevertheless, food imports have been insufficient to meet international standards of nutrition. In order to stimulate domestic production, the Government announced the liberalization of producer prices for most foodstuffs in 1985; in the case of rice, the major food grain, it authorized a substantial price increase early in 1986.

660. By the same token, production of cash crops (e.g. coffee, palm kernels, tropical fruit and groundnuts) also declined dramatically in recent years, due to non-remunerative prices; as a result, some small farmers produced for subsistence only, while those who continued producing exported their output clandestinely. By way of illustration, official exports of coffee amounted to 450 tons in 1984, while unrecorded exports were estimated at 2,000 to 3,000 tons in that year. In order to counteract these practices and encourage production, the Government more than quadrupled the official producer prices for coffee and palm kernels early in 1986, bringing them into line with levels in neighbouring countries.

661. As in other agricultural activities, official price policies also caused most of Guinea's important livestock to be marketed in neighbouring countries. The exploitation rate of the country's abundant fishery resources - the annual production potential is estimated at 200,000 tons - has been less than 10 per cent. Indiscriminate logging for sale of timber in Liberia and Côte d'Ivoire have severely reduced Guinea's commercial forestry resources.

662. Guinea's greatest source of potential wealth are its mineral resources, particularly bauxite, alumina and diamonds. According to some estimates, the country possesses a third of the world's high-grade bauxite reserves. At the same time, the level of bauxite and alumina production is a major determinant of the country's economic performance, accounting for 97 per cent of exports in 1984. Bauxite output decreased from 13,650 tons in 1984, the highest level since 1979, to 12,700 tons in 1985. The output of alumina also fell. Diamond production, on the other hand, is estimated to have jumped from 24,000 carats in 1983 to 47,000 carats in 1984 and to a record 180,000 carats in 1985. A major new diamond mine, which started production in 1984, is expected to add 10 per cent to Guinea's diamond export volume.

663. The manufacturing sector, which produces mainly processed agricultural products, construction material, chemical products and textiles, had been operating at only about 15 per cent of capacity, contributing no more than about 2 per cent of GDP until 1985.

664. The trade surplus which Guinea has consistently been able to achieve, due to relatively stable export earnings from bauxite and alumina, was again offset in 1984 by rising net service payments and private transfers abroad. A heavy capital flight from the country has worsened the situation. Net capital inflows have not been sufficient to offset the resulting current-account deficit. In fact, the country has suffered continual increases in its net foreign liabilities since 1979, which reached $205 million as of end-1984.

Environment and disasters

665. While the country continues to suffer under environmental degradation due to overgrazing, deforestation and resulting soil erosion, it was spared major disasters in 1984 and 1985.

Human resources and social development

666. The educational system is ill-adjusted to the country's manpower needs, as too high a share of resources is directed towards higher education as compared to basic education; vocational training has been particularly neglected. The quantity and quality of school buildings are not adequate and textbooks are in short supply, but the substantial investments needed to attain acceptable standards far exceed the country's resources. Pending the formulation of appropriate policies, the Government has decided to limit such expenditures to those for which external concessional finance is available.

667. In the health and population sectors, priority is being given to primary health care, nutrition and pharmaceutical programmes, the establishment and management of health services and training. As in the field of education, no new investments in the health sector are being undertaken until a suitable programme has been worked out, with the exception of those that complete almost-finished projects.

Development planning and policies

668. Following an intensive policy dialogue with the World Bank and IMF, the Guinean Government announced a broad range of structural reforms during 1984 and 1985, covering virtually all sectors of the economy. This Economic Reform Programme envisages a complete reorganization of the economy. Henceforth initiatives for economic development are to come mainly through the free expression of the private sector, which the Government will support and guide through appropriate laws and rules, without attempting to supplant it. The State is to remain dominant only in fields where private initiative is either unsuited or not forthcoming. Implementation of this Programme has begun with a reform of the public service, a major currency devaluation, and a substantial increase of agricultural producer prices to remunerative levels, and the restructuring of the public sector.

669. Until 1984 most enterprises were State-owned, suffered from poor management, lack of imported spare parts and raw materials, irregular electricity supply and inadequate maintenance. Their poor performance necessitated regular budgetary transfers, which absorbed between 30 and 40 per cent of the budget and as much as 10 per cent of the GDP in recent years. As a part of its reform programme, the Government has started drastic reductions of its holdings by liquidating poorly-performing enterprises and privatizing (partly or fully) most others; only enterprises considered to be of public interest are to remain in State hands and to be rehabilitated.

670. In order to establish an appropriate legal framework for the liberalization of the economy, the following laws for key areas of the economy have been adopted and/or revised: (a) the new Commercial Law, that came into effect in May 1985, is being revised to take account of the competition which

the Government is seeking to encourage; (b) the Investment Code of October 1984 is being modified in order to simplify its procedures and reinforce its effectiveness in promoting private investment, both Guinean and foreign; (c) a new Banking Law, that came into effect in March 1985, provided the basis for the liquidation of all State-owned banks in December 1985 and allows commercial banking with substantial private participation; (d) a new customs tariff, that came into effect early in 1986, simplified previous regulations and effected a reduction in nominal rates, thus counterbalancing the steep increase in the taxable base due to the price increases of imported goods following the currency devaluation and trade liberalization. A new Mining Code as well as a new Petroleum Code are under preparation.

671. On the external economic front, the single most important measure undertaken by the Government was a drastic currency devaluation in January 1986. Until then, the public sector and a small number of private clients were able to buy foreign exchange at the official rate of 24.69 sylis to the SDR (equivalent to 22.4 sylis to the dollar at end-1985), while most of the private sector had to secure its foreign currency on the parallel market, in which the dollar was traded at 370 to 400 sylis as of December 1985. The currency adjustment, undertaken in several steps, consisted of a significant devaluation of the syli, its replacement at par by the Guinean franc and the establishment of a two-tier exchange rate. The slightly more favourable first-window rate, applying to governmental transactions, the nationalized industry and the mining companies, was set at FG 300 per dollar, implying a 92.5 per cent devaluation, while the second-window rate (initially set at FG 340 per dollar), applies to all other private transactions. It was determined at weekly currency auctions open to all purchasers and sellers of foreign exchange (except those having access to the first window). Upon agreement with the IMF, the Government unified the two rates on 1 June 1986, the new exchange rate being in essence the former non-privileged second-window rate. As of 30 June 1986 the exchange rate as determined by the auction system was FG 360 per dollar, implying a 94.2 per cent devaluation against the SDR as compared to the December 1985 rate.

672. A short-term economic recovery plan under the title "Plan Intérimaire de Redressement National" (PIRN), covering the period 1985 to 1987, entered into force in July 1985. The Plan gives priority to infrastructural rehabilitation and reorganization rather than new investments, and stresses the role of the agricultural sector, which should become the basis for socio-economic development. Particular emphasis is given to food production.

## Mobilization of domestic resources for development

673. Public finances depend heavily on the performance of the mining sector, as corporate taxes and export duties paid by the joint-venture mining operations constitute almost half of public revenues. Most other revenues are provided by import duties. For many years, recurrent spending has outpaced recurrent revenues, mostly due to the bloated civil service on the one hand and losses of parastatals on the other. Both areas are prime targets of reforms that should go a long way towards the reduction of recurrent expenditures. On the receipts side, the reform of the customs schedule should also contribute to reducing the deficit, inasmuch as the increase of dutiable imports is expected to outweigh the reduction in nominal rates.

674. The streamlining of the civil service constitutes a major element of the government's reform programme.  In order to create an effective structure, a substantial reduction of government employees is envisaged in combination with a significant real increase of salaries for those remaining in service.  The number of civil servants currently estimated between 84,000 and 90,000 is to be reduced to around 40,000.  This reduction is to be achieved inter alia through financial incentives for voluntary departures, automatic retirement at age 55 and the removal of all fictitious and irregularly hired employees from the payroll.  The civil servants leaving the public sector are expected to find employment in the private sector.  However, the Government is preparing a public works programme to combat unemployment.

Transfer of external resources, debt, capital requirements

675. Following the satisfactory conclusion of negotiations on the Economic Reform Programme and first steps in its implementation, Guinea was granted an IMF stand-by credit of SDR 33 million ($38.1 million) in February 1986, as well as World Bank loans totalling SDR 38.5 million ($44.4 million).   Of these, SDR 22.9 million ($26.5 million) were in the form of a Structural Adjustment Loan under IDA conditions, while SDR 15.6 million ($18.8 million) represented a Sub-Saharan African Facility credit.   The assurance of the Bank Group credits has attracted special joint financing from Guinea's major donors in support of the Economic Reform Programme for a total of $65.9 million at the time (including Special Facility contributions).  France, which is Guinea's most important partner, is providing quick-disbursing assistance of FF 200 million ($25.3 million), Japan is contributing Yen 5,600 million ($27 million), the Federal Republic of Germany 23 million ($9 million) and Switzerland SF 10 million ($4.6 million).   Additional financing is being requested from the United States of America.   In early 1986 the World Bank estimated that, including the IMF Stand-by Credit, at least $147 million should become available in 1986 and 1987 in support of Guinea's Structural Adjustment Programme.

676. Confirmation of the IMF Stand-by credit opened the door for debt rescheduling negotiations in the framework of the Paris Club which were held in April 1986.  Public foreign debt, including short-term debt, amounted to $1.264 billion at the end of 1984 (equivalent to nearly 60 per cent of the 1984 GDP of $2.122 billion), of which $345 million was owed to CMEA and $375 million to OECD member countries.  The negotiations succeeded in alleviating considerably the burden connected with the latter debt.  The most important part of the rescheduling concerned payments arrears estimated at $120 million at the end of 1985, 95 per cent of which (amortization and interest) were rescheduled for repayment between 1990 and 1995, the remaining 5 per cent to be paid in three annual instalments, beginning 28 February 1987.   Similarly, 95 per cent of the debt service due between 1 January 1986 and 28 February 1987 (amounting to around $40 million) has been rescheduled for repayment between January 1992 and July 1996, with the remaining 5 per cent to be repaid concurrently with the respective 5 per cent of the payments arrears.

Follow-up of the SNPA

677. On 11 April 1986 a meeting between the Guinean authorities and the country's principal non-project aid donors took place in the World Bank's European Office in Paris.  Representatives from five countries (France, the Federal Republic of Germany, Japan, Switzerland and the United States) and four multilateral institutions (World Bank, IMF, OECD and UNDP) participated.  At the meeting the Guinean representatives stated their Government's intention to organize a Consultative Group under World Bank auspices.  The first meeting of this Group has been scheduled for December 1986 under joint World Bank/UNDP sponsorship.

18.  GUINEA-BISSAU

Economic performance

678. GDP at constant prices grew at 10.2 per cent in 1984 after an 8.1 per cent decline in the preceding year.

679. Four items (groundnuts, shrimps and fish, sawn wood and coconuts), account for an estimated 85 per cent of total exports.  During the period 1978-1985, the value of imports was four to five times greater than that of exports, while the deficit in the goods and services account averaged 36 per cent of GDP.  The deficit in the merchandise balance was reduced from $46 million in 1983 to $33 million in 1985, essentially on account of a 22 per cent compression of imports.  However, unrecorded exports, particularly of groundnuts, seem to be significant.

680. The country's fisheries resources are promising, and their contribution to GDP has been increasing.  Non-existent until 1976, exports of shrimps and fish now represent nearly 40 per cent of total exports.  The potential fish catch is estimated at 250,000 to 350,000 mt without endangering the ecological balance.

681. The country is heavily dependent on food imports, which represent nearly 30 per cent of total imports in normal crop years.  Local food production was affected by drought conditions and by insect outbursts.  With the increase in rainfall in 1985, production of cereals in 1985 has been estimated at a record 185,000 mt or 48 per cent above the average of the previous five years.  The cereal deficit for 1986 is estimated at 24,000 mt, of which 6,000 mt are covered by donor pledges.  However, the Government's declared inability to finance fully the remaining deficit implies correspondingly larger food aid requirements.

682. There are indications that mineral resources (including bauxite, phosphate and off-shore petroleum) may be commercially exploitable.  The maritime border dispute with Guinea concerning the sharing of some oil deposits is now settled.  The country's legislation on hydrocarbon mining was revised in 1985 with a view to encouraging exploration, and foreign oil companies have been invited to bid for off-shore exploration rights.

683. The country appears to be experiencing difficulties in securing fuel from suppliers within the region. The Bissau thermal-power station is being reinforced with the financial support of the Arab Bank for Economic Development in Africa ($4.7 million), which is expected to increase the country's production of electricity by 76 per cent.

684. Roads and ports are insufficient and in serious need of repair and maintenance. In 1981, less than 600 km of the 3,100 km road network were estimated to be paved.

## Environment and disasters

685. Recurrent drought affected the country several times between 1977 and 1983. Rains were favourable in 1984 and 1985, but a locust invasion devastated rice and millet crops in the north of the country in 1985. The United Nations Sudano-Sahelian Office estimates that at least one half of the national territory is vulnerable to forest fires during the dry season. The Government is encouraging reforestation and investing in irrigation schemes as a means of combating drought.

## Human resources and social development

686. An Action Plan for the Water Supply and Sanitation Sector has been prepared for the period 1987-1990.

## Development planning and policies

687. A four-year development plan for 1983-1986 favours investment in productive sectors such as agriculture, fisheries, forestry and mining.

688. During 1984, the Government took a number of measures aimed at improving efficiency and fostering production. These measures include: (i) a 50 per cent devaluation of the peso in December 1983, followed by further exchange-rate adjustments at relatively short intervals; (ii) increases in producer prices for traditional agricultural goods (averaging 70 per cent); (iii) assignment of a greater role to the private sector in the marketing of agricultural goods; (iv) reorganization and a more clearly defined role of the two State marketing organizations; and (v) the promotion of autonomous village associations announced in 1986 to develop food aid and other agricultural production. Measures aimed at facilitating customs transactions were approved at a meeting held in March 1986 by the Senegal-Gambia-Guinea Bissau customs assistance agreement. In January 1986, Guinea-Bissau became the ninth member of the Permanent Inter-State Committee on Drought Control in the Sahel (CILSS).

## Mobilization of domestic resources

689. For the first time since 1981, combined private and public consumption was compressed in 1984, when it fell to a level slightly below total GDP. Nevertheless, it follows that any capital accumulation still has to be entirely financed from external sources.

690. In 1983, the budget deficit reached 22.5 per cent of GDP, with current revenue insufficient even to cover government wages and salaries. Faced with this financial imbalance, the government launched an austerity programme in 1984 and again in 1985. Government revenue has been raised mainly through income tax reform, higher taxes on certain consumption goods, the effect of the exchange rate adjustment, and larger transfers from State enterprises engaged in exporting agricultural goods. Wage increases in 1984 did not exceed the 50 per cent average increase implemented at the beginning of that year, and the expansion of other current outlays did not exceed 60 per cent. As a result of all these measures, goverment revenue exceeded public wages and salaries in 1984; nevertheless, the budget deficit-GDP ratio fell by only 2 percentage points.

## Transfer of external resources, debt, capital requirements

691. The need to rely on foreign resources for development has brought about a serious deterioration in the country's payments position. Unrequited transfers, mainly in the form of official grants, financed about 50 per cent of the deficit in the goods and services account during the period 1980-83. But the absolute amount of concessional assistance fell from the 1981 peak of $68.0 million to $57.1 million in 1984.

692. Total external debt was estimated to amount to $164 million by the end of 1984. Debt service during that year was estimated at $5 million, or one half of total exports.

693. In September 1984, a stand-by arrangement amounting to SDR 1.875 million was agreed by the IMF. Financial support was granted by the World Bank in 1984 for strengthening the management capabilities of key economic ministries (SDR 6.0 million) and for facilitating imports of agricultural inputs and equipment material (SDR 10.1 million). Between 1978 and 1983, drawings from the EEC Stabex amounted to $11.8 million and from IMF's Compensatory Financing Facility to SDR 3 million.

## Mechanisms for monitoring and follow-up of the SNPA

694. A donors' round table was held in Lisbon in May 1984 with the participation of 27 countries and 23 international organizations. Total aid requirements submitted by Guinea-Bissau amounted to $249.1 million. Although commitments made are difficult to tabulate, they have been estimated at $161.9 million, i.e. 63 per cent of total requirements. Various countries also expressed readiness to renegotiate the country's external debt and to finance local costs of projects as well as other recurrent development expenses. The Government in turn announced the establishment of a Management Unit for Balance of Payments Assistance and offered to produce an annual report on aid utilization. The country's balance-of-payments needs were discussed at a meeting held between Guinea-Bissau and its partners under the auspices of the World Bank in Paris in February 1985. A second round table meeting was further held in Bissau in April 1985, where new pledges were made by donors.

695. As part of the follow-up to the round table process, review meetings are to be held periodically with representatives of donor countries under the aegis of UNDP.  A conference of non-governmental organizations supporting the country's development efforts was held in Bissau in 1985, in the context of the follow-up to the Lisbon Round Table.  Sectoral consultations for health were held in February 1986.

## 19.  HAITI

### Economic performance

696. In the 1970s the economy of Haiti had grown satisfactorily, inasmuch as real GDP grew by an average of almost 4 per cent per annum.  However, this expansion was reversed in the 1980s.  A substantial fall in GDP in 1981 and 1982 was followed by a very sluggish recovery in the period 1983-1985, during which GDP growth fell short of the rate of population growth.  This meant that in 1985 the level of per capita income was lower than that reached in 1980. Rural incomes, whose absolute levels are estimated at less than half the national average, declined even more sharply and were probably lower than their 1976 levels.  This poverty explains the internal and external migration that has taken place.  It is estimated that 38,000 persons are currently leaving the countryside each year on a net basis, while some 25,000 (about 0.5 per cent of the population) are leaving the country - mostly for the United States, Canada and the Dominican Republic.  This chronic poverty also contributed to the social disorders in 1984 and 1985, which eventually brought about the change in régime in early 1986.

697. Agriculture has been on a long-term decline, due to continued erosion, fragmentation of holdings and the low level of technology, which has remained virtually unchanged for two centuries.  The production of most locally-produced foodcrops (rice, corn, millet, beans, bananas) either stagnated or declined between 1980 and 1984, but some increases were reported in 1985.  Imports of food, including wheat, continue at a high level.  The production of coffee, the main agricultural export item, rose from around 33,000 mt in the crop year 1981/82 to 36,000-37,000 mt during the crop years 1982/83 through 1984/85.  Sugar cane production is also estimated to have increased slightly from 1981 to 1985, but deliveries to sugar factories have decreased, probably due to the low price paid to farmers.  A correspondingly high proportion of the cane was used for distillation into clairin.  From a net exporter of sugar throughout the 1970s, Haiti had become a net importer by 1985.

698. Manufacturing is a relatively important activity in Haiti, accounting for more than 16 per cent of GDP in the 1980s, possibly the highest figure amongst all LDCs.  The sector is divided between industries producing mostly for the local market and others - particularly assembling industries - which are almost exclusively export-oriented.  The import-substitution industries, which include State-owned enterprises, engaged in the production of flour, sugar, cement and edible oil, have not in general been performing well in the 1980s. These industries, which have enjoyed a high degree of protection, have often worked below capacity and sold at high prices.  On the other hand, the light industries manufacturing for export have been a major growth pole of the economy since the early 1970s.  After a pause in 1981-83, which may be

attributed to recession in the main export market - the United States - this growth had resumed, but is expected to be negative in 1986 in the wake of labour troubles associated with the political situation. In 1985, the value-added content of light manufactured exports represented more than 55 per cent of total exports. The main export industries are clothing, electrical and electronic equipment and sporting goods.

699. Bauxite, which accounted for 17 per cent of exports in late 1975, has not been mined since 1982. However, some encouraging prospects for mining copper, gold and lignite have been recently reported.

700. Although Haiti has a good tourist potential, earnings from this sector declined in the 1980s due to image problems.

## Environment and disasters

701. The ruggedness of the terrain makes fully two thirds of the land area unfit for cultivation. On the remaining area, soil erosion has been one of the reasons for the long-term decline of agriculture. It is estimated that 10-15,000 hectares are lost every year to soil erosion due to food crop plantings on steep slopes and felling of forests for fuel and construction. Erosion is further exacerbated by irregular and heavy rainfall. Meat production, for its part, is still affected by the destruction of most of the pig population following the swine fever outbreak of the late 1970s.

702. The civil disturbances from 1984 to 1986, which led to the change of régime, caused heavy damage to the country's already frail economy.

## Human resources and social development

703. The educational level of the population, particularly in the rural areas and among women, continues to be very low. In 1985, about 77 per cent of the population (90 per cent in rural areas) was considered to be illiterate, and the enrolment ratio in primary school was estimated at less than 50 per cent. In part, this reflects the fact that only four out of ten pupils entering primary education completed the course. A major curriculum revision being implemented is the use of creole in most primary schools. The education sector is supported by a number of donors, but progress is being hampered by the problem of recurrent costs. In fact, the expansion of enrolment in education has taken place mostly in the private sector. This is particularly striking in secondary schools.

### Number of pupils in secondary schools

| School year | Total | of which, share in: | |
| | | Public schools (Per cent) | Private schools (per cent) |
|---|---|---|---|
| 1979/80 | 87 680 | 20.9 | 79.1 |
| 1980/81 | 96 596 | 17.9 | 82.1 |
| 1981/82 | 98 570 | 16.1 | 83.9 |
| 1982/83 | 117 081 | 16.4 | 83.6 |
| 1983/84 | 128 900 | 17.8 | 82.2 |

704. Linked to the low educational level of the rural population, health indicators continue to be among the lowest in the world.

## Development planning and policies

705. The Third Five-Year Plan covered the period FY 1981/1982 to FY 1985/1986, 157/ but in view of the financial difficulties that occurred in the early part of its implementation, most of its targets have had to be abandoned. A Bi-Annual Plan for FY 1984/85-FY 1985/86 with more modest objectives than the Third Five-Year Plan was subsequently issued, but the social and political changes that have occurred since made the latter Plan inoperative as well. In July 1986 an Emergency Action Plan (Plan d'Action d'Urgence) was prepared with a view to mobilizing external assistance for a new Bi-Annual Plan 1986-88 scheduled to start in November 1986.

## Mobilization of domestic resources for development

706. The sharp recession of the economy of 1981 led to a financial crisis, which was to be overcome by a stabilization programme (including austerity measures on the part of the Government) supported by a stand-by agreement with the IMF (August 1982 - September 1983). This programme had succeeded in reducing the budget deficit. However, in spite of the increase in domestic revenue due to increased taxation and improved tax administration, the deficit widened again beginning in 1984, as current expenditure could not be contained. It has been repeatedly reported that certain long-standing "extra-budgetary" expenditures for undisclosed purposes had increased in 1984 and 1985. This meant that Haiti was not in a position to observe the performance criteria agreed with the IMF for a subsequent two-year stand-by agreement (November 1983 - October 1985), so that drawings under this agreement were suspended in early 1984.

### Fiscal year ending 30 September

|  | 1981 | 1982 | 1983 | 1984 | 1985 b/ |
|---|---|---|---|---|---|
|  | (In millions of gourdes) a/ | | | | |
| 1. Current domestic revenue | 660 | 749 | 847 | 914 | 1 120 |
| 2. Net transfers from public enterprises | -- | 75 | 74 | 91 | 73 |
| 3. Total domestic revenue (1 + 2) | 660 | 824 | 921 | 1 005 | 1 193 |
| 4. Current expenditure | 826 | 829 | 950 | 1 123 | 1 259 |
| 5. Deficit (3 - 4) | - 166 | - 5 | - 29 | - 118 | - 66 |

a/   1 dollar = 5 gourdes.
b/   Estimated.

It should be noted, however that surpluses from public enterprises were obtained by price increases, using the monopoly status enjoyed by most of them. Some of these prices were reduced by the new régime in 1986.

## Transfer of external resources and external debt

707. Available data indicate that net disbursements of grants and concessional assistance increased substantially in 1982 and 1983, but stagnated in 1984. Some donors are reported to have delayed aid disbursements in 1985. External public debt doubled between September 1980 and September 1985 to reach $689 million at the latter date. Most of this increase was due to the taking over by the Government of the debts of certain enterprises absorbed by the public sector. However, the structure of the debt has become more concessional. In FY 1984/85 debt servicing represented 12 per cent of exports of goods and services, compared to 7.8 per cent in 1981. The July 1986 Plan d'Action d'Urgence seeks the financing of projects for 1986-88 of a value of $460 million.

## Mechanisms for the monitoring and follow-up of the SNPA

708. There are two mechanisms in Haiti which may be considered in the context of monitoring and follow-up of the SNPA. Since 1976, there have been regular meetings of the Commission mixte pour l'implantation des programmes de coopération externe en Haiti initiated under the auspices of the Organization of American States. This Commission held its tenth session in July 1985. In 1982 Haiti joined the Caribbean Group for Co-operation in Economic Development organized by the World Bank, whose Haiti subgroup met for the third time in July 1985. In 1986, assistance for the Plan d'Action d'Urgence may lead to ad hoc arrangements between Haiti and its partners.

## 20. LAO PEOPLE'S DEMOCRATIC REPUBLIC

## Economic performance

709. Development in the Lao People's Democratic Republic has remained constrained by its small population, low rate of domestic savings, land-locked situation and shortage of educated and trained manpower at every level.

710. The main achievements during the 1980s have been the virtual attainment of self-sufficiency in rice production and the considerable progress made in the reconstruction of the economy after a period of conflict. The real annual rate of growth of the country's GDP averaged 6.1 per cent between 1980 and 1985, having fluctuated between a near-stagnant rate in 1983 to as much as 12.5 per cent in 1984. The latter improvement was largely due to a good harvest in that year, which yielded 1.3 million tons of rice according to official sources. Due to heavy rains, similarly good harvest results were produced in 1985, contributing heavily to the estimated 6.2 per cent growth of GDP in that year.

711. External trade is largely conducted by the Société du Commerce Lao (SCL), a State trading organization, which has a formal monopoly on all foreign trade, but in fact exercises it only on certain products, leaving others to the private sector. The country's exports in 1985 amounted to $29 million, of

which electricity exports to Thailand was a major part. Other commodities include timber and other wood products, tin, coffee and gypsum. The export earnings are greatly exceeded by the cost of imports, which were estimated at $160 million in 1985, composed mainly of foodstuffs, petroleum products, textiles, chemicals, metal manufactures and paper products.

712. The current account deficit of the balance of payments grew from $69.2 million in 1981 to an estimated $95.3 million in 1985. This was due primarily to a deteriorating trade balance caused by only modest gains in export earnings, which were more than offset by a rapid build-up of imports in support of development projects, particularly those financed by donors from the non-convertible area. Imports from the latter area more than doubled from $57.8 million in 1981 to an estimated $114.6 million in 1985. Vis-à-vis the convertible area, the poor performance of exports during the 1982-84 period, combined with a decline in long-term loans, led to reductions in imports in 1984 and 1985. Gross foreign-exchange reserves in convertible currencies fluctuated sharply from a low of $8.5 million at the end of 1982 to about $20 million in June 1984 (equivalent to about 8 months' imports from the convertible area).

713. The industrial sector is still at an early stage of development and its activities are limited to tin and gypsum mining, the processing of agricultural products, the small-scale manufacture of agricultural tools and construction material as well as the production of consumer goods. Growth in manufacturing is reported to have declined in 1983 and 1984, largely because of shortages of imported raw materials. However, the declining trend in industry was in fact reversed in 1985, during which a 13 per cent growth rate was estimated to have been achieved. Moreover, the Government adopted an industrial policy for the remainder of the 1980s, based on the processing of local raw materials in small-scale plants.

714. The Lao People's Democratic Republic being a land-locked country, its weak transport and communications network continues to hamper development. In the absence of a railway and access to the sea, the country depends on road, river, and air transport. The present road network consists of 1,138 km of asphalted, 5,293 km of gravelled and 3,838 km of dirt roads, giving it one of the lowest densities of road length per area in Asia. Most of the road network requires large-scale rehabilitation. River transport on the Mekong River has declined due to shortages of barges and inadequate port facilities, which in turn result from the absence of a programme to co-ordinate river and road transport. Air transport suffers from shortages of trained personnel and spare parts. The telecommunications network is inadequate to support the country's administrative, economic and social development needs and requires major improvements.

715. The Lao People's Democratic Republic is well endowed with hydroelectric, forest and mineral resources. Production of the forestry sector in 1985 was reported to have been over three times higher than in 1981. Exports of timber alone resulted in $8.6 million in foreign-exchange earnings in 1985, accounting for over 17 per cent of merchandise exports to the covertible area. As to minerals, tin has been found in Khammouane Province, gypsum near Savannakhet and gold in various rivers. Large deposits of potash and iron ore of high concentration have been identified, as well as smaller quantities of copper, lead, manganese, coal and limestone, but the net economic value of these minerals has yet to be assessed.

716. Since no oil has yet been discovered, petroleum products must be imported, accounting for about one fifth of imports from the convertible area. However, electricity generation largely depends on hydropower resources. While the country has a large hydropower potential (including that of the Mekong River estimated at over 18,000 MW), the total installed generating capacity amounts to no more than 170 MW. The Nam Ngum hydropower station (110 MW capacity) provides electricity mainly for export to Thailand. According to official sources, the Government has concentrated its efforts in the hydro-electric development programme on the rehabilitation of existing and the installation of additional small stations and the preparation of pre-investment studies on large electric power plants.

Environment and disasters

717. More than 90 per cent of all energy consumed in the Lao People's Democratic Republic comes from wood fuel, causing environmental concern on account of the danger of deforestation. Therefore, the Government has adopted policies to introduce alternative sources of energy for home consumption.

718. Although the Lao People's Democratic Republic did not experience any major disaster or serious political tension in 1985, refugees continued to leave the country, mostly for economic reasons, although at a lower scale than in 1984. Moreover, small groups of refugees voluntarily returned to Laos in 1985 bringing the total return flow since 1980 to nearly 3,000.

Human resources and social development

719. The Government has made some progress in the achievement of certain social development objectives, particularly in the educational sector. The attendance rate of primary-age children has reached approximately 80 per cent and progress in the campaign to abolish illiteracy is noteworthy. At the post-secondary level, new institutions have been established.

720. In spite of governmental efforts to create a proper physical and human infrastructure, health services are still deficient. In 1985, the infant mortality rate was reported at 120-130 per thousand and life expectancy at birth was estimated to be no more than 45 years. 158/ To overcome these difficulties, the Government has adopted a programme of rehabilitation of health services, upgrading the capability of the existing health personnel.

721. The Lao People's Democratic Republic carried out its first population census in March 1985, the preliminary results of which point to a total population of 3.6 million, growing at an annual rate of 2.9 per cent and having a density of 15 inhabitants per km$^2$. The fact that the population was lower than expected strengthened the government's opposition to family planning.

722. The Government introduced a new and substantially increased salary structure for its civil servants, containing more than 40 salary levels, but the bulk of salary payments are in the form of coupons for purchasing food and other consumer goods.

Development planning and policies

723. The Government organizes its economic planning and management within the framework of five-year and annual plans. However, the statistical and planning system in the Lao People's Democratic Republic has not yet reached the stage where consistent macro-economic projections backed by detailed sectoral data and interrelationships can be prepared. In fact, few in-depth sectoral analyses have been undertaken, but the Government wishes to prepare sectoral and subsectoral studies, in areas such as agriculture, forestry and industry.

724. The main objectives and priorities of the Second Five-Year Plan (1986-1990) are:  self-sufficiency in food production and establishment of a six-month food security reserve;  improvement of the transport and communications infrastructure;  development of natural resources, especially hydroelectricity and timber;  development of small-scale industries, processing locally available raw materials;  and expanded and improved educational and health services.

Mobilization of domestic resources for development

725. The main source of budget revenue are the surpluses accumulated by the State enterprises, part of which are transferred to the general government budget.  These surpluses accounted for approximately half of total fiscal receipts in the 1980s, of which with Electricité du Laos accounted for a very important component.  Investment capital is provided through budgetary allocations.

726. Recently, a number of measures were taken to increase financial discipline, such as price adjustments, stricter expenditure control, more rigid enforcement of the tax code, higher agricultural taxes and tighter supervision of the financial activities of both public and private enterprises.  According to official sources, 4,670 businesses were registered in 1984 and paid almost K 10 million ($285,000) in taxes. As a result, the country's budgetary performance has improved.  The ratio of fiscal revenue to GDP rose from 12 per cent in 1980 to 19.2 per cent in 1982, while current expenditures declined from 17 per cent to 12.1 per cent in the same period. However, in 1983 and 1984 the excess of domestic revenue over current expenditure declined, mainly because of lower profitability in public enterprises and the rising cost of consumer subsidies.  In 1984, the interest rate on private savings accounts was increased, so as to mobilize more domestic resources.

Transfer of external resources, debt, capital requirements

727. The Lao People's Democratic Republic relies heavily on foreign aid for its economic development.  Total gross receipts from abroad are reported to be in the range of $100 million a year (equivalent to $27 per capita based on a 3.6 million population), most of which comes from the socialist countries. The USSR is the major donor, contributing mainly project aid estimated at $50-60 million per annum.  Australia, India, Japan, the Netherlands and Sweden are also important donors.

728. In order to ensure that available external resources are used most effectively, the Government has intensified its aid co-ordination. Nevertheless, warnings that foreign assistance had not been "effectively managed and used" were made at the highest political level as late as 1986.

729. Outstanding disbursed debt, most of which is on highly concessional terms, amounted to an estimated $412.6 million in December 1984, of which $288 million was due to socialist countries and $124 million to countries with convertible currencies. The convertible-currency debt is roughly evenly divided between bilateral and multilateral creditors, particularly the Asian Development Bank, IDA and the IMF Trust Fund. The export-to-debt-service ratio with the convertible currency area is reported to have grown from 15.6 per cent in 1983 to 37.5 per cent in 1985, compared with 18.8 per cent vis-à-vis creditors in the non-convertible area in 1985.

## Mechanism for monitoring and follow-up of the SNPA

730. The Second Round Table Meeting for the Lao People's Democratic Republic was held in April 1986 in Geneva. The discussion focused on the future sectoral priorities namely, transport and communications, energy, agricultural diversification, forestry and the need to develop the country's managerial and technical human resources. The meeting concluded that further dialogue was needed between the Lao People's Democratic Republic and its major donors to define more precisely the priorities within each main sector. In addition to the various multilateral and bilateral donors, the Government addressed itself to non-governmental organizations in a position to assist in implementing small-scale projects in various sectors.

### 21.  LESOTHO

## Economic performance

731. Outstanding features in Lesotho's economy are the low level of merchandise exports, reliance on migrant labour for employment and as a source of purchasing power and foreign exchange, the government's dependence on customs revenue and foreign aid and the country's membership in the South African Customs Union (SACU) and the Common Monetary Area. 159/ Migrant labour, increases in customs revenue, and foreign aid have in the past provided the financial resources for rapid growth of national income. In the 1970s real GDP is estimated to have increased at a rate of close to 10 per cent per year and real GNP even faster. However, the factors mentioned above render the country vulnerable to external shocks. Lesotho is land-locked entirely surrounded by, and to a high degree dependent on, the Republic of South Africa (for imports, energy, transport and communications links). Thus, imports of goods and non-factor services exceed GDP since the mid-1970s.

732. In the early 1980s the pace of economic activity slackened in Lesotho. This was due to a combination of factors such as the spread of the international recession to the Southern African subregion, the onset of drought, and cutbacks in public sector expenditure as part of the efforts to contain a widening budget deficit. This affected, inter alia, agricultural output and building and construction, a sector largely upheld by government capital expenditure. Real GDP stagnated in 1981/82 and decreased during each of the following two years.

733. According to estimates by the Central Bank of Lesotho, real GDP rose by 3.7 per cent in 1984 and 2.4 per cent in 1985, the growth being attributed mainly to the recovery in agriculture and to manufacturing activity. A number of major building projects were completed in 1985, such as the new international airport, the government office complex, and a microwave telecommunications project. Other public projects continue, among them road building and road improvement programmes. In the early 1980s, manufacturing in Lesotho suffered as some enterprises relocated abroad. Since then, the Lesotho National Development Corporation (LNDC) has led an active investment promotion campaign and expansion in this sector has been encouraging, with extension of some existing enterprises and a number of new small and medium-sized ventures having started operations.

734. A salient feature in recent economic developments in Lesotho has been an acceleration of inflation, which is strongly influenced by price developments in South Africa. Goods and money flow freely between the two countries. Almost the totality of Lesotho's merchandise imports comes from the SACU area. With the rand, the loti has been depreciating strongly against the dollar. The annual rate of inflation in Lesotho had risen to 17 per cent in December 1985.

735. The overall balance of payments continued to show a surplus in 1985. Merchandise export values declined over the years 1981-1983 due to the decline and then almost complete cessation of diamond exports with the closure in 1982 of Lesotho's only diamond mine of significance. The performance of non-diamond exports improved in domestic currency terms during the first half of the decade, but fluctuated without any certain trend in dollar terms (between $22 and 29 million). Moreover, exports proceeds still finance only a small fraction of imports. Since the beginning of the decade, the trade deficit has been covered by migrants' remittances and aid and capital inflows.

736. The budgetary situation during the first two years of Lesotho's Third Plan period (1980/81-1984/85) was marked, inter alia, by the growth of recurrent expenditures and a widening deficit, which reached a level corresponding to over 15 per cent of GDP in 1981/82. This first expansionary phase was followed by a period of consolidation during the next three years, when expenditure was restrained, mainly through a clampdown on capital expenditures. The deficit was reduced and the government's cash position improved, largely due to buoyant customs revenue. However, budgetary pressure started building up again in mid-1985. Underlying factors were a slowdown in the growth of customs revenue, a rise in civil service salaries implemented in the beginning of the year, the need to step up maintenance expenditure and the effects of inflation on the cost of goods and services and of the falling loti on debt service. A sharp increase in the budget deficit for 1985/86 resulted, and a need for a tight budget policy over the medium term was foreseen.

737. The proposed Lesotho Highlands Water Scheme is a billion-dollar project holding the potential of transformational investment of the kind mentioned in the SNPA. Preliminary feasibility studies have been completed and detailed design, survey and preparatory engineering work was scheduled to start in 1986. The project involves the construction of a system of dams and tunnels for the transfer of water to South Africa. Construction would take place over several phases extending over a 30-year period. Apart from future royalty

income on water deliveries, Lesotho would gain an indigenous energy source through the project's hydroelectric power component, and reliable water supplies which could be used both to develop irrigated farming and to improve urban water supply. There are other possibilities as well for tapping the water resources in the highlands, such as the wholly domestic Oxbow multipurpose scheme, which also has a hydropower component.

## Disasters

738. Output of all main food crops has been on the decline in Lesotho since the mid-1970s, compounding the shortages that make the country largely dependent on imported food and food aid, even in normal years. Conditions worsened with the onset of severe drought in the subregion. A state of national food emergency was first declared in 1983, and continued into 1984 and 1985. There was some recovery in the 1984/85 agricultural season, but late rains and early frost again reduced 1985/86 crop yields. In mid-1986, Lesotho was one of seven African countries reported by FAO still to be suffering from abnormal food shortages.

## Human resources and social development

739. Employment is a major problem in Lesotho, greatly adding to the country's vulnerability. Currently nearly half of the male labour force finds employment in South Africa. By 1982/83, migrant labour income had already surpassed GDP. In the area of rural development various projects are underway including food-for-work schemes and programmes such as village water supplies, co-operative development and rural infrastructures. As regards the health situation, there were signs of overall deterioration and indications of an increased incidence of malnutrition among children, as a consequence of the drought.

## Development planning and policies

740. Lesotho's Third Five-Year Development Plan covered the fiscal years 1980/81-1984/85. The Fourth Development Plan was expected to be finalized at the end of 1986. Previous development plans have been largely a summation of investment projects. Preparations for the Fourth Plan aimed at a more comprehensive approach, with more emphasis on overall objectives and strategies, and sectoral programmes to be elaborated as instruments to fulfil these. As the government's financial situation is expected to remain tight, increased attention is being paid to recurrent cost implications and constraints.

741. Priority areas under the new Plan are likely to be agriculture, the development of water and energy resources, and industry. Domestic income generation and employment creation are all-important issues which will remain at the centre of the government's development strategy. A start has been made to address these issues, inter alia through the promotion of industry and of rural development. A major ongoing programme aiming at increasing agricultural output is the Food Self-Sufficiency Programme, concentrating on high productivity areas of maize and sorghum.

Mobilization of domestic resources

742. Customs revenue under the SACU agreement remains the government's main source of income, accounting in recent years for approximately two-thirds of receipts excluding foreign aid grants.  Among steps taken to broaden and expand the revenue base, the most important to date has been the introduction of a retail sales tax in late 1982.  The rate of sales tax has been raised several times, most recently under the 1986/87 budget to 12 per cent.  Income tax collection has been improved and efforts to further rationalize and intensify revenue collection are underway.

743. In Lesotho, high liquidity in the banking system coexists with scarcity of funds available for development purposes.  The Government has developed new financial instruments (treasury bills, government bonds) to tap domestic funds for its financing needs.  Ways are being sought to further develop the capital market and create domestic investment outlets to mobilize available resources for productive use.

744. Self-help traditionally plays an important role in rural development activities.  Private initiative is expected to continue to be encouraged under the new Plan.  A major role in investment promotion is played by the LNDC, dealing with both domestic and foreign investors.  Other institutions address themselves specifically to encouraging Basotho enterpreneurship.

Transfer of external resources, debt, capital requirements

745. The net annual inflow of concessional assistance disbursements to Lesotho fluctuated within the range of $90-105 million between 1980 and 1984.  New aid commitments picked up again in 1984 at a level of $122 million, as against an average of only $86 million in the two preceding years, implying a return to the average of $124 million registered in 1980-81.  Official capital on non-concessional terms, mostly from multilateral agencies, added some $6 million to the net inflow of resources in 1984.

746. Debt service has in recent years pre-empted a large share of government revenue and squeezed development expenditure.  Interest payments and debt amortization averaged some 25 per cent of total budget receipts in 1982/83-1984/85.  Since the beginning of that period, the Government has attempted to lessen the debt burden, in particular by clearing off short-term commercial debt.  However, the falling rand – and the consequent devaluation of the national currency – has recently been inflating the budgetary cost of foreign debt service.  At the end of 1985, Lesotho's external public debt amounted to Maloti 400 million ($156 million) as compared to Maloti 258 million ($130 million) one year earlier.

747. Development spending through the capital budget during Lesotho's Third Plan was well below Plan projections.  Capital expenditure more or less stagnated during the first four years of the Plan period, implying a substantial decrease in real terms. Spending was somewhat stepped up in 1984-85, but slackened again in the following year.  For 1986/87 capital expenditure of Maloti 198 million ($77 million at August 1986 exchange rates) was budgeted.  Expenditures were expected to be partly financed by foreign aid drawdowns of Maloti 93 million ($36.4 million) in grants and 50 million ($19.6 million) in loans.

Mechanisms for monitoring and follow-up of the SNPA

748. The Central Planning and Development Office (CPDO) in the Ministry of Planning Employment and Economic Affairs co-ordinates external assistance and serves as the focal point for SNPA follow-up. Round table meetings with donors have been held periodically since the early 1970s. The latest one, and the first to take place in the context of the SNPA, was the Donor Conference held in Maseru in May 1984. Meetings on special topics are arranged with donors on an ad hoc basis. For example, a donor consultative meeting was held in June 1985 in the context of the International Drinking Water Supply and Sanitation Decade. Regular meetings are also held between CPDO and donors represented locally. A joint government-donor co-ordinating committee on monitoring of food aid and other external assistance related to the effects of drought was to be set up in early 1986.

## 22. MALAWI

Economic performance

749. After an impressive overall economic performance in the 1970s - Malawi's GDP grew at an average annual rate of 6 per cent from 1973 to 1979 - a number of factors, such as drought, disruptions to external trade routes and sharply declining terms of trade, combined to give rise to severe imbalances in the economy at the turn of the decade. The budgetary position and the balance of payments deteriorated and indebtedness increased. Real GDP declined in 1980 and 1981. In the latter year, the Government adopted a stabilization and structural adjustment programme to restore internal and external balance to the economy and to create conditions for resumed growth. Real GDP growth did in fact resume in 1982, and in 1983 and 1984 growth rates of over 3 per cent were recorded. Factors explaining this performance were increased output in estate agriculture (in 1982 and 1983) and in smallholder agriculture. In 1984, there was a clear improvement in Malawi's external position, with improved export prices and earnings and, largely owing to drawings under the structural adjustment loan programme, an increased net inflow of long-term capital.

750. Overall economic developments in 1985 were decidedly less favorable. Total GDP was estimated to have increased by less than 3 per cent in real terms. Price developments for the main export crops - tea, tobacco and sugar - were on the whole unfavourable, while growth in agricultural output was sluggish. Performance in other sectors was mixed; growth in manufacturing output slowed down, while construction registered an upturn after a long slump. Inflation accelerated due, inter alia, to the rise in external transport costs and the depreciation of the kwacha.

751. The good export performance in 1984 had given rise to a substantial trade surplus, but in 1985 exports declined as import levels and transport costs went up, resulting in a sharply increased deficit on current account. Government drawings on loans dropped and high external debt service payments following two years of debt relief (1982/83 and 1983/84) put additional pressure on the balance of payments. The overall balance, which had been in surplus in 1984, turned around again to show a substantial deficit in 1985.

752. The World Bank in December 1985 accorded a third structural adjustment loan (SAL) to Malawi in support of the country's structural adjustment programme (see the section on Development planning and policies below). Earlier SALs accorded in 1981 and 1983 respectively totalled $100 million. The new loan, funded by resources from IDA and the special African Facility, amounted to $70 million and was to be accompanied by $44 million in joint and parallel financing from bilateral donors.

753. Projections for 1986 foresee a recovery in agricultural output and an acceleration of the real GDP growth rate to around 4 per cent. Budgetary and balance-of-payments constraints are expected to continue to be severe. Resumed drawings under the structural adjustment loan programme should ease the balance-of-payments situation in 1986. However, debt repayments will continue to weigh heavily on the budget and to drain resources out of the country during subsequent years. The extended facility accorded by the IMF in 1983 was due to expire in September 1986, requiring substantial repurchases at that time.

754. The Malawi kwacha, which is pegged to a basket of currencies, was devalued by 10 per cent in August 1986, the latest of a series of periodic exchange rate adjustments undertaken since 1982, for a cumulative devaluation of about 56 per cent vis-à-vis the SDR.

755. The difficult transport problems affecting Malawi as a land-locked country are epitomized by the severe disruptions leading to the virtual closure of the traditional rail links to the sea through Mozambique. These problems have compounded Malawi's economic difficulties since the beginning of the decade, and show no sign of abating; they have affected essential imports, such as fuel and fertilizers, and have imposed heavy additional costs on the economy for rerouting trade, thereby affecting the competitiveness of exports inter alia. The Government has initiated a programme to develop the country's own road haulage capacity and diversify its external trade routes. A new corridor to Dar-es-Salaam harbour has become operational and transport facilities along this route are being improved.

## Disasters

756. Since 1980 Malawi has not suffered from any major drought. Malawi was one of the very few African LDCs which did not face a food-related emergency in 1984. On the contrary, it was able to supply maize to neighbouring countries in the region under international food aid programmes.

## Human resources and social development

757. Important recent developments in the field of human resources and social development are the decisions to extend nation-wide a functional literacy programme, which was set up on a pilot basis in 1981, and the provision of child-spacing services within maternal and child health care, together with other population information and education. A national plan has been elaborated for the health sector for the decade 1985-1995. This plan aims, inter alia, at lowering child mortality through improving the health care delivery system and the development of a nutrition programme. A new national education plan has also been drawn up for the same period.

Development planning and policies

758. The stabilization and structural adjustment programme launched in 1981 adopted a two-pronged approach, encompassing demand restraint on the one hand and supply side measures on the other, with special emphasis on agriculture. A general aim under the programme has been to shift the main responsibility for growth to the private sector, through measures such as pricing policies, tariff reform, and appropriate interest and exchange-rate policies. Efforts to better mobilize and use domestic resources more efficiently have been pursued along several lines under the structural adjustment programme, such as revenue-raising measures, closer and more systematic control of government expenditure, improving the performance of the parastatal sector, and specific incentives and institutions for promoting industrial investment, notably by small-scale enterprises. The third phase of the programme foresees a range of new export-promoting measures.

759. In 1981, a rolling five-year development programme was introduced as a forward budgeting and planning device. The annual development budget represents the first year of this programme, which is revised and carried forward each year. Expansion of public investment has in recent years been restrained by: (a) the need to reduce the government share in total investment, in order to release resources for the private sector; (b) local resource and recurrent cost constraints: (c) the funding needs of existing programmes; and (d) foreign aid availability. Agriculture continues to be a key sector receiving an important share of public resources (with the inclusion of forestry, 28 per cent of planned central government development expenditure in 1986/87). High priority is also given to transportation (23 per cent in 1986/87). Under the current programme, the aim is to reach an average real GDP growth rate of 3.6 per cent during the period 1987-1991, implying only marginal growth in per capita income given a population growth rate estimated in the vicinity of 3 per cent.

760. The basic objectives of agricultural policy in Malawi are to maintain food self-sufficiency, expand exports and improve rural incomes. Apart from general measures, such as price incentives, the main instrument for supporting and seeking to increase smallholder agricultural output and productivity is the National Rural Development Programme. Complementing this Programme are other projects such as rural electrification, rural water supplies and the building of rural health centres. Programmes of self-help nature are traditionally important in rural development and have been intensified.

761. Malawi's resource base provides little scope for major transformational investment. Development efforts in future will, as in the past, have to be based mainly on agriculture and agro-industry. However, there are coal reserves which could be developed as an indigenous energy source, in addition to existing hydropower resources, as well as a range of other minerals which could provide raw materials for a domestic processing industry. Ongoing mineral development projects concern coal and gypsum mining, ceramics clay processing and graphite prospecting. A country-wide geophysical survey to locate new mineral exploration targets commenced in 1984. Energy supply problems have also been addressed through the start-up of domestic production of ethanol, marketed in a blend mixture with petrol in 1982, and through a programme for promoting fuelwood plantations.

Transfer of external resources, debt, capital requirements

762. The net inflow of concessional aid to Malawi declined steadily during the first four years of the decade, from $143 million in 1980 to $117 million in 1983. However, in 1984, the aid inflow reached a new peak level of $158 million. This turn-around was due to increased disbursements of multilateral aid, in particular to drawings under the World Banks SAL programme, which more than offset the decline of bilateral disbursements from $82 million in 1981 to $52 million in 1984. The net inflow of total official capital stayed below 1981 levels.

763. Malawi's external debt obligations rose steeply in 1979 and 1980, partly as a result of commercial borrowing. Such borrowing has since been restricted and debt rescheduling was negotiated in 1982 and 1983 both in the Paris Club and with private lenders. In those two years, debt service was estimated to have pre-empted a quarter of merchandise export earnings. Normal debt servicing has since resumed and is expected to exert considerable pressure on the balance of payments and constrain GDP growth during the rest of the decade. The Consultative Group for Malawi, which met in January 1986, noted that a capital inflow of at least $200 million per annum was needed over the period 1986-1989 to assist Malawi to continue its development strategy and maintain the restructuring process. The need for a high proportion of quick-disbursing programme assistance over the next few years was particularly emphasized.

Mechanisms for monitoring and follow-up of the SNPA

764. Since the adoption of the SNPA in 1981, a number of activities have been initiated in Malawi in the area of follow-up and aid co-ordination, including the establishment of a national focal point in the Ministry of Finance for the monitoring and follow-up of the SNPA. A first step in implementing the relevant provisions of the SNPA was the convening of an International Conference of Partners in Economic Development, held in Blantyre in February 1984 with the support of the UNDP. The main objective of the Conference was to initiate a policy dialogue with development partners and seek financial and technical assistance for the implementation of the country's public investment programme for the five-year period up to 1988/89. Following this meeting, a national Aid Co-ordination Committee was constituted and a project drawn up to further strengthen aid co-ordination activity and set up a supporting secretariat. Subsequently a Consultative Group under World Bank chairmanship was constituted for Malawi. The first meeting of the Group was held in Paris on 21 and 22 January 1986.

23. MALDIVES

Economic performance

765. Maldives, a country of over 1,200 tiny coral islands, occupies an estimated land area of only 298 km$^2$ spread over 90,000 km$^2$ in the Indian Ocean. The development activities, which began less than a decade ago, have emphasized investment in the development of the export-based sectors having a comparative advantage - fishing, tourism and international shipping.

766. The GDP in 1984 (excluding international shipping) amounted to
Rf 537 million ($76.1 million), corresponding to $430 per capita, of which
fisheries and tourism alone contributed 30 per cent.  The GDP growth rate of
12.9 per cent registered in 1984 represented a marked improvement over the
rates of 5.9 per cent and 9.6 per cent reported in 1983 and 1982
respectively.  The projections contained in the National Development Plan
foresee GDP growth rates averaging 9.6 per cent for 1985-1987, with the most
significant growth projected in the tertiary sectors:  tourism, construction,
transport, and governmental services.  The Government is the single largest
sector in the economy in terms of its contribution to GDP (17.6 per cent in
1984) and its share is expected to grow faster than any other, in both
absolute and relative terms, so as to exceed 20 per cent by 1987.  Due to the
relatively important earnings of foreign nationals resident in Maldives and
the losses incurred by the international shipping company (which is excluded
from GDP calculations), the absolute level and the trend of gross national
product (GNP) diverges significantly from that of gross domestic product
(GDP).  Thus, the two series moved in opposite directions in 1983, during
which the losses sustained by the shipping transactions more than offset gains
in GDP.

### Relationship of Gross Domestic Product and Gross National Product (1982-1984)
### (Million Rufiyaa at 1984 constant prices)

|  |  | 1982 | 1983 | 1984 (Est) |
|---|---|---|---|---|
| Gross Domestic Product (GDP) |  | 449 | 475 | 537 |
| Add: | Earnings of Maldivians abroad | 12 | 13 | 17 |
| Subtract: | Earnings of foreigners: |  |  |  |
|  | Wages | -44 | -66 | -70 |
|  | Profits | -18 | -59 | -64 |
| Adjust: | International Shipping transactions: |  |  |  |
|  | Wages and salaries of Maldivian employees | 12 | 11 | 5 |
|  | Surplus | 46 | -47 | -23 |
| Gross National Product |  | 365 | 327 | 402 |

Source:  Government of Maldives, National Development Plan 1985-1987,
Vol. I, p. 24.

767. The contribution of the fisheries sector to GDP amounted to 15.6 per cent
in 1983, but in 1984 the catch rose by over one half.  During the first half
of 1985 the catch of 31,000 tons was again one quarter higher than in the
corresponding period in 1984.  Fishing, the main traditional occupation,
employs an estimated 29 per cent of the labour force.  Although the present

catch has reached a level of self-sufficiency, the prospects of increasing the catch and the value-added component to a remunerative level in the fisheries sector depends largely on investments geared to improvements in technology related to the mechanization of the fleet, freezing and storage facilities; canning; and diversification of products and export outlets. In addition, exploitation of the Maldives' Exclusive Economic Zone (EEZ), could substantially increase the average yield in this sector.

768. Since the first tourist resort was established in 1972, the tourism sector has expanded to include over 5,000 beds with 83,214 tourists visiting in 1984 compared to some 1,096 in 1972. In the same year (1984), the estimated spending of tourists was about $30 million. In addition, the upgrading of the international airport on Hululé Island near Malé since 1981 has led to an increased number of tourist arrivals, with some of the major airlines now using Malé as a regular stopover. The share of tourism in GDP in 1984 (13.4 per cent) was little changed from that of previous years, but by 1987 its share is expected to rise to 15.2 per cent (to $15.2 million), making this the most dynamic sector of the current National Development Plan outside the Government itself.

769. The international shipping sector, traditionally engaged in "tramping trade" for over 90 per cent of its cargo earnings, used to contribute significantly to the country's GDP. However, since 1981, Maldives Shipping Limited (MSL) has been hit by recession in world cargo trade, which caused freight rates to drop from $47 per metric ton in 1980 to $25 in 1984. The technology of cargo traffic has changed significantly with the advent of refrigeration and containerization, changes which have narrowed MSL's competitive edge. Maldives shipping has undergone a programme of fleet rationalization, as the number of ships in operation was cut from 41 in 1981 to 19 by mid-1984, resulting in a reduction of the fleet capacity from 310,000 DWT in 1981 to about 177,000 DWT in 1984. The losses incurred by MSL between 1982 and 1984 are estimated at $16.5 million. These losses have lowered GDP by an average of 8 per cent and foreign-exchange earnings by 13 per cent during the period.

Human resources and social development

770. According to the March 1985 census, the population of Maldives was 181,453 persons, reflecting an annual growth rate of 3.3 per cent for the period 1977-1985. The population of Malé, the main island, was growing at an even faster rate (6.2 per cent) over the same period, of which migration from the outer atolls accounted for 3.7 per cent. This has contributed to housing shortages and deterioration of other social services and facilities in the capital, whose population of 46,000 is one of the densest in the world.

771. The labour force constitutes 78 per cent of the of working-age (15-59) population, partly due to a higher participation rate for women than in many developing countries. From 1980 to 1985, the country experienced an increase of 5 years in life expectancy at birth and a decline of over 4 percentage points in the infant mortality rate. This is evidence of improved health conditions in recent years although the situation is still far from satisfactory.

772. One of the major health hazards is the problem of proper drinking-water facilities, whereby water-borne diseases become epidemic. Efforts being made to provide essential health and social services are further hampered by scattered and isolated communities throughout the archipelago.

773. The literacy rate in Maldives may be high in terms of the country's traditional education system, but only 15 per cent of students receive a formal post-primary education in government schools. The country is faced with a lack of trained manpower, inasmuch as there were only 100 university graduates in the country in 1985, whereas some 3,800 persons were required for professional jobs. The policy of the Government is to increase the supply of skilled manpower by the end of the century, mainly through the introduction of a unified system of education, increased enrolment at home and provision of scholarships abroad, and by vocational and on-the-job training in the main areas of economic activities.

## Mobilization of domestic resources for development

774. Within its limited possibilities, the Government has made every effort to mobilize its domestic resources by adopting a number of policies including budgetary and balance-of-payments measures. The domestic savings rate increased to 13.7 per cent of GDP in 1983 and 18.9 per cent in 1984 as compared to negative savings in 1981 and 1982. Whereas overall savings had still been negative as late as 1981, domestic savings financed nearly one half of a vastly-expanded investment activity in 1983-84. Thus, of the 16 per cent increase in total available resources between the two-year periods 1981-82 and 1983-84, over three quarters were used for investment, while less than one quarter went into consumption. The Government accounted for a large and growing share of this investment (60 per cent in 1983-84).

775. Total government revenue at current prices and exchange rates increased from $9.3 million in 1981 to $19.2 million in 1984, largely due to higher tax revenues, whose ratio to GDP increased from 5.5 per cent to over 12.8 per cent between these two years. As from 1982, resource mobilization was enhanced by: (a) raising the accounting exchange rate used in the valuation of dutiable imports; (b) increased fees on some government-run service sectors; and (c) upward price adjustments on government real estate sales. In addition, higher tourism, transport and communications receipts have also helped increase total revenues in 1984.

## Development planning and policies

776. The long-term objectives of the National Development Plan for 1985-1987 are: (i) to raise the living standard of the people; (ii) to redress the economic and social imbalance between the capital (Malé) and the outer atolls; and (iii) to attain greater self-reliance for future growth. The Plan's development outlays for the period 1985-1987, as projected at current prices, are approximately $106.7 million, of which $29.6 million are to be invested through the private sector and $76.6 million by the Government and public enterprises. The Plan envisages 120 projects with a total cost of $117.8 million, of which $17.8 million are to be financed from national resources and the balance of $100 million from outside funding. Of the latter, $36.3 million was already committed as of the end of 1984. The

sectoral distribution of the projects as a share of total planned outlays is as follows:  agriculture and fisheries, 18.9 per cent;  transport and communications, 28.4 per cent;  health and sanitation, 19.4 per cent;  urban and atoll development, 24.7 per cent;  and education, 9.8 per cent.

## Transfer of external resources, debt, capital requirements

777. Concessional loans and grants steadily declined from $18.2 million in 1981 to $10.7 million and $7.5 million in 1982 and 1983 respectively and declined further to $6.4 million in 1984.  Projected external resource requirements for the period 1985-1987 are set at $55.6 million, compared to a total development outlay estimated at $106.2 million.  The ODA component is projected at $43.0 million, with the grant component expected to remain constant at $7 million annually.

778. The medium and long-term external debt outstanding of Maldives more than doubled from $24.8 million at the end of 1980 to $51.2 million by the end of 1984, but including short-term debt it stood at $65 million at that time.  The ratio of debt to GDP in 1984 was 67.3 per cent, but was expected to rise to 83.3 per cent in 1985.  The debt service to exports ratio increased from 3.2 per cent in 1981 to 28.2 per cent in 1984 and the estimate for 1985 was about 18.3 per cent.

779. In spite of the growing debt service payments, the country's balance-of-payments situation has remained fairly stable since 1981.  During the period 1981-1984, the current account deficit fluctuated around $20 million per year and is estimated to have declined to $12.9 million (equivalent to 14 per cent of GDP) in 1985.  Since net long-term capital inflows virtually ceased (and actually turned negative in 1985), the current account deficit had to be financed by short-term capital inflows and drawings on the country's exchange reserves, whose level fell from $8.4 million at the end of 1982 to $5.1 million at the end of 1984 (equivalent to less than one month's imports).  After a further decline in 1985, reserves recovered to about $7 million in mid-1986.  To the extent that the deficit was financed by increased reliance on commercial borrowing, this has resulted in continuously rising outflows on account of interest.  Thus, interest and other investment income outflows quadrupled from $3.5 million in 1981 to $14.0 million in 1985.  The projected annual current account deficit during the Plan period 1985-87 is estimated at $14.5 million, i.e. somewhat less than the level between 1981 and 1984.  In addition, the Government hopes to build up exchange reserves by $3 - 4 million per year.  These two items are to be financed with additional government and commercial bank borrowing of $6.4 million per year supplemented by the so co-called "balancing item" covering unidentified capital inflows as well as errors and omissions, which is estimated at $11.5 million per year.  This item is about 80 per cent as large as the expected current account deficit, representing a continuation of the trend recorded in recent years and presumably reflecting underreporting of tourist income and private remittances.

Mechanism for monitoring and follow-up of the SNPA

780. The first UNDP Round Table Meeting for Maldives in the context of the SNPA was held in Geneva in May 1983. At the request of the Government of Maldives, the World Bank convened a meeting of the development partners, which was held in Paris on 16 July 1984. At the second UNDP Round Table Meeting, held in Geneva in April 1986, several delegations commended the government's prudent policies and economic management. It was noted that the country's acute foreign exchange reserves position, resulting from increased debt service obligations and decreases in net external aid, required increased donor assistance to help ensure continued economic growth. The Meeting urged the Government: (a) to define clearer National Development Plan priorities, especially keeping in mind the manpower constraints and the limited domestic and external resources available; and (b) to improve the trade and payments accounts through a better investment strategy. As a follow-up to the Meeting, the Government has indicated its intention to start in-country sectoral meetings.

## 24. MALI

Recent economic performance

781. GDP in real terms remained virtually stagnant between 1980 and 1984, due principally to the drought and, in 1984, to the fall in export earnings.

782. Since cotton normally accounts for one half of total export earnings, developments in this field determine the overall export scene. Despite the severe drought of 1982-85, the cotton production was little affected during that period due to a large extent to its concentration in the southern parts of the country. A record cotton crop was registered in 1985/86 (20-30 per cent higher than the two previous harvests) following a 13.3 per cent increase in producer prices in June 1985. The expansion of cotton production, however, has been accompanied by a depressed world market: prices expressed in US dollars declined by around 50 per cent between August 1984 and March 1986. The loss was exacerbated in local-currency terms as the United States dollar depreciated vis-à-vis the CFA franc by 18 per cent between August 1985 and March 1986. Losses in public revenue resulting from the fall in cotton earnings were estimated at more than CFA 20 billion ($44.5 million) in 1985, which is equivalent to nearly one-third of the public budget.

783. Reckoned on an FOB basis, exports covered around two thirds of total imports in 1985. However, because of the extremely high transport costs (the CIF-FOB ratio is around 4:3, one of the highest among the LDCs), the export coverage on a FOB-CIF basis was only 47 per cent in 1985, i.e. lower than the 52 per cent recorded in 1984.

784. The drought raised the cereals deficit to 481,000 mt in the crop year November 1984/October 1985. As a result, food accounted for almost one third of total imports in 1985, as compared to 15.3 per cent in 1983 and 24 per cent in 1984. A good rainy season in 1985, coupled with higher producer prices, resulted in a substantial improvement in the 1985/86 crop, with yields close to the 1981 record. Thus, cereal production is estimated to have increased by

20 per cent to 1.4 million tons in 1985. Mali will have cereal import requirements of 275,000 mt in 1985/86, the lowest level in five years, of which 105,000 mt of food aid requirements are fully covered by donor pledges. Sugar production, basically oriented towards import substitution, has nearly trebled since 1982/83 to an estimated 18,000 mt.

785. The subsistence sector is very important and accounts for 48 per cent of total final consumption, according to ECA estimates.

786. The exploitation of gold and bauxite started recently, with production in 1985 estimated at 1,800 and 22,000 tons respectively. Gold has become the third export item of the country (12 per cent of total exports in 1984) and is expected to attain the second place in 1986 (27 per cent). Surveys have indicated the existence of oil at Agamor and Taoudénit and of uranium, diamonds, bauxite, iron ore and manganese in other regions.

787. Although the manufacturing sector contributed only 6.9 per cent of GDP in 1984, this represents a marked increase as compared to 4.2 per cent in 1981. Textiles, leather and processed food are the main industries of the country. State and parastatal enterprises contribute more than 70 per cent of manufacturing output, excluding handicraft production. Despite the entry into operation of the Selingue dam in 1981 and the implementation of a recovery plan at Mali's power corporation (Société d'énergie du Mali), value added of the electricity sector is estimated to have decreased by 12.8 per cent in 1984. Yet, prospects for this sector are good in view of the expected entry into operation of a second dam by 1988.

## Environment and disasters

788. The drought has had three major consequences on the domestic economy: increased food deficits; a decline in agricultural exports (groundnuts practically ceased to be an export line); and supply bottlenecks for the agro-industrial sector. As a result of the decrease in water levels, the fish catch was almost non-existent in 1985 as compared to a normal annual catch of 100,000 mt.

789. Rainfall in 1985 improved and was fairly well spread over the national territory. However, it arrived late and finished early in many regions. Water levels in rivers had started to fall again in 1986 and transport in the Niger river has again been occasionally interrupted. Moreover, rains caused swarms of grass-hoppers, locusts and grain-eating birds in several regions, which may have potentially devastating effects on the next harvest. A pest-control operation and a campaign against rinderpest were launched in 1985. Measures adopted in 1985 with a view to the preservation of the environment led to the drafting of a programme in early 1986 to counter the degradation of forests, which is to receive IDA support worth $6.3 million.

## Human resources and social development

790. The Government is conscious of the social costs borne by the adjustment policies which have been adopted to face external and internal imbalances. The number of employees in the public sector has been reduced by 25 per cent since 1979, while urban unemployment has been magnified by migration from

rural areas resulting from the drought. Average nominal salaries increased by less than 5 per cent during the entire period 1980-84, while prices rose at an average annual rate of 10 per cent. The cumulative real loss in purchasing power during that period has thus been estimated at 25 to 30 per cent. Public salaries were raised in nominal terms by 10 per cent in early 1985.

791. Due to very poor water supply and sanitation conditions relating to the drought, several regions were severely hit by cholera outbreaks in 1985. Information regarding the northern and western regions indicates that sanitary services presently cover only 5 per cent of the population of those regions. The first national centre for dental care, comprising seven clinic rooms and 40 beds, was opened in Bamako in April 1986.

Development planning and policies

792. A new development plan is under elaboration following the completion of the five-year plan for 1981-85. The new plan is expected to provide, inter alia, for greater decentralisation of the national planning system and for stronger incentives to the private sector.

793. A wide-ranging strategy aimed at attaining self-sufficiency in food and adequate nutritional levels has been in force since 1981/82. The cereals market has been reorganized, entailing the removal of market restrictions such as consumer price ceilings and the monopoly of the State in the marketing of cereals. Producer prices for a number of agricultural commodities have been raised during the past few years, but such increases were slowed down in 1985 in order to minimize inflationary pressures.

794. Unwieldy parastatal organizations have been or are being:  reorganized and streamlined (Office de Niger, the country's largest irrigated agriculture scheme;  and OPAM, the cereal marketing enterprise);  transferred to the private sector (SONAM, the maritime transport enterprise);  or abolished (Air Mali). A new airline is to be established with both public and private (domestic and foreign) participation. Austerity measures have been introduced in regard to public finance management, including limited increases in public salaries and personnel.  There was a considerable improvement in tax collection rates, which are estimated to have increased from 78 per cent of the full collection potential in 1981 to 98 per cent in 1985. The budget deficit was reduced from 3.2 per cent of GDP in 1980 to 1.3 per cent in 1984.

795. On 1 June 1984, Mali joined the West African Monetary Union (WAMU) and thereby adopted the CFA franc as its national currency, which is linked to the French franc at the rate of 50:1.

Mobilization of domestic resources

796. Participation of the local population in rural development has been promoted, notably through support of village mutual-aid associations (tons villageois). A financial network is being created with a view to channelling resources to such associations:  establishment of the aid fund for grass-roots ventures (Fonds d'assistance aux initiatives de base) and of the village mutual funds for grass-roots ventures (caisses villageoises d'initiatives de base). A food security fund (Fonds national d'autosuffisance alimentaire),

amounting to more than CFA 2 billion ($4.45 million) was established in February 1986 with a view to facilitating the activities of village associations regarding food production. More than 1,500 co-operatives and tons villageois were in operation as of January 1986.

## Transfer of external resources, debt, capital requirements

797. ODA disbursements increased to $322.9 million in 1984 from a trough of $195.4 million in 1982. Debt cancellation totalling $108.68 million has been granted by Canada, France, the Federal Republic of Germany and Italy. Total external public debt was estimated to be 109.1 per cent of total GDP in 1984. Debt-service is estimated at 12.7 per cent of export earnings in 1984. A 17-month stand-by arrangement, involving SDR 22.86 million, was entered into with IMF in November 1985. Between 1978 and 1983, drawings from the EEC Stabex scheme amounted to $20.9 million and those from IMF's Compensatory Financing Facility to SDR 5.1 million.

## Mechanisms for monitoring and follow-up of the SNPA

798. Two round tables were held respectively in Bamako (December 1982) and Geneva (November 1985), with a follow-up, in-country review meeting held in Bamako in December 1985. At the latter, follow-up groups were established with a view to improving co-ordination of aid in the following areas: food strategy; drought and desertification; employment, training and privatization; primary health care and population policy; and non-project assistance, recurrent costs and structural adjustment.

## 25. NEPAL

## Economic performance

799. Nepal recently completed its Sixth Five-Year Plan
(FY 1980/81-1984/85) 160/ with a GDP average annual growth rate estimated at 4.1 per cent in real terms compared to a target of 4.3 per cent. However, this trend rate masks a highly volatile year-to-year performance that ranged from over 8 per cent in 1981 to a negative rate in 1983. Economic performance during the FY 1984/85 was less than satisfactory, with GDP growth reported at only 2.8 per cent, i.e. far lower than the 7.4 per cent recorded in 1983/84. This poor performance was largely due to unfavourable weather conditions; thus, untimely monsoon rains diminished the rate of growth in agricultural production from 9.5 per cent in FY 1983/84 to 1.7 per cent in 1984/85.

800. The growing disequilibrium in the balances of trade and payments has been one of the major concerns of the country. The trade deficit registered sharp increases in the early 1980s, having risen from $229 million in 1981 to $307 million and $370 million in 1982 and 1983 respectively. But it fell again to less than the 1982 level in both 1984 and 1985. The current account, which had been almost in balance in 1981, deteriorated and then improved, reflecting partly the trade balance, but also a steady decline in official grant receipts from 1982 onwards. The overall balance of payments, which had been in surplus until 1982, moved into a small deficit in the following year, largely due to the sharply increased trade deficit in that year which was not fully offset by higher short-term capital inflows. The year 1984 witnessed a

considerable improvement in the trade deficit, which was, however, largely
negated by a large and unfavourable reversal in the net flow of short-term
capital.  As a result, monetary reserves fell by almost $45 million in 1984.
In 1985 the trade deficit continued close to the 1984 level, but the prior
trend for a slow but steady deterioration of the services account in
combination with a further growth of short-term outflows, left the overall
balance with a record deficit of almost $65 million.  Since at least one half
of this deficit was financed from drawings on the modest exchange reserves,
these fell to their lowest year-end level since 1968 ($56 million on 15
December 1985), but recovered to over $100 million by mid-1986.

801.  The export sector has been the most vulnerable sector of the economy.
This is due to its heavy dependence on the vagaries of the highly volatile
agricultural sector, whose heavy dependence on timely monsoon rains makes for
uneven export earnings.  This phenomenon was experienced both in 1980 and
1982.  However, a gradual change has been observed in the structural
composition of exports, particularly to countries other than India.  A
steadily increasing volume of manufactured goods is currently being exported
to countries other than India.  The composition of exports to India, however,
has remained the same.  On the import side, construction materials, such as
cement and iron rods, transport equipment, fertilizers, textiles, medicines,
industrial raw materials, machinery and petroleum products constitute a major
portion.  The increasing importation  of these items is mainly due to the lack
of major import substitution industries to meet demand for mass-consumption
items.  The growth of imports, in spite of the satisfactory export
performance, tendentially worsened the merchandise trade balance during the
Sixth Plan period.

802.  Exchange-rate adjustments were made to improve the competitiveness of
domestic exports and control import volume.  In this regard, the Nepalese
rupee was devalued vis-à-vis the currencies of all major trading partners,
including India, by 14.2 per cent.

803.  The performance of the manufacturing sector during the Sixth Plan period
has been satisfactory, with an average rate of growth estimated at
9 per cent.  Garment manufacturing has grown to become the country's
third-largest foreign-exchange earner.  However, policy-makers are concerned
about the fact that not all of this income has been surrendered to the Central
Bank.  Moreover, limited performance was noted in the production of
cigarettes, soap, leather, agricultural tools, textiles, etc.  Some of the
industries established have been joint ventures with foreign enterprises.  The
Government is determined to implement fully the New Industrial Enterprises Act
of 1982 designed to expand this sector.  Thus, the 1985/86 budget provides for
considerable assistance to the weak cloth and yarn industries, so as to reduce
the country's dependence on imports of these inputs for the country's
rapidly-growing and export-oriented garment industry.

804.  Of the total consumption of energy in Nepal, over 94 per cent is obtained
from traditional and 6 per cent from commercial sources, of which 64 per cent
is in the form of petroleum products.  The country has an enormous potential
for hydroelectric power generation.  However, the constraints in terms of
capital and skilled manpower requirements have constituted bottlenecks in its

development. Total installed electricity-generating capacity expanded from 138 MW at the end of 1982 to 172 MW in mid-1985, equivalent to an expansion of about 10 per cent per annum, but consumption grew at an average annual rate of 12 per cent in the meantime. The Government is in a continued process of implementing hydropower projects in rural and urban areas.

805. Under its many afforestation programmes, the Government has achieved annual increments of the forested area estimated at 2,500 hectares. However, due to heavy demand for wood fuel, this record has still been inadequate. The Government recognizes the magnitude of this ecological danger and has introduced measures placing greater emphasis on community involvement in plannning and implementation of afforestation programmes.

## Environment and disasters

806. The major disaster experienced during the 1980s were the floods of 1984 and 1985 which represent a major threat to the ecological balance of the country. The Government is determined to protect the country's environment and has not only introduced the reforestation and forest conservation programmes described above, but also launched a soil and watershed conservation programme on a massive scale. Moreover, the establishment of the Remote Sensing Centre for the purpose of keeping up-to-date environmental information on land, water and other natural resources; forest, hydrological and geological mapping; and the drafting of a National Environment Protection Act are all measures expected to help protect Nepal's natural environment.

## Human resources and social development

807. In spite of recent progress the country still faces daunting challenges in the fields of human resources and social development. Some progress has been made during the Sixth Plan period in the field of education. Efforts are underway to increase student enrolment at all levels and increase teacher training. Accordingly, additional primary, middle and high secondary schools were established in 1984/85 to meet the growing demands for student enrolment. Moreover, the country has trained its first though modest crop of engineers, doctors and high-level food technologists. However, the literacy rate, which was about 29 per cent during FY 1984/85 is viewed by the Government as unsatisfactory.

808. In the area of community health services, 467 health posts and 77 hospitals and laboratories had been established by 1985 since the beginning of the Sixth Plan period. Moreover, the number of medical doctors, nurses and other health personnel increased by about 6 per cent in 1984/85 in comparison with 1983/84. During the Sixth Plan period, the Water Supply and Sewerage Department made an additional 25 million litres of drinking water per day available in rural areas.

809. During the period 1971-81, population grew at an average annual rate of 2.6 per cent. It took 60 years for the population to double from 5.6 million in 1911 to 11.5 million in 1971. However, at the present rate, it will take 26 years to do so again. This poses a serious constraint both to poverty alleviation and the fulfilment of basic needs. Although family planning has been vigorously promoted by three organizations providing family planning services, little success has been noticed in this area so far.

Development planning and policies

810. The Seventh Five Year Plan (FY 1985/86-1989/90) envisages an overall annual growth rate of 4.5 per cent per annum, the agricultural sector is expected to grow at 3.5 per cent per annum, while non-agricultural sectors are expected to grow at 5.7 per cent on average. Growth in industrial production is targeted at an ambitious 12 per cent per annum. Cash crop production is expected to grow somewhat faster than food grain production. Other major sectors emphasized by the Plan are forest and soil conservation, development of water resources, export promotion, tourism development, population control, domestic resource mobilization, foreign trade and the strengthening of policy implementation capability through a decentralized development administration.

811. The Seventh Plan has placed increased emphasis on tax policies with a view to mobilizing increased resources for public sector investments and to promoting private investments. The Plan further aims to keep government expenditure, particularly recurrent expenditure, within specified limits and to improve the performance of public sector enterprises.

Mobilization of domestic resources

812. At 10.1 per cent of the GDP, the domestic savings rate over the Sixth Plan Period (FY 1980/81-1984/85) was well above the 7.7 per cent target. Nevertheless, even this rate of savings was considered insufficient in terms of the country's development needs inasmuch as the country still relied on capital inflows from abroad to cover 45 per cent of its investments. Thus, the fact that government revenue increased by 5 per cent in real terms over the Plan period, was considered inadequate. The reasons for this insufficiency were: the need to keep export taxes as low as possible, so as to keep exports competitive; import duty losses on an increasing number of items exempted due to their development impact; the difficulty of raising taxes from the key agricultural sector due to its subsistence nature and its declining productivity; and the large volume of uncontrollable border trade with India, abetted by the free mutual convertibility of the two countries' currencies. However, a slight improvement has been noted during the latter part of the Sixth Plan. Thus from 1983/84 to 1984/85 fiscal revenue grew by 9.5 per cent in real terms. This improvement, however small, reflects the government's determined efforts in mobilizing increased domestic resources. To this end, the Government introduced fiscal reforms, such as streamlining of the tax administration and launching a programme to minimize tax arrears. Moreover, the initiation of these measures in 1983/84 was further consolidated and extended in the economic policy package adopted in November 1985. These measures included lowering of government expenditures; limiting of the budget deficit and expansion of credit to the private sector.

Transfer of external resources, debt and capital requirement

813. The role of foreign aid in the economic development of Nepal is significant. Total commitments during the Sixth Five-Year Plan period amounted to $1.3 billion, 81 per cent of which was provided by bilateral and multilateral donors members of the Nepal Aid Group organized under the World Bank's auspices. Most of the remaining came from the United Nations system and other bilateral sources. Development assistance will remain

crucial for the foreseeable future.  Based on short-term balance-of-payments forecasts, the annual foreign financing required will increase from $313 million in 1985/86 to $413 million in 1987/88.  It is expected that 70 per cent of Nepal's development expenditure will be financed from foreign sources.  The remaining 30 per cent will be mobilized domestically.

814. During the past few years, foreign debt has been mounting steadily, but since foreign loans have been contracted almost entirely on concessional terms, debt service has been relatively light:  $12 million in 1983/84 and $17 million in 1984/85, representing 3.8 and 5.4 per cent of exports of goods and services respectively.

## Mechanism for monitoring and follow-up of the SNPA

815. Since the adoption of the SNPA in 1981, Nepal has had three meetings with its development partners.  These meetings have been organized under the World Bank's auspices.  The latest such meeting was held in January 1986 in Tokyo, in which discussions on problems facing Nepal's economy were discussed very frankly between the Government and the donor community.  At that occasion, the Government highlighted its efforts to mobilize both domestic and external resources to meet the financial gap.  The participants reaffirmed their continued support to Nepal's development efforts, including the need for increased amounts of quick-disbursing assistance to support stabilization measures initiated in December 1983 and further consolidated and extended the economy package of 1985.

26.  NIGER

## Recent economic performance

816. Real GDP fell in two years during the period 1981-1984, particularly in 1984 when a negative rate of 16 per cent was registered.  Real per capita output declined at an average rate of 5.4 per cent per annum during this period, as compared to an annual population growth rate gradually falling from 3 per cent. 161/  The fall in uranium export earnings and the drought are the determining factors of this persistent decline of economic activity during the 1980s.  Provisional estimates for 1985, however, point to a 7 per cent rise in real total GDP, implying only a partial recovery from the major decline suffered in 1984.

817. Niger is the world's fifth largest producer of uranium, which accounts for a decreasing but still dominant share of the country's exports (81 per cent in 1979 and 75 per cent in 1984).  Because of the depressed world market conditions, arising in particular from a glut the international, dollar-denominated spot market price for uranium has fallen sharply, and in late 1985 it stood at only one third of the high level prevailing in 1978.  The national authorities decided to cut back production of this item by about 20 per cent in 1983.  The annual production level was kept around 3,400 mt in 1983 and 1984 and estimates for 1985 point to an even lower level.  Niger's customers reduced the volume of purchases by 21 per cent in 1984-85 as compared to the 1983 level.  As a result both of the depreciation of the CFA franc vis-à-vis the dollar between 1980 and 1984 and of the preferential price accorded to Niger by the French purchasing company, export proceeds from

uranium expressed in CFA francs remained fairly stable during the period under review, fluctuating between CFA francs 91 billion and CFA francs 110 billion. In dollar terms, however, these proceeds have declined almost continuously from $460.1 million in 1980 to $230.2 million in 1984. Niger's uranium export earnings are likely to have deteriorated in 1986.

818. Live animals constitute the second main export item, even though its share declined from 16 per cent of total exports in 1983 to less than 13 per cent in 1985. This item now takes the place traditionally occupied by exports of groundnuts, which have virtually ceased. Cash crops represent merely 7 per cent of total export earnings.

819. As a result of the decline of uranium export receipts, total exports declined from $566 million in 1980 to $315 million in 1985. Imports have had to be compressed, notably those of capital equipment and household goods, from $594 million in 1980 to $330 million in 1984, but recovered to $400 million in 1985.

820. France is the main trading partner, accounting for around 35 per cent of both exports and imports in 1983. Subregional trade (principally with Nigeria) accounts for nearly one fifth of total exports and 15 per cent of imports.

821. Niger had achieved a high level of self-sufficiency in food by the beginning of the decade. Due to the drought, however, per capita food production declined at an annual rate of 7.2 per cent during the period 1980-1984. Food production fell by 21.2 per cent in 1984 alone; and the basic cereal production during the 1984/85 marketing year (October/September) was estimated at only 46 per cent of the 1983/84 level. With the increase in rainfall, food production improved significantly in 1985/86 and the production of cereals was estimated at 1.85 million tons, compared to 1.08 million tons in 1984/85 and to an annual average of 1.7 million tons during the period 1980-1984. In 1984/85 out-of-season crops were planted over 70,000 hectares and manioc was introduced. Such crops are being extended to all zones which have the required water resources. In 1985, production of such foodstuffs reached nearly 500,000 mt. No further food aid allocations are required, but external financial assistance is needed for the purchase of cereals in surplus regions and their redistribution in food deficit areas. Falling domestic prices for agricultural goods may act as a disincentive to future production.

822. In addition to uranium, mineral exploitation (still on a small scale) relates to coal, phosphates, cassiterite and salt. Deposits of iron ore, oil, and molybdenum have been discovered, but the quantities have not yet been accurately assessed.

823. Manufacturing output contributed merely 5.1 per cent of total GDP in 1983, as compared to 8.1 per cent in 1975 and 4.8 per cent in 1980. The country's first industrial trade fair was held in November 1985.

824. The decline in economic activity brought about a 40 per cent reduction of the number of wage-earners in private and parastatal enterprises between 1981 and 1984. However, employment in the government sector increased at an annual rate of 9 per cent over the same period.

Environment and disasters

825. The drought has adversely affected Niger since 1968, contributing to the above-mentioned decline in exports (e.g. groundnuts) and food crops, as well as to a 37 per cent loss of the national herd during the 1980s alone. During 1983/84, the rainfall was estimated at 30-50 per cent below the long-term average, bringing about a loss of 2 million hectares of arable land (13 per cent of total arable land). Well-distributed rains in 1985, however, led to an average harvest, even though such rainfall was still below the 30-year average. A grasshopper control programme is being implemented with FAO assistance.

826. Good ground-water levels are currently facilitating off-season crops in many low-lying areas. A wide-ranging, five-year programme to prevent deterioration of irrigation works, totalling $26.5 million, is being implemented with external assistance. Two major irrigation projects amounting to CFAF 9 billion (about $20 million) are already underway. A master plan to combat desertification (Plan directeur de lutte contre la désertification) was elaborated in 1985.

827. Firewood accounts for 90 per cent of the country's consumption of energy. This is a major factor explaining why an estimated 80,000 hectares of woodland disappear each year, while plantings are normally 2,200 hectares per annum.

Human resources and social development

828. Only 39 per cent of the population has access to drinking water within a range of 5 km. Between 1982 and 1984, 2,000 water points were created and 3,000 more are under construction. A $9.6 million programme to develop rural water points and to provide drinking water in five different regional administrative units (départements) is being implemented with financial assistance from Saudi Arabia.

Development policies and plans

829. At the end of the five-year development plan for 1979-1983, a wide institutional framework (conseils de développement) at the local, regional and national levels was established with a view to promoting economic development through the participation of the entire population. A two-year interim development programme (programme intérimaire de consolidation) was formulated for the period 1984-1985, as a transition to the next five-year plan and with a view to adapting the economic objectives and policies to prevailing conditions (depressed uranium market, external indebtedness, drought). The interim programme entailed a reorientation of public investment towards productive sectors, government expenditure cuts, measures to stimulate the participation of the private sector and improvements in economic management and planning.

830. A structural adjustment programme has been formulated for the period 1986-1988. The programme aims at improving the efficiency of the public

sector and encouraging the participation of the private sector in economic
activities, as well as in revitalizing food production. The tendency is
towards the elimination of public subsidies. The programme is being
implemented with support from structural adjustment loans of IDA ($20 million)
and the World Bank's Special Facility for Sub-Saharan Africa ($40 million). A
five-year national development plan for the period 1987-1991 is under
preparation.

831. Agricultural production and rural development are key policy priorities:
they are geared principally to developing dry-season production, rural water
supplies and irrigation, herd reconstitution, and reforestation.

832 In 1985, producer prices for a number of agricultural commodities were
raised and the marketing of agricultural commodities, including cereals, was
liberalized with a view to fostering production. A duty on imported rice was
introduced in March 1986 with a view to protecting domestic producers against
the fall in the price of imported rice (due to the decline of the dollar) and
thereby fostering local production of this item. Export duties on cattle have
been raised while the value-added tax on cattle has been reduced (from 25 to
15 per cent) as a means of encouraging both the reconstitution of the cattle
herd and the supply to the domestic market. A wide-ranging programme of herd
reconstitution is being prepared so as to profit from the 24-fold increase of
biomass production that has resulted from the rainfall improvement. The
Government is establishing cereal banks at the village level. Poultry farming
is being encouraged with a view to improving the nutritional intake of the
population. Other measures to ensure self-sufficiency in food include the
rehabilitation and protection of soils, development of seeds adapted to
special conditions, establishment of seed reserves based on local varieties,
better land management, and diversification of production.

833. The Government has taken measures to improve the efficiency of the public
sector and of parastatal organizations. These measures include the
reorganization of seven State companies operating in the fields of
electricity, foreign trade, grain marketing, coal extraction, underground
water exploration, irrigation, and development finance. Twelve other public
enterprises have been privatized or dismantled.

Mobilization of domestic resources for development

834. Fixed capital formation decreased its share in GDP from 25 per cent in
1978-80 to 13 per cent in 1983 and 1984. In real terms, it declined by
one-half between 1978 and 1984. A public investment programme amounting to
CFA francs 275 billion (about $800 million) has been adopted for 1986-88,
under which the level of public investment in 1988 is expected to be 50 per
cent higher than in 1985. For 1986, 45 per cent will be assigned to
productive sectors (particularly agriculture), 29 per cent to social sectors,
and 17 per cent to infrastructure.

835. The participation of the local population in rural development has been
promoted and has involved, _inter alia_, nation-wide reforestation campaigns.

An integrated rural development project is planned for the region of Zinder with French co-financing. The national youth movement, <u>Samariya</u>, was reorganized in 1986 to promote the role of the youth in economic and political development.

836. The fall in the proceeds from uranium exports and the public debt service have had an adverse effect on the governmental finances. Action has been taken to increase government revenue by means of: improved enforcement of existing taxes, limitations to the granting of tax exemptions and increased tax rates. On the expenditure side, austerity measures have been taken, and subsidies and transfers to parastatals have been reduced. The combined result of these measures was that the proportion of the budget deficit to the GDP was reduced from 6.8 per cent in 1984 to 5.5 per cent in 1985.

<u>Transfer of external resources, debt, capital requirements</u>

837. Total external debt amounted to $886 million at the end of 1984, equivalent to more than one half of GDP. Debt service represented 35 per cent of export earnings that year, as compared to 10 per cent in 1979.

838. Net disbursements of ODA reached a peak of $251.9 million in 1982 but fell to $177.6 million in 1983 and to $161.7 million in 1984. For the period 1980-84 the main bilateral ODA donors were France (37.8 per cent), the Federal Republic of Germany (24.0 per cent), the United States (13.6 per cent), Belgium (5.8 per cent) and Canada (5.0 per cent but which increased its share to 7.5 per cent in 1984). A 12-month stand-by arrangement of SDR 13.48 million was approved by the IMF in December 1985, following two successive arrangements. The above-mentioned structural adjustment loans granted by IDA and the World Bank for a total of $60 million carry the usual concessional terms of IDA. Debt cancellation for a total of $141.81 million has been accorded by Canada, France and the Federal Republic of Germany. Five multilateral reschedulings have been negotiated at both the Paris and London Clubs since 1983. The most recent reschedulings were negotiated in November 1985 at Paris, involving $35 million of officially-guaranteed debt due for repayment between 1 December 1985 and 4 December 1986, and in April 1986 at London in regard to payments of debt due to private banks between 1 October 1985 and 31 December 1986. The government did not resort to concessional borrowing from 1983 to at least 1985, and the country's net foreign asset position improved from minus 18.59 CFA francs billion ($44.5 million) in December 1983 to plus 8.98 CFA francs billion ($24.4 million) in May 1986. In 1983, Niger drew SDR 24 million from the IMF's Compensatory Financing Facility, an amount that was still outstanding by mid-1986 along with SDR 42 million of other drawings.

<u>Mechanisms for monitoring and follow-up of the SNPA</u>

839. A round table with donors has been tentatively scheduled for February 1987, with an in-country review meeting in September 1987.

27. RWANDA

## Economic performance

840. After a period of relative stability in the latter half of the 1970s, the economic situation of Rwanda deteriorated in the beginning of the 1980s as rapidly expanding public expenditures led to growing budget deficits on the one hand while falling export receipts as well as aid and capital inflows on the other caused real GDP growth to slow down. According to national sources, real GDP is estimated to have increased at an annual average rate of 5 to 6 per cent from 1979 to 1981. In contrast, the average growth rate between 1982 and 1984 is estimated at 2-3 per cent, i.e. lower than the estimated population growth rate of 3.6 per cent, implying a decrease in per capita income over this period. Mid-1984 was marked by drought conditions and a shortfall in output of some major food crops during the second, main crop season. Pressure on land remains a major development constraint in Rwanda and the overall economic situation is precarious. However, not all crops were affected by the drought - in fact, there was record output of the two main export crops, coffee and tea - and the secondary and tertiary sectors performed well on the whole in 1984.

841. In 1982 the Government introduced a programme to redress the economic situation, encompassing notably measures to strengthen the agricultural sector and to restore external balance. In this context steps were also taken to stabilize the Central Government's financial position. Substantial recurrent budget deficits accumulated in 1981-1983 and government cash balances were run down. Reinforced austerity measures were announced at the beginning of 1984. Expenditure growth has been restrained, rehabilitation of public enterprises begun, and a number of revenue-raising measures introduced. Thanks to these efforts and to an increase in external trade duties (the principal source of government revenue), the recurrent budget deficit narrowed and the overall Treasury position, which also reflects the development budget and special accounts, improved in 1984.

842. With regard to the balance of payments, import restrictions were introduced and the Rwanda franc was delinked from the United States dollar and tied to the SDR in September 1983, thereby mitigating the appreciation of the national currency vis-à-vis its European trading partners that had occurred in 1981-1982. The balance of payments subsequently started to improve, the trade and current account deficits narrowing somewhat in 1983. The amelioration continued in 1984 with increased coffee exports, improved prices for coffee and tea, and a recovery in capital inflows. The overall balance, which had been in deficit in 1981-83, turned around to show a surplus in 1984.

843. Mining, mainly of cassiterite (tin ore), has been an important source of export revenue and employment in Rwanda. The sector has, however, shown signs of decline since the late 1970s with overall output stagnating and its contribution to export receipts steadily declining. Rwanda's sole mining company was dissolved late in 1985. The manufacturing sector has been more buoyant and was estimated to have increased its share in GDP from 13 per cent

in the late 1970s to 15 per cent in 1983. The sector is largely composed of artisanal and small-scale industry producing for the domestic market, but in recent years the establishment of modern industry has also contributed to manufacturing expansion. Investigation is continuing of the possibilities to exploit the large reserves of methane gas under Lake Kivu which Rwanda shares with Zaire.

844. In August 1985 the Government began to prepare a new adjustment and recovery programme for the economy. Available indicators reflect a certain success in the government's adjustment efforts, notably in controlling public expenditure and improving the external position. However, the improvement in the overall economic situation in 1984 was largely aided by favourable export developments and improved terms of trade, and this illustrates Rwanda's vulnerability to fluctuations in external demand as well as to other exogenous factors such as weather conditions. Trends in external trade may have been less favourable during most of 1985, but the boom of coffee prices since late 1985 have considerably brightened the picture for 1986. Thus coffee wholesale prices during the first half of 1986 were almost 40 per cent above their levels one year earlier. With unchanged volumes, thus should translate into a massive gain in export earnings. Indeed, exchange reserves rose from $113 million to $145 million during the first eight months of 1986, to a level not seen since 1982.

## Disasters

845. In normal years Rwanda is not a food-aid dependent country. The 1984 drought put focus on the fragile balance between food supplies and population. Following that drought the country required emergency assistance to help feed the population. Rains were good and the food supply situation returned to normal in 1985. The vulnerability of the country's external trade links was demonstrated when the normal transit route through Uganda was blocked in mid-September 1985, requiring goods to be temporarily rerouted through the United Republic of Tanzania.

## Human resources and social development

846. A number of specific targets have been set in the field of human resources and social development, e.g. improved levels of primary school enrolment, health coverage and life expectancy. Some progress had been observed towards mid-1984. Thus the life expectancy target was estimated to have been achieved in 1984, an improvement in health conditions (e.g. a decrease in infant and child mortality) was observed, and the programme of expanding health infrastructure through building hospitals and health centres was well underway. On the other hand medical personnel and equipment were lacking, primary school enrolment stagnated and there was only modest progress in the functional literacy programme.

Development planning and policies

847. Rwanda's Third Five-Year Plan for Economic, Social and Cultural Development covered the years 1982-1986. The target GDP growth rate for this period was set at an average of 4.8 per cent a year. Total investment needs were estimated at RF 232 billion ($2.5 billion at the 1982 exchange rate). A package of priority projects, requiring RF 125 billion ($1,350 million) of financing up to 1986, was elaborated in more detail in the Plan. Of this priority investment package, 65 per cent was expected to be financed from external sources and 35 per cent domestically (the latter partly through the Umuganda self-help system).

848. Rwanda's overall development strategy places strong emphasis on rural development and an equitable distribution of social services and economic opportunities throughout the country. Food self-sufficiency was assigned top priority under the Third Plan, to which end a strategy is being pursued with support from EEC. In relation to the SNPA, the orientation of the Plan towards social development should be noted: besides food self-sufficiency, priority was given to human resources development through employment creation, education and training, and to improving health and housing conditions.

849. A mid-term evaluation of the implementation of the Third Plan was undertaken in the second half of 1984 to assess the realization of planned investment as well as progress towards physical output and social targets, and to serve as the basis for the preparations for the next five-year plan. Economic developments since the beginning of the Third Plan period have been less favourable than foreseen when the Plan was elaborated. Consequently the real GDP growth rate fell short of target in the first two years of the period. There was also a delay in the implementation of the planned investment programme, apparently due to inadequate project preparation in some instances, but also due to lack of financing. The implementation rate of the priority investment package during the first two years of the Plan period was estimated at 70-75 per cent. Externally-financed development expenditure during the biennium 1982-83 was lower than expected, partly due to problems in absorptive capacity, and government development expenditure was also below projections. Investment in agriculture and in industry lagged behind Plan projections while infrastructural investment in 1982-83 was close to target.

Transfer of external resources, debt, capital requirements

850. There was an upturn in the net inflow of concessional aid to Rwanda in 1984, when the inflow reached $165 million as compared to an average of $153 million in the period 1981-83. The upturn was due to increased disbursements from multilateral agencies and from OPEC donors, which more than offset the decline in bilateral aid from DAC donors during the period 1981-84.

851. About 20 per cent of the net aid inflow in 1981-84 was in the form of loans, whose share increased somewhat in the latter two years. On the whole, Rwanda has followed prudent borrowing policies, with little recourse to borrowing on non-concessional terms. Although the debt service ratio has increased in recent years, external debt service still remained well below 10 per cent of export earnings in 1984.

852. External financing requirements for the priority investment package under the Third Plan were calculated at RF 78 billion ($840 million at the 1982 exchange rate), but the amount effectively received from abroad during the first two years of the Plan period was estimated at RF 22 million, i.e. some 30 per cent below the expected level.

## Mechanisms for monitoring and follow-up of the SNPA

853. Rwanda was one of the first LDCs to arrange a country review meeting as a national follow-up to the SNPA. The Third Plan and associated external financing requirements were presented to aid donors at the Round Table Conference on External Aid held in Kigali in December 1982. Follow-up consultations for the water and sanitation sector were held in January 1986, and similar discussions on education were under preparation. Other initiatives have also been taken to strengthen co-ordination mechanisms. A meeting with non-governmental organizations was convened in June 1985, and consultations on the latest highway project were held in September 1985. Donors represented locally now meet regularly to exchange information among themselves and with the Government. Within the Government, interministerial co-ordination committees have been set up for key policy areas.

## 28. SAMOA

## Economic performance

854. Samoa is an island nation in central Polynesia with a total land area of 1,100 square miles and a population of 160,000 (1984 estimate). In 1984, total GDP was estimated at 183.5 million tala ($84.1 million), equivalent to $607 per capita. The small growth rates registered in 1983 and in 1984 (0.5 and 2.1 per cent respectively) did not suffice to recoup the losses suffered through negative growth rates between 1980 and 1982, with the result that per capita GDP measured in constant prices had declined by almost 10 per cent between 1980 and 1984.

855. A major sector of Samoa's economy is subsistence oriented. Agriculture contributed about 50 per cent of GDP and more than 70 per cent of export earnings. Moreover, the rural sector employed 80 per cent of the people. Nevertheless, international trade plays a dominant role in the economy: merchandise exports were estimated at 17 per cent of GDP in 1985, while merchandise imports were the equivalent of 52 per cent of GDP. Like many small LDCs, Samoa's merchandise exports were highly concentrated on a single commodity and its by-products. Thus, exports of coconut oil and copra constituted 62 per cent of total merchandise exports in 1984, while taro and cocoa accounted for another 11 per cent and 7 per cent respectively. Since the country's share in both world production and exports of coconut oil and related products is less than 1 per cent, it can exercise no influence on world market prices for these commodities. Thus, the economy is highly vulnerable to fluctuating prices for these exports in the international market.

856. Copra production during the 1980s averaged 28,000 long tons, as compared to a mere 16,000 tons during the period 1977-1979. Stimulated by an average export price increase from $314 in 1982 to $710 per ton in 1984, Western Samoa Trust Estates Corporation (WSTEC) increased its copra production well above the originally set target of 22,000 tons through better plantations. In the longer term, replacement of senile trees will further increase output prospects. The production of coconut oil for export is expected to increase further to 15,000 metric tonnes by 1990, 12,500 tonnes in 1985. However, the price for coconut oil began to decline as from early 1985 from its record high of $1,155 per tonne achieved in 1984 to an average price of $570 per tonne in 1985, i.e. roughly equal to 1981 prices. Furthermore, by mid-1986, these prices had been halved again.

857. At 645 metric tonnes in 1984, cocoa production was at its lowest level since 1980. The drop was particularly sharp compared to the high of 1,320 tons achieved in 1983. The Government has recently taken steps to increase cocoa production by providing loans under the Suspensory Loan Scheme, in which repayment of loan is waived in part or in full. The average export prices per metric tonne in 1983 and 1984 were $1,450 and $1,835 respectively, while the average producer price in Samoa, expressed in local currency, more than doubled between 1981 and 1984, i.e. well above the increase in the consumer price level during that period.

858. By 1984 exports of taro had recovered in dollar terms by 10.8 per cent from the 1983 level and were second only to coconut oil as a major foreign-exchange earner among the country's merchandise export items, even though it had been merely a subsistence crop ten years earlier. With improved credit lines by the Development Bank of Western Samoa to small farmers, taro production for export could increase. Development of the fisheries sector has achieved some success since the early 1970s, with catches increasing to 3,193 tons in 1983 compared to 1,560 tons in 1978. However, the catch in 1984 fell to only 1,579 tons owing to a shortage of fish-aggregating devices (fad).

859. The manufacturing sector does play a small but significant role in Samoa's economy: its share in GDP was 7.5 per cent in 1983, as compared to 5.5 per cent in 1980. However, since the late 1970s, the diversification process towards manufactured goods for export had virtually come to a halt, owing to the loss of its comparative advantage caused by high domestic price inflation.

860. The share of electricity in GDP was 3.8 per cent in 1983 as compared to 2 per cent in 1980, resulting in estimated foreign-exchange savings of almost $1.8 million due to reduced diesel oil imports for power generation since 1982, following the commissioning of three hydropower projects.

861. The tourism industry is beginning to play an important role, with total annual earnings rising from about $2.5 million during the period 1980-1982 to $6 million in 1984, reflecting an increase of tourist arrivals from 28,503 and 36,717 during 1982 and 1983 respectively to 40,043 in 1984.

Environment and disasters

862. In 1983, a fire in Asau destroyed about 1,600 hectares of forests. This constituted a serious setback for the forestry sector. Since then, the Government has initiated intensive reforestation programmes and nursery facilities, including a total ban on the export of logs.

Human resources and social development

863. In general, Samoa does not suffer from excessive population growth, acute hunger, endemic diseases or illiteracy, and further progress in the levels of health and education has been made in the 1980s.

864. In the field of health, the immunization of children aged less than one year has increased from 29 per cent in 1979 to 84 per cent in 1984; and almost all the population had access to piped water by 1984.

865. In education, the 1981 census recorded that 97.5 per cent of the 10-14 age group attended school. There has also been considerable improvement in curriculum development and in physical facilities; thus a Secondary Teachers' College was completed in 1981 and the National University was established in 1984. Adult literacy in Samoa is almost universal.

866. The annual growth rate of the population has dropped sharply from 2.8 per cent between 1961 and 1966 to around 0.6 per cent between 1976 and 1981. The main factors contributing to this decline are emigration and a low fertility rate. The fertility rate declined from 8.1 per cent in 1962 to 4.9 per cent in 1983. Data on emigration are incomplete, but according to UNFPA estimates, 14,225 Samoans emigrated between 1972 and 1976 alone. During the period 1974-1983, net outward migration is estimated to have averaged 2,776 per year (1.8 per cent). The combined effect of these two factors have caused the share of the population in the 0-14 years age bracket to decline from over 50 per cent in 1961 to 44.5 per cent in 1981, implying a smaller labour force for the future.

Development planning and policies

867. Samoa has had national development plans since the mid-1960s, and the present Fifth National Development Plan covers a period of three years (1985-1987). The Plan's primary strategy for achieving its objective of increased overall production is the better use of underutilized agricultural land that is controlled by the villages. Government policy is to encourage formation of joint ventures between villagers and outside partners, both local and overseas, for larger-scale commercial agriculture, as well as in the related areas of forestry, fisheries and agro-processing. The other Plan objectives are the attainment of a greater degree of economic self-reliance, greater participation of citizens in the development process, fair distribution of the fruits of development and the protection of the environment.

868. In the area of fiscal and monetary policy, the Government undertook a stabilization programme in 1983, of which the most important features were: (i) the increase of tax revenues (see paras. 870-871 below); and, (ii) a flexible exchange rate.

869. Domestic price inflation between 1979 and 1982 had approached 90 per cent while the exchange rate vis-à-vis the currency of its main trading partner - New Zealand - had remained virtually unchanged. However, the downward float of the New Zealand dollar, to which the tala was then pegged, had brought the value of the latter vis-à-vis the United States dollar down by 32.5 per cent between end-1980 and February 1983. Since this was deemed to be insufficient to overcome the erosion of its international competitiveness, Samoa instituted a series of devaluations against the New Zealand dollar, for a cumulative total of 12.8 per cent between February 1983 and March 1985. Subsequently, the tala was delinked and pegged to a basket of currencies of the country's five major trading partners. Between March 1985 and July 1986, devaluation vis-à-vis the SDR amounted to almost 16 per cent. Partly as the result of this series of measures, the current account deficit, which had amounted to about 14 per cent of GDP as late as 1981, was turned into a surplus from 1983 onwards. Consequently, exchange reserves have been steadily rising since 1982 to a level five times higher by September 1986. However, this equilibrium still depends on substantial unrequited private and official transfers amounting to $32-$35 million per year.

## Mobilization of domestic resources for development

870. Although the overall budgetary deficits as a share of GDP stopped growing after 1981, the stagnation in the receipts of foreign aid led to domestic credit expansion: domestic credit at the end of 1981 and 1982 rose from 39 per cent to 44 per cent of GDP. From 1983 onwards the stabilization programme adopted by the Government with the support of IMF succeeded in increasing the level of tax revenues, particularly import taxes, which are now levied on government imports that were formerly exempted. During the years 1983 and 1984, the government revenue increased by an average annual rate of 44 per cent in nominal terms, compared to an average rate of 7 per cent in the years 1981 and 1982. Although a part of this sudden increase was only nominal and the result of currency devaluation, tax revenues as a share of GDP did grow from 20 per cent in 1980-1981 to 27.1 per cent in 1984.

871. A positive factor in the mobilization of domestic resources was the government's policy to privatize most of the public enterprises which had a direct bearing on its budgetary deficits. The other factors were the utilization of reserve funds from social security institutions (National Provident Fund) for both the public and private sectors, and the changes in interest rate policy so as to attract private savings to the financial intermediaries. For example, in 1985 the interest rate on savings deposits was fixed at 7 per cent as compared to 4 per cent in 1980, while interest rates on term deposits were similarly increased. Likewise, the upper limit of lending rates was revised upwards to about 18 per cent compared to 12.5 per cent in 1980. As a result, real interest rates turned positive, helping to explain why term deposits with commercial banks rose by 77 per cent between end-1982 and end-1984.

## Transfer of external resources, debt and capital requirements

872. Samoa's major traditional donors are Australia, New Zealand, the European Economic Community, Japan and the United Nations agencies. Project grants by all donors combined ranged between $11.3 million and $13.7 million from 1980 to 1983, but fell to an estimated $8.5 million in 1984 and 1985. In addition, the Asian Development Bank and the World Bank have provided loans related to projects and the OPEC Fund has continued to provide balance-of-payments support. Under the STABEX scheme Samoa has drawn about ECU 2.9 million between 1982 and 1985.

873. Total net external assistance requirements for the 1985-1987 National Development Plan amounting to $28.7 million are well below the corresponding inflows of $45.3 million received from 1982 to 1984. The requirements for the six-year period 1985-1990, which constituted the basis for the presentation at the April 1986 Round Table Meeting, amount to $53.3 million. If loan repayments, IMF repurchases and foreign-exhange build-up requirements are taken into account, gross requirements for the six-year period amount to $95.1 million.

874. Samoa's outstanding external debt at the end of 1984 amounted to $61 million, excluding commercial debt and IMF drawings of $8 million. Despite the relative stabilization of total outstanding debt since 1981, debt service as a ratio to merchandise exports has been growing at a dangerously high pace; the ratio reached more than 40 per cent in 1985. This was mainly due to the accumulation of past borrowings, which rose by over 60 per cent between 1978 and 1983 and outstanding commercial loans of $4 million bearing high interest rates. The projections are relatively optimistic, with the debt-service ratio expected to decline to about 19.6 per cent by 1990 on the assumption that exports earnings, particularly earnings on coconut oil and related products, do not drop drastically and that no new borrowing occurs before 1990. In fact, neither of these conditions is likely to be fulfilled in view of the precipitous drop in coconut oil prices since early 1985, which is likely to require further borrowing to finance the balance-of-payments deficit resulting therefrom. It is evident, therefore, that debt service will reach unsustainable levels, unless debt rescheduling occurs and/or other sources of finance are forthcoming.

## Mechanism for monitoring and follow-up of the SNPA

875. After the first Round Table Meeting for Samoa which was held in May 1983, as a follow-up to the SNPA, the Second Round Table Meeting under the auspices of UNDP took place in Geneva in April 1986. The donors at the Meeting expressed their support to the Samoan Government for its efforts in trying to reach the Plan targets, particularly in the agriculture sector. Donors also stressed the critical need of the country to address itself to the problem of debt, and in this regard the Meeting noted that external assistance on a continuing basis would be needed in the form of grants and loans on highly concessional terms to meet the economic growth objectives. The Meeting stressed the need for greater efforts to co-ordinate external assistance at the project level and added that donors should consider co-financing arrangements for projects included in the National Development Plan.

### 29. SAO TOME AND PRINCIPE

Economic performance

876. Real gross domestic product declined from 1980 to 1984 and per capita incomes are estimated to have been reduced by one third during the same period. This negative evolution is largely due to the performance of the dominant cocoa sector. This crop occupies about half the country's cultivated area and one quarter of its total land area and provided between 80 and 90 per cent of exports over the period 1980-1984. Cocoa production, which exceeded 50,000 tons per annum in the first quarter of this century, had fallen to 7,000 tons by 1980 and continued to decline since then to less than 4,000 tons per annum in the middle of the decade. This performance of the cocoa sector has had an immediate impact on the country's balance of payments. The shortage of foreign exchange (only partially compensated by an increase in aid) has had a feedback effect on production (including cocoa production), by forcing the country to cut down on all imports including inputs for agriculture and the tiny industrial sector. Thus, in 1983 total merchandise imports were half the level (in current dobras) attained in 1982, and in 1984 and 1985 there were further cut-backs. Apart from the shortage of foreign exchange for inputs, the poor performance of the cocoa sector may be attributed to the lack of skilled manpower - the former owners left the estates upon their post-independence nationalization - and to the lack of motivation of the labour force in working under plantation-type conditions. Other factors have been the erratic rainfall pattern and the insufficient decentralization of management decisions from the Government to the State enterprises running the plantations. Production of other export products (copra, coconuts, coffee) have also had a tendency to decline over the period 1980-1984.

877. There is little tradition of food crop production in Sao Tome and Principe and efforts towards increased self-sufficiency, which is technically possible, have not yet borne fruit. On the other hand, fishing has progressed very satisfactorily since independence.

Fish production, 1975 and 1980-1984 (in tons)

| 1975 | 1980 | 1981 | 1982 | 1983 | 1984 |
|------|------|------|------|------|------|
| 377 | 1 848 | 2 158 | 1 690 | 3 599 | 4 289 |

One of the reasons for this increased output has been the availability of two trawlers as from 1980 and 1982 respectively. Fish provides most of the animal protein of the population, particularly since the pig population was wiped out in the early 1980s, following an epidemic of African swine fever.

878. Industrial activities are still modest, representing less than 10 per cent of GDP. Their development is constrained by the very small domestic market and the high cost of international transport. In this last respect, data indicate that for the years 1982 to 1984, transport costs of imports represented 31 per cent of their value, and absorbed 58.5 per cent of the export earnings. Tourism is not yet developed in Sao Tome and Principe. Even with the new hotel which opened in 1986, there are only 100 hotel rooms in the country.

## Human resources and social development

879. There has been a rapid increase in school attendance, with the introduction of free and compulsory education. However, the quality of education is very unsatisfactory. In fact, the rate of failures is so high that the numbers attending primary school were more than 150 per cent of the relevant age group (6-10 years old) in 1983/1984. This leads to a vicious circle of overcrowding of classrooms (56 per cent of which are used on a three-shift system) and correspondingly poor results. Health indicators are relatively satisfactory, particularly when compared to other least developed countries. Improvements have continued in the 1980s due to a large measure to outside aid. Thus, out of 53 doctors in 1985, 41 were expatriates.

## Development planning; new government policies

880. As regards the first Prospective Plan for socio-economic development for the period 1982-1985, it is estimated that only one third of the planned investments were realized. A new Plan for 1986-1990 is being finalized, the main elements of which were presented in the documentation for the December 1985 Round Table. Since 1985, the Government has decided to pursue a new economic policy whose primary objective is to restore the export capacity of the cocoa sector. The new policy envisages a greater role for individual initiative and the private sector. Thus, a number of State enterprises - including State farms - are being opened to joint ventures with overseas private investors, and the State monopoly in imports and exports of non-agricultural products has been abolished. An investment code was published in April 1986. A number of measures have also been taken to give incentives to agricultural workers; this includes allotment of parcels of land for their own use. As regards international economic relations, consideration is being given to closer links with the Central African Customs and Economic Union (UDEAC) and to reviewing the role of the dobra as a national currency.

## Mobilization of domestic resources for development

881. Due to the deteriorating economic situation, domestic resources were not sufficient to cover recurrent government expenditures from 1982 to 1984. In the context of the new economic policies adopted since 1985, a number of measures have been taken to increase the mobilization of domestic resources. Thus, the price of gasoline was increased in May 1985 from 11 to 30 dobras/litre. Other measures taken in 1985 include the raising of interest rates on savings accounts and a number of incentives to attract savings of the estimated 10,000 Sao Tomeans who reside abroad.

## Transfer of external resources, external debt

882. According to available data, concessional assistance to Sao Tome and Principe measured in current dollars quadrupled between 1979 and 1983 and increased slightly more in 1984. This has gone some way towards compensating for the substantial fall in export earnings. It was also necessary for the country to borrow on commercial terms to finance the purchase of essential items.

883. The amount of external indebtedness, which was negligible in the 1970s, has risen rapidly in the 1980s. According to national sources, it amounted to $65.8 million at the end of 1985, which is almost twice the GDP. Debt service payments have consequently started to increase, reaching 23.7 per cent of merchandise exports in 1984, and are projected to rise substantially. The Governor of the National Bank has stated that an attempt will be made to renegotiate debt service payments falling due in 1986 and 1987.

## Mechanism for monitoring and follow-up of the SNPA

884. Sao Tome and Principe met its development partners for the first time at a Round Table, with UNDP acting as lead agency, in December 1985 in Brussels. This was attended by delegations from 19 countries (5 as observers) and 11 intergovernmental organizations. During this meeting unanimous support was given to the orientations and programmes proposed by the Government. It is unofficially estimated that, following the Round Table, about $80 million of external financing (out of a total of $110 million requested) was secured for the five-year period 1986-1990. In 1984, a Ministry of Co-operation was created with a view to co-ordinating the implementation of external assistance programmes. In 1986, this Ministry was merged with the Ministry of Foreign Affairs. In May 1986, sectoral consultations were held in Sao Tome and Principe for rural development, including food strategy, fisheries and cocoa, together with consultations for energy and water, and transport problems. A meeting of non-governmental organizations is scheduled for November 1986 in Praia to discuss aid over the next five years.

### 30. SIERRA LEONE

## Economic performance

885. The economy of Sierra Leone has remained virtually stagnant over the last decade. Real GDP grew by about 1 per cent from FY 1978/1979 to FY 1983/1984. 162/ After a two-year period of export-led growth in FY 1978/1979 and FY 1979/1980, the annual rate of growth has been negative or nil. Between 1980 and 1984 the average rate of growth was about 0.3 per cent, but with an estimated population growth rate of at least 1.8 per cent per annum during this period, real per capita GDP fell.

886. The deterioration of the economy was a result of an interplay of factors. Firstly, the world economic recession reduced both demand and prices for the country's main exports of coffee, diamonds and cocoa, causing export earnings to remain well below the levels achieved in the late 1970s. Secondly, and more critical, however, is the secular dimension of the recession, namely the gradual depletion of Sierra Leone's major mineral resources, especially alluvial diamonds and iron ore during the 1970s. In recent years, the production of diamonds has fallen to less than one tenth of its level of a decade ago. The average annual exports of diamonds was about 1,700,000 carats between 1971 and 1975, 800,000 in 1976-1980 and 325,000 in 1981-1983. The production of iron ore, which comprised about 15 per cent of all exports as late as 1975, ceased altogether in 1976. Iron ore mining was resumed in 1983 on a small scale, but there are indications that its operation is uneconomic. In 1983, 420,000 tons of iron ore were exported, which paled against the level of 2.03 million tons in 1973. Last but not least, the

severe imbalance in the government budget must be noted as a contributing factor. However, the situation improved somewhat when stabilization measures were introduced during FY 1983/1984. The budget deficit, which had increased from 9.3 per cent of GDP in FY 1980/1981 to 14.1 per cent in FY 1982/1983, fell to 7 per cent of GDP and less in the two subsequent fiscal years. Likewise, gross foreign-exchange reserves, which had dropped sharply from $46.7 million at the end of 1979 to $1.3 million by June 1985, recovered to $9.5 million by June 1986.

887. The severe economic difficulties in the earlier years had led the Government to resort to external borrowing. The resulting debt burden has become a serious constraint to the country's economic recovery. The debt-to-GDP ratio rose from 35 per cent at the end of 1980 to 46 per cent at the end of 1984, but the immediate debt service burden has been alleviated by debt reschedulings covering payments originally due in the period 1977 to 1985. The government's deficit financing along with the massive devaluation of the currency have led to a consumer price inflation which averaged almost 70 per cent during the three-year period 1983-1985. The currency was devalued against the dollar by 49 per cent in July 1983 and by 57 per cent in February 1985, the latter being coupled with a switch of the peg from the dollar to the SDR. The currency suffered another effective devaluation of 59 per cent when it was floated in June 1986 (see below, section on mobilization of domestic resources for development).

888. Efforts are being made to revive the agricultural sector because of its important contribution to GDP, which was about 30 per cent in 1983, as well as its potential for assuring food self-sufficiency, thereby curbing the drain caused by food imports on foreign exchange. This, in combination with more favourable exchange-rate policies, caused an upsurge in the exports of coffee, which rose from $4.7 million in 1984 to $36 million in 1985.

889. While the industrial sector had weakened from the mid-1970s onwards, it rebounded in 1984, when its contribution to GDP rose to 25 per cent as compared to 20 per cent in 1983. The manufacturing sector is small, accounting for about 6 per cent of the GDP in 1984, its activities being confined mainly to food processing and beverages. Manufacturing is still highly import-intensive with a low value-added content. The share of the mining sector rose from less than 5 per cent in 1983 to more than 6 per cent in 1984. Since this sector has a high value-added content, the Government is taking measures to restore and expand it. Thus, new impetus is being given to gold extraction and the exploitation of the bauxite and rutile subsectors by attracting foreign investments to these activities. Production of rutile and bauxite became significant during the last few years. Rutile production rose from 37,000 tons in 1980 to 91,000 tons in 1984. During the first nine months of FY 1984/1985 it has emerged as the largest single source of official foreign-exchange earnings, even surpassing those from diamonds by $1 million. In the case of bauxite, a new investment programme has raised production to a new peak of 1 million tons in 1984. The other industrial sectors (mainly public utilities) contributed almost 7 per cent to GDP in 1984 as compared to 4.6 per cent in 1980. The country benefited from an expansion and improvement of its electricity supply, following the installation of two new generators in January 1985. Further improvement was expected in 1986 with the addition of two additional generators.

Human resources and social development

890. The nation's capability to provide social services to its population
(3.7 million according to the 1985 census) was seriously hampered by its
limited resources of domestic financing and of trained manpower.
Nevertheless, Sierra Leone's illiteracy rate of 15 per cent ranks among the
lowest in the LDCs. Primary school enrolment rose marginally from 39 per cent
in 1980 to 41 per cent in 1984. The government's educational strategy focuses
on providing non-formal education to a larger share of the population, but
primary school education will also continue to be emphasized. The new
Government indicated that the educational system would be made more relevant
to the country's needs and that greater emphasis would be placed on training
of farmers and craftsmen, such as electricians, carpenters and construction
workers. In line with its support for the World Health Assembly's resolution
on "Health For All by the Year 2000", the Government will direct its efforts
to improving the coverage of health services, raising life expectancy and
reducing infant mortality, which stood at 215 per 1,000 live births during the
period 1975-1980, a figure which is much higher than in neighbouring
countries. Four hospitals with at least 400 beds each are to be built in
Freetown and in major provincial centres with the support of a $6 million loan
from Saudi Arabia. In addition, an aid commitment worth $5 million in the
form of drugs has been made by the Iranian Government. The housing needs of
the low-income group in urban areas should receive greater attention with the
recent formation of a Housing Corporation.

Development planning and policies

891. During the last few years, the government's development programme
comprised essentially a series of stabilization programmes with the support of
IMF and the World Bank. Policy measures were directed towards placing public
finance on a sound basis and increasing budgetary resources, both foreign and
domestic, over the medium and long term. Concomitant measures undertaken
include the imposition of restrictions on the supply of credit both to the
private and public sectors and a ceiling on budget deficits. Subsidies on
certain consumer items were reduced while producer prices for agricultural
products were raised in 1983 and twice in 1984, so as to encourage
production. These measures helped to bring down the budget deficit in
FY 1983/1984 by 28 per cent compared to the preceding year. Although the
deficit rose again by 50 per cent in nominal terms in FY 1984/1985 as the
result of increases in public sector salaries as well as oil and rice
subsidies, this still represented a significant decline in terms of GDP. A
planned reduction of the budget deficit for FY 1985/1986 would probably
require a choice between retracting salary increases already granted or
shelving development projects.

892. Measures are being introduced by the new Government to place
Sierra Leone on a path of recovery and long-term growth. The two main
principles of the government's policies are to ensure that revenue is
channelled correctly through the Government, and to make institutions more
effective. To this end, the Government has concentrated on stamping out
smuggling, and weeding out ineffective management in parastatals, both of
which had plagued the country's development efforts. Beyond these measures,
the new economic reforms aim to bring about a sound monetary and fiscal

policy, a more equitable taxation policy, changes in the decision-making
machinery to make it more effective and responsive to popular needs,
anti-inflationary measures, sound mining and agricultural policies to improve
foreign-exchange earnings and reduce food imports, the use of foreign
investment to improve productive capacity, the development of small-scale
industries, a rational use of scarce foreign exchange and stronger Central
Bank control over foreign-exchange receipts and payments.  Top priority is to
be accorded to mining and agriculture, which are conceived as the
corner-stones to the country's economic development.  Other priority areas
would be education, health services and housing.  To ensure the effective
implementation of these measures, the Government has announced in the new
budget for FY 1986/1987 the establishment of a Presidential economic advisory
council, based at the State House and reporting directly to the President.  It
will maintain close liaison with the various ministries and planning bodies.

## Mobilization of domestic resources for development

893.  The government budget has been recording net dissavings since 1974
because of the continuous increase in recurrent expenditures and the relative
stagnation of public revenue.  Consequently, a part of recurrent expenditure
and all development expenditures had to be financed by a combination of
domestic credit creation and foreign inflows.  However, a turnaround occurred
in 1983, due in part to an improvement in the revenue position.  Between 1983
and 1984, the ratio of domestic revenues and foreign grants to GDP rose from
9.3 per cent to 12.7 per cent, while the corresponding ratios of recurrent and
development expenditure remained almost unchanged.  Data for private savings
are not available, but it is estimated that private investment had fallen from
about 14 per cent of GDP in 1970 to 4 per cent of GDP in 1980.  Under the
budget for FY 1986/1987, the Government will pursue a two-pronged approach to
mobilize domestic resources.  On the one hand, the huge recurrent public
expenditures would be pruned by reducing redundant labour.  Subsidies on
petroleum and rice are to be abolished and cost recovery of certain health
expenditure will be pursued.  On the other hand, revised tax policies and more
stringent administrative measures will be applied to augment revenue
collection.  Severe measures have been instituted to clamp down on smuggling,
above all the alignment of the official exchange rate with the internal
currency depreciation, so as to improve foreign exchange inflows and
collection of export and import duties.  The Government has established a Gold
and Diamond Office, which is to ensure that the exports proceeds from these
minerals are channelled through the local banking system.  Likewise,
unnumbered licences for imports have been banned, so as to force traders to
operate through the banking system.  To augment these measures, the Government
decided to float its currency as from June 1986.  In addition all foreign
exchange retention rights are to be removed.  During FY 1986/1987 two new
rural banks would be launched in an attempt to mobilize savings, especially
for agricultural development.

## Transfer of external resources, debt, capital requirements

894.  The weak internal financing capacity of Sierra Leone made the country
highly dependent on foreign aid and foreign borrowing.  Already before 1979, a
greater part of the country's debt was non-concessional.  Long-term debt has
risen only moderately since 1980, reaching $463 million by the end of 1984.

However, debt servicing will remain high in the future, because of the structure of the total debt: 45 per cent of the long-term debt was non-concessional, while short-term debt amounted to an additional $150 million at the end of 1984 (excluding IMF drawings of $75 million). Between 1975 and 1985, Sierra Leone held four rounds of debt renegotiations with the Paris Club, which resulted in the rescheduling of $68 million worth of debts between 1975 and 1981, and $88 million in 1984.

895. In 1985, Sierra Leone received food aid worth 200 million yen (about $1 million at the time) from the Japanese Government to finance imports of Burmese rice. China agreed to provide 3,000 tons of maize during FY 1986/1987. The country obtained debt relief from the Government of the Federal Republic of Germany, which wrote off DM 158 million ($48.4 million) in 1985. Sierra Leone also stands to receive additional compensatory financing from the EEC for losses in export earnings under the Lomé III Convention.

896. Under a World Bank Structural Adjustment Loan programme a "core programme" of development projects for 1986 to 1988, estimated at about Le 690 million ($115 million) was identified for implementation between FY 1986/1987 and FY 1987/1988. These projects were selected on the basis of their potential contribution to the country's development objectives and their impact on the balance of payments. It is envisaged that 85 per cent of the required financing will come from external sources.

## Mechanism for monitoring and follow-up of the SNPA

897. Sierra Leone planned to hold its first Round Table Meeting in Geneva early in 1987, with the assistance of UNDP.

## 31. SOMALIA

### Economic performance

898. The economic performance of Somalia has been uneven during the period 1981-1985, mainly due to fluctuations in livestock and crop production. After increasing by 5.6 per cent in 1982, real GDP grew by 1.4 per cent in 1983. Economic performance improved in 1984 and 1985, during which years the growth rate was estimated at 3.1 per cent and 4 per cent respectively.

899. The external sector was strongly affected by negative developments in the livestock subsector, which in normal years accounts for 85-90 per cent of export earnings. Thus, the precipitous fall of exports from their 1980-1982 levels 163/ to barely $100 million in 1983 and the further fall to around $45 million in 1984 was exclusively due to the fall of livestock and banana exports. The former was mainly explained by the ban of such exports to Saudi Arabia. In view of the export shortfall, the IMF approved a drawing of SDR 32.6 million for 1985 under its Compensatory Financing Facility (CFF). However in 1985, exports had recovered, due to increased livestock exports to Egypt, to their 1983 level. Annual imports (f.o.b.), as reported for balance-of-payments purposes, differ substantially from customs figures. The former have fluctuated between $370 million and $470 million during the

period 1981-1984, and were estimated to have declined by 16 per cent in 1985. Customs figures, on the other hand, show a continuing downward trend from $512 million in 1981 to $109 million in 1984, with a moderate recovery recorded during the first nine months of 1985.  However, it must be noted that customs figures cover only imports financed from official foreign-exchange holdings (estimated at 29 per cent of total imports in 1984), and exclude imports financed without official exchange cover (12 per cent in 1984) as well as the major grant and loan-financed imports (36 and 23 per cent respectively in 1984).  Consequently, the balance-of-payments series gives a more accurate reflection of the real trend of imports.  Since the services account is also structurally in deficit, transfers, both private and official have become the major sources of foreign-exchange finance in recent years.  After declining to less than $20 million both in 1982 and 1983, private transfers increased sharply to $163 million in 1984.  At $194 million in 1984, official transfers were well above their average level of $145 million for the period 1980-1983. In view of this higher inflow of transfers, the current account deficit of $146 million in 1984 remained virtually unchanged from its 1983 level, the sharp increase in the trade deficit.  In 1985, however, despite the one third cut of the trade deficit in 1985 ($279 million against $421 million in 1984), the current account deficit was estimated to have increased by $85 million (58 per cent) over the previous year's level, mainly due to increased interest payments.  The recovery of long-term inward capital movements to $111 million in 1984 and the positive balance of unrecorded transactions were not enough to prevent the virtual wiping out of international reserves by the end of that year, which also saw a further increase in the Central Bank's foreign 9iabilities.  The marginal recovery of gross reserves (excluding gold) to $2.5 million by the end of 1985 kept these at historically low levels both in absolute terms and in terms of import requirements (less than one week).

900.  During recent years, the livestock subsector has accounted on average for about 37 per cent of GDP and over 70 per cent of agricultural production, while crop production accounted for about 9 per cent and 17 per cent respectively.  Although no national livestock census has been carried out since 1975, official estimates credit Somalia with 4.1 million head of cattle, 4.8 million camels and 30.8 million small ruminants.  The drought in 1983 and the lateness of the rains in 1984 adversely affected this key subsector.  A $12 million livestock health scheme designed to improve disease control and research facilities, has been initiated with the help of IFAD and IDA. The EEC has also provided funds for the eradication of rinderpest.  After declining in 1983 as a result of the drought, crop production registered a 14 per cent increase in 1984 and was estimated to have increased by 23 per cent in 1985, due to above-average rainfall, increased producer prices and liberal marketing policies for agricultural commodities.  The fish catch amounted to 18,000 tons in 1984, representing an increase of 60 per cent over 1983, which was due to the establishment of joint ventures with foreign enterprises and higher prices.

901.  In the mining sector the government is proceeding with the exploration for metallic and non-metallic minerals.  On the basis of previous explorations it has been possible to establish cement, gypsum, ceramic clay and lime extraction plants.

902.  Aside from its meagre resource endowment, the manufacturing sector is constrained by shortages of skilled manpower, lack of spare parts and the poor performance of public sector enterprises.  Thus, due to the steadily decreasing utilization of manufacturing capacities, the share of manufacturing in GDP declined from 9.3 per cent in 1970 to 6.9 per cent in 1981 and 6 per cent in 1984.  Production in the sector is estimated to have declined by an annual average rate of 0.8 per cent during the period 1980-1982.  Incentives, including retention of a large part of foreign-exchange receipts, are being offered to the private sector to encourage production.

903.  High priority is accorded to the transport and communications sector, which claims an average of about 25 per cent of the resources of the Public Investment Programme.  At present, the road network comprises 4,965 km of primary roads as compared to 2,300 km in 1980, 4,346 km of secondary roads and an estimated 12,000 km network of rural/feeder roads.

## Environment and disasters

904.  The above-mentioned drought of 1983 and the late rains in 1984 adversely affected livestock off-take and agricultural production and thereby the almost 30 per cent of the population engaged in these activities.  However, the drought is now confined mainly to limited areas of the Sanag and Togdheer regions in the North.

905.  In addition to the standing refugee population of 700,000, the Government estimates the number of newcomers, who have entered from Ethiopia due to the drought, at 110,000, requiring additional food and non-food aid of about $15 million per annum.

## Human resources and social development

906.  The population of Somalia, excluding refugees, was estimated at 5.38 million in 1985, implying an annual growth rate of 2.9 per cent since 1981.  This high growth rate has put heavy pressure on the ability of the Government to provide adequate social services and is impeding efforts to raise living standards.  The situation has been aggravated by the presence of the high number of refugees.  Despite these difficulties the Government has made serious efforts to improve the situation.  As a result of educational reforms and campaigns to expand literacy and education, the adult literacy rate, mainly in the Somali language, was estimated at 60 per cent in 1985.  However, the corresponding figures in other languages is estimated at only about 12 per cent, as compared to an average of 35 per cent for all LDCs.  The official objective is to eradicate illiteracy by the year 2000.  Enrolment at the primary level increased almost twofold between 1982 and 1984 to a ratio of 21 per cent.  The government's strategy is to democratize access to basic education through universal, compulsory and free primary education, which was introduced in 1975;  qualitative improvements;  and expansion of post-primary education and training to meet the skilled manpower needs of the economy.  In the health sector the objective is to expand preventive services and improve access to curative health services.  Nevertheless, the past few years have

witnessed little improvement in the main health parameters of the country:
thus, between 1980 and 1985 the crude death rate and the infant mortality rate
have remained at about 21 per thousand population and 143 per thousand births
respectively.  About 25 per cent of children die before the age of five.
Modern health care is concentrated in urban areas and only about one third of
the population has access to safe drinking water.

## Development planning and policies

907.  In the face of the country's serious economic and financial crisis, the
Government initiated a stabilization programme in mid-1981, including policy
reforms in demand management, provision of incentives to productive sectors,
currency devaluation and fiscal and monetary restraint.  Beginning July 1982
the official exchange rate of the shilling was devalued at least 10 times for
a cumulative total of 90 per cent by May 1986 and an official secondary rate
was sanctioned for private imports and financial transactions, which was
25 per cent lower yet than the principal rate.  The Five-Year Development
Plan (FYDP), 1982-1986, was launched within the context of these policies.
The Plan gives high priority to the restoration of pre-existing capacity in
livestock raising and other agricultural activities.  In the livestock
subsector development efforts are concentrated on rangeland management and
livestock water supply programmes.  The development of the Juba Valley and the
construction of the Bardhere Dam, at a total cost of $306 million, is the
corner-stone in the government's strategy to achieve food self-sufficiency
through increasing the area under cultivation.  A technical review committee,
co-ordinated by the World Bank, has been established to assess the
pre-feasibility studies.  Within the Plan period a Three-Year Public
Investment Programme (1984-1986) was presented to a World Bank Consultative
Group meeting in 1983.   As the economic crisis re-emerged in 1984, the
Government adopted a new adjustment programme for 1985 under a new IMF
stand-by arrangement, which was presented to a special meeting of the
Consultative Group in January 1985.  The arrangement, which was to expire in
February 1986, was extended until June 1986.  The main objectives of the
latter programme were to achieve a GDP growth rate of 4 per cent, reduce
inflation from 90 per cent in 1984 to 20 per cent in 1985 and to reduce the
fiscal and balance-of-payments imbalances.  It also involved a 38 per cent
devaluation of the Somali shilling.  However, after four years of
implementation of stabilization programmes, the country is still facing
serious problems.   In 1984 the budget deficit increased by 56 per cent over
the previous year's level, inflation increased to 92 per cent against
36 per cent in 1983 and the current account deficit remained unchanged at
$146 million, equivalent to 8 per cent of GDP.  Although the rate of inflation
in 1985 fell back to its 1983 level, the current account deficit worsened.
Preparations for the Third Five-Year Development Plan (1987-1991) have already
started.

## Mobilization of domestic resources for development

908.  Several measures have been implemented since 1982 to increase the
mobilization of domestic resources.  A new Ministry of Revenue was established
to increase tax revenue through widening the tax base and improving tax
administration.  Other measures include the introduction of a sales tax on
selected items, increasing nominal interest rates and establishment of an

investment promotion unit in the Ministry of National Planning.  On the
expenditure side, subsidies are being gradually withdrawn on petroleum
products and have been eliminated in the case of agricultural products.
government domestic revenue, which is derived mainly from taxes on
international trade, declined from 14.8 per cent of GDP in 1981 to 13 per cent
in 1984, in view of the decline of export taxes resulting from lower exports
during that year.

## Transfer of external resources and debt

909.  Total financial flows reached their highest level in 1982, amounting to
$619.3 million, but declined by 49 per cent in 1983.  In 1984 they were
estimated to have increased to $405.8 million.

910.  Somalia's total external debt was estimated at about $1.51 billion at
the end of 1984, as compared to $1.2 billion at the end of 1982.  Debt service
payments amounted to $51 million in 1984, or about 19.6 per cent of exports of
goods and services, compared to 8.9 per cent in 1982.  A special debt
management unit has been established with the assistance of the IMF.

## Mechanism for the monitoring and follow-up of the SNPA

911.  Meetings of the World Bank's Consultative Group for Somalia were
convened in October 1983 and November 1985.  During both meetings the
Government presented its Three-Year Public Investment Programmes to its
development partners.  A special meeting of the Consultative Group was held in
January 1985 to review Somalia's adjustment and reform programmes and to
discuss the financing of the balance of payments for 1985.  At the local
level, the UNDP office organizes monthly meetings to ensure co-ordination
among donors.  The Ministry of Foreign Affairs established a Co-ordination
Unit in charge of co-ordination and monitoring of external resources,
including disaster relief.

### 32.  SUDAN

## Economic performance

912.  The overall performance of the economy, which depends largely on the
agricultural sector, was adversely affected by the severe drought during the
period 1982-1985, which caused sharp declines in agricultural production,
particularly in the rain-fed subsector.  Furthermore, contractions in
production and investment were also caused by foreign-exchange constraints and
economic adjustments required by the country's large external debt.  Thus,
with the onset of the drought, the record increase of real GDP of 7.4 per cent
in FY 1981/1982 164/ was followed by an estimated cumulatve decline of
4.7 per cent between 1981/1982 and 1983/1984 and by a further 1.7 per cent
decline of real GDP between 1983/1984 and 1984/1985.

913.  According to customs figures, the trade deficit reached a peak of
$920 million in 1981, equivalent to 8.5 per cent of GDP, but declined to
$450 million, or 5.9 per cent of GDP, in 1984.  However, in 1985, the deficit
increased to $750 million, or about 13.8 per cent of GDP.  Exports, which had
declined by 24 per cent between 1981 and 1982 to $499 million, more than

recovered the loss in the following two years to reach $629 million in 1984.
Their sharp decline in 1985 to $374 million was mainly attributable to
stagnation of cotton exports and the adverse effects of the drought on
livestock and groundnuts exports. Imports, on the other hand, which had
declined by 18 per cent in 1982 as a result of the implementation of control
and rationalization measures (from $1.6 billion to $1.3 billion) fluctuated
within a $100 million range of that depressed level through 1984, but declined
to only $771 million in 1985 despite the need for imports to meet the
requirements of the drought-affected population. The current account deficit,
which was estimated at 1.4 per cent of GDP in 1978, reached its highest level
in absolute and relative terms in 1981, amounting to $639.9 million,
equivalent to 5.9 per cent of GDP. The deficit then declined to $248 million
in 1982 and $219 million in 1983, and turned into a surplus of $25 million and
$151 million in 1984 and 1985 respectively, due to a decline of imports, a
significant improvement in the services account and an increase of official
transfer receipts. Long-term capital transfers, which had yielded $97 million
and $57 million in 1981 and 1982 respectively, declined to about $1 million in
1983 and were increasingly negative in 1984 and 1985, during which net
outflows exceeded $100 million. Net international reserves at the end of 1985
at $12.2 million were about one quarter of their 1980 level and were
equivalent to no more than one week's imports. During 1986, the reserve
situation improved moderately: by the end of August 1986 reserves had
recovered to $27.1 million.

914. In 1981/1982 agricultural production increased by 16 per cent over the
previous year's level, mainly on account of the increase in the production of
sorghum, sugar and cotton. This record growth rate was followed by negative
rates of 13.4 per cent and 4.9 per cent in 1982/1983 and 1983/1984
respectively as a result of the drought experienced during those years.
Production declined further by 6.7 per cent in 1984/1985. Cotton production,
which reached its lowest level in a decade in 1980/1981, has progressed
considerably since then, as production in 1984/1985 was more than double that
low level. Food production in 1984/1985 was about 1.5 million metric tons,
i.e. only one third of the average for the previous 10 years. The 1985/1986
rainy season was good in many parts of the country, particularly the
grain-growing areas of Central Sudan. This has resulted in a recovery of food
production to the pre-1984 average (4.6 million mt).

915. The contribution of the industrial sector to GDP declined from
10 per cent in 1970 to 8.6 per cent in 1985, in which year it employed only
about 4 per cent of the labour force. This was mainly due to the severe
balance-of-payments constraints faced by the country, which resulted in power
shortages, inadequate maintenance of transport facilities and equipment as
well as restrictions on the imports of industrial inputs and of spare parts.
Governmental rehabilitation efforts have focused on textiles, sugar and other
agro-industries and leather. To this end, the capital of the Industrial Bank
was increased sixfold to enable it to provide more credit to the private
sector.

916. In the transport sector the total length of the paved road network had
reached about 2,200 km by 1985 as compared to 375 km in 1970. The single
narrow-gauge track railway system runs for about 5,503 km, making it one of

the longest in Africa. A programme of modernizing the rolling stock of Sudan Railways at a cost of $700 million is being implemented over a 10-year period (1985-1995), with the assistance of the World Bank, the European Development Fund and Arab aid institutions. The seaport facilities at Port Sudan are being improved and modernized and the construction of a second port near Suakin has started. The main emphasis of the telecommunications development programme has been on a domestic satellite system, a microwave network and international telex and telephone services. However, these services are mainly concentrated in Khartoum.

917. With a contribution to GDP of about 0.1 per cent, mining has played only a marginal role in Sudan's economy so far, despite a wide variety of known or probable deposits. Extensive oil exploration has confirmed the presence of commercial oil deposits in the western and southern parts of the country. Production was scheduled to start in FY 1986/1987, but has been suspended due to lack of security in the South.

## Environment and disasters

918. Several parts of the Sudan, especially the western and eastern regions, have suffered from a serious drought during the last three years, resulting in local crop failures and food shortages affecting almost 8 million people, including 1.5 million displaced persons, at the climax of the emergency. Even after the rainy season of 1985 and the resulting sorghum surplus, 5 million people, constituting about one quarter of the population, are still affected by local crop failures, so that the emergency needs for 1986 are estimated at $130 million. The situation has been aggravated by the civil strife in the southern part of the country. The Sudan is also suffering from desert encroachment, which has advanced over 90 km within a 17-year period and is currently advancing at the rate of 5 km per year. In addition to these difficulties, the Sudan is hosting a refugee population of over 1 million from Ethiopia, Chad and Uganda, whose presence has considerably aggravated the pre-existing socio-economic problems of the country. In recognition of this, the General Assembly in its resolution 40/135, entitled "Situation of refugees in the Sudan", appealed to Member States and international organizations to provide assistance to the Sudan to deal with this problem.

## Human resources and social development

919. There have been significant cuts in expenditures for social services within the context of the stabilization and austerity programmes implemented since 1978 (see section entitled "Development planning and policies" below). This has led to a serious deterioration in educational and health facilities, the effects of which were only mitigated by self-help schemes. The objective of increasing the current 52 per cent enrolment ratio to universal primary enrolment by 1990, envisaged at the outset of the Six-Year Plan (1977/1978-1982/1983) has been modified. The adult literacy rate of 26 per cent is low compared to the 56 per cent average for all developing countries. There is an acute shortage of both teachers and teaching material, while the physical infrastructure has deteriorated considerably. In the health sector the cost recovery policy implemented in 1984 has substantially increased the cost of medicines and increased the burden on the poor segments

of the population. The deterioration in the health facilities has been further aggravated by the shortage of medical personnel. The drought and the large internal population displacement that resulted have added further constraints to the ability of the Government to provide the minimum required services.

## Development planning and policies

920. Faced with a serious economic and financial crisis, the government has implemented a series of economic stabilization and adjustment programmes since 1978, supported by the IMF and the World Bank. The Six-Year Plan (1977/1978-1982/1983) was replaced by rolling Three-Year Public Investment Programmes (TYPIP). Subsequently, four TYPIPs were launched - in 1978/1979, 1980/1981, 1982/1983 and 1983/1984 respectively. In accordance with the principle of rolling over the programmes every year, the first year covered is dropped and replaced by the financial year three years ahead and the two remaining years revised to reflect new developments. The main emphasis of these programmes has been on the efficient utilization of existing capacity through the completion of ongoing projects and rehabilitation of existing ones, rather than the creation of new capacities. Their objectives were to be achieved through mutually reinforcing policies affecting agriculture, the physical infrastructure and industry. These policies included a reorientation of production on the irrigated areas towards Sudan's most competitive crops, rehabilitation of installed equipment of public agricultural schemes, elimination of cost and price distortions, and liberalization of trade and exchange restrictions. In 1978, currency devaluation was used as a major policy instrument for the first time since independence. From mid-1978 until early 1985 the official exchange rate of the pound against the dollar was devalued five times for a cumulative total of 86 per cent, while the commercial rate at which all private trade is transacted fell by 91 per cent. The official and commercial rates were unified for a short period in 1981, but have diverged widely ever since. As of mid-1986 the official rate was LSd 2.5 per dollar, while the commercial rate was LSd 4.0 per dollar. However, despite the implementation of the stabilization and adjustment programmes and restrictive budgetary and exchange policy measures which accompanied them, the economic situation of the country continued to deteriorate and the cost of living increased sharply. These policies became politically unsustainable, and contributed to the overthrow of the régime in April 1985 and a rejection of its policies by the new administration, which adopted a Three-Year National Salvation Programme in March 1986.

## Mobilization of domestic resources for development

921. Domestic savings, which averaged about 10 per cent of GDP in the early 1970s, have become negative in recent years. The country relied heavily on external assistance and borrowing to finance both development and current expenditure. Several revenue-generating measures have been implemented since 1981, including elimination of subsidies, higher duties on imports and the reflection of the full effect of the successive devaluations on domestic prices. As a result, the budget deficit is estimated to have declined from 11 per cent of GDP in FY 1980/1981 to 7 per cent in FY 1982/1983. Additional measures announced in March 1986 include (a) a 10 per cent compulsory savings

levy from both public and private-sector employees, but this was later rescinded;  (b) the establishment of a two-tier pricing system for sugar and petroleum, involving additional taxes at the higher tier;  and (c) a 10 per cent reduction in public expenditure.  These measures are expected to save over LSd 180 million ($72 million) in FY 1985/1986.

## Transfer of external resources and external debt

922.  Total financial inflows amounted to $1.15 billion in 1983, a level 66.8 per cent higher than in 1981, but declined to $715 million in 1984.  The declining trend continued in 1985 as a result of the reaction of several bilateral and multilateral donors to the absence of an agreed programme with the IMF.

923.  Total external debt was estimated at about $6 billion at the end of 1984.  Debt service payments during that year, even after rescheduling, amounted to $211 million, equivalent to 19 per cent of exports of goods and services.  The Sudan has had four Paris Club meetings and one meeting of the London Club for debt rescheduling between 1979 and 1984, but these did not succeed in diminishing the payments arrears.

## Mechanisms for the monitoring and follow-up of the SNPA

924.  The Sudan has had four meetings with its development partners since 1981, including two World Bank Consultative Group meetings in 1983 and two special meetings concurrently with the United Nations Conference on the Emergency situation in Africa in March 1985 and the annual meeting of the IMF and the World Bank in Seoul in October 1985.  The Ministry of Finance and Economic Planning is the focal point for the monitoring and follow-up of the SNPA and co-ordinates external financial and technical assistance.  The Sixth Meeting of the Consultative Group, held in January 1983, established a Joint Monitoring Committee (JMC) comprising government officials and donor representatives to meet every three months to report on the progress in the implementation of the Recovery Programme.  Within the context of the Consultative Group meetings, subgroups were established to deal with sectoral issues.  Such subgroup meetings were convened to discuss the rehabilitation of the Gezira scheme, power rehabilitation, manpower development and training needs, and arrangements for petroleum imports.  A high-level interministerial committee was established to co-ordinate national and international relief efforts and a Commissioner for Rehabilitation and Development was appointed.

### 33.  TOGO

## Economic performance

925.  The years 1984 and 1985 have been positive for Togo's economy.  In both years there was good rainfall and, consequently, a good harvest.  The production of phosphates, which account for nearly half of the country's exports, rose by one third in 1984 and exports thereof in 1984 were 60 per cent higher than in 1983.  This improvement was the combined result of higher volumes and better prices.  As a result of a favourable price development in 1985, the values of phosphate exports exceeded the 1984 level, even though the volume decreased by over 12 per cent.

926. The GDP measured in current prices is reported to have grown by 3.8 and 7.1 per cent respectively in 1984 and 1985. Although the drop in food prices in 1984 and 1985 caused the consumer prices to fall in these two years, the overall GDP deflator is estimated to have risen by 2 per cent in both 1984 and 1985. This, combined with a population growth rate estimated at 2.8 per cent per annum, resulted in a fall of real GDP per capita of 1 per cent in 1984, followed by a real growth of 5.9 per cent in 1985, bringing it to $257. But this positive development must be set against the negative growth of the years 1981 to 1984.

927. Both the coffee and the cotton harvests more than doubled between 1983 and 1985, raising the production of these crops from very low to normal levels, while the production of food crops also recovered. Less favourable results were expected for the 1985/1986 harvest: decreases were likely in the production of sorghum/millet, maize and manioc, as well as of the cash crops of coffee and cocoa. But the production of groundnuts should continue to rise, while cotton production should have grown by over 30 per cent in 1985/1986. The production of the cash crops coffee, cocoa and cotton is likely to be stimulated in 1986/1987 by the 50 per cent average increase of producer prices decreed in 1986. No fixed prices exist for food crops.

928. As in most LDCs, Togolese exports are concentrated on a small number of products. Agricultural products (cotton, coffee and vegetable oil) make up almost 50 per cent, most of the rest coming from phosphates and cement. Preliminary figures for 1985 indicate that the combined value of exports of phosphates, cocoa and coffee declined by about 6 per cent. In combination with a 2.6 per cent rise in imports, f.o.b./f.o.b. trade deficit of CFAF 22 billion ($49 million) is estimated, as compared to CFAF 16.0 billion ($36.5 million) in 1984.

## Environment and disasters

929. Togo has not experienced a major environmental disaster in the last few years. However, like all sub-Sahelian countries, Togo suffered from the 1981-1983 drought. Agricultural production fell considerably, but not to the extent that food self-sufficiency was impaired.

## Human resources and social development

930. Education has long been high on the government's priority list. Thus schooling is compulsory for children up to the age of 15 years. A stronger impact of education is sought by improving the quality of the didactic material. A technical school has been installed to strengthen vocational training. Enrolment in the cities continues to be higher than in the countryside, but the government's new emphasis on rural development includes better education in the rural areas. The new rural development strategy not only aims to achieve better training and guidance of the farmers, but also seeks more intensive utilization of fertilizers and the use of improved seeds. The government plans to restructure the rural world by organizing producer groups and improving the infrastructure.

931. In the fields of health and social affairs, the government has set out to fight major endemic diseases, such as malaria, to reinforce the programmes of mother-and-children health, and to install a programme of primary health care.

## Development planning and policies

932. The government's development policies outlined for the 1985 Round Table Conference held in Lomé, contained the following elements.

933. First, the agricultural sector is to assure continued food self-sufficiency and is seen as the driving sector of the economy and a major foreign-exchange earner.

934. Secondly, the tourism sector has attracted the attention of the Government inasmuch as it is the country's third largest foreign-exchange earner, after phosphates and agriculture. But despite Togo's extensive and high-class hotel infrastructure, this sector has not yet fulfilled its potential so far. The government's objective is to increase its earning potential by improving and extending services.

935. Thirdly, the government's important philosophical shift, proposing the privatization of public and parastatal enterprises, marks a reversal from the policy followed in the period 1970-1975, when the Government took over loss-making private companies. The companies often continued to make losses, thereby representing a burden on the budget.

936. The IMF and the World Bank encouraged a withdrawal of the Government from parastatal enterprises. After 1974, when the phosphate market boomed, the Government committed major sums in equity participations in unprofitable companies. This trend is reversed now, as many of these enterprises are not yet profitable. Privatization is one of the government's priorities: it is also the strategy chosen by the Government to blow new life into the tourism sector. Thus the privatization of some luxury hotels, which had been taken over by the Government, producing a joint annual loss of over $1 million in the period 1977-1982, is expected to increase the occupancy rate and make them profitable again, thereby stimulating the tourism sector as a whole. As part of the privatization policy, three important companies have been returned to the private sector: the Sociéte Togolaise de Hydrocarbures (S.T.H.), a petrol refinery; the Sociéte Nationale de Sidérurgie (S.N.S.), a steel mill; and Soprolait, a dairy plant. The petrol refinery, which had started operations in 1977, was not profitable. It has been taken over by Shell which has transformed it into a storage facility. The S.N.S. steelmill has been taken over by an American group, which wants to improve the plant's operational efficiency and penetrate new markets (Nigeria). The plant's projected turnover for 1986 is CFA francs 2.2 billion ($6.1 million), against CFA francs 1.5 billion ($3.3 million) in 1985. The dairy farm Soprolait was taken over by a Danish group and now runs under the name FANMILK.

Mobilization of domestic resources for development

937. The Togolese Government has issued a new investment policy which aims to stimulate private investment. It gives guarantees and advantages to certain classes of investors. Whether an investor may benefit from these privileges depends on certain criteria, such as the level of invested capital, the company's estimated value added compared to its turnover, the number of jobs created by the firm, the share of risk capital provided by private Togolese shareholders and the training to be given to local executives.

938. Companies that meet these criteria receive guarantees, such as the right to repatriate capital and profits, and fiscal advantages, such as exemption from import duties and company tax, reduction of payroll taxes and reduction of "administrative formalities".

Natural resources

939. Togo is constructing a dam at Nangbeto on the Mono River, in co-operation with Benin. This dam, to be finished by mid-1987, will supply energy for an electricity plant of 60 MW. Heretofore electricity was partially imported from Ghana and generated from diesel oil. The Nangbeto Dam should make Togo largely self-sufficient for its energy needs, and will reduce its energy bill, which constituted over 10 per cent of total imports in 1984. The dam has additional advantages for Togo: an area of 42,000 hectares will be irrigated, the artificial lake will offer possibilities for fishing and tourism, and employment will be generated during the construction period.

940. Offshore prospecting for oil is being carried out, while onshore a Nigerian company has been charged with a cartographic survey of a part of Togolese territory, with the aim of developing the mining potential of the country.

Transfer of external resources, debt, capital requirements

941. Since 1980 Togo's total external debt has oscillated between $850 million and $1,020 million. Until 1982 this debt was exclusively of a long-term character, but from 1982 onwards a small but significant part ($75 million) has been of short-term nature. This was one factor that made debt service rise sharply from around $50 million before 1982 to a high of $103 million in 1984. Debt service in 1986 is expected to reach a high of $110 million, resulting in a debt-service-to-exports ratio of almost 50 per cent. France, the Federal Republic of Germany and Denmark have waived Togo's debt (CFA francs 2.2 billion, CFA francs 42.6 billion and CFA francs 4.0 billion respectively) for a total of CFA francs 48.8 billion ($100 million).

942. The IMF granted Togo a stand-by credit of SDR 20.04 million in support of its 1986-1987 economic programme. This economic programme aims at reducing fiscal deficits and at stimulating the private sector. The reduction of the fiscal deficit is to be achieved through the withdrawal of the Government from

public and parastatal enterprises. A stimulus to the private sector is given by the new investment policy and increased producer prices for the agricultural sector. The IMF credit is conditional on pursuit of the policy of privatization of public enterprises and of further measures to reduce the budget deficit.

## Follow-up of the SNPA

943. A Round Table Meeting was held in Lomé in June 1985, at which a 1985-1990 investment programme was presented. The distribution of planned investment over the five-year period between the rural sector, industry, infrastructure and socio-cultural development was 35, 5, 52 and 8 per cent respectively. The heavy share assigned to infrastructure is explained by the ongoing work on the Nangbeto Dam and by maintenance and extension of the road network. However, the part of the investment programme dedicated to rural development is expected to rise from 23 per cent in 1985 to 35 per cent in 1990. This growth will be offset by a declining expenditure on infrastructure after the completion of the Nangbeto Dam. It reflects the government's desire to achieve self-sufficiency in food, to increase the export of cash crops and to limit the rural exodus.

## 34. UGANDA

## Recent economic performance

944. The internal civil strife that raged in Uganda during much of 1985 has brought to a halt the economic recovery and rehabilitation programme that had been launched in 1981. Furthermore, towards the end of 1985 the performance of the formal Ugandan economy sharply declined largely as a result of the heavy damage suffered by its infrastructure. Inflation was soaring and the value of the Ugandan shilling against the United States dollar had fallen drastically. The number of displaced and disabled persons had risen dramatically and the flight of many qualified Ugandans had further reduced the country's already limited labour force. Gross foreign reserves were below $100 million and coffee exports had come to a virtual standstill. The political instability and insecurity in the country prompted international agencies and individual donor countries to hold back the assistance they had earmarked for Uganda.

945. Endowed with fertile soil and a mild tropical climate, and rarely suffering from drought, agriculture is the engine of growth of the economy. Most economic activities are closely linked to this sector which, besides feeding the urban population, provides most of the inputs for industry, is the most important source of taxation and produces most of the country's exports. Cultivable land constitutes around 70 per cent of the total area and land ownership is relatively evenly distributed. If Uganda was able to avoid a major economic catastrophe, it was largely thanks to its subsistence agriculture, which provided food for most of the population. In fact, Uganda was not only able to feed itself during the more than 15 years marked by recurrent internal strife, but also to export food, as it has done every year since independence. Even at the height of the civil war (roughly between mid-1985 and February 1986) barter deals were arranged with Rwanda and Zaire, under which beans and maize from Uganda were exchanged for soap and salt.

Food shortages did, however, arise in urban areas due to the breakdown of transport facilities. As a result, effective food prices far outpaced wages in the monetized sector, which, if they were paid at all, covered but a small fraction of the basic food requirements of a family.

946. According to the World Bank, Uganda is one of the few countries in Africa where food production is expected to grow faster than population over the next 10 years. Today it is self-sufficient in foodstuffs with the exception of wheat, rice, sugar and small amounts of dried milk and edible oil, and the country is judged to have the potential to produce considerable surpluses.

947. Uganda's principal cash crops are coffee, followed by cotton, maize and tea. As coffee is produced on a small-scale basis, the sector survived the civil strife reasonably well. Coffee accounted for no less than 95 per cent of foreign-exchange earnings in 1983. In recent years the unstable conditions of the country have often interrupted shipments to Mombasa; during the last part of 1985, official coffee trade stopped altogether. The coffee crop of early 1986 was good both in quantitative and qualitative terms. With the new Government installed in Kampala, the road to Mombasa was reopened and normal coffee trade resumed. Selling this coffee is a priority of the new Government, particularly since soaring world coffee prices are providing a financial foundation for reconstruction efforts. Cotton and tea yielded export receipts of $12.4 million and $3.2 million respectively in 1984.

948. Total exports fluctuated between $372 million and $399 million during the period 1983-1985, while imports decreased from $428 million in 1983 to around $370 million in 1984 and 1985, leaving a modest trade surplus ($28 million) in 1984 and a marginal one in 1985. The positive trade balances in 1984 and 1985 can be explained by rising world coffee prices on the one hand, and falling prices for petroleum products, which account for one quarter of Uganda's total imports, on the other. However, the balance on current account remained negative in 1984, owing to a structural deficit in services estimated at $75.9 million. A similar situation is likely to have recurred in 1985.

949. Despite measures to revive the stagnant industrial sector, growth since 1983 has been slow, owing mainly to problems of management, shortages of working capital, uncreditworthiness of enterprises and outdated equipment. Moreover, the complex and time-consuming ownership questions arising out of the reprivatization of enterprises undertaken since 1983 caused many business operations to be suspended. During the latter part of 1985, production in the monetized industrial sector came to an almost complete halt. Industrial rehabilitation depends critically on the availability of foreign exchange for imported inputs and spare parts promised by the new Government.

950. In the field of energy, more than 95 per cent of the country's requirements are met from fuelwood and charcoal. The former Government had given high priority to the optimum utilization of the hydroelectric power potential, estimated at 1955 MW. A major project in this respect is the capacity expansion of the Owen Falls Power Station from 135 MW to 172 MW, for which financing had been committed by the United Kingdom, the Commonwealth Development Corporation and the World Bank. In the second half of 1985 funding was suspended, but in June 1986 the United Kingdom unblocked its share of the funding ($10.8 million).

951. The Ugandan shilling has undergone repeated and drastic devaluations since 1980; by mid-1985 its effective exchange rate stood at barely one per cent of its 1980 level. Between September 1985 and in January 1986 it was devalued by a further 60 per cent to USh 1,470 per dollar. At the end of May 1986, a dual exchange rate was introduced, with a market rate of USh 5,000 per dollar for commercial transactions and a priority rate of USh 1,400 per dollar for essential imports, but in August 1986 the commercial rate was abolished in favour of the priority rate, which then became the sole official rate. Although the latter measure was officially justified as a way to combat the black market in foreign exchange, the gap between the rates on the official and black markets was reported to have widened to more than 400 per cent of the former by November 1986.

Environment and disasters

952. Uganda has been facing a serious refugee problem. More than half a million people are estimated to have been displaced by military and guerrilla operations.

953. As a consequence of the 15 years of civil strife, Ugandan wildlife has been seriously affected, in particular through poaching by undisciplined armed personnel. Moreover, the ecological balance of the fish population in Lake Victoria was upset by the introduction of Nile perches in the framework of a development project.

Human resources and social development

954. The population in 1984 was estimated at 14.3 million, with an annual growth rate estimated at 3.2 per cent. Educational services have expanded considerably since 1980, but have been affected by the civil strife, resulting in a general lack of maintenance of buildings and plants, a shortage of qualified teachers and in loss or damage to school facilities, equipment and supplies.

955. During recent years the Ugandan population has been receiving very poor health care. The country, which was considered to have had the best teaching hospital and medical care of Eastern Africa in the 1960s, spent only $1.7 per capita on health in 1984, one of the lowest rates in Eastern Africa. The recent internal strife has led to the destruction or insufficient maintenance of existing facilities, lack of essential supplies, the loss of numerous key professional and managerial staff as well as shortages of essential drugs. Moreover, safe water supplies have deteriorated. As a result, mortality rates are thought to have risen. Official estimates of infant mortality rates range between 100 and 120 per 1,000 live births, while the crude death rate might be close to 20 per 1,000 (June 1985). Owing to the fighting, the number of disabled persons who require urgent health care has increased. As government facilities have deteriorated, NGO-operated facilities, which constitute about 50 per cent of all health facilities, have been increasingly relied upon for essential services and have been operating beyond design capacity.

## Development planning and policies

956. A Revised Recovery Plan was instituted to prolong the pre-existing
recovery programme (FY 1981/82 - FY 1983/84) through FY 1984/85. 165/ Owing
to the unstable political situation, this Plan could no longer be implemented
during the second half of 1985.  By the end of 1985, a new national
development plan had been drafted, but it was never approved because of the
change in régime.

957. The President has stressed Uganda's need for economic independence and
self-reliance, warning against an economy which consumed what it did not
produce and produced what it did not consume.  He favours a mixture of State
and private enterprise.  Agriculture and construction are to receive priority
in the immediate reconstruction period, in particular with respect to imports
of agricultural and construction machinery.  In February 1986 a six-month
Emergency Relief and Rehabilitation Programme for war-ravaged areas was
launched, whose main objectives are the provision of emergency assistance to
displaced persons, the restoration of essential services and the provision of
emergency relief supplies, building materials and agricultural and industrial
inputs.  The cost of the Programme, for which the Government sought
international assistance, was set at $161 million.  In efforts to stimulate
exports, reduce the influence of parallel markets and control inflation, a
package of interim measures was introduced in May 1986, under which producer
prices for coffee, tea, tobacco and cocoa were almost doubled and interest
rates drastically increased.

## Mobilization of domestic resources

958. The country's financial administration has not been able to mobilize
effectively domestic savings and assure a sound, non-inflationary financing of
government deficits.  Until FY 1983/84, recurrent expenditures were largely
financed by current revenues. The government's overall budget deficit was
kept under control thanks mainly to drastic cuts of development expenditures
in real terms.  After June 1984, fiscal performance deteriorated sharply
following a large increase in current expenditures.  While the budget deficit
had been largely funded domestically until FY 1983/84, 86 per cent of the
deficit in FY 1984/85 was financed by external sources.  The fact that
domestic funding was mainly effected by credit creation on the part of the
banking system rather than through real savings had resulted in rampant
inflation, which was fueled by the breakdown of supplies in the monetized
economy during the 1985/1986 civil strife.  By mid-1985 it had attained an
annual rate of almost 150 per cent.

959. The share of government revenues in GDP is well below 10 per cent, its
key sources being export taxes on coffee, which provided an estimated
42 per cent of total revenues in FY 1983/84, followed by sales taxes and
customs-cum-excise duties, which accounted for an estimated 18 per cent.  The
contribution of income taxes is very low, even compared with neighbouring
countries, providing only 6.2 per cent of total tax revenues in FY 1982/83.
Owing to weak administrative services, tax collection rates are very low.

Transfer of external resources, debt, capital requirements

960. Total external debt amounted to $737 million at the end of 1984, rising to $1 billion by June 1986.  Of this amount, about $700 million is composed of medium and long-term loans on concessional terms, which can be rescheduled.  About $300 million is short-term debt, largely IMF drawings effected before the new Government took over, which cannot be rescheduled. Debt service payments have been absorbing nearly one half of the country's export revenues.  Uganda concluded two rescheduling agreements with the Paris Club of official creditors in FY 1981/82, covering only $56 million and $22 million respectively.  So far, debt cancellation by individual donors amounted to $64.9 million, of which $26.6 million was cancelled by the Federal Republic of Germany and $25.2 million by the United Kingdom.

961. In 1984 Uganda received $167.2 million in total net financial flows from abroad, of which 98.9 per cent were in the form of grants and concessional loans from DAC countries, mostly through multilateral institutions.  This flow represented a modest increase from the 1983 level of $151.1 million, but still fell short of the $171.7 million received in 1982.

962. For its rehabilitation and reconstruction, the country needs international assistance on a large scale.  Western donors had indicated their willingness to provide such assistance soon after the fall of President Obote, but most aid and development programmes were suspended during 1985.  Since the stabilization of the situation after the swearing in of President Museveni in January 1986, donor countries began unfreezing the considerable sums of aid earmarked for Uganda:  $50 million from UNDP, $70-$100 million from the World Bank, $125 million from the EEC under Lomé III, $8 million from the United States, $7 million from the United Kingdom, and $6.5 million from the Federal Republic of Germany.  By 31 July 1986 approximately $47.6 million had been pledged by the international community to the emergency relief and rehabilitation programme.

Monitoring and implementation of the SNPA

963. The internal political crisis has made the follow-up of the SNPA impossible.

### 35.  UNITED REPUBLIC OF TANZANIA

Economic performance

964. Real GDP growth has been officially estimated at 2.3 per cent in 1985 as against 3 per cent in 1984.  Given an annual population growth of 3.4 per cent, per capita growth has thus continued to decline.

965. The unsatisifactory growth is largely caused by the bad performance of agriculture, which remains the leading sector in terms of its contribution to GDP, foreign currency earnings and employment.  The agricultural sector has traditionally been vulnerable to drought and other natural calamities.  It has also been affected by the lack of physical infrastructure, particularly of

feeder roads and adequate storage facilities, a low level of technology, a
lack of skilled manpower and poor extension services.   Domestic food
production has not kept pace with demand.   The problem has been aggravated by
a pattern of urban consumption which leans towards maize, rice and wheat,
necessitating substantial cereal imports.

966. The year 1984 had been marked by drought, which made substantial food aid
necessary.   In 1985 rains were satisfactory and food output improved,
stimulated also by the large domestic producer price increases for food crops,
which became effective in June 1985.   The maize crop of crop year
1985/1986 166/ is estimated at 294,800 tons as against 160,000 tons in
1984/85, and the beans crop is estimated to have increased to 32,500 tons in
1985/86 against 23,000 tons in the previous crop year.   Output of wheat also
increased.   While the country did not need exceptional food aid during crop
year 1985/86, a structural deficit of 225,000 tons of cereals (maize, rice and
wheat) subsisted, which had to be covered by commercial imports and normal
food aid.   In 1985/86 100,000 tons of food were imported commercially,
leaving a structural food aid requirement of 125,000 tons.   By April 1986,
donor pledges amounted to 93,000 tons, of which 52,000 tons had been delivered.

967. Cash crop production as a whole declined by 28.6 per cent from 1984/1985
to 1985/1986 and that of cotton fell by as much as 62.5 per cent.   This was
due mainly to the lack of essential equipment and inputs, as well as transport
problems, but also to bad weather in some areas, despite the generally
favourable rainfall.   Consequently, the export volume of coffee and sisal
fell by 29 per cent and 48 per cent respectively between 1984 and 1985.

968. Underlying much of the recent difficulty of the Tanzanian economy have
been the severe foreign-currency constraints which have forced the country to
reduce imports substantially, with the effect that essential agricultural and
industrial inputs were not available and the necessary spare parts lacking.
At the end of 1984, 40 per cent of the country's 9,939 tractors were out of
action owing to the unavailability of imported spare parts.   Infrastructure
could not be appropriately maintained either.   Transport services had been
severely affected by the lack of spare parts, which prevented the necessary
maintenance of the vehicle fleet, and by insufficient imports of fuel for its
operation.   The lack of transport services had aggravated the shortages
caused by import constraints and the effects of the drought, which lasted
until 1984.   Shortages of seeds, fertilizers and insecticides as well as
agricultural implements had been experienced in many rural areas, while large
stockpiles of undistributed implements had been built up at factories and
ports.   With the return of rain in 1985, transport bottlenecks caused
agricultural products to accumulate in the villages, where they suffered from
pests and decay due to insufficient storage facilities.   The government is
now giving priority to secure the haulage of agricultural produce.

969. The balance of payments continued to deteriorate in 1985:   export
earnings in dollar terms declined by 25 per cent and imports increased by
21 per cent as against 1984, reducing the export-import coverage ratio to less
than 30 per cent.   The main reasons for the fall in export earnings were the
reductions in the volumes of commodities exported and the price declines for
Tanzanian commodities on world markets.   In an effort to restore the balance

of the external sector, the national currency was devalued by 60 per cent against the United States dollar between March and June 1986, a measure which went a long way towards correcting the pronounced overvaluation that had only been insufficiently corrected by the 1983 and 1984 devaluation of 21 and 27 per cent respectively.

970. Industrial output declined both in 1984 and in 1985, continuin the industrial decay which has marked each year since 1980 and reducing manufacturing output by more than 70 per cent since its 1979 peak. Shortages of foreign exchange, which have severely affected the highly import-dependent industrial structure, inadequate supplies of agricultural inputs, as well as infrastructural and transport problems have all contributed to the disastrous result, which has led to a temporary closure of many factories. The fall in industrial output together with the halt in imports of finished goods has caused severe shortages of basic essentials. In order to raise capacity utilization from the current low levels of between 20 and 30 per cent to 60 per cent, rehabilitation efforts are being undertaken and an export promotion scheme has been introduced under which selected industrial enterprises can draw on a special foreign-exchange account for importing their requirements in raw materials and spare parts. Initially the scheme benefited 12 companies, notably in the sectors of tyres, leather, textiles and metals. A further 25 companies are being considered for possible inclusion in the scheme.

971. The substantial energy resources of the country are largely undeveloped. In March 1986 the World Bank chaired a donor meeting to consider a three-year rehabilitation programme for the electricity sector, focusing on the rehabilitation of diesel power stations. A $22-million credit for the programme is under discussion in IDA.

## Environment and disasters

972. Deforestation continues to be a serious problem, with the country losing 4,000 hectares of forest cover annually, owing largely to overcutting of firewood for household purposes. Overgrazing also is a problem. DANIDA has committed about $5 million for the financing of projects for soil conservation and reforestation.

973. An outbreak of the "army worm pest" has affected maize crops in the Kilimanjaro area, pasture in Arusha and sorghum and millet in Dodoma. The United Republic of Tanzania is also among the East African countries whose crops are facing the danger of locust infestation.

974. An extensive operation covering the national parks of Serengeti, Mikumi, Manyara and Ruaha was undertaken by the Government to stop poaching. The poachers have operated in the national parks, where they have killed a great number of game, such as rhinoceros and elephants.

## Human resources and social development

975. The United Republic of Tanzania has placed great emphasis on meeting the health and educational needs of the population and has a well developed system of primary health care and basic education. The current government programme focuses on the provision of recurrent requirements and full utilization of

existing health facilities, stressing improvement of the quality of services and the need to consolidate the achievements so far. The same policy applies to basic education. While 98 per cent of children of the 7-13 age group are enrolled in primary schooling, its quality has recently suffered from the lack of textbooks, shortage of qualified teachers and the poor physical condition of schools.

## Development planning and policies

976. Development planning began after independence in 1964 with the preparation of a 15-year Perspective Plan (1965-1980) which included a five-year plan for the period from FY 1964/65 to FY 1968/69 167/ which was followed by two more five-year plans. Since 1981, when the Second Perspective Plan covering the 20-year period up to the year 2000 was drawn up, the five-year plans have included both the mainland and Zanzibar. The first five-year Union Development Plan ended in FY 1985/86; preparation of the Second Union Development Plan was delayed because of the 1985 elections and is to be presented early in 1987.

977. Annual planning designed to translate the long-term and medium-term goals into short-term operational programmes had already started in 1970/1971. To address the economic crisis, a National Economic Survival Plan was introduced in 1981, followed in 1982 by the Structural Adjustment Programme (SAP) for FY 1983/1984 and 1984/1985, whose main objectives were crisis management and structural adjustment. Based on the experience obtained in the implementation of the SAP, a special three-year Programme for Economic Recovery was announced in June 1986, covering the years 1986/1987 to 1988/1989, which was to be implemented as from July 1986. Major objectives of the Programme include an increase in the output of food and export crops through production incentives, improved marketing structures and more resources devoted to agriculture; an increase in export earnings, the rehabilitation of the country's physical infrastructure in support of directly productive activities, such as transport and communications, energy and water; an increase in the capacity utilization of existing industries and the restoration of the country's financial health through appropriate fiscal, monetary and trade policies.

978. For the stimulation of agricultural production, the Government has granted substantial producer price increases for both food and cash crops. For the crop year 1985/1986 producer prices for eight cash crops were raised by between 10 and 25 per cent, while for 1986/1987 even more important price rises have been announced. The Government intends to continue this incentive policy by setting producer prices at a level equivalent to 60 or 70 per cent of f.o.b. prices, or increasing them by 5 per cent annually in real terms, whichever is higher.

## Mobilization of domestic resources for development

979. Since 1979 the recurrent portion of the budget has shown continuing deficits, which have become a major source of inflation since they were largely financed by bank credit expansion. Ninety per cent of total recurrent revenues are provided by taxes, of which the sales and income taxes provided 55 per cent and 27 per cent respectively in FY 1982/83. The

effectiveness of tax collection has been greatly improved in recent years, but the real tax base has declined as sales, imports and profits have shrunk with the economic crisis. This prompted the introduction in July 1984 of a development levy, a form of flat-rate head tax, which every able-bodied adult is required to pay. In July 1985, the rate was increased. Export taxes were progressively removed in recent years to increase incentives to producers, while import taxes were increased in the face of a decline in the volume of imports. For FY 1986/87 the Government has announced its intention to increase revenues by adjusting sales and import tax levels, expanding the tax base and improving efficiency in revenue collection. Income taxes, on the other hand, were revised downwards from July 1986 onwards, in order to ease the burden on taxpayers who belonged to the world's most heavily-taxed persons, with marginal rates reaching 95 per cent. Development expenditures were expected to rise by 130 per cent in nominal terms, while the rise of recurrent expenditures was to be 53 per cent. The latter probably implies a sharp cut in real terms, inasmuch as the two thirds devaluation vis-à-vis the SDR will entail a substantially greater rise of the domestic price level.

## Transfer of external resources, debt, capital requirements

980. Efforts to reduce the budget deficit have largely fallen on the development budget, as the Government has limited the growth of development expenditures to the availability of project aid since 1979. This fiscal stringency was a sine qua non for obtaining a renewal of foreign assistance in 1986. Concessional loans and grants provided to the United Republic of Tanzania had shown a steady rise from 1970 to 1982, to reach a peak of $691.5 million, but these flows declined by 13.3 per cent in 1983 and 5.8 per cent in 1984. The decline affected both DAC and OPEC donors and was most marked with respect to bilateral flows. A number of donors have given emphasis to import support in their aid. A principal reason for the fall in concessional assistance from DAC countries was the lengthy disagreement with the IMF on policies to be adopted to restore the financial health of the country. Only the Scandinavian countries were ready to continue their assistance without prior agreement with the IMF.

981. The United Republic of Tanzania's medium and long-term outstanding debt, including undisbursed debt, stood at $2.9 billion at the end of 1984. Although over 62 per cent of this debt was concessional, the country has made extensive use of suppliers' and commercial banking credits since 1979, the servicing of which has added considerable weight to its debt burden. Thus, interest payments have increased every year from an estimated 13 per cent of total export earnings in 1980 to about 55 per cent in 1985. However, the debt burden was significantly eased by debt relief amounting to $406.6 million given by a number of DAC donors in response to UNCTAD Trade and Development Board resolution 165 (S-IX).

## Monitoring and follow-up of the SNPA

982. The United Republic of Tanzania is covered by a Consultative Group Arrangement chaired by the World Bank. In June 1986 a meeting under World Bank auspices between the United Republic of Tanzania and all its major bilateral and multilateral donors took place in Paris. It was the first meeting of this Group since the adoption of the SNPA.

983. Donors, representing 27 countries and international organizations, agreed that about $800 million a year would be needed for the country's economic recovery and noted that the United Republic of Tanzania would require debt relief on the most generous terms. They also concluded that efforts should be made to improve aid co-ordination through regular meetings of the Group, more informal meetings of donors in the United Republic of Tanzania, and bilateral aid consultations.

36. VANUATU

## Economic performance

984. The economy has gradually recovered from the setback that followed the pre-independence disturbances of 1980 and since 1981 it has expanded steadily. GDP growth in real terms is estimated to have accelerated from about 2 per cent in 1981 to nearly 4 per cent in 1983 and 4.5 per cent in 1984. Estimates by the National Planning and Statistical Office (NPSO) indicate that the cash income per head of the ni-Vanuatu (name of the indigenous population) was about $235 in 1983, a figure which would rise to $356 if food grown for subsistence were taken into account. Economic activity in 1985 has been affected by relief work and reconstruction following two major cyclones in January 1985. Incomes are not likely to increase because of the widespread damage to agricultural crops including copra, the major export and foreign-exchange earner.

985. Vanuatu's external transactions in recent years have been characterized by large deficits in the commodity trade account which were more than offset by surpluses in the services and transfer accounts. The net inflow of long-term capital in 1983 and 1984 would have produced sizeable surpluses in the overall balance of payments but for the correspondingly large outflows of short-term capital and unexplained transactions. Nevertheless, it did allow monetary reserves to rise moderately to a level roughly equal to two months' imports.

986. The value of Vanuatu's exports dropped by more than 50 per cent between 1979, the last year before independence, and 1982. The 1984 recovery was short-lived and largely due to copra, which accounted for over 60 per cent of export earnings in that year. Exports of copra had risen to over 46,000 metric tons in 1984, an increase of nearly 20 per cent over the preceding year, while prices were also relatively high, resulting in more than a twofold increase of export earnings from copra. However in 1985, earnings from exports of copra fell back to less than their 1983 level in dollar terms, partly because of extensive cyclone damage to coconut trees in the northern islands of Vanuatu in January 1985 (which brought the export volume back to its 1982-83 average), but more importantly due to the precipitous fall in copra prices, which dropped by 46 per cent on average between 1984 and 1985. By April 1986 copra prices had fallen to one quarter of their average 1984 levels to nominal prices not seen since 1972. Imports in 1985 in dollar terms had barely recovered their 1979/1980 levels after a severe contraction in the intervening years. Consumer goods, such as foodstuffs, mineral fuels and lubricants accounted for almost two thirds of total import spending during 1981-1983. However, the country has made notable progress in import substitution, although the scope for such substitution tends to be limited by the small size of the domestic market.

987. Tourism, the most important source of earnings on the services account, suffered considerably in 1985. However, in order to encourage tourists, the Government devalued the national currency by an accumulative total of 17.5 per cent in first quarter of 1985 and of 1986. Also, a major step taken to maximize the economic benefits of tourism was the establishment of Air Vanuatu and greater ni-Vanuatu participation in tourist projects and increased hotel construction.

988. The international assistance which Vanuatu has received has helped the country maintain a surplus in its overall balance of payments. The budgetary contribution from the French Government for 1985 remained at the VT 185 million ($1.74 million) level originally expected from each of the two ex-colonial powers, but the British contribution was reduced to VT 100 million ($0.94 million). Special cyclone relief and reconstruction assistance from many aid donors during the first half of 1985 also supported the balance of payments.

989. Agriculture is the major sector of the economy in terms of employment and accounts for over 80 per cent of the country's total visible exports, but it contributes only one fifth of the countrys's monetized GDP, reflecting the dual nature of the economy and the chasm separating the urban from the rural sectors. In forestry, 1,200 hectares had been reforested or newly planted between 1976 and December 1983. The Government is now seeking to set aside 10,000 hectares over a 20-year period to produce high-quality sawn and veneer logs for export.

990. The manufacturing sector presents particular problems for small island economies, especially those located at great distances from major markets such as Vanuatu. With over 800 jobs and a value added contribution to GDP of VT 613 million ($6.17 million) in 1983, the manufacturing sector, although small, is of growing importance to the domestic economy: a 38 per cent growth in employment from 1980 to 1983 and more importantly, an 88 per cent growth in value added (at current prices) was reported for the same period. A cement factory and other import-substituting plants established in 1985 included a project to process papaya for export, which provided 300 jobs, mainly for female workers.

991. The guiding principle of transport planning in Vanuatu is the integration of the three modes of transport: land, sea and air. To this end, a number of investments were made in the transport infrastructures including marine and inter-island transport and roads over the first half of the Plan period (1982-1986). With the opening of airfields on the outer islands since 1982, the country's internal air network has been considerably expanded.

992. Vanuatu enjoys good internal and international communications. The first half of the Plan period saw the completion of a big telecommunication project. This provided communications to a number of villages and rural subscribers throughout the archipelago.

993. Vanuatu has diverse and extensive indigenous energy resources. During the period since 1982 biomass, hydropower and geothermal prospects have been identified as possibilities for electric power generation. Of these, biomass

already provides three quarters of the country's energy requirements.
However, the modern sector remains totally dependent upon petroleum imports,
which amounted to VT 535 million ($5.38 million) in 1983, accounting for
8.5 per cent of total imports in that year.  Over the remainder of the Plan
period the Government has attached high priority to developing alternative
renewable energy sources.

994. The last census taken in January 1979 set the population at 111,251, of
whom 94 per cent were ni-Vanuatu.  The annual rate of population growth for
the ni-Vanuatu population is currently estimated at 3.2 per cent, implying a
doubling of the population every 22 years.

Environment and disaster

995. Located in the Pacific tropical cyclone belt, the country is also prone
to occasional earthquakes, droughts, floods, tidal waves and volcanic
eruptions.  In January 1985 a major cyclone caused considerable damage to
coconut trees and other agricultural crops in the northern islands, but no
exact data thereon are available.  A national disaster warning and relief
Plan, which was drawn up in 1980 and covered the whole range of possible
national disasters, was never officially approved and the planned systems have
been only partly established.

Human resources and social development

996. The scarcity of skilled labour and of indigenous professional and
managerial personnel represents a serious constraint for the country's
development.  Only 13.1 per cent of the indigenous labour force, of which just
over one third are female, had any formal education, according to the 1979
census.  Since independence, the Government has instituted a number of major
reforms in the educational system, such as the integration of the English and
French systems in many spheres, including a unified school administration, an
integrated teacher training programme and a single primary-school curriculum.

997. In the health sector, the main problem has been that of making health
services available to a widely scattered population, within the limitations of
a small budget.  The major development in this sector since 1982 has been a
policy shift towards a preventive health care programme.  Greater emphasis has
been placed on mother and child health care, immunizations, health education
and malaria control.  Although life expectancy at birth is still relatively
low (56 and 54 years for ni-Vanuatu men and women respectively) it is
undoubtedly higher than it was 30 or 40 years ago.  The implementation of the
rural water supplies programme remains one of the highest priorities of the
Government's rural development programme.  The proportion of the rural
population with access to potable water has increased from 31 per cent in 1978
to 54 per cent in 1984.

Development planning and policies

998. The development objectives and strategies of the Government contained in
the First National Development Plan (FNDP) for 1982-1986, as updated following
a mid-term review in January 1985, are:  (a) promoting balanced regional and
rural growth; (b)  promoting fuller utilization of the country's agricultural,

human and other resources, including the mobilization of the private sector;
(c) encouraging a spirit of national self-reliance. The proposed allocation
of resources to development programmes closely reflects official objectives
and strategies. Agriculture (including forestry and fisheries) was expected
to absorb 29 per cent of planned capital expenditures over the Plan period.
The other major sectors and their respective shares in planned FNDP outlays
were: education (11.5 per cent), land transport (10.5 per cent), forestry
(7.1 per cent), manufacturing and finance (about 6 per cent each); and air
transport (5.3 per cent).

## Mobilization of domestic resources for development

999. Over the first half of the Plan period, the recurrent budget remained in
surplus largely thanks to foreign grants. The proportion of the recurrent
budget financed from domestic resources increased from 62.1 per cent in 1981
to an estimated 82.7 per cent in 1984. It is expected that Vanuatu will fund
its total recurrent budget from domestic sources by 1987/1988. For 1984 and
1985, increases in domestic revenue of 23.4 per cent and 13.6 per cent
respectively have been estimated. Although the tax base has been widened over
the 1982-1984 period (notably with the introduction of the 10 per cent hotel
turnover tax), the need to further widen and deepen the tax base remains a
major objective. Although the introduction of income tax remains a medium-
term objective, both the administrative costs of introducing any such scheme
and the smallness of the formal sector preclude this for the foreseeable
future. The Government would also wish to ensure that the "tax-haven" status
of Vanuatu remain unchanged, by excluding the offshore income component from
taxation.

## Transfer of external resources, debt, capital requirements

1000. In order to implement the development strategy outlined in the FNDP, it
was estimated that the total capital requirements over the five-year period
were VT 11,500 million (in 1981 prices), equivalent to $130.9 million at the
average 1981 exchange rate. This figure is clearly no more than an estimate
of the broad magnitude of resources required to meet national and sectoral
objectives. The status report of the Development Fund shows that in 1982
total contributions received were $4.65 million, the largest contribution
coming from the European Development Fund. In 1983, total receipts were
$4.58 million, the United Kingdom being the major source of funds.
Preliminary estimates for 1984 and 1985 set external contributions at
$5.36 million and $4.72 million respectively.

1001. At the end of 1984, Vanuatu's external publicly guranteed debt was
$5.1 million, which is a relatively modest amount, equivalent to less than
two months' imports in 1985.

## Mechanism for monitoring and follow-up of the SNPA

1002. At its twenty-first session (New York, April 1985), the Committee for
Development Planning recommended the inclusion of Vanuatu in the
United Nations list of the least developed countries, a recommendation
accepted by the Economic and Social Council on 25 July 1985 and by the

General Assembly in December 1985. Thereupon, and in pursuance of Trade and Development Board resolution 311 (XXX) entitled "Assistance to Cape Verde, Vanuatu and Uganda", an UNCTAD mission was sent to Vanuatu in October/November 1985 to identify the assistance needs of Vanuatu within UNCTAD's field of competence. Moreover, an informal Vanuatu aid co-ordination meeting had been tentatively scheduled for late 1986, but further information thereon had not been released by November 1986.

## 37. YEMEN

### Economic performance

1003. The economic performance of Yemen during the first two years of the decade was impressive. This was mainly due to the rapidly rising services and construction sectors made possible by workers' remittances and ODA flows. Gross domestic product increased in real terms by 9.6 per cent and 10.0 per cent in 1981 and 1982 respectively. However, the decline in agricultural production caused by the earthquake in 1982, the decline in workers' remittances, and the drought of 1983 and 1984 reversed this upward trend, depressing the growth rate to 3.5 and 2.4 per cent in 1983 and 1984 respectively. Further reductions in remittances and development assistance have further depressed economic performance in 1985.

1004. The trade balance of Yemen continues to face a serious structural imbalance due to the extremely low level of exports, averaging about $44 million during the period 1981-1984 (although increasing sharply in 1984 and in 1985), and the very high level of imports, which reached $1.8 billion in 1981. However, as a result of adjustment measures adopted in 1983 imports declined, by 9.4 per cent and 5.9 per cent in 1983 and 1984 respectively compared to the 1981 peak, and were projected to decline by 9 per cent of that level in 1985. The large trade deficit, estimated at 32 per cent of GDP in 1984, had been mainly financed by workers' remittances, which have been declining since 1979 and were estimated at less than $1 billion in 1985. After an upsurge in official transfers up to 1982 and of long-term capital transfers in 1980, both declined consistently thereafter to a quarter and a sixth of their respective record levels by 1985. The above-mentioned cuts in imports helped to cut the current account deficit by 50 per cent and 61 per cent in 1984 and 1985 respectively compared to the 1980-1983 average. Net international reserves, which reached their highest level in terms of imports in 1976 (equivalent to 69 weeks of imports), have consistently declined ever since to a mere quarter of their 1979 record, being $356 million by June 1986. This was the equivalent of 15 weeks of imports at their sharply-reduced current levels.

1005. An important factor which had contributed to the more than eleven-fold increase in food imports between 1973 and 1982 was the poor performance of the agricultural sector. This was caused by the massive emigration from rural areas which was not accompanied by an increase in productivity, but did result in increased labour costs, making local produce less competitive vis-à-vis imports; and the shift from recorded coffee and cotton production to unrecorded but profitable qat production. During the period 1981-1985 food production per capite of the population declined by an annual average rate of 1.9 per cent. Yemen imports at present about 600,000 tons of wheat compared to a maximum domestic production of about 70,000 tons. In order to encourage agricultural production, several measures, including subsidization of agricultural inputs and protection of agriculture, were implemented under a policy which declared the year 1984 to be the "Year of Agricultural Development". During that year the Government embarked on the development of extension services and even more important work started on the construction of the Marib dam and an irrigation scheme dependent on it. The dam, financed by the United Arab Emirates, will cost about $95 million and will have the capacity to retain 300 million $m^3$ of water and irrigate an initial area of about 20,000 hectares. The accumulation of silt is expected to provide a fertile soil suitable for the cultivation of a wide variety of grains, vegetables and fruits. In a move designed to encourage local production and save foreign exchange, the Government banned imports of fruits and vegetables, which had amounted to a total of $273 million during the period 1981-1983. This has had a positive effect, inasmuch as the country now approaches self-sufficiency in these items.

1006. The industrial sector, which accounts for about 16 per cent of GDP, continues to face several constraints, e.g. scarcity of natural resources, shortages of skilled manpower, high labour costs and an insufficient infrastructure. The private sector is particularly active, especially in food processing, which accounts for about 45 per cent of value added in manufacturing. The public sector has concentrated on the production of cement, which is still below demand, but which is projected to increase substantially with the entry into operation of the third cement factory in the early years of the Third Five-Year Development Plan 1987-1991.

1007. Although deposits of copper, iron, coal, lead, nickel, gold, silver and sulphur have been found, extraction is limited at present to salt and quarrying. Petroleum has been discovered in commercial quantities in the Al-Jawf basin, one of whose four fields is expected to have a production capacity of 50,000-100,000 b/d over 20 years. The revenue generated from its exploitation is expected to be a major source of income during the Third Five-Year Plan (1987-1992). A refinery with a capacity of 10,000 b/d, one third of domestic needs, became operational in April 1986. Exports are expected once the construction of a 400 km pipeline from the oil fields to the Red Sea is completed in 1988.

## Environment and disasters

1008. Dhamar Province was struck by a severe earthquake in December 1982 which caused extensive loss of life and damage to property. About 3,000 people were killed and 150,000 were left homeless. Assistance was received from bilateral and multilateral sources for the rehabilitation and reconstruction programme, including temporary housing. In March 1986, 1,200 permanent housing units were distributed to affected people as the second phase of reconstruction.

## Human resources and development

1009. According to the 1986 census, the country's population is about 9.3 million, implying an annual growth rate of 3 per cent since 1975. The Government, assisted by bilateral and multilateral donors, has made significant progress in developing education and health facilities and providing public services during the Second Five-Year Plan (1982-1986). In the education sector an adult literacy programme is being implemented.

However, the adult literacy rate, at 14 per cent in 1985, is low compared to
the 35 per cent average for all LDCs. The number of primary schools increased
by 46 per cent between 1980 and 1983 and more schools are being established in
remote areas. Thus, the primary school enrolment ratio increased from
29 per cent in 1975 to 65 per cent in 1985. On-the-job training is strongly
emphasized in the implementation of development projects. Education is free
at all levels. However, these efforts are being partially frustrated by a
brain drain and emigration of the working population, which constitute one of
the major constraints to development in Yemen. In the health sector the
number of hospitals increased by 21 per cent and that of health centres almost
threefold between 1978 and 1982. The emphasis is on extending primary health
care (PHC) services with a view to eradicating endemic diseases. In 1985
about 25 per cent of the rural population was covered with PHC services
through 184 PHC units and 15 rural health centres. Other measures include
promoting health and nutrition education.

## Development planning and policies

1010. The main emphasis in the Second Five-Year Development Plan (1982-1986)
was on the productive sectors of the economy, especially agriculture, industry
and mining. The Plan called for better co-ordination and use of the available
human, natural and financial resources in order to attain continuous and
self-sustained development. However, the implementation of the Plan faced
several constraints, particularly the shortage of skilled manpower, the Dhamar
earthquake in 1982, the shortage of rainfall in 1982/1983, the decline in real
terms of workers' remittances, insufficient domestic savings, and declining
external assistance, which had been expected to finance 73 per cent of planned
investment. Thus in 1983 the Government reviewed the strategies and
priorities of the Plan and decided to concentrate on the agricultural sector.
Nevertheless, the Government has enacted favourable legislation and introduced
several monetary and fiscal incentives to encourage the participation of the
foreign and domestic private sectors in industrial development. A rebate of
25 per cent on duties on all imported raw materials for industry and a tax
holiday for the first five years of operation is granted. The Industrial Bank
of Yemen provides soft loans to finance viable projects. Measures were
initiated with the objective of limiting both the budgetary and external
payments imbalances. These included tighter fiscal and monetary policies; a
phased devaluation of the rial, amounting to a cumulative cut of 37 per cent
vis-à-vis the dollar between November 1983 and January 1986; rationalizing
imports; and substantial reductions in current and development expenditures
of the Government, resulting in substantial cuts of the budget deficits (see
below). The Third Five-Year Development Plan (1987-1991) will have to be
formulated in the context of continuing declining private as well as official
transfers. In addition to the revenue expected from oil exports, further
efforts will need to be made to increase the mobilization of domestic
resources.

## Mobilization of domestic resources for development

1011. Concerned by the poor fiscal performance during the period 1980-1982, with the budget deficit representing 48 per cent of total government expenditures and 33 per cent of GDP in 1982, the Government implemented several revenue-generating and expenditure-reducing measures during the period 1983-1985. These included: increasing tariff rates, improving tax collection, increasing prices of public services and imposing new taxes on real estate and undeveloped land. To reduce current expenditures a freeze was imposed on wages and the recruitment of foreign labour, while capital expenditures, except for health and construction, were reduced. Thus, between 1982 and 1984 domestic revenue increased by 26 per cent, while current expenditures increased by only 13 per cent and capital expenditures declined by 23 per cent. As a result, the budget deficit declined by 12.4 per cent between 1982 and 1984, despite a 64 per cent decline in grants. Notwithstanding these improvements, domestic savings continued to be negative, equivalent to about -22 per cent of GDP in 1984. However, these negative domestic savings were more than offset by the substantial net factor income and unrequited emigrant transfers, which were equivalent to 34 per cent of GDP during the same year.

## Transfer of external resources and external debt

1012. Net disbursements of all financial flows, which amounted to $504 million in 1982, declined in the following years and were estimated at only $325 million in 1984, thus affecting the implementation of the Second Five-Year Plan. Total external debt is estimated to have increased to $2.08 billion at the end of 1984 from $1.57 billion at the end of 1982. Debt service payments amounted to $142 million in 1984, representing 13 per cent of exports of goods and services, as compared to 6.8 per cent in 1982.

## Mechanism for the follow-up and monitoring of the SNPA

1013. The Central Planning Organization is the central authority responsible for the co-ordination of all external development assistance. Yemen convened its Second International Conference in 1982 and used the occasion to launch its Second Five-Year Development Plan. In 1985 two sectoral aid co-ordination meetings, for water resources and agriculture, were convened in collaboration with the local UNDP Office and attended by representatives of bilateral and multilateral donors. The aim of these meetings is to improve the efficiency of aid utilization. An example of effective aid co-ordination is provided by a project on Drought Relief Assistance for Sana'a and Hodeidah Governorates. The funds for the project were provided by the Netherlands, UNDP and FAO. Co-ordination at the field level is ensured by UNDP.

## Notes

<u>1/</u>  Before its 1986 session the General Assembly had identified
37 countries as least developed among the developing countries on the basis of
their very low per capita income, very low literacy rate and low contribution
of manufacturing industries to GDP.  These countries are Afghanistan,
Bangladesh, Benin, Bhutan, Botswana, Burkina Faso, Burundi, Cape Verde,
Central African Republic, Chad, Comoros, Democratic Yemen, Djibouti,
Equatorial Guinea, Ethiopia, Gambia, Guinea, Guinea-Bissau, Haiti, Lao
People's Democratic Republic, Lesotho, Malawi, Maldives, Mali, Nepal, Niger,
Rwanda, Samoa, Sao Tome and Principe, Sierra Leone, Somalia, Sudan, Togo,
Uganda, United Republic of Tanzania, Vanuatu and Yemen.  Three countries added
by the General Assembly to the list at its 1986 session are not covered by
this report (Kiribati, Mauritania and Tuvalu).

<u>2/</u>  Because of increased interest payments and the deteriorating terms
of trade, growth of national income in the early 1980s fell short of GDP
growth rates for LDCs as a group.

<u>3/</u>  This concept is used to take into account changes in the terms of
trade combined with the volume of exports.

<u>4/</u>  UNCTAD/ST/LDC/3, p.32.

<u>5/</u>  UNCTAD/ST/LDC/2, paras. 115-125, table 7.

<u>6/</u>  Ibid., paras. 160-177.

<u>7/</u>  Ibid., para. 171.

<u>8/</u>  See UNCTAD/ST/LDC/2, pp.24-25.

<u>9/</u>  Ibid., pp.37-39.

<u>10/</u>  See, for example, UNCTAD/ST/LDC/2, paras. 36-49.

<u>11/</u>  Food is defined as agricultural commodities that are considered
edible and contain nutrients.  Accordingly, together with inedible
commodities, coffee and tea are excluded because, although edible, they have
practically no nutritive value (cf. <u>FAO Bulletin of Statistics</u>, notes on the
tables).  Cassava, potatoes and yams are among the rootcrops which constitute,
in addition to cereals, the basic dietary elements in a number of LDCs.

<u>12/</u>  The 1986 grain harvest in Botswana is expected to be below normal
for the fifth consecutive year.

<u>13/</u>  The 1985 production of cereals in Cape Verde amounted to only 1,300
tons, compared to annual consumption requirements of over 77,000 tons.

<u>14/</u>  External assistance is required in Sudan for the geographical
redistribution of food surpluses into food-deficit areas.

15/ An FAO document entitled African Agriculture - the next 25 years (ARC/86/3) contains a detailed, in-depth analysis of the various factors (exogenous and endogenous) that have contributed to Africa's current agricultural crisis, and suggest a strategy to overcome the crisis (cf. subsection C below). The document is of direct relevance to least developed countries.

16/ For detailed analysis of the adverse effects that some domestic policies of developing countries (including LDCs) may have on agricultural and food production, see World Bank, World Development Report 1986, chaps. 4 and 5.

17/ Ibid., p.66.

18/ Economist Intelligence Unit, Benin - Annual Supplement 1985, p.46; Togo - Annual supplement 1985, p.11.

19/ On recent policy improvements in this regard see sub-section B.1. below.

20/ "Contribution of the Food and Agriculture Organization", (TD/B/AC.17/26/Add.7), para. 19.

21/ FAO, African agriculture: the next 25 years (ARC/86/3), annex III, para. 1.3.

22/ Industry in the 1980s (UNIDO,1985), p.196.

23/ UNIDO, "Industry and general debt in Africa: a preliminary analysis", in Industry and Development, No. 17, pp.20 and 21.

24/ Economic Commission for Africa report (E/ECA/LDCs.5/4), March 1985, p.5.

25/ Quoted in West Africa, 31 March 1986.

26/ UNIDO, Bulletin of the Industrial Development Decade for Africa, vol.I, No.2, 1985.

27/ This problem was highlighted in the conclusions and recommendations of the Mid-term Global Review of the Implementation of the SNPA, which was held in Geneva in late 1985 (see TD/B/1078-TD/B/AC.17/28, paragraph 28).

28/ Southern African Development Co-ordination Conference, Harare, 30-31/1/86, document on energy, p.4.

29/ UNEP, Assessment of desertification in the Sudan-Sahelian region, 1978-1984 (UNEP/C.12/Background paper 1, 16 May 1984).

30/ See Energy exploration and development trends in developing countries - report of the Secretary-General of the United Nations (A/41/383/E/1986/101), 10 June 1986.  Table 1 of this document contains a list of developing countries (including LDCs) in which exploratory drilling was carried out during 1982-1984.

31/ Cf. James Walls, In Combat with Droughts and Deserts (United Nations Sudano-Sahelian Office).

32/ For further details, see United Nations United Nations Transport and Communications Decade for Africa, 1978-1988, volume 1, Global Strategy and Plan for Action, First Phase 1980-1983, (E/CN.14/726 - E/CN.14/Trans/147), pp.3-5, Transport and Communications Decade in Africa, Report by the Secretary-General, (A/41/382 - E/1986/99), 1986; Transport and Communications Decade for Asia and the Pacific, Report of the Secretary-General, (E/1986/66, 1986).

33/ Desertification affects more than one half of the LDCs (see table 16).  Of the 22 African countries which are covered by the mandate given to the United Nations Sudano-Sahelian Office (UNSO) in regard to drought and desertification, 16 are least developed countries.

34/ Tropical Forests:  A Call for Action, report of an International Task Force convened by the World Resources Institute, the World Bank and the UNDP, World Resources Institute, Washington D.C..

35/ Le Monde, 9 April 1986.

36/ Cf. El Khalifa, 1983, as mentioned in UNEP, Assessment of desertification in the Sudano-Sahelian Region 1978-1984 (UNEP/GC.12/Background paper 1, 16 May 1984, paragraph 79).

37/ UNDRO, Disaster prevention and mitigation, vol. 12, 1986.

38/ See Countries stricken by desertification and drought - report of the Secretary-General of the United Nations (A/41/346;  E/1986/96), 9 June 1986, paragraphs 27-40.  Because of difficulties in quantifying hydrological and agricultural drought, operating definitions of drought derive mainly from the meteorological point of view.

39/ These two countries are not subject, strictly speaking, to desertification but are affected by other environmental degradation problems, particularly erosion on the slopes of the Fouta Djallon Massif, which is located in Guinea and borders on Guinea-Bissau.  Such degradation problems affect the flooding patterns of the Senegal, Gambia and Niger rivers, which originate in the massif, and thus Western Sahelian countries into which these rivers flow.

40/   The surface area of Lake Chad shrank to 3,000 km$^2$ at the end of 1984, while the normal area varies between 13,000 and 28,000 km$^2$ (cf. study prepared by S.I. Sok, National Weather Bureau of Chad, as mentioned in the documentation prepared for the International Conference for the Economic Development of Chad, 1985, vol.1, page 33 of the English version).  The Lake Chad basin was declared a disaster area at a meeting of Heads of State of the Lake Chad Basin Commission held in May 1985.

41/   General Assembly/Economic and Social Council, document A/40/392, E/1985/117, paragraph 14.

42/   See "The drought and the external trade of the countries members of the Permanent Inter-State Committee on Drought Control in the Sahel (CILSS)," report by the UNCTAD secretariat (TD/B/1082), 19 December 1985.

43/   CILSS comprises nine countries of which seven are LDCs:  Burkina Faso, Cape Verde, Chad, Gambia, Guinea-Bissau, Mali, Mauritania, Niger and Senegal.

44/   CILSS/Club du Sahel document SAHEL D(84) 251, November 1984.

45/   This picture is heavily influenced, however, by the pronounced upward shift in the value of the United States dollar vis-à-vis most major currencies during the period 1981-1985.  If LDC export values are expressed in SDRs, the upward trend continues until 1984.

46/   The 18 commodities covered by the Integrated Programme for Commodities (IPC) and listed in UNCTAD resolution 93 (IV) are bananas, cocoa, coffee, cotton and cotton yarn, hard fibres and products, jute and jute manufactures, bovine meat, rubber, sugar, tea, tropical timber, vegetable oils and oil-seeds, bauxite, copper, iron ore, manganese, phosphates and tin.  In fact, however, in most LDCs only 3 to 5 products account for the indicated share in total exports.

47/   Over the period 1980 to 1985, it is estimated that the cumulative loss in foreign-exchange earnings (total value of exports in the five years 1981-1985 less five times the export value in 1980) amounted to a total of $2.8 billion, equivalent to two fifths of the 1985 export value.

48/   For more information, see "Commodities earnings shortfalls and an additional compensatory financing facility" (TD/B/AC.43/2), Geneva 1986.

49/   Measured in terms of SDRs, so as to reduce the impact of the fluctuation of the dollar, the increasing trend was broken in 1983, after which the level of imports virtually stagnated above the level of 1980.

50/   Trade and Development Report, 1986 (UNCTAD/TDR/6) (United Nations publication, Sales No. E.86.II.D.5), p.1, first paragraph.

51/ Marie Angélique Savane, "Migration" in ILO, Rural development and women in Africa, Geneva 1984.

52/ One example is the Grameen Bank project in Bangladesh. The members of the Bank have to make a weekly deposit which goes into the "group fund". When a group member receives a loan, an obligatory deduction of 5 per cent of the loan amount is made, and this paid into the "group fund". Rural women are actively involved in decision-making as each group elects its own chairman and secretary and must hold its weekly meetings. Several groups in the same village also hold joint meetings weekly. The group's strong savings programme helps to promote self-reliance as it reduces their dependence on bank loans, and the existence of a common fund gives the members experience in money management. This project has proved to be an important measure in improving the rural poor women's self-reliance, not only in terms of resource availability but also in building confidence and ability in management of funds and in planning for investments through a group approach to savings and credit. Women were able to participate both as beneficiaries and decision makers and the project demonstrated that, given access to financial resources, the poor rural women were able to transform their economic base and therefore increase their income. By May 1983, of the total loans amounting to about $US 5 million granted to 40,000 landless men and women, 40 per cent of the beneficiaries were women.

53/ In contrast, earlier projects on women such as rural women's co-operatives were self-limiting and they tended to perpetuate dependency. The co-operatives concentrated mainly on skill development, giving women training especially in home economics, sewing, knitting, weaving and kitchen gardening; and also production with emphasis on handicrafts. Women were paid for the products made by them while the marketing of the products was handled by the co-operatives. Giving training in sewing for women in Bangladesh, for example, has been found to have little value when the poor women cannot afford sewing machines. Although these rural co-operatives also provide financial credit and women are included as a target group, poorer women have not been able to avail themselves of these services because of collateral and complex procedural requirements.

54/ A Commission on Women in Botswana, for example, which included all ministries or their representatives, demonstrated the influence of such machinery by successfully blocking the licensing of a factory which would have thrown 10,000 women out of work.

55/ The areas identified are employment; education; energy; the environment; food, water and agriculture; housing, settlement, community development and transport; trade and commercial services; science and technology, and communications.

56/ In replies to the 1986 UNCTAD questionnaire on the implementation of the SNPA.

57/  The World Bank Annual Report, 1984. An adviser on women in development was appointed in its operation policy unit in 1977.

58/  Press release Press/A(83)62.  The OECD Development Assistance Committee adopted a set of Guiding Principles in November 1983 to aid agencies for supporting the role of women in development.

59/  Indeed many development programmes and projects, ranging from population control to (for example) maintaining village wells, have been impaired by women's low standard of living.  For instance, in Bangladesh, the decline in fertility rates has been slow despite the Population Control Programme carried out by the Government since 1976, mainly because of the poverty levels.  Unless parents can earn enough from their own labour and are assured of support in their old age, they will not limit the size of their families.

60/  See OECD Press Release, "Financial resources for developing countries:  1985 and recent trends" (PRESS/A/(86)27), 18 June 1986, and OECD, Financing and external debt of developing countries, 1985 survey (Paris, 1986), tables III.3 and III.4.

61/  The advantages of foreign direct investment and donors' incentives in promoting it in LDCs were discussed in UNCTAD, "The least developed countries - 1985 report" Addendum:  Chapter II.  Review of international support measures (TD/B/AC.17/25/Add(2)A), paras. A21 and A22.

62/  A questionnaire on action in response to policy recommendations contained in chapters II and III of the SNPA was addressed to countries other than LDCs as well as to international institutions and organizations in 1982, 1984 and 1986.

63/  Switzerland indicated in its reply to the UNCTAD questionnaire that it aims at doubling its ODA to LDCs in Swiss francs by 1985.

64/  Report of the United Nations Conference on the Least Developed Countries, Paris, 1 to 14 September 1981 (A/CONF.104/22/Rev.1) (United Nations publication, Sales No. E.82.I.8), para. 49.

65/  Statement by the representative of the USSR, speaking on behalf of Group D.  See TD/B/C.3(XI)/Misc.6.

66/  For comparison see table 33.

67/  See UNCTAD, "Financial solidarity for development, 1986 supplement" (TAD/INF/1797).

68/  See OECD Press Release (PRESS/A(86)27), op. cit., p.3.

69/  In replies to the UNCTAD questionnaire.

70/ STABEX (the European Communities' export earnings stabilization scheme), which applies to all African LDCs under the Lomé Conventions, is being extended to the remaining nine non-African LDCs in accordance with the commitment made during the mid-term global review of the SNPA. Sectoral import support programmes, now being prepared under Lomé III, are a new measure which will benefit LDCs.

71/ See A/36/689, part two, para. 31.

72/ This estimate is based on the assumption that all those donor countries which either considerably exceeded the 0.15 per cent target or did not accept any target will continue to give the same percentage of their GNP as ODA to LDCs as in 1982-1984 and that other donor countries will fulfil either the 0.15 per cent target or that of doubling ODA to LDCs compared with its level in 1976-1980.

73/ See "The least developed countries ..." (op. cit.), Addendum Chapter II (cont.) (TD/B/AC.17/25/Add.2(C)), in particular paras. C6 to C10.

74/ The major revisions adopted for the reassessment of the projected capital requirements are a drop in the oil price level from $26 to $15 a barrel and a decrease in international interest rates from 10 to 7 per cent, while at the same time private transfers, which are mainly remittances from workers in oil exporting countries, are assumed to be lower by 25 per cent. (Because of the sharp fall in oil prices, it can be expected that remittances from workers in oil-exporting countries will record a major downward shift in the near future.)

75/ The modified price projections (see footnote 73/ above) have a considerable impact; in fact, the current account deficit in the three scenarios is reduced by $2.2, $2.8 and $3.1 billion respectively. The changes in reserves are the same as those in TD/B/AC.17/25/Add.2(C). If the assumption with respect to the accumulation of reserves had also been lowered, the overall reduction would have increased correspondingly.

76/ For example, the United States has indicated that it places high priority on LDCs' implementation of effective and efficient policies which promote an open economic system and self-sustaining economic growth - the establishment of an ongoing dialogue between the United States and recipients aimed at improving their policy environment and development prospects is an important aspect of the United States' overall assistance programme - and that its levels of assistance would be affected by whether the recipient policy environment was conducive to effective aid utilization. Hungary has expressed the view that external assistance proved to be most effective in countries which took steps towards more equitable ownership and revenue distribution, developed their economies on a planned basis and strengthened the collective sector of their economy. As regards the World Bank, policy-based sector lending is becoming an increasingly prominent feature of its operations, focusing in particular on improvements in pricing and marketing policies, budgeting and investment programming. Every loan is designed on a case-by-case basis depending on the loan objective and the country circumstances. The types of reform addressed range from major changes in macro-economic policies to in-depth restructuring of sectoral investments and incentive programmes.

77/ Needed improvements in these respects were reviewed and further identified by government experts of donor countries and multilateral and bilateral financial and technical assistance institutions with representatives of the LDCs at a meeting in May 1985 (see TD/B/1055 - TD/B/AC.41/6, op. cit.) and at the mid-term global review of the implementation of the SNPA. See also Chapter II below.

In the submission to the special session of the United Nations General Assembly on Africa's economic and social crisis (which covered 26 LDCs) the focus was on the following proposals (see OAU/ECA/2AU/Rev.2):

(i)    Non-project aid, particularly balance-of-payments support, to African countries should be greatly expanded during the period 1986-1990;

(ii)   Donor countries and agencies should agree to ease procurement requirements and administrative procedures to ensure fast disbursement to African countries for production inputs and for policy support assistance;

(iii)  Donor countries and agencies should substantially increase their aid budgets as well as speed up the disbursement of funds in support of policy reforms; and

(iv)   There should be non-politicization of aid.

78/ See TD/B/1055 - TD/B/AC.41/6, op.cit., para. 56.

79/ According to OECD sources, there are prospects for a recovery of financial flows to developing countries in 1986 and beyond, and a number of DAC countries have indicated their intention of increasing their ODA. See OECD, "Financial resources for developing countries: 1985 and recent trends", (Press/A(86)27).

80/ See IMF, World economic outlook (April 1986).

81/ See below, chapter IV on "The debt situation of the LDCs", paras. 328 to 330.

82/ See World Bank Development Committee, Report of the Task Force on Concessional Flows (October 1985), para. 19. See also the World Bank, Financing adjustment with growth in sub-Saharan Africa, 1986-90 (1986).

83/ See, in particular, OECD, Twenty-five years of development co-operation, A review, (Paris, 1985) and World Bank Development Committee, Report of the Task Force on Concessional Flows (October 1985).

84/ See the report of the intergovernmental Group (TD/B/1078 - TD/B/AC.17/28).

85/ See, inter alia, the SNPA, paragraph 70(a), Conference resolution 98(IV). See also chapter IV below on the debt situation of the LDCs.

86/ The standard measure of concessionality of aid programmes is the overall grant element, which reflects the grant share as well as the financial terms of loans (i.e., their interest rate, maturity and grace period). As regards ODA loans, the extent of the benefit depends on the difference between the ODA interest rate and the market rate and the length of time the funds are available to the borrower. To calculate this benefit, the present value at the market rate of interest of each repayment is ascertained. The excess of the loan's face value over the sum of these present values, expressed as a percentage of the face value, is the "grant element" of the loan. Conventionally, the market rate is taken as 10 per cent. Thus, the grant element is nil for a loan carrying an interest rate of 10 per cent; it is 100 per cent for a grant and it lies between these two limits for a soft loan. Generally speaking, a loan will not convey a grant element of over 25 per cent if its maturity is less than 10 years, unless its interest is well below 5 per cent (see OECD, Development co-operation, 1982 review (Paris), 1982, p.171).

87/ Of these three, Italy has introduced new policies to soften the terms of its aid loans and increase the share of grants in aid to lower-income countries, and consequently it is expected that Italian aid to the LDCs will be in compliance with the DAC Terms Recommendation. As regards France, the DAC, at its latest aid review of this country, noted "the development of means aiming at a softening of the financial terms of aid to the least-developed countries". (See OECD, Twenty-five years of development co-operation ... (op.cit.), p.107, and OECD press releases PRESS/A(85)37 and PRESS/A(86)21 of 31 May 1985 and 16 May 1986.) Indeed, the grant element of concessional loans to LDCs further increased in 1985 (to 55.7 per cent as compared with 54 per cent in 1984 and 48 per cent in 1983). In its reply to the UNCTAD questionnaire, France reported its intention of increasing the share of grant financing in its aid to LDCs. The most recent DAC member, Ireland, which joined in 1985, extends all its bilateral aid in grant form.

88/ Shifts also occur from non-concessional to concessional financing. For example, in its reply to the UNCTAD questionnaire, France reported that the terms of its structural adjustment loans to LDCs have been continuously softening and that in 1986 they were for the first time extended on ODA terms.

89/ OECD, Development co-operation, 1984 review (Paris 1985), p.110, and Twenty-five years of development co-operation ... (op.cit.), p.245.

90/ For the same reason, no data on tying status are available for 1983.

91/ TD/276, para. 94.

92/ France reported doubling the percentage share of untied economic and financial assistance in its bilateral aid to LDCs in 1984 as compared to 1983.

93/ Since early 1982, half of the LDCs have at some point in time elaborated economic and financial programmes supported by stand-by arrangements with the IMF. Eight such agreements, plus one for an extended IMF facility, were in force by the end of the first half of 1986.

94/ The Intergovernmental Group on the LDCs at the mid-term global review of the SNPA recommended, with regard to different types and forms of aid, that, particularly in support of domestic adjustment measures of LDCs, donors should provide aid in more flexible forms, especially balance-of-payments support, and at a sectoral level for rehabilitation and maintenance, as well as for longer-term objectives (see the report of the Group, sect.II, A.4).

95/ The category of general economic support may be taken as a broad measure of the amount of programme aid extended to the LDCs, although it would exclude such flexible forms of aid as rehabilitation and maintenance assistance allocated to specific projects or sectors, and other sectoral aid.

96/ See OECD Press release (PRESS/A/(86)27), op.cit.

97/ Cf. "Conclusions for aid policies emerging from a review of aid experience", OECD Press Release (PRESS/A(85)74) of 3 December 1985.

98/ At the mid-term global review of the implementation of the SNPA, it was noted that the provision of aid for the local costs of investments could facilitate the financing of recurrent costs, particularly in the social sectors, from domestic resources. Nevertheless, the importance of aid also for recurrent costs in appropriate cases was recognized. It was recommended that donors should further increase, where appropriate, their participation in local and recurrent cost financing with adequate provisions for allowing a progressive take-over of recurrent costs by LDCs.

99/ Cf. TD/B/1055 - TD/B/AC.41/6, op.cit., and OECD Press Release (PRESS/A(85)74), op.cit.

100/ Virtually all LDCs have put increasing food self-sufficiency among their foremost development objectives. See also chapter III A on "Food and agriculture".

101/ The share of rural development measures in bilateral commitments extended to LDCs by the Federal Republic of Germany has been considerably extended, reaching 32 per cent in 1984. Food strategies and food security were supported by the EC under the Second Lomé Convention (e.g. in Mali and Rwanda), and this approach has now become a regular feature of the more concentrated Lome III resources. Among bilateral donors, Denmark plans to apply an integrated food strategy approach and has supported the establishment of national food strategies in some LDCs, including Bangladesh and the United Republic of Tanzania.

102/ Haiti now participates also in the World Bank-chaired Caribbean Group for Co-operation in Economic Development.

103/ Of these, some had already convened their second round table meeting (Bhutan, Chad, Lao People's Democratic Republic, Maldives, Mali and Samoa). New consultative groups sponsored by the World Bank had been set up for Somalia and Malawi, the first meeting of such a group for Guinea was under preparation, and the consultative groups for Uganda and the United Republic of Tanzania had been reconvened. Moreover, the Second Yemen International Development Conference was held in 1982 (outside the round table framework).

104/ They have, however, been dealt with to a certain extent in the GATT Sub-Committee on Trade of Least-Developed Countries, which has a programme of ad hoc consultations under which individual LDCs can consult their developed trading partners.

105/ See the "Report of the Intergovernmental Group on the Least Developed Countries on its sixth session" (TD/B/1078-TD/B/AC.17/28), part one, III, para. 76.

106/ Several donors have also stressed the need for improving local co-ordination in that process.

107/ See UNDP, "Evaluation of the round table experience in the Africa region", Final report (April 1985), p.vii.  See also "Review and assessment of the SNPA round table meeting process for the Asia and Pacific least developed countries", (September 1984).

108/ Of more than 20 Bank-led consultative and aid groups, only 8, including the group being set up for Guinea, are concerned with LDCs.

109/ See "Implementation of the Substantial New Programme of Action for the 1980s for the Least Developed Countries", Report of the Administrator to the Governing Council of the UNDP (DP/1986/17), June 1986.

110/ See Toward sustained development in sub-Saharan Africa:  A joint programme of action (1984) and Financing adjustment with growth in Sub-Saharan Africa, 1986-1990, op.cit.

111/ The question of donor influence on development policy remains a particularly sensitive aspect of the aid co-ordination process.

112/ The positive contribution of non-governmental organizations to the development of LDCs was recognized at the mid-term review of the SNPA. Several LDC Governments have already, with UNDP support, convened special consultations with NGOs.

113/ Offers of technical or other co-operation were in many instances made by these countries at the early round tables and were greatly appreciated by the LDCs.

114/ According to data from the World Bank's Debtor Reporting System, LDCs' external debt outstanding increased almost ten-fold between 1970 and 1980.

115/ The overall balance-of-payments surplus of $364 million in 1979 turned into a deficit of $406 million in 1980.  This deficit climbed to $1.2 billion in 1982.

116/ To some $200 million.

117/ See part one, Chapter I.

118/ Conversely the reported increases in LDCs' debt in preceding years are somewhat understated because of the appreciation of the United States dollar during those years.

119/ "Beyond increases in total reported debt, the fall in the dollar value had a number of other statistical impacts. In particular it increases de facto the share in total debt of aggregates principally denominated in non-United States dollars e.g. ODA, export credits, Sub-Saharan African debt, fixed interest rate debt, and has the opposite effect for bank lending, Western Hemisphere debt and floating rate debt. It also generally increases debt to export ratios." See Financing and external debt of developing countries, 1985 Survey, op.cit. p.50. See also Lancaster and Williamson, African debt and financing. (Washington, IIE, May 1986).

120/ See below chapter IV C (a).

121/ There was an effective softening of the average terms for export credits and bank lending as well as for lending by multilateral institutions. See Financing and external debt ..., op.cit., 1983 Survey, p.51.

122/ Unlike the case of debt stocks, in 1985 the exchange rate effect was modest on debt service aggregates (but will be significant in the case of the reported amounts for 1986). Debt stocks are expressed at year-end exchange rates while debt service payments are expressed at average annual exchange rates. The latter were relatively closer to 1984 exchange rates because the value of the United States dollar started falling steadily only in March 1985.

123/ The majority of these countries have a debt/GDP ratio close to or exceeding 50 per cent. Half of them have a debt service/exports ratio close to or over 30 per cent (see table 42).

124/ To ease LDCs' payments, the United States has allowed, on a case-by-case basis, repayment in local currency of the dollar debt obligation arising from purchases of agricultural commodities. Japan gives the LDCs cash grants to offset debt servicing of ODA loans on which the exchange of notes was concluded before 31 March 1978.

125/ See the report of the Intergovernmental Group, op.cit., part one, section B.XII.2.

126/ In the majority of cases the ratio of debt service (actually paid) to exports, was less than one third, yet generally equal to or higher than the average ratio for LDCs (see table 42).

127/ The conclusions and recommendations of the mid-term global review specifically invite "creditors of official and officially guaranteed loans to LDCs, when concluding a debt rescheduling arrangement for a least developed country, to give due consideration to, inter alia, the debtor country's adjustment measures for restoration of its debt-servicing capacity and long-term growth" (see the report of the Intergovernmental Group, op.cit., section B.XII.3).

128/ See the SNPA, op.cit., para. 113 (c), and the conclusions and recommendations of the mid-term global review (Ibid., Section B.XVII.17 (a)).

129/ The text reads as follows: "Recommends that in the context of a review of the economic and financial situation of a least developed country, country review meetings may also take into account its debt situation". (Ibid., section B.XII.5).

130/ Ibid., 4.

131/ These proposals can be classified into three main categories: (i) those involving a change in the character of claims held by creditors (interest capitalization schemes and conversion of debt into equity-like claims); (ii) those involving a change in the ownership of claims and (iii) those involving a change in the value of claims. For a detailed discussion of these proposals, see UNCTAD, Trade and Development Report, 1986 (UNCTAD/TDR/6 and Corr.1) United Nations publication Sales No. E.86.II.D.5, annex to chapter VI.

132/ Proposals along similar lines can be found in the "Special Memorandum by the ECA Conference of Ministers on Africa's Economic and Social Crisis adopted in May 1984" (E/ECA/CM.10/37/Rev.2) and in the "Draft Recommendations of the Steering Committee on Economic Issues for the 21st Assembly of Heads of State and Government" (CM/133(XL11) Rev.2).

133/ This proposal was put forward by F. Rohatyn of Lazard Frères. See Euromoney Trade Finance Report (November 1985).

134/ See World Bank, Development Committee Communiqué issued in Washington following the meeting of 10-11 April 1968.

135/ The Baker initiative consists of three elements: first, the adoption by principal debtor countries of comprehensive macro-economic and structural policies, geared to combining growth with adjustment; second, a continued central role for the Fund, in conjunction with increased and more effective structural adjustment lending by multilateral development banks, in support of these policies; and third, a call on commercial banks to support these policies by lending new money - to the tune of $20 billion over the next three years - to an indicative group of 15 major debtor countries. See IMF Survey (31 March 1986), p.108.

136/ See Part two, Chapter I.

137/ See The Substantial New Programme of Action for the 1980s for the Least Developed Countries, paras. 76 and 77, in the Report of the United Nations Conference on the Least Developed Countries, Paris, 1 to 14 September 1981 (United Nations publication, Sales No. E.82.I.8), and Mid-term Global Review of Progress Towards the Implementation of the Substantial New Programme of Action for the Least Developed Countries, paras. 65-67 (TD/B/1078-TD/B/AC.17/28), 30 October 1985.

138/ See report of the Special Committee on Preferences on its fourteenth session, TD/B/C.5(XIV)/Misc.2.

139/ Carpets with surface of jute and/or other textile bast fibres and/or Manila hemps, or of sisal and/or other fibres of agave family (tariff sub-item ex. 58.02).

140/ Tariff item 57.10.

141/ For a detailed discussion of the effect of RBPs in LDCs see UNCTAD, The Least Developed Countries, 1985 Report, op.cit. paras. D37 and D32.

142/ See also Chapter IV, para. 151 and table 20.

143/ UNCTAD, Compensatory financing of export earnings shortfalls (TD/B/1029/Rev.1).

144/ Ibid., annex VII-A, pp.2-6.

145/ For the report of the Intergovernmental Group, see TD/B/1078.

146/ Calculated on the basis of Handbook of International Trade and Development Statistics, 1985 Supplement, 4.3(D), pp.196-224.

147/ Tentative estimates.

148/ The fiscal year ends on 21 March.

149/ The fiscal year (FY) ends on 30 June.

150/ In the past Cotonou has also handled the overflow traffic for the Port of Lagos, when the latter was congested.

151/ The fiscal year ends on 31 March.

152/ The pula had been devalued by 5 per cent and 15 per cent against the basket of currencies to which it is pegged, in July 1984 and January 1985 respectively. This had followed a persistent strengthening of the pula against the South African rand. To counteract such a development in the future, the weight of the rand in the basket was increased in January 1985. From end-1982 to end-1985 the value of the pula halved in relation to the dollar, most of this depreciation taking place in 1984 and 1985.

153/ The season extends from October to June for the main cash crops coffee and cotton.

154/ The conversion rate was fixed at a ratio of 4 Bipkwele for 1 CFA franc, although the nominal official rate of the former had been 347.66 per dollar against CFA francs 479.60 per dollar.

155/ The fiscal year ends on 7 July.

156/ Fiscal year ends on 30 June.

157/ The fiscal year (FY) ends 30 September.

158/ It should be noted, however, that both of these rates are close to the average for all LDCs.

159/ Formerly the Rand Monetary Area. Lesotho's currency - the loti - is pegged to a parity rate with the South African rand, which circulates freely in the country.

160/ The fiscal year ends on 15 July.

161/ In dollar terms, this translates into a per capita GDP of $236 in 1984 as against $471 in 1980. However, this decline is amplified by the rise of the exchange rate of the dollar during the period under consideration.

162/ The fiscal year ends 30 June.

163/ Due to the use of multiple exchange rates during that period the dollar equivalent of this series ranges between an average of $128 million and $161 million, depending on the source consulted.

164/ The fiscal year (FY) ends on 30 June.

165/ The fiscal year ends on 30 June.

166/ The crop year ends on 31 March.

167/ The fiscal year ends on 30 June.

ANNEX

BASIC DATA ON THE LEAST DEVELOPED COUNTRIES

ANNEXE

DONNEES DE BASE RELATIVES AUX PAYS LES MOINS AVANCES

| CONTENTS | | | TABLE DES MATIERES | |
|---|---|---|---|---|
| | | Page | | Page |

| Explanatory Notes | v -xi | | Notes explicatives | xii-xviii |
|---|---|---|---|---|

**Table**

**Tableaux**

| 1. | Real GDP, total and per capita: annual average growth rates, 1970-1984 | 2-3 |
|---|---|---|
| 2. | Per capita GDP and population: levels and growth | 4 |
| 3. | Total agricultural production and total food production: annual average growth rates 1970-1985 | 5 |
| 4. | The agricultural sector | 6-7 |
| 5. | The manufacturing sector | 8-9 |
| 6. | Investment | 10-11 |
| 7. | Exports and imports:  basic comparisons | 12 |
| 8. | Unit value indices of imports: tentative estimates 1970-1985 | 13 |
| 9. | Export value and purchasing power : growth 1970-1985 | 14 |
| 10. | Import value and volume : growth 1970-1985 | 15 |
| 11. | Commodity structure of exports, by main category (1984 or latest year available) | 16 |
| 12. | Commodity structure of imports, by main category (1984 or latest year available) | 17 |
| 13. | Main markets for exports : relative shares in 1984 (or latest year available) | 18 |
| 14. | Main sources of imports : relative shares in 1984 (or latest year available) | 19 |
| 15. | Leading exports in 1982 | 20-22 |
| 16. | Leading exports of LDCs as a group in 1982 | 23 |
| 17. | Foreign exchange receipts and import volume expressed in constant 1980 dollars per capita, 1970 and 1975-1984 | 24-28 |
| 18. | External assistance, exports and imports 1983 and 1984 | 29-30 |
| 19. | External assistance, exports and imports per capita, 1983 and 1984 | 31-32 |
| 20. | Percentage distribution of financial flows to all LDCs and to all developing countries, by type of flow, 1970, 1975 and 1980-1984 | 33 |
| 21A. | Composition of total financial flows in current dollars, 1970 and 1975-1984: all LDCs | 34 |
| 21B. | Composition of total financial flows in current dollars, 1970and 1975-1984: all developing countries | 35 |
| 22A. | Composition of total financial flows in constant dollars, 1970 and 1975-1984: all LDCs | 36 |
| 22B. | Composition of total financial flows in constant dollars, 1970 and 1975-1984: all developing countries | 37 |
| 22A. | Composition of total financial flows in constant dollars per capita, 1970 and 1975-1984: all LDCs | 38 |
| 23B. | Composition of total financial flows in constant dollars per capita, 1970 and 1975-1984: all developing countries | 39 |

| 1. | Produit intérieur brut réel, total et par habitant: taux annuels moyens d'accroissement 1970 à 1984 | 2-3 |
|---|---|---|
| 2. | PIB par habitant et population: niveaux et croissance | 4 |
| 3. | Production agricole totale et production vivrière totale: taux moyens de croissance annuelle 1970-1985 | 5 |
| 4. | Le secteur agricole | 6-7 |
| 5. | Le secteur manufacturier | 8-9 |
| 6. | Investissement | 10-11 |
| 7. | Exportations et importations: comparaisons de base.. | 12 |
| 8. | Indices de la valeur unitaire des importations : estimations approximatives, 1970-1985 | 13 |
| 9. | Valeur et pouvoir d'achat des exportations : évolution 1970-1985 | 14 |
| 10. | Valeur et volume des importations : évolution 1970-1985 | 15 |
| 11. | Composition des exportations des PMA, par principales catégories de produits (1984 ou année disponible la plus récente) | 16 |
| 12. | Composition des importations, par principales catégories de produits (1984 ou année disponible la plus récente) | 17 |
| 13. | Principaux marchés aux exportations : parts relatives en 1984 (ou année disponible la plus récente) | 18 |
| 14. | Principales sources d'importations : parts relatives en 1984 (ou année disponible la plus récente) | 19 |
| 15. | Principales exportations en 1982 | 20-22 |
| 16. | Principales exportations de l'ensemble des PMA en 1982 | 23 |
| 17. | Rentrées de devises et volume des importations, en dollars constants de 1980 par habitant, 1970 et 1975-1984 | 24-28 |
| 18. | Aide extérieure, exportations et importations 1983 et 1984 | 29-30 |
| 19. | Aide extérieure, exportations et importations par habitant, 1983 et 1984 | 31-32 |
| 20. | Répartition en pourcentage des apports financiers à l'ensemble des PMA et à l'ensemble des pays en développement, par catégories d'apports, 1970, 1975 et 1980-1984 | 33 |
| 20A. | Composition des courants financiers en dollars courants, 1970 et 1975-1984: ensemble des PMA | 34 |
| 21B. | Composition des courants financiers en dollars courants, 1970 et 1975-1984: ensemble des pays en développement | 35 |
| 22A. | Composition des courants financiers en dollars constants, 1970 et 1975-1984: ensemble des PMA | 36 |
| 22B. | Composition des courants financiers en dollars constants, 1970 et 1975-1984: ensemble des pays en développement | 37 |
| 23A. | Composition des courants financiers en dollars constants par habitant, 1970 et 1975-1984: ensemble des PMA | 38 |
| 23B. | Composition des courants financiers en dollars constants par habitant, 1970 et 1975-1984: ensemble des pays en développement | 39 |

| Table | | Page |
|---|---|---|
| 24. | Share of LDCs in flows to all developing countries, by type of flow, 1970 and 1975-1984 | 40 |
| 25A. | Bilateral ODA from individual DAC member countries and total financial flows from individual multilateral agencies mainly financed by them, to all LDCs, in <u>current</u> dollars 1975-1984 ...................................... | 41 |
| 25B. | Bilateral ODA from individual DAC member countries and total financial flows from individual multilateral agencies mainly financed by them, to all LDCs, in <u>constant</u> dollars, 1975-1984 ...................................... | 42 |
| 25C. | Bilateral ODA from individual DAC member countries and total financial flows from individual multilateral agencies mainly financed by them: main LDC recipients in 1984 ........... | 43 |
| 26. | Concessional assistance to LDCs from individual DAC member countries and multilateral agencies mainly financed by them: relative importance and relative shares as compared to all developing countries, 1970, 1975 and 1980-1984 | 44 |
| 27. | Concessional assistance from DAC member countries and multilateral agencies mainly financed by them, to individual LDCs, 1970 and 1975-1984 and leading donors in 1984 ........... | 45-46 |
| 28. | Bilateral grants from DAC member countries to individual LDCs, 1970 and 1975-1984 ............ | 47 |
| 29. | Bilateral ODA from DAC member countries to individual LDCs, 1970 and 1975-1984 ............ | 48-49 |
| 30. | Grants from multilateral agencies mainly financed by DAC member countries to individual LDCs, 1970 and 1975-1984 ...................... | 50 |
| 31. | Concessional assistance from multilateral agencies mainly financed by DAC member countries to individual LDCs, 1970 and 1975-1984 ......... | 51 |
| 32. | Non-concessional assistance from multilateral agencies mainly financed by DAC member countries to individual LDCs, 1970 and 1975-1984 ......... | 52 |
| 33. | Technical assistance disbursements to individual LDCs, 1970 and 1975-1984 ...................... | 53 |
| 34. | Net ODA as per cent of donor's GNP, from individual DAC member countries to LDCs as a group, 1975-1984 .............................. | 54 |
| 35. | ODA commitments from individual DAC member countries and multilateral agencies mainly financed by them, to all LDCs, 1975-1984 ....... | 55 |
| 36. | ODA commitments from DAC member countries and multilateral agencies mainly financed by them, to individual LDCs, 1975-1984 ................. | 56 |
| 37. | Grant element of ODA commitments from individual DAC member countries to LDCs and to all developing countries, 1975-1984 ............... | 57 |
| 38A. | ODA commitments from individual DAC member countries and multilateral agencies mainly financed by them, to LDCs as a group, by purpose, average 1981-1984 ................... | 58 |
| 38B. | ODA commitments from DAC member countries and multilateral agencies mainly financed by them, to individual LDCs, by purpose, average 1981-1984 ...................................... | 59 |

| Tableaux | | Page |
|---|---|---|
| 24. | Parts des PMA dans les apports financiers à l'ensemble des pays en développement, par catégories d'apports, 1970 et 1975-1984 ............. | 40 |
| 25A. | APD bilatérale de chaque pays membre du CAD et apports financiers totaux de chaque institution multilatérale essentiellement financée par ceux-ci, à l'ensemble des PMA, en dollars <u>courants</u> 1975-1984 | 41 |
| 25B. | APD bilatérale de chaque pays membre du CAD et apports financiers totaux de chaque institution multilatérale essentiellement financée par ceux-ci, à l'ensemble des PMA, en dollars <u>constants</u>, 1975-1984 ............................................. | 42 |
| 25C. | APD bilatérale de chaque pays membre du CAD et apports financiers totaux de chaque institution multilatérale essentiellement financée par ceux-ci: principaux PMA bénéficiaires en 1984 ................. | 43 |
| 26. | Aide concessionnelle aux PMA en provenance des pays membres du CAD et des institutions multilatérales essentiellement financées par ceux-ci: importance relative et parts relatives par rapport à l'ensemble des pays en développement, 1970, 1975 et 1980-1984 .. | 44 |
| 27. | Aide concessionnelle reçue par chacun des PMA en provenance des pays du CAD et des institutions multilatérales essentiellement financées par ceux-ci, 1970 et 1975-1984 et principaux donneurs en 1984 .... | 45-46 |
| 28. | Dons reçus par chacun des PMA en provenance des pays membres du CAD, 1970 et 1975-1984 .............. | 47 |
| 29. | APD bilatérale reçue par chacun des PMA en provenance des pays membres du CAD, 1970 et 1975-1984 | 48-49 |
| 30. | Dons reçus par chacun des PMA en provenance des institutions multilatérales essentiellement financées par les pays membres du CAD, 1970 et 1975-1984 ...... | 50 |
| 31. | Aide concessionnelle reçue par chacun des PMA en provenance des institutions multilatérales essentiellement financées par les pays membres du CAD, 1970 et 1975-1984 ................................. | 51 |
| 32. | Aide non-concessionnelle reçue par chacun des PMA en provenance des institutions multilatérales essentiellement financées par les pays membres du CAD, 1970 et 1975-1984 ................................. | 52 |
| 33. | Versements au titre de l'assistance technique en faveur des PMA, 1970 et 1975-1984 ................... | 53 |
| 34. | Apports nets de l'APD accordée par chaque pays membre du CAD à l'ensemble des PMA, en pourcentage du PNB du pays donneur, 1975-1984 ................... | 54 |
| 35. | Engagements de l'APD de chaque pays membre du CAD et de chaque institution multilatérale essentiellement financée par ceux-ci, en faveur de l'ensemble des PMA 1975-1984 ............................................. | 55 |
| 36. | Engagements de l'APD à chacun des PMA en provenance des pays membres du CAD et des institutions multilatérales essentiellement financées par ceux-ci, 1975-1984 ............................................. | 56 |
| 37. | Elément de libéralité des engagements de l'APD de chaque pays membre du CAD aux PMA et à l'ensemble des pays en développement, 1975-1984 ................... | 57 |
| 38A. | Engagements de l'APD de chaque pays membre du CAD et chaque institution multilatérale essentiellement financée par ceux-ci, en faveur de l'ensemble des PMA, par objet, moyenne 1981-1984 ...................... | 58 |
| 38B. | Engagements de l'APD à chacun des PMA, en provenance des pays membres du CAD et des institutions multilatérales essentiellement financées par ceux-ci, par objet, moyenne 1981-1984 ........................... | 59 |

| Table | | Page |
|---|---|---|
| 39. | Tying status of bilateral ODA from individual DAC member countries to all LDCs, 1981, 1982 and 1984 ..................................... | 60 |
| 40A. | Bilateral ODA from individual OPEC member countries and total financial flows from individual multilateral agencies mainly financed by them, to LDCs as a group, in <u>current</u> dollars 1975-1984 ..................................... | 61 |
| 40B. | Bilateral ODA from individual OPEC member countries and total financial flows from individual multilateral agencies mainly financed by them, to LDCs as a group, in <u>constant</u> dollars, 1975-1984 .......................... | 62 |
| 41. | Concessional assistance from OPEC member countries and multilateral agencies mainly financed by them, to individual LDCs, 1970 and 1975-1984 ..................................... | 63 |
| 42. | Concessional assistance from OPEC member countries to individual LDCs, 1970 and 1975-1984 | 64-65 |
| 43. | Grants from OPEC member countries to individual LDCs, 1970 and 1975-1984 ........... | 66 |
| 44. | Concessional assistance from multilateral agencies mainly financed by OPEC member countries, to individual LDCs, 1975-1984 ...... | 67 |
| 45. | Non-concessional flows from multilateral agencies mainly financed by OPEC member countries to individual LDCs, 1977-1984 ....... | 68 |
| 46. | Net ODA as per cent of donor's GNP, from individual OPEC member countries to LDCs as a group, 1975-1984 .......................... | 69 |
| 47. | ODA commitments from individual OPEC member countries and multilateral agencies mainly financed by them to LDCs as a group, 1975-1984 ..................................... | 70 |
| 48. | ODA commitments from OPEC member countries and multilateral agencies mainly financed by them, to individual LDCs, 1975-1984 ................ | 71 |
| 49. | Grant element of ODA commitments from individual OPEC member countries and multilateral agencies mainly financed by them, to LDCs as a group, 1977-1984 ..................................... | 72 |
| 50. | Balance of payments summary, 1970, 1973, 1975 and 1978-1984 ................................. | 73 |
| 51. | External debt outstanding, 1975 and 1979-1984.. | 74-75 |
| 52. | Debt service payments of LDCs, 1975 and 1979-1984 ..................................... | 76-77 |
| 53. | Other selected economic and social indicators: | 78-84 |
| | A.  Area and population distribution .......... | 78 |
| | B.  Birth and death rates, life expectancy .... | 79 |
| | C.  Health at birth ........................... | 80 |
| | D.  Food and water ............................ | 81 |
| | E.  Education and literacy .................... | 82 |
| | F.  Communications and media .................. | 83 |
| | G.  Energy .................................... | 84 |

| Tableaux | | Page |
|---|---|---|
| 39. | Etats de déliement de l'APD bilatérale à l'ensemble des PMA, en provenance de chaque pays membre du CAD, 1981, 1982 et 1984 ..................................... | 60 |
| 40A. | APD bilatérale de chaque pays membre de l'OPEP et apports financiers totaux de chaque institution multilatérale essentiellement financée par ceux-ci, en faveur de l'ensemble des PMA, en dollars <u>courants</u> 1975-1984 ......................................... | 61 |
| 40B. | APD bilatérale de chaque pays membre de l'OPEP et apports financiers totaux de chaque institution multilatérale essentiellement financée par ceux-ci, en faveur de l'ensemble des PMA, en dollars <u>constants</u>, 1975-1984 .............................. | 62 |
| 41. | Aide concessionnelle reçue par chacun des PMA, en provenance de l'OPEP et des institutions multila- térales essentiellement financées par ceux-ci, 1970 et 1975-1984 ................................. | 63 |
| 42. | Aide concessionnelle reçue par chacun des PMA en provenance des pays membres de l'OPEP, 1970 et 1975-1984 ................................... | 64-65 |
| 43. | Dons reçus par chacun des PMA, en provenance des pays membres de l'OPEP, 1970 et 1975-1984 ........... | 66 |
| 44. | Aide concessionnelle reçue par chacun des PMA, en provenance des institutions multilatérales essentiellement financées par les pays membres de l'OPEP, 1975-1984 ................................. | 67 |
| 45. | Apports non-concessionnels reçus par chacun des PMA en provenance des institutions multilatérales essentiellement financées par les pays membres de l'OPEP, 1977-1984 ................................. | 68 |
| 46. | Apports nets de l'APD accordée par chaque pays membre de l'OPEP à l'ensemble des PMA en pourcentage du PNB du pays donneur, 1975-1984 ................... | 69 |
| 47. | Engagements de l'APD de chaque pays membre de l'OPEP et de chaque institution multilatérale essentiellement financée par ceux-ci, en faveur de l'ensemble des PMA, 1975-1984 ................................. | 70 |
| 48. | Engagements de l'APD à chacun des PMA, en provenance des pays membres de l'OPEP et des institutions multilatérales essentiellement financées par ceux-ci, 1975-1984 ............................. | 71 |
| 49. | Elément de libéralité des engagements de l'APD de chaque pays membre de l'OPEP et de chaque institution multilatérale essentiellement financée par ceux-ci, à l'ensemble des PMA, 1977-1984 ..................... | 72 |
| 50. | Situation récapitulative de la balance des paiements, 1970, 1973, 1975 et 1978-1984 ............ | 73 |
| 51. | Encours de la dette extérieure, 1975 et 1979-1984 ... | 74-75 |
| 52. | Paiements effectués au titre du service de la dette, 1975 et 1979-1984 ................................. | 76-77 |
| 53. | Quelques autres indicateurs économiques et sociaux: | 78-84 |
| | A.  Superficie et répartition de la population..... | 78 |
| | B.  Taux de natalité et de mortalité, espérance de vie ................................................ | 79 |
| | C.  Santé à la naissance ........................... | 80 |
| | D.  Alimentation et eau ............................ | 81 |
| | E.  Enseignement et alphabétisme ................... | 82 |
| | F.  Communications et médias ....................... | 83 |
| | G.  Energie ........................................ | 84 |

EXPLANATORY NOTES

A.  Definition of country groupings

Least developed countries :

In this document, the 37 countries identified by the United Nations as least developed are: Afghanistan, Bangladesh, Benin, Bhutan, Botswana, Burkina Faso, Burundi, Cape Verde, Central African Republic, Chad, Comoros, Democratic Yemen, Djibouti, Equatorial Guinea, Ethiopia, Gambia, Guinea, Guinea-Bissau, Haiti, Lao People's Democratic Republic, Lesotho, Malawi, Maldives, Mali, Nepal, Niger, Rwanda, Samoa, Sao Tome and Principe, Sierra Leone, Somalia, Sudan, Togo, Uganda, United Republic of Tanzania, Vanuatu and Yemen. Except where otherwise indicated, the totals and the tables for least developed countries as a group refer to these 37 countries. The United Nations General Assembly at its 41st session in December 1986 has approved the inclusion of three additional countries, Kiribati, Mauritania and Tuvalu, which will be covered in the next isse of the Basic Data.

Major economic areas :

The classification of countries and territories according to main economic areas used in this document has been adopted for purposes of statistical convenience only and follows that in the UNCTAD Handbook of International Trade and Development Statistics, Supplement 1986. Countries and territories are classified according to main economic areas as follows :

Developed market-economy countries : United States, Canada, EEC (Belgium, Denmark, France, Germany, Federal Republic of, Greece, Ireland, Italy, Luxembourg, Netherlands, Portugal, Spain, United Kingdom), EFTA (Austria, Finland, Iceland, Norway, Sweden, Switzerland), Faeroe Islands, Gibraltar, Israel, Japan, Australia, New Zealand, South Africa.

Socialist countries of Eastern Europe : Albania, Bulgaria, Czechoslovakia, German Democratic Republic, Hungary, Poland, Romania, USSR.

Socialist countries of Asia : China, Democratic People's Republic of Korea, Mongolia, Viet Nam.

Developing countries and territories : All other countries, territories and areas in Africa, Asia, America, Europe and Oceania not specified above.

In some tables the group of all developing countries excludes, as indicated, major petroleum exporters. Major petroleum exporters are defined as those countries for which petroleum and petroleum products accounted for more than 50 per cent of their total exports in 1978, namely, Algeria, Angola, Bahrain, Brunei, Congo, Ecuador, Gabon, Indonesia, Iran, (Islamic Republic of), Iraq, Kuwait, Libyan Arab Jamahiriya, Mexico, Nigeria, Oman, Qatar, Saudi Arabia, Syrian Arab Republic, Trinidad and Tobago, United Arab Emirates and Venezuela.

Other country groupings :

DAC member countries : In this document, the countries members of the OECD Development Assistance Committee are Australia, Austria, Belgium, Canada, Denmark, Finland, France, Germany, Federal Republic of, Italy, Japan, Netherlands, New Zealand, Norway, Sweden, Switzerland, United Kingdom and United States. Ireland, which became a DAC member in 1986, will be included with other DAC member countries in the next issue of the Basic Data.

OPEC member countries : The countries members of the Organization of the Petroleum Exporting Countries are Algeria, Ecuador, Gabon, Indonesia, Iran, (Islamic Republic of), Iraq, Kuwait, Libyan Arab Jamahiriya, Nigeria, Qatar, Saudi Arabia, United Arab Emirates and Venezuela.


B.     Terms, definitions and sources used

The estimates of population are for mid-year and are primarily based on data from the Population Division of the Department of International Economic and Social Affairs of the United Nations Secretariat.

National accounts data are mainly based on information from the United Nations Statistical Office, the United Nations Economic Commission for Africa, the World Bank and national sources.

The estimates relating to agricultural production, food and nutrition, are derived mainly from information provided by FAO.

Trade data are estimates by the UNCTAD secretariat mainly derived from the UNCTAD Handbook of International Trade and Development Statistics, Supplement 1986. Exports are valued f.o.b. and imports c.i.f.

The figures concerning aid flows are mainly based on information provided by the OECD secretariat. Following the DAC definitions[1] concessional assistance refers to flows which qualify as official development assistance (ODA), i.e., grants or loans undertaken by the official sector, with promotion of economic development and welfare as main objectives, and at concessional financial terms (if a loan, at least 25 per cent grant element). Non-concessional flows include grants from private agencies (private aid) and transactions at commercial terms : export credits, bilateral portfolio investment (including bank lending) by residents or institutions in donor countries; direct investment (including reinvested earnings); and purchases of securities of international organisations active in development. Figures for commitments reflect a firm obligation to furnish assistance specified as to volume, purpose, financial terms and conditions, while figures for disbursements represent the actual provision of funds. Unless otherwise specified, disbursement figures are shown net, i.e., less capital repayments on earlier loans. Grants, loans and credits for military purposes and loans and credits with a maturity of less than one year, are excluded from aid flows.

---

1/     See, OECD Development Co-operation, 1983 Review , (Paris, 1983) p. 176.

The data for the years 1977-1984 concerning aid flows from OPEC member countries and multilateral agencies mainly financed by them have been supplied directly by the donors to the UNCTAD secretariat. In a few cases the figures represent estimates by the UNCTAD secretariat based on secondary sources.

Tables 34 and 46 present data for individual DAC and OPEC member countries respectively, on the estimated amount of official development assistance provided to LDCs expressed as a percentage of the GNP of each donor. So as to give a clear picture of the total flow, an attempt has been made to estimate the share of multilateral flows to LDCs which is provided by each donor. In order to do so, the share of each agency's disbursements to LDCs, expressed as a percentage of its total disbursements to developing countries, was applied to the donor's contributions to the agency in question; the sum for all agencies thus calculated was then added to the donor's bilateral ODA and expressed as a percentage of its GNP.

Balance of payments data are estimates by the UNCTAD secretariat based on the IMF balance of payments tapes and other information mainly provided by the IMF.

Debt data cover total external long-term and medium-term debt (incuding private debt) and are based on information provided by the OECD secretariat.

With regard to other economic and social indicators, data on area are from the United Nations, Demographic Yearbook 1984[2]/ and the FAO, Production Yearbook 1984.

The estimates relating to urban population are not strictly comparable from country to country because of differences in definitions and coverage. They have been mainly derived from the United Nations, World Population Chart 1985.[3]/

The labour force participation rate refers to economicaly active population as a percentage of total population of sex(es) specified of all ages, as shown in the World Bank, Social Indicators Data Sheets (June 1985).

Crude birth rates and crude death rates indicate respectively the number of births and deaths per thousand of population. Together with life expectancy at birth and infant mortality rates, crude birth and death rates have been derived mainly from the United Nations, Demographic Yearbook 1984; United Nations, Demographic indicators of countries: estimates and projections as assessed in 1984 and United Nations, World Population Chart 1985.

Life expectancy at birth indicates the average number of years the newly born children would live, if subject to the same mortality conditions in the year(s) to which the life expectancy refers, while the infant mortality rate is the number of infants who die before reaching one year of age per thousand live births in the reference year.

---

2/    ST/ESA/STAT/SER.R/14, United Nations publication, Sales No. E/F. 85. XIII.1.

3/    ST/ESA/SER.A/98/Add.1, United Nations Publication, Sales no. E.85.XIII.A.

Under the heading health at birth, low birth weight directly reflects the nutritional status of mothers and indirectly, mediated through the status of women, that of the population in general. The figures are drawn from WHO, World Health Statistics Quarterly 33(3)(1980) and Weekly Epidemiological Record, No. 27, 6 July 1984.

The percentage of women attended during childbirth by trained personnel is a good indicator of the availability of medical services. It reflects the geographical distribution of the facilities and hence their accessibility, and indeed whether the hospitals had the equipment and supplies to dispense effective medical care. The percentage of women attended during childbirth by trained personnel also to a degree reflects the status of women. Data are drawn from WHO, World Health Statistics Quarterly, 38(3)(1985).

The estimates of average daily calorie intake per capita was calculated by dividing the calorie equivalent of the food supplies in an economy by the population. Food supplies comprise domestic production, imports less exports, and changes in stocks; they exclude animal feed, seeds for use in agriculture, and food lost in processing and distribution. The daily calorie requirements used as a basis for calculating average daily calorie intake as a percentage of requirements refers to the calories needed to sustain a person at normal levels of activity and health taking into account age and sex distributions, average body weights, and environmental temperatures. The data in this table are weighted by population and are taken from World Bank, World Development Report 1986.

The percentage of population with access to safe water or adequate sanitation are estimates by WHO. The percentage with access to safe water refers to the share of people with "reasonable" access to treated surface waters or untreated but uncontaminated water, such as that from protected boreholes, springs and sanitary wells, as percentage of their respective populations. In an urban area a public fountain or standpost located not more than 200 metres from a house is considered as being within "reasonable" access to that house; in rural areas, "reasonable" access would imply that the housewife or members of the household do not spend a disproportionate part of the day in fetching the family's water needs.

The percentage of population with access to adequate sanitation includes the share of urban population served by connexions to public sewers or by systems (pit privies, pour flush latrines, septic tanks, communal toilets, etc.) and the share of rural population with adequate disposal such as pit privies, pour-flush latrines, etc.

With respect to both water and sanitation, the figures are derived from The International drinking water supply and sanitation decade: review of national progress (as at 31 December 1983).

Data relating to education and literacy are mainly derived from information provided by UNESCO. The adult literacy rate is the percentage of people aged 15 and over who can read and write. The data on school enrolment ratios refer to estimates of total, male, and female, enrolment of students of all ages in primary/secondary school, expressed as percentages of the total, male, and female, population of primary/secondary school age.

Newsprint consumption is estimated from imports, except in Bangladesh, which also produces newsprint for domestic consumption. The estimates are based on information provided by FAO.

Data on mail traffic cover letters, postcards, printed matter, merchandise samples, small packets and photopost packets. The figures are from the Universal Postal Union, Statistiques des services postaux 1980 and 1984.

Data on circulation of daily newspapers per 1000 inhabitants, refer to circulation of "daily general interest newspaper" and are based on data from UNESCO, Statistical Yearbook 1985.

Data on telephones per 1000 inhabitants are based on ITU, Yearbook of Common Carrier Telecommunication Statistics (13th edition) and ITU, Telecommunications for all, November 1983.

Data on radio receivers per 1000 inhabitants are based on information provided by UNESCO. The ratio uses the number of receivers in use and/or licenses issued, depending on the method of estimation used in each reporting country.

Data on energy consumption per capita refer, on the one hand, to forms of primary energy, including hard coal, lignite, peat and oil shale, crude petroleum and natural gas liquids, natural gas, and primary electricity (nuclear, geomethermal, and hydroelectric power) - often called "commercial energy" - and on the other hand, to the use of fuelwood, charcoal and bagasse. All data are converted into coal equivalent and are based on information from United Nations, Energy Statistics Yearbook 1984[4/] and on the World Bank, Social Indicators Data Sheets (various issues).

The data on installed electricity capacity are also derived from United Nations, Energy Statistics Yearbook 1984.

## C.    Other notes

"Dollars" ($) refer to United States dollars, unless otherwise stated.

Annual rates of growth and change refer to compound rates.

Details and percentages in tables do not necessarily add to totals, because of rounding.

The following symbols have been used :

A dash (-) or a zero (0) indicates that the amount is nil or negligible.

Two dots (..) indicate that the data are not available or are not separately reported.

Use of a hyphen (-) between dates representing years, e.g. 1970-1980, signifies the full period involved, including the initial and final years.

4/ ST/ESA/STAT/SER.J/28, United Nations publications, Sales No. E/F.86 XVII.2.

D.    Abbreviations used

| | |
|---|---|
| AfDB | African Development Bank |
| AfDF | African Development Fund |
| AFESD | Arab Fund for Economic and Social Development |
| AsDB | Asian Development Bank |
| BADEA | Arab Bank for Economic Development in Africa |
| CMEA | Council for Mutual Economic Assistance |
| CRS | Creditor Reporting System (OECD) |
| DAC | Development Assistance Committee (of OECD) |
| DRS | Debtor Reporting System (World Bank) |
| EDF | European Development Fund |
| EEC | European Economic Community |
| EIB | European Investment Bank |
| FAO | Food and Agriculture Organization of the United Nations |
| IBRD | International Bank for Reconstruction and Development (World Bank) |
| IDA | International Development Association |
| IDB | Inter-American Development Bank |
| IFAD | International Fund for Agricultural Development |
| IFC | International Finance Corporation |
| IMF | International Monetary Fund |
| LDCs | Least Developed Countries |
| mill. | Millions |
| OAPEC | Organization of Arab Petroleum Exporting Countries |
| ODA | Official development assistance |
| OECD | Organisation for Economic Co-operation and Development |
| OPEC | Organisation of Petroleum Exporting Countries |
| SAAFA | Special Arab Aid Fund for Africa |
| SITC | Standard International Trade Classification, Revision 1 |

SNPA    Substantial New Programme of Action for the 1980s for the
        Least Developed Countries

UN      United Nations

UNDP    United Nations Development Programme

UNHCR   Office of the United Nations High Commissioner for Refugees

UNICEF  United Nations Children's Fund

UNTA    United Nations Technical Assistance

WFP     World Food Programme

NOTES EXPLICATIVES

## A. Définition des groupements de pays

### Pays en développement les moins avancés :

Les 37 pays ainsi identifiés par l'Organisation des Nations Unies qui figurent dans ce document sont les suivants : Afghanistan, Bangladesh, Bénin, Bhoutan, Botswana, Burkina Faso, Burundi, Cap-Vert, Comores, Djibouti, Ethiopie, Gambie, Guinée, Guinée-Bissau, Guinée équatoriale, Haïti, Lesotho, Malawi, Maldives, Mali, Népal, Niger, Ouganda, République centrafricaine, République démocratique populaire lao, République-Unie de Tanzanie, Rwanda, Samoa, Sao Tomé-et-Principe, Sierra Leone, Somalie, Soudan, Tchad, Togo, Vanuatu, Yémen, et Yémen démocratique. Les totaux et les tableaux concernant l'ensemble des pays les moins avancés se rapportent à ces 37 pays. L'Assemblée générale des Nations Unies, au cours de sa 41ème session en décembre 1986, a approuvé l'inclusion de trois pays additionnels, Kiribati, la Mauritanie et Tuvalu, qui seront compris dans la prochaine édition des Données de base.

### Grandes zones économiques :

Le classement des pays et territoires par grandes zones économiques, utilisé dans ce document, n'a été adopté qu'aux fins de présentation des statistiques et il suit celui qui est utilisé dans le Manuel de statistiques du commerce international et du développement, Supplément 1986. Les pays et territoires sont classés en grandes zones économiques, constituées comme suit :

Les pays développés à économie de marché : Etats-Unis, Canada, Communauté économique européenne (Allemagne, République fédérale d', Belgique, Danemark, Espagne, France, Grèce, Irlande, Italie, Luxembourg, Pays-Bas, Portugal, Royaume-Uni), AELE (Autriche, Finlande, Islande, Norvège, Suède, Suisse), Gibraltar, îles Féroé, Israël, Japon, Australie, Nouvelle-Zélande, Afrique du Sud.

Les pays socialistes d'Europe orientale : Albanie, Bulgarie, Hongrie, Pologne, République démocratique allemande, Roumanie, Tchécoslovaquie, URSS.

Les pays socialistes d'Asie : Chine, Mongolie, République populaire démocratique de Corée, Viet Nam.

Les pays et territoires en développement : tous les autres pays, terrritoires et zones d'Afrique, d'Asie, d'Amérique, d'Europe et d'Océanie non mentionnés ci-dessus.

Dans certains tableaux, il est indiqué que l'ensemble des pays en développement ne comprend pas les principaux pays exportateurs de pétrole. Par principaux pays exportateurs de pétrole, on entend les pays pour lesquels les exportations de pétrole et de produits pétroliers ont représenté plus de 50 pour cent de leurs exportations totales en 1978, c'est-à-dire : Algérie, Angola, Arabie saoudite, Bahrein, Brunéi, Congo, Emirats arabes unis, Equateur, Gabon, Indonésie, Iraq, Iran, République islamique d', Jamahiriya arabe libyenne, Koweit, Mexique, Nigeria, Oman, Qatar, République arabe syrienne, Trinité-et-Tobago et Venezuela.

Autres groupements de pays :

Les pays membres du Comité d'aide au développement (CAD) qui figurent dans ce document sont les suivants : Allemagne, République fédérale d', Australie, Autriche, Belgique, Canada, Danemark, Etats-Unis, Finlande, France, Italie, Japon, Norvège, Nouvelle-Zélande, Pays-Bas, Royaume-Uni, Suède et Suisse. L'Irlande, qui est devenue membre du CAD en 1986, figurera avec les autres pays membres du CAD dans la prochaine édition des Données de base.

Les pays membres de l'Organisation des pays exportateurs de pétrole (OPEP) sont les suivants : Algérie, Arabie saoudite, Emirats arabes unis, Equateur, Gabon, Indonésie, Iraq, Iran, République islamique d', Koweit, Jamahiriya arabe libyenne, Nigéria, Qatar et Venezuela.

B.    Définitions, terminologie et sources utilisées

Les estimations de la population sont des estimations de milieu d'année fondées essentiellement sur des données fournies par la Division de la population du Département des affaires économiques et sociales internationales de l'ONU.

Les données se rapportant aux comptes nationaux ont été établies principalement d'après des informations provenant du Bureau de statistique des Nations Unies, de la Commission économique pour l'Afrique et de la Banque mondiale, ainsi que de sources nationales.

Les estimations concernant la production agricole, l'alimentation et la nutrition, sont surtout tirées d'informations communiquées par la FAO.

Les données se rapportant au commerce sont des estimations du secrétariat de la CNUCED tirées en grande partie du Manuel de statistiques du commerce international et du développement, Supplément 1986. Les exportations sont données en valeur f.o.b. et les importations en valeur c.a.f.

Les chiffres se rapportant aux apports d'aide sont principalement fondés sur des informations communiquées par le secrétariat de l'OCDE. Suivant les définitions du CAD,[1] l'aide concessionnelle désigne les apports qui sont considérés comme une "aide publique au développement" (APD), c'est-à-dire les dons ou les prêts accordés par le secteur public, dans le but essentiel d'améliorer le développement économique et le niveau de vie, et assortis de conditions financières libérales (dans le cas des prêts, 25 pour cent au moins d'élément de don).

Les apports non-concessionnels comprennent les dons des organismes privés (aide privée) et les transactions assorties de conditions commerciales : crédits à l'exportation, investissements bilatéraux de portefeuille (prêts bancaires compris) effectués par des résidents ou des institutions des pays donneurs; investissements directs (bénéfices réinvestis compris) et achats de titres d'organisations internationales s'occupant du développement. Les données concernant les engagements se rapportent au moment où le donneur prend l'engagement ferme de fournir une aide déterminée quant à son volume, sa destination, ses conditions financières et ses modalités, tandis que les données concernant les versements correspondent à la fourniture effective des fonds. Sauf indication contraire, les chiffres des versements

_____

1/    Voir OCDE, Coopération pour le développement, examen 1983 (Paris 1983), p.200.

sont indiqués "nets", c'est-à-dire déduction faite des remboursements effectués au titre de prêts antérieurs. Les dons, les prêts et les crédits de caractère militaire, ainsi que les prêts et les crédits dont la durée de remboursement est inférieure à un an, sont exclus.

Les données pour les années 1977-1984, concernant l'aide en provenance des pays membres de l'OPEP et des institutions multilatérales essentiellement financées par ceux-ci, ont été généralement fournies directement par les donneurs eux-mêmes. Dans quelques cas, les chiffres sont des estimations du secrétariat de la CNUCED à partir de sources secondaires.

Les tableaux 34 et 46 présentent des estimations, pour les divers pays membres du CAD et de l'OPEP, sur le montant de l'aide publique au développement qui a été fourni aux PMA, exprimé en pourcentage du PNB de chaque donneur. Afin de donner un aperçu précis des apports totaux, on a essayé d'estimer la part des apports multilatéraux qui a été fournie par chaque donneur aux PMA. A cette fin, on a appliqué aux contributions du pays donneur à chacune des institutions multilatérales, la part respective des versements nets de chacune de ces institutions aux PMA exprimée en pourcentage des versements nets correspondant à l'ensemble des pays en développement. La somme ainsi obtenue pour l'ensemble des institutions est ajoutée à l'aide bilatérale du pays donneur et exprimée en pourcentage de son PNB.

Les données concernant la <u>balance des paiements</u> sont des estimations du secrétariat de la CNUCED d'après les bandes magnétiques de la balance des paiements du FMI et d'autres renseignements fournis surtout par le FMI.

Les données concernant la <u>dette</u> recouvrent la dette extérieure totale à long et moyen terme (y compris la dette privée) et sont fondées sur des renseignements communiqués par le secrétariat de l'OCDE.

En ce qui concerne les autres indicateurs économiques et sociaux, les données relatives aux <u>superficies</u> sont tirées de l'<u>Annuaire démographique 1984</u> des Nations Unies[2] et de l'<u>Annuaire de la production 1984</u> de la FAO.

Les estimations concernant la <u>population urbaine</u> ne sont pas toujours comparables d'un pays à l'autre en raison des différences qui existent dans les définitions et la couverture. Elles sont principalement tirées du <u>World Population Chart 1985</u> des Nations Unies.[3]

Le <u>taux d'activité</u> est le rapport (en pourcentage) entre la population active et la population du ou des sexes indiqués, tous âges confondus. Les chiffres sont tirés des <u>Social Indicators Data Sheets</u>, (juin 1985), de la Banque mondiale.

Les <u>taux bruts de natalité et de mortalité</u> indiquent respectivement le nombre de naissances vivantes et de décès pour mille habitants. Ces taux, ainsi que l'<u>espérance de vie à la naissance</u> et les <u>taux de mortalité infantile</u>, sont principalement tirés de l'<u>Annuaire démographique 1984</u>; de <u>Demographic indicators of countries : estimates and projections as assessed in 1984</u>, et de <u>World Population Chart 1985</u> des Nations Unies.

---

[2]    ST/ESA/STAT/SER.R./14, Publication des Nations Unies, no. de vente E/F.85.XIII.1.

[3]    ST/ESA/SER.A/98/Add.1, Publication des Nations Unies, no. de vente E.85.XIII.A.

L'espérance de vie à la naissance indique le nombre moyen d'années que vivrait un nouveau-né pour autant que les conditions de mortalité ne changent pas, alors que le taux de mortalité infantile exprime le nombre de décès d'enfants de moins d'un an pour mille naissances vivantes survenus pendant l'année de référence.

Sous la rubrique santé à la naissance, le poids insuffisant à la naissance reflète directement le statut nutritionnel des mères et indirectement, compte tenu du statut de la femme, celui de la population en général. Les chiffres sont tirés du Rapport trimestriel de statistiques sanitaires mondiales, 33(3) (1980), et du Relevé épidémiologique hebdomadaire no. 27, du 6 juillet 1984 de l'OMS.

Le pourcentage de femmes ayant reçu des soins prodigués par du personnel qualifié pendant l'accouchement constitue un indicateur de la disponibilité des services médicaux. Il reflète la distribution géographique de l'équipement et par conséquent leur accessibilité et dans quelle mesure les hôpitaux disposent du matériel et des fournitures qu'il faut pour offrir des soins médicaux efficaces. Le pourcentage de femmes ayant reçu des soins prodigués par du personnel qualifié pendant l'accouchement reflète aussi dans une certaine mesure le statut de la femme. Les données sont tirées du Rapport trimestriel de statistiques sanitaires mondiales, 38(3)(1985) de l'OMS.

On a calculé les disponibilités alimentaires en divisant l'équivalent en calorie de l'offre de denrées alimentaires disponible dans un pays par sa population totale. Cette offre comprend la production intérieure, les importations diminuées des exportations et les variations de stocks; elle ne recouvre ni l'alimentation du bétail, ni les semences utilisées dans l'agriculture, ni les pertes en cours de traitement et de distribution. Les besoins caloriques par habitant et par jour ayant servis à calculer les disponibilités alimentaires en pourcentage des besoins expriment le nombre de calories nécessaires pour maintenir une population dans un état d'activité et de santé normal, compte tenu de sa structure par âge et par sexe, du poids moyen des habitants, et des températures ambiantes. Les chiffres présentés sur ce tableau sont pondérés par la population. Les données sont tirées du Rapport sur le développement dans le monde 1986 de la Banque mondiale.

Les pourcentages de la population disposant d'eau saine ou de mesures suffisantes d'hygiène du milieu sont des estimations de l'OMS. Le pourcentage de la population disposant d'eau saine indique la part en pourcentage de personnes jouissant d'un accès "raisonnable" aux eaux superficielles traitées ou à une eau non traitée mais non contaminée, provenant par exemple de forages, de sources et de puits protégés, par rapport à la population en question. Dans une zone urbaine, une fontaine publique ou une borne-fontaine située dans un rayon de 200 mètres est considérée comme étant d'accès "raisonnable". Dans les zones rurales, pour que l'accès soit "raisonnable" il faut que la ménagère ou toute autre personne faisant partie du ménage ne passe pas une trop grande partie de la journée à se procurer l'eau nécessaire à la famille.

Le pourcentage de la population disposant de mesures suffisantes d'hygiène du milieu comprend la part de la population urbaine jouissant de raccordements aux égouts publics ou de systèmes ménagers (cabinets à fosse, latrines à entraînement par eau, fosses septiques, toilettes communales, etc.) et la part de la population rurale jouissant de moyens suffisants d'évacuation (cabinets à fosses, latrinements à entraînement par eau, etc.).

Tant pour l'eau que pour l'hygiène du milieu, les données se basent sur The International drinking water supply and sanitation decade : review of national progress (as at 31 December 1983).

Les données concernant l'enseignement et l'alphabétisme sont principalement tirées de renseignements fournis par l'UNESCO. Le taux d'alphabétisation des adultes est le pourcentage de la population âgée de 15 ans ou plus, sachant lire et écrire. Les données concernant les taux d'inscription scolaire sont des estimations du nombre total de garçons et du nombre de filles inscrits à l'école primaire et secondaire, de tous âges, exprimées en pourcentage de la population totale, masculine et féminine en âge de fréquenter l'école primaire ou secondaire.

La consommation de papier journal est estimée à partir d'importations, à l'exception du Bangladesh qui produit, en outre des importations, du papier journal pour la consommation intérieure. Les estimations sont établies d'après des données de la FAO.

Les données relatives au trafic postal couvrent les lettres, les cartes postales, les imprimés, les échantillons, les petits colis et les colis renfermant des travaux photographiques. Les données sont tirées des Statistiques des services postaux, 1980 et 1984 de l'Union Postale Universelle.

Les données sur la circulation des journaux quotidiens pour 1000 habitants se rapportent à "la circulation des journaux quotidiens d'information générale" et sont établies d'après des données de l'Annuaire statistique 1985 de l'UNESCO.

Les données sur les téléphones pour mille habitants se basent sur l'Annuaire statistique des télécommunications du secteur public (13ème édition) et Telecommunications for all, (novembre 1983) de l'UIT.

Les données sur les postes récepteurs de radio pour 1000 habitants sont établies d'après des renseignements fournis par l'UNESCO. Le rapport est calculé à partir du nombre de postes récepteurs en service et/ou de licenses délivrées selon la méthode d'estimation employée dans chaque pays qui fournit des données.

Les données concernant la consommation d'énergie par habitant se rapportent, d'une part, aux formes d'énergie primaire (houille, lignite, tourbe et schiste bitumineux, pétrole brut et liquides extraits du gaz naturel, et électricité primaire (nucléaire, géothermique et hydraulique) - souvent appelées "énergie commerciale" - et, d'autre part, à l'utilisation de bois de chauffage, de charbon de bois et de bagasse. Toutes les données sont converties en équivalent charbon et ont été établies d'après l'Annuaire des statistiques de l'énergie 1984 des Nations Unies[4] et les Social Indicators Data Sheets de la Banque mondiale (divers numéros).

Les données sur la puissance électrique installée sont également tirées de l'Annuaire des statistiques de l'énergie 1984 des Nations Unies.

_____

[4]    ST/ESA/STAT/SER.J./28, Publication des Nations Unies, no. de vente E/F/86.XVII.2.

C.    Autres notes

Sauf indication contraire, le terme "dollar" s'entend du dollar des Etats-Unis d'Amérique.

Les taux annuels de croissance et de variation sont des taux composés.

Les chiffres étant arrondis, les totaux indiqués ne correspondent pas toujours à la somme des composantes et des pourcentages portés dans les tableaux.

Les symboles suivants ont été utilisés :

Un tiret (-) ou un zéro (0) signifient que le montant est nul ou négligeable.

Deux points (..) signifient que les données ne sont pas disponibles ou ne sont pas montrées séparément.

Le trait d'union (-) entre deux millésimes, par exemple (1970-1980), indique qu'il s'agit de la période tout entière (y compris la première et la dernière année mentionnée).

D.    Abréviations utilisées

| | |
|---|---|
| AID | Association internationale de développement |
| APD | Aide publique au développement |
| ATNU | Assistance technique des Nations Unies |
| BADEA | Banque arabe pour le développement économique de l'Afrique |
| BAfD | Banque africaine de développement |
| BAsD | Banque asiatique de développement |
| BEI | Banque européenne d'investissement |
| BID | Banque interaméricaine de développement |
| BIRD | Banque internationale pour la reconstruction et le développement (Banque mondiale) |
| CAD | Comité d'aide au développement (de l'OCDE) |
| CAEM | Conseil d'assistance économique mutuelle |
| CEE | Communauté économique européenne |
| CTCI | Classification type pour le commerce international (révision 1) |
| FADES | Fonds arabe de développement économique et social |
| FAfD | Fonds africain de développement |

| | |
|---|---|
| FAO | Organisation des Nations Unies pour l'alimentation et l'agriculture |
| FSAAA | Fonds spécial d'aide arabe à l'Afrique |
| FED | Fonds européen de développement |
| FIDA | Fonds international pour le développement agricole |
| FMI | Fonds monétaire international |
| mill. | Millions |
| NPSA | Nouveau programme d'action pour les années 80 en faveur des pays les moins avancés |
| OCDE | Organisation de coopération et de développement économique |
| ONU | Organisation des Nations Unies |
| OPAEP | Organisation des pays arabes exportateurs de pétrole |
| OPEP | Organisation des pays exportateurs de pétrole |
| PAM | Programme alimentaire mondial |
| PMA | Les pays les moins avancés |
| PNUD | Programme des Nations Unies pour le développement |
| SFI | Société financière internationale |
| SNPC | "Système de notification des pays créanciers" de l'OCDE |
| SNPD | "Système de notification des pays débiteurs" de la Banque mondiale |
| UNHCR | Haut Commissariat des Nations Unies pour les réfugiés |
| UNICEF | Fonds des Nations Unies pour l'enfance |

TABLES

TABLEAUX

Table 1
Real GDP, total and per capita : annual average growth rates, 1970-1984

Percentages

Tableau 1
Produit intérieur brut réel, total et par habitant : taux annuels moyens d'accroissement, 1970-1984

En pourcentage

| Country | Total real product / Produit réel total | | | | | | Per capita real product / Produit réel par habitant | | | | Pays |
|---|---|---|---|---|---|---|---|---|---|---|---|
| | 1970-1980 a/ | 1980-1984 | 1980-1981 | 1981-1982 | 1982-1983 | 1983-1984 | 1980-1981 | 1981-1982 | 1982-1983 | 1983-1984 | |
| Afghanistan b/ | 3.7 | 2.7 | 1.8 | 2.0 | 4.8 | 2.1 | -0.8 | -0.5 | 2.1 | -0.5 | Afghanistan b/ |
| Bangladesh c/ | 3.7 | 3.8 | 6.8 | 0.8 | 3.6 | 4.2 | 4.7 | -1.5 | 1.4 | 2.0 | Bangladesh c/ |
| Benin | 3.4 | 3.6 | 10.9 | 4.0 | -1.9 | 1.6 | 7.5 | 0.9 | -4.9 | -1.5 | Bénin |
| Bhutan d/ | .. | 7.0 | 9.0 | 10.8 | 6.1 | 2.6 | 6.7 | 8.6 | 4.0 | 0.5 | Bhoutan d/ |
| Botswana c/ | 9.0 | 11.8 | 8.6 | -2.5 | 23.6 | 19.4 | 4.3 | -6.4 | 19.0 | 15.0 | Botswana c/ |
| Burkina Faso | 4.0 | -1.4 | 3.5 | 0.0 | -4.8 | -3.9 | 0.9 | -2.4 | -7.0 | -6.1 | Burkina Faso |
| Burundi | 3.1 | 0.6 | 10.5 | -3.2 | 1.1 | -5.2 | 7.3 | -6.0 | -1.7 | -7.7 | Burundi |
| Cape Verde | 0.3 | 7.6 | 7.3 | 4.8 | 0.7 | 18.4 | 5.1 | 2.7 | -1.2 | 16.2 | Cap-Vert |
| Cent.African Rep. | 2.2 | -0.2 | -2.3 | 0.4 | -2.3 | 3.6 | -4.6 | -1.9 | -4.5 | 1.3 | Rép. centrafricaine |
| Chad | 1.8 | -7.0 | -9.0 | -7.3 | -7.0 | -4.6 | -11.1 | -9.4 | -9.1 | -6.7 | Tchad |
| Comoros | -0.9 | 4.3 | 3.6 | 5.9 | 3.7 | 3.9 | 0.2 | 2.7 | 0.5 | 1.0 | Comores |
| Democratic Yemen | 2.6 | 1.9 | 6.6 | -4.6 | 4.0 | 2.0 | 3.5 | -7.3 | 1.2 | -0.7 | Yémen démocratique |
| Djibouti | 3.0 | 1.5 | -8.0 | 13.6 | 0.9 | 0.5 | -11.9 | 9.9 | -2.0 | -2.0 | Djibouti |
| Equatorial Guinea | .. | 1.3 | 2.3 | 3.8 | -3.0 | 2.3 | 0.1 | 1.6 | -5.1 | 0.2 | Guinée équatoriale |
| Ethiopia e/ | 2.6 | 1.5 | 2.5 | 1.4 | 4.7 | -2.4 | -0.3 | -1.3 | 1.9 | -5.0 | Ethiopie e/ |
| Gambia c/ | 4.1 | 1.6 | -8.2 | 9.5 | 14.7 | -7.5 | -10.3 | 7.1 | 12.2 | -9.5 | Gambie c/ |
| Guinea | 4.3 | 1.3 | 0.6 | 1.8 | 1.3 | 1.6 | -1.9 | -0.6 | -1.0 | -0.7 | Guinée |
| Guinea-Bissau | 2.5 | 6.1 | 18.2 | 6.0 | -8.1 | 10.2 | 15.9 | 4.0 | -9.8 | 8.2 | Guinée-Bissau |
| Haiti f/ | 3.8 | -0.9 | -2.7 | -3.9 | -0.3 | 2.7 | -4.1 | -5.3 | -1.0 | 1.3 | Haïti f/ |
| Lao People's D.R. | -0.1 | 3.2 | 6.6 | 1.9 | -3.3 | 8.1 | 4.3 | -0.6 | -5.4 | 5.8 | Rép. dém. pop. lao |
| Lesotho d/ | 9.6 | -0.5 | -0.4 | -3.6 | -1.4 | 3.7 | -3.0 | -6.1 | -3.8 | 1.2 | Lesotho d/ |
| Malawi | 6.0 | 2.3 | -5.1 | 2.5 | 4.4 | 7.7 | -8.2 | -0.7 | 1.2 | 4.5 | Malawi |
| Maldives | 13.6 h/ | 9.0 | 7.9 | 9.6 | 5.9 | 12.9 | 4.7 | 6.4 | 2.8 | 9.5 | Maldives |
| Mali | 3.8 | -0.1 | -1.8 | 5.9 | -4.1 | -0.1 | -4.6 | 2.9 | -6.8 | -2.8 | Mali |
| Nepal g/ | 2.7 | 4.5 | 8.3 | 3.8 | -1.4 | 7.4 | 5.7 | 1.4 | -3.6 | 5.0 | Népal g/ |
| Niger | 5.0 | -2.0 | -5.3 | -2.7 | 7.2 | -6.7 | -8.0 | -5.5 | 4.2 | -9.2 | Niger |
| Rwanda | 8.0 | 2.3 | 8.1 | 1.1 | 3.0 | -2.8 | 4.7 | -2.2 | -0.3 | -6.0 | Rwanda |
| Samoa | .. | -1.9 | -9.0 | -1.0 | 0.4 | 2.1 | -9.6 | -1.6 | -0.2 | 1.5 | Samoa |
| Sao Tome & Principe | 1.1 | -6.9 | -13.8 | 3.3 | -11.9 | -4.3 | -15.8 | -1.0 | -14.7 | -6.4 | Sao Tomé-et-Principe |
| Sierra Leone c/ | 1.8 | 0.3 | 1.3 | -0.2 | -0.3 | 0.5 | -0.5 | -2.0 | -2.1 | -1.3 | Sierra Leone c/ |
| Somalia | 2.7 | 4.2 | 6.7 | 5.6 | 1.4 | 3.1 | 3.7 | 2.7 | -1.4 | 0.2 | Somalie |
| Sudan c/ | 6.7 | 1.4 | 3.2 | 7.4 | -3.0 | -1.7 | 0.1 | 4.3 | -5.7 | -4.4 | Soudan c/ |
| Togo | 2.3 | -3.3 | -3.5 | -3.7 | -5.4 | -0.7 | -6.5 | -6.6 | -8.1 | -3.5 | Togo |
| Uganda | -2.4 | 7.1 | 5.7 | 9.1 | 8.8 | 4.7 | -2.3 | 5.5 | 5.3 | 1.3 | Ouganda |
| U.Rep.of Tanzania | 4.5 | 1.4 | 2.1 | 1.3 | -0.4 | 2.5 | -1.3 | -2.1 | -3.7 | -0.9 | Rép.-Unie de Tanzanie |
| Vanuatu | .. | 3.0 | 2.0 | 2.0 | 3.0 | 5.0 | -0.8 | -0.8 | 0.2 | 2.1 | Vanuatu |
| Yemen c/ | 9.9 | 6.3 | 9.6 | 10.0 | 3.5 | 2.4 | 6.8 | 7.2 | 0.9 | -0.2 | Yémen c/ |
| All LDCs | 3.9 | 2.4 | 3.5 | 2.5 | 1.8 | 1.7 | 0.9 | -0.2 | -0.8 | -0.8 | Ensemble des PMA |
| All developing countries | 5.8 | 1.0 | 1.3 | 0.9 | -0.5 | 2.5 | -1.2 | -1.5 | -2.8 | 0.2 | Ensemble des pays en développement |
| Developed market economy countries | 3.2 | 2.1 | 1.6 | -0.2 | 2.4 | 4.5 | 1.0 | -0.9 | 1.8 | 3.9 | Pays développés à économie de marché |
| Socialist countries of Eastern Europe | 5.3 | 3.4 | 2.4 | 3.0 | 4.2 | 3.8 | 1.6 | 2.1 | 3.3 | 2.9 | Pays socialistes d'Europe orientale |

Table 1 (continued)

Source: UNCTAD secretariat calculations based on data from the
United Nations Statistical Office, the Economic Commission
for Africa, the World Bank and other international
and national sources.

a/ Exponential trend function.
b/ Years beginning 21 March.
c/ Years ending 30 June.
d/ Years beginning 1 April.
e/ Years ending 7 July.
f/ Years ending 30 September.
g/ Years ending 15 July.
h/ 1974-1980.

Tableau 1 (suite)

Source: Chiffres calculés par le secrétariat de la CNUCED
d'après des données du Bureau de statistique des
Nations Unies, de la Commission économique pour
l'Afrique, de la Banque Mondiale et d'autres
sources internationales et nationales.

a/ Fonction exponentielle de tendance.
b/ Années commençant le 21 mars.
c/ Années finissant le 30 juin.
d/ Années commençant le 1er avril.
e/ Années finissant le 7 juillet.
f/ Années finissant le 30 septembre.
g/ Années finissant le 15 juillet.
h/ 1974-1980.

Table 2                 Tableau 2

Per capita GDP and population: levels and growth      PIB par habitant et population: niveaux et croissance

| Country | Per capita GDP in 1984 dollars PIB par habitant en dollars de 1984 | | | | Annual average growth rates of per capita real product (%) Taux annuels moyens d'accroissement du PIB par habitant (%) | | Population | | | Pays |
|---|---|---|---|---|---|---|---|---|---|---|
| | Estimated Estimation | Actual Réel | Projected Projection 1990 | | | | Total Totale (mill.) | Growth rate (% per annum) Taux de croissance (% par année) | | |
| | 1970 | 1984 | A a/ | B b/ | 1970-1980 c/ | 1980-1984 | 1984 | 1970-1980 c/ | 1980-1984 | |
| Afghanistan d/ | 212 | 210 i/ | 208 | 312 | 1.2 | 0.1 | 17.7 | 2.5 | 2.6 | Afghanistan d/ |
| Bangladesh e/ | 141 | 145 | 147 | 189 | 1.0 | 1.6 | 96.7 | 2.7 | 2.2 | Bangladesh e/ |
| Benin | 222 | 241 | 250 | 314 | 0.7 | 0.4 | 3.9 | 2.7 | 3.1 | Bénin |
| Bhutan f/ | .. | 122 | .. | 159 | .. | 4.9 | 1.4 | 2.0 | 2.0 | Bhoutan f/ |
| Botswana e/ | 409 | 1041 | 1553 | 1356 | 4.9 | 7.5 | 1.1 | 3.9 | 4.0 | Botswana e/ |
| Burkina Faso | 131 | 133 | 134 | 173 | 2.0 | -3.7 | 6.8 | 2.0 | 2.4 | Burkina Faso |
| Burundi | 209 | 209 | 209 | 272 | 1.4 | -2.2 | 4.6 | 1.7 | 2.9 | Burundi |
| Cape Verde | 261 | 296 | 312 | 385 | -0.6 | 5.5 | 0.3 | 0.9 | 2.0 | Cap-Vert |
| Central African Rep. | 276 | 236 | 221 | 307 | 0.0 | -2.4 | 2.5 | 2.1 | 2.3 | République centrafricaine |
| Chad | 203 | 118 | 94 | 154 | -0.2 | -9.1 | 4.9 | 2.1 | 2.3 | Tchad |
| Comoros | 253 | 208 | 191 | 271 | -4.2 | 1.1 | 0.4 | 3.5 | 3.1 | Comores |
| Democratic Yemen | 547 | 449 | 412 | 585 | 0.3 | -0.9 | 2.1 | 2.2 | 2.8 | Yémen démocratique |
| Djibouti | 892 | 574 k/ | 475 | 748 | -3.8 | -1.8 | 0.4 | 7.0 | 3.4 | Djibouti |
| Equatorial Guinea | .. | 213 | .. | 277 | .. | -0.9 | 0.4 | 1.9 | 2.2 | Guinée équatorial |
| Ethiopia g/ | 118 | 116 l/ | 115 | 158 | -0.1 | -1.2 | 42.0 | 2.7 | 2.7 | Ethiopie g/ |
| Gambia e/ | 272 | 288 | 295 | 375 | 0.6 | -0.6 | 0.7 | 3.6 | 2.2 | Gambie e/ |
| Guinea | 315 | 357 | 377 | 465 | 2.2 | -1.0 | 5.9 | 2.1 | 2.4 | Guinée |
| Guinea-Bissau | 208 | 176 | 164 | 229 | -1.8 | 4.1 | 0.9 | 4.4 | 1.9 | Guinée-Bissau |
| Haiti h/ | 292 | 350 | 378 | 456 | 2.3 | -2.3 | 5.2 | 1.4 | 1.4 | Haïti h/ |
| Lao People's Dem. Rep. | 212 | 203 | 199 | 264 | -1.9 | 1.0 | 3.7 | 1.9 | 2.2 | Rép. Dém. populaire lao |
| Lesotho f/ | 114 | 195 | 245 | 254 | 7.1 | -3.0 | 1.5 | 2.3 | 2.6 | Lesotho f/ |
| Malawi | 135 | 178 | 200 | 232 | 3.1 | -0.9 | 6.7 | 2.8 | 3.2 | Malawi |
| Maldives | .. | 432 | .. | 562 | .. | 5.8 | 0.2 | 3.1 | 3.0 | Maldives |
| Mali | 133 | 137 | 139 | 178 | 1.6 | -2.9 | 7.9 | 2.1 | 2.9 | Mali |
| Nepal i/ | 149 | 155 | 158 | 202 | 0.2 | 2.0 | 16.1 | 2.5 | 2.4 | Népal i/ |
| Niger | 279 | 279 | 279 | 363 | 2.4 | -4.8 | 6.0 | 2.5 | 2.9 | Niger |
| Rwanda | 200 | 282 | 327 | 367 | 4.5 | -1.0 | 5.9 | 3.3 | 3.3 | Rwanda |
| Samoa | .. | 619 | .. | 806 | .. | -2.5 | 0.2 | 0.7 | 0.6 | Samoa |
| Sao Tome & Principe | 530 | 388 | 340 | 505 | -0.3 | -9.2 | 0.1 | 1.4 | 2.5 | Sao Tomé-et-Principe |
| Sierra Leone e/ | 283 | 283 | 283 | 368 | 0.3 | -1.5 | 3.5 | 1.5 | 1.8 | Sierra Leone e/ |
| Somalia | 280 | 261 | 253 | 453 | -0.3 | 1.3 | 5.2 | 3.0 | 2.9 | Somalie |
| Sudan e/ | 318 | 366 | 388 | 477 | 3.6 | -1.5 | 21.0 | 3.0 | 2.9 | Soudan e/ |
| Togo | 287 | 232 | 212 | 302 | 0.0 | -6.2 | 2.9 | 2.4 | 3.0 | Togo |
| Uganda | 332 | 220 m/ | 184 | 286 | -5.2 | 3.6 | 15.0 | 3.0 | 3.4 | Ouganda |
| United Rep. of Tanzania | 246 | 250 | 252 | 326 | 1.1 | -2.0 | 21.5 | 3.3 | 3.5 | Rép.-Unie de Tanzanie |
| Vanuatu | .. | 683 n/ | .. | 971 | .. | 0.2 | 0.1 | 3.0 | 2.8 | Vanuatu |
| Yemen e/ | 212 | 480 | 681 | 625 | 6.7 | 3.6 | 7.8 | 3.0 | 2.6 | Yémen e/ |
| All LDCs | 197 | 206 | 209 | 268 | 1.2 | -0.2 | 323.1 | 2.6 | 2.6 | Ensemble des PMA |
| All developing countries | 681 | 870 l/ | 992 | 1184 | 3.3 | -1.3 | 2471.7 | 2.4 | 2.4 | Ensemble des pays en développement |
| Developed market economy countries | 7713 | 10106 l/ | 11688 | n.a. | 2.3 | 1.4 | 787.7 | 0.9 | 0.6 | Pays développés à économie de marché |
| Socialist countries of Eastern Europe | 1685 | 2606 n/ | 3485 | n.a. | 4.4 | 2.5 | 390.7 | 0.8 | 0.9 | Pays socialistes d'Europe orientale |

Source: UNCTAD secretariat calculations based on data from the United Nations Statistical Office, the Economic Commission for Africa, the World Bank and other international and national sources.

a/ At 1970-1984 growth rate. b/ Based on the target rate of 4.5 per cent as called for by the International Development Strategy for the Third United Nations Development Decade. c/ Exponential trend function. d/ Years beginning 21 March. e/ Years ending 30 June. f/ Years beginning 1 April. g/ Years ending 7 July. h/ Years ending 30 September. i/ Years ending 15 July. j/ 1981. k/ Adjusted data, (i.e. excluding income accruing to non-national residents). l/ 1983. m/ Tentative estimates of GNP per capita. Source: The World Bank Atlas 1986. n/ 1982.

Source: Chiffres calculés par le secrétariat de la CNUCED d'après des données du Bureau de statistique des Nations Unies, de la Commission Economique pour l'Afrique, de la Banque mondiale et d'autres sources internationales et nationales.

a/ D'après le taux de croissance 1970-1984. b/ D'après l'objectif de 4,5 pour cent prévu dans la Stratégie internationale du développement pour la Troisième Décennie de développement des Nations Unies. c/ Fonction exponentielle de de tendance. d/ Années commençant le 21 mars. e/ Années finissant le 30 juin. f/ Années commençant le 1er avril. g/ Années finissant le 7 juillet. h/ Années finissant le 30 septembre. i/ Années finissant le 15 juillet. j/ 1981. k/ Données ajustées (c.à.d. ne tenant pas compte du revenu des résidents non-nationaux). l/ 1983. m/ Estimations approximatives du PNB par habitant. Source: The World Bank Atlas 1986. n/ 1982.

Table 3
Total agricultural production and food production:
annual average growth rates 1970-1985

Tableau 3
Production agricole totale et production vivrière totale:
taux annuels moyens d'accroissement 1970-1985

Percentages / En pourcentage

| Country | Total agricultural production / Production agricole totale | | | | | | | Total food production / Production vivrière totale | | | | | | | Pays |
|---|---|---|---|---|---|---|---|---|---|---|---|---|---|---|---|
| | 1970-1980a | 1980-1985 | 1980-1981 | 1981-1982 | 1982-1983 | 1983-1984 | 1984-1985 | 1970-1980a | 1980-1985 | 1980-1981 | 1981-1982 | 1982-1983 | 1983-1984 | 1984-1985 | |
| Afghanistan | 2.4 | 0.9 | 2.1 | 0.0 | 2.4 | -0.2 | 0.2 | 2.2 | 0.9 | 2.4 | 0.6 | 1.7 | -0.5 | 0.3 | Afghanistan |
| Bangladesh | 2.4 | 1.8 | -0.2 | 3.6 | 3.0 | 0.3 | 2.6 | 2.5 | 1.7 | -0.0 | 3.5 | 2.7 | 1.0 | 1.3 | Bangladesh |
| Benin | 2.3 | 7.7 | 0.4 | 3.0 | 3.8 | 18.8 | 13.5 | 2.5 | 7.0 | -0.1 | 2.3 | 3.4 | 17.3 | 13.2 | Bénin |
| Bhutan | 2.5 | 2.3 | 1.7 | 2.6 | 2.8 | 2.2 | 2.4 | 2.5 | 2.4 | 1.7 | 2.6 | 2.9 | 2.2 | 2.4 | Bhoutan |
| Botswana | -2.3 | 2.8 | 18.9 | -0.4 | -6.1 | -1.9 | 5.1 | -2.3 | 2.8 | 19.1 | -0.6 | -6.2 | -1.8 | 5.1 | Botswana |
| Burkina Faso | 1.3 | 4.2 | 7.2 | -0.8 | -2.0 | -1.6 | 19.5 | 1.1 | 4.3 | 8.1 | -0.2 | -2.9 | -1.8 | 20.4 | Burkina Faso |
| Burundi | 2.5 | 3.9 | 19.1 | -7.3 | 5.1 | -3.1 | 7.9 | 2.7 | 3.0 | 11.0 | -0.2 | -0.0 | -0.5 | 5.4 | Burundi |
| Cape Verde | 4.0b/ | -5.7 | -26.3 | -7.5 | -11.5 | 21.6 | 1.5 | 3.9b/ | -5.9 | -26.9 | -7.6 | -11.6 | 22.0 | 1.5 | Cap-Vert |
| Central African Rep. | 2.1 | 1.9 | -0.1 | 3.9 | -3.1 | 5.1 | 3.8 | 2.1 | 1.4 | 0.6 | 2.6 | -1.8 | 2.9 | 2.6 | Rép. centrafricaine |
| Chad | 1.6 | 1.7 | -6.9 | 4.1 | 6.4 | -11.9 | 19.9 | 1.5 | 1.5 | -6.4 | 2.0 | 4.4 | -9.9 | 20.0 | Tchad |
| Comoros | 2.2b/ | 1.5 | -4.1 | 4.3 | 4.3 | -0.3 | 3.5 | 2.4b/ | 1.4 | -4.3 | 4.1 | 4.3 | -0.4 | 3.3 | Comores |
| Democratic Yemen | 2.3 | 0.8 | 1.9 | -5.2 | 7.0 | 0.2 | 0.6 | 2.6 | 0.5 | 1.8 | -5.4 | 5.4 | 0.3 | 0.6 | Yémen démocratique |
| Djibouti | .. | .. | | | | | | .. | .. | | | | | | Djibouti |
| Equatorial Guinea | 1.5 | 0.5 | -0.3 | 8.4 | -5.5 | -4.6 | 5.5 | 1.5 | 0.1 | -1.0 | 9.4 | -6.6 | -6.3 | 5.7 | Guineé équatoriale |
| Ethiopia | -2.4 | 8.1 | 32.3 | 18.9 | -30.2 | 9.4 | 23.0 | -2.6 | 8.1 | 31.5 | 19.4 | -30.1 | 9.0 | 23.1 | Ethiopie |
| Gambia | -0.6 | 3.1 | 10.5 | 1.3 | -1.8 | 1.6 | 4.3 | 0.6 | 3.2 | 11.1 | 1.3 | -1.9 | 1.6 | 4.6 | Gambie |
| Guinea | 1.8 | 7.9 | 21.3 | 17.6 | -14.9 | 1.6 | 1.8 | 1.5 | 7.9 | 21.4 | 17.7 | -14.9 | 18.4 | 1.8 | Guinée |
| Guinea-Bissau | 1.4 | 0.4 | 1.2 | 2.3 | 1.9 | 18.4 | -5.1 | 1.5 | 6.6 | 1.2 | 1.8 | 0.9 | 3.1 | -5.7 | Guinée-Bissau |
| Haiti | 2.1 | 6.6 | 8.9 | 0.4 | 0.7 | 16.6 | 7.3 | 2.1 | 6.6 | 9.0 | 0.1 | 0.7 | 16.6 | 7.0 | Haïti |
| Lao People's Dem.Rep. | 0.7 | 2.6 | 2.3 | -9.5 | 7.2 | 1.7 | 12.5 | 1.3 | 2.6 | 2.4 | -10.4 | 6.8 | 1.9 | 13.8 | Rép. dém. pop. lao |
| Lesotho | 3.5 | 3.0 | 4.3 | 6.5 | -1.0 | 1.7 | 3.9 | 2.7 | 2.2 | 4.4 | 4.3 | -0.8 | 0.4 | 3.0 | Lesotho |
| Malawi | 1.6b/ | 2.6 | 0.7 | 4.2 | 5.0 | 0.6 | 2.4 | 1.6b/ | 2.6 | 0.7 | 4.2 | 5.0 | 0.6 | 2.4 | Malawi |
| Maldives | 3.0 | 2.8 | 8.9 | 3.8 | -4.6 | -2.0 | 8.6 | 2.6 | 2.8 | 11.0 | 4.2 | -5.8 | -2.4 | 8.2 | Maldives |
| Mali | 0.9 | 2.6 | 3.0 | -7.3 | 17.9 | -0.6 | 1.8 | 0.9 | 2.9 | 3.4 | -7.0 | 18.2 | -0.3 | 1.7 | Mali |
| Nepal | 3.7 | 0.8 | -0.8 | -0.4 | 2.1 | -18.9 | 27.4 | 3.7 | 0.8 | -0.8 | -0.5 | 2.1 | -18.9 | 27.5 | Népal |
| Niger | 4.4 | 1.9 | 10.0 | 3.6 | 7.4 | -16.2 | 7.0 | 4.1 | 1.4 | 8.0 | 5.6 | 7.0 | -18.5 | 7.7 | Niger |
| Rwanda | 2.3b/ | -0.1 | 0.8 | -2.4 | -1.3 | 3.6 | -1.2 | 2.4b/ | -0.1 | 0.9 | -2.5 | -1.4 | 3.8 | -1.2 | Rwanda |
| Samoa | -4.3b/ | -0.9 | 7.3 | -7.5 | 1.2 | -7.7 | 3.2 | -4.3b/ | -0.9 | 7.4 | -7.6 | 1.2 | -7.7 | 3.2 | Samoa |
| Sao Tome and Principe | 1.6 | 1.3 | 0.4 | 9.6 | 1.5 | -11.4 | 7.6 | 1.3 | 1.4 | 1.0 | 10.3 | 3.0 | -13.7 | 8.0 | Sao Tomé-et-Principe |
| Sierra Leone | 0.6 | 0.4 | 0.6 | 4.1 | -4.6 | 0.1 | 1.9 | 0.7 | 0.4 | 0.7 | 4.3 | -4.6 | -0.1 | 1.9 | Sierra Leone |
| Somalia | 2.1 | 5.3 | 13.1 | -7.1 | 3.1 | -6.0 | 27.2 | 3.2 | 5.0 | 15.0 | -9.9 | -4.6 | -7.5 | 31.8 | Somalie |
| Sudan | 1.1 | 1.2 | 1.5 | -2.3 | -1.7 | 5.4 | 3.6 | 1.2 | 0.8 | 1.5 | -2.5 | -1.6 | 6.8 | 0.1 | Soudan |
| Togo | -0.4 | 6.4 | 11.1 | 10.3 | 5.2 | -0.3 | 6.0 | 0.4 | 6.3 | 12.1 | 9.3 | 5.1 | -1.0 | 6.2 | Togo |
| Uganda | 3.8 | 1.6 | 2.9 | -4.0 | 3.0 | 5.0 | 1.6 | 4.9 | 2.1 | 2.9 | -2.5 | 3.4 | 4.9 | 1.8 | Ouganda |
| Un. Rep. of Tanzania | 3.8 | 5.2 | 24.9 | -14.2 | 4.8 | 13.4 | 0.9 | 3.9 | 5.3 | 25.1 | -13.8 | 4.5 | 13.8 | 0.9 | Rép.-Un. de Tanzanie |
| Vanuatu | 3.4 | 1.8 | 5.2 | 2.0 | -9.1 | 3.3 | 8.4 | 3.0 | 1.8 | 5.3 | 2.0 | -9.3 | 3.4 | 8.6 | Vanuatu |
| Yemen | | | | | | | | | | | | | | | Yémen |
| All LDCs | 1.8 | 2.4 | 3.1 | 2.2 | 1.7 | -0.8 | 5.8 | 2.1 | 2.1 | 3.5 | 1.7 | 1.0 | -1.2 | 5.6 | Ensemble des PMA |
| All developing countries | 2.9 | 2.9 | 5.0 | 1.0 | 2.7 | 1.9 | 3.9 | 3.1 | 2.9 | 4.9 | 1.7 | 2.7 | 1.6 | 3.5 | Ensemble des pays en développement |

Source: UNCTAD secretariat calculations, based on data from FAO.
a/ Exponential trend function.
b/ 1973-1980.

Source: Chiffres calculés par le secrétariat de la CNUCED, d'après des données de la FAO.
a/ Fonction exponentielle de tendance.
b/ 1973-1980.

Table 4
The agricultural sector

| Country | Labor force (% in agri.) Main d'oeuvre (% dans l'agri.) 1984 | % share of agri. in GDP Part en % de l'agri. dans le PIB 1984 | Agricultural production Annual average growth rates per capita (%) Production agricole Taux annuels moyens d'accroissement par habitant (%) | | | | | |
|---|---|---|---|---|---|---|---|---|
| | | | 1970-1980a/ | 1980-1981 | 1981-1982 | 1982-1983 | 1983-1984 | 1984-1985 |
| Afghanistan | 76 | (59) | -0.1 | -0.4 | -2.5 | -0.2 | -2.7 | -2.3 |
| Bangladesh | 82 | 48 | -0.3 | -2.2 | 1.2 | 0.7 | -1.9 | 0.4 |
| Benin | 44 | 43 | -0.3 | -2.6 | -0.1 | 0.6 | 15.2 | 10.0 |
| Bhutan | 93 | 50 | 0.5 | -0.4 | 0.6 | 0.8 | 0.1 | 0.3 |
| Botswana | 77 | 6 | -6.0 | 14.2 | -4.3 | -9.6 | -5.5 | 1.5 |
| Burkina Faso | 79 | 42 | -0.7 | 4.6 | -3.2 | -4.3 | -3.9 | 16.8 |
| Burundi | 81 | 58 b/ | 0.8 | 15.6 | -10.0 | 2.2 | -5.7 | 5.1 |
| Cape Verde | 54 | 20 | 3.1f/ | -27.9 | -9.3 | -13.1 | 19.3 | -0.4 |
| Central Afr.Rep. | 85 | 39 | 0.0 | -2.3 | 1.6 | -5.3 | 2.8 | 1.5 |
| Chad | 80 | 45 | -0.4 | -9.1 | 1.7 | 4.0 | -13.8 | 17.3 |
| Comoros | 62 | 43 | -1.2f/ | -7.3 | 1.2 | 1.1 | -3.1 | 0.4 |
| Democratic Yemen | 56 | 10 | 0.0 | -1.0 | -7.9 | 4.1 | -2.4 | -2.0 |
| Djibouti | (2) | 6 | .. | .. | .. | .. | .. | .. |
| Eq. Guinea | 72 | 43 | .. | .. | .. | .. | .. | .. |
| Ethiopia | 77 | 48 b/ | -1.1 | -2.9 | 5.5 | -8.0 | -7.2 | 2.7 |
| Gambia | 76 | 32 | -5.8 | 29.3 | 16.2 | -31.7 | 7.1 | 20.2 |
| Guinea | 78 | 41 | -1.5 | 7.9 | -1.0 | -4.0 | -0.7 | 2.1 |
| Guinea-Bissau | 80 | 43 b/ | -2.5 | 19.0 | 15.4 | -16.5 | 16.2 | -0.0 |
| Haiti | 63 | (32) | 0.0 | -0.2 | 0.9 | 0.6 | 0.5 | -6.4 |
| Lao P.D.R. | 72 | (60) | 0.2 | 6.6 | -1.8 | -1.5 | 14.0 | 5.0 |
| Lesotho | 81 | 17 | -1.6 | -0.4 | -11.8 | 4.5 | -0.7 | 9.8 |
| Malawi | 81 | 37 | 0.7 | 0.9 | 3.1 | -4.1 | -1.3 | 0.9 |
| Maldives | 54 b/ | 29 | -1.4f/ | -2.3 | 1.1 | 1.9 | -2.4 | -0.7 |
| Mali | 85 | 52 | 0.8 | 5.7 | 0.9 | -7.2 | -4.6 | 5.8 |
| Nepal | 92 | 56 b/ | -1.5 | 0.6 | -9.5 | 15.2 | -2.9 | -0.5 |
| Niger | 85 | 47 | 1.2 | -3.8 | -3.3 | -0.7 | -21.1 | 24.1 |
| Rwanda | 88 | 43 | 1.1 | 6.5 | 0.3 | 3.9 | -18.9 | 3.4 |
| Samoa | 75b/c/ | 51 b/ | 1.7f/ | 0.2 | -3.0 | -1.9 | 3.0 | -1.8 |
| Sao Tome & Prin. | (56) | 26 | -5.5f/ | 4.9 | -9.6 | -2.1 | -9.6 | 0.0 |
| Sierra Leone | 62 | 35 | 0.1 | -1.4 | 7.6 | -0.3 | -12.9 | 5.8 |
| Somalia | 78 | 50 d/ | -2.3 | -2.2 | 1.5 | -7.3 | -2.7 | -0.9 |
| Sudan | 74 | 30 | -0.9 | 9.7 | -9.8 | 0.2 | -8.6 | 23.8 |
| Togo | 66 | 32 | -1.2 | -1.6 | -5.2 | -4.6 | 2.4 | 0.7 |
| Uganda | 78 | 82 e/ | -3.2 | 7.5 | 6.7 | 1.8 | -3.6 | 2.5 |
| U.R. of Tanzania | 79 | 55 | 0.4 | -0.5 | -7.2 | -0.5 | 1.5 | -1.8 |
| Vanuatu | (79) | .. | 0.8 | 21.5 | -16.5 | 2.0 | 10.3 | -1.8 |
| Yemen | 73 | 24 | 0.4 | 2.6 | -0.6 | -11.4 | 0.8 | 5.7 |
| All LDCs | 79 | 45 | -0.8 | 0.5 | -0.5 | -0.9 | -3.2 | 3.2 |
| All developing countries | 56 | 17 b/ | 0.5 | 2.5 | -1.4 | 0.4 | -0.4 | 1.6 |

Source: UNCTAD secretariat calculations based on data from FAO, the Economic Commission for Africa, the World Bank and other international and national sources.

a/ Exponential trend function.
b/ 1983.
c/ In subsistence agriculture.
d/ 1982.
e/ 1981.
f/ 1973-1980.

Tableau 4
Le secteur agricole

| Food production<br>Annual average growth rates<br>per capita (%)<br><br>Production vivrière<br>Taux annuels moyens d'accroissement<br>par habitant (%) | | | | | | Pays |
| 1970-<br>1980a/ | 1980-<br>1981 | 1981-<br>1982 | 1982-<br>1983 | 1983-<br>1984 | 1984-<br>1985 | |
|---|---|---|---|---|---|---|
| -0.3 | -0.1 | -2.0 | -0.8 | -3.0 | -2.3 | Afghanistan |
| -0.2 | -2.0 | 1.1 | 0.5 | -1.2 | -0.9 | Bangladesh |
| -0.1 | -3.1 | -0.8 | 0.3 | 13.7 | 9.7 | Bénin |
| 0.4 | -0.4 | 0.6 | 0.8 | 0.1 | 0.3 | Bhoutan |
| -6.0 | 14.4 | -4.3 | -9.6 | -5.5 | 1.5 | Botswana |
| -0.8 | 5.4 | -3.0 | -5.2 | -4.1 | 17.7 | Burkina Faso |
| 1.0 | 7.7 | -3.0 | -2.8 | -3.2 | 2.6 | Burundi |
| 3.0f/ | -28.4 | -9.4 | -13.3 | 19.7 | -0.3 | Cap-Vert |
| 0.0 | -1.8 | 0.3 | -4.0 | 0.7 | 0.3 | Rép. centrafricaine |
| -0.1 | -8.6 | -0.3 | 2.0 | -11.9 | 17.4 | Tchad |
| -1.0f/ | -7.4 | 1.1 | 1.1 | -3.1 | 0.3 | Comores |
| 0.3 | -1.1 | -8.1 | 2.6 | -2.4 | -2.0 | Yémen démocratique |
| .. | .. | .. | .. | .. | .. | Djibouti |
| .. | .. | .. | .. | .. | .. | Guineé équatoriale |
| -1.2 | -3.6 | 6.5 | -9.1 | -8.8 | 3.0 | Ethiopie |
| -5.9 | 28.5 | 16.8 | -31.6 | 6.7 | 20.4 | Gambie |
| -1.5 | 8.4 | -1.1 | -4.1 | -0.7 | 2.3 | Guinée |
| -2.4 | 19.0 | 15.4 | -16.5 | 16.2 | -0.0 | Guinée-Bissau |
| 0.0 | -0.2 | -1.3 | 0.4 | 1.7 | -7.0 | Haïti |
| 0.2 | 6.6 | -2.0 | -1.2 | 14.1 | 4.7 | Rép. dém. pop. lao |
| -1.0 | -0.3 | -12.7 | 4.1 | -0.5 | 11.0 | Lesotho |
| -0.1 | 1.1 | 1.0 | -3.8 | -2.6 | 0.1 | Malawi |
| -1.4f/ | -2.3 | 1.1 | 1.9 | -2.4 | -0.7 | Maldives |
| 0.5 | 7.8 | 1.2 | -8.4 | -5.1 | 5.4 | Mali |
| -1.5 | 0.9 | -9.2 | 15.5 | -2.6 | -0.6 | Népal |
| 1.2 | -3.7 | -3.3 | -0.8 | -21.1 | 24.1 | Niger |
| 0.8 | 4.6 | 2.2 | 3.5 | -21.2 | 4.0 | Rwanda |
| 1.7f/ | 0.3 | -3.1 | -2.0 | 3.2 | -1.8 | Samoa |
| -5.5f/ | 4.9 | -9.7 | -2.1 | -9.7 | 0.0 | Sao Tomé-et-Principe |
| -0.2 | -0.9 | 8.3 | 1.2 | -15.2 | 6.2 | Sierra Leone |
| -2.3 | -2.1 | 1.4 | -7.2 | -2.7 | -0.9 | Somalie |
| 0.2 | 11.5 | -12.5 | -1.8 | -10.1 | 28.3 | Soudan |
| -1.2 | -1.6 | -5.4 | -4.5 | 3.8 | -2.6 | Togo |
| -2.4 | 8.5 | 5.7 | 1.7 | -4.2 | 2.6 | Ouganda |
| 1.5 | -0.5 | -5.8 | 0.0 | 1.4 | -1.6 | Rép.-Un. de Tanzanie |
| 0.9 | 21.7 | -16.2 | 1.6 | 10.7 | -1.9 | Vanuatu |
| 0.0 | 2.6 | -0.6 | -11.6 | 0.8 | 5.9 | Yémen |
| -0.5 | 0.9 | -0.9 | -1.5 | -3.7 | 3.0 | Ensemble des PMA |
| 0.7 | 2.4 | -0.7 | 0.4 | -0.7 | 1.2 | Ensemble des pays<br>en développement |

Source: Chiffres calculés par le secrétariat de la CNUCED, d'après
des données de la FAO, de la Commission économique pour
l'Afrique, de la Banque Mondiale, et d'autres sources
internationales et nationales.

a/ Fonction exponentielle de tendance.
b/ 1983.
c/ Dans l'agriculture de subsistence.
d/ 1982.
e/ 1981.
f/ 1973-1980.

Table 5
The manufacturing sector

Tableau 5
Le secteur manufacturier

| Country | % share in GDP 1984 / Part en % dans le PIB 1984 | 1970-1980 b/ | 1980-1984 | 1980-1981 | 1981-1982 | 1982-1983 | 1983-1984 | Pays |
|---|---|---|---|---|---|---|---|---|
| | | Annual average growth rates a/ / Taux annuels moyens d'accroissement a/ | | | | | | |
| Afghanistan c/ | (28) | 3.2 | 4.5 | -1.7 | 3.2 | 11.8 | 5.3 | Afghanistan c/ |
| Bangladesh | 9 | 11.8 | 2.2 | 5.4 | 1.5 | -1.6 | 3.7 | Bangladesh |
| Benin | 10 | 2.3 g/ | 24.2 | 29.3 | 5.9 | 39.7 | 24.4 | Bénin |
| Bhutan | 4 | .. | .. | .. | .. | .. | .. | Bhoutan |
| Botswana | 7 | 13.3 | 8.2 | 26.7 | 23.8 | -7.4 | -5.7 | Botswana |
| Burkina Faso | 15 | 5.1 | 2.8 | 0.5 | 8.1 | 3.7 | -0.9 | Burkina Faso |
| Burundi | 9 d/ | 3.7 | 5.7 h/ | 14.1 | -2.9 | 6.6 | | Burundi |
| Cape Verde | 5 | 1.6 | 4.7 | 6.9 | 4.3 | 2.9 | 4.8 | Cap-Vert |
| Central African Rep. | 8 | -9.2 | -3.2 | -9.8 | -5.4 | 1.4 | 1.4 | Rép. centrafricaine |
| Chad | 9 | -0.5 | -8.1 | -12.6 | -6.8 | -7.6 | -5.2 | Tchad |
| Comoros | 6 | -4.9 | 5.0 | 6.5 | 5.0 | 4.0 | 4.5 | Comores |
| Democratic Yemen | 11 | .. | 4.4 i/ | 22.6 | -11.2 | | | Yémen démocratique |
| Djibouti | 10 | 6.3 | 0.6 | -0.3 | 3.3 | 0.9 | -1.6 | Djibouti |
| Equatorial Guinea | 5 | .. | 1.7 | 3.7 | 3.3 | -6.4 | 6.8 | Guineé équatoriale |
| Ethiopia | 11 d/ | 2.3 | 4.1 h/ | 4.1 | 3.4 | 4.9 | | Ethiopie |
| Gambia | 10 | .. | 11.2 c/ | 47.7 c/ | 7.6 c/ | -4.6 c/ | 1.0 c/ | Gambie |
| Guinea | 2 | 0.8 | 0.6 h/ | 0.8 | -2.0 | 3.0 | | Guinée |
| Guinea-Bissau | 4 d/ | 2.1 | -6.0 h/ | -4.0 | 7.9 | -19.9 | | Guinée-Bissau |
| Haiti | (17) | 8.5 | -3.1 | -11.6 | -3.9 | 5.6 | -1.6 | Haïti |
| Lao People's Dem.Rep. c/ | (7) | | 2.2 | -7.6 | 17.4 | -0.7 | 1.1 | Rép. dém. pop. lao c/ |
| Lesotho | 7 | 17.3 | 3.7 | -3.4 | 27.5 | -25.4 | 25.9 | Lesotho |
| Malawi | 12 | 6.0 | 3.3 | 3.4 | -0.2 | 7.1 | 3.3 | Malawi |
| Maldives | 5 | .. | 14.6 | 26.2 | 21.9 | 6.3 | 5.5 | Maldives |
| Mali | 7 | .. | .. | .. | .. | .. | | Mali |
| Nepal | 4 d/ | .. | .. | .. | .. | | | Népal |
| Niger | 4 | 1.8 | -1.6 | -4.0 | -1.2 | 7.5 | -8.1 | Niger |
| Rwanda | 18 | 26.7 | 5.5 | 7.5 | 1.3 | 8.7 | 4.7 | Rwanda |
| Samoa | 6 d/ | .. | 9.4 h/ | 7.2 | 3.6 | 17.7 | | Samoa |
| Sao Tome and Principe | 10 | 2.3 | -3.3 | -26.3 | 13.4 | 2.4 | 2.3 | Sao Tomé-et-Principe |
| Sierra Leone | 6 | 4.6 | -3.1 | -3.1 | 1.8 | -4.9 | -5.9 | Sierra Leone |
| Somalia | 6 e/ | 3.1 | -0.8 i/ | -0.8 | -0.7 | | | Somalie |
| Sudan | 9 | 5.7 | 3.3 | 4.0 | 4.1 | 1.6 | 3.4 | Soudan |
| Togo | 7 | -3.1 | -5.2 | 4.4 | 4.2 | -7.4 | -19.7 | Togo |
| Uganda | 4 f/ | -9.1 | -3.6 h/ | -5.4 | 14.2 | 2.8 | | Ouganda |
| Un. Rep. of Tanzania | 7 | 6.0 | -4.7 | -10.7 | -3.0 | -3.4 | -1.4 | Rép.-Unie de Tanzanie |
| Vanuatu | .. | .. | .. | .. | .. | .. | .. | Vanuatu |
| Yemen | 9 | 12.2 | 18.2 | 19.2 | 20.4 | 23.2 | 10.6 | Yémen |
| All LDCs | 9 | (5.3) | (2.6) | (3.0) | (2.7) | (2.4) | (3.0) | Ensemble des PMA |
| All developing countries | 18 d/ | 7.2 | 0.6 h/ | 1.2 | 1.0 | -1.8 | .. | Ensemble des pays en développement |

Table 5 (continued)

Source: UNCTAD secretariat calculations based on data from the United Nations Statistical Office, the Economic Commission for Africa, the World Bank and other international and national sources.

a/ Value-added at constant prices.
b/ Exponential trend function.
c/ Total industry.
d/ 1983.
e/ 1982.
f/ 1981.
g/ 1972-1980.
h/ 1980-1983.
i/ 1980-1982.

Tableau 5 (suite)

Source: Chiffres calculés par le secrétariat de la CNUCED d'après des données du Bureau de statistique des Nations Unies, de la Commission économique pour l'Afrique, de la Banque Mondiale et d'autres sources internationales et nationales.

a/ Valeur ajoutée aux prix constants.
b/ Fonction exponentielle de tendance.
c/ Ensemble des activités industrielles.
d/ 1983.
e/ 1982.
f/ 1981.
g/ 1972-1980.
h/ 1980-1983.
i/ 1980-1982.

Table 6
Investment a/

Tableau 6
Investissement a/

| Country / Pays | Per capita levels ($) Niveaux par habitant ($) 1984 | % share in GDP Part en % dans le PIB 1984 | 1970-1980 c/ | 1980-1984 | 1980-1981 | 1981-1982 | 1982-1983 | 1983-1984 |
|---|---|---|---|---|---|---|---|---|
| | | | Annual average growth rates b/ — Taux annuels moyens d'accroissement b/ | | | | | |
| Afghanistan | .. | .. | 0.3 | .. | .. | .. | .. | 43.1 |
| Bangladesh | 19 | 13 | 8.9 | 7.8 | 2.8 | -5.7 | -2.7 | -42.9 |
| Benin / Bénin | 16 | 7 | .. | -23.1 | 62.2 | 10.2 | -65.9 | .. |
| Bhutan / Bhoutan | .. | .. | .. | .. | .. | .. | .. | .. |
| Botswana | 215 | 21 | 4.6 | -13.8 | 1.8 | -3.5 | -31.2 | -18.2 |
| Burkina Faso | 19 | 14 | 5.2 | -3.0 | -17.2 | -9.8 | 10.8 | 6.7 |
| Burundi | (44) | 21 e/ | 16.2 | 22.0 g/ | 37.6 | -25.0 | 75.8 | .. |
| Cape Verde / Cap-Vert | 83 | 28 | -0.3 | 6.5 | 6.9 | 3.8 | -11.3 | 30.7 |
| Central African Rep. / Rép. centrafricaine | 28 | 12 | -9.7 | 15.9 | 21.7 | -8.9 | 47.8 | 10.3 |
| Chad / Tchad | 8 | 7 | -0.8 | -21.1 | -32.6 | -29.4 | -13.6 | -5.5 |
| Comoros / Comores | 98 | 47 | -1.0 | 10.8 | -16.2 | 1.4 | 11.6 | 58.7 |
| Democratic Yemen / Yémen démocratique | .. | .. | .. | .. | .. | .. | .. | .. |
| Djibouti | 139 | 24 | -1.4 | 7.7 | 27.8 | 10.1 | 1.8 | -6.1 |
| Equatorial Guinea / Guineé équatoriale | 34 | 16 | .. | 1.2 | 5.2 | 3.6 | -7.0 | 3.3 |
| Ethiopia / Ethiopie | 12 e/ | 11 e/ | -1.1 | 4.4 g/ | 3.4 | 9.2 | 0.7 | -32.6 |
| Gambia / Gambie | 46 | 16 | .. | -12.6 | -2.3 | -17.6 | 7.6 | .. |
| Guinea / Guinée | 34 | 10 | -1.4 | -2.7 g/ | -9.1 | -1.3 | 2.8 | .. |
| Guinea-Bissau / Guinée-Bissau | 54 | 30 | -1.7 | 1.0 g/ | -16.5 | 28.1 | -3.6 | .. |
| Haiti / Haïti | 55 | 16 | 13.6 | 0.9 | 0.7 | -6.8 | 5.4 | 4.8 |
| Lao People's Dem.Rep. / Rép. dém. pop. lao | .. | .. | .. | .. | .. | .. | .. | .. |
| Lesotho | 74 | 38 | 23.3 | 3.4 | 2.4 | -2.1 | 4.3 | 9.5 |
| Malawi | 29 | 16 | 3.2 | -5.8 | -32.8 | 33.4 | 14.9 | -23.6 |
| Maldives | 133 | 31 | .. | .. | .. | 0.9 | 62.4 | -6.8 |
| Mali | 42 | 31 | .. | .. | .. | .. | .. | .. |
| Nepal / Népal | 30 | 19 | 23.1 | 6.0 | 4.3 | -0.6 | 18.4 | 3.0 |
| Niger | 42 | 15 | 14.3 | -17.2 | -37.9 | -12.2 | -5.8 | -8.5 |
| Rwanda | 33 | 12 | .. | 2.9 | -6.8 | 14.2 | -4.0 | 9.8 |
| Samoa | 187 | 30 | .. | -13.1 g/ | 5.3 | -33.7 | -5.9 | .. |
| Sao Tome and Principe / Sao Tomé-et-Principe | 103 | 26 | 15.8 | -11.9 | -36.9 | 73.8 | -57.5 | 29.1 |
| Sierra Leone | 25 | 9 | -1.5 | -10.3 g/ | -15.9 | -13.0 | -0.4 | .. |
| Somalia / Somalie | (52) | 20 f/ | -4.7 | 88.3 h/ | 261.8 | -2.0 | .. | .. |
| Sudan / Soudan | 51 | 14. | 10.8 | -4.1 | -4.2 | 9.2 | -17.8 | -1.6 |
| Togo | 55 | 24 | .. | .. | .. | .. | .. | .. |
| Uganda / Ouganda | (18) | 8 e/ | -11.1 | 21.4 h/ | 22.3 | 20.5 | .. | .. |
| Un. Rep. of Tanzania / Rép.-Unie de Tanzanie | 36 | 14 | 2.5 | -6.2 | 12.3 | -4.7 | -19.2 | -10.6 |
| Vanuatu | .. | .. | .. | .. | .. | .. | .. | .. |
| Yemen / Yémen | 100 | 21 | 24.9 | -14.9 | -13.9 | -6.8 | -28.7 | -8.2 |
| All LDCs / Ensemble des PMA d/ | 31 | 15 | 4.6 | -3.8 | -0.4 | -0.8 | -10.8 | 4.0 |
| All developing countries / Ensemble des pays en développement | 209 e/ | 24 e/ | 8.8 | -3.6 g/ | 0.8 | -7.0 | -4.5 | .. |

Table 6 (continued)

Source: UNCTAD secretariat calculations based on data from the United Nations Statistical Office, the Economic Commission for Africa, the World Bank and other international and national sources.

a/ Gross fixed capital formation plus increase in stocks.

b/ Real investment.
c/ Exponential trend function.
d/ Only includes countries for which data are shown above.

e/ 1983.
f/ 1982.
g/ 1980-1983.
h/ 1980-1982.

Tableau 6 (suite)

Source: Chiffres calculés par le secrétariat de la CNUCED d'après des données du Bureau de statistique des Nations Unies, de la Commission économique pour l'Afrique, de la Banque Mondiale et d'autres sources internationales et nationales.

a/ Formation brute de capitale fixe plus variation des stocks.
b/ Investissements réels.
c/ Fonction exponentielle de tendance.
d/ Ne comprend que les pays pour lesquels des données figurent ci-dessus.
e/ 1983.
f/ 1982.
g/ 1980-1983.
h/ 1980-1982.

Table 7

Tableau 7

Exports and imports: basic comparisons

Exportations et importations: comparaisons de base

| Country | Exports in 1984 / Exportations en 1984 | | | Annual average growth rates of purchasing power of exports per capita (%) / Taux moyens de croissance annuelle du pouvoir d'achat des exportations par hab. (%) | | Imports in 1984 / Importations en 1984 | | | Annual average growth rates of import volume per capita (%) / Taux moyens de croissance annuelle des importations par habitant (%) | | Pays |
|---|---|---|---|---|---|---|---|---|---|---|---|
| | Value ($ million) / Valeur (millions de dollars) | % of GDP / En % du PIB | Exports per cap. ($) / Exportations par hab. (dollars) | 1970-1980a/ | 1980-1985 | Value ($ million) / Valeur (millions de dollars) | % of GDP / En % du PIB | Imports per cap. ($) / Importations par hab. (dollars) | 1970-1980a/ | 1980-1985 | |
| Afghanistan | 735 | 21.4b/ | 41.6 | 5.1 | 0.4 | 800 | 23.3b/ | 45.3 | 3.4 | 7.2 | Afghanistan |
| Bangladesh | 934 | 6.7 | 9.7 | -8.9 | 6.9 | 2042 | 14.6 | 21.1 | -0.2 | 4.1 | Bangladesh |
| Benin | 33 | 3.5 | 8.4 | -12.8 | -9.3 | 310 | 32.8 | 79.1 | 2.3 | 3.2 | Bénin |
| Bhutan | .. | .. | .. | .. | .. | .. | .. | .. | .. | .. | Bhoutan |
| Botswana | 674 | 60.5 | 630.5 | 13.6 | 6.6 | 679 | 61.0 | 635.2 | 8.4 | -3.9 | Botswana |
| Burkina Faso | 80 | 8.9 | 11.8 | 2.8 | -5.9 | 211 | 23.3 | 31.1 | 5.7 | -8.8 | Burkina Faso |
| Burundi | 98 | 10.2 | 21.3 | 1.2 | 11.1 | 186 | 19.4 | 40.5 | 5.7 | 2.0 | Burundi |
| Cape Verde | 5 | 5.3 | 15.6 | -9.5 | 5.5 | 84 | 88.8 | 262.5 | -2.7 | 11.6 | Cap-Vert |
| Central African Rep. | 86 | 14.5 | 34.1 | -1.1 | 0.3 | 87 | 14.6 | 34.5 | -5.0 | 8.5 | Rép. centrafricaine |
| Chad | 111 | 19.2 | 22.6 | -1.2 | 2.1 | 171 | 29.6 | 34.8 | -6.8 | 20.4 | Tchad |
| Comoros | 21 | 23.4 | 48.7 | -4.0 | 4.3 | 30 | 33.4 | 69.6 | -5.1 | -2.1 | Comores |
| Democratic Yemen | 645 | 69.0 | 309.8 | 0.9 | -2.4 | 1543 | 165.0 | 741.1 | -0.7 | 14.7 | Yémen démocratique |
| Djibouti | 26 | 12.8 | 73.4 | -20.0 | 6.0 | 110 | 54.1 | 310.7 | -10.2 | -2.9 | Djibouti |
| Equatorial Guinea | 20 | 24.4 | 52.1 | -17.6 | 8.1 | 30 | 36.6 | 78.1 | -19.7 | 3.6 | Guinée équatoriale |
| Ethiopia | 417 | 8.8c/ | 9.9 | -4.6 | -3.6 | 942 | 19.9c/ | 22.4 | -2.5 | 4.4 | Ethiopie |
| Gambia | 47 | 22.9 | 66.0 | -5.1 | 8.4 | 98 | 47.7 | 137.6 | 6.4 | -9.9 | Gambie |
| Guinea | 430 | 20.3 | 72.4 | 10.5 | 2.5 | 360 | 17.0 | 60.6 | 2.1 | 9.8 | Guinée |
| Guinea Bissau | 18 | 11.7 | 20.6 | -2.2 | 5.9 | 48 | 31.2 | 55.0 | -11.0 | 2.7 | Guinée-Bissau |
| Haiti | 179 | 9.8 | 34.4 | 3.6 | -3.1 | 472 | 25.9 | 90.8 | 5.9 | 7.3 | Haïti |
| Lao People's Dem. Rep. | 20 | 2.6 | 5.4 | 2.7 | -0.7 | 145 | 19.1 | 38.8 | -11.7 | 4.7 | Rép. dém. pop. lao |
| Lesotho | 21 | 7.3 | 14.2 | 8.2 | -18.2 | 312 | 108.1 | 210.4 | 12.2 | -11.4 | Lesotho |
| Malawi | 313 | 26.1 | 46.4 | 0.0 | -3.5 | 269 | 22.4 | 39.9 | 0.7 | -9.3 | Malawi |
| Maldives | 25 | 32.8 | 141.8 | -8.3 | 25.9 | 53 | 69.6 | 300.7 | 6.8 | 12.6 | Maldives |
| Mali | 181 | 16.8 | 23.0 | 4.5 | -3.4 | 368 | 34.2 | 46.8 | 6.4 | -1.2 | Mali |
| Nepal | 128 | 5.1 | 7.9 | -5.9 | 15.6 | 416 | 16.6 | 25.8 | 1.6 | 6.6 | Nepal |
| Niger | 228 | 13.7 | 38.3 | 15.3 | -17.7 | 330 | 19.9 | 55.4 | 9.9 | -8.4 | Niger |
| Rwanda | 145 | 8.8 | 24.7 | 3.9 | -0.4 | 295 | 17.8 | 50.3 | 8.3 | -3.0 | Rwanda |
| Samoa | 19 | 19.3 | 119.3 | -1.1 | -0.3 | 50 | 50.7 | 313.9 | 3.4 | -2.0 | Samoa |
| Sao Tome and Principe | 7 | 19.2 | 74.5 | -2.7 | -24.1 | 12 | 32.9 | 127.7 | -4.3 | -7.2 | Sao Tomé-et-Principe |
| Sierra Leone | 148 | 14.8 | 41.8 | -8.3 | -5.1 | 166 | 16.6 | 46.9 | -3.5 | -17.7 | Sierra Leone |
| Somalia | 45 | 3.3 | 8.6 | -1.8 | -7.6 | 109 | 8.0 | 20.8 | 3.3 | -20.3 | Somalie |
| Sudan | 629 | 8.2 | 30.0 | -8.7 | -7.3 | 1147 | 14.9 | 54.7 | 1.7 | -13.4 | Soudan |
| Togo | 191 | 28.6 | 66.3 | 3.9 | -11.3 | 271 | 40.6 | 94.1 | 8.9 | -14.2 | Togo |
| Uganda | 399 | 12.1d/ | 26.7 | -10.2 | 0.6 | 371 | 11.3d/ | 24.8 | -11.7 | 3.7 | Ouganda |
| U.-R. of Tanzania | 377 | 7.0 | 17.5 | -9.3 | -11.9 | 847 | 15.8 | 39.4 | -3.7 | -4.4 | Rép. Unie de Tanzanie |
| Vanuatu | 44 | 53.3e/ | 344.5 | -2.5 | -3.0 | 67 | 81.2e/ | 524.6 | -0.2 | 0.0 | Vanuatu |
| Yemen | 65 | 1.7 | 8.3 | -0.4 | 36.1 | 1655 | 44.3 | 212.5 | 32.5 | -2.7 | Yémen |
| All LDCs | 7544 | 11.5 | 23.4 | -3.2 | -1.3 | 15086 | 23.0 | 46.9 | 1.5 | -0.9 | Ensemble des PMA |
| All developing countriesf/ | 275153 | 22.0c/ | 138.2 | 2.1 | 3.0 | 306099 | 24.5c/ | 153.8 | 2.5 | -1.4 | Ensemble des pays en développementf/ |

Source: UNCTAD secretariat mainly based on UNCTAD Handbook of International Trade and Development Statistics, Supplement 1986.

a/ Exponential trend function. b/ Per cent of GDP in 1981. c/ Per cent of GDP in 1983. d/ Per cent of GNP. e/ Per cent of GDP in 1982. f/ Excluding major petroleum exporters.

Source: Calculs du secrétariat de la CNUCED principalement d'après le "Manuel de statistiques du commerce international et du développement, supplément 1986, de la CNUCED.

a/ Fonction exponentielle de tendance. b/ En pourcentage du PIB en 1981. c/ En pourcentage du PIB en 1983. d/ En pourcentage du PNB. e/ En pourcentage du PIB en 1982. f/ Non compris les principaux pays exportateurs de pétrole.

Table 8 / Tableau 8

Unit value indices of imports : 1970-1985 / Indices de valeur unitaire des importations : 1970-1985

( 1980 = 100 )

| Country | 1970 | 1971 | 1972 | 1973 | 1974 | 1975 | 1976 | 1977 | 1978 | 1979 | 1981 | 1982 | 1983 | 1984 | 1985 | Pays |
|---|---|---|---|---|---|---|---|---|---|---|---|---|---|---|---|---|
| Afghanistan | 29.3 | 31.0 | 33.0 | 40.8 | 53.1 | 55.5 | 56.1 | 61.8 | 68.0 | 84.0 | 95.8 | 91.4 | 87.4 | 86.6 | 86.7 | Afghanistan |
| Bangladesh | 27.5 | 29.0 | 31.4 | 40.0 | 56.0 | 58.2 | 58.0 | 63.7 | 70.2 | 83.1 | 92.7 | 85.7 | 83.3 | 82.0 | 80.8 | Bangladesh |
| Benin | 27.2 | 28.7 | 31.2 | 38.9 | 51.1 | 55.6 | 56.2 | 61.7 | 68.5 | 83.0 | 98.2 | 95.2 | 90.5 | 88.6 | 88.5 | Bénin |
| Burkina Faso | 28.6 | 30.6 | 32.8 | 40.7 | 52.5 | 56.0 | 56.6 | 62.2 | 68.9 | 84.0 | 97.0 | 93.7 | 89.5 | 88.1 | 88.2 | Burkina Faso |
| Central African Rep. | 31.3 | 33.5 | 36.6 | 44.6 | 57.8 | 60.9 | 61.3 | 67.2 | 75.9 | 89.4 | 93.8 | 91.0 | 88.4 | 87.0 | 88.0 | Rép. centrafricaine |
| Chad | 28.1 | 30.2 | 31.6 | 39.2 | 50.4 | 53.6 | 54.5 | 60.0 | 65.8 | 82.5 | 99.2 | 96.4 | 91.2 | 90.3 | 90.5 | Tchad |
| Ethiopia | 21.8 | 23.4 | 25.4 | 31.4 | 44.7 | 48.4 | 49.9 | 54.0 | 58.2 | 74.8 | 104.3 | 100.6 | 94.0 | 91.8 | 91.2 | Ethiopie |
| Gambia | 26.9 | 28.3 | 30.7 | 38.8 | 52.0 | 56.0 | 56.5 | 62.0 | 68.8 | 83.0 | 97.0 | 93.1 | 88.8 | 87.0 | 86.8 | Gambie |
| Malawi | 28.3 | 30.3 | 32.7 | 40.3 | 51.4 | 55.6 | 56.4 | 62.0 | 68.9 | 84.3 | 98.4 | 96.1 | 91.5 | 89.9 | 90.3 | Malawi |
| Mali | 27.6 | 29.5 | 31.6 | 39.3 | 52.4 | 55.1 | 55.8 | 61.5 | 67.4 | 83.5 | 96.9 | 93.0 | 89.0 | 88.2 | 88.1 | Mali |
| Niger | 27.7 | 29.5 | 31.9 | 39.0 | 51.2 | 53.9 | 55.1 | 60.6 | 65.6 | 82.3 | 99.1 | 95.7 | 91.7 | 91.2 | 90.7 | Niger |
| Rwanda | 28.9 | 30.6 | 32.8 | 40.8 | 53.4 | 56.3 | 57.2 | 62.8 | 68.9 | 84.6 | 97.1 | 93.7 | 90.4 | 89.6 | 89.5 | Rwanda |
| Sierra Leone | 24.5 | 26.1 | 28.4 | 35.5 | 47.2 | 50.7 | 51.8 | 56.2 | 61.3 | 77.0 | 101.3 | 97.0 | 91.1 | 88.9 | 88.4 | Sierra Leone |
| Somalia | 27.6 | 29.2 | 31.5 | 40.0 | 53.8 | 57.4 | 57.8 | 63.4 | 70.4 | 86.3 | 96.2 | 92.4 | 88.9 | 87.3 | 87.0 | Somalie |
| Sudan | 27.8 | 29.6 | 32.0 | 40.0 | 54.6 | 59.1 | 59.4 | 65.1 | 73.4 | 86.3 | 95.5 | 92.5 | 89.0 | 86.8 | 87.1 | Soudan |
| Togo | 27.3 | 28.9 | 31.4 | 39.3 | 52.4 | 56.8 | 57.5 | 63.0 | 70.3 | 84.4 | 97.6 | 94.9 | 90.7 | 88.8 | 88.9 | Togo |
| Uganda | 29.6 | 31.7 | 34.0 | 41.4 | 56.4 | 60.2 | 61.0 | 66.8 | 75.4 | 89.6 | 95.3 | 93.6 | 90.8 | 89.3 | 90.4 | Ouganda |
| Un. Rep. of Tanzania | 23.8 | 25.8 | 28.0 | 34.3 | 48.2 | 52.0 | 53.0 | 57.5 | 63.0 | 78.1 | 101.0 | 97.0 | 91.5 | 89.3 | 88.8 | Rép.-Un. de Tanzanie |
| All LDCs a/ | 26.7 | 28.5 | 30.5 | 38.2 | 51.9 | 55.7 | 56.2 | 61.6 | 67.7 | 82.4 | 97.0 | 93.0 | 89.0 | 87.1 | 86.9 | Ensemble des PMA a/ |
| All developing countries b/ | 22.0 | 23.7 | 25.4 | 31.6 | 46.1 | 49.7 | 50.9 | 55.5 | 59.7 | 75.9 | 102.2 | 97.8 | 92.1 | 90.2 | 89.5 | Ensemble des pays en développement b/ |
| All developing countries c/ | 23.5 | 25.3 | 27.4 | 34.3 | 48.5 | 53.1 | 54.4 | 59.8 | 65.4 | 80.2 | 99.1 | 95.3 | 91.0 | 89.1 | 88.9 | Ensemble des pays en développement c/ |

Source: UNCTAD secretariat estimates.

a/ This index is based on the indices for individual countries shown above. It has been applied to obtain the data on import volume, export purchasing power and aid in constant prices in the case of individual LDCs for which such index was not available.

b/ Excluding major petroleum exporters.

c/ Including major petroleum exporters.

Source: Estimations du secrétariat de la CNUCED.

a/ Cet indice est basé sur les indices pour les pays individuels qui figurent ci-dessus. On l'a utilisé pour obtenir les données concernant le volume des importations, le pouvoir d'achat des exportations et l'aide en prix constants dans les cas des PMA pour lesquels un tel indice n'était pas disponible.

b/ Non compris les principaux pays exportateurs de pétrole.

c/ Y compris les principaux pays exportateurs de pétrole.

Table 9
Export value and purchasing power : annual average growth rates 1970-1985

Tableau 9
Valeur et pouvoir d'achat des exportations : taux annuels moyens d'accroissement 1970-1985

Percentages — En pourcentage

| Country | Export value / Valeur des exportations | | | | | | Purchasing power of exports / Pouvoir d'achat des exportations | | | | | | Pays |
|---|---|---|---|---|---|---|---|---|---|---|---|---|---|
| | 1970-1980a/ | 1980-1981 | 1981-1982 | 1982-1983 | 1983-1984 | 1984-1985 | 1970-1980a/ | 1980-1981 | 1981-1982 | 1982-1983 | 1983-1984 | 1984-1985 | |
| Afghanistan | 21.4 | -1.6 | 2.0 | 3.1 | 0.7 | -3.4 | 7.7 | 2.8 | 6.9 | 7.8 | 1.7 | -3.5 | Afghanistan |
| Bangladesh | 6.3 | -10.3 | 0.8 | 3.4 | 35.4 | -0.7 | -6.4 | -3.2 | 8.9 | 6.4 | 37.5 | 0.7 | Bangladesh |
| Benin | 1.8 | -46.0 | -29.4 | 33.3 | 3.1 | 21.2 | -10.5 | -45.0 | -27.2 | 40.3 | 5.4 | 21.3 | Bénin |
| Bhutan | .. | .. | .. | .. | .. | .. | .. | .. | .. | .. | .. | .. | Bhoutan |
| Botswana | 34.4 | -24.9 | 20.9 | 39.2 | 6.0 | 7.9 | 18.0 | -22.6 | 26.2 | 45.4 | 8.2 | 8.1 | Botswana |
| Burkina Faso | 18.4 | -16.7 | -25.3 | 1.8 | 40.4 | -17.5 | 4.8 | -14.1 | -22.6 | 6.5 | 42.6 | -17.6 | Burkina Faso |
| Burundi | 17.2 | 9.2 | 23.9 | -9.1 | 22.5 | 12.2 | 3.0 | 12.6 | 29.4 | -5.0 | 25.1 | 12.5 | Burundi |
| Cape Verde | 4.0 | -25.0 | 33.3 | 25.0 | 0.0 | 0.0 | -8.7 | -22.7 | 39.2 | -30.6 | 2.1 | 0.2 | Cap-Vert |
| Central African Rep. | 13.4 | -31.3 | 38.0 | -31.2 | 14.7 | 33.7 | 0.9 | -26.7 | 42.1 | -29.2 | 16.5 | 32.3 | Rép. centrafricaine |
| Chad | 14.0 | 16.9 | -30.1 | 27.6 | 50.0 | -27.9 | 0.9 | 17.9 | -28.1 | 34.8 | 51.6 | -28.1 | Tchad |
| Comoros | 13.0 | -20.0 | 25.0 | 0.0 | 5.0 | 19.0 | -0.7 | -17.6 | 30.5 | 4.5 | 7.3 | 19.3 | Comores |
| Democratic Yemen | 17.5 | -44.8 | 84.9 | -15.2 | -4.3 | 7.0 | 3.2 | -43.1 | 93.0 | -11.4 | -2.2 | 7.2 | Yémen démocratique |
| Djibouti | -2.6 | 10.5 | -4.8 | 25.0 | 4.0 | 0.0 | -14.4 | 13.9 | -0.6 | 30.6 | 6.2 | 0.2 | Djibouti |
| Equatorial Guinea | -4.4 | 14.3 | 6.2 | 17.6 | 0.0 | 0.0 | -16.0 | 17.8 | 10.9 | 22.9 | 2.1 | 0.2 | Guineé équatoriale |
| Ethiopia | 13.3 | -8.5 | 3.9 | -0.5 | 3.7 | -11.3 | -2.0 | -12.2 | 7.7 | 6.5 | 6.2 | -10.7 | Ethiopie |
| Gambia | 11.9 | -12.9 | 63.0 | 9.1 | -2.1 | -4.3 | -1.7 | -10.2 | 69.7 | 14.4 | -0.0 | -4.0 | Gambie |
| Guinea | 28.5 | 25.6 | -16.3 | -2.4 | 7.5 | 0.0 | 12.8 | 29.5 | -12.7 | 1.9 | 9.8 | 0.2 | Guinée |
| Guinea-Bissau | 16.3 | 27.3 | -14.3 | 91.7 | -21.7 | -22.2 | 2.1 | 31.1 | -10.5 | 100.3 | -20.1 | -22.1 | Guinée-Bissau |
| Haiti | 19.6 | -33.2 | 7.9 | -5.5 | 16.2 | 0.6 | 5.0 | -31.2 | 12.7 | -1.3 | 18.7 | 0.8 | Haïti |
| Lao People's Dem.Rep. | 19.1 | 6.5 | 21.2 | -45.7 | -50.0 | 45.0 | 4.6 | 9.7 | 26.5 | 4.5 | -48.9 | 45.3 | Rép. dém. pop. lao |
| Lesotho | 26.1 | -13.8 | -30.0 | 10.5 | 10.5 | 0.0 | 10.8 | -11.2 | -26.9 | -43.3 | 12.9 | 0.2 | Lesotho |
| Malawi | 16.4 | -5.3 | -8.9 | -6.9 | 36.7 | -19.5 | 2.8 | -3.7 | -6.7 | -2.2 | 39.1 | -19.8 | Malawi |
| Maldives | 7.7 | 10.0 | 27.3 | 35.7 | 31.6 | 28.0 | -5.5 | 13.3 | 32.8 | 41.8 | 34.4 | 28.3 | Maldives |
| Mali | 21.1 | -24.9 | -5.2 | 13.0 | 9.7 | -3.3 | 6.8 | -22.5 | -1.2 | 18.1 | 10.7 | -3.2 | Mali |
| Nepal | 9.8 | 75.0 | -37.1 | 6.8 | 36.2 | 25.8 | -3.5 | 80.3 | -34.4 | 11.6 | 39.1 | 26.1 | Népal |
| Niger | 33.8 | -19.6 | -26.8 | -13.5 | -20.8 | -2.2 | 18.2 | -18.9 | -24.2 | -19.7 | -20.4 | -1.6 | Niger |
| Rwanda | 21.3 | -1.8 | -6.4 | 17.5 | 19.8 | -20.0 | 7.3 | 1.1 | -3.0 | 21.8 | 20.8 | -19.8 | Rwanda |
| Samoa | 13.3 | -35.3 | 18.2 | 46.2 | 0.0 | -21.1 | -0.5 | -33.3 | 23.4 | 52.7 | 2.1 | -20.9 | Samoa |
| Sao Tome and Principe | 12.4 | -30.0 | -35.7 | -33.3 | 16.7 | -28.6 | -1.3 | -27.9 | -32.9 | -30.3 | 19.2 | -28.4 | Sao Tomé-et-Principe |
| Sierra Leone | 6.4 | -25.0 | -41.8 | 3.4 | 60.9 | 2.7 | -6.9 | -26.0 | -39.2 | 10.0 | 64.8 | 3.3 | Sierra Leone |
| Somalia | 15.0 | 14.3 | 30.9 | -49.7 | -55.0 | 100.0 | 1.2 | 18.8 | 36.3 | -47.8 | -54.2 | 100.6 | Somalie |
| Sudan | 7.0 | 21.2 | -24.2 | 25.1 | 0.8 | -40.5 | 6.4 | 26.9 | -21.7 | 30.0 | 3.4 | -40.8 | Soudan |
| Togo | 21.1 | -36.7 | -16.5 | -8.5 | 17.9 | -0.5 | 6.4 | -35.1 | -14.1 | -4.3 | 20.4 | -0.7 | Togo |
| Uganda | 4.6 | -29.9 | 43.4 | 7.2 | 7.3 | -4.8 | -7.6 | -26.4 | 45.9 | 10.6 | 9.0 | -5.9 | Ouganda |
| Un. Rep. of Tanzania | 7.5 | 20.7 | -25.8 | -19.6 | 3.0 | -24.7 | -6.3 | 19.5 | -22.7 | -14.8 | 5.6 | -24.3 | Rép.-Un. de Tanzanie |
| Vanuatu | 14.3 | -8.6 | -28.1 | 26.1 | 51.7 | -31.8 | 0.4 | -5.8 | -25.0 | 31.8 | 55.0 | -31.7 | Vanuatu |
| Yemen | 16.7 | 104.3 | -17.0 | -30.8 | 140.7 | 63.1 | 2.5 | 110.6 | -13.4 | -27.7 | 145.9 | 63.4 | Yémen |
| All LDCs | 13.1 | -10.1 | -1.1 | 0.1 | 9.1 | -4.4 | -0.7 | -7.4 | 3.2 | 4.6 | 11.4 | -4.2 | Ensemble des PMA |
| All developing countries b/ | 20.9 | 5.2 | -4.7 | 3.4 | 12.6 | -0.6 | 4.5 | 2.9 | -0.5 | 9.8 | 14.9 | 0.2 | Ensemble des pays en développement b/ |

For source and notes see table 10 page 15.

Pour la source et les notes se référer au tableau 10 page 15.

Table 10 / Tableau 10
Import value and volume : annual average growth rates 1970-1985
Valeur et volume des importations : taux annuels moyens d'accroissement 1970-1985

Percentages / En pourcentage

| Country | Import value / Valeur des importations | | | | | | Import volume / Volume des importations | | | | | | Pays |
|---|---|---|---|---|---|---|---|---|---|---|---|---|---|
| | 1970-1980a/ | 1980-1981 | 1981-1982 | 1982-1983 | 1983-1984 | 1984-1985 | 1970-1980a/ | 1980-1981 | 1981-1982 | 1982-1983 | 1983-1984 | 1984-1985 | |
| Afghanistan | 19.4 | 12.7 | 11.7 | 12.2 | 2.6 | -3.8 | 5.9 | 17.7 | 17.1 | 17.3 | 3.5 | -3.8 | Afghanistan |
| Bangladesh | 16.4 | -8.1 | -4.2 | -8.6 | 28.7 | 6.3 | 2.5 | -0.9 | 3.6 | -6.0 | 30.7 | 7.9 | Bangladesh |
| Benin | 19.5 | 63.7 | -14.4 | -31.0 | -3.1 | 29.0 | 5.1 | 66.8 | -11.7 | -27.5 | -1.0 | 29.1 | Bénin |
| Bhutan | .. | .. | .. | .. | .. | .. | .. | .. | .. | .. | .. | .. | Bhoutan |
| Botswana | 28.2 | 15.6 | -14.1 | 7.3 | -7.7 | -12.2 | 12.6 | 19.1 | -10.4 | 12.1 | -5.8 | -12.0 | Botswana |
| Burkina Faso | 21.8 | -5.6 | 2.4 | -16.8 | -26.7 | 6.6 | 7.8 | -2.7 | 6.0 | -12.9 | -25.6 | 6.5 | Burkina Faso |
| Burundi | 22.4 | -4.2 | 32.9 | -14.5 | 1.6 | 0.0 | 7.5 | -1.3 | 38.7 | -10.6 | 3.8 | 0.2 | Burundi |
| Cape Verde | 11.8 | 2.9 | 0.0 | 14.3 | 5.0 | 34.5 | -1.8 | 6.1 | 4.4 | 19.4 | 7.3 | 34.8 | Cap-Vert |
| Central African Rep. | 8.9 | 17.3 | 33.7 | -59.1 | 67.3 | 37.9 | -3.1 | 25.1 | 37.7 | -57.9 | 70.0 | 36.4 | Rép. centrafricaine |
| Chad | 7.5 | 45.9 | 0.9 | 44.0 | 8.9 | 11.1 | -4.9 | 47.1 | 3.9 | 52.2 | 10.1 | 10.8 | Tchad |
| Comoros | 11.8 | 3.0 | -5.9 | 0.0 | -6.3 | 0.4 | -1.8 | 6.2 | -1.8 | 4.5 | -4.2 | 0.2 | Comores |
| Democratic Yemen | 15.6 | 3.2 | 137.6 | -7.3 | 4.0 | -16.4 | 6.4 | 6.4 | 148.0 | -3.1 | 6.3 | -16.2 | Yémen démocratique |
| Djibouti | 9.4 | -4.0 | -4.2 | 0.0 | -4.3 | 0.0 | -3.9 | -1.1 | 0.0 | 4.5 | -2.3 | 0.2 | Djibouti |
| Equatorial Guinea | -6.8 | 19.2 | 35.5 | -28.6 | 0.0 | 0.0 | -18.2 | 22.9 | 41.4 | -25.4 | 2.1 | 0.2 | Guineé équatoriale |
| Ethiopia | 15.7 | 2.4 | 6.5 | 11.3 | 7.5 | -0.7 | 0.1 | -1.9 | 10.4 | 19.1 | 10.1 | -0.1 | Ethiopie |
| Gambia | 25.5 | -25.2 | -20.5 | 18.6 | -14.8 | -4.1 | 10.2 | -22.8 | -17.2 | 24.3 | -13.0 | -3.8 | Gambie |
| Guinea | 18.7 | 18.5 | -3.1 | -3.2 | 20.0 | 16.7 | 4.2 | 22.1 | 1.1 | 1.1 | 22.6 | 16.9 | Guinée |
| Guinea-Bissau | 5.8 | -9.1 | 0.0 | 30.0 | -26.2 | 25.0 | -7.1 | -6.3 | 4.4 | 35.8 | -24.6 | 25.3 | Guinée-Bissau |
| Haiti | 22.3 | 26.6 | -13.6 | 13.7 | 7.3 | -0.4 | 7.4 | 30.4 | -9.8 | 18.8 | 9.6 | -0.2 | Haïti |
| Lao People's Dem.Rep. | 2.4 | -4.6 | 4.0 | 7.7 | 3.6 | 10.3 | -10.0 | -1.7 | 8.6 | 12.5 | 5.8 | 10.6 | Rép. dém. pop. lao |
| Lesotho | 30.8 | 13.8 | -0.2 | 11.4 | -46.8 | -19.9 | 14.8 | 17.3 | 4.2 | 16.4 | -45.7 | -19.7 | Lesotho |
| Malawi | 17.1 | -20.5 | -11.1 | 0.0 | -13.5 | 5.6 | 3.5 | -19.1 | -9.1 | 5.1 | -12.0 | 5.1 | Malawi |
| Maldives | 25.3 | 6.9 | 38.7 | 32.6 | -7.0 | 0.0 | 10.1 | 10.1 | 44.8 | 38.5 | -5.0 | 0.2 | Maldives |
| Mali | 23.2 | -12.5 | -13.8 | 3.9 | 6.7 | 14.4 | 8.6 | -9.7 | -10.1 | 8.6 | 7.6 | 14.5 | Mali |
| Nepal | 18.6 | 7.9 | 7.0 | 17.5 | -10.3 | 10.6 | 4.2 | 11.2 | 11.7 | 22.7 | -8.4 | 10.8 | Népal |
| Niger | 27.5 | -14.1 | -13.3 | -20.8 | -5.7 | 21.2 | 12.6 | -13.4 | -10.3 | -17.3 | -5.2 | 21.9 | Niger |
| Rwanda | 26.4 | 5.3 | 7.8 | -2.5 | 9.7 | -25.4 | 11.8 | 8.5 | 11.7 | 1.1 | 10.6 | -25.3 | Rwanda |
| Samoa | 18.5 | 6.3 | -25.4 | 12.0 | -10.7 | 2.0 | 4.1 | 9.6 | -22.1 | 17.0 | -8.8 | 2.2 | Samoa |
| Sao Tome and Principe | 10.5 | -10.5 | -11.8 | -33.3 | 20.0 | 8.3 | -2.9 | -7.8 | -7.9 | -30.3 | 22.6 | 8.6 | Sao Tomé-et-Principe |
| Sierra Leone | 12.0 | -24.6 | -23.1 | -30.8 | 0.0 | -9.0 | -2.0 | -25.6 | -19.6 | -26.4 | 2.4 | -8.5 | Sierra Leone |
| Somalia | 21.0 | 47.1 | -35.5 | -45.8 | -39.1 | -2.8 | 6.5 | 53.0 | -32.9 | -43.7 | -38.0 | 3.0 | Somalie |
| Sudan | 19.2 | 0.1 | -18.6 | 5.4 | -15.3 | -32.8 | 11.5 | 4.9 | -16.0 | 9.5 | -13.1 | -33.0 | Soudan |
| Togo | 26.9 | -20.9 | -10.1 | -27.4 | -4.6 | -2.6 | -9.1 | -18.9 | -7.6 | -24.0 | -2.5 | -2.7 | Togo |
| Uganda | 2.9 | 32.4 | 10.1 | 0.2 | -13.3 | 1.1 | -0.5 | 39.0 | 12.0 | 3.4 | -11.9 | -0.2 | Ouganda |
| Un. Rep. of Tanzania | 14.2 | -1.1 | -6.7 | -27.3 | 3.0 | 21.4 | 2.8 | -2.1 | -2.8 | -23.0 | 5.6 | 22.0 | Rép.-Un. de Tanzanie |
| Vanuatu | 17.1 | -18.3 | 1.7 | 6.8 | 6.3 | 6.0 | 2.8 | -15.8 | 6.2 | 11.6 | 8.6 | 6.2 | Vanuatu |
| Yemen | 55.3 | -5.1 | -13.5 | 4.7 | 3.9 | -3.4 | 36.4 | -2.2 | -9.7 | 9.4 | 6.1 | -3.2 | Yémen |
| All LDCs | 18.7 | 1.2 | -1.3 | -4.2 | -0.2 | -1.3 | 4.2 | 4.2 | 3.0 | 0.2 | 1.9 | -1.1 | Ensemble des PMA |
| All developing countries b/ | 21.3 | 5.7 | -7.9 | -3.1 | 3.6 | -4.8 | 4.9 | 3.4 | -3.7 | 2.9 | 5.8 | -4.0 | Ensemble des pays en développement b/ |

Source: UNCTAD secretariat calculations, based on UNCTAD Handbook of International Trade and Development Statistics, Supplement 1986.
a/ Exponential trend function.
b/ Excluding major petroleum exporters.

Source: Calculs du secrétariat de la CNUCED, d'après le Manuel de statistiques du Commerce International et du Développement. Supplément 1986, de la CNUCED.
a/ Fonction exponentielle de tendance.
b/ Non compris les principaux pays exportateurs de pétrole.

Table 11 / Tableau 11

Commodity structure of exports of LDCs by main category (1984 or latest year available)
Composition des exportations des PMA, par principales catégories de produits (1984 ou année disponible la plus récente)

| Country / SITC | Year / Année | Total value ($ million) / Valeur totale (million de $) | All food items / Produits alimentaires (0+1+22+4) | Agricultural raw materials / Matières premières d'origine agricole (2-22-27-28) | Fuels / Combustibles (3) | Ores and metals / Minerais et métaux (27+28+67+68) | Manufactured goods / Produits manufacturés (5+6+7+8-67-68) | Un-allocated / Non-distribués (9) | Memo item: Textiles fibres, yarn and clothing / Fibres textiles, filés, tissus et vêtements (26+65+84) | Pays / CTCI |
|---|---|---|---|---|---|---|---|---|---|---|
| Afghanistan | 1983 | 730 | 30.5 | 9.6 | 45.5 | - | 10.5a/ | 3.9 | 12.8 | Afghanistan |
| Bangladesh | 1985 | 927 | 17.9 | 13.3 | 2.6 | - | 65.8b/ | 0.4 | 67.5 | Bangladesh |
| Benin | 1979 | 46 | 70.7 | 12.8 | 2.3 | 0.4 | 10.8 | 3.0 | 13.4 | Bénin |
| Bhutan | 1983 | 14 | 25.2 | 6.8 | 0.0 | - | 46.8 | 21.2 | - | Bhoutan |
| Botswana | 1984 | 674 | 8.7 | 2.0 | 0.0 | 8.4 | 80.4c/ | 0.5 | 4.9 | Botswana |
| Burkina Faso | 1983 | 57 | 33.5 | 56.0 | - | 0.4 | 10.1 | - | 56.8 | Burkina Faso |
| Burundi | 1983 | 80 | 77.0 | 5.3 | - | 1.7 | 11.0 | 4.9 | 1.8 | Burundi |
| Cape Verde | 1984 | 5 | 84.3 | 1.4 | 2.8 | 8.7 | 2.9 | 0.0 | 0.1 | Cap-Vert |
| Central African Rep. | 1983 | 75 | 37.2 | 26.5 | - | 3.1 | 32.6 | 0.5 | 9.2 | Rép. centrafricaine |
| Chad | 1984 | 111 | (18.7) | (81.3) | - | - | - | - | (81.3) | Tchad |
| Comoros | 1983 | 20 | 79.2 | 0.6 | 0.0 | 1.4 | 16.9d/ | 1.8 | 0.1 | Comores |
| Democratic Yemen | 1981 | 430 | 4.0 | 0.8 | 93.4e/ | 0.2 | 1.5 | 0.1 | 0.7 | Yémen démocratique |
| Djibouti | 1983 | 25 | 39.4 | 5.8 | 5.2 | 1.8 | 45.3 | 2.7 | 25.0 | Djibouti |
| Equatorial Guinea | 1984 | 20 | 74.4 | 23.9 | - | - | - | 1.7 | .. | Guinée équatoriale |
| Ethiopia | 1983 | 402 | 73.1 | 14.6 | 0.5 | 0.1 | 10.0 | 1.7 | 1.4 | Ethiopie |
| Gambia | 1983 | 48 | 74.3 | 3.4 | 0.3 | 2.1 | 17.3 | 2.6 | 3.2 | Gambie |
| Guinea | 1983 | 400 | 3.4 | 0.4 | - | 95.0g/ | 0.5 | 0.7 | 0.0 | Guinée |
| Guinea-Bissau | 1983 | 23 | 73.0 | 2.0 | - | 7.8 | 4.9 | 12.2 | 0.1 | Guinée-Bissau |
| Haiti | 1984/85 | 227 | 52.7 | 0.2 | 0.1 | - | 47.1i/ | 0.0 | - | Haïti |
| Lao P.D.R. | 1985 | 29 | (7.6) | (18.0) | (57.4)h/ | 8.8 | .. | (8.2) | .. | Rép. dém. pop. lao |
| Lesotho | 1982 | 35 | 12.1 | 12.1 | 0.1 | 8.8 | 71.5 | 4.2 | 16.0 | Lesotho |
| Malawi | 1983 | 229 | 94.8 | 0.4 | - | 0.3 | 3.2 | 1.3 | 2.6 | Malawi |
| Maldives | 1983 | 19 | 45.9 | 0.3 | 0.0 | 0.1 | 53.1 | 0.6 | 47.1 | Maldives |
| Mali | 1984 | 181 | 34.7 | 49.8 | - | - | 3.1 | 12.4 | 49.7 | Mali |
| Nepal | 1985 | 161 | 35.1 | 5.6 | - | 0.3 | 59.0 | 0.0 | 45.3 | Népal |
| Niger | 1981 | 455 | 16.3 | 5.6 | 0.9 | 79.8 | 2.1 | 0.1 | 1.2 | Niger |
| Rwanda | 1984 | 145 | 84.4 | 4.7 | 0.1 | 10.1 | 0.7 | 0.5 | 0.0 | Rwanda |
| Samoa | 1983 | 19 | 91.5 | 4.0 | - | 0.4 | 3.7 | - | 0.2 | Samoa |
| Sao Tome & Principe | 1983 | 6 | 91.3 | 2.2 | 0.1 | 0.2 | 6.3 | 0.0 | 1.0 | Sao Tomé-et-Principe |
| Sierra Leone | 1983 | 92 | 32.7 | 0.6 | 3.9 | 33.7 | 29.3c/ | - | 0.1 | Sierra Leone |
| Somalia | 1981 | 152 | 97.5 | 1.9 | 0.2 | 0.0 | 0.4 | - | 0.0 | Somalie |
| Sudan | 1983 | 624 | 53.7 | 40.6 | 1.6 | 0.3 | 2.7 | 1.1 | 26.3 | Soudan |
| Togo | 1981 | 212 | 26.1 | 6.4 | 1.3 | 51.5 | 14.6 | 0.0 | 7.6 | Togo |
| Uganda | 1983 | 372 | 94.5 | 4.4 | 0.4 | 0.0 | 0.6 | 0.1 | 2.9 | Ouganda |
| U.R. of Tanzania | 1982 | 455 | 70.8 | 18.3 | 2.0 | 2.5 | 5.3 | 1.0 | 18.9 | R.-U. de Tanzanie |
| Vanuatu | 1983 | 29 | 96.5 | 2.9 | - | - | 0.6 | - | 4.2 | Vanuatu |
| Yemen | 1983 | 27 | 75.0 | 4.7 | 0.4 | - | 11.6 | 8.2 | 4.2 | Yémen |
| All LDCs | 1984 | | 39.9 | 12.3 | 10.7 | 13.0 | 22.7 | 1.4 | 18.3 | Ensemble des PMA |
| All developing countries f/ | 1984 | 275153 | 20.6 | 5.1 | 19.1 | 8.0 | 45.2 | 2.0 | .. | Ensemble des pays en développement f/ |

Source : UNCTAD Handbook of International Trade and Development Statistics, Supplement 1986; and other international and national sources.

Source : CNUCED, Manuel de statistiques du commerce international et du développement, Supplément 1986, et autres sources internationales et nationales.

a/ Mainly carpets, etc. (SITC 657.5).
b/ Mainly jute fabrics woven (SITC 653.4) and textile products n.e.s. (SITC 656).
c/ Mainly diamonds.
d/ Essential oils (SITC 551.1).
e/ Excluding OPEC countries.
h/ Electricity.
g/ Bauxite and concentrate of aluminium (SITC 287.32).
i/ Mainly sporting goods.

a/ Principalement les tapis, etc. (CTCI 657.5).
b/ Principalement les tissus de jute (CTCI 653.4) et les produits textiles etc. non classés ailleurs (CTCI 656).
c/ Principalement les diamants.
e/ Produits pétroliers.
g/ Bauxite et concentrés d'aluminium (CTCI 287.31) et alumina (CTCI 287.32).
d/ Essences (CTCI 551.1).
f/ non compris les pays de l'OPEP.
h/ Electricité.
i/ Principalement les articles de sport.

Table 12 / Tableau 12

Commodity structure of imports of LDCs by main category (1984 or latest year available)

Composition des importations des PMA, par principales catégories de produits (1984 ou année la plus récente disponible)

| Country | Year | Total value ($mill.) | All food items | Agricultural raw materials | Fuels | Ores and metals | Manufactured goods | Un-allocated | Crude and manufactured fertilizers | Cereals | Transport equipment | Pays |
|---|---|---|---|---|---|---|---|---|---|---|---|---|
| SITC/CTCI | | | 0+1+22+4 | 2-22-27-28 | 3 | 27+28+67+68 | 5+6+7+8 -67-68 | 9 | 271+56 | 04 | 73 | |
| Afghanistan | 1983 | 780 | 12.1 | - | 21.4 | - | 56.3 | 10.2 | 0.5 | - | (30.8) | Afghanistan |
| Bangladesh | 1983 | 1587 | 20.0 | 7.3 | 10.7 | 8.3 | 53.5 | 0.2 | 8.1 | 9.3 | 5.4 | Bangladesh |
| Benin | 1983 | 320 | 14.8 | 2.5 | 5.2 | 1.8 | 75.5 | 0.3 | 0.5 | 3.6 | 5.0 | Bénin |
| Bhutan | 1983 | 36 | 15.3 | - | 23.0 | 3.1 | 48.2 | 10.4 | 0.0 | 6.5 | 16.2 | Bhoutan |
| Botswana | 1984 | 679 | 18.3 | 5.4 | 10.3 | 8.0a/ | 52.9 | 5.1 | 0.2 | 6.3 | 12.8 | Botswana |
| Burkina Faso | 1983 | 288 | 25.5 | 2.1 | 17.1 | 4.1 | 51.2 | - | 2.0 | 10.9 | 11.3 | Burkina Faso |
| Burundi | 1984 | 186 | 14.5 | - | 19.0 | 8.6 | 53.9 | 3.9 | 1.2 | 6.0 | 9.4 | Burundi |
| Cape Verde | 1983 | 80 | 32.6 | 0.8 | 13.9 | 2.2 | 50.3 | 0.2 | 0.0 | 8.5 | 8.4 | Cap-Vert |
| Central African Rep. | 1981 | 95 | 15.9 | 0.6 | 1.5 | 3.5 | 78.0 | 0.5 | 0.0 | 6.2 | 8.4 | Rép.centrafricaine |
| Chad | 1983 | 157 | (18.1) | (1.0) | (1.2) | (1.5) | (77.9) | (0.3) | (4.3) | (9.7) | (21.4) | Tchad |
| Comoros | 1983 | 32 | 22.2 | 1.0 | 7.2 | 3.1 | 61.8 | 4.7 | 0.0 | 14.7 | 13.4 | Comores |
| Democratic Yemen | 1981 | 673 | 20.7 | (1.2) | (44.3) | (1.4) | (32.3) | (0.1) | (0.2) | (7.5) | (4.2) | Yémen démocratique |
| Djibouti | 1983 | 115 | (24.5) | (7.1) | (29.1) | (1.1) | (37.7) | (0.5) | - | (4.2) | (6.7) | Djibouti |
| Equatorial Guinea | 1982 | 42 | 22.9 | 0.1 | 10.4 | 1.6 | 64.8 | 0.2 | 0.2 | 3.3 | 13.2 | Guinée équatoriale |
| Ethiopia | 1982 | 787 | 9.8 | 2.7 | 24.6 | 4.2 | 58.7 | - | 0.8 | 5.6 | 12.2 | Ethiopie |
| Gambia | 1982 | 97 | 28.2 | 2.0 | 9.7 | 3.3 | 56.4 | 0.4 | 0.2 | 6.9 | 14.3 | Gambie |
| Guinea | 1983 | 300 | 12.8 | 0.7 | 29.2 | 2.9 | 53.9 | 0.5 | 0.3 | 5.3 | 7.8 | Guinée |
| Guinea-Bissau | 1983 | 65 | 39.7 | 1.2 | 10.5 | 0.9 | 47.1 | 0.6 | 0.0 | 31.3 | 9.4 | Guinée-Bissau |
| Haiti | 1984/85 | 449 | 28.1 | 2.7 | 14.2 | - | 54.1 | 0.9 | .. | .. | 18.4 | Haïti |
| Lao P.D.R. | 1981 | 125 | (20.8) | (0.1) | (18.9) | (3.6) | (53.5) | (3.1) | (3.3) | (16.2) | (14.1) | Rép.dém.pop. lao |
| Lesotho | 1982 | 527 | 25.1 | 0.4 | 7.6 | 2.8 | 61.5 | 2.6 | 1.5 | 7.1 | 10.0 | Lesotho |
| Malawi | 1981 | 350 | 11.0 | 0.8b/ | 16.9 | 4.3 | 66.7 | 0.3 | 8.3 | 5.5 | 6.6 | Malawi |
| Maldives | 1983 | 57 | 16.9 | 1.7b/ | 25.0 | (2.6) | 52.9 | 1.0 | - | 4.7 | 2.4 d/ | Maldives |
| Mali | 1983 | 345 | 15.4 | 0.7 | 17.6 | 2.6 | 63.1 | 0.4 | 7.0 | 5.4 | 10.0 | Mali |
| Nepal | 1985 | 460 | 14.0 | 2.2 | 11.6 | 7.5 | 64.7 | 0.0 | 4.7 | 0.8 | 5.2 | Népal |
| Niger | 1981 | 510 | 23.5 | 1.3 | 14.8 | 4.0 | 55.5 | 0.8 | 0.4 | 11.8 | 8.1 | Niger |
| Rwanda | 1984 | 295 | 16.5 | 11.6 | 17.0 | 14.0 | 40.8c/ | 0.1 | 0.7 | 5.5 | 8.4 | Rwanda |
| Samoa | 1983 | 56 | 25.2 | 0.7 | 13.1 | 3.1 | 54.9 | 3.0 | 0.8 | 4.0 | 18.3 | Samoa |
| Sao Tome & Principe | 1983 | 10 | 36.3 | 0.5 | 1.8 | 4.4 | 56.8 | 0.2 | 0.1 | 15.3 | 10.7 | Sao Tomé-et-Principe |
| Sierra Leone | 1983 | 166 | 27.6 | 0.9 | 34.7 | 2.2 | 34.2 | 0.4 | 0.3 | 11.4 | 7.0 | Sierra Leone |
| Somalia | 1981 | 512 | 20.3 | 6.3 | 2.2 | 1.5 | 69.0 | 0.7 | 0.3 | 13.3 | 22.2 | Somalie |
| Sudan | 1983 | }1354 | 13.0 | 1.2 | 21.4 | 3.1 | 60.9 | 0.4 | 2.7 | 5.1 | 12.6 | Soudan |
| Togo | 1981 | 435 | 25.7 | 1.7 | 8.4 | 3.1 | 61.1 | .. | 0.2 | 5.2 | 7.3 | Togo |
| Uganda | 1983 | 428 | (13.1) | (0.3) | (27.7) | (2.5) | (56.1) | (0.3) | .. | (3.1) | 11.1 | Ouganda |
| U.R. of Tanzania | 1983 | 822 | (10.1) | (1.1) | (10.8) | (7.3) | (69.4) | (1.3) | (1.4) | (6.3) | (14.4) | R.-U. de Tanzanie |
| Vanuatu | 1983 | 63 | 25.8 | 0.7 | 11.0 | 1.8 | 58.1 | 2.5 | 0.1 | 7.8 | 7.8 | Vanuatu |
| Yemen | 1983 | 1593 | 25.8 | 2.2 | 14.4 | 4.1 | 53.3 | 0.1 | 0.5 | 7.9 | 13.1 | Yémen |
| All LDCs e/ | | | 18.5 | 2.6 | 16.5 | 4.3 | 56.9 | 1.3 | 2.1 | 6.6 | 11.7 | Ensemble des PMA |
| All developing countries e/ | 1984 | 306099 | 11.5 | 3.5 | 21.3 | 6.1 | 54.0 | 3.8 | .. | .. | .. | Ensemble des pays en développement e/ |

Source : UNCTAD Handbook of International Trade and Development Statistics, Supplement 1986, and other international and national sources.

Source : CNUCED, Manuel de statistiques du commerce international et du développement, Supplément 1986, et autres sources internationales et nationales.

a/ Including metal products. / Y compris les produits métalliques.
b/ SITC 2. / CTCI 2.
c/ SITC 5+6+7+8. / CTCI 5+6+7+8.
d/ SITC 7. / CTCI 7.
e/ Excluding OPEC countries. / Non compris les pays de l'OPEP.

Table 13 / Tableau 13

**Main markets for exports of LDCs : relative shares in 1984 (or latest year available)**
**Principaux marchés aux exportations des PMA : parts relatives en 1984 (ou année disponible la plus récente)**

Percentages — En pourcentage

| Country / Pays | Year / Année | Developed market economy countries — Pays développés à économie de marché | | | | | Socialist countries — Pays socialistes | | Developing Countries — Pays en développement | | | Unallocated — Non-distribués |
|---|---|---|---|---|---|---|---|---|---|---|---|---|
| | | Total | EEC / CEE | Japan / Japon | USA and Canada / Etats-Unis et Canada | Other a/ / Autres a/ | Eastern Europe / Europe orientale | Asia / Asie | Total | OPEC / OPEP | Other / Autres | |
| Afghanistan | 1984 | 17.6 | 13.6 | 0.2 | 2.0 | 1.8 | 67.1 | .. | 4.5 | 0.5 | 4.0 | 10.8 |
| Bangladesh | 1985 | 48.8 | 16.9 | 7.2 | 21.9 | 2.8 | 6.0 | 1.2 | 43.9 | 8.7 | 35.2 | 0.1 |
| Benin / Bénin | 1982 | 70.6 | 58.4 | 12.2 | 0.0 | 0.0 | - | - | 28.8 | 11.1 | 17.7 | 0.6 |
| Bhutan / Bhoutan | 1984/85 | - | - | - | - | - | - | - | 100.0 | - | 100.0 | - |
| Botswana | 1984 | 94.7 | 5.7 | 0.1 | 8.2 | 80.7 | - | - | 4.7 | - | 4.7 | 0.6 |
| Burkina Faso | 1984 | 48.0 | 38.1 | 7.2 | 1.1 | 1.6 | - | 4.7 | 30.0 | 0.4 | 29.6 | 17.3 |
| Burundi | 1985 | 77.1 | 41.6 | 1.1 | 5.9 | 28.5 | - | - | 21.9 | 0.1 | 21.8 | 1.0 |
| Cape Verde / Cap-Vert | 1984 | 48.4 | 47.4 | - | 1.1 | - | .. | - | 47.9 | 21.3 | 26.6 | 3.7 |
| Central African Rep. / Rép. centrafricaine | 1984 | 78.2 | 77.2 | 0.1 | 0.9 | 0.3 | - | - | 16.9 | - | 16.9 | 4.9 |
| Chad / Tchad | 1982 | 65.4 | 63.3 | 1.6 | 0.2 | 0.3 | - | - | 27.5 | 0.0 | 27.5 | 7.1 |
| Comoros / Comores | 1983 | 94.7 | 66.7 | 0.5 | 24.3 | 3.2 | - | - | 2.6 | 0.0 | 2.6 | 2.7 |
| Democratic Yemen / Yémen démocratique | 1982 | 52.3 | 48.7 | 2.5 | 0.1 | 1.0 | - | - | 21.1 | 0.5 | 20.6 | 26.6 |
| Djibouti | 1983 | (25.6) | (25.3) | - | - | (0.3) | - | - | (72.6) | (5.4) | (67.2) | (1.8) |
| Equatorial Guinea / Guinée équatoriale | 1983 | 94.1 | 92.5 | - | 0.4 | 1.2 | - | - | 5.5 | - | 5.5 | 0.4 |
| Ethiopia / Ethiopie | 1984 | 70.8 | 41.3 | 7.5 | 19.5 | 2.5 | 7.7 | 0.5 | 20.6 | 4.2 | 16.4 | 0.4 |
| Gambia / Gambie | 1983 | 68.7 | 52.9 | - | 0.4 | 15.4 | - | - | 31.3 | 1.4 | 29.9 | - |
| Guinea / Guinée | 1984 | 88.5 | 58.9 | 0.1 | 28.8 | 0.7 | - | - | 11.4 | 0.2 | 11.2 | 0.1 |
| Guinea-Bissau / Guinée-Bissau | 1984 | 51.0 | 50.4 | - | - | 0.6 | 35.3 | 9.2 | 4.5 | - | 4.5 | 0.1 |
| Haiti / Haïti | 1983/84 | 94.7 | 36.5 | 0.3 | 56.5 | 1.3 | - | - | 5.3 | - | 5.3 | - |
| Lao People's Dem.Rep. / Rép.dém.populaire lao | 1983 | 21.5 | 3.0 | .. | 9.9 | 8.6 | - | - | 75.9 | - | 75.9 | 2.6 |
| Lesotho | 1982 | 94.9 | 14.2 | - | 0.4 | 80.3 | - | - | 5.1 | - | 5.1 | - |
| Malawi | 1984 | 75.9 | 58.1 | 3.0 | 9.1 | 5.7 | - | - | 22.4 | 0.1 | 22.3 | 1.7 |
| Maldives | 1983 | 38.2 | 4.0 | 4.5 | 29.1 | 0.6 | - | - | 61.8 | - | 61.8 | - |
| Mali | 1983 | (57.2) | (47.8) | (7.6) | (0.7) | (1.1) | 4.2 | 2.6 | (15.2) | (0.8) | (14.4) | (27.6) |
| Nepal / Népal | 1985 | 39.1 | 15.2 | 0.5 | 21.9 | 1.5 | - | - | 54.2 | 0.0 | 54.2 | 0.0 |
| Niger | 1984 | 80.6 | 78.8 | 1.5 | 0.3 | 0.0 | - | - | 17.0 | 14.0 | 3.0 | 2.4 |
| Rwanda | 1984 | 92.2 | 80.8 | 0.6 | 7.2 | 3.6 | - | - | 7.8 | 0.1 | 7.7 | - |
| Samoa | 1984 | 81.7 | 21.1 | 3.2 | 28.1 | 29.3 | - | - | 18.0 | - | 18.0 | 0.3 |
| Sao Tome & Principe / Sao Tomé-et-Principe | 1984 | 100.0 | 95.8 | - | - | 4.2 | - | - | 0.0 | - | - | - |
| Sierra Leone | 1984 | 65.4 | 56.1 | - | 8.8 | 0.5 | - | - | 5.7 | 3.9 | 1.8 | 28.9 |
| Somalia / Somalie | 1982 | 11.6 | 10.8 | - | 0.7 | 0.1 | - | - | 60.4 | 48.7 | 11.7 | 28.0 |
| Sudan / Soudan | 1983 | 30.3 | 22.3 | 4.4 | 2.6 | 1.0 | - | - | 54.3 | 36.5 | 17.8 | 15.4 |
| Togo | 1984 | 66.2 | 62.7 | 0.7 | 0.8 | 2.0 | 10.6 | 1.4 | 21.9 | 1.8 | 20.1 | 0.0 |
| Uganda / Ouganda | 1984 | 87.2 | 55.5 | 6.5 | 21.8 | 3.4 | - | - | 12.8 | 1.6 | 11.2 | 0.0 |
| U.R. of Tanzania / R.-U. de Tanzanie | 1985 | 70.8 | 59.3 | 3.8 | 2.9 | 4.8 | 1.2 | 0.7 | 24.4 | 7.7 | 16.7 | 2.9 |
| Vanuatu | 1984 | 62.9 | 53.2 | 9.3 | - | 0.4 | - | - | 8.9 | - | 8.9 | 28.2 |
| Yemen / Yémen | 1984 | 35.0 | 21.7 | 1.1 | 12.1 | 0.1 | - | 0.2 | 62.3 | 17.6 | 44.7 | 2.5 |
| **All LDCs / Ensemble des PMA** | 1984 | 60.0 | 36.7 | 3.0 | 11.0 | 9.9 | 7.2 | 0.4 | 24.5 | 6.9 | 17.6 | 7.3 |
| **All developing countries c/ / Ensemble des pays en développement c/** | 1984 | 63.6 | 16.7 d/ | 8.9 | 32.0 | 6.0 d/ | 4.8 | 2.6 | 27.5 | 6.6 | 20.9 | 1.5 |

Source : UNCTAD, Handbook of International Trade and Development Statistics, Supplement 1986; IMF, Direction of Trade Yearbook 1986 and other international and national souces.

Source : CNUCED, Manuel de statistiques du commerce international et du développement, Supplément 1986; FMI, Direction of Trade Yearbook 1986 et autres sources internationales et nationales.

a/ Including EFTA. — Y compris l'AELE.
b/ Including the South African Customs Union. — Y compris l'Union douanière de l'Afrique du sud.
c/ Excluding OPEC countries. — Non compris les pays de l'OPEP.
d/ Spain and Portugal are included with "other developed market economy countries". — L'Espagne et le Portugal sont compris avec les "autres pays développés à économie de marché".

Table 14

Tableau 14

Main sources of imports of LDCs : relative shares in 1984
(or latest year available)

Principales sources d'importation des PMA : parts relatives en 1984
(ou année disponible la plus récente)

Percentages — En pourcentage

| Country / Pays | Year / Année | Developed market economy countries / Pays développés à économie de marché | | | | | Socialist countries / Pays socialistes | | Developing Countries / Pays en développement | | | Un-allocated / Non-distribués | Pays |
|---|---|---|---|---|---|---|---|---|---|---|---|---|---|
| | | Total | CEE | Japan / Japon | USA and Canada / Etats-Unis et Canada | Other a/ / Autres a/ | Eastern Europe / Europe orientale | Asia / Asie | Total | OPEC / OPEP | Other / Autres | | |
| Afghanistan | 1984 | 21.1 | 7.3 | 11.7 | 0.8 | 1.3 | 51.2 | 0.8 | 12.8 | 0.1 | 12.7 | 14.1 | Afghanistan |
| Bangladesh | 1985 | 42.9 | 12.6 | 12.2 | 14.1 | 4.0 | 3.9 | 4.2 | 49.1 | 10.9 | 38.2 | - | Bangladesh |
| Benin | 1983 | 60.8 | 51.7 | 2.8 | 3.7 | 2.6 | - | - | 11.8 | 0.1 | 11.7 | 27.4 | Bénin |
| Bhutan | 1984/85 | - | - | - | - | - | - | - | 87.9 | - | - | 12.1 | Bhoutan |
| Botswana | 1984 | 89.3 | 8.6 | 0.3 | 2.2 | 78.3 | - | - | 8.9 | - | 8.9 | 1.8 | Botswana |
| Burkina Faso | 1983 | 61.2 | 44.9 | 4.3 | 10.8 | 1.2 | 0.3 | 2.2 | 36.0 | 2.4 | 33.6 | 0.3 | Burkina Faso |
| Burundi | 1984 | 57.5 | 45.6 | 5.3 | 5.6 | 1.0 | 0.5 | 6.3 | 33.4 | - | 33.4 | 2.3 | Burundi |
| Cape Verde | 1985 | 84.3 | 81.0 | - | - | 3.3 | 0.5 | - | 14.0 | 0.8 | 13.2 | 1.2 | Cap-Vert |
| Central African Rep. | 1984 | 69.2 | 59.3 | 5.3 | 4.6 | - | - | - | 7.8 | - | 7.8 | 23.0 | Rép. centrafricaine |
| Chad | 1983 | 38.0 | 28.5 | 0.1 | 8.6 | 0.8 | - | 0.3 | 57.2 | 0.7 | 56.5 | 4.5 | Tchad |
| Comoros | 1983 | (81.5) | (53.8) | (4.4) | (23.3) | - | - | - | (16.7) | - | (16.7) | (1.8) | Comores |
| Democratic Yemen | .. | .. | .. | .. | .. | .. | .. | .. | .. | .. | .. | .. | Yémen démocratique |
| Djibouti | 1983 | (65.1) | (53.1) | (7.6) | (2.1) | (2.3) | - | .. | (27.0) | - | (27.0) | (7.9) | Djibouti |
| Equatorial Guinea | 1984 | 78.2 | 70.9 | 0.8 | 0.6 | 5.9 | - | 8.9 | 12.7 | 0.8 | 11.9 | 0.2 | Guinée équatoriale |
| Ethiopia | 1984 | 64.0 | 34.9 | 6.6 | 17.7 | 4.8 | 26.1 | 0.5 | 8.9 | 0.6 | 8.3 | 0.5 | Ethiopie |
| Gambia | 1984 | 61.7 | 41.6 | 4.0 | 13.6 | 2.5 | 6.7 | 7.5 | 20.2 | 3.7 | 16.5 | 3.9 | Gambie |
| Guinea | 1984 | 78.6 | 61.6 | 1.5 | 12.2 | 3.3 | - | 0.5 | 20.3 | 0.1 | 20.2 | 0.6 | Guinée |
| Guinea-Bissau | 1984 | 75.2 | 71.3 | 0.2 | - | 3.7 | 5.2 | 2.3 | 13.3 | 0.1 | 13.2 | 4.0 | Guinée-Bissau |
| Haiti | 1983/84 | 78.2 | 11.5 | 6.5 | 56.5 | 3.7 | - | - | 21.5 | - | 21.5 | 0.2 | Haïti |
| Lao People's Dem.Rep. | 1982 | 32.8 | 18.2 | 12.4 | 0.4 | 1.8 | - | - | 66.0 | - | 66.0 | 1.2 | Rép.dém.populaire lao |
| Lesotho | 1982 | 99.4 | 0.9 | - | 0.4 | 98.1 | - | - | 0.6 | - | 0.6 | - | Lesotho |
| Malawi | 1984 | 38.8 | 23.6 | 8.3 | 4.2 | 2.7 | - | - | 59.4 | - | 59.4 | 1.8 | Malawi |
| Maldives | 1983 | 20.8 | 5.8 | 11.6 | 3.2 | 2.2 | - | - | 79.7 | - | 79.7 | - | Maldives |
| Mali | 1984 | 61.4 | 53.6 | 1.1 | 5.0 | 1.7 | 0.8 | 2.2 | 34.5 | 0.2 | 34.3 | 1.1 | Mali |
| Nepal | 1985 | 22.2 | 7.0 | 11.8 | 1.5 | 1.9 | 0.7 | 5.5 | 71.7 | 0.1 | 71.6 | - | Népal |
| Niger | 1984 | 56.5 | 50.8 | 2.9 | 0.6 | 2.2 | 0.6 | 1.4 | 34.6 | 17.2 | 17.4 | 6.9 | Niger |
| Rwanda | 1984 | 58.2 | 40.4 | 8.7 | 7.4 | 1.7 | 0.2 | 9.1 | 32.4 | - | 32.4 | 0.1 | Rwanda |
| Samoa | 1985 | 73.0 | 3.6 | 13.7 | 3.7 | 52.0 | 0.1 | 1.6 | 23.7 | - | 23.7 | 1.6 | Samoa |
| Sao Tome & Principe | 1984 | 84.3 | 72.7 | 3.3 | - | 8.3 | - | - | 15.7 | - | 15.7 | - | Sao Tomé-et-Principe |
| Sierra Leone | 1984 | 52.7 | 40.5 | 6.1 | 4.2 | 1.9 | 1.1 | 2.3 | 41.1 | 36.6 | 4.5 | 2.8 | Sierra Leone |
| Somalia | 1983 | (68.2) | (42.9) | (3.9) | (18.8) | (2.6) | - | - | (30.6) | (24.6) | 6.0 | (1.2) | Somalie |
| Sudan | 1983 | 53.6 | 38.3 | 3.2 | 9.6 | 2.5 | 5.1 | 2.4 | 36.8 | 18.8 | 18.0 | 2.1 | Soudan |
| Togo | 1984 | 77.0 | 63.3 | 5.3 | 6.0 | 2.4 | 0.9 | 2.0 | 18.2 | 2.4 | 15.8 | 1.9 | Togo |
| Uganda | 1984 | 44.2 | 34.0 | 5.7 | 1.4 | 3.1 | - | 1.0 | 54.6 | 2.3 | 52.3 | 0.2 | Ouganda |
| U.R. of Tanzania | 1985 | 64.9 | 42.6 | 9.4 | 5.4 | 7.5 | 1.1 | 1.6 | 32.3 | 16.0 | 16.3 | 0.1 | R.-U. de Tanzanie |
| Vanuatu | 1983 | 61.3 | 12.9 | 9.8 | 1.0 | 37.6 | - | 4.2 | 18.7 | .. | 18.7 | 20.0 | Vanuatu |
| Yemen | 1984 | 54.8 | 33.5 | 11.9 | 5.0 | 4.4 | 1.2 | 4.2 | 32.0 | 11.3 | 20.7 | 7.8 | Yémen |
| All LDCs | 1984 | 55.7 | 29.3 | 7.4 | 8.8 | 10.3 | 6.6 | 2.2 | 31.9 | 7.3 | 24.6 | 3.6 | Ensemble des PMA |
| All developing countries c/ | 1984 | 56.6 | 17.3 d/ | 14.3 d/ | 18.7 | 6.3 d/ | 7.1 | 3.2 | 33.2 | 14.2 | 19.0 | - | Ensemble des pays en développement c/ |

Source : UNCTAD, Handbook of International Trade and Development Statistics, Supplement 1986; IMF, Direction of Trade Statistics, Supplement 1986; IMF, Direction of Trade Yearbook 1986 and other international and national sources.

a/ Including EFTA.
b/ Including the South African Customs Union.
c/ Excluding OPEC countries.
d/ Spain and Portugal are included with "other" developed market economy countries.

Source : CNUCED, Manuel de statistiques du commerce international et du développement, Supplément 1986; FMI, Direction of Trade Yearbook 1986 et autres sources internationales et nationales.

a/ Y compris l'AELE.
b/ Y compris l'Union douanière de l'Afrique du sud.
c/ Non compris les pays de l'OPEP.
d/ L'Espagne et le Portugal sont compris avec les "autres" pays développés à économie de marché.

Table 15                                                        Tableau 15

Leading exports of individual LDCs, 1982                        Principales exportations des PMA, par pays individuels, 1982
(or latest year available)                                      (ou année la plus récente disponible)

| SITC CTCI | Country and leading export commodity[a] | Value of exports in $ million / Valeur des exportations en millions de dollars | As % of country total / En % du total du pays | As % of all developing countries / En % de l'ensemble des pays en développement | As % of World / En % du Monde | Pays et principaux produits exportés[a] |
|---|---|---|---|---|---|---|
| | | (1) | (2) | (3) | (4) | |
| | **Afghanistan** | | | | | **Afghanistan** |
| | All commodities | 757.0 | 100.00 | 0.16 | 0.04 | Ensemble des produits |
| 341 | Gas, natural | 283.6 | 35.47 | 2.37 | 0.80 | Gaz, naturel |
| 051 | Fresh fruit | 154.0 | 20.34 | 3.97 | 1.63 | Fruits frais |
| 657 | Floor coverings, tapestries | 80.8 | 10.67 | 4.45 | 1.75 | Tapis et tapisseries |
| | **Bangladesh** | | | | | **Bangladesh** |
| | All commodities | 671.1 | 100.00 | 0.14 | 0.04 | Ensemble des produits |
| 656 | Textiles, etc. products | 163.3 | 24.33 | 12.28 | 4.77 | Articles en textiles, etc. |
| 653 | Woven textiles, non-cotton | 125.1 | 18.64 | 4.04 | 0.89 | Tissus autres que les tissus de coton |
| 264 | Jute | 100.1 | 14.92 | 82.26 | 78.89 | Jute |
| 031 | Fresh fish, simply preserved | 66.4 | 9.90 | 1.40 | 0.60 | Poisson frais, conservé de façon simple |
| 611 | Leather | 56.5 | 8.41 | 5.06 | 1.70 | Cuirs |
| 074 | Tea and mate | 50.4 | 7.51 | 4.12 | 3.54 | Thé et maté |
| | **Benin** | | | | | **Bénin** |
| | All commodities | 22.0 | 100.00 | 0.00 | 0.00 | Ensemble des produits |
| 072 | Cocoa | 7.5 | 34.05 | 0.30 | 0.23 | Cacao |
| 422 | Fixed vegetable oil, non-soft | 5.1 | 23.03 | 0.20 | 0.17 | Huiles végétales fixes, non fluides |
| 263 | Cotton | 2.9 | 13.38 | 0.11 | 0.04 | Coton |
| 221 | Oil seeds, nuts, kernels | 1.4 | 6.34 | 0.12 | 0.02 | Graines, noix, amandes oléagineuses |
| 661 | Cement, etc. building products | 1.3 | 5.74 | 0.09 | 0.03 | Ciment, etc., produits de construction |
| | **Burkina Faso** | | | | | **Burkina Faso** |
| | All commodities | 56.2 | 100.00 | 0.01 | 0.00 | Ensemble des produits |
| 263 | Cotton | 23.6 | 41.92 | 0.89 | 0.36 | Coton |
| 221 | Oil seeds, nuts, kernels | 9.0 | 16.01 | 0.75 | 0.10 | Graines, noix, amandes oléagineuses |
| 001 | Live animals | 7.1 | 12.66 | 0.80 | 0.14 | Animaux vivants |
| 629 | Articles of rubber, n.e.s. | 2.9 | 5.10 | 0.39 | 0.03 | Articles en caoutchouc, n.d.a. |
| | **Burundi** | | | | | **Burundi** |
| | All commodities | 88.0 | 100.00 | 0.02 | 0.00 | Ensemble des produits |
| 071 | Coffee | 60.1 | 68.29 | 0.66 | 0.60 | Café |
| | **Cape Verde** | | | | | **Cap-Vert** |
| | All commodities | 5.0 | 100.00 | 0.00 | 0.00 | Ensemble des produits |
| 031 | Fresh fish, simply preserved | 2.1 | 42.14 | 0.04 | 0.02 | Poisson frais, conservé de façon simple |
| 276 | Other crude minerals | 1.1 | 21.91 | 0.13 | 0.03 | Autres minéraux bruts |
| 032 | Fish etc. tinned, prepared | 0.7 | 14.40 | 0.08 | 0.03 | Préparation et conserves de poissons |
| 051 | Fresh fruit | 0.3 | 5.40 | 0.01 | 0.00 | Fruits frais |
| | **Central African Republic** | | | | | **République centrafricaine** |
| | All commodities | 107.9 | 100.00 | 0.02 | 0.01 | Ensemble des produits |
| 071 | Coffee | 35.8 | 33.17 | 0.39 | 0.36 | Café |
| 667 | Pearls, precious and semi-precious stones (diamonds) | 26.3 | 24.39 | 1.82 | 0.26 | Perles fines, pierres gemmes et similaires (diamants) |
| 242 | Wood rough | 14.0 | 12.98 | 0.53 | 0.25 | Bois bruts |
| 243 | Wood shaped | 7.7 | 7.16 | 0.45 | 0.08 | Bois équarris |
| 263 | Cotton | 6.9 | 6.36 | 0.26 | 0.10 | Coton |
| 291 | Crude animal materials, n.e.s. | 6.3 | 5.84 | 1.53 | 0.50 | Matières brutes d'origine animale, n.d.a. |
| | **Chad** | | | | | **Tchad** |
| | All commodities | 58.0 | 100.00 | 0.01 | 0.00 | Ensemble des produits |
| 263 | Cotton | 43.2 | 74.46 | 1.74 | 0.70 | Coton |
| 652 | Cotton fabrics, woven | 10.0 | 17.16 | 0.47 | 0.15 | Tissus de coton |
| | **Comoros** | | | | | **Comores** |
| | All commodities | 11.0 | 100.00 | 0.00 | 0.00 | Ensemble des produits |
| 075 | Spices | 5.5 | 49.94 | 0.65 | 0.55 | Epices |
| 551 | Essential oils, perfumes, etc. | 2.2 | 19.65 | 1.06 | 0.14 | Huiles essentielles, produits utilisés en parfumerie, etc. |
| 283 | Non-ferrous metal ores | 1.6 | 14.15 | 0.03 | 0.02 | Minerais de métaux communs non-ferreux |
| 221 | Oil seeds, nuts, kernels | 0.6 | 5.28 | 0.05 | 0.01 | Graines, noix, amandes oléagineuses |
| | **Democratic Yemen** | | | | | **Yémen démocratique** |
| | All commodities | 737.0 | 100.00 | 0.16 | 0.04 | Ensemble des produits |
| 332 | Petroleum products | 507.5 | 68.86 | 1.25 | 0.53 | Produits dérivés du pétrole |
| 031 | Fresh fish, simply preserved | 80.6 | 10.94 | 1.70 | 0.73 | Poisson frais, conservé de façon simple |
| 331 | Crude petroleum, etc. | 55.9 | 7.58 | 0.03 | 0.02 | Pétrole brut, etc. |
| | **Equatorial Guinea** | | | | | **Guinée équatoriale** |
| | All commodities | 25.3 | 100.00 | 0.01 | 0.00 | Ensemble des produits |
| 072 | Cocoa | 13.6 | 53.61 | 0.55 | 0.42 | Cacao |
| 242 | Wood rough | 7.3 | 28.96 | 0.28 | 0.13 | Bois bruts |
| 283 | Non-ferrous metal ores | 1.3 | 5.15 | 0.02 | 0.01 | Minerais de métaux communs non-ferreux |

Table 15 (continued)                    Tableau 15 (suite)                    TD/B/1120 Annex
                                                                                 page 21

Leading exports of individual LDCs, 1982          Principales exportations des PMA, par pays individuels, 1982
(or latest year available)                        (ou année la plus récente disponible)

|       |                                         | (1)   | (2)    | (3)   | (4)  |                                                      |
|-------|-----------------------------------------|-------|--------|-------|------|------------------------------------------------------|
|       | Ethiopia                                |       |        |       |      | Ethiopie                                             |
|       | All commodities                         | 404.3 | 100.00 | 0.09  | 0.02 | Ensemble des produits                                |
| 071   | Coffee                                  | 248.7 | 61.53  | 2.73  | 2.47 | Café                                                 |
| 211   | Hides, skins, undressed                 | 41.2  | 10.19  | 11.81 | 1.55 | Cuirs et peaux non apprêtés                          |
| 332   | Petroleum products                      | 30.9  | 7.65   | 0.08  | 0.03 | Produits dérivés du pétrole                          |
|       | Gambia                                  |       |        |       |      | Gambie                                               |
|       | All commodities                         | 44.0  | 100.00 | 0.01  | 0.00 | Ensemble des produits                                |
| 221   | Oil seeds, nuts, kernels                | 18.6  | 42.32  | 1.56  | 0.20 | Graines, noix, amandes oléagineuses                  |
| 421   | Fixed vegetable oils, soft              | 13.6  | 31.00  | 1.29  | 0.41 | Huiles végétales fixes, fluides                      |
| 081   | Animal feeding stuff                    | 5.4   | 12.24  | 0.16  | 0.05 | Nourriture destinée aux animaux                      |
|       | Guinea                                  |       |        |       |      | Guinée                                               |
|       | All commodities                         | 420.5 | 100.00 | 0.09  | 0.02 | Ensemble des produits                                |
| 283   | Non-ferrous metal ores                  | 399.3 | 94.96  | 6.98  | 4.29 | Minerais de métaux communs non-ferreux               |
|       | Guinea-Bissau                           |       |        |       |      | Guinée-Bissau                                        |
|       | All commodities                         | 12.0  | 100.00 | 0.00  | 0.00 | Ensemble des produits                                |
| 221   | Oil seeds, nuts, kernels                | 5.2   | 43.52  | 0.44  | 0.06 | Graines, noix, amandes oléagineuses                  |
| 031   | Fresh fish, simply preserved            | 2.9   | 24.56  | 0.06  | 0.03 | Poisson frais, conservé de façon simple              |
| 276   | Other crude minerals                    | 1.0   | 8.69   | 0.12  | 0.03 | Autres minéraux bruts                                |
| 263   | Cotton                                  | 0.6   | 5.19   | 0.02  | 0.01 | Coton                                                |
| 243   | Wood shaped                             | 0.6   | 5.12   | 0.04  | 0.01 | Bois équarris                                        |
|       | Haiti                                   |       |        |       |      | Haïti                                                |
|       | All commodities                         | 162.0 | 100.00 | 0.03  | 0.01 | Ensemble des produits                                |
| 071   | Coffee                                  | 36.4  | 22.47  | 0.40  | 0.36 | Café                                                 |
| 841   | Clothing (except fur clothing)          | 29.5  | 18.23  | 0.18  | 0.08 | Vêtements (à l'exclusion des vêtements de fourrure)  |
| 894   | Toys, sporting goods, etc.              | 19.1  | 11.77  | 0.51  | 0.22 | Jouets, articles pour divertissements, etc.          |
| 722   | Electric power machinery, etc.          | 8.7   | 5.39   | 0.37  | 0.03 | Machines électriques génératrices, etc.              |
|       | Lao People's Democratic Republic        |       |        |       |      | République démocratique populaire lao                |
|       | All commodities                         | 18.0  | 100.00 | 0.00  | 0.00 | Ensemble des produits                                |
| 242   | Wood rough                              | 5.4   | 30.07  | 0.20  | 0.10 | Bois bruts                                           |
| 673   | Iron and steel shapes                   | 2.8   | 15.78  | 0.22  | 0.02 | Profilés, en fer ou en acier                         |
| 071   | Coffee                                  | 1.5   | 8.15   | 0.02  | 0.01 | Café                                                 |
| 243   | Wood shaped                             | 1.4   | 7.66   | 0.08  | 0.01 | Bois équarris                                        |
|       | Malawi                                  |       |        |       |      | Malawi                                               |
|       | All commodities                         | 259.0 | 100.00 | 0.05  | 0.01 | Ensemble des produits                                |
| 121   | Tobacco, unmanufactured                 | 128.2 | 49.51  | 6.50  | 3.01 | Tabacs bruts                                         |
| 074   | Tea and mate                            | 48.9  | 18.88  | 4.00  | 3.43 | Thé et maté                                          |
| 061   | Sugar and honey                         | 40.5  | 15.65  | 0.53  | 0.36 | Sucre et miel                                        |
|       | Maldives                                |       |        |       |      | Maldives                                             |
|       | All commodities                         | 10.0  | 100.00 | 0.00  | 0.00 | Ensemble des produits                                |
| 031   | Fresh fish, simply preserved            | 5.4   | 54.52  | 0.12  | 0.15 | Poisson frais, conservé de façon simple              |
| 032   | Fish etc. tinned, prepared              | 2.6   | 25.74  | 0.27  | 0.10 | Préparation et conserves de poisson                  |
| 074   | Tea and mate                            | 0.5   | 5.40   | 0.04  | 0.04 | Thé et maté                                          |
|       | Mali                                    |       |        |       |      | Mali                                                 |
|       | All commodities                         | 146.0 | 100.00 | 0.03  | 0.01 | Ensemble des produits                                |
| 263   | Cotton                                  | 66.9  | 45.80  | 2.52  | 1.01 | Coton                                                |
| 221   | Oil seeds, nuts, kernels                | 23.7  | 16.26  | 1.99  | 0.26 | Graines, noix, amandes oléagineuses                  |
| 001   | Live animals                            | 9.7   | 6.66   | 1.09  | 0.19 | Animaux vivants                                      |
|       | Nepal                                   |       |        |       |      | Nepal                                                |
|       | All commodities                         | 87.0  | 100.00 | 0.02  | 0.00 | Ensemble des produits                                |
| 611   | Leather                                 | 16.5  | 18.91  | 1.47  | 0.49 | Cuirs                                                |
| 657   | Floor coverings, tapestries             | 14.1  | 16.23  | 0.78  | 0.31 | Tapis et tapisseries                                 |
| 042   | Rice                                    | 9.6   | 11.03  | 0.54  | 0.27 | Riz                                                  |
| 653   | Woven textiles, non-cotton              | 6.8   | 7.81   | 0.22  | 0.05 | Tissus autres que les tissus de coton                |
| 291   | Crude animal materials, n.e.s.          | 6.4   | 7.38   | 1.56  | 0.51 | Matières brutes d'origine animale, n.d.a.            |
| 054   | Vegetables, fresh, frozen or simple preserved | 6.4 | 7.31 | 0.24 | 0.08 | Légumes frais, congelés ou simplement en conserve |
| 656   | Textiles, etc. products                 | 4.8   | 5.51   | 0.36  | 0.14 | Articles en textiles, etc.                           |
| 264   | Jute                                    | 4.6   | 5.32   | 3.80  | 3.65 | Jute                                                 |
|       | Niger                                   |       |        |       |      | Niger                                                |
|       | All commodities                         | 333.0 | 100.00 | 0.07  | 0.02 | Ensemble des produits                                |
| 515   | Radioactive and associated materials    | 299.3 | 89.89  | 91.16 | 7.56 | Matières radioactives, produits associés             |
| 331   | Crude petroleum, etc.                   | 19.6  | 5.88   | 0.01  | 0.01 | Pétrole brut, etc.                                   |
|       | Rwanda                                  |       |        |       |      | Rwanda                                               |
|       | All commodities                         | 89.0  | 100.00 | 0.02  | 0.00 | Ensemble des produits                                |
| 071   | Coffee                                  | 65.9  | 74.01  | 0.72  | 0.65 | Café                                                 |
| 283   | Non-ferrous metal ores  tin and tungsten) | 9.0 | 10.11  | 0.16  | 0.10 | Minerais de métaux communs non-ferreux (étain et tungstène) |
| 074   | Tea and mate                            | 6.2   | 6.98   | 0.51  | 0.44 | Thé et maté                                          |
|       | Samoa                                   |       |        |       |      | Samoa                                                |
|       | All commodities                         | 13.0  | 100.00 | 0.00  | 0.00 | Ensemble des produits                                |
| 221   | Oil seeds, nuts, kernels                | 7.0   | 53.71  | 0.58  | 0.08 | Graines, noix, amandes oléagineuses                  |
| 072   | Cocoa                                   | 2.4   | 18.41  | 0.10  | 0.07 | Cacao                                                |
| 054   | Vegetables, fresh, frozen or simply preserved | 1.1 | 8.35 | 0.04 | 0.01 | Légumes frais, congelés ou simplement en conserve |

Table 15 (continued)

Tableau 15 (suite)

Leading exports of individual LDCs, 1982 (or latest year available)

Principales exportations des PMA, par pays individuels, 1982 (ou année la plus récente disponible)

| SITC / CTCI | Country and leading export commodity[a/] / Valeur des exportations en millions de dollars | Value of exports in $ million | As % of country total / En % du total du pays | As % of all developing countries / En % de l'ensemble des pays en développement | As % of World / En % du Monde | Pays et principaux produits exportés[a/] |
|---|---|---|---|---|---|---|
| | | (1) | (2) | (3) | (4) | |
| | Sao Tome and Principe | | | | | Sao Tomé-et-Principe |
| | All commodities | 7.4 | 100.00 | 0.00 | 0.00 | Ensemble des produits |
| 072 | Cocoa | 5.1 | 69.20 | 0.21 | 0.16 | Cacao |
| 221 | Oil seeds, nuts, kernels | 1.5 | 19.66 | 0.12 | 0.02 | Graines, noix, amandes oléagineuses |
| | Sierra Leone | | | | | Sierra Leone |
| | All commodities | 125.0 | 100.00 | 0.03 | 0.01 | Ensemble des produits |
| 667 | Pearls, precious and semi-precious stones | 48.4 | 38.70 | 3.35 | 0.47 | Perles fines, pierres gemmes et similaires |
| 275 | Natural abrasives | 28.3 | 22.67 | 34.39 | 5.75 | Abrasifs naturels |
| 283 | Non-ferrous metal ores | 13.1 | 10.48 | 0.23 | 0.14 | Minerais de métaux communs non-ferreux |
| 072 | Cocoa | 11.2 | 8.98 | 0.45 | 0.35 | Cacao |
| 071 | Coffee | 11.2 | 8.96 | 0.12 | 0.11 | Café |
| | Somalia | | | | | Somalie |
| | All commodities | 212.0 | 100.00 | 0.04 | 0.01 | Ensemble des produits |
| 001 | Live animals | 162.0 | 76.42 | 18.23 | 3.17 | Animaux vivants |
| 051 | Fresh fruit (bananas) | 12.0 | 5.66 | 0.31 | 0.13 | Fruits frais (bananes) |
| 211 | Hides, skins, undressed | 11.4 | 5.36 | 3.26 | 0.43 | Cuirs et peaux non apprêtés |
| | Sudan | | | | | Soudan |
| | All commodities | 499.0 | 100.00 | 0.11 | 0.03 | Ensemble des produits |
| 263 | Cotton | 130.0 | 26.06 | 4.90 | 1.96 | Coton |
| 044 | Maize (corn), unmilled | 75.0 | 15.03 | 6.10 | 0.85 | Maïs non moulu |
| 001 | Live animals | 64.0 | 12.83 | 7.20 | 1.25 | Animaux vivants |
| 292 | Crude vegetable materials, n.e.s. | 40.3 | 8.07 | 3.45 | 0.88 | Matières brutes d'origine végétale, n.d.a. |
| 221 | Oil seeds, nuts, kernels | 35.4 | 7.09 | 2.96 | 0.38 | Graines, noix, amandes oléagineuses |
| 081 | Animal feeding stuff | 26.2 | 5.26 | 0.80 | 0.26 | Nourriture destinée aux animaux |
| | Togo | | | | | Togo |
| | All commodities | 126.0 | 100.00 | 0.03 | 0.01 | Ensemble des produits |
| 271 | Fertilizers, crude | 64.6 | 51.25 | 5.67 | 3.15 | Engrais bruts |
| 332 | Petroleum products | 20.5 | 16.30 | 0.05 | 0.02 | Produits dérivés du pétrole |
| 072 | Cocoa | 15.4 | 12.21 | 0.62 | 0.47 | Cacao |
| 071 | Coffee | 12.2 | 9.66 | 0.13 | 0.12 | Café |
| | Uganda | | | | | Ouganda |
| | All commodities | 354.2 | 100.00 | 0.07 | 0.02 | Ensemble des produits |
| 071 | Coffee | 340.3 | 96.09 | 3.73 | 3.38 | Café |
| | United Republic of Tanzania | | | | | République-Unie de Tanzanie |
| | All commodities | 427.0 | 100.00 | 0.09 | 0.02 | Ensemble des produits |
| 071 | Coffee | 131.3 | 30.76 | 1.44 | 1.30 | Café |
| 263 | Cotton | 56.4 | 13.21 | 2.12 | 0.85 | Coton |
| 075 | Spices | 50.5 | 11.82 | 5.99 | 5.11 | Spices |
| 074 | Tea and mate | 22.6 | 5.28 | 1.84 | 1.58 | Thé et maté |
| | Vanuatu | | | | | Vanuatu |
| | All commodities | 10.7 | 100.00 | 0.00 | 0.00 | Ensemble des produits |
| 321 | Oil seeds, nuts, kernels | 7.4 | 69.10 | 0.62 | 0.08 | Graines, noix, amandes oléagineuses |
| 011 | Meat, fresh, chilled or frozen | 1.3 | 12.13 | 0.06 | 0.01 | Viande fraîche, réfrigérée ou congelée |
| | Yemen | | | | | Yémen |
| | All commodities | 18.0 | 100.00 | 0.00 | 0.00 | Ensemble des produits |
| 276 | Other crude minerals | 3.6 | 19.98 | 0.42 | 0.09 | Autres minéraux bruts |
| 211 | Hides, skins, undressed | 3.1 | 17.00 | 0.88 | 0.12 | Cuirs et peaux non apprêtés |
| 332 | Petroleum products | 2.4 | 13.15 | 0.01 | 0.00 | Produits dérivés du pétrole |
| 071 | Coffee | 2.2 | 12.16 | 0.02 | 0.02 | Café |

Source : UNCTAD Handbook of International Trade and Development Statistics, Supplement 1985.

Source : CNUCED Manuel de statistiques du commerce international et du développement, Supplément 1985.

Note : Column (1) shows export values f.o.b. in millions of dollars. Column (2) shows for each commodity presented its percentage share in the individual country export total, while columns (3) and (4) show the relative importance of each commodity shown expressed as a percentage of the relevant total group for that commodity (i.e. "all developing countries" and "world" respectively).

a/ A "leading export commodity" is one which accounts for at least 5 per cent of the country's total exports.

Note : La colonne (1) montre la valeur des exportations f.o.b. en millions de dollars. La colonne (2) montre, pour chaque produit indiqué, sa part en pourcentage dans le total des exportations du pays concerné, alors que les colonnes (3) et (4) montrent l'importance relative de chaque produit indiqué présenté comme part en pourcentage du total du groupe de produits auquel il se rapporte (total se référant respectivement à "l'ensemble des pays en développement" et au "monde").

a/ Par "principaux produits exportés" on entend les produits équivalent chacun à 5 pour cent au moins du total des exportations du pays concerné.

Table 16 / Tableau 16

Leading exports of LDCs as a group (Ranked according to 1982 value in $ million)a/

Principales exportations de l'ensemble des PMA (Classées selon leur valeur en millions de dollars en 1982) a/

| SITC CTCI | Item | Value of exports in $ million / Valeur des exportations en millions de dollars | As % of total exports of LDCs / En % du total des exportations des PMA | As % of all developing countries, exports of products shown / En % du total des exportations des produits indiqués effectuées par l'ensemble des pays en développement | As % of world exports of products shown / En % du total des exportations des produits indiqués effectuées par le monde | Produit |
|---|---|---|---|---|---|---|
| | All commodities | 6349.9 | 100.00 | 1.34 | 0.34 | Ensemble des produits |
| 071 | Coffee | 967.2 | 15.23 | 10.60 | 9.61 | Café |
| 332 | Petroleum products | 604.3 | 9.52 | 1.49 | 0.63 | Produits dérivés du pétrole |
| 283 | Ores & concentrates of non-ferrous base metals | 432.7 | 6.81 | 7.56 | 4.65 | Minerais de métaux communs non-ferreux & concentrés |
| 263 | Cotton | 389.7 | 6.14 | 14.68 | 5.88 | Coton |
| 515 | Radioactive and associated materials | 299.3 | 4.71 | 91.16 | 7.56 | Matières radioactives et produits associés |
| 341 | Gas, natural and manufactured | 286.7 | 4.52 | 2.39 | 0.81 | Gaz naturel et gaz manufacturé |
| 001 | Live animals | 252.8 | 3.98 | 28.45 | 4.94 | Animaux vivants |
| 051 | Fruit, fresh and nuts, fresh or dried | 191.7 | 3.02 | 4.94 | 2.03 | Fruits frais et noix fraîches ou sèches |
| 656 | Made-up articles, of textile materials,n.e.s. | 176.4 | 2.78 | 13.26 | 5.15 | Articles façonnés en textiles, n.d.a. |
| 031 | Fish, fresh and simply preserved | 172.4 | 2.71 | 3.64 | 1.55 | Poisson frais ou conservé de façon simple |
| 121 | Tobacco, unmanufactured | 154.4 | 2.43 | 7.83 | 3.63 | Tabacs bruts |
| 221 | Oil seeds, nuts and kernels | 147.4 | 2.32 | 12.33 | 1.59 | Graines, noix et amandes oléagineuses |
| 653 | Textile fabrics, other than cotton fabrics | 134.3 | 2.12 | 4.34 | 0.96 | Tissus autres que les tissus de coton |
| 074 | Tea and Mate | 133.2 | 2.10 | 10.89 | 9.34 | Thé et maté |
| 264 | Jute | 105.4 | 1.66 | 86.60 | 83.04 | Jute |
| 211 | Hides and skins, undressed | 105.3 | 1.66 | 30.20 | 3.98 | Cuirs et peaux, non-apprêtés |
| 667 | Pearls, precious and semi-precious stones | 98.2 | 1.55 | 6.79 | 0.96 | Perles fines, pierres gemmes et similaires |
| 657 | Floor coverings, tapestries, etc. | 97.8 | 1.54 | 5.39 | 2.12 | Tapis et tapisseries, etc. |
| 292 | Crude vegetable materials, n.e.s. | 96.3 | 1.52 | 8.25 | 2.11 | Matières brutes d'origine végétale, n.d.a. |
| 611 | Leather | 92.8 | 1.46 | 8.31 | 2.79 | Cuirs |
| 044 | Maize (corn.), unmilled | 77.4 | 1.22 | 6.29 | 0.87 | Maïs, non moulu |
| 331 | Crude petroleum, etc. | 75.5 | 1.19 | 0.04 | 0.03 | Pétrole brut, etc. |
| 841 | Clothing (except fur clothing) | 75.3 | 1.19 | 0.46 | 0.21 | Vêtements(à l'exclusion des vêtements de fourrure) |
| 054 | Vegetables, fresh, frozen or simply preserved | 74.4 | 1.17 | 2.76 | 0.96 | Légumes frais, congelés ou simplement en conserve |
| 075 | Spices | 70.5 | 1.11 | 8.36 | 7.13 | Epices |
| 061 | Sugar and honey | 66.3 | 1.04 | 0.86 | 0.59 | Sucre et miel |
| 271 | Fertilizers, crude | 64.6 | 1.02 | 5.67 | 3.15 | Engrais bruts |
| 072 | Cocoa | 61.8 | 0.97 | 2.48 | 1.90 | Cacao |
| 081 | Feeding-stuff for animals | 59.8 | 0.94 | 1.82 | 0.60 | Nourriture destinée aux animaux |
| 291 | Crude animal materials, n.e.s. | 50.6 | 0.80 | 12.26 | 4.01 | Matières brutes d'origine animale, n.d.a. |
| 242 | Wood, rough | 38.0 | 0.60 | 1.43 | 0.69 | Bois bruts |
| 275 | Natural abrasives | 34.6 | 0.54 | 41.97 | 7.01 | Abrasifs naturels |
| 042 | Rice | 26.5 | 0.42 | 1.49 | 0.74 | Riz |
| 655 | Special textile fabrics and related products | 22.6 | 0.36 | 3.91 | 0.52 | Textiles spéciaux et produits connexes |
| 212 | Fur skins, undressed | 21.9 | 0.35 | 49.93 | 1.52 | Pelleteries, non-apprêtées |
| 718 | Machines for special industries | 21.9 | 0.34 | 2.46 | 0.07 | Machines pour industries spécialisées |
| 421 | Fixed vegetable oils, soft | 21.8 | 0.34 | 2.06 | 0.65 | Huiles végétales fixes, fluides |
| 652 | Cotton fabrics, woven | 21.3 | 0.34 | 1.02 | 0.33 | Tissus de coton |
| 894 | Toys, sporting goods, etc. | 20.8 | 0.33 | 0.55 | 0.24 | Jouets, articles pour divertissements, etc. |
| 265 | Vegetable fibres, except cotton and jute | 20.7 | 0.33 | 14.48 | 6.98 | Fibres végétales autres que le coton et le jute |
| 651 | Textile yarn and thread | 19.4 | 0.31 | 0.75 | 0.17 | Filés et fils textiles |
| 243 | Wood, shaped or simply worked | 19.1 | 0.30 | 1.11 | 0.21 | Bois équarris ou dégrossis |
| 422 | Other fixed vegetable oils | 13.6 | 0.21 | 0.55 | 0.46 | Autres huiles végétales fixes |
| 722 | Electric power machinery, etc. | 13.3 | 0.21 | 0.57 | 0.05 | Machines électriques génératrices, etc. |
| 276 | Other crude minerals | 11.4 | 0.18 | 1.32 | 0.30 | Autres minéraux bruts |
| 724 | Telecommunications apparatus | 11.2 | 0.18 | 0.19 | 0.04 | Appareils de télécommunications |
| 732 | Road motor vehicles | 10.3 | 0.16 | 0.35 | 0.01 | Véhicules automobiles routiers |

Source : UNCTAD secretariat computations based on data of the United Nations Statistical Office.

a/ Data for 34 LDCs (i.e., excluding Botswana and Lesotho) accounting for over 90 per cent of the total exports of LDCs. "Leading exports" refer to exports exceeding $ 10 million in 1982.

Source : Calculs du secrétariat de la CNUCED basés sur des données du Bureau de statistique des Nations Unies.

a/ Les données se rapportent à 34 PMA (c.à.d. à l'exclusion du Botswana et du Lesotho) dont les exportations représentent plus de 90 pour cent du total des exportations des PMA. Par "principales exportations", on entend les exportations de produits atteignant plus de 10 millions de $ en 1982.

Table 17
Foreign exchange receipts and import volume expressed in
constant 1980 dollars a/ per capita, 1970 and 1975-1984

Tableau 17
Rentrées de devises et volume des importations, en dollars
constants de 1980 a/ par habitant, 1970 et 1975-1984

A. Export purchasing power per capita
A. Pouvoir d'achat des exportations, par habitant

| Country | 1970 | 1975 | 1976 | 1977 | 1978 | 1979 | 1980 | 1981 | 1982 | 1983 | 1984 | Pays |
|---|---|---|---|---|---|---|---|---|---|---|---|---|
| Afghanistan | 23.6 | 28.6 | 37.0 | 34.4 | 31.2 | 37.8 | 44.2 | 44.3 | 46.1 | 48.5 | 48.0 | Afghanistan |
| Bangladesh | 27.7 | 6.6 | 9.2 | 8.6 | 9.3 | 8.9 | 8.3 | 7.9 | 8.4 | 8.7 | 11.8 | Bangladesh |
| Benin | 45.7 | 19.0 | 13.2 | 20.8 | 12.0 | 16.5 | 18.2 | 9.7 | 6.8 | 9.3 | 9.5 | Bénin |
| Bhutan | ... | ... | ... | ... | ... | ... | ... | ... | ... | ... | ... | Bhoutan |
| Botswana | 132.4 | 337.8 | 397.7 | 356.6 | 385.2 | 598.9 | 549.7 | 408.7 | 495.5 | 693.9 | 723.8 | Botswana |
| Burkina Faso | 12.4 | 14.1 | 16.8 | 15.2 | 10.5 | 15.2 | 14.6 | 12.2 | 9.2 | 9.6 | 13.4 | Burkina Faso |
| Burundi | 26.0 | 15.3 | 25.6 | 37.1 | 25.7 | 31.3 | 15.9 | 17.3 | 21.8 | 20.1 | 24.5 | Burundi |
| Cape Verde | 27.7 | 12.7 | 12.4 | 16.9 | 10.1 | 10.2 | 13.5 | 10.2 | 14.0 | 17.9 | 17.2 | Cap-Vert |
| Central African Rep. | 52.8 | 38.3 | 44.9 | 56.7 | 43.1 | 39.3 | 50.0 | 35.8 | 49.7 | 34.4 | 39.2 | Rép. centrafricaine |
| Chad | 29.3 | 22.2 | 26.3 | 42.4 | 35.0 | 24.3 | 15.9 | 18.3 | 12.8 | 16.9 | 25.0 | Tchad |
| Comoros | 69.2 | 55.8 | 47.9 | 42.3 | 37.2 | 55.9 | 52.5 | 41.8 | 53.0 | 53.6 | 55.9 | Comores |
| Democratic Yemen | 338.0 | 186.8 | 185.7 | 169.1 | 160.3 | 311.2 | 418.6 | 231.2 | 433.6 | 373.7 | 355.6 | Yémen démocratique |
| Djibouti | 491.9 | 302.1 | 276.0 | 244.6 | 97.3 | 45.5 | 61.3 | 66.8 | 64.2 | 81.4 | 84.3 | Djibouti |
| Equatorial Guinea | 322.0 | 146.4 | 54.7 | 68.4 | 74.0 | 102.0 | 39.8 | 45.8 | 49.7 | 59.8 | 59.8 | Guineé équatoriale |
| Ethiopia | 19.4 | 15.1 | 17.3 | 18.6 | 14.9 | 15.2 | 11.3 | 9.6 | 10.1 | 10.5 | 10.8 | Ethiopie |
| Gambia | 135.9 | 159.8 | 111.3 | 133.7 | 94.0 | 111.4 | 47.5 | 41.7 | 69.3 | 77.6 | 75.9 | Gambie |
| Guinea | 35.9 | 52.9 | 77.8 | 82.5 | 83.7 | 72.6 | 72.1 | 91.1 | 77.7 | 77.4 | 83.1 | Guinée |
| Guinea-Bissau | 28.5 | 20.0 | 13.4 | 23.2 | 20.1 | 22.0 | 13.6 | 17.5 | 15.3 | 30.2 | 23.7 | Guinée-Bissau |
| Haiti | 36.0 | 31.8 | 47.9 | 49.3 | 49.2 | 37.1 | 46.0 | 31.2 | 34.7 | 33.8 | 39.5 | Haïti |
| Lao People's Dem.Rep. | 9.2 | 6.5 | 6.8 | 5.1 | 5.4 | 12.7 | 9.0 | 9.7 | 12.0 | 12.3 | 6.1 | Rép. dém. pop. lao |
| Lesotho | 21.1 | 19.7 | 24.8 | 18.2 | 37.0 | 41.7 | 43.3 | 37.5 | 26.7 | 14.8 | 16.3 | Lesotho |
| Malawi | 46.9 | 48.4 | 55.2 | 58.9 | 47.6 | 45.7 | 47.9 | 44.6 | 40.3 | 38.2 | 51.6 | Malawi |
| Maldives | 97.4 | 53.4 | 51.3 | 56.8 | 40.1 | 48.0 | 64.0 | 70.4 | 90.7 | 124.8 | 162.8 | Maldives |
| Mali | 21.0 | 15.6 | 23.6 | 30.9 | 24.7 | 25.6 | 29.2 | 22.0 | 21.1 | 24.2 | 26.1 | Mali |
| Nepal | 15.7 | 13.8 | 11.7 | 12.5 | 9.3 | 9.2 | 5.5 | 9.6 | 6.1 | 6.7 | 9.1 | Népal |
| Niger | 27.9 | 36.2 | 50.8 | 53.6 | 85.4 | 105.0 | 106.6 | 83.9 | 61.8 | 54.2 | 42.0 | Niger |
| Rwanda | 23.3 | 17.1 | 31.4 | 32.0 | 21.0 | 28.0 | 21.8 | 21.3 | 20.0 | 23.6 | 27.6 | Rwanda |
| Samoa | 128.7 | 83.4 | 82.0 | 159.3 | 105.7 | 141.2 | 109.3 | 72.5 | 88.8 | 134.9 | 136.0 | Samoa |
| Sao Tome and Principe | 405.2 | 157.1 | 175.6 | 455.0 | 373.6 | 317.7 | 235.3 | 165.8 | 108.8 | 73.3 | 85.5 | Sao Tomé-et-Principe |
| Sierra Leone | 145.3 | 78.4 | 63.7 | 68.4 | 82.3 | 82.4 | 61.9 | 45.0 | 26.9 | 29.0 | 47.0 | Sierra Leone |
| Somalia | 32.4 | 37.7 | 38.9 | 22.9 | 34.2 | 29.1 | 28.5 | 32.9 | 43.6 | 22.1 | 9.9 | Somalie |
| Sudan | 77.4 | 46.2 | 56.4 | 59.5 | 41.2 | 34.1 | 29.1 | 35.8 | 27.2 | 34.4 | 34.5 | Soudan |
| Togo | 99.8 | 98.4 | 79.0 | 106.3 | 140.9 | 103.5 | 131.2 | 82.5 | 68.7 | 63.8 | 74.7 | Togo |
| Uganda | 97.2 | 39.7 | 51.0 | 71.1 | 37.6 | 38.3 | 26.3 | 18.8 | 26.5 | 28.3 | 29.9 | Ouganda |
| Un. Rep. of Tanzania | 80.4 | 44.9 | 56.1 | 55.4 | 43.0 | 36.0 | 27.1 | 31.3 | 23.4 | 19.2 | 19.6 | Rép.-Unie de Tanzanie |
| Vanuatu | 527.8 | 181.8 | 262.2 | 557.2 | 574.4 | 512.5 | 306.0 | 280.5 | 204.7 | 262.3 | 395.5 | Vanuatu |
| Yemen | 2.1 | 3.3 | 2.3 | 2.8 | 1.6 | 2.5 | 3.3 | 6.7 | 5.7 | 4.0 | 9.6 | Yémen |
| All LDCs | 41.0 | 24.9 | 29.8 | 31.9 | 27.8 | 28.7 | 26.8 | 24.2 | 24.3 | 24.8 | 26.9 | Ensemble des PMA |
| All developing countries b/ | 116.7 | 115.0 | 132.5 | 140.4 | 144.7 | 141.1 | 129.8 | 130.5 | 127.0 | 136.3 | 153.2 | Ensemble des pays en développement b/ |

For source and notes see page 28.

Pour la source et les notes se référer à la page 28.

Table 17 (continued)
Foreign exchange receipts and import volume expressed in
constant 1980 dollars a/ per capita, 1970 and 1975-1984

Tableau 17 (suite)
Rentrées de devises et volume des importations, en dollars
constants de 1980 a/ par habitant, 1970 et 1975-1984

B. External assistance per capita c/
B. Aide extérieure, par habitant c/

| Country | 1970 | 1975 | 1976 | 1977 | 1978 | 1979 | 1980 | 1981 | 1982 | 1983 | 1984 | Pays |
|---|---|---|---|---|---|---|---|---|---|---|---|---|
| Afghanistan | 14.1 | 13.6 | 14.8 | 13.8 | 13.2 | 12.9 | 21.0 | 17.6 | 11.1 | 22.9 | 13.6 | Afghanistan |
| Bangladesh | 13.6 | 24.6 | 12.2 | 12.4 | 17.1 | 16.4 | 14.0 | 13.0 | 17.6 | 15.4 | 16.0 | Bangladesh |
| Benin | 20.8 | 35.5 | 32.8 | 33.0 | 34.4 | 35.7 | 113.4 | 33.8 | 55.2 | 32.5 | 49.2 | Bénin |
| Bhutan | 0.7 | 3.3 | 4.8 | 3.9 | 3.8 | 5.7 | 6.5 | 7.7 | 9.1 | 10.7 | 14.8 | Bhoutan |
| Botswana | 86.0 | 204.6 | 122.3 | 79.0 | 37.0 | 192.7 | 58.4 | 119.6 | 128.5 | 141.7 | 194.3 | Botswana |
| Burkina Faso | 15.2 | 28.5 | 27.4 | 31.6 | 39.7 | 43.3 | 38.1 | 36.1 | 41.8 | 33.0 | 29.4 | Burkina Faso |
| Burundi | 19.1 | 25.3 | 21.7 | 25.6 | 28.2 | 31.3 | 32.3 | 33.4 | 39.9 | 46.9 | 37.9 | Burundi |
| Cape Verde | - | 54.6 | 164.2 | 149.8 | 179.1 | 142.0 | 211.4 | 177.2 | 234.5 | 235.5 | 236.4 | Cap-Vert |
| Central African Rep. | 22.8 | 46.3 | 30.7 | 29.9 | 30.6 | 42.7 | 55.4 | 47.1 | 46.7 | 46.5 | 52.8 | Rép. centrafricaine |
| Chad | 21.9 | 35.9 | 28.6 | 35.4 | 48.9 | 23.4 | 7.6 | 11.9 | 13.2 | 21.4 | 25.5 | Tchad |
| Comoros | 109.3 | 111.6 | 136.3 | 152.4 | 52.5 | 56.5 | 112.3 | 131.2 | 97.8 | 117.3 | 112.3 | Comores |
| Democratic Yemen | 64.5 | 90.5 | 229.2 | 128.6 | 82.9 | 71.5 | 133.0 | 78.4 | 110.1 | 84.7 | 86.6 | Yémen démocratique |
| Djibouti | 295.2 | 282.0 | 217.7 | 352.1 | 516.5 | 90.7 | 229.4 | 208.9 | 188.5 | 222.8 | 467.3 | Djibouti |
| Equatorial Guinea | - | 2.3 | -7.7 | -14.2 | 5.7 | 6.7 | 28.4 | 31.8 | 36.1 | 62.6 | 79.5 | Guineé équatoriale |
| Ethiopia | 8.2 | 8.4 | 8.5 | 6.3 | 7.0 | 8.9 | 7.2 | 7.8 | 9.7 | 11.6 | 14.8 | Ethiopie |
| Gambia | 12.0 | 27.3 | 39.1 | 74.4 | 94.0 | 88.1 | 132.4 | 132.1 | 72.3 | 61.4 | 101.4 | Gambie |
| Guinea | 37.9 | 9.2 | 7.6 | 14.6 | 26.6 | 15.9 | 28.1 | 22.4 | 14.7 | 15.1 | 26.4 | Guinée |
| Guinea-Bissau | 11.4 | 56.6 | 69.9 | 93.7 | 109.3 | 90.7 | 88.5 | 91.9 | 83.5 | 88.8 | 84.0 | Guinée-Bissau |
| Haiti | 6.2 | 23.4 | 28.0 | 30.3 | 28.7 | 31.6 | 24.0 | 23.4 | 27.8 | 27.7 | 29.8 | Haïti |
| Lao People's Dem.Rep. | 91.4 | 28.6 | 31.4 | 29.9 | 50.6 | 34.3 | 25.6 | 27.1 | 29.5 | 26.2 | 24.3 | Rép. dém. pop. lao |
| Lesotho | 35.2 | 46.0 | 43.9 | 50.8 | 59.8 | 57.5 | 67.7 | 78.2 | 71.4 | 82.7 | 72.1 | Lesotho |
| Malawi | 33.5 | 31.0 | 26.2 | 33.6 | 31.5 | 42.9 | 31.6 | 31.8 | 22.0 | 17.6 | 26.5 | Malawi |
| Maldives | 6.5 | 72.1 | 74.4 | 56.8 | 97.3 | 54.4 | 145.9 | 110.0 | 13.6 | 62.4 | 48.8 | Maldives |
| Mali | 23.5 | 42.1 | 26.1 | 31.2 | 40.2 | 38.6 | 38.3 | 35.0 | 29.5 | 32.3 | 45.6 | Mali |
| Nepal | 8.0 | 6.4 | 6.7 | 13.7 | 8.2 | 11.9 | 11.0 | 12.5 | 14.1 | 14.2 | 14.4 | Népal |
| Niger | 40.4 | 60.2 | 63.4 | 46.6 | 66.3 | 62.3 | 47.4 | 68.5 | 54.4 | 39.7 | 25.7 | Niger |
| Rwanda | 21.1 | 37.1 | 33.7 | 33.6 | 37.6 | 38.2 | 30.3 | 29.8 | 29.9 | 32.2 | 30.8 | Rwanda |
| Samoa | 38.6 | 163.4 | 137.0 | 259.2 | 223.9 | 262.1 | 160.8 | 162.9 | 163.0 | 223.6 | 96.6 | Samoa |
| Sao Tome and Principe | - | 20.2 | 256.9 | 61.3 | 72.9 | 43.3 | 45.9 | 72.2 | 119.6 | 147.8 | 150.2 | Sao Tomé-et-Principe |
| Sierra Leone | -3.3 | 17.5 | 24.0 | 25.2 | 27.2 | 24.9 | 28.1 | 19.6 | 27.8 | 21.3 | 23.0 | Sierra Leone |
| Somalia | 33.7 | 82.4 | 54.6 | 151.3 | 75.7 | 67.8 | 113.5 | 79.4 | 135.6 | 69.4 | 88.9 | Somalie |
| Sudan | 6.9 | 61.9 | 56.1 | 36.1 | 38.3 | 41.8 | 45.3 | 37.7 | 43.2 | 63.6 | 39.3 | Soudan |
| Togo | 29.2 | 43.6 | 53.6 | 80.7 | 157.4 | 100.6 | 69.5 | 19.5 | 37.3 | 43.3 | 45.3 | Togo |
| Uganda | 14.9 | 7.6 | 7.0 | 4.0 | -14.8 | 3.5 | 10.4 | 11.9 | 13.1 | 11.5 | 12.5 | Ouganda |
| Un. Rep. of Tanzania | 21.6 | 51.9 | 39.4 | 44.5 | 46.7 | 51.7 | 44.8 | 43.0 | 38.6 | 30.4 | 31.9 | Rép.-Unie de Tanzanie |
| Vanuatu | 140.7 | 300.0 | 718.3 | 256.9 | 324.1 | 471.0 | 369.9 | 258.5 | 286.5 | 313.0 | 408.1 | Vanuatu |
| Yemen | 12.0 | 56.9 | 75.5 | 91.0 | 71.2 | 62.1 | 77.2 | 59.8 | 73.2 | 69.6 | 47.9 | Yémen |
| All LDCs | 17.1 | 29.6 | 25.0 | 25.9 | 26.9 | 27.2 | 28.0 | 24.7 | 27.4 | 26.9 | 26.5 | Ensemble des PMA |
| All developing countries b/ | 44.9 | 52.6 | 54.1 | 51.1 | 58.5 | 45.8 | 40.7 | 42.6 | 38.9 | 52.5 | 32.8 | Ensemble des pays en développement b/ |

For source and notes see page 28.

Pour la source et les notes se référer à la page 28.

Table 17 (continued)
Foreign exchange receipts and import volume expressed in
constant 1980 dollars a/ per capita, 1970 and 1975-1984

Tableau 17 (suite)
Rentrées de devises et volume des importations, en dollars
constants de 1980 a/ par habitant, 1970 et 1975-1984

**C. Total receipts d/, per capita**
**C. Total des rentrées de devises d/, par habitant**

| Country | 1970 | 1975 | 1976 | 1977 | 1978 | 1979 | 1980 | 1981 | 1982 | 1983 | 1984 | Pays |
|---|---|---|---|---|---|---|---|---|---|---|---|---|
| Afghanistan | 37.7 | 42.2 | 51.8 | 48.2 | 44.5 | 50.7 | 65.2 | 61.9 | 57.2 | 71.4 | 61.7 | Afghanistan |
| Bangladesh | 41.3 | 31.2 | 21.5 | 20.9 | 26.4 | 25.3 | 22.3 | 20.9 | 26.0 | 24.1 | 27.7 | Bangladesh |
| Benin | 66.4 | 54.5 | 46.0 | 53.8 | 46.5 | 52.1 | 131.6 | 43.5 | 62.0 | 41.8 | 58.7 | Bénin |
| Bhutan | .. | .. | .. | .. | .. | .. | .. | .. | .. | .. | .. | Bhoutan |
| Botswana | 218.4 | 542.4 | 520.0 | 435.6 | 422.1 | 791.7 | 608.1 | 528.3 | 623.9 | 835.7 | 918.1 | Botswana |
| Burkina Faso | 27.6 | 42.6 | 44.2 | 46.8 | 50.2 | 58.5 | 52.7 | 48.3 | 51.0 | 42.6 | 42.7 | Burkina Faso |
| Burundi | 45.1 | 40.7 | 47.3 | 62.7 | 53.9 | 62.6 | 48.1 | 50.7 | 61.7 | 67.0 | 62.4 | Burundi |
| Cape Verde | .. | 67.3 | 176.6 | 166.7 | 189.2 | 150.3 | 224.9 | 187.4 | 248.5 | 253.4 | 254.2 | Cap-Vert |
| Central African Rep. | 75.6 | 84.6 | 75.6 | 86.7 | 73.7 | 82.0 | 105.5 | 82.9 | 96.4 | 80.9 | 92.1 | Rép. centrafricaine |
| Chad | 51.1 | 58.1 | 54.9 | 77.7 | 83.8 | 47.7 | 23.4 | 30.1 | 26.0 | 38.3 | 50.5 | Tchad |
| Comoros | 178.4 | 167.3 | 184.2 | 194.7 | 89.7 | 112.4 | 164.8 | 173.0 | 150.8 | 170.9 | 168.2 | Comores |
| Democratic Yemen | 402.6 | 277.2 | 415.0 | 297.6 | 243.1 | 382.7 | 551.6 | 309.6 | 543.7 | 458.4 | 442.3 | Yémen démocratique |
| Djibouti | 787.1 | 584.1 | 493.7 | 596.8 | 613.8 | 136.2 | 290.6 | 275.7 | 252.7 | 304.3 | 551.6 | Djibouti |
| Equatorial Guinea | .. | 148.6 | 47.1 | 54.2 | 79.8 | 108.6 | 68.2 | 77.6 | 85.7 | 122.4 | 139.3 | Guinée équatoriale |
| Ethiopia | 27.6 | 23.5 | 25.8 | 24.9 | 21.9 | 24.2 | 18.5 | 17.5 | 19.8 | 22.1 | 25.6 | Ethiopie |
| Gambia | 147.9 | 187.1 | 150.4 | 208.1 | 188.0 | 199.5 | 180.0 | 173.9 | 141.6 | 138.9 | 177.3 | Gambie |
| Guinea | 73.8 | 62.1 | 85.4 | 97.1 | 110.3 | 88.5 | 100.2 | 113.5 | 92.4 | 92.5 | 109.4 | Guinée |
| Guinea-Bissau | 39.9 | 76.6 | 83.3 | 116.8 | 129.3 | 112.7 | 102.1 | 109.4 | 98.9 | 118.9 | 107.7 | Guinée-Bissau |
| Haiti | 42.2 | 55.2 | 75.8 | 79.5 | 77.0 | 68.7 | 70.0 | 54.6 | 62.5 | 61.5 | 69.4 | Haïti |
| Lao People's Dem.Rep. | 100.6 | 35.1 | 38.2 | 34.9 | 56.0 | 47.0 | 34.7 | 36.8 | 41.5 | 38.4 | 30.5 | Rép. dém. pop. lao |
| Lesotho | 56.4 | 65.7 | 68.8 | 69.0 | 96.8 | 99.2 | 111.1 | 115.6 | 98.1 | 97.5 | 88.4 | Lesotho |
| Malawi | 80.4 | 79.3 | 81.4 | 92.5 | 79.1 | 88.6 | 79.5 | 76.4 | 62.3 | 55.8 | 78.1 | Malawi |
| Maldives | 103.9 | 125.6 | 125.7 | 113.6 | 137.4 | 102.4 | 209.8 | 180.4 | 104.3 | 187.3 | 211.7 | Maldives |
| Mali | 44.5 | 57.6 | 49.8 | 62.1 | 64.9 | 64.2 | 67.5 | 56.9 | 50.6 | 56.5 | 71.7 | Mali |
| Nepal | 23.7 | 20.2 | 18.4 | 26.2 | 17.5 | 21.1 | 16.5 | 22.1 | 20.2 | 20.9 | 23.5 | Népal |
| Niger | 68.2 | 96.4 | 114.2 | 100.2 | 151.7 | 167.3 | 154.0 | 152.4 | 116.1 | 93.9 | 67.7 | Niger |
| Rwanda | 44.4 | 54.3 | 65.1 | 65.6 | 58.6 | 66.2 | 52.0 | 51.1 | 49.9 | 55.8 | 58.4 | Rwanda |
| Samoa | 167.3 | 246.8 | 219.0 | 418.5 | 329.6 | 403.3 | 270.1 | 235.3 | 251.8 | 358.5 | 233.5 | Samoa |
| Sao Tome and Principe | 177.4 | 177.4 | 432.5 | 516.4 | 446.5 | 361.0 | 281.2 | 238.3 | 228.4 | 221.1 | 235.7 | Sao Tomé-et-Principe |
| Sierra Leone | 142.0 | 95.9 | 87.7 | 93.6 | 109.4 | 107.4 | 90.0 | 64.6 | 54.7 | 50.3 | 70.0 | Sierra Leone |
| Somalia | 66.1 | 120.1 | 93.5 | 174.3 | 109.9 | 97.0 | 141.9 | 112.3 | 179.2 | 91.5 | 98.7 | Somalie |
| Sudan | 84.3 | 108.2 | 112.5 | 95.6 | 79.5 | 76.0 | 74.4 | 73.5 | 70.4 | 97.9 | 73.8 | Soudan |
| Togo | 129.0 | 142.0 | 132.6 | 187.0 | 298.3 | 204.1 | 200.6 | 102.0 | 106.0 | 107.2 | 120.0 | Togo |
| Uganda | 112.0 | 47.2 | 57.9 | 75.1 | 22.8 | 41.7 | 36.7 | 30.6 | 39.6 | 39.8 | 42.4 | Ouganda |
| Un. Rep. of Tanzania | 102.0 | 96.8 | 95.6 | 99.9 | 89.7 | 87.7 | 71.9 | 74.2 | 61.9 | 49.6 | 51.5 | Rép.-Unie de Tanzanie |
| Vanuatu | 668.5 | 481.7 | 980.5 | 814.2 | 898.6 | 983.5 | 675.9 | 539.0 | 491.2 | 575.3 | 803.5 | Vanuatu |
| Yemen | 14.1 | 60.1 | 77.8 | 93.8 | 72.8 | 64.6 | 80.5 | 66.5 | 78.9 | 73.6 | 57.5 | Yémen |
| All LDCs | 57.9 | 54.4 | 54.7 | 57.6 | 54.6 | 55.8 | 54.7 | 48.8 | 51.6 | 51.5 | 53.3 | Ensemble des PMA |
| All developing countries b/ | 161.6 | 167.5 | 186.6 | 191.5 | 203.2 | 186.9 | 170.5 | 173.1 | 165.8 | 188.8 | 186.0 | Ensemble des pays en développement b/ |

For source and notes see page 28.

Pour la source et les notes se référer à la page 28.

Table 17 (continued)
Foreign exchange receipts and import volume expressed in
constant 1980 dollars a/ per capita, 1970 and 1975-1984

Tableau 17 (suite)
Rentrées de devises et volume des importations, en dollars
constants de 1980 a/ par habitant, 1970 et 1975-1984

D. Import volume per capita
D. Volume des importations par habitant

| Country | 1970 | 1975 | 1976 | 1977 | 1978 | 1979 | 1980 | 1981 | 1982 | 1983 | 1984 | Pays |
|---|---|---|---|---|---|---|---|---|---|---|---|---|
| Afghanistan | 30.7 | 44.8 | 41.4 | 54.6 | 57.3 | 52.5 | 34.6 | 39.7 | 45.3 | 51.8 | 52.3 | Afghanistan |
| Bangladesh | 40.5 | 19.0 | 16.8 | 22.4 | 22.7 | 21.3 | 22.2 | 21.6 | 21.9 | 20.1 | 25.7 | Bangladesh |
| Benin | 88.6 | 116.9 | 125.3 | 124.9 | 138.9 | 114.6 | 95.6 | 154.5 | 132.3 | 93.0 | 89.3 | Bénin |
| Bhutan | ... | ... | ... | ... | ... | ... | ... | ... | ... | ... | ... | Bhoutan |
| Botswana | 294.8 | 518.6 | 472.3 | 546.7 | 612.4 | 715.7 | 755.2 | 863.9 | 743.7 | 803.1 | 729.2 | Botswana |
| Burkina Faso | 33.7 | 48.4 | 44.7 | 57.9 | 54.9 | 59.3 | 58.1 | 55.2 | 57.1 | 48.5 | 35.3 | Burkina Faso |
| Burundi | 23.9 | 29.7 | 30.3 | 30.9 | 36.5 | 45.8 | 41.0 | 39.3 | 52.9 | 46.0 | 46.4 | Burundi |
| Cape Verde | 221.3 | 253.8 | 186.5 | 247.9 | 218.2 | 169.7 | 230.0 | 238.8 | 244.4 | 286.3 | 301.3 | Cap-Vert |
| Central African Rep. | 57.9 | 55.1 | 41.8 | 44.2 | 32.9 | 34.8 | 35.2 | 43.0 | 57.9 | 23.9 | 39.7 | Rép. centrafricaine |
| Chad | 59.5 | 61.6 | 52.5 | 74.8 | 76.7 | 23.5 | 16.5 | 23.7 | 24.1 | 35.8 | 38.6 | Tchad |
| Comoros | 124.5 | 128.3 | 69.2 | 84.6 | 78.6 | 92.0 | 86.6 | 88.9 | 84.8 | 85.8 | 79.9 | Comores |
| Democratic Yemen | 500.8 | 350.7 | 432.3 | 508.1 | 477.5 | 261.9 | 350.3 | 361.9 | 872.1 | 822.2 | 850.8 | Yémen démocratique |
| Djibouti | 1147.9 | 1233.7 | 873.6 | 676.0 | 508.4 | 430.6 | 403.2 | 381.6 | 369.2 | 374.6 | 356.7 | Djibouti |
| Equatorial Guinea | 309.1 | 112.6 | 21.9 | 48.9 | 39.2 | 66.8 | 73.9 | 88.7 | 122.7 | 89.7 | 89.7 | Guineé équatoriale |
| Ethiopia | 27.3 | 18.6 | 21.1 | 20.9 | 25.1 | 20.6 | 19.1 | 18.3 | 19.7 | 22.8 | 24.4 | Ethiopie |
| Gambia | 143.9 | 199.8 | 235.3 | 217.3 | 241.1 | 270.9 | 250.0 | 188.6 | 152.7 | 185.8 | 158.3 | Gambie |
| Guinea | 47.0 | 61.1 | 46.2 | 53.4 | 66.6 | 57.7 | 49.9 | 59.5 | 58.8 | 58.0 | 69.6 | Guinée |
| Guinea-Bissau | 192.4 | 105.8 | 99.1 | 71.8 | 84.3 | 95.7 | 68.0 | 62.4 | 63.9 | 85.2 | 63.1 | Guinée-Bissau |
| Haïti | 45.7 | 56.1 | 79.3 | 71.7 | 68.3 | 66.6 | 72.1 | 92.7 | 82.4 | 96.5 | 104.3 | Haïti |
| Lao People's Dem.Rep. | 150.0 | 25.2 | 23.9 | 29.9 | 34.3 | 34.0 | 38.2 | 36.8 | 39.1 | 43.0 | 44.5 | Rép. dém. pop. lao |
| Lesotho | 112.7 | 242.1 | 302.2 | 297.7 | 315.4 | 333.6 | 346.5 | 395.7 | 401.7 | 455.9 | 241.5 | Lesotho |
| Malawi | 67.2 | 87.4 | 68.5 | 68.6 | 87.1 | 81.5 | 73.9 | 57.9 | 51.0 | 51.9 | 44.3 | Malawi |
| Maldives | 65.0 | 40.1 | 38.5 | 45.4 | 120.4 | 159.9 | 185.5 | 198.3 | 278.6 | 374.5 | 345.2 | Maldives |
| Mali | 29.9 | 51.1 | 41.7 | 39.3 | 62.9 | 62.5 | 62.7 | 54.9 | 48.0 | 50.6 | 53.0 | Mali |
| Nepal | 27.4 | 23.6 | 28.5 | 29.0 | 23.3 | 21.5 | 23.3 | 25.3 | 27.6 | 33.1 | 29.6 | Népal |
| Niger | 50.5 | 40.2 | 48.1 | 65.7 | 92.3 | 108.3 | 111.8 | 94.0 | 82.0 | 65.9 | 60.7 | Niger |
| Rwanda | 27.0 | 39.1 | 39.9 | 38.8 | 53.8 | 45.5 | 47.2 | 49.6 | 53.6 | 52.5 | 56.1 | Rwanda |
| Samoa | 360.4 | 440.7 | 351.4 | 435.5 | 509.3 | 572.8 | 405.1 | 441.3 | 341.7 | 397.5 | 360.4 | Samoa |
| Sao Tome and Principe | 455.9 | 246.9 | 197.6 | 277.0 | 391.3 | 288.8 | 223.5 | 201.3 | 181.3 | 122.2 | 146.5 | Sao Tomé-et-Principe |
| Sierra Leone | 166.9 | 119.8 | 96.8 | 102.3 | 132.9 | 118.8 | 125.6 | 91.7 | 72.4 | 52.4 | 52.7 | Sierra Leone |
| Somalia | 47.0 | 65.6 | 63.9 | 83.0 | 77.1 | 64.0 | 74.5 | 110.7 | 72.3 | 39.6 | 23.9 | Somalie |
| Sudan | 73.8 | 109.1 | 99.7 | 97.3 | 92.7 | 70.8 | 84.4 | 85.8 | 70.0 | 74.5 | 63.0 | Soudan |
| Togo | 117.9 | 135.9 | 140.0 | 189.9 | 263.1 | 245.9 | 215.3 | 169.2 | 151.7 | 111.9 | 106.0 | Togo |
| Uganda | 59.3 | 29.7 | 24.1 | 23.8 | 27.4 | 17.3 | 22.4 | 30.1 | 32.6 | 32.6 | 27.8 | Ouganda |
| Un. Rep. of Tanzania | 98.7 | 93.3 | 74.0 | 76.4 | 103.1 | 75.9 | 65.4 | 61.8 | 58.1 | 43.2 | 44.1 | Rép.-Unie de Tanzanie |
| Vanuatu | 571.8 | 618.1 | 524.3 | 804.9 | 848.0 | 795.9 | 620.8 | 508.3 | 525.0 | 569.9 | 602.2 | Vanuatu |
| Yemen | 22.8 | 86.9 | 116.6 | 261.9 | 285.5 | 264.9 | 263.2 | 250.9 | 220.9 | 235.7 | 243.9 | Yémen |
| All LDCs | 55.2 | 50.7 | 48.4 | 56.9 | 62.6 | 54.8 | 54.4 | 55.3 | 55.5 | 54.2 | 53.8 | Ensemble des PMA |
| All developing countries b/ | 142.8 | 165.8 | 164.7 | 173.6 | 183.7 | 177.3 | 172.1 | 173.9 | 163.6 | 164.7 | 170.5 | Ensemble des pays en développement b/ |

For source and notes see page 28.

Pour la source et les notes se référer à la page 28.

Table 17 (end)

Source: UNCTAD secretariat estimates mainly based on UNCTAD Handbook of International Trade and Development Statistics, Supplement 1986.

a/ Exports, external assistance and total receipts in all years are expressed in terms of their command over imports at 1980 prices. (For the deflators used, see table 8).

b/ Excluding major petroleum exporters.

c/ Total financial flows as in table 23A.

d/ Export purchasing power plus external assistance.

Tableau 17 (fin)

Source: Estimations du secrétariat de la CNUCED d'après le Manuel de statistiques du Commerce international et du Développement, Supplément 1986, de la CNUCED.

a/ Les recettes d'exportations, les rentrées au titre de l'aide extérieure et le total des rentrées de devises pour toutes les années sont exprimés en pouvoir d'achat à l'importation au prix de 1980. (Pour les déflateurs utilisés, se reporter au tableau 8).

b/ Non compris les principaux pays exportateurs de pétrole.

c/ Total des apports financiers comme au tableau 23A.

d/ Pouvoir d'achat des exportations plus aide extérieure.

Table 18

External assistance (net disbursements), exports and imports, 1983

$ million

Tableau 18

Aide extérieure (versements nets), exportations et importations 1983

Millions de dollars

| Country | Technical assistance DAC | Total concessional assistance a/ — All sources | Of which: DAC | Of which: OPEC | Non-concessional b/ assistance | Exports (f.o.b.) | Imports (c.i.f.) | Total concessional assistance from all sources as % of imports | Pays |
|---|---|---|---|---|---|---|---|---|---|
| Afghanistan | 15.2 | 344.8 | 15.9 | -2.1 | -0.2 | 730 | 780 | 44.2 | Afghanistan |
| Bangladesh | 176.3 | 1137.9 | 957.4 | 123.8 | 75.5 | 690 | 1587 | 71.7 | Bangladesh |
| Benin | 25.8 | 106.6 | 80.3 | 6.4 | 5.3 | 32 | 320 | 33.3 | Bénin |
| Bhutan | 7.2 | 12.9 | 12.9 | - | - | - | - | - | Bhutan |
| Botswana | 40.5 | 103.4 | 91.2 | 12.2 | 26.5 | 636 | 736 | 14.0 | Botswana |
| Burkina Faso | 65.3 | 184.1 | 181.2 | 2.9 | 11.8 | 57 | 288 | 63.9 | Burkina Faso |
| Burundi | 45.4 | 151.3 | 133.4 | 4.9 | 35.4 | 80 | 183 | 82.7 | Burundi |
| Cape Verde | 17.4 | 61.7 | 59.5 | 0.2 | 4.1 | 5 | 80 | 77.1 | Cap-Vert |
| Central African Rep. | 29.3 | 94.8 | 92.9 | 0.3 | 6.6 | 75 | 52 | 182.3 | Rép. centrafricaine |
| Chad | 21.7 | 95.5 | 95.3 | 0.2 | -1.6 | 74 | 157 | 60.8 | Tchad |
| Comoros | 10.1 | 42.3 | 29.5 | 9.8 | 1.4 | 20 | 32 | 132.2 | Comores |
| Democratic Yemen | 14.3 | 177.6 | 57.3 | 40.0 | -24.9 | 674 | 1483 | 12.0 | Yémen démocratique |
| Djibouti | 29.2 | 66.9 | 52.1 | 14.8 | 1.5 | 25 | 115 | 58.2 | Djibouti |
| Equatorial Guinea | 3.9 | 19.9 | 10.7 | 0.5 | 1.0 | 20 | 30 | 66.5 | Guinée équatoriale |
| Ethiopia | 63.8 | 430.1 | 269.3 | - | 17.6 | 402 | 876 | 49.1 | Ethiopie |
| Gambia | 15.8 | 42.3 | 40.9 | 1.4 | -4.3 | 48 | 115 | 36.8 | Gambie |
| Guinea | 14.4 | 75.5 | 67.4 | 1.0 | 2.6 | 400 | 300 | 25.2 | Guinée |
| Guinea-Bissau | 16.2 | 65.7 | 57.8 | 6.9 | 2.0 | 23 | 65 | 101.1 | Guinée-Bissau |
| Haiti | 32.2 | 134.1 | 132.5 | 1.6 | -7.6 | 154 | 440 | 30.5 | Haïti |
| Lao P.D.R. | 10.7 | 84.8 | 29.3 | 0.5 | 0.3 | 40 | 140 | 60.6 | Rép. dém. pop. lao |
| Lesotho | 33.0 | 104.5 | 96.3 | 7.7 | 2.0 | 19 | 587 | 17.8 | Lesotho |
| Malawi | 34.8 | 116.9 | 116.9 | - | -11.6 | 229 | 311 | 37.6 | Malawi |
| Maldives | 3.8 | 11.4 | 6.9 | 4.5 | -1.9 | 19 | 57 | 20.0 | Maldives |
| Mali | 53.7 | 220.0 | 168.3 | 48.9 | 0.4 | 165 | 345 | 63.8 | Mali |
| Nepal | 68.1 | 202.1 | 200.3 | 1.3 | -3.4 | 94 | 464 | 43.6 | Népal |
| Niger | 61.0 | 177.6 | 158.2 | 18.3 | 33.5 | 288 | 350 | 50.7 | Niger |
| Rwanda | 53.8 | 155.0 | 149.5 | 1.6 | 10.2 | 121 | 269 | 57.6 | Rwanda |
| Samoa | 7.4 | 27.1 | 27.1 | - | 4.4 | 19 | 56 | 48.4 | Samoa |
| Sao Tome & Principe | 1.6 | 12.1 | 11.1 | 0.5 | -0.0 | 6 | 10 | 121.0 | Sao Tomé-et-Principe |
| Sierra Leone | 19.3 | 67.4 | 64.6 | 1.7 | -21.6 | 92 | 166 | 40.6 | Sierra Leone |
| Somalia | 113.6 | 335.4 | 284.1 | 48.0 | -21.6 | 100 | 179 | 187.4 | Somalie |
| Sudan | 127.4 | 993.4 | 599.0 | 354.5 | 161.7 | 624 | 1354 | 73.4 | Soudan |
| Togo | 27.7 | 111.7 | 106.6 | 5.1 | -1.7 | 162 | 284 | 39.3 | Togo |
| Uganda | 34.0 | 136.4 | 124.4 | 11.0 | 14.7 | 372 | 428 | 31.9 | Uganda |
| U. R. of Tanzania | 173.4 | 599.6 | 563.4 | 32.5 | -22.2 | 366 | 822 | 72.9 | Rép.-Unie de Tanzanie |
| Vanuatu | 16.1 | 26.9 | 26.9 | - | 7.7 | 29 | 63 | 42.7 | Vanuatu |
| Yemen | 59.9 | 318.2 | 124.2 | 193.3 | 151.9 | 27 | 1593 | 20.0 | Yémen |
| All LDCs | 1543.3 | 7049.4 | 5294.6 | 955.6 | 477.0 | 6917 | 15117 | 46.6 | Ensemble des PMA |
| All developing countries c/ | 7133.1 | 28569.5 | 22138.7 | 4171.1 | 65619.1 | 244470 | 295459 | 9.7 | Ensemble des pays en développement c/ |

Source: UNCTAD secretariat estimates mainly based on data from the OECD/DAC secretariat, the World Bank and UNCTAD, Handbook of International Trade and Development, Statistics, Supplement 1986.

a/ Including technical assistance. b/ From all sources; including private flows from DAC member countries. c/ Excluding major petroleum exporters.

Source: Estimations du secrétariat de la CNUCED principalement d'après des données du secrétariat de l'OCDE/CAD et de la Banque mondiale et du Manuel de statistiques du commerce international et du développement, Supplément 1986, de la CNUCED.

a/ Y compris l'assistance technique. b/ De toutes provenances; y compris les apports privés en provenance des pays membres du CAD. c/ Non compris les principaux pays exportateurs de pétrole.

Table 18 (continued)

External assistance (net disbursements), exports and imports, 1984

$ million

Tableau 18 (suite)

Aide extérieure (versements nets), exportations et importations, 1984

Millions de dollars

| Country | Technical assistance / Assistance technique DAC/CAD | Total concessional assistance / Total de l'aide concessionnelle — All sources / Toutes provenances | Of which / DAC/CAD | Of which / OPEC/OPEP | Non-concessional[b] assistance / Aide non-concessionnelle[b] | Exports / Exportations (f.o.b.) | Imports / Importations (c.i.f.) | Total concessional assistance from all sources as % of imports / Total de l'aide concessionnelle de toutes provenances en % des importations | Pays |
|---|---|---|---|---|---|---|---|---|---|
| Afghanistan | 12.4 | 209.8 | 7.5 | -0.7 | -1.0 | 735 | 800 | 26.2 | Afghanistan |
| Bangladesh | 157.9 | 1232.0 | 1174.8 | 32.4 | 34.3 | 934 | 2042 | 60.3 | Bangladesh |
| Benin | 28.1 | 79.8 | 77.1 | 0.3 | 91.2 | 33 | 310 | 25.7 | Bénin |
| Bhutan | 8.8 | 17.9 | 17.6 | 0.3 | - | - | - | - | Bhutan |
| Botswana | 34.8 | 102.4 | 91.7 | 10.7 | 78.5 | 674 | 679 | 15.1 | Botswana |
| Burkina Faso | 71.5 | 177.4 | 178.4 | -1.0 | -1.9 | 80 | 211 | 84.1 | Burkina Faso |
| Burundi | 44.4 | 136.7 | 127.4 | 9.3 | 15.1 | 98 | 186 | 73.5 | Burundi |
| Cape Verde | 17.1 | 65.2 | 59.4 | 3.8 | 0.7 | 5 | 84 | 77.6 | Cap-Vert |
| Central African Rep. | 38.5 | 114.4 | 111.6 | 2.1 | 1.4 | 86 | 87 | 131.5 | Rép. centrafricaine |
| Chad | 18.8 | 114.9 | 114.6 | 0.3 | -2.0 | 111 | 171 | 67.2 | Tchad |
| Comoros | 9.3 | 40.3 | 33.8 | 4.9 | 1.8 | 21 | 30 | 134.5 | Comores |
| Democratic Yemen | 9.9 | 161.0 | 46.1 | 39.1 | -3.9 | 645 | 1543 | 10.4 | Yémen démocratique |
| Djibouti | 29.7 | 115.5 | 58.8 | 48.0 | 28.6 | 26 | 110 | 105.0 | Djibouti |
| Equatorial Guinea | 6.7 | 23.8 | 15.1 | -0.0 | 2.8 | 20 | 30 | 79.3 | Guinée équatoriale |
| Ethiopia | 80.8 | 517.7 | 362.9 | -0.2 | 53.8 | 417 | 942 | 55.0 | Ethiopie |
| Gambia | 14.8 | 55.2 | 53.9 | 1.3 | 7.6 | 47 | 98 | 56.3 | Gambie |
| Guinea | 18.0 | 131.1 | 88.7 | 34.4 | 5.4 | 430 | 360 | 36.4 | Guinée |
| Guinea-Bissau | 11.8 | 57.1 | 52.8 | 3.3 | 6.8 | 18 | 48 | 119.0 | Guinée-Bissau |
| Haiti | 33.5 | 134.7 | 134.3 | 0.4 | 0.2 | 179 | 472 | 28.5 | Haïti |
| Lao P.D.R. | 12.3 | 78.1 | 33.0 | 1.1 | 1.1 | 20 | 145 | 53.9 | Rép. dém. pop. lao |
| Lesotho | 31.7 | 97.7 | 92.1 | 4.8 | -4.5 | 21 | 312 | 31.3 | Lesotho |
| Malawi | 39.6 | 158.5 | 158.6 | -0.1 | 2.2 | 313 | 269 | 58.9 | Malawi |
| Maldives | 3.6 | 7.6 | 6.5 | 1.1 | -0.1 | 25 | 53 | 14.3 | Maldives |
| Mali | 59.8 | 322.9 | 309.5 | 10.4 | -6.3 | 181 | 368 | 87.7 | Mali |
| Nepal | 68.4 | 198.7 | 199.1 | -0.9 | 3.2 | 128 | 416 | 47.8 | Népal |
| Niger | 61.5 | 161.7 | 155.5 | 6.2 | -22.0 | 228 | 330 | 49.0 | Niger |
| Rwanda | 52.8 | 164.6 | 158.5 | 6.1 | -2.6 | 145 | 295 | 55.8 | Rwanda |
| Samoa | 6.9 | 20.0 | 20.2 | -0.2 | -6.6 | 19 | 50 | 40.0 | Samoa |
| Sao Tome & Principe | 2.3 | 12.3 | 10.9 | 0.4 | - | 7 | 12 | 102.5 | Sao Tomé-et-Principe |
| Sierra Leone | 19.4 | 60.8 | 44.3 | 16.1 | 11.7 | 148 | 166 | 36.6 | Sierra Leone |
| Somalia | 107.4 | 393.3 | 333.8 | 59.5 | 12.5 | 45 | 109 | 360.8 | Somalie |
| Sudan | 121.7 | 643.1 | 499.9 | 109.4 | 71.9 | 629 | 1147 | 56.1 | Soudan |
| Togo | 29.9 | 109.6 | 106.2 | 3.4 | 6.2 | 191 | 271 | 40.4 | Togo |
| Uganda | 32.4 | 165.2 | 165.2 | -1.4 | 2.0 | 399 | 371 | 44.5 | Uganda |
| U. R. of Tanzania | 138.1 | 563.8 | 540.6 | 17.6 | 48.1 | 377 | 847 | 66.6 | Rép.-Unie de Tanzanie |
| Vanuatu | 13.1 | 24.5 | 24.5 | - | 20.9 | 44 | 67 | 36.6 | Vanuatu |
| Yemen | 61.5 | 324.9 | 135.4 | 176.2 | 0.1 | 65 | 1655 | 19.6 | Yémen |
| All LDCs | 1509.2 | 6996.0 | 5800.3 | 600.1 | 457.2 | 7544 | 15086 | 46.4 | Ensemble des PMA |
| All developing countries[c] | 7193.8 | 28463.8 | 23619.6 | 2680.6 | 30366.5 | 275153 | 306099 | 9.3 | Ensemble des pays en développement[c] |

For sources and notes, see Table 18 p.29.

Pour les sources et les notes, se référer au tableau 18 p.29.

Table 19
External assistance (net disbursements), exports and imports per capita, 1983

Tableau 19
Aide extérieure (versements nets), exportations et importations par habitant, 1983

$ Dollars

| Country | Technical assistance / Assistance technique | Total concessional assistance a/ — Total de l'aide concessionnelle / All sources — Toutes provenances | of which/dont: / of which: — DAC CAD | OPEC OPEP | Non-concessional assistance b/ / Aide non-con-cessionnelle | Exports / Exporta-tions (f.o.b.) | Imports / Importa-tions (c.i.f.) | Pays |
|---|---|---|---|---|---|---|---|---|
| Afghanistan | 0.9 | 20.0 | 0.9 | -0.1 | -0.0 | 42.4 | 45.3 | Afghanistan |
| Bangladesh | 1.9 | 12.0 | 10.1 | 1.3 | 0.8 | 7.3 | 16.8 | Bangladesh |
| Benin | 6.8 | 28.1 | 21.1 | 1.7 | 1.4 | 8.4 | 84.2 | Bénin |
| Bhutan | 5.3 | 9.5 | 9.5 | - | - | - | - | Bhoutan |
| Botswana | 39.3 | 100.4 | 88.5 | 11.8 | 25.7 | 617.5 | 714.6 | Botswana |
| Burkina Faso | 9.9 | 27.8 | 27.3 | 0.4 | 1.8 | 8.6 | 43.5 | Burkina Faso |
| Burundi | 10.1 | 33.8 | 29.8 | 1.1 | 7.9 | 17.9 | 40.9 | Burundi |
| Cape Verde | 55.4 | 196.5 | 189.5 | 0.6 | 13.1 | 15.9 | 254.8 | Cap-Vert |
| Central African Rep. | 11.9 | 38.5 | 37.7 | 0.1 | 2.7 | 30.4 | 21.1 | Rép. centrafricaine |
| Chad | 4.5 | 19.9 | 19.8 | 0.0 | -0.3 | 15.4 | 32.7 | Tchad |
| Comoros | 24.1 | 101.0 | 70.4 | 23.4 | 3.3 | 47.7 | 76.4 | Comores |
| Democratic Yemen | 7.1 | 87.6 | 28.3 | 19.7 | -12.3 | 332.5 | 731.6 | Yémen démocratique |
| Djibouti | 84.6 | 193.9 | 151.0 | 42.9 | 4.3 | 72.5 | 333.3 | Djibouti |
| Equatorial Guinea | 10.4 | 53.1 | 28.5 | 1.3 | 2.7 | 53.2 | 79.8 | Guineé équatoriale |
| Ethiopia | 1.6 | 10.5 | 6.6 | - | 0.4 | 9.8 | 21.4 | Ethiopie |
| Gambia | 22.7 | 60.7 | 58.7 | 2.0 | -6.2 | 68.9 | 165.0 | Gambie |
| Guinea | 2.5 | 13.0 | 11.6 | 0.2 | 0.4 | 68.9 | 51.7 | Guinée |
| Guinea-Bissau | 18.9 | 76.7 | 67.4 | 8.1 | 2.3 | 26.8 | 75.8 | Guinée-Bissau |
| Haiti | 6.3 | 26.2 | 25.9 | 0.3 | -1.5 | 30.1 | 85.9 | Haïti |
| Lao People's Dem.Rep. | 2.9 | 23.2 | 8.0 | 0.1 | 0.1 | 10.9 | 38.3 | Rép. dém. pop. lao |
| Lesotho | 22.8 | 72.2 | 66.6 | 5.3 | 1.4 | 13.1 | 405.7 | Lesotho |
| Malawi | 5.3 | 17.9 | 17.9 | - | -1.8 | 35.0 | 47.5 | Malawi |
| Maldives | 22.2 | 66.6 | 40.3 | 26.3 | -11.1 | 111.1 | 333.2 | Maldives |
| Mali | 7.0 | 28.7 | 22.0 | 6.4 | 0.0 | 21.5 | 45.0 | Mali |
| Nepal | 4.3 | 12.8 | 12.7 | 0.1 | -0.2 | 6.0 | 29.4 | Népal |
| Niger | 10.5 | 30.7 | 27.3 | 3.2 | 5.8 | 49.7 | 60.4 | Niger |
| Rwanda | 9.5 | 27.3 | 26.3 | 0.3 | 1.8 | 21.3 | 47.4 | Rwanda |
| Samoa | 46.7 | 171.2 | 171.2 | - | 27.8 | 120.0 | 353.7 | Samoa |
| Sao Tome and Principe | 17.4 | 131.5 | 120.7 | 5.4 | - | 65.2 | 108.7 | Sao Tomé-et-Principe |
| Sierra Leone | 5.5 | 19.4 | 18.6 | 0.5 | -0.0 | 26.4 | 47.7 | Sierra Leone |
| Somalia | 22.3 | 65.9 | 55.9 | 9.4 | -4.2 | 19.7 | 35.2 | Somalie |
| Sudan | 6.2 | 48.7 | 29.4 | 17.4 | 7.9 | 30.6 | 66.4 | Soudan |
| Togo | 9.9 | 39.9 | 38.1 | 1.8 | -0.6 | 57.9 | 101.5 | Togo |
| Uganda | 2.3 | 9.4 | 8.6 | 0.8 | 1.0 | 25.7 | 29.6 | Ouganda |
| Un. Rep. of Tanzania | 8.3 | 28.9 | 27.1 | 1.6 | -1.0 | 17.6 | 39.6 | Rép.-Unie de Tanzanie |
| Vanuatu | 129.6 | 216.5 | 216.5 | - | 62.0 | 233.4 | 507.1 | Vanuatu |
| Yemen | 7.9 | 41.9 | 16.4 | 25.5 | 20.0 | 3.6 | 209.7 | Yémen |
| All LDCs | 4.9 | 22.4 | 16.8 | 3.0 | 1.5 | 22.1 | 48.2 | Ensemble des PMA |
| All developing countries c/ | 3.7 | 14.7 | 11.4 | 2.1 | 33.7 | 125.5 | 151.7 | Ensemble des pays en développement c/ |

For sources and notes, see table 18 page 29.

Pour les sources et les notes, se référer au tableau 18 page 29.

Table 19 (continued)
External assistance (net disbursements), exports and imports per capita, 1984

Tableau 19 (suite)
Aide extérieure (versements nets), exportations et importations par habitant, 1984

Dollars

| Country / Pays | Technical assistance / Assistance technique | Total concessional assistance a/ Total de l'aide concessionnelle — All sources / Toutes provenances | of which/dont: DAC CAD | of which/dont: OPEC OPEP | Non-concessional assistance b/ Aide non-concessionnelle | Exports / Exportations (f.o.b.) | Imports / Importations (c.i.f.) |
|---|---|---|---|---|---|---|---|
| Afghanistan | 0.7 | 11.9 | 0.4 | -0.0 | -0.1 | 41.6 | 45.3 |
| Bangladesh | 1.6 | 12.7 | 12.1 | 0.3 | 0.4 | 9.7 | 21.1 |
| Benin / Bénin | 7.2 | 20.3 | 19.7 | 0.1 | 23.3 | 8.4 | 79.1 |
| Bhutan / Bhoutan | 6.3 | 12.9 | 12.7 | 0.2 | - | - | - |
| Botswana | 32.6 | 95.8 | 85.8 | 10.0 | 73.4 | 630.5 | 635.2 |
| Burkina Faso | 10.5 | 26.1 | 26.3 | -0.1 | -0.3 | 11.8 | 31.1 |
| Burundi | 9.7 | 29.7 | 27.7 | 2.0 | 3.3 | 21.3 | 40.5 |
| Cape Verde / Cap-Vert | 53.4 | 203.7 | 185.6 | 11.9 | 2.2 | 15.6 | 262.5 |
| Central African Rep. / Rép. centrafricaine | 15.3 | 45.4 | 44.3 | 0.8 | 0.6 | 34.1 | 34.5 |
| Chad / Tchad | 3.8 | 23.4 | 23.3 | 0.1 | -0.4 | 22.6 | 34.8 |
| Comoros / Comores | 21.6 | 93.6 | 78.4 | 11.4 | 4.2 | 48.7 | 69.6 |
| Democratic Yemen / Yémen démocratique | 4.8 | 77.3 | 22.1 | 18.8 | -1.9 | 309.8 | 741.1 |
| Djibouti | 83.9 | 326.3 | 166.1 | 135.6 | 80.8 | 73.4 | 310.7 |
| Equatorial Guinea / Guineé équatoriale | 17.4 | 62.0 | 39.3 | -0.0 | 7.3 | 52.1 | 78.1 |
| Ethiopia / Ethiopie | 1.9 | 12.3 | 8.6 | -0.0 | 1.3 | 9.9 | 22.4 |
| Gambia / Gambie | 20.8 | 77.5 | 75.7 | 1.8 | 10.7 | 66.0 | 137.6 |
| Guinea / Guinée | 3.0 | 22.1 | 14.9 | 5.8 | 0.9 | 72.4 | 60.6 |
| Guinea-Bissau / Guinée-Bissau | 13.5 | 65.4 | 60.5 | 3.8 | 7.8 | 20.6 | 55.0 |
| Haiti / Haïti | 6.4 | 25.9 | 25.8 | 0.1 | 0.0 | 34.4 | 90.8 |
| Lao People's Dem.Rep. / Rép. dém. pop. lao | 3.3 | 20.9 | 8.8 | 0.3 | 0.3 | 5.4 | 38.8 |
| Lesotho | 21.4 | 65.9 | 62.1 | 3.2 | -3.0 | 14.2 | 210.4 |
| Malawi | 5.9 | 23.5 | 23.5 | -0.0 | -0.3 | 46.4 | 39.9 |
| Maldives | 20.4 | 43.1 | 36.9 | 6.2 | -0.6 | 141.8 | 300.7 |
| Mali | 7.6 | 41.0 | 39.3 | 1.3 | -0.8 | 23.0 | 46.8 |
| Nepal / Népal | 4.2 | 12.3 | 12.4 | -0.1 | -0.2 | 7.9 | 25.8 |
| Niger | 10.3 | 27.2 | 26.1 | 1.0 | -3.7 | 38.3 | 55.4 |
| Rwanda | 9.0 | 28.1 | 27.0 | 1.0 | -0.4 | 24.7 | 50.3 |
| Samoa | 43.3 | 125.6 | 126.8 | -1.3 | -41.4 | 119.3 | 313.9 |
| Sao Tome and Principe / Sao Tomé-et-Principe | 24.5 | 130.9 | 116.0 | 4.3 | - | 74.5 | 127.7 |
| Sierra Leone | 5.5 | 17.2 | 12.5 | 4.5 | 3.3 | 41.8 | 46.9 |
| Somalia / Somalie | 20.5 | 75.2 | 63.8 | 11.4 | 2.4 | 8.6 | 20.8 |
| Sudan / Soudan | 5.8 | 30.7 | 23.8 | 5.2 | 3.4 | 30.0 | 54.7 |
| Togo | 10.4 | 38.1 | 36.9 | 1.2 | 2.2 | 66.3 | 94.1 |
| Uganda / Ouganda | 2.2 | 11.0 | 11.0 | -0.1 | 0.1 | 26.7 | 24.8 |
| Un. Rep. of Tanzania / Rép.-Unie de Tanzanie | 6.4 | 26.2 | 25.2 | 0.8 | 2.2 | 17.5 | 39.4 |
| Vanuatu | 102.6 | 191.8 | 191.8 | - | 163.6 | 344.5 | 524.6 |
| Yemen / Yémen | 7.9 | 41.7 | 17.4 | 22.6 | 0.0 | 8.3 | 212.5 |
| All LDCs / Ensemble des PMA | 4.7 | 21.7 | 18.0 | 1.9 | 1.4 | 23.4 | 46.9 |
| All developing countries c/ / Ensemble des pays en développement c/ | 3.6 | 14.3 | 11.9 | 1.3 | 15.3 | 138.2 | 153.8 |

For sources and notes, see table 18 page 29.   Pour les sources et les notes, se référer au tableau 18 page 29.

Table 20

Tableau 20

Percentage distribution of financial flows to all LDCs and to all developing countries by type of flow, 1970, 1975 and 1980-1984

Répartition en pourcentage des apports financiers à l'ensemble des PMA et à l'ensemble des pays en développement, par catégorie d'apports, 1970, 1975 et 1980-1984

Percentages

En pourcentage

| | Least developed countries / Pays les moins avancés | | | | | | | All developing countries / Ensemble des pays en développement | | | | | | | |
|---|---|---|---|---|---|---|---|---|---|---|---|---|---|---|---|
| | 1970 | 1975 | 1980 | 1981 | 1982 | 1983 | 1984 | 1970 | 1975 | 1980 | 1981 | 1982 | 1983 | 1984 | |
| I. Concessional loans and grants | 90.0 | 86.4 | 85.4 | 91.9 | 90.1 | 93.7 | 93.9 | 46.2 | 37.5 | 41.5 | 35.0 | 36.6 | 29.3 | 37.9 | I. Prêts concessionnels et dons |
| Of which : | | | | | | | | | | | | | | | Dont : |
| DAC | 80.1 | 65.1 | 66.1 | 72.9 | 69.4 | 70.3 | 77.8 | 39.0 | 24.0 | 28.2 | 24.3 | 27.3 | 22.2 | 30.6 | CAD |
| - Bilateral | 61.9 | 43.2 | 41.8 | 45.2 | 44.3 | 42.4 | 45.4 | 32.7 | 17.2 | 19.6 | 17.3 | 19.3 | 15.6 | 21.7 | - Apports bilatéraux |
| - Multilateral a/ | 18.2 | 21.9 | 24.3 | 27.7 | 25.1 | 27.9 | 32.4 | 6.2 | 6.8 | 8.6 | 7.0 | 8.0 | 6.6 | 8.9 | - Apports multilatéraux a/ |
| - Grants | 52.3 | 40.3 | 58.6 | 57.7 | 51.6 | 52.0 | 55.2 | 23.4 | 14.7 | 19.2 | 16.2 | 18.2 | 15.3 | 21.7 | - Dons |
| - Loans | 27.8 | 24.8 | 7.5 | 15.1 | 17.8 | 18.3 | 22.6 | 15.6 | 9.3 | 9.0 | 8.1 | 9.1 | 6.9 | 8.9 | - Prêts |
| - Technical Assistance | 27.5 | 14.7 | 17.8 | 21.2 | 19.1 | 20.5 | 20.2 | 11.2 | 7.4 | 8.4 | 7.4 | 8.4 | 7.2 | 9.5 | - Assistance technique |
| - Other | 52.6 | 50.4 | 48.2 | 51.6 | 50.3 | 49.8 | 57.6 | 27.8 | 16.6 | 19.7 | 16.9 | 18.9 | 15.0 | 21.1 | - Autres |
| OPEC | 0.6 | 15.5 | 12.5 | 12.2 | 13.7 | 12.7 | 8.1 | 2.3 | 10.8 | 10.7 | 8.4 | 6.7 | 4.9 | 4.6 | OPEP |
| - Bilateral | 0.6 | 13.6 | 10.9 | 9.4 | 11.6 | 10.8 | 7.0 | 2.3 | 10.5 | 10.4 | 8.0 | 6.3 | 4.6 | 4.4 | - Apports bilatéraux |
| - Multilateral b/ | - | 1.9 | 1.6 | 2.8 | 2.1 | 1.9 | 1.1 | - | 0.3 | 0.3 | 0.4 | 0.4 | 0.3 | 0.2 | - Apports multilatéraux b/ |
| - Grants | 0.0 | 10.3 | 5.3 | 3.4 | 7.1 | 8.2 | 4.9 | 2.1 | 5.9 | 4.7 | 3.5 | 3.4 | 2.3 | 2.5 | - Dons |
| - Loans | 0.5 | 5.2 | 7.3 | 8.7 | 6.6 | 4.5 | 3.1 | 0.2 | 4.9 | 6.0 | 4.9 | 3.3 | 2.6 | 2.1 | - Prêts |
| II. Non-concessional flows | 10.0 | 13.6 | 14.6 | 8.1 | 9.9 | 6.3 | 6.1 | 53.8 | 62.5 | 58.5 | 65.0 | 63.4 | 70.7 | 62.1 | II. Courants financiers non-concessionnels |
| Of which : | | | | | | | | | | | | | | | Dont : |
| DAC | 10.0 | 10.4 | 14.0 | 7.8 | 10.9 | 5.8 | 6.2 | 51.9 | 56.1 | 57.6 | 63.7 | 62.1 | 70.1 | 61.2 | CAD |
| - Bilateral official | -0.1 | 0.1 | 2.8 | 2.1 | 2.4 | 2.9 | 3.5 | 4.2 | 3.3 | 5.1 | 4.1 | 5.9 | 3.2 | 6.5 | - Apports publics bilatéraux |
| - Multilateral a/ | 5.2 | 2.5 | 1.1 | 0.9 | 0.8 | 1.1 | 0.9 | 4.1 | 4.6 | 5.3 | 5.5 | 7.3 | 6.6 | 9.7 | - Apports multilatéraux a/ |
| - Export credits c/ | 3.3 | 5.0 | 10.7 | 2.8 | 2.3 | 1.2 | 1.1 | 11.9 | 7.8 | 13.0 | 8.8 | 7.4 | 4.5 | 5.6 | - Crédits à l'exportation c/ |
| - Direct investment | 1.2 | 1.3 | 0.7 | 1.5 | 2.2 | 0.4 | 0.4 | 19.9 | 19.7 | 11.7 | 16.3 | 13.5 | 8.5 | 12.1 | - Investissements directs |
| - Other d/ | 0.4e/ | 1.4e/ | -1.3e/ | 0.5e/ | 3.3e/ | 0.2e/ | 0.3e/ | 11.9 | 20.6 | 22.4 | 29.0 | 28.0 | 47.3 | 27.4 | - Autres d/ |
| TOTAL FINANCIAL FLOWS | 100.0 | 100.0 | 100.0 | 100.0 | 100.0 | 100.0 | 100.0 | 100.0 | 100.0 | 100.0 | 100.0 | 100.0 | 100.0 | 100.0 | TOTAL DES APPORTS FINANCIERS |

For source and notes see table 21A.

Pour les sources et les notes, se référer au tableau 21A.

Table 21A
Composition of total financial flows in current dollars,
1970 and 1975-1984 : all LDCs

Net disbursements in $ million

Tableau 21A
Composition des courants financiers en dollars courants,
1970 et 1975-1984 : ensemble des PMA

Versements nets en millions de dollars

| | 1970 | 1975 | 1976 | 1977 | 1978 | 1979 | 1980 | 1981 | 1982 | 1983 | 1984 |
|---|---|---|---|---|---|---|---|---|---|---|---|
| Concessional loans & grants — Prêts concessionnels et dons | (921) | 3659 | 3296 | 3797 | 4697 | 5571 | 6970 | 6587 | 7051 | 7049 | 6996 |
| of which / Dont: | | | | | | | | | | | |
| DAC — CAD | (820) | 2755 | 2323 | 2608 | 3755 | 4551 | 5392 | 5224 | 5437 | 5295 | 5800 |
|   - Bilateral a/ — Apports bilatéraux | (634) | 1827 | 1439 | 1635 | 2326 | 2885 | 3409 | 3242 | 3472 | 3192 | 3386 |
|   - Multilateral a/ — Apports multilatéraux a/ | (186) | 928 | 884 | 973 | 1429 | 1667 | 1983 | 1982 | 1965 | 2102 | 2414 |
|   - Grants — Dons | (535) | 1704 | 1513 | 1718 | 2866 | 3443 | 4781 | 4138 | 4039 | 3916 | 4113 |
|   - loans — Prêts | (284) | 1051 | 810 | 890 | 889 | 1108 | 611 | 1086 | 1397 | 1379 | 1687 |
|   - Technical assistance — Assistance technique | (281) | 621 | 642 | 655 | 889 | 1134 | 1456 | 1522 | 1495 | 1543 | 1509 |
|   - Other — Autres | (539) | 2134 | 1681 | 1953 | 2866 | 3417 | 3936 | 3702 | 3941 | 3751 | 4291 |
| OPEC — OPEP | (6) | 656 | 760 | 959 | 737 | 792 | 1021 | 873 | 1073 | 956 | 600 |
|   - Bilateral — Apports bilatéraux | (6) | 576 | 677 | 852 | 647 | 695 | 887 | 674 | 909 | 813 | 519 |
|   - Multilateral b/ — Apports multilatéraux b/ | (-) | 81 | 83 | 108 | 90 | 96 | 134 | 199 | 164 | 143 | 81 |
|   - Grants — Dons | (0) | 436 | 396 | 705 | 380 | 233 | 429 | 247 | 557 | 617 | 368 |
|   - Loans — Prêts | (6) | 220 | 364 | 255 | 356 | 558 | 592 | 626 | 516 | 339 | 232 |
| Non-concessional flows — Courants financiers non-concessionnels | (103) | 574 | 411 | 519 | 365 | 800 | 1192 | 581 | 779 | 477 | 457 |
| of which / Dont: | | | | | | | | | | | |
| DAC — CAD | (103) | 439 | 370 | 516 | 406 | 779 | 1143 | 558 | 853 | 434 | 460 |
|   - Bilateral official — Apports publics bilatéraux | (-2) | 6 | 35 | 33 | 18 | 122 | 228 | 151 | 188 | 216 | 261 |
|   - Multilateral a/ — Apports multilatéraux a/ | (54) | 107 | 22 | 41 | 66 | 91 | 89 | 64 | 65 | 82 | 66 |
|   - Export credits c/ — Crédits à l'exportation c/ | (34) | 211 | 215 | 330 | 249 | 403 | 873 | 201 | 177 | 93 | 81 |
|   - Direct investment — Investissements directs | (12) | 57 | 74 | 116 | 56 | 40 | 55 | 107 | 169 | 30 | 32 |
|   - Other d/ e/ — Autres d/ e/ | (4) | 59 | 23 | -4 | 17 | 124 | -103 | 35 | 255 | 13 | 20 |
| TOTAL FINANCIAL FLOWS — TOTAL DES APPORTS FINANCIERS | (1024) | 4233 | 3708 | 4316 | 5062 | 6371 | 8162 | 7169 | 7830 | 7526 | 7453 |

Source: UNCTAD secretariat calculations mainly based on OECD/DAC and UNCTAD data.

a/ From multilateral agencies mainly financed by DAC member countries.
b/ From multilateral agencies mainly financed by OPEC member countries.
c/ Guaranteed private.
d/ Bilateral financial flows originating in DAC countries and their capital markets in the form of bond lending and bank lending (either directly or through syndicated "Eurocurrency credits").
e/ Only flows allocated by individual recipient country.

Source: Chiffres calculés par le secrétariat de la CNUCED d'après des données de l'OCDE/CAD et de la CNUCED.

a/ En provenance des institutions multilatérales essentiellement financées par les pays membres du CAD.
b/ En provenance des institutions multilatérales essentiellement financées par les pays membres de l'OPEP.
c/ Privés garantis.
d/ Apports financiers bilatéraux provenant des pays membres du CAD ou passant par leurs marchés de capitaux, sous forme d'émissions d'obligations et de prêts bancaires (soit directement, soit comme crédits consortiaux en euromonnaies).
e/ Uniquement les apports alloués par pays bénéficiaires.

Table 21B
Composition of total financial flows in current dollars, 1970 and 1975-1984 : all developing countries

Tableau 21B
Composition des courants financiers en dollars courants, 1970 et 1975-1984 : ensemble des pays en développement

Net disbursements in $ million / Versements nets en millions de dollars

| | 1970 | 1975 | 1976 | 1977 | 1978 | 1979 | 1980 | 1981 | 1982 | 1983 | 1984 |
|---|---|---|---|---|---|---|---|---|---|---|---|
| **Concessional loans & grants** / Prêts concessionnels et dons | 7898 | 20174 | 19101 | 18489 | 25752 | 29480 | 35701 | 34662 | 32085 | 31233 | 31053 |
| of which: DAC / Dont: CAD | 6658 | 12917 | 12077 | 12633 | 16738 | 20593 | 24240 | 24107 | 23941 | 23682 | 25032 |
| – Bilateral / Apports bilatéraux | 5591 | 9246 | 8658 | 8978 | 11869 | 14777 | 16877 | 17144 | 16931 | 16638 | 17720 |
| – Multilateral a/ / Apports multilatéraux a/ | 1067 | 3671 | 3419 | 3655 | 4869 | 5816 | 7363 | 6963 | 7010 | 7044 | 7312 |
| – Grants / Dons | 3994 | 7893 | 7532 | 8211 | 10915 | 13760 | 16525 | 16090 | 15945 | 16297 | 17769 |
| – loans / Prêts | 2664 | 5023 | 4546 | 4422 | 5822 | 6833 | 7715 | 8017 | 7996 | 7385 | 7264 |
| – Technical assistance / Assistance technique | 1910 | 3971 | 3807 | 4076 | 4998 | 6248 | 7250 | 7379 | 7359 | 7705 | 7760 |
| – Other / Autres | 4748 | 8946 | 8270 | 8557 | 11740 | 14345 | 16990 | 16728 | 16583 | 15977 | 17273 |
| OPEC / OPEP | 391 | 5797 | 5579 | 4470 | 7549 | 7157 | 9200 | 8297 | 5871 | 5196 | 3776 |
| – Bilateral / Apports bilatéraux | 391 | 5638 | 5160 | 4249 | 7248 | 6906 | 8912 | 7930 | 5517 | 4872 | 3634 |
| – Multilateral b/ / Apports multilatéraux b/ | - | 159 | 418 | 221 | 301 | 251 | 287 | 367 | 354 | 324 | 143 |
| – Grants / Dons | 364 | 3166 | 2602 | 3017 | 2262 | 3751 | 4016 | 3473 | 2971 | 2406 | 2061 |
| – Loans / Prêts | 27 | 2631 | 2977 | 1453 | 5287 | 3406 | 5184 | 4824 | 2900 | 2790 | 1716 |
| **Non-concessional flows** / Courants financiers non-concessionnels | 9185 | 33625 | 36000 | 40821 | 51699 | 46322 | 50385 | 64472 | 55695 | 75469 | 50793 |
| of which: DAC / Dont: CAD | 8865 | 30177 | 33251 | 39387 | 50661 | 45927 | 49546 | 63129 | 54514 | 74790 | 50088 |
| – Bilateral official / Apports publics bilatéraux | 715 | 1780 | 2057 | 1848 | 2951 | 2605 | 4415 | 4105 | 5220 | 3448 | 5325 |
| – Multilateral a/ / Apports multilatéraux a/ | 694 | 2480 | 2468 | 2625 | 2878 | 3838 | 4574 | 5414 | 6381 | 7018 | 7913 |
| – Export credits c/ / Crédits à l'exportation c/ | 2032 | 4222 | 6037 | 8310 | 9494 | 8410 | 11159 | 8752 | 6501 | 4802 | 4567 |
| – Direct investment / Investissements directs | 3391 | 10597 | 7881 | 9321 | 10974 | 11633 | 10084 | 16111 | 11841 | 9036 | 9887 |
| – Other d/ / Autres d/ | (2032 | 11098 | 14808 | 17282 | 24364 | 19441 | 19313 | 28746 | 24570 | 50486 | 22397) |
| **TOTAL FINANCIAL FLOWS** / TOTAL DES APPORTS FINANCIERS | 17083 | 53799 | 55101 | 59310 | 77451 | 75802 | 86086 | 99133 | 87779 | 106702 | 81845 |

For sources and notes, see table 21A.

Pour les sources et les notes, se référer au tableau 21A.

Table 22A
Composition of total financial flows in constant dollars,
1970 and 1975-1984 : all LDCs

Tableau 22A
Composition des courants financiers en dollars constants,
1970 et 1975-1984 : ensemble des PMA

Net disbursements in millions of 1980 dollars
Versements nets en millions de dollars de 1980

| | 1970 | 1975 | 1976 | 1977 | 1978 | 1979 | 1980 | 1981 | 1982 | 1983 | 1984 | |
|---|---|---|---|---|---|---|---|---|---|---|---|---|
| Concessional loans & grants | (3453) | 6572 | 5862 | 6159 | 6935 | 6758 | 6970 | 6787 | 7584 | 7922 | 8031 | Prêts concessionnels et dons |
| of which : | | | | | | | | | | | | Dont : |
| DAC | (3073) | 4949 | 4131 | 4231 | 5545 | 5521 | 5392 | 5383 | 5847 | 5950 | 6659 | CAD |
| - Bilateral | (2376) | 3281 | 2560 | 2652 | 3434 | 3499 | 3409 | 3341 | 3734 | 3588 | 3888 | - Apports bilatéraux |
| - Multilateral a/ | (697) | 1668 | 1572 | 1579 | 2110 | 2022 | 1983 | 2042 | 2113 | 2363 | 2771 | - Apports multilatéraux a/ |
| - Grants | (2007) | 3061 | 2690 | 2788 | 4232 | 4177 | 4781 | 4264 | 4344 | 4401 | 4722 | - Dons |
| - loans | (1066) | 1888 | 1441 | 1443 | 1312 | 1344 | 611 | 1119 | 1503 | 1550 | 1937 | - Prêts |
| - Technical assistance | (1054) | 1116 | 1141 | 1062 | 1313 | 1376 | 1456 | 1568 | 1608 | 1734 | 1733 | - Assistance technique |
| - Other | (2019) | 3833 | 2990 | 3169 | 4232 | 4145 | 3936 | 3815 | 4239 | 4216 | 4926 | - Autres |
| OPEC | (22) | 1179 | 1352 | 1557 | 1088 | 960 | 1021 | 899 | 1154 | 1074 | 689 | OPEP |
| - Bilateral | (22) | 1034 | 1205 | 1382 | 955 | 843 | 887 | 694 | 977 | 914 | 596 | - Apports bilatéraux |
| - Multilateral b/ | - | 145 | 148 | 174 | 133 | 117 | 134 | 205 | 176 | 160 | 93 | - Apports multilatéraux b/ |
| - Grants | (1) | 783 | 704 | 1143 | 562 | 283 | 429 | 254 | 599 | 693 | 423 | - Dons |
| - Loans | (21) | 395 | 648 | 413 | 526 | 677 | 592 | 645 | 555 | 381 | 266 | - Prêts |
| Non-concessional flows | (385) | 1030 | 731 | 843 | 539 | 970 | 1192 | 599 | 837 | 536 | 525 | Courants financiers non-concessionnels |
| of which : | | | | | | | | | | | | Dont : |
| DAC | (385) | 789 | 657 | 837 | 600 | 945 | 1143 | 575 | 918 | 488 | 527 | CAD |
| - Bilateral official | (-6) | 10 | 63 | 53 | 27 | 148 | 228 | 156 | 202 | 243 | 300 | - Apports publics bilatéraux |
| - Multilateral a/ | (201) | 191 | 39 | 66 | 98 | 110 | 89 | 66 | 69 | 92 | 76 | - Apports multilatéraux a/ |
| - Export credits c/ | (127) | 379 | 383 | 536 | 367 | 488 | 873 | 207 | 191 | 105 | 93 | - Crédits à l'exportation c/ |
| - Direct investment | (45) | 102 | 131 | 188 | 83 | 48 | 55 | 110 | 182 | 34 | 37 | - Investissements directs |
| - Other d/ e/ | (16) | 106 | 41 | -6 | 25 | 151 | -103 | 36 | 274 | 15 | 22 | - Autres d/ e/ |
| TOTAL FINANCIAL FLOWS | (3838) | 7602 | 6594 | 7002 | 7474 | 7728 | 8162 | 7386 | 8421 | 8459 | 8556 | TOTAL DES APPORTS FINANCIERS |

For sources and notes, see table 21A.

Pour les sources et les notes, se référer au tableau 21A.

Table 22B
Composition of total financial flows in constant dollars,
1970 and 1975-1984 : all developing countries

Net disbursements in millions of 1980 dollars

Tableau 22B
Composition des courants financiers en dollars constants,
1970 et 1975-1984 : ensemble des pays en développement

Versements nets en millions de dollars de 1980

| | 1970 | 1975 | 1976 | 1977 | 1978 | 1979 | 1980 | 1981 | 1982 | 1983 | 1984 | |
|---|---|---|---|---|---|---|---|---|---|---|---|---|
| Concessional loans & grants of which: | 33650 | 37964 | 35100 | 30933 | 39377 | 36753 | 35701 | 34980 | 33667 | 34329 | 34863 | Prêts concessionnels et dons Dont: |
| DAC | 28369 | 24307 | 22193 | 21136 | 25593 | 25674 | 24240 | 24328 | 25122 | 26030 | 28104 | CAD |
| - Bilateral | 23824 | 17399 | 15910 | 15021 | 18148 | 18423 | 16877 | 17301 | 17766 | 18288 | 19895 | - Apports bilatéraux |
| - Multilateral a/ | 4545 | 6908 | 6283 | 6115 | 7444 | 7251 | 7363 | 7027 | 7356 | 7743 | 8210 | - Apports multilatéraux a/ |
| - Grants | 17017 | 14854 | 13840 | 13738 | 16690 | 17155 | 16525 | 16237 | 16731 | 17912 | 19949 | - Dons |
| - loans | 11352 | 9453 | 8353 | 7398 | 8903 | 8519 | 7715 | 8091 | 8391 | 8118 | 8155 | - Prêts |
| - Technical assistance | 8138 | 7473 | 6996 | 6819 | 7642 | 7789 | 7250 | 7446 | 7722 | 8469 | 8712 | - Assistance technique |
| - Other | 20231 | 16835 | 15198 | 14317 | 17950 | 17885 | 16990 | 16882 | 17401 | 17562 | 19392 | - Autres |
| OPEC | 1664 | 10909 | 10251 | 7479 | 11543 | 8923 | 9200 | 8374 | 6161 | 5711 | 4240 | OPEP |
| - Bilateral | 1664 | 10610 | 9483 | 7109 | 11083 | 8611 | 8912 | 8003 | 5789 | 5355 | 4080 | - Apports bilatéraux |
| - Multilateral b/ | - | 299 | 768 | 369 | 461 | 312 | 287 | 371 | 372 | 357 | 160 | - Apports multilatéraux b/ |
| - Grants | 1550 | 5957 | 4781 | 5048 | 3459 | 4676 | 4016 | 3505 | 3118 | 2644 | 2314 | - Dons |
| - Loans | 115 | 4951 | 5470 | 2431 | 8085 | 4246 | 5184 | 4869 | 3043 | 3067 | 1926 | - Prêts |
| Non-concessional flows | 39135 | 63277 | 66153 | 68297 | 79050 | 57751 | 50385 | 65064 | 58442 | 82951 | 57026 | Courants financiers non-concessionnels Dont: |
| DAC | 37771 | 56787 | 61102 | 65898 | 77464 | 57258 | 49546 | 63708 | 57203 | 82205 | 56235 | CAD |
| - Bilateral official | 3046 | 3350 | 3781 | 3092 | 4512 | 3248 | 4415 | 4143 | 5478 | 3790 | 5978 | - Apports publics bilatéraux |
| - Multilateral a/ | 2959 | 4667 | 4534 | 4392 | 4401 | 4785 | 4574 | 5464 | 6696 | 7714 | 8884 | - Apports multilatéraux a/ |
| - Export credits c/ | 8660 | 7945 | 11093 | 13904 | 14516 | 10485 | 11159 | 8832 | 6821 | 5279 | 5127 | - Crédits à l'exportation c/ |
| - Direct investment | 14449 | 19941 | 14482 | 15595 | 16780 | 14503 | 10084 | 16259 | 12425 | 9932 | 11100 | - Investissements directs |
| - Other d/ | ( 8658 | 20884 | 27211 | 28915 | 37254 | 24237 | 19313 | 29010 | 25782 | 55491 | 25145) | - Autres d/ |
| TOTAL FINANCIAL FLOWS | 72785 | 101240 | 101232 | 99230 | 112486 | 94504 | 86086 | 100044 | 92019 | 117280 | 91889 | TOTAL DES APPORTS FINANCIERS |

For sources and notes, see table 21A.

Pour les sources et les notes, se référer au tableau 21A.

**Table 23A**
Composition of total financial flows in constant dollars per capita, 1970 and 1975-1984 : all LDCs
Net disbursements in 1980 dollars

**Tableau 23A**
Composition des courants financiers en dollars constants par habitant, 1970 et 1975-1984 : ensemble des PMA
Versements nets en dollars de 1980

| | 1970 | 1975 | 1976 | 1977 | 1978 | 1979 | 1980 | 1981 | 1982 | 1983 | 1984 |
|---|---|---|---|---|---|---|---|---|---|---|---|
| Concessional loans & grants / Prêts concessionnels et dons | (15.4) | 25.6 | 22.3 | 22.8 | 25.0 | 23.8 | 23.9 | 22.7 | 24.7 | 25.2 | 24.9 |
| of which: / Dont: — DAC / CAD | (13.7) | 19.3 | 15.7 | 15.7 | 20.0 | 19.4 | 18.5 | 18.0 | 19.0 | 18.9 | 20.6 |
|   — Bilateral / Apports bilatéraux | (10.6) | 12.8 | 9.7 | 9.8 | 12.4 | 12.3 | 11.7 | 11.2 | 12.2 | 11.4 | 12.0 |
|   — Multilateral a/ / Apports multilatéraux a/ | (3.1) | 6.5 | 6.0 | 5.8 | 7.6 | 7.1 | 6.8 | 6.8 | 6.9 | 7.5 | 8.6 |
|   — Grants / Dons | (8.9) | 11.9 | 10.2 | 10.3 | 15.3 | 14.7 | 16.4 | 14.3 | 14.2 | 14.0 | 14.6 |
|   — loans / Prêts | (4.7) | 7.4 | 5.5 | 5.3 | 4.7 | 4.7 | 2.1 | 3.7 | 4.9 | 4.9 | 6.0 |
|   — Technical assistance / Assistance technique | (4.7) | 4.4 | 4.3 | 3.9 | 4.7 | 4.8 | 5.0 | 5.2 | 5.2 | 5.5 | 5.4 |
|   — Other / Autres | (9.0) | 14.9 | 11.4 | 11.7 | 15.3 | 14.6 | 13.5 | 12.8 | 13.8 | 13.4 | 15.2 |
| OPEC / OPEP | (0.1) | 4.6 | 5.1 | 5.8 | 3.9 | 3.4 | 3.5 | 3.0 | 3.8 | 3.4 | 2.1 |
|   — Bilateral / Apports bilatéraux | (0.1) | 4.0 | 4.6 | 5.1 | 3.4 | 3.0 | 3.0 | 2.3 | 3.2 | 2.9 | 1.8 |
|   — Multilateral b/ / Apports multilatéraux b/ | - | 0.6 | 0.6 | 0.6 | 0.5 | 0.4 | 0.5 | 0.7 | 0.6 | 0.5 | 0.3 |
|   — Grants / Dons | (0.0) | 3.1 | 2.7 | 4.2 | 2.0 | 1.0 | 1.5 | 0.8 | 2.0 | 2.2 | 1.3 |
|   — Loans / Prêts | (0.1) | 1.5 | 2.5 | 1.5 | 1.9 | 2.4 | 2.0 | 2.2 | 1.8 | 1.2 | 0.8 |
| Non-concessional flows / Courants financiers non-concessionnels | (1.7) | 4.0 | 2.8 | 3.1 | 1.9 | 3.4 | 4.1 | 2.0 | 2.7 | 1.7 | 1.6 |
| of which: / Dont: — DAC / CAD | (1.7) | 3.1 | 2.5 | 3.1 | 2.2 | 3.3 | 3.9 | 1.9 | 3.0 | 1.5 | 1.6 |
|   — Bilateral official / Apports publics bilatéraux | (0.9) | - | 0.2 | 0.2 | 0.1 | 0.5 | 0.8 | 0.5 | 0.7 | 0.8 | 0.9 |
|   — Multilateral a/ / Apports multilatéraux a/ | (0.6) | 0.7 | 0.1 | 0.2 | 0.4 | 0.4 | 0.3 | 0.2 | 0.2 | 0.3 | 0.2 |
|   — Export credits c/ / Crédits à l'exportation c/ | (0.2) | 1.5 | 1.5 | 2.0 | 1.3 | 1.7 | 3.0 | 0.7 | 0.6 | 0.3 | 0.3 |
|   — Direct investment / Investissements directs | (0.1) | 0.4 | 0.5 | 0.7 | 0.3 | 0.2 | 0.2 | 0.4 | 0.6 | 0.1 | 0.1 |
|   — Other d/ e/ / Autres d/ e/ | | 0.4 | 0.2 | - | 0.1 | 0.5 | -0.4 | 0.1 | 0.9 | - | - |
| TOTAL FINANCIAL FLOWS / TOTAL DES APPORTS FINANCIERS | (17.1) | 29.6 | 25.0 | 25.9 | 26.9 | 27.2 | 28.0 | 24.7 | 27.4 | 26.9 | 26.5 |

For sources and notes, see table 21A.

Pour les sources et les notes, se référer au tableau 21A.

Table 23B
Composition of total financial flows in constant dollars
per capita, 1970 and 1975-1984 : all developing countries

Net disbursements in 1980 dollars

Tableau 23B
Composition des courants financiers en dollars constants
par habitant, 1970 et 1975-1984 : ensemble des pays en développement

Versements nets en dollars de 1980

| | 1970 | 1975 | 1976 | 1977 | 1978 | 1979 | 1980 | 1981 | 1982 | 1983 | 1984 | |
|---|---|---|---|---|---|---|---|---|---|---|---|---|
| Concessional loans & grants | 19.0 | 19.0 | 17.1 | 14.7 | 18.3 | 16.7 | 15.9 | 15.2 | 14.3 | 14.2 | 14.1 | Prêts concessionnels et dons |
| of which : DAC | 16.1 | 12.2 | 10.8 | 10.1 | 11.9 | 11.7 | 10.8 | 10.6 | 10.6 | 10.8 | 11.4 | Dont : CAD |
| – Bilateral | 13.5 | 8.7 | 7.8 | 7.2 | 8.4 | 8.4 | 7.5 | 7.5 | 7.5 | 7.6 | 8.0 | – Apports bilatéraux |
| – Multilateral a/ | 2.6 | 3.5 | 3.1 | 2.9 | 3.5 | 3.3 | 3.3 | 3.0 | 3.1 | 3.2 | 3.3 | – Apports multilatéraux a/ |
| – Grants | 9.6 | 7.4 | 6.8 | 6.5 | 7.8 | 7.8 | 7.3 | 7.0 | 7.1 | 7.4 | 8.1 | – Dons |
| – loans | 6.4 | 4.7 | 4.1 | 3.5 | 4.1 | 3.9 | 3.4 | 3.5 | 3.6 | 3.4 | 3.3 | – Prêts |
| – Technical assistance | 4.6 | 3.7 | 3.4 | 3.2 | 3.6 | 3.5 | 3.2 | 3.2 | 3.3 | 3.5 | 3.5 | – Assistance technique |
| – Other | 11.5 | 8.4 | 7.4 | 6.8 | 8.4 | 8.1 | 7.5 | 7.3 | 7.4 | 7.3 | 7.8 | – Autres |
| OPEC | 0.9 | 5.5 | 5.0 | 3.6 | 5.4 | 4.1 | 4.1 | 3.6 | 2.6 | 2.4 | 1.7 | OPEP |
| – Bilateral | 0.9 | 5.3 | 4.6 | 3.4 | 5.2 | 3.9 | 4.0 | 3.5 | 2.5 | 2.2 | 1.7 | – Apports bilatéraux |
| – Multilateral b/ | – | 0.1 | 0.4 | 0.2 | 0.2 | 0.1 | 0.1 | 0.2 | 0.2 | 0.1 | 0.1 | – Apports multilatéraux b/ |
| – Grants | 0.9 | 3.0 | 2.3 | 2.4 | 1.6 | 2.1 | 1.8 | 1.5 | 1.3 | 1.1 | 0.9 | – Dons |
| – Loans | 0.1 | 2.5 | 2.7 | 1.2 | 3.8 | 1.9 | 2.3 | 2.1 | 1.3 | 1.3 | 0.8 | – Prêts |
| Non-concessional flows | 22.2 | 31.7 | 32.3 | 32.5 | 36.8 | 26.3 | 22.4 | 28.2 | 24.8 | 34.3 | 23.1 | Courants financiers non-concessionnels |
| of which : DAC | 21.4 | 28.4 | 29.8 | 31.4 | 36.0 | 26.0 | 22.0 | 27.6 | 24.2 | 34.0 | 22.8 | Dont : CAD |
| – Bilateral official | 1.7 | 1.7 | 1.8 | 1.5 | 2.1 | 1.5 | 2.0 | 1.8 | 2.3 | 1.6 | 2.4 | – Apports publics bilatéraux |
| – Multilateral a/ | 1.7 | 2.3 | 2.2 | 2.1 | 2.0 | 2.2 | 2.0 | 2.4 | 2.8 | 3.2 | 3.6 | – Apports multilatéraux a/ |
| – Export credits c/ | 4.9 | 4.0 | 5.4 | 6.6 | 6.8 | 4.8 | 5.0 | 3.8 | 2.9 | 2.2 | 2.1 | – Crédits à l'exportation c/ |
| – Direct investment | 8.2 | 10.0 | 7.1 | 7.4 | 7.8 | 6.6 | 4.5 | 7.1 | 5.3 | 4.1 | 4.5 | – Investissements directs |
| – Other d/ | (4.9) | (10.5) | (13.3) | (13.8) | (17.3) | (11.0) | (8.6) | (12.6) | (10.9) | (23.0) | (10.2) | – Autres d/ |
| TOTAL FINANCIAL FLOWS | 41.2 | 50.7 | 49.4 | 47.3 | 55.1 | 43.0 | 38.3 | 43.4 | 39.0 | 48.5 | 37.2 | TOTAL DES APPORTS FINANCIERS |

For sources and notes, see table 21A.

Pour les sources et les notes, se référer au tableau 21A.

Table 24
Share of LDCs in flows to all developing countries, by type of flow, 1970 and 1975-1984

Tableau 24
Part des PMA dans les apports financiers à l'ensemble des pays en développement, par catégories d'apports, 1970 et 1975-1984

Percentages / En pourcentage

| | 1970 | 1975 | 1976 | 1977 | 1978 | 1979 | 1980 | 1981 | 1982 | 1983 | 1984 | |
|---|---|---|---|---|---|---|---|---|---|---|---|---|
| Concessional loans & grants | (11.7) | 18.1 | 17.3 | 20.5 | 18.2 | 18.9 | 19.5 | 19.0 | 22.0 | 22.6 | 22.5 | Prêts concessionnels et dons |
| of which: / DAC | (12.3) | 21.3 | 19.2 | 20.6 | 22.4 | 22.1 | 22.2 | 21.7 | 22.7 | 22.4 | 23.2 | Dont: / CAD |
| - Bilateral | (11.3) | 19.8 | 16.6 | 18.2 | 19.6 | 19.5 | 20.2 | 18.9 | 20.5 | 19.2 | 19.1 | - Apports bilatéraux |
| - Multilateral a/ | (17.4) | 25.3 | 25.8 | 26.6 | 29.4 | 28.7 | 26.9 | 28.5 | 28.0 | 29.8 | 33.0 | - Apports multilatéraux a/ |
| - Grants | (13.4) | 21.6 | 20.1 | 20.9 | 26.3 | 25.0 | 28.9 | 25.7 | 25.3 | 24.0 | 23.1 | - Dons |
| - Loans | (10.7) | 20.9 | 17.8 | 20.1 | 15.3 | 16.2 | 7.9 | 13.5 | 17.5 | 18.7 | 23.2 | - Prêts |
| - Technical assistance | (14.7) | 15.6 | 16.9 | 16.1 | 17.8 | 18.2 | 20.1 | 20.6 | 20.3 | 20.0 | 19.4 | - Assistance technique |
| - Other | (11.3) | 23.9 | 20.3 | 22.8 | 24.4 | 23.8 | 23.2 | 22.1 | 23.8 | 23.5 | 24.8 | - Autres |
| OPEC | (1.5) | 11.3 | 13.6 | 21.5 | 9.8 | 11.1 | 11.1 | 10.5 | 18.3 | 18.4 | 15.9 | OPEP |
| - Bilateral | (1.5) | 10.2 | 13.1 | 20.1 | 8.9 | 10.1 | 9.9 | 8.5 | 16.5 | 16.7 | 14.3 | - Apports bilatéraux |
| - Multilateral b/ | - | 50.9 | 19.8 | 48.7 | 29.9 | 38.4 | 46.6 | 54.2 | 46.3 | 44.0 | 56.9 | - Apports multilatéraux b/ |
| - Grants | (0.1) | 13.8 | 15.2 | 23.4 | 16.8 | 6.2 | 10.7 | 7.1 | 18.7 | 25.6 | 17.9 | - Dons |
| - Loans | (20.8) | 8.4 | 12.2 | 17.5 | 6.7 | 16.4 | 11.4 | 13.0 | 17.8 | 12.1 | 13.5 | - Prêts |
| Non-concessional flows | (1.1) | 1.7 | 1.1 | 1.3 | 0.7 | 1.7 | 2.4 | 0.9 | 1.4 | 0.6 | 0.9 | Courants financiers non-concessionnels |
| of which: / DAC | (1.2) | 1.5 | 1.1 | 1.3 | 0.8 | 1.7 | 2.3 | 0.9 | 1.6 | 0.6 | 0.9 | Dont: / CAD |
| - Bilateral official | .. | 0.3 | 1.7 | 1.8 | 0.6 | 4.7 | 5.2 | 3.7 | 3.6 | 6.3 | 4.9 | - Apports publics bilatéraux |
| - Multilateral a/ | (7.7) | 4.3 | 0.9 | 1.6 | 2.3 | 2.4 | 2.0 | 1.2 | 1.0 | 1.2 | 0.8 | - Apports multilatéraux a/ |
| - Export credits c/ | (1.7) | 5.0 | 3.6 | 4.0 | 2.6 | 4.8 | 7.8 | 2.3 | 2.7 | 1.9 | 1.8 | - Crédits à l'exportation c/ |
| - Direct investment | (0.4) | 0.5 | 0.9 | 1.2 | 1.5 | 0.3 | 0.5 | 0.7 | 1.4 | 0.3 | 0.3 | - Investissements directs |
| - Other d/ e/ | (0.2) | (0.5) | (0.2) | .. | (0.1) | (0.6) | .. | (0.1) | (1.0) | (0.0) | (0.0) | - Autres d/ e/ |
| TOTAL FINANCIAL FLOWS | (6.0) | 7.9 | 6.7 | 7.3 | 6.5 | 8.4 | 9.5 | 7.2 | 8.9 | 7.1 | 9.1 | TOTAL DES APPORTS FINANCIERS |

Note : No percentage is shown when either the net flow to all LDCs or the net flow to all developing countries in a particular year is negative. For other notes and sources, see table 21A.

Note : Aucune donnée n'est indiquée dans les cas où dans une année quelconque, les versements nets, soit aux PMA soit aux pays en développement dans leur ensemble, sont négatifs. Pour les autres notes et sources, se référer au tableau 21A.

Table 25A
Bilateral ODA from DAC member countries and total financial flows from multilateral agencies a/ to all LDCs, 1975-1984

Tableau 25A
APD bilatérale des pays membres du CAD et apports financiers totaux des institutions multilatérales a/ à l'ensemble des PMA, 1975-1984

Net disbursements in $ million / Versements nets en millions de dollars

| | 1975 | 1976 | 1977 | 1978 | 1979 | 1980 | 1981 | 1982 | 1983 | 1984 |
|---|---|---|---|---|---|---|---|---|---|---|
| **A. Bilateral donors / A. Donneurs bilatéraux** | | | | | | | | | | |
| Australia / Australie | 30.0 | 15.1 | 18.4 | 30.5 | 51.5 | 34.0 | 59.1 | 85.3 | 53.0 | 68.9 |
| Austria / Autriche | 0.6 | 1.5 | 2.4 | 3.1 | 2.9 | 5.7 | 9.0 | 7.1 | 7.1 | 5.5 |
| Belgium / Belgique | 52.5 | 54.3 | 58.9 | 75.1 | 101.5 | 96.3 | 85.4 | 69.3 | 61.5 | 51.4 |
| Canada / Canada | 166.1 | 125.4 | 110.3 | 170.0 | 185.9b/ | 166.0b/ | 168.2 | 224.7 | 228.0 | 230.7 |
| Denmark / Danemark | 48.7 | 47.2 | 60.9 | 77.3 | 94.4 | 116.0 | 74.6 | 84.1 | 97.2 | 77.9 |
| Finland / Finlande | 12.6 | 15.9 | 11.3 | 10.5 | 14.9 | 22.1 | 23.9 | 21.6 | 32.7 | 37.8 |
| France / France | 255.2 | 246.2 | 222.0 | 260.8 | 371.1b/ | 430.7 | 488.6 | 415.5 | 390.0 | 505.6 |
| Germany,Fed.Rep.of / Allemagne, Rép. Féd. d' | 252.6 | 237.2 | 256.7 | 383.7 | 526.2 | 580.6 | 528.1 | 541.0 | 441.8 | 411.4 |
| Italy / Italie | 12.3 | 9.8 | 11.5 | 13.1 | 17.0 | 37.3 | 60.6 | 112.1 | 165.0 | 248.6 |
| Japan / Japon | 69.7 | 59.8 | 105.1 | 216.9 | 330.4 | 362.9 | 293.7 | 407.7 | 265.4 | 278.5 |
| Netherlands / Pays-Bas | 62.7 | 81.5 | 156.4 | 217.6 | 260.8 | 308.1 | 285.2 | 254.6 | 202.9 | 236.0 |
| New Zealand / Nouvelle-Zélande | 10.3 | 4.8 | 5.1 | 5.7 | 6.3 | 6.3 | 5.3 | 4.4 | 4.8 | 4.8 |
| Norway / Norvège | 38.2 | 39.1 | 61.8 | 77.4 | 90.5 | 94.6 | 90.4 | 121.9 | 120.2 | 100.9 |
| Sweden / Suède | 120.9 | 115.3 | 142.0 | 149.8 | 216.5 | 198.5 | 180.7 | 167.5 | 147.7 | 124.8 |
| Switzerland / Suisse | 13.5 | 11.6 | 20.0 | 42.1 | 28.8 | 57.3 | 55.7 | 58.7 | 66.0 | 68.6 |
| United Kingdom / Royaume-Uni | 116.9 | 108.5 | 128.6 | 212.7 | 280.8 | 354.2 | 304.2 | 258.3 | 215.7 | 198.7 |
| United States / Etats-Unis | 564.0 | 266.0 | 263.0 | 380.0 | 388.0 | 558.0 | 529.0 | 638.0 | 693.0 | 736.0 |
| Total bilateral concessional / Total des apports bilatéraux concessionnels | 1826.8 | 1439.2 | 1634.4 | 2326.3 | 2967.5 | 3428.6 | 3241.7 | 3471.3 | 3192.0 | 3386.1 |
| **B. Multilateral donors / B. Donneurs multilatéraux** | | | | | | | | | | |
| **1. Concessional / 1. Apports concessionnels** | | | | | | | | | | |
| AfDF / FAfD | 3.9 | 10.5 | 22.3 | 34.1 | 52.8 | 80.6 | 76.1 | 82.9 | 113.6 | 75.2 |
| AsDB / BAsD | 26.6 | 15.6 | 24.0 | 56.2 | 58.7 | 75.4 | 64.5 | 59.1 | 81.3 | 121.7 |
| EEC/EDF / CEE/FED | 288.6 | 183.7 | 213.2 | 291.8 | 365.7 | 444.4 | 485.9 | 389.7 | 370.9 | 456.2 |
| IBRD / BIRD | - | 0.1 | 6.1 | 13.3 | 19.5 | 18.7 | 9.8 | 3.0 | 2.5 | 0.5 |
| IDA / AID | 270.8 | 352.5 | 358.6 | 372.9 | 472.6 | 493.8 | 572.4 | 696.3 | 739.4 | 879.6 |
| IDB / BID | 14.6 | 15.7 | 21.3 | 16.9 | 15.9 | 8.9 | 10.0 | 12.5 | 14.9 | 16.2 |
| IFAD / FIDA | - | - | - | - | 1.1 | 12.9 | 22.6 | 27.8 | 50.3 | 50.3 |
| IMF Trust fund / Fonds fiduciaire du FMI | - | - | 37.7 | 239.9 | 198.4 | 246.7 | 2.6 | - | - | - |
| UN / ONU | 323.6 | 305.5 | 290.3 | 404.4 | 482.0 | 601.3 | 738.1 | 693.7 | 729.4 | 814.0 |
| of which:UNDP / dont : PNUD | 92.8 | 95.3 | 90.5 | 113.9 | 142.0 | 176.3 | 261.5 | 228.8 | 197.6 | 202.0 |
| UNHCR / UNHCR | 9.0 | 10.0 | 7.6 | 18.0 | 35.8 | 96.9 | 100.9 | 88.6 | 111.1 | 133.2 |
| UNICEF / UNICEF | 26.6 | 23.9 | 32.7 | 49.4 | 66.8 | 71.9 | 65.5 | 62.1 | 77.9 | 80.2 |
| UNTA / ATNU | 14.9 | 16.9 | 21.2 | 26.6 | 23.5 | 6.7 | 30.7 | 28.2 | 41.2 | 31.6 |
| WFP / PAM | 120.5 | 95.6 | 116.3 | 151.9 | 172.1 | 168.2 | 217.2 | 217.9 | 229.5 | 290.5 |
| Total | 928.1 | 883.6 | 973.5 | 1429.5 | 1666.7 | 1982.9 | 1982.0 | 1965.0 | 2102.3 | 2413.7 |
| **2. Non-concessional / 2. Apports non-concessionnels** | | | | | | | | | | |
| AfDB / BAfD | 14.6 | 15.9 | 20.2 | 18.1 | 25.4 | 32.1 | 26.2 | 36.3 | 50.8 | 37.8 |
| AsDB / BAsD | 1.1 | - | -0.2 | -0.7 | -0.7 | 0.2 | -0.6 | -1.0 | -0.7 | -0.7 |
| EEC/EDF / CEE/FED | - | - | -0.1 | 12.5 | 15.2 | 18.9 | 4.6 | 5.7 | 10.9 | 3.9 |
| IBRD / BIRD | 91.8 | 0.3 | 14.1 | 19.8 | 37.7 | 31.8 | 31.2 | 15.9 | 13.1 | 7.9 |
| IFC / SFI | -1.0 | 5.6 | 6.6 | 16.2 | 13.2 | 6.4 | 2.5 | 7.7 | 7.5 | 17.1 |
| Total | 106.5 | 21.8 | 40.6 | 65.9 | 90.8 | 89.4 | 63.9 | 64.6 | 81.6 | 66.0 |
| Total concessional (A + B.1) / Total des apports concessionnels (A + B.1) | 2754.9 | 2322.8 | 2607.9 | 3755.8 | 4634.2 | 5411.5 | 5223.7 | 5436.8 | 5294.3 | 5799.8 |
| GRAND TOTAL / TOTAL GENERAL | 2861.4 | 2344.6 | 2648.5 | 3821.7 | 4725.0 | 5500.9 | 5287.6 | 5501.4 | 5375.9 | 5865.8 |

For source and notes see page 43.    Pour la source et les notes se référer à la page 43.

Table 25B
Bilateral ODA from DAC member countries and total financial flows from multilateral agencies a/ to all LDCs, 1975-1984

Tableau 25B
APD bilatérale des pays membres du CAD et apports financiers totaux des institutions multilatérales a/ à l'ensemble des PMA, 1975-1984

Net disbursements in millions of constant 1980 dollars c/
Versements nets en millions de dollars constants de 1980 c/

| | | 1975 | 1976 | 1977 | 1978 | 1979 | 1980 | 1981 | 1982 | 1983 | 1984 |
|---|---|---|---|---|---|---|---|---|---|---|---|
| **A. Bilateral donors** | **A.Donneurs bilatéraux** | | | | | | | | | | |
| Australia | Australie | 53.9 | 26.9 | 29.9 | 45.0 | 62.5 | 34.0 | 60.9 | 91.7 | 59.6 | 79.1 |
| Austria | Autriche | 1.1 | 2.7 | 3.9 | 4.6 | 3.5 | 5.7 | 9.3 | 7.6 | 8.0 | 6.3 |
| Belgium | Belgique | 94.3 | 96.6 | 95.6 | 110.9 | 123.1 | 96.3 | 88.0 | 74.5 | 69.1 | 59.0 |
| Canada | Canada | 298.3 | 223.0 | 178.9 | 251.0 | 225.5b/ | 166.0b/ | 173.3 | 241.7 | 256.2 | 264.8 |
| Denmark | Danemark | 87.5 | 83.9 | 98.8 | 114.1 | 114.5 | 116.0 | 76.9 | 90.4 | 109.2 | 89.4 |
| Finland | Finlande | 22.6 | 28.3 | 18.3 | 15.5 | 18.1 | 22.1 | 24.6 | 23.2 | 36.7 | 43.4 |
| France | France | 458.3 | 437.8 | 360.2 | 385.1 | 450.1b/ | 430.7 | 503.5 | 446.9 | 438.3 | 580.4 |
| Germany,Fed.Rep.of | Allemagne, Rép. Féd. d' | 453.7 | 421.8 | 416.5 | 566.5 | 638.3 | 580.6 | 544.2 | 581.8 | 496.5 | 472.3 |
| Italy | Italie | 22.1 | 17.4 | 18.7 | 19.3 | 20.6 | 37.3 | 62.4 | 120.6 | 185.4 | 285.4 |
| Japan | Japon | 125.2 | 106.3 | 170.5 | 320.2 | 400.8 | 362.9 | 302.6 | 438.5 | 298.3 | 319.7 |
| Netherlands | Pays-Bas | 112.6 | 144.9 | 253.7 | 321.3 | 316.4 | 308.1 | 293.9 | 273.8 | 228.0 | 270.9 |
| New Zealand | Nouvelle-Zélande | 18.5 | 8.5 | 8.3 | 8.4 | 7.6 | 6.3 | 5.5 | 4.7 | 5.4 | 5.5 |
| Norway | Norvège | 68.6 | 69.5 | 100.3 | 114.3 | 109.8 | 94.6 | 93.1 | 131.1 | 135.1 | 115.8 |
| Sweden | Suède | 217.1 | 205.1 | 230.4 | 221.2 | 262.6 | 198.5 | 186.2 | 180.1 | 166.0 | 143.3 |
| Switzerland | Suisse | 24.2 | 20.6 | 32.4 | 62.2 | 34.9 | 57.3 | 57.4 | 63.1 | 74.2 | 78.8 |
| United Kingdom | Royaume-Uni | 209.9 | 193.0 | 208.6 | 314.0 | 340.6 | 354.2 | 313.4 | 277.8 | 242.4 | 228.1 |
| United States | Etats-Unis | 1012.9 | 473.1 | 426.7 | 561.1 | 470.6 | 558.0 | 545.1 | 686.2 | 778.8 | 844.9 |
| Total bilateral concessional | Total des apports bilatéraux concessionnels | 3280.9 | 2559.5 | 2651.5 | 3434.7 | 3599.6 | 3428.6 | 3340.2 | 3733.9 | 3587.3 | 3887.2 |
| **B. Multilateral donors** | **B.Donneurs multilatéraux** | | | | | | | | | | |
| **1. Concessional** | **1.Apports concessionnels** | | | | | | | | | | |
| AfDF | FAfD | 7.0 | 18.7 | 36.2 | 50.3 | 64.0 | 80.6 | 78.4 | 89.2 | 127.7 | 86.3 |
| AsDB | BAsD | 47.8 | 27.7 | 38.9 | 83.0 | 71.2 | 75.4 | 66.5 | 63.6 | 91.4 | 139.7 |
| EEC/EDF | CEE/FED | 518.3 | 326.7 | 345.9 | 430.8 | 443.6 | 444.6 | 500.7 | 419.7 | 416.8 | 523.7 |
| IBRD | BIRD | - | 0.2 | 9.9 | 19.6 | 23.7 | 18.7 | 10.1 | 3.2 | 2.8 | 0.6 |
| IDA | AID | 486.3 | 626.9 | 581.8 | 550.6 | 573.3 | 493.8 | 589.8 | 748.9 | 831.0 | 1009.8 |
| IDB | BID | 26.2 | 27.9 | 34.6 | 25.0 | 19.3 | 8.9 | 10.3 | 13.4 | 16.7 | 18.6 |
| IFAD | FIDA | - | - | - | - | 1.3 | 12.9 | 23.3 | 29.9 | 56.5 | 57.7 |
| IMF Trust fund | Fonds fiduciaire du FMI | - | - | 61.2 | 354.2 | 240.7 | 246.7 | 2.7 | - | - | - |
| UN | ONU | 581.2 | 543.3 | 471.0 | 597.1 | 584.7 | 601.3 | 760.5 | 746.1 | 819.7 | 934.5 |
| of which:UNDP | dont : PNUD | 166.7 | 169.5 | 146.8 | 146.2 | 172.2 | 176.3 | 269.4 | 246.1 | 222.1 | 231.9 |
| UNHCR | UNHCR | 16.2 | 17.8 | 12.3 | 26.6 | 43.4 | 96.9 | 104.0 | 95.3 | 124.9 | 152.9 |
| UNICEF | UNICEF | 47.8 | 42.5 | 53.0 | 72.9 | 81.0 | 71.9 | 67.5 | 66.8 | 87.5 | 92.1 |
| UNTA | ATNU | 26.8 | 30.1 | 34.4 | 39.3 | 28.5 | 6.7 | 31.6 | 30.3 | 46.3 | 36.3 |
| WFP | PAM | 216.4 | 170.0 | 188.7 | 224.3 | 208.8 | 168.2 | 223.8 | 234.4 | 257.9 | 333.5 |
| Total | Total | 1666.8 | 1571.4 | 1579.3 | 2110.6 | 2021.7 | 1982.9 | 2042.2 | 2113.4 | 2362.7 | 2770.9 |
| **2. Non-concessional** | **2.Apports non-concessionnels** | | | | | | | | | | |
| AfDB | BAfD | 26.2 | 28.3 | 32.8 | 26.7 | 30.8 | 32.1 | 27.0 | 39.0 | 57.1 | 43.4 |
| AsDB | BAsD | 2.0 | - | -0.3 | -1.0 | -0.8 | 0.2 | -0.6 | -1.1 | -0.8 | -0.8 |
| EEC/EDF | CEE/FED | - | - | -0.2 | 18.5 | 18.4 | 18.9 | 4.7 | 6.1 | 12.2 | 4.5 |
| IBRD | BIRD | 164.9 | 0.5 | 22.9 | 29.2 | 45.7 | 31.8 | 32.1 | 17.1 | 14.7 | 9.1 |
| IFC | SFI | -1.8 | 10.0 | 10.7 | 23.9 | 16.0 | 6.4 | 2.6 | 8.3 | 8.4 | 19.6 |
| Total | Total | 191.3 | 38.8 | 65.9 | 97.3 | 110.1 | 89.4 | 65.8 | 69.5 | 91.7 | 75.8 |
| Total concessional (A + B.1) | Total des apports concessionnels (A + B.1) | 4947.7 | 4130.9 | 4230.9 | 5545.3 | 5621.3 | 5411.5 | 5382.5 | 5847.3 | 5950.0 | 6658.0 |
| GRAND TOTAL | TOTAL GENERAL | 5139.0 | 4169.7 | 4296.7 | 5642.5 | 5731.4 | 5500.9 | 5448.3 | 5916.8 | 6041.7 | 6733.8 |

For source and notes see page 43.　　Pour la source et les notes se référer à la page 43.

Table 25C

Bilateral ODA from DAC member countries and total financial flows from multilateral agencies a/ to all LDCs : main recipients in 1984b/

| | Main recipients in 1984d/ |
|---|---|
| **A. Bilateral donors** | |
| Australia | Bangladesh, Ethiopia, U.-R. of Tanzania. |
| Austria | Cape Verde, U.-R. of Tanzania, Ethiopia. |
| Belgium | Rwanda, Burundi. |
| Canada | Bangladesh, U.R. of Tanzania. |
| Denmark | U.-R. of Tanzania, Bangladesh. |
| Finland | U.-R. of Tanzania. |
| France | Mali, Central African Republic. |
| Germany, Fed.Rep. of | U.-R. of Tanzania, Sudan, Bangladesh. |
| Italy | Somalia, Ethiopia, U.-R. of Tanzania. |
| Japan | Bangladesh, Sudan, Nepal. |
| Netherlands | Bangladesh, U.-R. of Tanzania, Sudan. |
| New Zealand | Samoa, Vanuatu. |
| Norway | U.-R. of Tanzania, Bangladesh. |
| Sweden | U.-R. of Tanzania, Ethiopia. |
| Switzerland | Nepal, Rwanda. |
| United Kingdom | Bangladesh, Sudan, U.-R. of Tanzania. |
| United States | Bangladesh, Sudan. |
| **B. Multilateral donors** | |
| **1. Concessional flows** | |
| AfDF | - |
| AsDB | Bangladesh, Nepal. |
| EEC/EDF | Ethiopia, Bangladesh. |
| IBRD | U.-R. of Tanzania. |
| IDA | Bangladesh. |
| IDB | Haïti. |
| IFAD | Yemen, Bangladesh. |
| UN | Bangladesh, Somalia, Sudan. |
| of which: UNDP | Bangladesh. |
| UNHCR | Sudan, Somalia, Ethiopia. |
| UNICEF | Bangladesh, Ethiopia, U.-R. of Tanzania. |
| UNTA | - |
| WFP | Bangladesh, Somalia. |
| Other UN | U.-R. of Tanzania. |
| **2. Non-concessional flows** | |
| AfDB | Burundi, Malawi, Uganda, Guinea, Lesotho. |
| AsDB | Bangladesh. |
| EEC/EDF | Botswana, Burkina Faso, Niger. |
| IBRD | Botswana, U.-R. of Tanzania. |
| IFC | Guinea, Gambia, Nepal. |

Source : UNCTAD secretariat, based on information from the OECD/DAC secretariat.

a/ Multilateral agencies mainly financed by DAC member countries.
b/ Including flows to LDCs not allocated by recipient country.
c/ Actual disbursements were converted to 1980 prices using the index for LDCs in Table 8.
d/ Accounting each for 10 per cent or more of the total provided to all LDCs.

---

Tableau 25C

APD bilatérale des pays membres du CAD et apports financiers totaux des institutions multilatéralesa/ à l'ensemble des PMA : principaux bénéficiaires en 1984b/

| | Principaux pays bénéficiaires en 1984d/ |
|---|---|
| **A. Donneurs bilatéraux** | |
| Australie | Bangladesh, Ethiopie, R.-U. de Tanzanie |
| Autriche | Cap-Vert, R.U. de Tanzanie, Ethiopie. |
| Belgique | Rwanda, Burundi. |
| Canada | Bangladesh, R.-U. de Tanzanie. |
| Danemark | R.-U. de Tanzanie, Bangladesh. |
| Finlande | R.-U. de Tanzanie. |
| France | Mali, République centrafricaine. |
| Allemagne, Rép.féd.d' | R.-U. de Tanzanie, Soudan, Bangladesh. |
| Italie | Somalie, Ethiopie, R.-U. de Tanzanie. |
| Japon | Bangladesh, Soudan, Népal. |
| Pays-Bas | Bangladesh, R.-U. de Tanzanie, Soudan. |
| Nouvelle-Zélande | Samoa, Vanuatu. |
| Norvège | R.-U. de Tanzanie, Bangladesh. |
| Suède | R.-U. de Tanzanie, Ethiopie. |
| Suisse | Népal, Rwanda. |
| Royaume-Uni | Bangladesh, Soudan, R.-U. de Tanzanie. |
| Etats-Unis | Bangladesh, Soudan. |
| **B. Donneurs multilatéraux** | |
| **1. Apports concessionnels** | |
| FAfD | - |
| BAsD | Bangladesh, Népal. |
| CEE/FED | Ethiopie, Bangladesh. |
| BIRD | R.-U. de Tanzanie |
| AID | Bangladesh. |
| BID | Haïti. |
| FIDA | Yémen, Bangladesh. |
| ONU | Bangladesh, Somalie, Soudan. |
| dont : PNUD | Bangladesh. |
| UNHCR | Soudan, Somalie, Ethiopie. |
| UNICEF | Bangladesh, Ethiopie, R.-U. de Tanzanie. |
| ATNU | - |
| PAM | Bangladesh, Somalie. |
| Autres ONU | R.-U. de Tanzanie. |
| **2. Apports non-concessionnels** | |
| BAfD | Burundi, Malawi, Ouganda, Guinée, Lesotho. |
| BAsD | Bangladesh. |
| CEE/FED | Botswana, Burkina Faso, Niger. |
| BIRD | Botswana, R.-U. de Tanzanie. |
| SFI | Guinée, Gambie, Népal. |

Source : Secrétariat de la CNUCED, d'après des renseignements du secrétariat de l'OCDE/CAD.

a/ Institutions multilatérales essentiellement financées par les pays membres du CAD.
b/ Y compris les apports aux PMA non alloués par pays bénéficiaires.
c/ Les versements effectifs ont été convertis aux prix de 1980 en utilisant l'indice pour les PMA qui figure au tableau 8.
d/ Recevant individuellement 10 pour cent ou davantage du total accordé à l'ensemble des PMA.

Table 26

Concessional assistance to LDCs from individual DAC member countries and multilateral agencies mainly financed by them:

Relative importance and relative shares as compared to all developing countries, 1970, 1975 and 1980-1984

Percentages

Table 26

Aide concessionnelle aux PMA en provenance des pays membres du CAD et des institutions multilatérales essentiellement financées par ceux-ci:

Importance relative et parts relatives par rapport à l'ensemble des pays en développement, 1970, 1975 et 1980-1984

En pourcentage

| | Relative importance of individual DAC countries and multilateral agencies in all their ODA flows to LDCs — Importance relative des différents pays du CAD et institutions multilatérales dans l'ensemble de leurs apports concessionnels aux PMA | | | | | | | Share of LDCs in ODA flows to all developing countries — Parts des PMA dans le total des apports concessionnels aux pays en développement | | | | | | | |
|---|---|---|---|---|---|---|---|---|---|---|---|---|---|---|---|
| | 1970 | 1975 | 1980 | 1981 | 1982 | 1983 | 1984 | 1970 | 1975 | 1980 | 1981 | 1982 | 1983 | 1984 | Donneurs bilatéraux |
| **A. Bilateral donors** | | | | | | | | | | | | | | | **A. Donneurs bilatéraux** |
| Australia | 0.5 | 1.1 | 0.6 | 1.1 | 1.6 | 1.0 | 1.2 | 2.2 | 6.9 | 7.0 | 10.8 | 15.2 | 10.0 | 11.5 | Australie |
| Austria | 0.4 | 0.0 | 0.1 | 0.2 | 0.1 | 0.1 | 0.0 | 87.8 | 1.2 | 3.9 | 5.7 | 4.4 | 5.8 | 4.2 | Autriche |
| Belgium | 2.8 | 1.9 | 1.8 | 1.6 | 1.3 | 1.2 | 0.9 | 24.6 | 21.0 | 21.7 | 23.8 | 24.3 | 21.8 | 20.3 | Belgique |
| Canada | 4.3 | 6.0 | 3.1 | 3.2 | 4.1 | 4.3 | 4.0 | 13.1 | 27.1 | 25.2 | 22.6 | 27.3 | 27.0 | 22.4 | Canada |
| Denmark | 0.9 | 1.8 | 2.1 | 1.4 | 1.5 | 1.8 | 1.3 | 20.0 | 45.7 | 45.8 | 36.9 | 27.9 | 38.5 | 35.6 | Danemark |
| Finland | - | 0.5 | 0.4 | 0.5 | 0.4 | 0.6 | 0.7 | - | 51.4 | 40.0 | 35.9 | 27.9 | 41.2 | 36.4 | Finlande |
| France | 10.2 | 9.3 | 8.0 | 9.4 | 7.6 | 7.4 | 8.7 | 9.9 | 14.3 | 12.5 | 13.8 | 12.6 | 12.5 | 16.1 | France |
| Germany, Federal Republic of | 8.6 | 9.2 | 10.7 | 10.1 | 10.0 | 8.3 | 7.1 | 16.5 | 23.2 | 27.1 | 24.1 | 25.9 | 22.9 | 23.9 | Allemagne, Rép. fédérale d' |
| Italy | 3.0 | 0.4 | 0.7 | 1.2 | 2.1 | 3.1 | 4.3 | 38.6 | 37.6 | 44.8 | 36.6 | 20.4 | 37.8 | 40.5 | Italie |
| Japan | 3.6 | 2.5 | 6.7 | 5.6 | 7.5 | 5.0 | 4.8 | 8.0 | 8.2 | 18.1 | 13.2 | 20.4 | 12.8 | 13.7 | Japon |
| Netherlands | 0.7 | 2.3 | 5.7 | 5.5 | 4.7 | 3.8 | 4.1 | 3.9 | 17.6 | 25.3 | 25.5 | 24.3 | 25.3 | 27.2 | Pays-Bas |
| New Zealand | - | 0.4 | 0.1 | 0.1 | 0.0 | 0.0 | 0.0 | - | 12.0 | 12.0 | 10.5 | 10.1 | 10.1 | 11.0 | Nouvelle-Zélande |
| Norway | 0.5 | 1.4 | 1.7 | 1.7 | 2.2 | 2.3 | 1.7 | 29.4 | 43.1 | 35.0 | 36.1 | 38.3 | 37.5 | 34.6 | Norvège |
| Sweden | 2.6 | 4.4 | 3.7 | 3.5 | 3.1 | 2.8 | 2.2 | 33.9 | 36.2 | 32.0 | 34.3 | 32.6 | 31.0 | 27.0 | Suède |
| Switzerland | 0.3 | 0.5 | 1.1 | 1.1 | 1.1 | 1.2 | 1.2 | 14.0 | 19.5 | 32.6 | 34.3 | 32.1 | 30.4 | 31.6 | Suisse |
| United Kingdom | 7.6 | 4.2 | 6.5 | 5.8 | 4.8 | 4.1 | 3.4 | 15.8 | 27.0 | 27.0 | 23.0 | 25.1 | 25.1 | 26.0 | Royaume-Uni |
| United States | 31.2 | 20.5 | 10.3 | 10.1 | 11.7 | 13.1 | 12.7 | 9.7 | 22.3 | 15.8 | 15.0 | 15.7 | 16.2 | 14.1 | États-Unis |
| **Total bilateral concessional** | 77.3 | 66.3 | 63.4 | 62.1 | 63.9 | 60.3 | 58.4 | 11.3 | 19.8 | 20.3 | 18.9 | 20.5 | 19.2 | 19.1 | **Total des apports bilatéraux concessionnels** |
| **B. Multilateral donors** | | | | | | | | | | | | | | | **B. Donneurs multilatéraux** |
| AfDF | - | 0.1 | 1.5 | 1.5 | 1.5 | 2.1 | 1.3 | - | 100.0 | 84.1 | 84.1 | 67.8 | 72.0 | 67.6 | FafD |
| AsDB | 0.1 | 1.0 | 1.4 | 1.2 | 1.1 | 1.5 | 2.1 | 46.7 | 35.0 | 53.0 | 45.2 | 33.4 | 36.6 | 40.1 | BAsD |
| EEC/EDF | 6.7 | 10.5 | 8.2 | 9.3 | 7.2 | 7.0 | 7.9 | 29.9 | 40.0 | 42.8 | 34.0 | 34.3 | 30.8 | 35.9 | CEE/FED |
| IBRD | - | - | 0.3 | 0.2 | 0.0 | 0.0 | 0.0 | - | - | 17.5 | 11.1 | 5.2 | 5.3 | 1.2 | BIRD |
| IDA | 6.1 | 9.8 | 9.1 | 11.0 | 12.8 | 14.0 | 15.2 | 30.9 | 24.9 | 32.1 | 30.0 | 29.5 | 32.6 | 37.2 | AID |
| IDB | 0.1 | 0.5 | 0.2 | 0.2 | 0.2 | 0.3 | 0.3 | 0.4 | 4.6 | 2.7 | 2.3 | 3.4 | 4.1 | 3.7 | BID |
| IFAD | - | - | 0.2 | 0.4 | 0.5 | 1.0 | 0.9 | - | - | 24.0 | 30.2 | 27.6 | 35.7 | 31.4 | FIDA |
| IMF Trust Fund | - | - | 4.6 | 0.0 | - | - | - | - | - | 15.1 | 9.5 | - | - | - | Fonds fiduciaire du FMI |
| UN | 9.6 | 11.7 | 11.1 | 14.1 | 12.8 | 13.8 | 14.0 | 16.0 | 22.3 | 25.3 | 27.1 | 26.2 | 28.0 | 31.2 | ONU |
| **Total multilateral concessional** | 22.7 | 33.7 | 36.6 | 37.9 | 36.1 | 39.7 | 41.6 | 17.4 | 25.3 | 26.9 | 28.5 | 28.0 | 29.8 | 33.0 | **Total des apports multilatéraux concessionnels** |
| **Total concessional flows** | 100.0 | 100.0 | 100.0 | 100.0 | 100.0 | 100.0 | 100.0 | 12.3 | 21.3 | 22.3 | 21.7 | 22.7 | 22.4 | 23.2 | **Total des apports concessionnels** |

Source: UNCTAD secretariat, based on information from the OECD/DAC secretariat.

Source: Secrétariat de la CNUCED, d'après des renseignements du secrétariat de l'OCDE/CAD.

Table 27
Concessional assistance from DAC member countries and
multilateral agencies a/ to individual LDCs, 1970 & 1975-1984

Tableau 27
Aide concessionelle reçue par chacun des PMA en provenance des pays
du CAD et des institutions multilatérales a/, 1970 et 1975-1984

Net disbursements in $ million — Versements nets en millions de dollars

| Country | 1970 | 1975 | 1976 | 1977 | 1978 | 1979 | 1980 | 1981 | 1982 | 1983 | 1984 | Pays |
|---|---|---|---|---|---|---|---|---|---|---|---|---|
| Afghanistan | 28.4 | 53.5 | 63.9 | 75.3 | 76.4 | 99.5 | 30.8 | 2.6 | 9.0 | 15.9 | 7.5 | Afghanistan |
| Bangladesh | 227.4 | 956.4 | 521.1 | 586.0 | 961.7 | 1132.0 | 1208.0 | 1014.9 | 1197.8 | 957.4 | 1174.8 | Bangladesh |
| Benin | 14.9 | 52.0 | 50.9 | 45.0 | 57.7 | 81.1 | 86.3 | 77.6 | 76.0 | 80.3 | 77.1 | Bénin |
| Bhutan | 0.2 | 2.1 | 3.2 | 2.9 | 3.2 | 5.9 | 8.3 | 9.8 | 11.3 | 12.9 | 17.6 | Bhoutan |
| Botswana | 14.2 | 45.9 | 47.6 | 47.5 | 68.8 | 99.1 | 103.9 | 96.5 | 92.9 | 91.2 | 91.7 | Botswana |
| Burkina Faso | 22.0 | 86.1 | 83.1 | 107.4 | 157.9 | 193.4 | 205.4 | 208.2 | 201.0 | 181.2 | 178.4 | Burkina Faso |
| Burundi | 17.9 | 47.1 | 44.5 | 46.8 | 71.4 | 88.6 | 109.1 | 117.9 | 120.6 | 133.4 | 127.4 | Burundi |
| Cape Verde | - | 8.7 | 13.1 | 24.4 | 32.5 | 32.5 | 60.4 | 49.3 | 53.2 | 59.5 | 59.4 | Cap-Vert |
| Central African Rep. | 14.4 | 55.4 | 38.1 | 40.4 | 51.3 | 82.3 | 108.9 | 101.6 | 88.7 | 92.9 | 111.6 | Rép. centrafricaine |
| Chad | 22.3 | 57.1 | 60.9 | 81.9 | 117.8 | 79.7 | 35.3 | 59.8 | 60.9 | 95.3 | 114.6 | Tchad |
| Comoros | 7.9 | 21.7 | 11.6 | 8.6 | 7.6 | 13.5 | 25.4 | 32.1 | 26.1 | 29.5 | 33.8 | Comores |
| Democratic Yemen | 4.3 | 20.2 | 23.2 | 32.1 | 47.0 | 39.7 | 38.6 | 36.1 | 57.4 | 57.3 | 46.1 | Yémen démocratique |
| Djibouti | 11.8 | 34.4 | 28.1 | 34.5 | 32.0 | 23.1 | 40.6 | 50.1 | 54.8 | 52.1 | 58.8 | Djibouti |
| Equatorial Guinea | - | 0.7 | 0.4 | 0.4 | 0.6 | 2.7 | 9.3 | 9.8 | 13.0 | 10.7 | 15.1 | Guinée équatoriale |
| Ethiopia | 40.0 | 119.1 | 140.5 | 111.7 | 137.1 | 174.3 | 211.8 | 226.7 | 199.8 | 269.3 | 362.9 | Ethiopie |
| Gambia | 1.3 | 7.7 | 9.8 | 17.8 | 26.7 | 30.0 | 40.2 | 45.2 | 43.0 | 40.9 | 53.9 | Gambie |
| Guinea | 10.3 | 9.4 | 11.5 | 17.1 | 48.3 | 48.5 | 84.9 | 79.6 | 60.2 | 67.4 | 88.7 | Guinée |
| Guinea-Bissau | 0.1 | 15.5 | 18.7 | 35.9 | 47.7 | 49.8 | 55.6 | 63.7 | 59.7 | 57.8 | 52.8 | Guinée-Bissau |
| Haiti | 7.8 | 59.3 | 71.7 | 84.5 | 92.9 | 92.7 | 105.1 | 105.6 | 125.7 | 132.5 | 134.3 | Haïti |
| Lao People's Dem.Rep. | 69.4 | 38.9 | 28.4 | 30.2 | 71.8 | 49.9 | 40.1 | 34.9 | 37.9 | 29.3 | 33.0 | Rép. dém. pop. lao |
| Lesotho | 10.0 | 27.4 | 30.1 | 36.9 | 50.0 | 63.9 | 90.8 | 100.1 | 86.8 | 96.3 | 92.1 | Lesotho |
| Malawi | 36.9 | 63.9 | 63.3 | 79.4 | 98.5 | 141.7 | 142.0 | 137.3 | 121.2 | 116.9 | 158.6 | Malawi |
| Maldives | 0.2 | 3.0 | 1.5 | 2.0 | 4.8 | 2.5 | 5.5 | 5.0 | 3.0 | 6.9 | 6.5 | Maldives |
| Mali | 21.3 | 115.3 | 86.0 | 97.1 | 151.4 | 179.7 | 224.5 | 210.2 | 159.3 | 168.3 | 309.5 | Mali |
| Nepal | 23.6 | 45.4 | 50.0 | 71.4 | 75.1 | 133.3 | 156.2 | 169.2 | 195.3 | 200.3 | 199.1 | Népal |
| Niger | 31.7 | 124.1 | 125.4 | 91.0 | 134.9 | 167.6 | 161.6 | 164.3 | 167.6 | 158.2 | 155.5 | Niger |
| Rwanda | 21.8 | 81.6 | 78.9 | 90.5 | 121.1 | 145.4 | 148.1 | 145.2 | 148.9 | 149.5 | 158.5 | Rwanda |
| Samoa | 1.5 | 13.4 | 11.7 | 19.0 | 19.7 | 29.4 | 24.9 | 24.0 | 21.9 | 27.1 | 20.2 | Samoa |
| Sao Tome and Principe | - | 0.3 | 1.7 | 3.0 | 4.0 | 3.0 | 3.9 | 5.6 | 9.4 | 11.1 | 10.9 | Sao Tomé-et-Principe |
| Sierra Leone | 7.0 | 16.3 | 15.0 | 25.0 | 40.0 | 48.2 | 84.0 | 57.9 | 80.8 | 64.6 | 44.3 | Sierra Leone |
| Somalia | 27.9 | 72.7 | 67.4 | 68.2 | 88.0 | 101.9 | 290.2 | 307.2 | 279.0 | 284.1 | 333.8 | Somalie |
| Sudan | 6.6 | 110.3 | 115.6 | 109.4 | 224.2 | 261.7 | 441.1 | 482.8 | 554.4 | 599.0 | 499.9 | Soudan |
| Togo | 17.0 | 39.8 | 40.5 | 64.2 | 102.4 | 109.7 | 87.4 | 62.4 | 106.6 | 106.6 | 106.2 | Togo |
| Uganda | 33.1 | 13.3 | 20.1 | 14.1 | 17.1 | 41.3 | 112.1 | 135.5 | 127.4 | 124.4 | 165.2 | Ouganda |
| Un. Rep. of Tanzania | 51.3 | 288.2 | 267.0 | 327.3 | 421.9 | 583.5 | 646.5 | 649.3 | 656.6 | 563.4 | 540.6 | Rép.-Un. de Tanzanie |
| Vanuatu | 3.2 | 12.6 | 31.0 | 14.7 | 18.8 | 38.4 | 44.0 | 30.5 | 26.0 | 26.9 | 24.5 | Vanuatu |
| Yemen | 12.2 | 36.6 | 47.5 | 64.6 | 73.0 | 81.7 | 121.2 | 115.8 | 136.6 | 124.2 | 135.4 | Yémen |
| All LDCs | 819.9 | 2755.4 | 2323.0 | 2608.2 | 3755.3 | 4551.2 | 5392.0 | 5224.3 | 5436.6 | 5294.6 | 5800.3 | Ensemble des PMA |
| All developing countries | 6658.1 | 12917 | 12077 | 12633 | 16738 | 20593 | 24240 | 24107 | 23941 | 23682 | 25032 | Ensemble des pays en développement |

Source: UNCTAD secretariat, based on information from the
OECD/DAC secretariat.

a/ Multilateral institutions mainly financed by
DAC countries.

Source: Secrétariat de la CNUCED, d'après des renseignements du
secrétariat de l'OCDE/CAD.

a/ Institutions multilatérales essentiellement financées
par les pays du CAD.

Table 27 (continued)

Concessional assistance from DAC member countries and multilateral agencies[a]/ to individual LDCs : Leading donors [b]/ in 1984

| Country | Leading donors |
|---|---|
| Afghanistan | UNDP, Sweden, UNICEF, UNTA. |
| Bangladesh | IDA, USA, Japan. |
| Benin | France, IDA, Germany, Federal Republic of. |
| Bhutan | UNDP, WFP, Japan. |
| Botswana | Germany, Fed. Rep. of, USA, UK, Sweden, WFP. |
| Burkina Faso | USA, France. |
| Burundi | IDA, France, Belgium, Germany, Fed.Rep. of. |
| Cape Verde | EEC, Italy, Sweden. |
| Central African Rep. | France, EEC, IDA. |
| Chad | France, EEC, WFP. |
| Comoros | France, AfDF, IDA. |
| Democratic Yemen | IDA, WFP. |
| Djibouti | France. |
| Equatorial Guinea | France, UNDP, WFP. |
| Ethiopia | EEC, Italy, IDA. |
| Gambia | USA, Germany, Fed. Rep. of. |
| Guinea | IDA, EEC, Canada, France. |
| Guinea-Bissau | Netherlands, EEC, Sweden. |
| Haiti | USA, IDA, IDB. |
| Lao People's Dem.Rep. | IDA, Sweden, UNDP. |
| Lesotho | USA, Germany, Fed. Rep. of. |
| Malawi | IDA. |
| Maldives | Japan, UNDP. |
| Mali | France. |
| Nepal | AsDB, IDA, Japan, USA. |
| Niger | France, USA, IDA, EEC. |
| Rwanda | IDA, Belgium, Germany, Fed.Rep.of, USA. |
| Samoa | New Zealand, AsDB, EEC, Australia. |
| Sao Tome and Principe | EEC, France. |
| Sierra Leone | USA, Germany, Fed. Rep. of, EEC, IDA. |
| Somalia | Italy, USA, UNHCR, WFP. |
| Sudan | USA, IDA. |
| Togo | France, IDA, EEC, Germany, Fed. Rep. of. |
| Uganda | IDA, EEC. |
| United Rep.of Tanzania | IDA, Sweden. |
| Vanuatu | U.K., France, Australia. |
| Yemen | USA, IDA. |

Source : UNCTAD secretariat, based on information from the OECD/DAC secretariat.

a/ Multilateral institutions mainly financed by DAC countries.

b/ Accounting for 10 per cent or more of total concessional assistance received by the given LDC.

---

Tableau 27 (suite)

Aide concessionnelle reçue par chacun des PMA en provenance des pays du CAD et des institutions multilatérales[a]/: Principaux donneurs [b]/ en 1984

| Principaux donneurs | Pays |
|---|---|
| PNUD, Suède, UNICEF, ATNU. | Afghanistan |
| AID, Etats-Unis, Japon. | Bangladesh |
| France, AID, Allemagne, République fédérale d'. | Bénin |
| PNUD, PAM, Japon. | Bhoutan |
| Allemagne,R.F.d', Etats-Unis, Royaume-Uni, Suède, PAM. | Botswana |
| Etats-Unis, France. | Burkina Faso |
| AID, France, Belgique, Allemagne, Rép. féd. d'. | Burundi |
| CEE, Italie, Suède. | Cap-Vert |
| France, CEE, AID. | République centrafricaine |
| France, CEE, PAM. | Tchad |
| France, FAfD, AID. | Comores |
| AID, PAM. | Yémen démocratique |
| France. | Djibouti |
| France, PNUD, PAM. | Guinée équatoriale |
| CEE, Italie, AID. | Ethiopie |
| Etats-Unis, Allemagne, Rép. féd. d'. | Gambie |
| AID, CEE, Canada, France. | Guinée |
| Pays-Bas, CEE, Suède. | Guinée-Bissau |
| Etats-Unis, AID, BID. | Haïti |
| AID, Suède, PNUD. | République dém. pop. lao |
| Etats-Unis, Allemagne, Rép. féd. d'. | Lesotho |
| AID. | Malawi |
| Japon, PNUD. | Maldives |
| France. | Mali |
| BAsD, AID, Japon, Etats-Unis. | Népal |
| France, Etats-Unis, AID, CEE. | Niger |
| AID, Belgique, Allemagne, Rép. féd. d', Etats-Unis. | Rwanda |
| Nouvelle-Zélande, BAsD, CEE, Australie. | Samoa |
| CEE, France. | Sao Tomé-et-Principe |
| Etats-Unis, Allemagne, Rép. féd. d', CEE, AID. | Sierra Leone |
| Italie, Etats-Unis, UNHCR, PMA. | Somalie |
| Etats-Unis, AID. | Soudan |
| France, AID, CEE, Allemagne, Rép. féd. d'. | Togo |
| AID, CEE. | Ouganda |
| AID, Suède. | Rép. Unie de Tanzanie |
| Royaume-Uni, France, Australie. | Vanuatu |
| Etats-Unis, AID. | Yémen |

Source : Secrétariat de la CNUCED, d'après des renseignements du secrétariat de l'OCDE/CAD.

a/ Institutions multilatérales essentiellement financées par les pays du CAD.

b/ Donnant 10 pour cent ou davantage de l'aide concessionnelle totale reçue par le PMA en question.

Table 28
Bilateral grants from DAC member countries to individual LDCs, 1970 and 1975-1984

Tableau 28
Dons reçus par chacun des PMA en provenance des pays membres du CAD, 1970 et 1975-1984

Net disbursements in $ million

Versements nets en millions de dollars

| Country | 1970 | 1975 | 1976 | 1977 | 1978 | 1979 | 1980 | 1981 | 1982 | 1983 | 1984 | Pays |
|---|---|---|---|---|---|---|---|---|---|---|---|---|
| Afghanistan | 20.2 | 19.6 | 18.8 | 27.9 | 31.8 | 42.7 | 17.5 | 1.9 | 7.0 | 11.8 | 5.4 | Afghanistan |
| Bangladesh | .. | 255.0 | 147.5 | 222.3 | 531.2 | 538.3 | 1044.7 | 542.7 | 617.6 | 480.3 | 573.0 | Bangladesh |
| Benin | 8.9 | 22.4 | 16.1 | 16.9 | 36.4 | 33.3 | 42.0 | 41.3 | 36.4 | 33.6 | 37.0 | Bénin |
| Bhutan | 0.2 | 0.6 | 1.0 | 0.6 | 0.7 | 1.2 | 1.7 | 2.6 | 3.2 | 2.9 | 4.8 | Bhoutan |
| Botswana | 8.7 | 24.8 | 31.5 | 31.6 | 86.2 | 69.9 | 81.3 | 76.4 | 83.9 | 75.8 | 66.3 | Botswana |
| Burkina Faso | 12.9 | 47.0 | 48.1 | 62.0 | 91.8 | 165.9 | 133.2 | 161.4 | 125.9 | 105.7 | 110.2 | Burkina Faso |
| Burundi | 11.4 | 26.5 | 26.0 | 27.5 | 36.5 | 42.7 | 56.9 | 64.8 | 60.6 | 60.6 | 61.0 | Burundi |
| Cape Verde | - | 2.1 | 6.8 | 15.8 | 25.0 | 27.2 | 38.9 | 35.8 | 42.5 | 44.8 | 38.7 | Cap-Vert |
| Central African Rep. | 9.5 | 33.4 | 24.0 | 30.8 | 29.0 | 52.9 | 71.9 | 58.5 | 60.7 | 51.0 | 65.0 | Rép. centrafricaine |
| Chad | 14.0 | 27.4 | 40.3 | 45.7 | 64.7 | 51.3 | 20.4 | 46.5 | 35.3 | 50.0 | 59.7 | Tchad |
| Comoros a/ | 6.8 | 16.9 | 8.0 | 1.1 | 0.6 | 7.5 | 14.0 | 22.7 | 11.9 | 14.3 | 14.6 | Comores a/ |
| Democratic Yemen | 1.3 | 4.1 | 8.5 | 6.0 | 6.6 | 4.9 | 7.6 | 5.1 | 5.8 | 5.2 | 3.5 | Yémen démocratique |
| Djibouti | 9.6 | 25.6 | 26.3 | 29.7 | 30.3 | 20.5 | 34.1 | 37.8 | 44.3 | 37.7 | 41.6 | Djibouti |
| Equatorial Guinea | - | - | - | - | - | 0.1 | 1.2 | 4.3 | 5.1 | 4.0 | 8.0 | Guineé équatoriale |
| Ethiopia | 21.2 | 42.6 | 47.1 | 55.1 | 60.9 | 65.7 | 87.6 | 78.3 | 71.8 | 95.3 | 157.4 | Ethiopie |
| Gambia | 0.6 | 1.9 | 3.7 | 10.4 | 11.4 | 10.8 | 23.9 | 17.6 | 20.7 | 21.9 | 30.2 | Gambie |
| Guinea | 1.3 | 0.2 | 0.3 | 2.6 | 9.2 | 12.7 | 14.7 | 21.8 | 17.4 | 14.4 | 29.5 | Guinée |
| Guinea-Bissau | - | 8.1 | 11.8 | 25.2 | 34.9 | 33.5 | 31.8 | 39.7 | 33.3 | 31.9 | 29.3 | Guinée-Bissau |
| Haiti | 4.2 | 21.8 | 24.7 | 26.5 | 32.5 | 35.7 | 48.2 | 53.8 | 64.1 | 67.0 | 57.5 | Haïti |
| Lao People's Dem.Rep. | 66.9 | 27.3 | 13.8 | 14.0 | 28.7 | 23.9 | 16.8 | 17.0 | 22.0 | 13.3 | 15.0 | Rép. dém. pop. lao |
| Lesotho | 6.1 | 14.7 | 17.8 | 20.6 | 29.0 | 40.5 | 60.4 | 59.0 | 53.3 | 61.4 | 62.6 | Lesotho |
| Malawi | 14.3 | 16.4 | 27.3 | 21.3 | 78.8 | 120.3 | 58.2 | 78.3 | 64.2 | 56.5 | 50.3 | Malawi |
| Maldives | 0.1 | 0.8 | 0.6 | 1.2 | 2.6 | 0.6 | 1.9 | 3.0 | 2.3 | 3.6 | 3.7 | Maldives |
| Mali | 9.4 | 52.0 | 42.4 | 49.1 | 74.7 | 146.3 | 120.2 | 133.0 | 90.7 | 90.8 | 121.5 | Mali |
| Nepal | 20.9 | 25.9 | 27.6 | 38.7 | 40.5 | 69.8 | 95.3 | 84.3 | 108.8 | 103.9 | 90.8 | Népal |
| Niger | 17.5 | 61.4 | 58.7 | 41.4 | 91.8 | 125.9 | 86.9 | 104.9 | 116.9 | 102.1 | 87.8 | Niger |
| Rwanda | 16.8 | 52.4 | 50.4 | 56.5 | 75.6 | 101.3 | 91.6 | 92.5 | 93.8 | 93.4 | 93.7 | Rwanda |
| Samoa | 0.3 | 7.6 | 7.2 | 11.0 | 11.3 | 21.7 | 13.6 | 14.2 | 15.4 | 16.7 | 11.0 | Samoa |
| Sao Tome and Principe | - | - | 0.7 | 1.6 | 1.8 | 1.4 | 1.2 | 1.8 | 3.8 | 3.4 | 4.0 | Sao Tomé-et-Principe |
| Sierra Leone | 4.8 | 6.5 | 6.9 | 8.8 | 12.8 | 22.1 | 27.5 | 22.9 | 22.6 | 22.3 | 17.8 | Sierra Leone |
| Somalia | 12.3 | 24.2 | 18.5 | 25.9 | 27.2 | 39.4 | 157.0 | 117.1 | 105.2 | 110.0 | 107.9 | Somalie |
| Sudan | 1.4 | 27.4 | 27.5 | 43.1 | 92.9 | 112.1 | 376.9 | 273.6 | 336.9 | 368.7 | 268.7 | Soudan |
| Togo | 6.7 | 19.9 | 19.9 | 24.8 | 25.1 | 32.0 | 31.0 | 33.2 | 31.8 | 36.3 | 38.3 | Togo |
| Uganda | 12.6 | 3.5 | 3.1 | 4.0 | 8.6 | 27.5 | 41.3 | 90.9 | 54.2 | 69.1 | 47.0 | Ouganda |
| Un. Rep. of Tanzania | 23.6 | 152.0 | 169.4 | 191.9 | 420.3 | 438.6 | 607.4 | 442.1 | 427.8 | 375.9 | 361.0 | Rép.-Unie de Tanzanie |
| Vanuatu | 2.9 | 10.6 | 29.3 | 12.0 | 17.9 | 36.3 | 43.7 | 25.0 | 23.8 | 24.9 | 21.9 | Vanuatu |
| Yemen | 5.6 | 11.1 | 8.1 | 22.4 | 30.3 | 44.0 | 150.8 | 54.6 | 59.8 | 77.6 | 70.1 | Yémen |
| All LDCs | (401.7) | 1093.7 | 1019.7 | 1226.0 | 2189.6 | 2620.5 | 3753.3 | 2960.4 | 2980.8 | 2838.1 | 2865.8 | Ensemble des PMA |
| All developing countries | 3325.4 | 5752.6 | 5895.2 | 6396.0 | 8575.9 | 10785 | 13182 | 12141 | 12339 | 12631 | 13955 | Ensemble des pays en développement |

Source: UNCTAD secretariat, based on information from the OECD/DAC secretariat.

Source: Secrétariat de la CNUCED, d'après des renseignements du secrétariat de l'OCDE/CAD.

a/ Excluding grants from France to Mayotte.

a/ Non compris l'aide versée au titre de dons par la France à Mayotte.

Table 29
Bilateral ODA from DAC member countries
to individual LDCs, 1970 and 1975-1984

Net disbursements in $ million

Tableau 29
APD bilatérale reçue par chacun des PMA en provenance des pays
membres du CAD, 1970 et 1975-1984

Versements nets en millions de dollars

| Country | Pays | 1970 | 1975 | 1976 | 1977 | 1978 | 1979 | 1980 | 1981 | 1982 | 1983 | 1984 |
|---|---|---|---|---|---|---|---|---|---|---|---|---|
| Afghanistan | Afghanistan | 21.4 | 32.5 | 34.8 | 27.6 | 32.0 | 47.0 | 11.4 | -7.9 | 0.4 | 5.4 | -1.0 |
| Bangladesh | Bangladesh | .. | 703.9 | 319.8 | 384.0 | 666.5 | 774.8 | 850.2 | 672.0 | 822.0 | 582.4 | 674.7 |
| Benin | Bénin | 8.2 | 29.1 | 27.5 | 26.6 | 30.3 | 48.6 | 35.7 | 45.0 | 40.9 | 41.5 | 39.5 |
| Bhutan | Bhoutan | 0.2 | 0.6 | 1.0 | 0.6 | 0.7 | 1.2 | 1.5 | 2.6 | 3.2 | 2.9 | 4.8 |
| Botswana | Botswana | 9.3 | 38.5 | 40.6 | 38.1 | 55.1 | 73.6 | 83.5 | 75.9 | 83.2 | 74.5 | 64.8 |
| Burkina Faso | Burkina Faso | 13.7 | 53.1 | 60.1 | 71.7 | 96.6 | 132.0 | 151.1 | 158.0 | 147.0 | 127.9 | 122.0 |
| Burundi | Burundi | 11.6 | 26.4 | 25.9 | 28.8 | 38.6 | 44.1 | 59.7 | 64.9 | 75.2 | 70.7 | 69.5 |
| Cape Verde | Cap-Vert | - | 2.1 | 6.8 | 15.8 | 25.0 | 27.2 | 39.0 | 36.2 | 42.6 | 44.9 | 38.8 |
| Central African Rep. | Rép. centrafricaine | 9.2 | 33.3 | 25.7 | 30.2 | 29.7 | 51.2 | 75.1 | 72.8 | 68.8 | 65.0 | 68.2 |
| Chad | Tchad | 14.7 | 28.2 | 43.2 | 49.6 | 70.9 | 49.4 | 20.2 | 31.3 | 35.3 | 51.4 | 58.9 |
| Comoros a/ | Comores a/ | 6.8 | 17.5 | 8.4 | 1.8 | 1.8 | 6.3 | 13.4 | 17.8 | 14.2 | 15.7 | 18.1 |
| Democratic Yemen | Yémen démocratique | 1.3 | 6.1 | 9.0 | 6.9 | 12.9 | 4.7 | 4.1 | 4.7 | 9.7 | 6.6 | 5.2 |
| Djibouti | Djibouti | 10.9 | 34.1 | 28.1 | 32.7 | 29.3 | 19.0 | 32.0 | 36.3 | 44.4 | 41.2 | 48.3 |
| Equatorial Guinea | Guineé équatoriale | - | - | - | - | - | 0.1 | 1.2 | 4.3 | 5.1 | 4.0 | 8.0 |
| Ethiopia | Ethiopie | 32.7 | 72.9 | 72.8 | 59.0 | 56.0 | 70.5 | 91.4 | 76.2 | 76.9 | 93.1 | 187.0 |
| Gambia | Gambie | 1.0 | 3.5 | 5.4 | 12.6 | 14.8 | 13.2 | 16.5 | 19.2 | 23.6 | 21.4 | 34.7 |
| Guinea | Guinée | 7.0 | 5.5 | 4.4 | 5.1 | 5.0 | 14.2 | 32.5 | 31.2 | 26.8 | 26.6 | 42.1 |
| Guinea-Bissau | Guinée-Bissau | - | 8.1 | 11.8 | 26.1 | 36.8 | 33.9 | 34.4 | 41.4 | 33.7 | 32.2 | 30.4 |
| Haïti | Haïti | 5.2 | 24.8 | 32.1 | 39.6 | 49.8 | 48.5 | 62.8 | 67.0 | 78.7 | 79.0 | 70.9 |
| Lao People's Dem.Rep. | Rép. dém. pop. lao | 68.5 | 32.6 | 24.0 | 26.7 | 42.6 | 26.4 | 16.7 | 16.8 | 21.3 | 12.6 | 13.8 |
| Lesotho | Lesotho | 6.2 | 14.7 | 18.0 | 20.7 | 29.1 | 43.7 | 60.2 | 59.2 | 53.4 | 61.3 | 62.7 |
| Malawi | Malawi | 25.9 | 47.1 | 46.2 | 54.1 | 56.4 | 92.0 | 75.6 | 82.1 | 65.0 | 56.2 | 51.7 |
| Maldives | Maldives | 0.1 | 2.0 | 0.6 | 1.2 | 3.7 | 0.9 | 1.9 | 2.8 | 0.9 | 3.2 | 3.4 |
| Mali | Mali | 9.8 | 55.7 | 53.3 | 60.9 | 93.0 | 93.9 | 131.4 | 133.0 | 96.3 | 96.6 | 223.1 |
| Nepal | Népal | 20.4 | 28.6 | 29.2 | 37.5 | 39.6 | 82.4 | 84.0 | 88.0 | 111.4 | 109.6 | 98.4 |
| Niger | Niger | 21.2 | 80.2 | 80.1 | 59.4 | 77.7 | 116.7 | 105.0 | 122.5 | 123.6 | 107.4 | 101.9 |
| Rwanda | Rwanda | 16.7 | 53.7 | 56.6 | 61.4 | 78.9 | 88.4 | 96.6 | 102.6 | 99.0 | 95.8 | 95.8 |
| Samoa | Samoa | 0.3 | 8.8 | 7.3 | 11.1 | 11.3 | 20.7 | 13.7 | 14.2 | 15.4 | 16.7 | 11.0 |
| Sao Tome and Principe | Sao Tomé-et-Principe | - | - | 0.7 | 1.6 | 1.8 | 1.4 | 1.2 | 1.8 | 3.8 | 3.4 | 4.0 |
| Sierra Leone | Sierra Leone | 5.2 | 9.8 | 7.5 | 12.0 | 13.5 | 28.4 | 56.8 | 33.7 | 55.7 | 35.7 | 22.4 |
| Somalia | Somalie | 17.9 | 23.3 | 20.1 | 25.2 | 46.8 | 49.8 | 139.3 | 139.8 | 141.6 | 152.2 | 193.1 |
| Sudan | Soudan | -0.1 | 60.2 | 54.4 | 55.8 | 113.0 | 149.3 | 271.6 | 294.7 | 357.3 | 438.2 | 308.6 |
| Togo | Togo | 7.7 | 23.5 | 20.5 | 42.4 | 66.5 | 68.9 | 52.1 | 36.9 | 50.4 | 49.0 | 52.8 |
| Uganda | Ouganda | 24.4 | 4.7 | 9.6 | 3.8 | 7.5 | 16.1 | 42.3 | 78.6 | 52.8 | 43.7 | 47.3 |
| Un. Rep. of Tanzania | Rép.-Unie de Tanzanie | 37.9 | 234.7 | 212.0 | 257.3 | 332.3 | 457.4 | 523.1 | 484.7 | 483.7 | 427.7 | 407.2 |
| Vanuatu | Vanuatu | 3.2 | 12.1 | 30.5 | 12.6 | 18.4 | 37.7 | 43.3 | 24.4 | 23.3 | 24.4 | 22.2 |
| Yemen | Yémen | 7.9 | 15.0 | 11.3 | 34.2 | 37.1 | 51.0 | 78.5 | 77.4 | 85.1 | 72.1 | 82.2 |
| ALL LDCs | Ensemble des PMA | (634.0) | 1826.9 | 1439.3 | 1634.7 | 2325.9 | 2884.6b/ | 3409.2c/ | 3242.1 | 3471.7 | 3192.2 | 3386.5 |
| All developing countries | Ensemble des pays en développement | 5591.4 | 9245.7 | 8658.3 | 8977.9 | 11869 | 14777 | 16877 | 17144 | 16931 | 16638 | 17720 |

Table 29 (continued)

Source: UNCTAD secretariat, based on information from the OECD/DAC secretariat.

a/ Excluding grants from France to Mayotte.

b/ Excluding $31.8 million and $69.7 million from Canada and France respectively, not allocated by recipient country.

c/ Excluding $19.5 million from Canada not allocated by recipient country.

Tableau 29 (suite)

Source: Secrétariat de la CNUCED, d'après des renseignements du secrétariat de l'OCDE/CAD.

a/ Non compris l'aide versée au titre de dons par la France à Mayotte.

b/ Non compris 13,8 millions de dollars et 69,7 millions de dollars, en provenance du Canada et de la France respectivement, non alloués par pays bénéficiaires.

c/ Non compris 19,5 millions de dollars en provenance du Canada, non alloués par pays bénéficiaires.

Table 30
Grants from multilateral agencies mainly financed by
DAC member countries to individual LDCs, 1970 and 1975-1984

Tableau 30
Dons reçus par chacun des PMA en provenance des institutions
multilatérales essentiellement financées par les pays membres
du CAD, 1970 et 1975-1984

Net disbursements in $ million — Versements nets en millions de dollars

| Country | 1970 | 1975 | 1976 | 1977 | 1978 | 1979 | 1980 | 1981 | 1982 | 1983 | 1984 | Pays |
|---|---|---|---|---|---|---|---|---|---|---|---|---|
| Afghanistan | 7.0 | 16.4 | 13.5 | 20.2 | 21.9 | 34.0 | 9.4 | 9.5 | 9.2 | 11.0 | 9.2 | Afghanistan |
| Bangladesh | .. | 107.4 | 82.3 | 87.4 | 107.8 | 105.2 | 95.7 | 130.6 | 153.3 | 123.0 | 169.6 | Bangladesh |
| Benin | 6.6 | 17.3 | 16.9 | 10.4 | 17.5 | 23.4 | 24.9 | 19.3 | 17.1 | 15.6 | 17.8 | Bénin |
| Bhutan | - | 1.5 | 2.2 | 2.3 | 2.5 | 4.7 | 6.6 | 6.9 | 7.4 | 9.3 | 12.1 | Bhoutan |
| Botswana | 3.3 | 6.2 | 5.5 | 7.4 | 11.0 | 20.8 | 16.8 | 17.4 | 9.6 | 16.1 | 21.4 | Botswana |
| Burkina Faso | 8.3 | 26.6 | 15.7 | 17.4 | 37.3 | 32.2 | 27.3 | 32.6 | 40.4 | 32.2 | 41.4 | Burkina Faso |
| Burundi | 5.9 | 20.4 | 17.4 | 12.0 | 16.6 | 24.9 | 26.9 | 38.6 | 18.9 | 25.9 | 22.7 | Burundi |
| Cape Verde | - | 6.6 | 6.3 | 8.6 | 7.5 | 5.1 | 10.9 | 9.3 | 8.5 | 12.9 | 17.7 | Cap-Vert |
| Central African Rep. | 5.0 | 21.4 | 12.1 | 9.1 | 11.2 | 18.0 | 18.0 | 20.7 | 14.0 | 18.3 | 24.3 | Rép. centrafricaine |
| Chad | 7.4 | 23.6 | 12.5 | 13.6 | 21.6 | 19.4 | 13.1 | 26.7 | 25.1 | 42.8 | 49.7 | Tchad |
| Comoros | 1.1 | 4.2 | 3.2 | 6.8 | 5.2 | 4.8 | 7.1 | 11.2 | 9.6 | 9.6 | 7.1 | Comores |
| Democratic Yemen | 3.0 | 12.3 | 7.3 | 17.2 | 15.1 | 17.3 | 19.0 | 22.2 | 29.6 | 24.0 | 19.4 | Yémen démocratique |
| Djibouti | 0.9 | 0.3 | - | 1.8 | 2.7 | 3.7 | 8.0 | 13.0 | 9.4 | 9.6 | 9.4 | Djibouti |
| Equatorial Guinea | - | 0.7 | 0.4 | 0.4 | 0.6 | 2.6 | 2.2 | 5.5 | 7.8 | 6.0 | 6.5 | Guineé équatoriale |
| Ethiopia | 4.5 | 27.5 | 30.7 | 18.3 | 33.0 | 42.4 | 81.1 | 111.0 | 87.9 | 117.5 | 127.8 | Ethiopie |
| Gambia | 0.3 | 3.3 | 3.4 | 2.2 | 7.5 | 11.2 | 16.0 | 22.0 | 14.6 | 10.2 | 13.5 | Gambie |
| Guinea | 3.3 | 3.9 | 5.9 | 5.7 | 18.5 | 17.1 | 28.9 | 21.5 | 20.0 | 16.9 | 23.0 | Guinée |
| Guinea-Bissau | 0.1 | 7.4 | 6.9 | 9.8 | 10.6 | 14.4 | 16.9 | 13.0 | 13.2 | 11.2 | 15.6 | Guinée-Bissau |
| Haiti | 1.6 | 10.9 | 9.3 | 7.6 | 13.1 | 13.7 | 14.3 | 12.7 | 18.5 | 13.1 | 19.5 | Haïti |
| Lao People's Dem.Rep. | 0.9 | 3.8 | 4.0 | 3.6 | 20.3 | 16.6 | 13.2 | 11.5 | 8.2 | 8.2 | 10.2 | Rép. dém. pop. lao |
| Lesotho | 3.8 | 10.9 | 9.8 | 10.4 | 14.8 | 14.4 | 20.1 | 28.1 | 16.1 | 22.9 | 20.3 | Lesotho |
| Malawi | 1.4 | 5.3 | 4.8 | 9.0 | 13.8 | 17.4 | 26.7 | 25.6 | 21.9 | 17.5 | 24.5 | Malawi |
| Maldives | 0.1 | 1.0 | 0.9 | 0.8 | 1.1 | 1.6 | 2.0 | 1.7 | 2.0 | 2.6 | 2.6 | Maldives |
| Mali | 10.3 | 45.1 | 17.0 | 19.7 | 31.9 | 49.0 | 56.4 | 49.3 | 39.0 | 39.6 | 61.3 | Mali |
| Nepal | 3.0 | 10.7 | 10.5 | 14.7 | 13.6 | 20.1 | 33.9 | 32.1 | 29.8 | 36.3 | 31.5 | Népal |
| Niger | 8.2 | 41.6 | 41.6 | 24.1 | 41.2 | 38.0 | 24.9 | 26.5 | 30.6 | 29.5 | 34.2 | Niger |
| Rwanda | 5.0 | 22.3 | 13.7 | 17.6 | 28.1 | 32.3 | 30.6 | 32.3 | 32.6 | 25.9 | 28.6 | Rwanda |
| Samoa | 0.7 | 1.8 | 2.5 | 4.0 | 2.4 | 4.3 | 5.1 | 5.2 | 3.8 | 5.2 | 4.0 | Samoa |
| Sao Tome and Principe | - | 0.3 | 1.0 | 1.4 | 2.2 | 1.6 | 2.7 | 1.8 | 3.0 | 6.0 | 6.7 | Sao Tomé-et-Principe |
| Sierra Leone | 1.8 | 4.1 | 5.1 | 7.9 | 6.6 | 7.9 | 14.1 | 17.7 | 13.5 | 18.3 | 12.4 | Sierra Leone |
| Somalia | 6.8 | 39.7 | 39.2 | 32.6 | 30.5 | 43.8 | 125.6 | 146.0 | 112.4 | 105.0 | 109.1 | Somalie |
| Sudan | 6.7 | 35.0 | 22.3 | 28.3 | 34.5 | 56.5 | 104.5 | 105.4 | 102.2 | 96.1 | 108.0 | Soudan |
| Togo | 8.2 | 14.2 | 15.6 | 11.7 | 16.1 | 14.0 | 13.0 | 14.5 | 8.7 | 23.0 | 26.4 | Togo |
| Uganda | 3.3 | 5.9 | 7.9 | 9.3 | 8.1 | 24.2 | 39.9 | 43.2 | 30.8 | 41.1 | 51.4 | Ouganda |
| Un. Rep. of Tanzania | 4.0 | 36.0 | 26.3 | 23.5 | 36.3 | 48.4 | 50.3 | 66.4 | 60.9 | 52.3 | 65.8 | Rép.-Unie de Tanzanie |
| Vanuatu | 0.0 | 0.5 | 0.5 | 2.1 | 0.4 | 0.7 | 0.7 | 6.1 | 2.3 | 2.4 | 1.7 | Vanuatu |
| Yemen | 4.3 | 14.5 | 18.3 | 13.6 | 13.7 | 17.0 | 20.5 | 20.9 | 26.7 | 20.4 | 21.0 | Yémen |
| All LDCs | (133.8) | 610.6 | 492.9 | 492.5 | 676.8 | 822.7 | 1027.3 | 1178.0 | 1058.6 | 1077.5 | 1247.4 | Ensemble des PMA |
| All developing countries | 668.4 | 2140.7 | 1636.5 | 1815.0 | 2339.2 | 2974.8 | 3342.2 | 3949.0 | 3605.9 | 3666.0 | 3813.3 | Ensemble des pays en développement |

Source: UNCTAD secretariat, based on information from the OECD/DAC secretariat.

Source: Secrétariat de la CNUCED, d'après des renseignements du secrétariat de l'OCDE/CAD.

Table 31
Concessional assistance from multilateral agencies mainly financed by DAC member countries to individual LDCs. 1970 and 1975-1984

Tableau 31
Aide concessionnelle reçue par chacun des PMA en provenance des institutions multilatérales essentiellement financées par les pays membres du CAD, 1970 et 1975-1984

Net disbursements in $ million — Versements nets en millions de dollars

| Country | 1970 | 1975 | 1976 | 1977 | 1978 | 1979 | 1980 | 1981 | 1982 | 1983 | 1984 | Pays |
|---|---|---|---|---|---|---|---|---|---|---|---|---|
| Afghanistan | 7.0 | 21.0 | 29.1 | 47.7 | 44.4 | 52.5 | 19.4 | 10.5 | 8.6 | 10.5 | 8.5 | Afghanistan |
| Bangladesh | .: | 252.5 | 201.3 | 202.0 | 295.2 | 357.2 | 357.8 | 342.9 | 375.8 | 375.0 | 500.1 | Bangladesh |
| Benin | 6.7 | 22.9 | 23.4 | 18.4 | 27.4 | 32.5 | 50.6 | 32.6 | 35.1 | 38.8 | 37.6 | Bénin |
| Bhutan | - | 1.5 | 2.2 | 2.3 | 2.5 | 4.7 | 6.6 | 7.2 | 8.1 | 10.0 | 12.8 | Bhoutan |
| Botswana | 4.9 | 7.4 | 7.0 | 9.4 | 13.7 | 25.5 | 20.4 | 20.6 | 9.7 | 16.7 | 26.9 | Botswana |
| Burkina Faso | 8.3 | 33.0 | 23.0 | 35.7 | 61.3 | 61.4 | 54.3 | 50.2 | 54.0 | 53.3 | 56.4 | Burkina Faso |
| Burundi | 6.3 | 20.7 | 18.6 | 18.0 | 32.8 | 44.5 | 49.4 | 53.0 | 45.4 | 62.7 | 57.9 | Burundi |
| Cape Verde | - | 6.6 | 6.3 | 8.6 | 7.5 | 5.3 | 21.4 | 13.1 | 10.6 | 14.6 | 20.6 | Cap-Vert |
| Central African Rep. | 5.2 | 22.1 | 12.4 | 10.2 | 21.6 | 31.1 | 33.8 | 28.8 | 19.9 | 27.9 | 43.4 | Rép. centrafricaine |
| Chad | 7.6 | 28.9 | 17.7 | 32.3 | 46.9 | 30.3 | 15.1 | 28.5 | 25.6 | 43.9 | 55.7 | Tchad |
| Comoros | 1.1 | 4.2 | 3.2 | 6.8 | 5.8 | 7.2 | 12.0 | 14.3 | 11.9 | 13.8 | 15.7 | Comores |
| Democratic Yemen | 3.0 | 14.1 | 14.2 | 25.2 | 34.1 | 35.0 | 34.5 | 31.4 | 47.7 | 50.7 | 40.9 | Yémen démocratique |
| Djibouti | 0.9 | 0.3 | - | 1.8 | 2.7 | 4.1 | 8.6 | 13.8 | 10.9 | 10.7 | 10.5 | Djibouti |
| Equatorial Guinea | - | 0.7 | 0.4 | 0.4 | 0.6 | 2.6 | 8.1 | 5.5 | 7.9 | 6.7 | 7.1 | Guineé équatoriale |
| Ethiopia | 7.3 | 46.2 | 67.7 | 52.7 | 81.1 | 103.8 | 120.4 | 150.5 | 122.9 | 176.2 | 175.9 | Ethiopie |
| Gambia | 0.3 | 4.2 | 4.4 | 5.2 | 11.9 | 16.8 | 23.7 | 26.0 | 19.4 | 19.5 | 19.2 | Gambie |
| Guinea | 3.3 | 3.9 | 7.1 | 12.0 | 38.4 | 34.3 | 52.4 | 48.4 | 33.4 | 40.8 | 46.6 | Guinée |
| Guinea-Bissau | 0.1 | 7.4 | 6.9 | 9.8 | 10.9 | 15.9 | 21.2 | 22.3 | 26.0 | 25.6 | 22.4 | Guinée-Bissau |
| Haiti | 2.6 | 34.5 | 39.6 | 44.9 | 43.1 | 44.2 | 42.3 | 38.6 | 47.0 | 53.5 | 63.4 | Haïti |
| Lao People's Dem.Rep. | | 6.3 | 4.4 | 3.5 | 29.2 | 23.5 | 23.4 | 18.1 | 16.6 | 16.7 | 19.2 | Rép. dém. pop. lao |
| Lesotho | 3.8 | 12.7 | 12.1 | 16.2 | 20.9 | 20.2 | 30.6 | 40.9 | 33.4 | 35.0 | 29.4 | Lesotho |
| Malawi | 11.0 | 16.8 | 17.1 | 25.3 | 42.1 | 49.7 | 66.4 | 55.2 | 56.2 | 60.7 | 106.9 | Malawi |
| Maldives | 0.1 | 1.0 | 0.9 | 0.8 | 1.1 | 1.6 | 3.6 | 2.2 | 2.1 | 3.7 | 3.1 | Maldives |
| Mali | 11.5 | 59.6 | 32.7 | 36.2 | 58.4 | 85.8 | 93.1 | 77.2 | 63.0 | 71.7 | 86.4 | Mali |
| Nepal | 3.2 | 16.8 | 20.8 | 33.9 | 35.5 | 50.9 | 72.2 | 81.2 | 83.9 | 90.7 | 100.7 | Népal |
| Niger | 10.5 | 43.9 | 45.3 | 31.6 | 57.2 | 50.9 | 56.6 | 41.8 | 44.0 | 50.8 | 53.6 | Niger |
| Rwanda | 5.1 | 27.9 | 22.3 | 29.1 | 42.2 | 57.0 | 51.5 | 42.6 | 49.9 | 53.7 | 62.7 | Rwanda |
| Samoa | 1.2 | 4.6 | 4.4 | 7.9 | 8.4 | 8.7 | 11.2 | 9.8 | 6.5 | 10.4 | 9.2 | Samoa |
| Sao Tome and Principe | - | 0.3 | 1.0 | 1.4 | 2.2 | 1.6 | 2.7 | 3.8 | 5.6 | 7.7 | 6.9 | Sao Tomé-et-Principe |
| Sierra Leone | 1.8 | 6.5 | 7.5 | 13.0 | 26.5 | 19.8 | 27.2 | 24.2 | 25.1 | 28.9 | 21.9 | Sierra Leone |
| Somalia | 10.0 | 49.4 | 47.3 | 43.0 | 41.2 | 52.1 | 150.9 | 167.4 | 137.4 | 131.9 | 140.7 | Somalie |
| Sudan | 6.7 | 50.1 | 61.2 | 53.6 | 111.2 | 112.4 | 169.5 | 188.1 | 197.1 | 160.8 | 191.3 | Soudan |
| Togo | 9.3 | 16.3 | 20.0 | 21.8 | 35.9 | 40.8 | 35.3 | 25.5 | 23.0 | 57.6 | 53.4 | Togo |
| Uganda | 8.7 | 8.6 | 10.5 | 10.3 | 9.6 | 25.2 | 69.8 | 56.9 | 74.6 | 80.7 | 117.9 | Ouganda |
| Un. Rep. of Tanzania | 13.4 | 53.5 | 55.0 | 70.0 | 89.6 | 126.1 | 123.4 | 164.6 | 172.9 | 135.7 | 133.4 | Rép.-Unie de Tanzanie |
| Vanuatu | - | 0.5 | 0.5 | 2.1 | 0.4 | 0.7 | 0.7 | 6.1 | 2.7 | 2.5 | 2.3 | Vanuatu |
| Yemen | 4.3 | 21.6 | 36.2 | 30.4 | 35.9 | 30.7 | 42.7 | 38.4 | 51.5 | 52.1 | 53.2 | Yémen |
| All LDCs | (185.9) | 928.5 | 883.7 | 973.5 | 1429.4 | 1666.6 | 1982.8 | 1982.2 | 1964.9 | 2102.4 | 2413.8 | Ensemble des PMA |
| All developing countries | 1066.7 | 3671.1 | 3419.2 | 3654.9 | 4868.6 | 5816.1 | 7362.7 | 6963.2 | 7010.5 | 7044.2 | 7312.3 | Ensemble des pays en développement |

Source: UNCTAD secretariat, based on information from the OECD/DAC secretariat.

Source: Secrétariat de la CNUCED, d'après des renseignements du secrétariat de l'OCDE/CAD.

Table 32
Non-concessional assistance from multilateral agencies mainly financed by DAC member countries to individual LDCs.
1970 and 1975-1984

Net disbursements in $ million

Tableau 32
Aide non-concessionnelle reçue par chacun des PMA en provenance des institutions multilatérales essentiellement financées par les pays membres du CAD, 1970 et 1975-1984

Versements nets en millions de dollars

| Country | 1970 | 1975 | 1976 | 1977 | 1978 | 1979 | 1980 | 1981 | 1982 | 1983 | 1984 | Pays |
|---|---|---|---|---|---|---|---|---|---|---|---|---|
| Afghanistan | - | - | - | - | - | - | - | - | - | - | - | Afghanistan |
| Bangladesh | .. | 55.9 | 0.2 | 0.0 | -0.5 | -0.5 | 1.3 | -0.3 | 0.4 | -0.7 | -0.7 | Bangladesh |
| Benin | - | 0.1 | 1.1 | 3.5 | 2.5 | 1.2 | 3.4 | 2.5 | -0.4 | -0.1 | -0.4 | Bénin |
| Bhutan | - | - | - | - | - | - | - | - | - | - | - | Bhoutan |
| Botswana | - | 2.7 | 2.1 | 2.9 | 2.5 | 5.5 | 3.3 | 9.7 | 16.6 | 18.5 | 23.0 | Botswana |
| Burkina Faso | - | - | 1.0 | -0.2 | 0.7 | -0.5 | 0.0 | -0.5 | -0.4 | 2.6 | 1.8 | Burkina Faso |
| Burundi | -0.3 | 0.3 | 1.5 | 1.1 | 0.2 | -0.2 | 0.3 | 0.3 | 0.9 | 9.9 | 10.5 | Burundi |
| Cape Verde | - | - | - | - | - | - | - | - | 7.0 | 4.1 | 0.7 | Cap-Vert |
| Central African Rep. | - | 0.6 | 0.2 | - | 0.0 | -0.1 | 0.2 | 0.0 | -0.1 | 0.8 | 1.6 | Rép. centrafricaine |
| Chad | - | - | - | - | - | - | - | - | - | - | - | Tchad |
| Comoros | - | - | - | - | - | - | - | - | 1.1 | 2.6 | 2.6 | Comores |
| Democratic Yemen | - | - | - | - | - | - | - | - | - | - | - | Yémen démocratique |
| Djibouti | - | - | - | - | - | - | - | - | - | - | - | Djibouti |
| Equatorial Guinea | 2.9 | 2.1 | -1.8 | -3.7 | -3.9 | -4.0 | 0.7 | 1.5 | 2.6 | 1.2 | 0.3 | Guineé équatoriale |
| Ethiopia | - | - | - | 0.0 | 0.1 | 0.8 | -2.2 | -1.3 | -1.9 | -1.3 | -1.8 | Ethiopie |
| Gambia | - | - | - | -0.3 | -1.8 | -1.4 | 5.7 | 2.1 | 1.3 | 1.2 | 4.1 | Gambie |
| Guinea | 15.2 | 1.3 | -2.1 | - | - | - | -2.5 | - | 0.6 | 2.1 | 12.9 | Guinée |
| Guinea-Bissau | - | - | - | - | - | - | 0.0 | 0.4 | 2.0 | 4.0 | 2.8 | Guinée-Bissau |
| Haiti | -0.2 | - | - | - | - | - | - | - | - | 0.7 | - | Haïti |
| Lao People's Dem.Rep. | - | - | - | - | - | - | - | - | - | - | - | Rép. dém. pop. lao |
| Lesotho | - | - | - | - | 0.3 | - | - | 0.2 | 2.1 | 2.4 | 4.7 | Lesotho |
| Malawi | - | 0.4 | 3.0 | 8.7 | 11.9 | 21.8 | 15.8 | 26.7 | 22.0 | 2.5 | 1.4 | Malawi |
| Maldives | - | - | - | - | - | - | - | - | - | - | - | Maldives |
| Mali | - | -0.1 | -0.1 | 0.5 | 2.6 | 1.6 | 1.1 | 0.4 | 1.6 | 0.8 | - | Mali |
| Nepal | - | 0.1 | -0.1 | 2.1 | 0.5 | -0.2 | -0.3 | -0.4 | -0.3 | - | 2.4 | Népal |
| Niger | - | 0.2 | -0.1 | -0.1 | 0.9 | 7.4 | 6.8 | 3.8 | 0.7 | 14.5 | 0.6 | Niger |
| Rwanda | - | - | - | -0.3 | 0.2 | - | 0.2 | 0.1 | 1.2 | 0.6 | -0.3 | Rwanda |
| Samoa | - | - | - | - | - | - | - | - | - | - | - | Samoa |
| Sao Tome and Principe | 3.0 | 3.9 | 1.3 | 0.8 | -0.1 | 2.1 | 3.3 | 1.3 | 0.3 | -0.9 | -3.6 | Sao Tomé-et-Principe |
| Sierra Leone | - | 1.5 | 0.1 | 0.0 | 0.0 | -0.2 | - | 0.2 | -0.1 | -0.4 | -0.6 | Sierra Leone |
| Somalia | 5.6 | -2.9 | 0.4 | -3.1 | 3.7 | 2.7 | -2.4 | -0.5 | -3.1 | -5.4 | -8.5 | Somalie |
| Sudan | - | -0.1 | 0.8 | 1.8 | 29.8 | 29.0 | 31.8 | -2.6 | -2.5 | -1.1 | -1.0 | Soudan |
| Togo | - | - | - | - | - | - | - | - | - | - | - | Togo |
| Uganda | -0.5 | 0.9 | 2.6 | 2.5 | 0.5 | 3.1 | 1.8 | 4.8 | 6.0 | 6.6 | 5.4 | Ouganda |
| Un. Rep. of Tanzania | 1.2 | 39.6 | 11.7 | 24.0 | 16.0 | 20.2 | 21.0 | 17.8 | 6.9 | 17.3 | 7.5 | Rép.-Unie de Tanzanie |
| Vanuatu | - | - | - | - | - | - | - | - | - | - | - | Vanuatu |
| Yemen | - | - | - | - | - | 2.4 | - | - | - | -0.9 | -0.5 | Yémen |
| All LDCs | (53.7) | 106.5 | 21.8 | 40.8 | 66.1 | 90.7 | 89.3 | 63.8 | 64.5 | 81.8 | 66.1 | Ensemble des PMA |
| All developing countries | 694.5 | 2480.0 | 2467.6 | 2625.2 | 2878.1 | 3837.7 | 4574.1 | 5414.1 | 6381.4 | 7017.9 | 7913.3 | Ensemble des pays en développement |

Source: UNCTAD secretariat, based on information from the OECD/DAC secretariat.

Source: Secrétariat de la CNUCED, d'après des renseignements du secrétariat de l'OCDE/CAD.

Table 33
Technical assistance disbursements to individual LDCS, a/
1970 and 1975-1984

Tableau 33
Versements au titre de l'assistance technique en faveur des PMA, a/
1970 et 1975-1984

$ million

Millions de dollars

| Country | 1970 | 1975 | 1976 | 1977 | 1978 | 1979 | 1980 | 1981 | 1982 | 1983 | 1984 | Pays |
|---|---|---|---|---|---|---|---|---|---|---|---|---|
| Afghanistan | 20.9 | 25.1 | 20.3 | 28.1 | 31.1 | 37.8 | 21.8 | 14.8 | 13.9 | 15.2 | 12.4 | Afghanistan |
| Bangladesh | .. | 58.3 | 60.0 | 27.3 | 99.7 | 148.2 | 158.9 | 147.1 | 133.1 | 176.3 | 157.9 | Bangladesh |
| Benin | 6.1 | 19.8 | 16.0 | 13.7 | 16.9 | 20.4 | 25.9 | 25.1 | 27.9 | 25.8 | 28.1 | Bénin |
| Bhutan | 0.1 | 1.8 | 2.7 | 2.1 | 2.2 | 4.8 | 6.0 | 7.4 | 6.2 | 7.2 | 8.8 | Bhoutan |
| Botswana | 2.7 | 13.7 | 15.5 | 18.0 | 23.0 | 36.3 | 47.5 | 48.0 | 42.8 | 40.5 | 34.8 | Botswana |
| Burkina Faso | 8.2 | 32.6 | 37.5 | 37.6 | 49.1 | 60.7 | 73.0 | 72.0 | 73.7 | 65.3 | 71.5 | Burkina Faso |
| Burundi | 10.5 | 23.2 | 23.0 | 25.6 | 30.4 | 35.7 | 45.0 | 44.2 | 46.8 | 45.4 | 44.4 | Burundi |
| Cape Verde | - | 1.0 | 2.2 | 5.6 | 5.6 | 6.2 | 11.9 | 11.4 | 20.6 | 17.4 | 17.1 | Cap-Vert |
| Central African Rep. | 8.1 | 19.5 | 19.4 | 20.8 | 24.6 | 32.9 | 34.1 | 33.6 | 31.2 | 29.3 | 38.5 | Rép. centrafricaine |
| Chad | 9.9 | 25.4 | 22.0 | 24.6 | 29.2 | 21.4 | 11.9 | 16.8 | 15.3 | 21.7 | 18.8 | Tchad |
| Comoros | 4.8 | 7.0 | 2.2 | 2.3 | 1.3 | 2.9 | 7.0 | 10.1 | 9.6 | 10.1 | 9.3 | Comores |
| Democratic Yemen | 2.3 | 9.2 | 11.3 | 10.6 | 10.8 | 7.9 | 11.6 | 12.6 | 14.8 | 14.3 | 9.9 | Yémen démocratique |
| Djibouti | 6.2 | 11.1 | 14.0 | 15.2 | 14.3 | 19.0 | 27.8 | 29.8 | 30.8 | 29.2 | 29.7 | Djibouti |
| Equatorial Guinea | - | 0.7 | 0.4 | 0.4 | 0.6 | 2.2 | 2.0 | 4.5 | 4.1 | 3.9 | 6.7 | Guineé équatoriale |
| Ethiopia | 19.6 | 36.1 | 31.5 | 30.3 | 26.5 | 29.2 | 44.2 | 63.9 | 53.1 | 63.8 | 80.8 | Ethiopie |
| Gambia | 0.7 | 2.7 | 4.3 | 3.3 | 6.8 | 9.6 | 12.7 | 13.8 | 17.4 | 15.8 | 14.8 | Gambie |
| Guinea | 4.1 | 3.4 | 5.5 | 6.0 | 10.3 | 11.1 | 18.7 | 21.4 | 20.5 | 14.4 | 18.0 | Guinée |
| Guinea-Bissau | 0.1 | 2.5 | 7.0 | 4.6 | 6.7 | 9.0 | 12.1 | 12.7 | 15.2 | 16.2 | 11.8 | Guinée-Bissau |
| Haiti | 3.6 | 11.8 | 13.5 | 13.6 | 20.5 | 24.0 | 32.3 | 32.8 | 34.1 | 32.2 | 33.5 | Haïti |
| Lao People's Dem.Rep. | 39.6 | 15.0 | 4.5 | 5.0 | 11.8 | 12.0 | 14.0 | 13.3 | 11.3 | 10.7 | 12.3 | Rép. dém. pop. lao |
| Lesotho | 2.6 | 8.7 | 12.0 | 12.7 | 16.3 | 19.9 | 29.1 | 31.2 | 32.3 | 33.0 | 31.7 | Lesotho |
| Malawi | 9.1 | 16.3 | 17.4 | 17.6 | 24.0 | 30.0 | 36.4 | 38.1 | 37.2 | 34.8 | 39.6 | Malawi |
| Maldives | 0.2 | 0.8 | 1.0 | 1.0 | 1.5 | 2.2 | 2.8 | 2.5 | 3.6 | 3.8 | 3.6 | Maldives |
| Mali | 8.1 | 24.6 | 23.2 | 25.6 | 35.4 | 49.5 | 76.9 | 63.0 | 55.0 | 53.7 | 59.8 | Mali |
| Nepal | 8.0 | 24.7 | 20.4 | 26.0 | 30.6 | 38.1 | 50.5 | 52.7 | 63.8 | 68.1 | 68.4 | Népal |
| Niger | 11.7 | 29.2 | 27.9 | 30.5 | 38.4 | 47.3 | 62.1 | 59.2 | 68.3 | 61.0 | 61.5 | Niger |
| Rwanda | 11.7 | 31.4 | 32.3 | 41.2 | 42.8 | 50.9 | 54.5 | 53.2 | 49.6 | 53.8 | 52.8 | Rwanda |
| Samoa | 0.9 | 4.7 | 4.7 | 5.6 | 6.8 | 6.1 | 9.8 | 10.8 | 7.6 | 7.4 | 6.9 | Samoa |
| Sao Tome and Principe | - | 0.3 | 0.5 | 0.9 | 1.5 | 1.3 | 1.3 | 1.4 | 2.8 | 1.6 | 2.3 | Sao Tomé-et-Principe |
| Sierra Leone | 5.3 | 7.9 | 10.4 | 10.4 | 13.2 | 14.9 | 21.4 | 21.7 | 21.3 | 19.3 | 19.4 | Sierra Leone |
| Somalia | 10.6 | 19.6 | 16.0 | 19.4 | 21.5 | 32.1 | 92.9 | 103.2 | 92.0 | 113.6 | 107.4 | Somalie |
| Sudan | 6.5 | 28.1 | 30.9 | 37.7 | 60.3 | 69.1 | 102.4 | 131.5 | 117.9 | 127.4 | 121.7 | Soudan |
| Togo | 7.7 | 16.9 | 16.9 | 18.9 | 21.9 | 25.0 | 28.9 | 30.4 | 30.3 | 27.7 | 29.9 | Togo |
| Uganda | 14.4 | 9.0 | 8.4 | 7.7 | 12.0 | 16.4 | 21.0 | 33.8 | 29.5 | 34.0 | 32.4 | Ouganda |
| Un. Rep. of Tanzania | 21.4 | 60.2 | 76.7 | 80.2 | 106.0 | 138.2 | 172.6 | 176.4 | 180.7 | 173.4 | 138.1 | Rép.-Unie de Tanzanie |
| Vanuatu | 0.6 | 2.1 | 14.5 | 2.3 | 2.7 | 22.4 | 24.7 | 17.2 | 16.1 | 16.1 | 13.1 | Vanuatu |
| Yemen | 2.6 | 17.0 | 15.6 | 25.2 | 32.8 | 39.5 | 50.3 | 60.6 | 64.7 | 59.9 | 61.5 | Yémen |
| All LDCs | (281.3) | 621.4 | 641.6 | 654.8 | 889.1 | 1134.1 | 1456.0 | 1522.2 | 1495.1 | 1543.3 | 1509.2 | Ensemble des PMA |
| All developing countries | 1909.9 | 3970.9 | 3807.0 | 4075.8 | 4998.1 | 6247.9 | 7249.7 | 7378.7 | 7358.8 | 7704.7 | 7759.6 | Ensemble des pays en développement |

Source: UNCTAD secretariat, based on information from the OECD/DAC secretariat.
a/ Bilateral contributions from DAC member countries plus contributions from multilateral agencies mainly financed by them.

Source: Secrétariat de la CNUCED, d'après des renseignements du secrétariat de l'OCDE/CAD.
a/ Somme des contributions bilatérales des pays membres du CAD et des contributions des institutions multilatérales essentiellement financées par ceux-ci.

Table 34

Net ODA as per cent of donor's GNP from individual DAC
member countries to LDCs as a group, 1975-1984

Percentages

Tableau 34

Apports nets de l'APD accordée par chaque pays membre du CAD à
l'ensemble des PMA, en pourcentage du PNB du pays donneur,1975-1984

En pourcentage

| Country | 1975 | 1976 | 1977 | 1978 | 1979 | 1980 | 1981 | 1982 | 1983 | 1984 | Pays |
|---|---|---|---|---|---|---|---|---|---|---|---|
| | Bilateral ODA | | | | | APD bilatérale | | | | | |
| Australia | 0.04 | 0.02 | 0.02 | 0.03 | 0.04 | 0.02 | 0.04 | 0.05 | 0.03 | 0.04 | Australie |
| Austria | 0.00 | 0.00 | 0.01 | 0.01 | 0.00 | 0.01 | 0.01 | 0.01 | 0.01 | 0.01 | Autriche |
| Belgium | 0.08 | 0.08 | 0.07 | 0.08 | 0.09 | 0.08 | 0.09 | 0.08 | 0.08 | 0.07 | Belgique |
| Canada | 0.10 | 0.06 | 0.06 | 0.08 | 0.08 | 0.06 | 0.06 | 0.08 | 0.07 | 0.07 | Canada |
| Denmark | 0.14 | 0.12 | 0.14 | 0.15 | 0.16 | 0.18 | 0.13 | 0.16 | 0.18 | 0.15 | Danemark |
| Finland | 0.05 | 0.05 | 0.04 | 0.03 | 0.04 | 0.04 | 0.05 | 0.04 | 0.07 | 0.08 | Finlande |
| France | 0.08 | 0.07 | 0.06 | 0.06 | 0.06 | 0.06 | 0.08 | 0.08 | 0.08 | 0.10 | France |
| Germany, Fed.Rep. of | 0.06 | 0.05 | 0.05 | 0.06 | 0.07 | 0.07 | 0.08 | 0.08 | 0.07 | 0.07 | Allemagne, Rép.féd.d' |
| Italy | 0.01 | 0.01 | 0.01 | 0.01 | 0.01 | 0.01 | 0.02 | 0.03 | 0.05 | 0.07 | Italie |
| Japan | 0.01 | 0.01 | 0.02 | 0.02 | 0.03 | 0.04 | 0.03 | 0.04 | 0.02 | 0.02 | Japon |
| Netherlands | 0.08 | 0.09 | 0.15 | 0.17 | 0.17 | 0.18 | 0.20 | 0.19 | 0.15 | 0.19 | Pays-Bas |
| New Zealand | 0.08 | 0.04 | 0.04 | 0.04 | 0.03 | 0.03 | 0.02 | 0.02 | 0.02 | 0.02 | Nouvelle-Zélande |
| Norway | 0.14 | 0.13 | 0.17 | 0.20 | 0.20 | 0.17 | 0.16 | 0.22 | 0.23 | 0.19 | Norvège |
| Sweden | 0.18 | 0.16 | 0.18 | 0.17 | 0.21 | 0.16 | 0.16 | 0.17 | 0.16 | 0.14 | Suède |
| Switzerland | 0.02 | 0.02 | 0.03 | 0.05 | 0.03 | 0.05 | 0.06 | 0.06 | 0.06 | 0.07 | Suisse |
| United Kingdom | 0.05 | 0.05 | 0.05 | 0.07 | 0.07 | 0.07 | 0.06 | 0.05 | 0.05 | 0.05 | Royaume-Uni |
| United States | 0.04 | 0.02 | 0.01 | 0.02 | 0.02 | 0.02 | 0.02 | 0.02 | 0.02 | 0.02 | Etats-Unis |
| Total DAC countries | 0.05 | 0.03 | 0.04 | 0.04 | 0.05 | 0.05 | 0.04 | 0.05 | 0.04 | 0.04 | Total pays du CAD |
| | Total ODA a/ | | | | | APD totale a/ | | | | | |
| Australia | 0.06 | 0.03 | 0.03 | 0.08 | 0.09 | 0.06 | 0.06 | 0.10 | 0.08 | 0.07 | Australie |
| Austria | 0.01 | 0.01 | 0.01 | 0.03 | 0.04 | 0.01 | 0.04 | 0.04 | 0.03 | 0.03 | Autriche |
| Belgium | 0.15 | 0.13 | 0.12 | 0.15 | 0.14 | 0.13 | 0.16 | 0.15 | 0.15 | 0.14 | Belgique |
| Canada | 0.15 | 0.11 | 0.12 | 0.14 | 0.15 | 0.11 | 0.11 | 0.11 | 0.13 | 0.13 | Canada |
| Denmark | 0.21 | 0.19 | 0.21 | 0.25 | 0.26 | 0.30 | 0.25 | 0.29 | 0.29 | 0.28 | Danemark |
| Finland | 0.07 | 0.08 | 0.06 | 0.06 | 0.07 | 0.08 | 0.08 | 0.08 | 0.11 | 0.12 | Finlande |
| France | 0.11 | 0.10 | 0.09 | 0.08 | 0.10 | 0.11 | 0.12 | 0.12 | 0.13 | 0.16 | France |
| Germany, Fed.Rep. of | 0.10 | 0.09 | 0.09 | 0.10 | 0.12 | 0.13 | 0.12 | 0.12 | 0.13 | 0.12 | Allemagne, Rép.féd.d' |
| Italy | 0.04 | 0.03 | 0.03 | 0.05 | 0.03 | 0.06 | 0.06 | 0.07 | 0.08 | 0.13 | Italie |
| Japan | 0.03 | 0.03 | 0.04 | 0.05 | 0.06 | 0.08 | 0.05 | 0.05 | 0.06 | 0.07 | Japon |
| Netherlands | 0.16 | 0.16 | 0.21 | 0.22 | 0.26 | 0.27 | 0.29 | 0.29 | 0.25 | 0.29 | Pays-Bas |
| New Zealand | 0.10 | 0.05 | 0.06 | 0.04 | 0.05 | 0.04 | 0.04 | 0.03 | 0.03 | 0.03 | Nouvelle-Zélande |
| Norway | 0.21 | 0.22 | 0.26 | 0.31 | 0.30 | 0.29 | 0.29 | 0.37 | 0.38 | 0.31 | Norvège |
| Sweden | 0.25 | 0.23 | 0.27 | 0.27 | 0.31 | 0.23 | 0.26 | 0.31 | 0.26 | 0.21 | Suède |
| Switzerland | 0.04 | 0.04 | 0.06 | 0.07 | 0.06 | 0.08 | 0.08 | 0.08 | 0.10 | 0.10 | Suisse |
| United Kingdom | 0.08 | 0.08 | 0.11 | 0.13 | 0.14 | 0.10 | 0.11 | 0.11 | 0.10 | 0.09 | Royaume-Uni |
| United States | 0.05 | 0.03 | 0.04 | 0.05 | 0.02 | 0.05 | 0.03 | 0.04 | 0.04 | 0.04 | Etats-Unis |
| Total DAC countries | 0.07 | 0.06 | 0.07 | 0.08 | 0.08 | 0.09 | 0.08 | 0.08 | 0.08 | 0.08 | Total pays du CAD |

Source: UNCTAD secretariat, based on information from
the OECD/DAC secretariat.

a/ Including imputed flows to LDCs through
multilateral channels.

Source: Secrétariat de la CNUCED, d'après des renseignements du
secrétariat de l'OCDE/CAD.

a/ Y compris le montant imputé de l'APD fournie aux PMA
à travers les voies multilatérales.

Table 35
ODA commitments from individual DAC member countries and individual multilateral agencies a/ to all LDCs, 1975-1984
$ million

Tableau 35
Engagements de l'APD de chaque pays membre du CAD et de chaque institution multilatérale a/ en faveur de l'ensemble des PMA, 1975-1984
Millions de dollars

| | 1975 | 1976 | 1977 | 1978 | 1979 | 1980 | 1981 | 1982 | 1983 | 1984 |
|---|---|---|---|---|---|---|---|---|---|---|
| **A. Bilateral donors / A. Donneurs bilatéraux** | | | | | | | | | | |
| Australia / Australie | 28.2 | 10.6 | 45.2 | 45.5 | 35.9 | 51.2 | 72.3 | 60.4 | 54.3 | 48.5 |
| Austria / Autriche | 0.5 | 0.8 | 0.3 | 2.4 | 0.3 | 0.9 | 1.0 | 6.2 | 5.6 | 4.9 |
| Belgium / Belgique | 62.9 | 68.4 | 76.1 | 101.0 | 104.8 | 112.9 | 89.8 | 72.1 | 65.3 | 51.3 |
| Canada | 185.5 | 138.8 | 349.1 | 509.2 | 197.4 | 121.3 | 203.5 | 236.7 | 304.8 | 336.7 |
| Denmark / Danemark | 34.4 | 46.2 | 49.7 | 217.9 | 117.5 | 108.5 | 58.2 | 113.1 | 88.1 | 153.6 |
| Finland / Finlande | 20.7 | 10.6 | 9.7 | 8.2 | 41.4 | 38.7 | 38.4 | 34.9 | 21.1 | 42.6 |
| France | 293.0 | 287.6 | 223.3 | 218.2 | 344.5 | 577.6 | 561.4 | 511.0 | 484.2 | 598.6 |
| Germany, Fed. Rep. of / Allemagne, Rép. Féd. d' | 308.0 | 362.3 | 343.9 | 506.8 | 1000.2 | 1835.3 | 711.0 | 477.2 | 488.7 | 483.2 |
| Italy / Italie | 14.7 | 11.9 | 16.5 | 15.7 | 19.4 | 43.9 | 225.5 | 207.4 | 281.6 | 292.9 |
| Japan / Japon | 154.9 | 108.5 | 162.6 | 348.3 | 329.0 | 386.6 | 362.4 | 451.6 | 305.8 | 377.9 |
| Netherlands / Pays-Bas | 107.9 | 146.2 | 256.5 | 417.8 | 320.0 | 358.5 | 315.8 | 204.6 | 251.8 | 201.1 |
| New Zealand / Nouvelle-Zélande | 6.7 | 1.8 | 3.5 | 7.7 | 4.8 | 9.2 | 8.8 | 3.8 | 3.0 | 4.4 |
| Norway / Norvège | 47.6 | 34.9 | 57.0 | 71.5 | 67.8 | 67.9 | 121.0 | 101.8 | 85.3 | 109.5 |
| Sweden / Suède | 151.1 | 130.0 | 265.3 | 224.8 | 285.7 | 164.3 | 192.5 | 167.6 | 145.2 | 145.5 |
| Switzerland / Suisse | 14.4 | 7.7 | 34.6 | 41.5 | 24.0 | 56.3 | 101.4 | 35.7 | 80.1 | 50.0 |
| United Kingdom / Royaume-Uni | 217.3 | 240.9 | 118.7 | 426.3 | 445.8 | 429.0 | 227.1 | 147.0 | 183.2 | 230.3 |
| United States / Etats-Unis | 524.1 | 384.5 | 383.8 | 439.8 | 511.6 | 630.9 | 702.6 | 811.8 | 868.7 | 1135.3 |
| Total bilateral concessional / Total des apports bilatéraux concessionnels | 2172.0 | 1991.7 | 2395.7 | 3602.6 | 3850.2 | 4993.0 | 3992.8 | 3642.8 | 3716.8 | 4266.3 |
| **B. Multilateral donors / B. Donneurs multilatéraux** | | | | | | | | | | |
| AfDB/AfDF / BAfD/FAfD | 95.2 | 77.5 | 121.9 | 132.2 | 159.2 | 190.3 | 217.9 | 207.3 | 243.6 | 173.5 |
| AsDB / BAsD | 70.9 | 125.6 | 128.2 | 130.9 | 178.5 | 204.3 | 241.2 | 256.7 | 378.2 | 390.3 |
| EEC/EDF / CEE/FED | 172.9 | 375.1 | 463.2 | 360.8 | 421.9 | 474.6 | 580.1 | 574.9 | 463.1 | 517.8 |
| IBRD / BIRD | - | 62.7 | 31.5 | - | - | - | - | - | - | - |
| IDA / AID | 599.3 | 536.1 | 607.2 | 769.8 | 678.3 | 1222.8 | 1001.8 | 1180.2 | 1287.4 | 1362.5 |
| IDB / BID | 41.1 | 5.0 | 15.7 | 43.5 | 4.1 | 9.1 | 32.6 | 17.4 | - | |
| IFAD / FIDA | - | - | - | 62.3 | 120.1 | 134.9 | 154.8 | 58.3 | 82.8 | 89.6 |
| UN / ONU | 323.6 | 305.6 | 290.2 | 404.3 | 481.9 | 601.2 | 738.0 | 693.8 | 729.4 | 813.9 |
| Total multilateral concessional / Total des apports multilatéraux concessionnels | 1303.0 | 1487.6 | 1657.9 | 1903.7 | 2043.9 | 2837.2 | 2933.8 | 3003.7 | 3201.9 | 3347.6 |
| GRAND TOTAL / TOTAL GENERAL | 3475.0 | 3479.3 | 4053.6 | 5506.3 | 5894.1 | 7830.3 | 6926.6 | 6646.5 | 6918.7 | 7613.9 |

Source: UNCTAD secretariat based on information from the OECD/DAC secretariat.

a/ Multilateral agencies mainly financed by DAC member countries.

Source: Secrétariat de la CNUCED, d'après des renseignements du secrétariat de l'OCDE/CAD.

a/ Institutions multilatérales essentiellement financées par les pays membres du CAD.

Table 36
ODA commitments from DAC member countries
and multilateral agencies mainly financed by them
to individual LDCs, 1975-1984
$ million

Tableau 36
Engagements de l'APD à chacun des PMA, en provenance des pays
membres du CAD et des institutions multilatérales
essentiellement financées par ceux-ci, 1975-1984
Millions de dollars

| Country | 1975 | 1976 | 1977 | 1978 | 1979 | 1980 | 1981 | 1982 | 1983 | 1984 | Pays |
|---|---|---|---|---|---|---|---|---|---|---|---|
| Afghanistan | 71.8 | 117.3 | 112.1 | 134.8 | 148.0 | 17.3 | 13.9 | 14.5 | 17.0 | 13.8 | Afghanistan |
| Bangladesh | 1215.5 | 877.6 | 892.4 | 1411.3 | 1216.1 | 2007.0 | 1502.9 | 1598.0 | 1413.6 | 1688.9 | Bangladesh |
| Benin | 47.3 | 57.7 | 73.7 | 120.7 | 78.8 | 99.0 | 118.7 | 154.6 | 55.4 | 151.1 | Bénin |
| Bhutan | 1.8 | 3.6 | 3.0 | 3.1 | 5.3 | 15.4 | 11.8 | 12.4 | 24.8 | 28.2 | Bhoutan |
| Botswana | 54.0 | 52.7 | 58.1 | 153.8 | 123.5 | 126.5 | 112.5 | 101.0 | 95.4 | 108.1 | Botswana |
| Burkina Faso | 111.6 | 134.2 | 139.7 | 202.0 | 255.5 | 244.8 | 318.3 | 268.6 | 194.2 | 202.3 | Burkina Faso |
| Burundi | 61.2 | 68.4 | 75.9 | 78.4 | 127.5 | 170.9 | 222.0 | 97.7 | 183.6 | 114.1 | Burundi |
| Cape Verde | 16.7 | 20.1 | 36.9 | 47.6 | 59.3 | 56.5 | 71.2 | 59.5 | 74.1 | 93.2 | Cap-Vert |
| Central African Rep. | 57.2 | 32.4 | 61.6 | 62.4 | 85.3 | 129.9 | 85.4 | 145.8 | 137.7 | 97.0 | Rép. centrafricaine |
| Chad | 73.6 | 113.5 | 86.4 | 134.5 | 50.6 | 35.2 | 96.1 | 67.9 | 95.8 | 136.5 | Tchad |
| Comoros | 20.9 | 11.6 | 15.8 | 15.7 | 22.0 | 35.4 | 56.0 | 43.9 | 28.8 | 49.9 | Comores |
| Democratic Yemen | 37.2 | 17.4 | 25.4 | 45.3 | 31.4 | 56.4 | 56.5 | 114.0 | 55.6 | 53.1 | Yémen démocratique |
| Djibouti | 34.8 | 26.4 | 32.7 | 23.6 | 31.5 | 46.2 | 55.6 | 71.3 | 70.6 | 76.2 | Djibouti |
| Equatorial Guinea | 0.7 | -1.6 | 0.4 | 0.6 | 3.2 | 19.7 | 18.5 | 13.6 | 17.2 | 25.2 | Guinée équatoriale |
| Ethiopia | 195.2 | 132.1 | 177.5 | 117.9 | 145.3 | 227.2 | 295.9 | 295.7 | 428.1 | 597.1 | Ethiopie |
| Gambia | 9.2 | 29.3 | 13.6 | 35.2 | 66.8 | 72.7 | 64.6 | 48.3 | 50.0 | 83.3 | Gambie |
| Guinea | 36.4 | 17.4 | 45.8 | 95.9 | 90.1 | 148.5 | 69.7 | 106.4 | 115.3 | 175.4 | Guinée |
| Guinea-Bissau | 23.8 | 41.8 | 47.2 | 65.6 | 64.3 | 63.5 | 59.8 | 57.8 | 91.2 | 75.2 | Guinée-Bissau |
| Haiti | 95.8 | 102.1 | 104.7 | 130.3 | 86.6 | 76.5 | 136.8 | 195.9 | 142.8 | 134.3 | Haïti |
| Lao People's Dem.Rep. | 37.3 | 30.6 | 36.1 | 68.7 | 65.5 | 81.0 | 46.6 | 19.4 | 53.9 | 37.7 | Rép. dém. pop. lao |
| Lesotho | 38.7 | 53.1 | 81.0 | 58.9 | 125.0 | 119.4 | 108.5 | 67.8 | 95.4 | 120.2 | Lesotho |
| Malawi | 85.4 | 69.5 | 145.8 | 266.7 | 185.2 | 143.4 | 210.8 | 71.1 | 270.3 | 142.7 | Malawi |
| Maldives | 2.4 | 1.8 | 8.3 | 2.9 | 6.5 | 5.9 | 4.8 | 7.2 | 15.6 | 13.7 | Maldives |
| Mali | 146.7 | 163.1 | 154.1 | 165.6 | 249.2 | 158.8 | 264.2 | 223.1 | 270.3 | 379.0 | Mali |
| Nepal | 53.7 | 161.9 | 128.7 | 184.5 | 207.0 | 270.1 | 249.6 | 210.0 | 280.6 | 393.3 | Népal |
| Niger | 109.6 | 180.4 | 117.4 | 171.0 | 250.0 | 184.7 | 239.4 | 209.2 | 230.4 | 308.0 | Niger |
| Rwanda | 97.9 | 116.2 | 147.1 | 141.1 | 161.4 | 207.1 | 207.5 | 196.7 | 194.2 | 163.3 | Rwanda |
| Samoa | 17.8 | 8.0 | 21.9 | 32.0 | 29.1 | 24.9 | 45.7 | 14.1 | 17.7 | 21.0 | Samoa |
| Sao Tome and Principe | 0.3 | 1.6 | 3.8 | 14.1 | 3.6 | 4.4 | 7.9 | 7.4 | 9.6 | 13.9 | Sao Tomé-et-Principe |
| Sierra Leone | 33.6 | 17.2 | 51.6 | 42.7 | 108.1 | 67.3 | 114.8 | 74.0 | 58.4 | 66.2 | Sierra Leone |
| Somalia | 78.5 | 100.4 | 79.9 | 109.1 | 184.0 | 366.5 | 457.7 | 307.4 | 302.2 | 341.0 | Somalie |
| Sudan | 167.0 | 129.3 | 155.7 | 413.5 | 428.3 | 967.3 | 553.5 | 534.5 | 679.6 | 639.3 | Soudan |
| Togo | 43.1 | 66.8 | 150.9 | 61.7 | 77.9 | 137.2 | 75.3 | 111.7 | 156.2 | 113.5 | Togo |
| Uganda | 9.1 | 17.8 | 17.1 | 17.2 | 75.5 | 209.9 | 195.5 | 199.4 | 293.0 | 294.7 | Ouganda |
| Un. Rep. of Tanzania | 307.7 | 404.1 | 626.2 | 757.0 | 847.2 | 890.5 | 637.6 | 706.3 | 510.4 | 500.0 | Rép.-Un. de Tanzanie |
| Vanuatu | 15.5 | 26.2 | 12.6 | 22.0 | 39.7 | 72.9 | 30.8 | 32.5 | 30.7 | 22.7 | Vanuatu |
| Yemen | 65.8 | 77.2 | 112.7 | 98.8 | 159.7 | 270.4 | 110.4 | 187.9 | 158.9 | 140.9 | Yémen |
| All LDCs | 3474.9 | 3479.3 | 4053.6 | 5506.2 | 5893.9 | 7830.3 | 6926.4 | 6646.4 | 6918.2 | 7613.8 | Ensemble des PMA |

Source: UNCTAD secretariat, based on information from the OECD/DAC secretariat.

Source: Secrétariat de la CNUCED, d'après des renseignements du secrétariat de l'OCDE/CAD.

Table 37

Grant element of ODA commitments from individual DAC member
countries to LDCs and to all developing countries, 1975-1984[a]/

Tableau 37

Élément de libéralité des engagements de l'APD
de chaque pays membre du CAD aux PMA et à
l'ensemble des pays en développement, 1975-1984[a]/

| Country | | 1975 | 1976 | 1977 | 1978 | 1979 | 1980 | 1981 | 1982 | 1983 | 1984 | | Pays |
|---|---|---|---|---|---|---|---|---|---|---|---|---|---|
| Australia | A | 100.0 | 100.0 | 100.0 | 100.0 | 100.0 | 100.0 | 100.0 | 100.0 | 100.0 | 100.0 | A | Australie |
| | B | 100.0 | 100.0 | 100.0 | 100.0 | 100.0 | 100.0 | 100.0 | 100.0 | 100.0 | 100.0 | B | |
| Austria | A | 100.0 | 100.0 | 35.5 | 99.0 | 95.9 | 93.2 | 93.9 | 94.9 | 99.4 | 100.0 | A | Autriche |
| | B | 94.8 | 97.3 | 67.5 | 65.8 | 86.1 | 70.3 | 55.1 | 58.8 | 61.1 | 82.1 | B | |
| Belgium | A | 100.0 | 99.0 | 98.7 | 98.9 | 98.4 | 98.1 | 98.5 | 98.3 | 98.2 | 98.8 | A | Belgique |
| | B | 98.1 | 98.2 | 98.3 | 98.6 | 98.0 | 97.9 | 97.6 | 98.6 | 97.3 | (98.1) | B | |
| Canada | A | 94.7 | 98.3 | 100.0 | 100.0 | 100.0 | 100.0 | 100.0 | 100.0 | 100.0 | 100.0 | A | Canada |
| | B | (96.4) | 97.3 | 97.5 | 96.6 | 97.2 | 98.0 | 97.2 | 98.8 | 99.3 | 98.6 | B | |
| Denmark | A | 88.6 | 91.5 | 94.9 | 96.4 | 96.8 | 93.5 | 95.2 | 96.9 | 99.1 | 100.0 | A | Danemark |
| | B | 96.0 | 96.6 | 97.3 | 95.3 | 96.7 | 97.3 | 95.4 | 95.7 | 96.4 | 98.0 | B | |
| Finland | A | 87.8 | 84.8 | 100.0 | 100.0 | 100.0 | 100.0 | 95.0 | 99.0 | 100.0 | 100.0 | A | Finlande |
| | B | 91.5 | 90.8 | 97.5 | 99.0 | 97.7 | 97.5 | 95.6 | 95.9 | 99.7 | 95.6 | B | |
| France | A | 97.0 | 87.9 | 94.6 | (95.0) | (95.0) | 79.2 | 89.0 | 81.7 | 79.6 | 78.0 | A | France |
| | B | (90.9) | 90.9 | 93.4 | 92.3 | (93.5) | 90.0 | 89.5 | 90.0 | 89.3 | (88.4) | B | |
| Germany, Fed.Rep.of | A | 93.0 | 91.1 | 93.8 | 92.7 | 97.8 | 98.8 | 99.3 | 99.4 | 96.2 | 99.4 | A | Allemagne, Rép.féd. |
| | B | 88.3 | (86.8) | 86.0 | 86.6 | 85.1 | 89.3 | 84.9 | 88.9 | 88.8 | 84.6 | B | |
| Italy [b]/ | A | 100.0 | 100.0 | 100.0 | 100.0 | 100.0 | 90.0 | 54.7 | 71.1 | 89.5 | 80.0 | A | Italie [b]/ |
| | B | 98.4 | (97.3) | 99.2 | 98.7 | 99.6 | 98.8 | 91.4 | 91.4 | (90.7) | 91.2 | B | |
| Japan | A | 86.0 | 72.7 | 72.5 | 76.2 | 75.4 | 80.2 | 85.4 | 82.2 | 87.9 | 88.9 | A | Japon |
| | B | (69.5) | 75.8 | 70.2 | 75.0 | 77.7 | 74.3 | 75.3 | 74.2 | 79.8 | 73.7 | B | |
| Netherlands | A | 95.0 | 93.1 | 97.2 | 99.3 | 98.5 | 99.8 | 98.2 | 99.5 | 99.1 | 100.0 | A | Pays-Bas |
| | B | 93.8 | 86.5 | 90.8 | 93.3 | 92.5 | 91.6 | 95.1 | 93.9 | 95.1 | 93.4 | B | |
| New Zealand | A | 100.0 | 100.0 | 100.0 | 100.0 | 100.0 | 100.0 | 100.0 | 100.0 | 100.0 | 100.0 | A | Nouvelle-Zélande |
| | B | 99.1 | 97.4 | 99.8 | 100.0 | 100.0 | 100.0 | 100.0 | 100.0 | 100.0 | 100.0 | B | |
| Norway | A | 100.0 | 100.0 | 100.0 | 100.0 | 100.0 | 100.0 | 100.0 | 100.0 | 99.9 | 97.9 | A | Norvège |
| | B | 100.0 | 100.0 | 100.0 | 100.0 | 100.0 | 100.0 | 99.7 | 99.2 | 98.1 | 99.4 | B | |
| Sweden | A | 100.0 | 100.0 | 100.0 | 100.0 | 100.0 | 100.0 | 100.0 | 100.0 | 100.0 | 100.0 | A | Suède |
| | B | 99.2 | 99.9 | 99.8 | 99.9 | 100.0 | 99.0 | 99.7 | 99.8 | 99.8 | 100.0 | B | |
| Switzerland | A | 100.0 | 98.2 | 100.0 | 100.0 | 100.0 | 100.0 | 100.0 | 100.0 | 100.0 | 100.0 | A | Suisse |
| | B | 93.0 | 92.1 | 96.9 | 95.1 | 95.8 | 96.9 | 97.0 | 96.6 | 98.5 | 98.1 | B | |
| United Kingdom | A | 99.0 | 99.7 | 93.6 | (99.2) | 99.0 | 99.7 | 100.0 | 100.0 | 100.0 | 100.0 | A | Royaume-Uni |
| | B | (96.9) | 97.5 | 96.7 | 93.9 | 96.1 | 96.4 | 96.9 | 98.5 | 98.3 | (99.4) | B | |
| United States | A | 92.0 | 82.7 | 90.0 | 92.1 | 96.5 | 95.0 | 96.3 | 97.6 | 95.7 | 97.4 | A | États-Unis |
| | B | 85.7 | 86.4 | 89.9 | 89.4 | 91.5 | 90.5 | 93.4 | 93.8 | 94.7 | 93.7 | B | |
| Total DAC countries | A | 95.4 | 92.1 | 94.2 | 93.9 | 95.7 | 94.7 | 93.5 | 92.8 | 93.9 | 93.7 | A | Total des pays du CAD |
| | B | 89.4 | 89.3 | 89.4 | 89.9 | 90.8 | 89.9 | 89.6 | 90.5 | 91.3 | 90.0 | B | |

Source : OECD, Development Co-operation (various issues)
and information from the OECD/DAC Secretariat.

A = Commitments to LDCs excluding Djibouti, Equatorial Guinea,
Sao Tome & Principe, Sierra Leone, Togo and Vanuatu
(1975-1980); Guinea-Bissau (1975-1978); Bangladesh,
Central African Republic, Gambia and Democratic Yemen
(1975-1976); and Cape Verde and Comoros (1975).
The DAC target norm for LDCs is 90 per cent. The SNPA,
para. 70(a), calls upon donor countries and institutions to provide as a general rule assistance to LDCS
as grants.

B = Commitments to all developing countries and territories,
as well as to Gibraltar, Greece, Israel, Portugal,
Yugoslavia and Viet Nam. The DAC target norm for all
developing countries is 84 per cent.

a/ Excluding debt reorganisation.

b/ Italy has not subscribed to the 1972 DAC Terms
Recommendations.

Source : OCDE, Coopération pour le développement (divers numéros)
et renseignements du secrétariat de l'OCDE/CAD.

A = Engagements aux PMA, non compris Djibouti, la Guinée
équatoriale, Sao Tomé-et-Principe, Sierra Leone, le Togo
et Vanuatu (1975 à 1980); la Guinée-Bissau (1975 à 1978);
le Bangladesh, la République centrafricaine, la Gambie et
le Yémen démocratique (1975 à 1976); et le Cap-Vert et
les Comores (1975). L'objectif du CAD pour les PMA
a pour norme 90 pour cent. Le NPSA, au paragraphe 70(a),
demande aux pays et aux institutions donateurs de fournir
en règle générale, sous forme de dons, l'aide aux PMA.

B = Engagements à l'ensemble des pays en développement, ainsi
qu'à Gibraltar, la Grèce, Israël, le Portugal, la
Yougoslavie et le Viet-Nam. L'objectif du CAD pour
l'ensemble des pays en développement a pour norme 84 pour
cent.

a/ Non compris la réorganisation de la dette.

b/ L'Italie n'a pas souscrit aux Recommandations des
Conditions de l'Aide du CAD de 1972.

Table 38A

ODA commitments from DAC member countries and multilateral agencies a/ to LDCs as a group, by purpose, average 1981-1984

Tableau 38A

Engagements de l'APD de chaque pays membre du CAD et de chaque institution multilatérale, a/ en faveur de l'ensemble des PMA, par objet, moyenne 1981-1984

| Donors / Donneurs | Agriculture | Industry, mining, construction / Industries manufacturières, extraction, construction | Energy / Energie | Transport and communication / Transports et communications | Health / Santé | Education / Enseignement | Social infrastructure / Infrastructure sociale | Trade, banking, tourism and other services / Commerce, banques, tourisme, et autres services | General economic support b/ / Soutien économique général b/ | Technical cooperation / Coopération technique | Total c/ (in $ m. / en m.$) |
|---|---|---|---|---|---|---|---|---|---|---|---|
| | Per cent of total / En pourcentage du total | | | | | | | | | | |
| **A. Bilateral donors / Donneurs bilatéraux** | | | | | | | | | | | |
| Australia / Australie | 6.4 | - | 0.0 | 8.4 | 0.5 | 0.5 | - | 0.0 | 69.0 | 15.3 | 236 |
| Austria / Autriche | - | 0.0 | - | - | - | - | - | 0.0 | - | 77.8 | 18 |
| Belgium / Belgique | - | - | - | - | - | - | - | - | 100.0 | - | 278 |
| Canada / Canada | 29.4 | 13.8 | 10.1 | 18.2 | 4.5 | 5.5 | 1.4 | 0.5 | 2.4 | 9.8 | 1082 |
| Denmark / Danemark | 32.3 | 0.5 | 9.2 | 8.3 | 21.8 | 3.2 | - | 0.0 | 3.4 | 14.2 | 413 |
| Finland / Finlande | 10.0 | 5.0 | 0.8 | 0.0 | 0.8 | - | - | - | 10.0 | 54.2 | 137 |
| France / France | 14.0 | 0.8 | 8.4 | 15.5 | 4.6 | 0.8 | 1.6 | 1.4 | 13.3 | 35.2 | 2155 |
| Germany, Fed.Rep.of / Allemagne, Rép.féd.d' | 5.2 | 0.8 | 9.6 | 14.6 | 4.6 | 0.0 | 0.3 | 0.2 | 18.5 | 45.0 | 2160 |
| Italy / Italie | 10.8 | 8.9 | 18.8 | 12.1 | 4.3 | 0.9 | 0.6 | - | 16.1 | 29.0 | 1007 |
| Japan / Japon | 17.4 | 0.2 | 11.4 | 10.1 | 10.3 | 0.9 | 1.5 | - | 39.8 | 8.4 | 1498 |
| Netherlands / Pays-Bas | 23.4 | 1.8 | 2.8 | 6.0 | 6.5 | 0.9 | 1.5 | 0.4 | 26.2 | 26.7 | 973 |
| New Zealand / Nouvelle-Zélande | 27.8 | - | 0.0 | 0.0 | 0.0 | 0.0 | 0.0 | 0.0 | 0.0 | 50.0 | 20 |
| Norway / Norvège | 13.2 | 7.1 | 7.1 | 12.0 | 16.0 | 3.7 | 8.0 | 0.6 | 11.4 | 20.6 | 418 |
| Sweden / Suède | 18.4 | 7.8 | 1.9 | 3.5 | 7.6 | 10.5 | 1.6 | 0.2 | 25.8 | 19.2 | 651 |
| Switzerland / Suisse | 33.0 | 1.1 | 1.1 | 11.2 | 12.0 | 10.9 | 3.0 | 2.6 | 0.4 | 22.1 | 267 |
| United Kingdom / Royaume-Uni | 2.4 | 0.0 | 10.8 | 9.8 | 0.3 | 0.9 | - | - | 33.4 | 40.4 | 788 |
| United States / Etats-Unis | 14.9 | 0.1 | 1.9 | 2.5 | 6.4 | 2.4 | 0.5 | 0.5 | 39.1 | 31.6 | 3518 |
| **Total bilateral / Total bilatéral** | 15.0 | 2.7 | 6.8 | 9.1 | 6.5 | 2.2 | 0.9 | 0.5 | 25.9 | 28.9 | 15619 |
| **B. Multilateral donors / Donneurs multilatéraux** | | | | | | | | | | | |
| AfDF / FAfD | 30.1 | 4.7 | 3.5 | 23.8 | 27.4 | 8.5 | 2.0 | - | - | - | 842 |
| AsDB / BAsD | 32.5 | 1.3 | 43.0 | 6.8 | 4.8 | 5.5 | - | 0.7 | 3.7 | - | 1266 |
| EEC/EDF / CEE/FED | 35.4 | 3.8 | 4.1 | 23.6 | 9.6 | 2.9 | 0.7 | 0.9 | 26.0 | 1.2 | 2136 |
| IDA / AID | 34.3 | 4.7 | 14.4 | 19.8 | 3.8 | 9.2 | 3.1 | 0.8 | 8.6 | - | 4832 |
| IDB / BID | 76.7 | 13.3 | - | - | - | - | - | - | 10.0 | - | 50 |
| UN / ONU | .. | .. | .. | .. | .. | .. | .. | .. | .. | 67.9 | 2975 |
| IFAD / FIDA | 100.0 | .. | .. | .. | .. | .. | .. | .. | .. | - | 386 |
| **Total multilateral / Total multilatéral** | 27.7 | 3.0 | 10.5 | 12.3 | 5.3 | 5.2 | 1.5 | 0.5 | 8.3 | 16.8 | 12487 |
| **GRAND TOTAL (A+B) / TOTAL GENERAL (A+B)** | 20.6 | 2.8 | 8.5 | 10.6 | 5.9 | 3.5 | 1.2 | 0.5 | 18.1 | 23.5 | 28106 |

Source : OECD "Creditor Reporting System".

Note : For technical reasons the amounts to sectors may be understated.

a/ Multilateral agencies mainly financed by DAC member countries.
b/ Including current imports financing, emergency and disaster relief, budget support, balance of payments support and debt re-organisation.
c/ Including unallocated and other commitments.

Source : "Système de notification des pays créanciers" de l'OCDE.

Note : Pour des raisons techniques les données pour les secteurs peuvent être sous-estimées.

a/ Institutions multilatérales essentiellement financées par les pays membres du CAD.
b/ Comprend les contributions destinées à financer des importations courantes, le secours d'urgence, le soutien budgétaire, le soutien à la balance des paiements et le réaménagement de la dette.
c/ Y compris les engagements non-ventilés et autres.

Table 38B

ODA commitments from DAC member countries and multilateral agencies a/ to individual LDCs, by purpose, average 1981-1984

Tableau 38B

Engagements de l'APD à chacun des PMA en provenance des pays membres du CAD et des institutions multilatérales, a/ par objet, moyenne 1981-1984

Per cent of total / En pourcentage du total

| Recipient country / Pays bénéficiaire | Agriculture | Industry, mining, construction / Industries manufacturières, extraction, construction | Energy / Energie | Transport and communication / Transports et communications | Health / Santé | Education / Enseignement | Social infrastructure / Infrastructure sociale | Trade, banking, tourism and other services / Commerce, banques, tourisme et autres services b/ | General economic support b/ / Soutien économique général b/ | Technical cooperation / Coopération technique | Total c/ (in $ m. / en m.$) |
|---|---|---|---|---|---|---|---|---|---|---|---|
| Afghanistan | 0.0 | - | - | - | 1.8 | 0.0 | - | - | 3.5 | 93.0 | 59 |
| Bangladesh | 28.9 | 4.1 | 16.3 | 4.1 | 3.9 | 2.1 | 0.4 | 0.0 | 27.9 | 11.5 | 6203 |
| Benin / Bénin | 22.6 | 0.7 | 16.1 | 16.1 | 7.2 | 6.3 | 1.4 | 0.9 | 2.7 | 25.3 | 480 |
| Bhutan / Bhoutan | 29.2 | - | 4.2 | 0.0 | 4.2 | 1.4 | - | - | - | 44.4 | 77 |
| Botswana | 13.5 | 2.4 | 8.4 | 10.2 | 4.2 | 10.6 | 0.7 | 0.9 | 6.9 | 40.1 | 417 |
| Burkina Faso | 25.8 | 2.1 | 5.1 | 17.4 | 5.2 | 1.2 | 0.5 | 0.3 | 7.5 | 32.5 | 983 |
| Burundi | 23.0 | 2.9 | 13.0 | 11.9 | 6.9 | 4.6 | 2.5 | 1.1 | 5.2 | 27.4 | 617 |
| Cape Verde / Cap-Vert | 11.5 | 8.1 | 4.2 | 8.1 | 8.5 | 3.1 | 1.2 | 0.0 | 25.4 | 28.1 | 298 |
| Central African R. / Rép. centrafricaine | 23.3 | 1.0 | 2.4 | 18.8 | 3.2 | 4.0 | 0.5 | 0.8 | 7.1 | 37.6 | 466 |
| Chad / Tchad | 15.8 | 1.2 | 0.4 | 9.3 | 5.0 | 1.9 | 10.4 | 0.8 | 25.1 | 28.6 | 396 |
| Comoros / Comores | 16.4 | 1.5 | 6.0 | 26.9 | 4.5 | 5.2 | 0.0 | 3.0 | 6.0 | 30.6 | 179 |
| Democratic Yemen / Yémen démocratique | 25.6 | 3.4 | 15.5 | 9.7 | 9.2 | 7.1 | 0.0 | - | 5.0 | 23.5 | 279 |
| Djibouti | 1.7 | 0.0 | 11.7 | 13.5 | 8.3 | 1.3 | 1.3 | 0.0 | 5.7 | 55.2 | 274 |
| Equatorial Guinea / Guinée équatoriale | 11.4 | 0.0 | 6.8 | 2.3 | 0.0 | - | 2.3 | 4.5 | 2.3 | 56.8 | 74 |
| Ethiopia / Ethiopie | 17.0 | 4.6 | 3.6 | 17.7 | 9.2 | 5.0 | 1.7 | 2.1 | 18.6 | 19.8 | 1617 |
| Gambia / Gambie | 32.4 | 0.8 | 2.5 | 13.7 | 4.6 | 1.2 | 5.0 | 0.8 | 8.3 | 30.7 | 246 |
| Guinea / Guinée | 8.1 | 11.8 | 13.1 | 27.8 | 2.3 | 5.6 | 3.1 | 0.0 | 9.1 | 16.8 | 467 |
| Guinea-Bissau / Guinée-Bissau | 21.9 | 4.5 | 6.9 | 11.5 | 8.0 | 3.5 | 3.1 | - | 18.0 | 20.5 | 284 |
| Haiti / Haïti | 20.1 | 2.3 | 10.4 | 11.1 | 5.9 | 2.9 | 6.0 | 0.8 | 16.7 | 23.5 | 610 |
| Lao P.D.R. / Rép.dém.pop.Lao | 32.5 | 2.5 | 14.4 | 8.8 | 5.9 | 0.0 | 0.0 | - | 4.4 | 26.9 | 158 |
| Lesotho | 10.7 | 0.2 | 0.5 | 18.8 | 10.9 | 10.2 | 2.0 | 0.3 | 10.9 | 35.3 | 392 |
| Malawi | 13.7 | 1.4 | 0.3 | 24.6 | 8.6 | 13.5 | 0.4 | 0.6 | 10.8 | 25.3 | 695 |
| Maldives | 15.6 | 0.0 | 0.0 | 3.1 | 15.6 | 9.4 | 0.0 | - | 6.2 | 43.8 | 41 |
| Mali | 25.4 | 0.4 | 4.7 | 12.7 | 9.7 | 3.5 | 0.4 | 0.2 | 17.8 | 24.8 | 1137 |
| Nepal / Népal | 25.6 | 2.3 | 18.7 | 10.4 | 7.1 | 5.2 | 0.5 | 0.2 | 2.0 | 25.8 | 1134 |
| Niger | 18.2 | 2.8 | 3.7 | 16.6 | 10.0 | 5.4 | 1.4 | 1.4 | 8.5 | 31.5 | 987 |
| Rwanda | 24.7 | 0.3 | 6.2 | 16.3 | 9.0 | 3.3 | 1.2 | 2.8 | 7.6 | 26.7 | 762 |
| Samoa | 21.3 | - | 9.6 | 11.7 | 8.5 | 2.1 | 0.0 | 8.5 | 2.1 | 34.0 | 98 |
| Sao Tome & Principe / Sao Tomé et Principe | 37.8 | - | - | 10.8 | 0.0 | 8.1 | - | - | 13.5 | 29.7 | 39 |
| Sierra Leone | 40.2 | - | 1.6 | 5.9 | 0.6 | 8.7 | 0.0 | - | 16.2 | 26.8 | 313 |
| Somalia / Somalie | 9.9 | 1.5 | 2.1 | 10.1 | 4.8 | 1.0 | 0.2 | 0.3 | 28.0 | 41.6 | 1408 |
| Sudan | 23.0 | 0.5 | 5.1 | 7.4 | 2.5 | 1.0 | 1.1 | 0.0 | 34.7 | 24.1 | 2407 |
| Togo | 19.5 | 3.8 | 7.9 | 11.3 | 9.6 | 1.1 | 0.1 | 0.2 | 16.5 | 28.5 | 457 |
| Uganda / Ouganda | 19.7 | 5.3 | 0.5 | 11.3 | 8.9 | 3.9 | 1.9 | 1.0 | 28.9 | 17.3 | 983 |
| U.R. of Tanzania / Rép.-U. de Tanzanie | 16.0 | 5.2 | 9.2 | 11.6 | 8.3 | 2.9 | 0.6 | 0.2 | 17.4 | 25.0 | 2354 |
| Vanuatu | 0.9d/ | - | - | 0.1d/ | 0.6d/ | 4.8d/ | - | 0.7d/ | 22.7d/ | 69.6d/ | 117 |
| Yemen / Yémen | 15.1 | 0.3 | 6.5 | 8.0 | 8.9 | 9.2 | 4.1 | - | 5.3 | 41.3 | 598 |
| All LDCs / Ensemble des PMA | 21.4 | 2.9 | 8.6 | 11.0 | 6.2 | 3.6 | 1.2 | 0.5 | 18.7 | 24.5 | 28105 |

Source : OECD "Creditor Reporting System".
Note : For technical reasons the amounts to sectors may be understated.

Source : "Système de notification des pays créanciers" de l'OCDE.
Note : Pour des raisons techniques les données techniques les données pour les secteurs peuvent être sous-estimées.

a/ Multilateral agencies mainly financed by DAC member countries.
b/ Including current imports financing, emergency and disaster relief, budget support, balance of payments support and debt re-organisation.
c/ Including unallocated and other commitments.
d/ Per cent of total in 1984.

a/ Institutions multilatérales essentiellement financées par les pays membres du CAD.
b/ Comprend les contributions destinées à financer des importations courantes, le secours d'urgence, le soutien budgétaire, le soutien à la balance des paiements et le réaménagement de la dette.
c/ Y compris les engagements non-ventilés et autres.
d/ En pourcentage du total en 1984.

Table 39

Table 39

**Tying status of bilateral ODA from individual DAC member countries to all LDCs, 1981, 1982 and 1984ª/**

**État de déliement de l'APD bilatérale à l'ensemble des PMA, en provenance de chaque pays membre du CAD, 1981, 1982 et 1984 a/**

Commitments

Engagements

| Donor country | Year Année | Total ($ million) (millions de dollars) | Untied b/ Aide non-liée b/ | Partially tied b/ Aide partielle- ment liée b/ | Tied c/ Aide liée c/ Including all technical co-operation Y compris l'ensemble de la coopération technique | Tied c/ Aide liée c/ Excluding all technical co-operation Non compris l'ensemble de la coopération technique | Pays donneur |
|---|---|---|---|---|---|---|---|
| Australia | 1981 | 67 | 13 | – | 87 | 75 | Australie |
| | 1982 | 55 | 2 | 2 | 96 | 87 | |
| | 1984 | 48 | 19 | – | 81 | 58 | |
| Austria | 1981 | 1 | .. | .. | .. | .. | Austria |
| | 1982 | 6 | .. | .. | .. | .. | |
| | 1984 | 5 | .. | .. | .. | .. | |
| Belgium | 1981 | 90 | 41 | – | 59 | 9 | Belgique |
| | 1982 | 72 | 40 | – | 60 | 10 | |
| | 1984 | 51 | .. | .. | .. | .. | |
| Canada | 1981 | 204 | (13) | – | (87) | (76) | Canada |
| | 1982 | 237 | 15 | – | 85 | 65 | |
| | 1984 | 337 | 15 | 1 | 84 | 74 | |
| Denmark | 1981 | 60 | (53) | – | 47 | (35) | Danemark |
| | 1982 | 127 | 19 | – | 81 | 72 | |
| | 1984 | 154 | 37 | 19 | 44 | 32 | |
| Finland | 1981 | 38 | 32 | 32 | 36 | – | Finlande |
| | 1982 | 35 | 32 | 32 | 36 | – | |
| | 1984 | 43 | .. | .. | .. | .. | |
| France | 1981 | 570 | – | 31 | 69 | 43 | France |
| | 1982 | 501 | – | 37 | 63 | 45 | |
| | 1984 | 599 | 20 | 45 | 35 | 8 | |
| Germany, Fed. Rep. of | 1981 | 711 | 45 | – | 55 | 9 | Allemagne, Rép. Féd. d' |
| | 1982 | 477 | 42 | – | 58 | 10 | |
| | 1984 | 483 | 35 | 5 | 60 | 21 | |
| Italy | 1981 | 188 | (35) | – | (65) | (45) | Italie |
| | 1982 | 245 | 25 | – | 75 | 45 | |
| | 1984 | 293 | 8 | 1 | 91 | 60 | |
| Japan | 1981 | 365 | 67 | 13 | 20 | 10. | Japon |
| | 1982 | 450 | 48 | 22 | 30 | 22 | |
| | 1984 | 378 | 45 | 28 | 27 | 20 | |
| Netherlands | 1981 | 321 | 12 | 57 | 31 | 3 | Pays-Bas |
| | 1982 | 205 | 15 | 48 | 37 | 1 | |
| | 1984 | 201 | 11 | 57 | 32 | 4 | |
| New Zealand | 1981 | 8 | 25 | – | 75 | 38 | Nouvelle-Zélande |
| | 1982 | 2 | 50 | – | 50 | – | |
| | 1984 | 4 | .. | .. | .. | .. | |
| Norway | 1981 | 121 | 73 | – | 27 | 8 | Norvège |
| | 1982 | 102 | 75 | – | 25 | 10 | |
| | 1984 | 110 | 74 | 4 | 22 | 7 | |
| Sweden | 1981 | 228 | 61 | 23 | 16 | – | Suède |
| | 1982 | 210 | 55 | 9 | 36 | 16 | |
| | 1984 | 146 | 58 | – | 42 | 16 | |
| Switzerland | 1981 | 110 | 62 | – | 38 | 18 | Suisse |
| | 1982 | 36 | 65 | – | 35 | 20 | |
| | 1984 | 50 | 66 | – | 34 | 22 | |
| United Kingdom | 1981 | 220 | 17 | 7 | 76 | 35 | Royaume-Uni |
| | 1982 | 140 | 9 | 1 | 90 | 36 | |
| | 1984 | 230 | 32 | 2 | 66 | 36 | |
| United States | 1981 | 632 | 2 | – | 98 | 58 | Etats-Unis |
| | 1982 | 705 | 5 | – | 95 | 55 | |
| | 1984 | 1135 | 1 | 1 | 98 | 62 | |
| Total DAC countries | 1981 | 3934 | 29 | 12 | 59 | 30 | Total des pays du CAD |
| | 1982 | 3605 | 24 | 12 | 64 | 35 | |
| | 1984 | 4266 | 22 | 14 | 64 | 37 | |

Source: UNCTAD secretariat estimates based on data provided by by the OECD secretariat.

Source: Estimations du secrétariat de la CNUCED d'après des données fournies par le secrétariat de l'OCDE.

a/ Due to a change in reporting methods, 1984 figures are not directly comparable with those for 1981 and 1982. Figures for 1984 include commitments to Vanuatu.

a/ A cause d'un changement dans les méthodes de notification, les données pour 1984 ne sont pas directement comparables avec celles se rapportant aux années 1981 et 1982. Les données pour 1984 comprennent les engagements à Vanuatu.

b/ Excluding technical co-operation.

b/ Non compris la coopération technique.

c/ Including food aid and, for a number of countries, local costs when these are not separately identified at commitment stage.

c/ Y compris l'aide alimentaire et, pour certains pays, les coûts locaux quand ceux-ci ne sont pas identifiés séparément au stade des engagements.

Table 40A
Bilateral ODA from OPEC member countries and total financial flows from multilateral agencies mainly financed by them, to LDCs as a group, 1975-1984

Tableau 40A
APD bilatérale des pays membres de l'OPEP at apports financiers totaux des institutions multilatérales essentiellement financées par ceux-ci, en faveur de l'ensemble des PMA, 1975-1984

Net disbursements in $ million / Versements nets en millions de dollars

| | 1975 | 1976 | 1977 | 1978 | 1979 | 1980 | 1981 | 1982 | 1983 | 1984 |
|---|---|---|---|---|---|---|---|---|---|---|
| **A. Bilateral donors / A. Donneurs bilatéraux** | | | | | | | | | | |
| Algeria / Algérie | 2.6 | 4.9 | 2.5 | 0.5 | 14.4 | 20.0 | 9.6 | 0.2 | - | - |
| Iran (Islamic Rep.) / Iran (Rép. Islamique) | 3.1 | 5.7 | - | 15.0 | - | - | - | - | - | - |
| Iraq / Iraq | 32.4 | 50.2 | 25.0 | 42.5 | 22.5 | 48.7 | - | - | - | - |
| Kuwait / Koweit | 47.4 | 70.1 | 122.4 | 110.8 | 127.6 | 169.0 | 167.7 | 110.6 | 153.9 | 144.2 |
| Libyan Arab Jamahiriya / Jamahiriya arabe Libyenne | 40.8 | 12.5 | 0.8 | 10.4 | 0.0 | 8.1 | 23.1 | - | - | - |
| Nigeria / Nigéria | 2.2 | 3.5 | 1.3 | - | 0.1 | 0.1 | - | - | - | - |
| Qatar / Qatar | 32.8 | 12.9 | 5.0 | 8.4 | 3.8 | 38.3 | 23.2 | 7.7 | 7.4 | 2.0 |
| Saudi Arabia / Arabie saoudite | 271.0 | 432.8 | 579.5 | 305.5 | 421.9 | 450.2 | 382.7 | 721.0 | 612.4 | 342.5 |
| United Arab Emirates / Emirats arabes unis | 143.4 | 84.8 | 115.1 | 153.3 | 104.7 | 152.0 | 67.2 | 69.2 | 39.2 | 30.2 |
| Total bilateral concessional / Total des apports bilatéraux concessionnels | 575.7 | 677.4 | 851.6 | 646.4 | 695.0 | 886.4 | 673.5 | 908.7 | 812.9 | 518.9 |
| **B. Multilateral donors / B. Donneurs multilatéraux** | | | | | | | | | | |
| **1. Concessional / 1. Apports concessionnels** | | | | | | | | | | |
| BADEA | - | - | 4.5 | 19.7 | 15.9 | 18.5 | 15.1 | 15.5 | 20.5 | 12.0 |
| AFESD / FADES | 15.8 | 18.5 | 23.2 | 48.3 | 34.3 | 45.7 | 58.5 | 38.9 | 36.8 | 26.5 |
| Islamic Dev. Bank / Banque islamique de dév. | - | - | - | 4.9 | 11.2 | 5.4 | 17.1 | 8.2 | 14.2 | 13.0 |
| OPEC Fund / Fonds de l'OPEP | - | - | 79.7 | 17.2 | 34.8 | 64.4 | 108.2 | 101.4 | 71.0 | 29.6 |
| OAPEC Special Account / Compte spécial de l'OPAEP | 64.9 | 33.5 | - | - | - | - | - | - | - | - |
| SAAFA / FSAAA | - | 31.0 | - | - | - | - | - | - | - | - |
| Total | 80.7 | 83.0 | 107.4 | 90.1 | 96.2 | 134.0 | 198.9 | 164.0 | 142.5 | 81.1 |
| **2. Non-concessional / 2. Apports non-concessionnels** | | | | | | | | | | |
| BADEA | - | - | - | 8.1 | 4.2 | 8.8 | 1.2 | 2.3 | -0.3 | 0.9 |
| Islamic Dev. Bank / Banque Islamique de dév. | - | - | 4.9 | 8.7 | 104.0 | 95.0 | 95.3 | -55.5 | 18.6 | -3.2 |
| Total | - | - | 4.9 | 16.8 | 108.2 | 103.8 | 96.5 | -53.2 | 18.3 | -2.3 |
| Total concessional (A+B1) / Total des apports concessionnels (A+B1) | 656.4 | 760.4 | 959.0 | 736.5 | 791.2 | 1020.4 | 872.4 | 1072.7 | 955.4 | 600.0 |
| GRAND TOTAL a/ / TOTAL GENERAL a/ | 656.4 | 760.4 | 966.0 | 753.3 | 899.4 | 1124.2 | 968.9 | 1029.4 | 1003.7 | 597.7 |

Source: UNCTAD secretariat estimates.
Note: The figures include only those amounts allocated to a specific country and therefore understate financial flows to the extent that certain donors have recorded disbursements in favour of groups of countries including some LDCs. For abbreviations see pages x and xi.

a/ Including bilateral non-concessional flows.

Source: Estimations du secrétariat de la CNUCED. Pour 1975-1976: estimations du secrétariat de l'OCDE.
Note: Les données ne comprennent que les montants imputables à un pays bénéficiaire déterminé. Par conséquent, les apports financiers sont sous-estimés dans la mesure où certains donneurs ont alloué des versements à des groupes de pays comprenant des PMA. Se reporter, pour les abréviations aux pages xvii et xviii.

a/ Y compris des apports bilatéraux non-concessionnels.

Table 40B
Bilateral ODA from OPEC member countries and total financial flows from multilateral agencies mainly financed by them, to LDCs as a group, 1975-1984

Tableau 40B
APD bilatérale des pays membres de l'OPEP et apports financiers totaux des institutions multilatérales essentiellement financées par ceux-ci, en faveur de l'ensemble des PMA, 1975-1984

Net disbursements in millions of constant 1980 dollars a/

Versements nets en millions de dollars constants de 1980 a/

| Donor / Donneur | 1975 | 1976 | 1977 | 1978 | 1979 | 1980 | 1981 | 1982 | 1983 | 1984 |
|---|---|---|---|---|---|---|---|---|---|---|
| A. Bilateral donors / A. Donneurs bilatéraux | | | | | | | | | | |
| Algeria / Algérie | 4.7 | 8.7 | 4.1 | 0.7 | 17.5 | 20.0 | 9.9 | 0.2 | - | - |
| Iran (Islamic Rep.) / Iran (Rép. Islamique) | 5.6 | 10.1 | - | 22.1 | - | - | - | - | - | - |
| Iraq | 58.2 | 89.3 | 40.6 | 62.7 | 27.3 | 48.7 | - | - | - | - |
| Kuwait / Koweit | 85.1 | 124.7 | 198.6 | 163.6 | 154.8 | 169.0 | 172.8 | 119.0 | 173.0 | 165.5 |
| Libyan Arab Jamahiriya / Jamahiriya arabe Libyenne | 73.3 | 22.2 | 1.3 | 15.4 | 0.1 | 8.1 | 23.8 | - | - | - |
| Nigeria / Nigéria | 4.0 | 6.2 | 2.1 | 2.1 | 0.0 | 0.1 | - | - | - | - |
| Qatar | 58.9 | 22.9 | 8.1 | 12.4 | 4.6 | 38.3 | 23.9 | 8.3 | 8.3 | 2.3 |
| Saudi Arabia / Arabie saoudite | 486.7 | 769.7 | 940.1 | 451.1 | 511.8 | 450.2 | 394.3 | 775.4 | 688.2 | 393.2 |
| United Arab Emirates / Emirats arabes unis | 257.5 | 150.8 | 186.7 | 226.3 | 127.0 | 152.0 | 69.2 | 74.4 | 44.1 | 34.7 |
| Total bilateral concessional / Total des apports bilatéraux concessionnels | 1034 | 1205 | 1382 | 954.4 | 843.0 | 886.4 | 694.0 | 977.3 | 913.6 | 595.7 |
| B. Multilateral donors / B. Donneurs multilatéraux | | | | | | | | | | |
| 1. Concessional / 1. Apports concessionnels | | | | | | | | | | |
| BADEA | 28.4 | - | 7.3 | 29.1 | 19.3 | 18.5 | 15.6 | 16.7 | 23.0 | 13.8 |
| AFESD / FADES | - | 32.9 | 37.6 | 71.3 | 41.6 | 45.7 | 60.3 | 41.8 | 41.4 | 30.4 |
| Islamic Dev. Bank / Banque islamique de dév. | - | - | - | 7.2 | 13.6 | 5.4 | 17.6 | 8.8 | 16.0 | 14.9 |
| OPEC Fund / Fonds de l'OPEP | - | 59.6 | 129.3 | 25.4 | 42.2 | 64.4 | 111.5 | 109.1 | 79.8 | 34.0 |
| OAPEC Special Account / Compte spécial de l'OPAEP | 116.6 | 55.1 | - | - | - | - | - | - | - | - |
| SAAFA / FSAAA | - | - | - | - | - | - | - | - | - | - |
| Total | 144.9 | 147.6 | 174.2 | 133.0 | 116.7 | 134.0 | 204.9 | 176.4 | 160.1 | 93.1 |
| 2. Non-concessional / 2. Apports non-concessionnels | | | | | | | | | | |
| BADEA | - | - | - | 12.0 | 5.1 | 8.8 | 1.2 | 2.5 | -0.3 | 1.0 |
| Islamic Dev. Bank / Banque Islamique de dév. | - | - | 7.9 | 12.8 | 126.2 | 95.0 | 98.2 | -59.7 | 20.9 | -3.7 |
| Total | - | - | 7.9 | 24.8 | 131.2 | 103.8 | 99.4 | -57.2 | 20.6 | -2.6 |
| Total concessional (A+B1) / Total des apports concessionnels (A+B1) | 1179 | 1352 | 1556 | 1087 | 959.7 | 1020 | 898.9 | 1154 | 1074 | 688.8 |
| GRAND TOTAL b/ / TOTAL GENERAL b/ | 1179 | 1352 | 1567 | 1112 | 1091 | 1124 | 998.4 | 1107 | 1128 | 686.1 |

Source: Table 40A.

Source: Tableau 40A.

a/ Actual disbursements were converted to 1980 prices using the index for LDCs in Table 8.

b/ Including bilateral non-concessional flows.

a/ Les versements effectifs ont été convertis aux prix de 1980 en utilisant l'indice pour les PMA qui figure au tableau 8.

b/ Y compris des apports bilatéraux non-concessionnels.

Table 41
Concessional assistance from OPEC member countries
and multilateral agencies mainly financed by them a/
to individual LDCs, 1970 and 1975-1984

Tableau 41
Aide concessionnelle reçue par chacun des PMA, en provenance
des pays membres de l'OPEP et des institutions multilatérales
essentiellement financées par ceux-ci a/, 1970 et 1975-1984

Net disbursements in $ million

Versements nets en millions de dollars

| Country | 1970 | 1975 | 1976 | 1977 | 1978 | 1979 | 1980 | 1981 | 1982 | 1983 | 1984 | Pays |
|---|---|---|---|---|---|---|---|---|---|---|---|---|
| Afghanistan | - | 21.6 | 14.7 | 4.3 | 15.5 | 8.3 | 1.4 | 20.4 | 0.4 | -2.1 | -0.7 | Afghanistan |
| Bangladesh | - | 61.1 | 10.9 | 39.7 | 45.7 | 23.6 | 55.2 | 77.6 | 149.4 | 123.8 | 32.4 | Bangladesh |
| Benin | - | 2.4 | 3.6 | 4.6 | 5.4 | 3.4 | 2.4 | 3.9 | 1.6 | 6.4 | 0.3 | Bénin |
| Bhutan | - | - | - | - | - | - | - | - | - | - | 0.3 | Bhoutan |
| Botswana | - | 5.4 | - | 0.1 | 0.1 | 0.5 | 2.7 | 0.4 | 8.5 | 12.2 | 10.7 | Botswana |
| Burkina Faso | - | 2.9 | 1.0 | 3.0 | 2.7 | 5.8 | 7.9 | 10.6 | 8.7 | 2.9 | -1.0 | Burkina Faso |
| Burundi | - | 1.0 | 0.1 | 1.2 | 2.8 | 6.1 | 7.3 | 3.9 | 6.4 | 4.9 | 9.3 | Burundi |
| Cape Verde | - | 0.1 | 11.8 | 2.2 | 0.6 | 1.0 | 2.1 | 1.3 | 0.1 | 0.2 | 3.8 | Cap-Vert |
| Central African Rep. | - | 1.4 | - | 1.7 | - | 1.3 | 2.1 | 0.0 | 1.1 | 0.3 | 2.1 | Rép. centrafricaine |
| Chad | - | 8.1 | 1.5 | 1.6 | 7.5 | 6.0 | 0.0 | 0.6 | 0.5 | 0.2 | 0.3 | Tchad |
| Comoros | - | - | 13.8 | 22.5 | 2.6 | 3.0 | 16.4 | 12.9 | 10.4 | 9.8 | 4.9 | Comores |
| Democratic Yemen | 4.1 | 31.3 | 146.9 | 93.1 | 43.2 | 32.4 | 65.5 | 62.7 | 69.0 | 40.0 | 39.1 | Yémen démocratique |
| Djibouti | - | - | - | 19.7 | 64.0 | - | 30.6 | 13.2 | 3.6 | 14.8 | 48.0 | Djibouti |
| Equatorial Guinea | - | 1.5 | - | 0.5 | - | - | - | - | 1.0 | 0.5 | -0.0 | Guinée équatoriale |
| Ethiopia | - | 15.4 | - | 3.3 | 2.6 | 0.9 | 0.1 | 10.3 | 0.2 | - | -0.2 | Ethiopie |
| Gambia | - | 0.4 | 2.1 | 2.6 | 8.9 | 6.4 | 14.2 | 16.2 | 3.7 | 1.4 | 1.3 | Gambie |
| Guinea | - | 5.9 | 0.4 | 15.6 | 14.0 | 12.2 | 4.5 | 2.5 | 2.5 | 1.0 | 34.4 | Guinée |
| Guinea-Bissau | - | 3.2 | 3.8 | 2.2 | 2.5 | 2.8 | 3.8 | 1.8 | 3.8 | 6.9 | 3.3 | Guinée-Bissau |
| Haiti | - | - | - | 3.1 | - | - | - | 0.6 | 2.0 | 1.6 | 0.4 | Haïti |
| Lao People's Dem.Rep. | - | - | - | 2.1 | - | 4.2 | 0.7 | 0.0 | 0.5 | 0.5 | 1.1 | Rép. dém. pop. lao |
| Lesotho | - | 2.8 | - | 1.9 | 0.0 | 0.3 | 0.0 | 1.0 | 2.9 | 7.7 | 4.8 | Lesotho |
| Malawi | - | - | - | - | - | - | 1.3 | 0.3 | 0.0 | - | -0.1 | Malawi |
| Maldives | - | - | - | - | - | - | 17.4 | 7.3 | 2.5 | 4.5 | 1.1 | Maldives |
| Mali | - | 0.2 | 2.9 | 1.5 | 3.3 | 4.0 | 29.3 | 21.1 | 32.8 | 48.9 | 10.4 | Mali |
| Nepal | - | 29.4 | 3.0 | 16.8 | 11.9 | 24.7 | 6.8 | 9.0 | 5.5 | 1.3 | -0.9 | Népal |
| Niger | - | 0.4 | 0.2 | 41.5 | 1.6 | 3.5 | 8.1 | 32.6 | 82.7 | 18.3 | 6.2 | Niger |
| Rwanda | - | 16.8 | 4.1 | 8.8 | 21.4 | 7.1 | 7.2 | 8.3 | 1.7 | 1.6 | 6.1 | Rwanda |
| Samoa | - | 9.2 | 0.4 | 5.8 | 4.0 | 2.7 | 0.8 | 1.0 | 1.0 | 0.5 | -0.2 | Samoa |
| Sao Tome and Principe | - | 0.6 | 10.0 | 0.1 | 0.5 | 0.5 | - | 0.5 | 0.5 | 0.5 | 0.4 | Sao Tomé-et-Principe |
| Sierra Leone | - | 1.8 | 0.2 | 1.0 | 0.3 | 5.2 | 6.6 | 2.1 | 1.2 | 1.7 | 16.1 | Sierra Leone |
| Somalia | - | 79.3 | 41.5 | 213.8 | 113.9 | 106.2 | 143.7 | 53.4 | 182.3 | 48.0 | 59.5 | Somalie |
| Sudan | 1.5 | 178.2 | 267.5 | 129.8 | 115.9 | 303.9 | 241.6 | 201.8 | 161.9 | 354.5 | 109.4 | Soudan |
| Togo | - | 2.0 | 2.6 | 0.1 | 7.2 | 7.4 | 0.0 | 0.1 | 2.7 | 5.1 | 3.4 | Togo |
| Uganda | - | 25.7 | 5.2 | 9.5 | 2.0 | 4.7 | 0.2 | 0.2 | 5.9 | 11.0 | -1.4 | Ouganda |
| Un. Rep. of Tanzania | - | 7.3 | 0.6 | 12.8 | - | - | 19.7 | 24.0 | 29.1 | 32.5 | 17.6 | Rép.-Un. de Tanzanie |
| Vanuatu | - | - | - | - | - | - | - | - | - | - | - | Vanuatu |
| Yemen | 0.3 | 141.1 | 211.8 | 289.3 | 234.2 | 201.5 | 320.1 | 269.5 | 285.7 | 193.3 | 176.2 | Yémen |
| All LDCs | 5.9 | 656.4 | 760.4 | 959.5 | 736.8 | 791.6 | 1020.6 | 872.7 | 1072.9 | 955.6 | 600.1 | Ensemble des PMA |
| All developing countries | 390.6 | 5797.0 | 5578.6 | 4470.0 | 7549.4 | 7157.0 | 9199.8 | 8297.5 | 5871.3 | 5196.0 | 3776.5 | Ensemble des pays en développement |

For sources and notes see page 65.

Pour les sources et les notes se référer à la page 65.

Table 42
Concessional assistance from OPEC member countries
to individual LDCs, 1970 and 1975-1984 a/

Net disbursements in $ million

Tableau 42
Aide concessionnelle reçue par chacun des PMA, en provenance
des pays membres de l'OPEP, 1970 et 1975-1984 a/

Versements nets en millions de dollars

| Country | 1970 | 1975 | 1976 | 1977 | 1978 | 1979 | 1980 | 1981 | 1982 | 1983 | 1984 | Pays |
|---|---|---|---|---|---|---|---|---|---|---|---|---|
| Afghanistan | - | 21.6 | 14.7 | 0.6 | 15.5 | 8.3 | 1.4 | 20.4 | 0.4 | -2.1 | -0.6 | Afghanistan |
| Bangladesh | - | 61.1 | 10.9 | 25.8 | 44.6 | 13.2 | 51.1 | 47.2 | 126.8 | 110.0 | 20.3 | Bangladesh |
| Benin | - | - | 3.6 | 1.2 | - | 2.1 | 1.8 | 1.2 | 0.0 | 2.1 | -0.3 | Bénin |
| Bhutan | - | - | - | - | - | - | - | - | - | - | 0.3 | Bhoutan |
| Botswana | - | - | - | - | - | - | 0.0 | - | 6.1 | 8.1 | 10.1 | Botswana |
| Burkina Faso | - | 0.2 | 1.0 | 0.1 | 0.9 | 0.9 | 1.0 | 2.0 | - | 0.3 | 1.4 | Burkina Faso |
| Burundi | - | - | 0.1 | 0.4 | 2.0 | 1.7 | 2.8 | 2.0 | 5.9 | 3.3 | 9.4 | Burundi |
| Cape Verde | - | 0.1 | 1.3 | 0.7 | - | - | - | - | - | 0.2 | 1.2 | Cap-Vert |
| Central African Rep. | - | 0.2 | - | - | - | 1.3 | 2.1 | 0.0 | 1.1 | 0.3 | 0.5 | Rép. centrafricaine |
| Chad | - | 3.7 | 1.5 | 0.4 | 6.0 | 6.0 | 0.0 | - | 0.2 | 0.2 | - | Tchad |
| Comoros | 4.1 | - | 3.3 | 22.3 | 2.1 | 2.8 | 15.8 | 11.4 | 7.9 | 6.3 | 2.3 | Comores |
| Democratic Yemen | - | 31.1 | 140.2 | 88.6 | 28.9 | 23.8 | 53.2 | 44.2 | 56.5 | 23.2 | 26.9 | Yémen démocratique |
| Djibouti | - | - | - | 19.7 | 64.0 | - | 30.6 | 12.4 | 1.6 | 11.5 | 38.5 | Djibouti |
| Equatorial Guinea | - | 1.2 | - | - | - | - | - | - | - | - | - | Guinée équatoriale |
| Ethiopia | - | 1.2 | - | 0.9 | 0.2 | 0.9 | 0.1 | 10.1 | - | - | - | Ethiopie |
| Gambia | - | - | 2.1 | 1.0 | 7.5 | 4.1 | 7.0 | 14.0 | 2.3 | 0.9 | 0.7 | Gambie |
| Guinea | - | 5.9 | 0.4 | 13.2 | 9.1 | 9.2 | 0.1 | -0.2 | 0.7 | -0.5 | 29.7 | Guinée |
| Guinea-Bissau | - | 3.2 | 3.8 | 0.6 | 1.9 | 1.8 | 1.3 | 0.0 | 2.7 | 6.1 | 3.2 | Guinée-Bissau |
| Haiti | - | - | - | - | - | - | - | - | - | - | - | Haïti |
| Lao People's Dem.Rep. | - | - | - | - | 0.0 | 0.3 | 0.0 | 0.2 | 0.0 | 2.5 | 2.7 | Rép. dém. pop. lao |
| Lesotho | - | - | - | - | - | - | - | - | - | - | - | Lesotho |
| Malawi | - | - | - | - | - | - | - | - | - | - | - | Malawi |
| Maldives | - | 0.2 | 2.9 | 1.3 | 3.1 | 3.6 | 16.6 | 5.7 | 1.6 | 3.9 | 0.6 | Maldives |
| Mali | - | 25.5 | 3.0 | 12.4 | 5.2 | 21.3 | 19.0 | 7.0 | 20.4 | 32.3 | 5.6 | Mali |
| Nepal | - | 0.4 | 0.2 | 37.4 | 1.6 | 3.5 | 6.8 | 8.7 | 0.0 | -0.9 | -0.9 | Népal |
| Niger | - | 14.1 | 4.1 | 5.9 | 16.1 | 0.7 | 1.6 | 23.7 | 82.1 | 18.1 | 7.8 | Niger |
| Rwanda | - | 8.2 | 0.4 | 5.0 | 1.1 | 0.5 | 1.2 | 0.5 | 0.0 | 1.6 | 5.9 | Rwanda |
| Samoa | - | - | - | - | - | - | - | - | - | - | - | Samoa |
| Sao Tome and Principe | - | 0.1 | 0.2 | - | - | - | - | 0.0 | - | 0.0 | - | Sao Tomé-et-Principe |
| Sierra Leone | - | - | - | - | - | 4.0 | 4.0 | - | 0.2 | 0.0 | 13.5 | Sierra Leone |
| Somalia | 1.5 | 71.8 | 37.3 | 208.2 | 106.0 | 95.7 | 127.6 | 38.1 | 160.7 | 26.2 | 49.8 | Somalie |
| Sudan | - | 164.1 | 239.0 | 114.3 | 97.5 | 288.2 | 218.7 | 175.0 | 141.5 | 352.8 | 105.1 | Soudan |
| Togo | - | 2.0 | 2.6 | 0.1 | - | - | 0.0 | 0.1 | 2.7 | 2.3 | 1.9 | Togo |
| Uganda | - | 20.0 | 5.2 | 5.0 | 7.2 | 7.4 | 0.1 | 0.0 | 1.0 | 2.4 | -1.5 | Ouganda |
| Un. Rep. of Tanzania | - | 0.2 | 0.6 | 6.9 | 1.0 | 3.5 | 15.5 | 15.3 | 14.3 | 18.2 | 10.9 | Rép.-Un. de Tanzanie |
| Vanuatu | - | - | - | - | - | - | - | - | - | - | - | Vanuatu |
| Yemen | 0.3 | 139.5 | 199.2 | 278.8 | 223.9 | 189.4 | 306.2 | 233.3 | 271.4 | 182.6 | 173.0 | Yémen |
| ALL LDCs | 5.9 | 575.7 | 677.4 | 852.0 | 646.6 | 695.3 | 886.7 | 673.7 | 908.8 | 813.0 | 518.9 | Ensemble des PMA |
| All developing countries | 390.6 | 5638.3 | 5160.4 | 4249.2 | 7248.2 | 6906.5 | 8912.4 | 7930.1 | 5516.9 | 4871.6 | 3633.9 | Ensemble des pays en développement |

For sources and notes see page 65.

Pour les sources et les notes se référer à la page 65.

Table 41 and 42 (continued)

Source: UNCTAD secretariat estimates.
For 1970 and 1975-1976 : OECD secretariat estimates.

Note: The figures relating to LDCs include only those amounts allocated to a specific recipient country and therefore understate financial flows to the extent that certain donors have recorded disbursements in favour of groups of countries including some LDCs.

a/ The members of OPEC and the multilateral agencies financed by them included here and providing assistance to LDCs are listed in table 40A.

Tableau 41 et 42 (suite)

Source: Estimations du secrétariat de la CNUCED.
Pour 1970 et 1975-1976 : estimations du secrétariat de l'OCDE.

Note: Les données se rapportant aux PMA ne comprennent que les montants imputables à un pays bénéficiaire déterminé. Par conséquent, les apports financiers sont sous-estimés dans la mesure où certains donneurs ont alloué des versements à des groupes de pays comprenant des PMA.

a/ La liste des membres de l'OPEP et des institutions multilatérales financées par ceux-ci qui sont inclus ici et qui fournissent de l'aide aux PMA figure au tableau 40A.

Table 43
Grants from OPEC member countries
to individual LDCs, 1970 and 1975-1984 a/

Tableau 43
Dons reçus par chacun des PMA, en provenance
des pays membres de l'OPEP, 1970 et 1975-1984 a/

Net disbursements in $ million

Versements nets en millions de dollars

| Country | 1970 | 1975 | 1976 | 1977 | 1978 | 1979 | 1980 | 1981 | 1982 | 1983 | 1984 | Pays |
|---|---|---|---|---|---|---|---|---|---|---|---|---|
| Afghanistan | - | 13.8 | 2.7 | 0.1 | 5.0 | - | - | 1.0 | - | - | 0.1 | Afghanistan |
| Bangladesh | - | 10.7 | 2.5 | 10.8 | 6.7 | - | 20.4 | 5.8 | 90.6 | 80.0 | 10.0 | Bangladesh |
| Benin | - | - | - | 0.5 | - | - | - | - | - | 0.0 | 0.0 | Bénin |
| Bhutan | - | - | - | - | - | - | - | - | - | - | - | Bhoutan |
| Botswana | - | - | - | - | - | - | - | - | - | - | - | Botswana |
| Burkina Faso | - | 0.2 | 1.0 | 0.1 | 0.9 | 0.9 | 0.0 | 2.0 | - | 0.3 | 0.0 | Burkina Faso |
| Burundi | - | - | 0.0 | 0.0 | - | - | 1.0 | - | - | 0.0 | 0.0 | Burundi |
| Cape Verde | - | 0.1 | 1.3 | 0.7 | - | - | - | - | - | 0.2 | - | Cap-Vert |
| Central African Rep. | - | - | - | - | - | - | - | - | - | - | - | Rép. centrafricaine |
| Chad | - | 3.7 | 1.5 | 0.4 | 6.0 | 6.0 | 0.0 | - | - | 0.2 | 0.0 | Tchad |
| Comoros | - | - | 2.3 | 19.7 | 0.6 | 1.1 | 1.9 | 7.5 | 0.7 | 1.9 | 0.7 | Comores |
| Democratic Yemen | 0.1 | 27.6 | 128.8 | 76.5 | 8.8 | 17.6 | 34.2 | 20.4 | 31.1 | 13.2 | 21.2 | Yémen démocratique |
| Djibouti | - | - | - | 19.7 | 64.0 | - | 25.0 | 12.2 | 0.1 | 5.7 | 25.0 | Djibouti |
| Equatorial Guinea | - | - | - | - | - | - | - | - | - | - | - | Guinée équatoriale |
| Ethiopia | - | 1.2 | - | 0.9 | 0.2 | 0.9 | - | - | - | 0.4 | 0.1 | Éthiopie |
| Gambia | - | 1.2 | 2.1 | 0.2 | 0.2 | 0.0 | 0.0 | 3.1 | 0.9 | 0.7 | - | Gambie |
| Guinea | - | 1.9 | 0.4 | 0.6 | - | 0.3 | 0.1 | 0.0 | - | - | - | Guinée |
| Guinea-Bissau | - | 1.2 | 3.8 | 0.6 | 2.1 | 0.0 | 0.0 | - | 0.0 | 0.5 | 25.1 | Guinée-Bissau |
| Haiti | - | - | - | - | - | - | - | - | - | - | - | Haïti |
| Lao People's Dem.Rep. | - | - | - | - | - | - | - | - | - | - | - | Rép. dém. pop. lao |
| Lesotho | - | - | - | - | - | - | - | - | - | - | - | Lesotho |
| Malawi | - | - | - | - | - | - | - | - | 0.0 | - | - | Malawi |
| Maldives | - | 0.2 | 1.8 | 1.2 | 0.0 | 1.0 | 1.1 | 1.2 | 0.1 | 0.8 | 0.8 | Maldives |
| Mali | - | 24.5 | 3.0 | 5.1 | 1.0 | 11.5 | 5.1 | 0.0 | 0.0 | 0.5 | 0.0 | Mali |
| Nepal | - | 0.4 | 0.2 | 33.0 | - | - | - | - | - | 0.0 | 0.0 | Népal |
| Niger | - | 14.1 | 3.1 | 3.0 | 15.9 | 0.4 | 1.6 | 1.9 | 1.7 | 0.8 | 0.0 | Niger |
| Rwanda | - | 5.2 | 0.1 | 0.6 | - | - | - | 0.1 | - | 0.1 | 0.0 | Rwanda |
| Samoa | - | - | - | - | - | - | - | - | - | - | - | Samoa |
| Sao Tome and Principe | - | 0.1 | 0.2 | 0.0 | 0.0 | - | - | - | - | - | - | Sao Tomé-et-Principe |
| Sierra Leone | - | 0.0 | - | - | - | - | 4.0 | 0.0 | 0.2 | 0.0 | 13.5 | Sierra Leone |
| Somalia | - | 52.3 | 14.4 | 191.3 | 50.7 | 32.4 | 78.7 | 24.0 | 148.7 | 3.9 | 0.3 | Somalie |
| Sudan | - | 120.1 | 42.4 | 82.9 | 36.9 | 12.1 | 27.8 | 15.7 | 104.9 | 338.3 | 102.5 | Soudan |
| Togo | - | 2.0 | 2.6 | 0.1 | - | - | 0.0 | 0.0 | 0.0 | 0.0 | 0.0 | Togo |
| Uganda | - | 20.0 | 2.2 | 0.0 | 4.8 | 0.1 | 0.0 | 0.0 | - | 0.2 | 0.1 | Ouganda |
| Un. Rep. of Tanzania | - | 0.2 | - | - | 0.0 | - | - | - | - | 0.0 | 0.0 | Rép.-Un. de Tanzanie |
| Vanuatu | - | - | - | - | - | - | - | - | - | - | - | Vanuatu |
| Yemen | 0.2 | 135.4 | 179.7 | 255.5 | 175.9 | 148.1 | 226.8 | 149.6 | 175.4 | 166.1 | 166.0 | Yémen |
| All LDCs | 0.3 | 436.2 | 395.9 | 704.6 | 380.4 | 233.1 | 428.4 | 245.5 | 555.1 | 615.1 | 366.4 | Ensemble des PMA |
| All developing countries | 363.7 | 3164.7 | 2594.1 | 3015.3 | 2261.4 | 3750.3 | 4014.7 | 3471.1 | 2967.6 | 2399.6 | 2054.8 | Ensemble des pays en développement |

Source: UNCTAD secretariat estimates.
For 1970 and 1975-1976: OECD secretariat estimates.

Source: Estimations du secrétariat de la CNUCED.
Pour 1970 et 1975-1976: estimations du secrétariat
de l'OCDE.

Table 44
Concessional assistance from multilateral agencies a/ mainly financed by OPEC countries, to individual LDCs, 1975-1984

Net disbursements in $ million

Tableau 44
Aide concessionnelle reçue par chacun des PMA, en provenance des institutions multilatérales a/ essentiellement financées par les pays membres de l'OPEP, 1975-1984

Versements nets en millions de dollars

| Country | 1975 | 1976 | 1977 | 1978 | 1979 | 1980 | 1981 | 1982 | 1983 | 1984 | Pays |
|---|---|---|---|---|---|---|---|---|---|---|---|
| Afghanistan | - | - | 3.7 | - | - | - | - | - | - | -0.1 | Afghanistan |
| Bangladesh | - | - | 13.9 | 1.1 | 10.4 | 4.1 | 30.4 | 22.6 | 13.8 | 12.1 | Bangladesh |
| Benin | 2.4 | - | 3.4 | 5.4 | 1.3 | 0.6 | 2.7 | 1.6 | 4.3 | 0.6 | Bénin |
| Bhutan | - | - | - | - | - | - | - | - | - | - | Bhoutan |
| Botswana | 5.4 | - | 2.9 | 0.1 | 0.5 | 2.7 | 0.4 | 2.4 | 4.1 | 0.6 | Botswana |
| Burkina Faso | 2.7 | - | 0.8 | 1.8 | 4.9 | 6.9 | 8.6 | 8.7 | 2.6 | -2.4 | Burkina Faso |
| Burundi | 1.0 | - | 1.5 | 0.8 | 4.4 | 4.5 | 1.9 | 0.5 | 1.6 | -0.0 | Burundi |
| Cape Verde | - | 10.5 | 1.7 | 0.6 | 1.0 | 2.0 | 1.3 | 0.3 | - | 2.6 | Cap-Vert |
| Central African Rep. | 1.2 | - | 1.2 | 1.5 | - | 0.0* | 0.6 | 0.5 | 0.0 | 1.6 | Rép. centrafricaine |
| Chad | 4.4 | - | 0.2 | 0.5 | 0.2 | 0.6 | 1.5 | 2.5 | 3.5 | 0.3 | Tchad |
| Comoros | - | 10.5 | 0.2 | 0.5 | 0.2 | 0.6 | 1.5 | 2.5 | 3.5 | 2.6 | Comores |
| Democratic Yemen | 0.2 | 6.7 | 4.5 | 14.3 | 8.6 | 12.3 | 18.5 | 12.5 | 16.8 | 12.2 | Yémen démocratique |
| Djibouti | - | - | 0.5 | - | - | - | 0.8 | 2.0 | 3.3 | 9.5 | Djibouti |
| Equatorial Guinea | 0.3 | - | - | 2.4 | - | 0.0* | - | 1.0 | 0.5 | -0.0 | Guinée équatoriale |
| Ethiopia | 14.2 | - | 2.4 | 1.4 | 2.3 | 7.2 | 0.2 | 0.2 | 0.5 | -0.2 | Ethiopie |
| Gambia | 0.4 | - | 1.6 | - | 3.0 | 4.4 | 2.2 | 1.4 | 0.5 | 0.6 | Gambie |
| Guinea | - | - | 2.4 | 4.9 | 1.0 | 2.5 | 2.7 | 1.8 | 1.5 | 4.7 | Guinée |
| Guinea-Bissau | - | - | 1.6 | 0.6 | - | - | 1.8 | 1.1 | 0.8 | 0.1 | Guinée-Bissau |
| Haiti | - | - | 3.1 | - | 4.2 | 0.7 | 0.6 | 2.0 | 1.6 | 0.4 | Haïti |
| Lao People's Dem.Rep. | 2.8 | - | 2.1 | - | - | - | 0.0 | 0.5 | 0.5 | 1.1 | Rép. dém. pop. lao |
| Lesotho | - | - | 1.9 | 0.0 | - | 1.3 | 0.0 | 2.9 | 5.2 | 2.1 | Lesotho |
| Malawi | - | - | - | - | - | 0.8 | 0.3 | - | 0.6 | -0.1 | Malawi |
| Maldives | - | - | 0.2 | 0.2 | 0.4 | - | 1.6 | 0.9 | 0.6 | 0.5 | Maldives |
| Mali | 3.9 | - | 4.4 | 6.7 | 3.4 | 10.3 | 14.1 | 12.4 | 16.6 | 4.8 | Mali |
| Nepal | - | - | 4.1 | 4.1 | - | 6.5 | 0.3 | 5.5 | 2.2 | 0.0 | Népal |
| Niger | 2.7 | - | 2.9 | 5.3 | 6.4 | 6.0 | 8.9 | 0.6 | 0.2 | -1.6 | Niger |
| Rwanda | 1.0 | - | 0.8 | 2.9 | 2.2 | 0.8 | 7.8 | 1.7 | 0.0 | -0.2 | Rwanda |
| Samoa | - | - | 1.6 | 0.5 | 0.5 | - | 1.0 | 1.0 | - | -0.2 | Samoa |
| Sao Tome and Principe | 0.5 | 10.0 | 0.1 | 0.1 | 1.2 | 2.6 | 0.5 | 0.5 | 0.5 | 0.4 | Sao Tomé-et-Principe |
| Sierra Leone | 1.8 | 4.2 | 1.0 | 0.3 | 10.5 | 16.1 | 2.1 | 1.0 | 1.7 | 2.6 | Sierra Leone |
| Somalia | 7.5 | 28.5 | 5.6 | 7.9 | 15.7 | 22.9 | 15.3 | 21.6 | 21.8 | 9.7 | Somalie |
| Sudan | 14.1 | - | 15.5 | 18.4 | - | - | 26.8 | 20.4 | 1.7 | 4.3 | Soudan |
| Togo | - | - | - | 0.0* | 0.0* | 0.1 | - | - | 2.8 | 1.5 | Togo |
| Uganda | 5.7 | - | 4.5 | 1.0 | 1.2 | 4.2 | 0.2 | 4.9 | 8.6 | 0.1 | Ouganda |
| Un. Rep. of Tanzania | 7.1 | 0.0 | 5.9 | - | - | - | 8.7 | 14.8 | 14.3 | 6.7 | Rép.-Un. de Tanzanie |
| Vanuatu | - | - | - | - | - | - | - | - | - | - | Vanuatu |
| Yemen | 1.6 | 12.6 | 10.5 | 10.3 | 12.1 | 13.9 | 36.2 | 14.3 | 10.7 | 3.2 | Yémen |
| All LDCs | 80.7 | 83.0 | 107.5 | 90.2 | 96.3 | 133.9 | 199.0 | 164.1 | 142.6 | 81.2 | Ensemble des PMA |
| All developing countries | 158.7 | 418.2 | 220.8 | 301.2 | 250.5 | 287.4 | 367.4 | 354.4 | 324.4 | 142.6 | Ensemble des pays en développement |

Source: UNCTAD secretariat estimates. For 1975-1976 : OECD secretariat estimates.
a/ For the list of multilateral agencies included here, providing concessional assistance to LDCs, see table 40A.

Source: Estimations du secrétariat de la CNUCED. Pour 1975-1976 : estimations du secrétariat de l'OCDE.
a/ Pour la liste des institutions multilatérales qui sont incluses ici et qui fournissent de l'aide concessionnelle aux PMA, se référer au tableau 40A.

Table 45
Non-concessional flows from multilateral agencies a/ mainly financed by OPEC countries, to individual LDCs, 1977-1984

Tableau 45
Apports non-cessionnels reçus par chacun des PMA, en provenance des institutions multilatérales a/ essentiellement financées par les pays membres de l'OPEP, 1977-1984

Net disbursements in $ million / Versements nets en millions de dollars

| Country | 1977 | 1978 | 1979 | 1980 | 1981 | 1982 | 1983 | 1984 | Pays |
|---|---|---|---|---|---|---|---|---|---|
| Afghanistan | - | - | - | - | - | - | - | - | Afghanistan |
| Bangladesh | - | - | 37.1 | -14.7 | 34.1 | -11.4 | 38.9 | -6.6 | Bangladesh |
| Benin | - | 0.1 | 1.7 | 1.8 | 0.7 | 2.1 | -0.0 | -0.3 | Bénin |
| Bhutan | - | - | - | - | - | - | - | - | Bhoutan |
| Botswana | - | - | - | - | - | - | - | - | Botswana |
| Burkina Faso | - | - | - | 2.6 | 2.5 | 0.3 | 0.2 | -2.3 | Burkina Faso |
| Burundi | - | - | - | - | - | - | - | - | Burundi |
| Cape Verde | - | - | - | - | - | - | - | - | Cap-Vert |
| Central African Rep. | - | - | - | - | - | - | - | - | Rép. centrafricaine |
| Chad | - | - | - | - | - | - | - | - | Tchad |
| Comoros | - | - | - | - | 3.7 | -0.4 | -2.4 | -0.7 | Comores |
| Democratic Yemen | - | - | - | 12.8 | 1.2 | 5.0 | -20.4 | - | Yémen démocratique |
| Djibouti | - | - | - | - | - | - | - | - | Djibouti |
| Equatorial Guinea | - | - | - | - | - | - | - | - | Guinée équatoriale |
| Ethiopia | - | - | - | - | - | - | - | - | Ethiopie |
| Gambia | - | - | - | - | 6.6 | -2.3 | 1.1 | -1.2 | Gambie |
| Guinea | - | 2.3 | 10.5 | 18.0 | 3.6 | -8.6 | -2.3 | -2.0 | Guinée |
| Guinea-Bissau | - | - | - | 8.5 | 5.0 | - | - | 1.0 | Guinée-Bissau |
| Haiti | - | - | - | - | - | - | - | - | Haïti |
| Lao People's Dem.Rep. | - | - | - | - | - | - | - | - | Rép. dém. populaire lao |
| Lesotho | - | - | - | - | - | - | - | - | Lesotho |
| Malawi | - | - | - | - | - | - | - | - | Malawi |
| Maldives | - | - | - | - | 3.3 | - | - | - | Maldives |
| Mali | - | - | 2.7 | -0.3 | -2.0 | - | - | - | Mali |
| Nepal | - | - | - | - | - | - | - | - | Népal |
| Niger | - | 4.6 | 10.1 | 7.1 | 14.6 | -14.6 | -4.0 | -0.0 | Niger |
| Rwanda | - | - | - | - | - | - | - | - | Rwanda |
| Samoa | - | - | - | - | - | - | - | - | Samoa |
| Sao Tome and Principe | - | - | - | - | - | - | - | - | Sao Tomé-et-Principe |
| Sierra Leone | - | - | - | - | - | - | - | - | Sierra Leone |
| Somalia | 4.9 | 1.7 | 3.9 | 15.0 | 12.6 | -6.2 | -4.6 | - | Somalie |
| Sudan | - | 2.2 | 39.0 | 32.6 | 7.2 | -2.9 | -7.2 | -7.7 | Soudan |
| Togo | - | - | 1.0 | 0.0 | - | -0.1 | -0.1 | - | Togo |
| Uganda | - | 5.8 | 1.4 | 0.5 | 0.0 | 0.4 | 2.5 | -0.2 | Ouganda |
| Un. Rep. of Tanzania | - | - | - | - | - | 0.5 | -0.0 | 0.3 | Rép.-Unie de Tanzanie |
| Vanuatu | - | - | - | - | - | - | - | - | Vanuatu |
| Yemen | - | - | 0.4 | 19.8 | 3.4 | -15.0 | 16.7 | 17.4 | Yémen |
| All LDCs | 4.9 | 16.9 | 108.3 | 103.8 | 96.5 | -53.2 | 18.3 | -2.3 | Ensemble des PMA |
| All developing countries | 38.7 | 155.1 | 258.6 | 104.3 | 328.0 | -2.7 | 131.6 | 207.6 | Ensemble des pays en développement |

Source: UNCTAD secretariat estimates.
a/ For the list of multilateral agencies included here, providing concessional assistance to LDCs, see table 40A.

Source: Estimations du secrétariat de la CNUCED.
a/ Pour la liste des institutions multilatérales qui sont incluses ici et qui fournissent de l'aide concessionnelle aux PMA, se référer au tableau 40A.

Table 46                                                     Tableau 46

Net ODA as per cent of donor's GNP from individual OPEC      Apports nets de l'APD accordée par chaque pays membre de l'OPEP à
member countries to LDCs as a group, 1975-1984              l'ensemble des PMA, en pourcentage du PNB du pays donneur, 1975-1984

Percentages                                                                                              En pourcentage

| Country | 1975 | 1976 | 1977 | 1978 | 1979 | 1980 | 1981 | 1982 | 1983 | 1984 | Pays |
|---|---|---|---|---|---|---|---|---|---|---|---|
| | Bilateral ODA | | | | APD bilatérale | | | | | | |
| Algeria | 0.02 | 0.03 | 0.01 | 0.00 | 0.05 | 0.05 | 0.02 | 0.00 | - | - | Algérie |
| Iran (Islamic Rep. of) | 0.01 | 0.01 | - | 0.02 | - | - | - | - | - | - | Iran (Rép. islamique) |
| Iraq | 0.21 | 0.32 | 0.14 | 0.19 | 0.07 | 0.13 | - | - | - | - | Iraq |
| Kuwait | 0.36 | 0.48 | 0.77 | 0.61 | 0.46 | 0.52 | 0.53 | 0.44 | 0.59 | 0.54 | Koweit |
| Libyan Arab Jamahiriya | 0.36 | 0.08 | 0.00 | 0.06 | 0.00 | 0.02 | 0.08 | - | - | - | Jamahiriya arabe libyenne |
| Nigeria | 0.01 | 0.01 | 0.00 | - | 0.00 | 0.00 | - | - | - | - | Nigéria |
| Qatar | 1.30 | 0.39 | 0.16 | 0.24 | 0.07 | 0.58 | 0.32 | 0.12 | 0.12 | 0.03 | Qatar |
| Saudi Arabia | 0.76 | 0.92 | 0.98 | 0.47 | 0.55 | 0.39 | 0.24 | 0.47 | 0.55 | 0.34 | Arabie saoudite |
| United Arab Emirates | 1.60 | 0.74 | 0.79 | 1.10 | 0.55 | 0.55 | 0.22 | 0.24 | 0.15 | 0.11 | Emirats arabes unis |
| Venezuela | - | - | - | - | - | - | - | - | - | - | Venezuela |
| Total OPEC countries | 0.27 | 0.26 | 0.28 | 0.20 | 0.17 | 0.17 | 0.12 | 0.16 | 0.14 | 0.10 | Total des pays l'OPEP |
| | Total ODA a/ | | | | APD totale a/ | | | | | | |
| Algeria | 0.01 | 0.05 | 0.09 | 0.06 | 0.10 | 0.11 | 0.08 | 0.08 | 0.04 | 0.06 | Algérie |
| Iran (Islamic Rép. of) | 0.01 | 0.01 | 0.04 | 0.05 | 0.01 | 0.01 | 0.00 | 0.00 | 0.00 | - | Iran (Rép. islamique) |
| Iraq | 0.22 | 0.44 | 0.22 | 0.23 | 0.10 | 0.18 | 0.06 | 0.06 | 0.01 | 0.00 | Iraq |
| Kuwait | 0.43 | 0.71 | 1.21 | 0.99 | 0.72 | 0.72 | 0.71 | 0.84 | 0.98 | 0.92 | Koweit |
| Libyan Arab Jamahiriya | 0.55 | 0.16 | 0.16 | 0.31 | 0.16 | 0.12 | 0.21 | 0.08 | 0.15 | 0.02 | Jamahiriya arabe libyenne |
| Nigeria | 0.03 | 0.10 | 0.10 | 0.03 | 0.02 | 0.01 | 0.12 | 0.03 | 0.02 | 0.05 | Nigéria |
| Qatar | 1.57 | 0.42 | 0.29 | 0.49 | 0.20 | 0.77 | 0.41 | 0.29 | 0.23 | 0.10 | Qatar |
| Saudi Arabia | 0.90 | 1.00 | 1.06 | 0.60 | 0.83 | 0.48 | 0.31 | 0.59 | 0.71 | 0.51 | Arabie saoudite |
| United Arab Emirates | 1.76 | 0.77 | 0.86 | 1.25 | 0.74 | 0.64 | 0.29 | 0.35 | 0.22 | 0.12 | Emirats arabes unis |
| Venezuela | 0.02 | 0.02 | 0.06 | 0.04 | 0.03 | 0.03 | 0.04 | 0.04 | 0.06 | 0.01 | Venezuela |
| Total OPEC countries | 0.32 | 0.32 | 0.37 | 0.29 | 0.27 | 0.23 | 0.19 | 0.23 | 0.22 | 0.17 | Total des pays de l'OPEP |

Source:  UNCTAD secretariat estimates.  For 1975-1976,
         the estimates are based on information from
         the OECD secretariat.

   a/  Including imputed flows to LDCs through
       multilateral channels.

Source:  Estimations du secrétariat de la CNUCED.  Pour 1975-1976,
         les estimations sont établies d'après des renseignements
         du secrétariat de l'OCDE.

   a/  Y compris le montant imputé de l'APD fournie aux PMA
       à travers les voies multilatérales.

Table 47
ODA commitments from individual OPEC member countries
and individual multilateral agencies mainly financed
by them, to LDCs as a group, 1975-1984
$ million

Tableau 47
Engagements de l'APD de chaque pays membre de l'OPEP et de chaque
institution multilatérale essentiellement financée par ceux-ci,
en faveur de l'ensemble des PMA, 1975-1984
Millions de dollars

| | 1975 | 1976 | 1977 | 1978 | 1979 | 1980 | 1981 | 1982 | 1983 | 1984 | |
|---|---|---|---|---|---|---|---|---|---|---|---|
| **A. Bilateral donors** | | | | | | | | | | | **A. Donneurs bilatéraux** |
| Algeria | 3.6 | 4.9 | 2.5 | 0.5 | 34.4 | - | 20.0 | 0.2 | - | - | Algérie |
| Iran (Islamic Rep.) | 16.6 | 20.9 | - | - | - | - | - | - | - | - | Iran (Rép. Islamique) |
| Iraq | 51.1 | 64.0 | 1.3 | 53.5 | 324.5 | 289.4 | 48.8 | 37.3 | - | - | Iraq |
| Kuwait | 189.4 | 138.6 | 161.6 | 116.7 | 106.8 | 207.9 | 257.4 | 265.0 | 165.5 | 125.6 | Koweit |
| Libyan Arab Jamahiriya | 36.1 | 6.5 | 0.8 | 25.4 | 0.0 | 8.7 | 23.1 | - | - | - | Jamahiriya arabe Libyenne |
| Nigeria | 3.0 | 0.2 | 0.1 | 0.9 | 1.6 | 2.5 | - | - | - | - | Nigéria |
| Qatar | 19.9 | 17.5 | 4.6 | 10.7 | 3.0 | 37.3 | 22.6 | 7.6 | 7.4 | 2.0 | Qatar |
| Saudi Arabia | 397.5 | 509.4 | 847.4 | 783.8 | 347.0 | 360.5 | 425.7 | 842.9 | 1073 | 436.0 | Arabie saoudite |
| United Arab Emirates | 157.9 | 140.6 | 253.2 | 135.9 | 58.1 | 287.8 | 36.0 | 83.0 | 7.1 | 102.8 | Emirats arabes unis |
| Total bilateral concessional | 875.1 | 902.6 | 1271 | 1127 | 875.4 | 1194.1 | 833.6 | 1236.0 | 1253.3 | 666.4 | Total des apports bilatéraux concessionnels |
| **B. Multilateral donors** | | | | | | | | | | | **B. Donneurs multilatéraux** |
| BADEA | - | 42.6 | 29.8 | 22.6 | 8.2 | 44.8 | 10.0 | 32.0 | 20.5 | 0.2 | BADEA |
| AFESD | 65.9 | 103.6 | 95.0 | 0.5 | 14.4 | 43.6 | 68.6 | 65.7 | 145.4 | 110.4 | FADES |
| Islamic Dev. Bank | - | - | 30.6 | 12.8 | 18.3 | 11.9 | 19.0 | 39.6 | 8.0 | 86.8 | Banque islamique de dév. |
| OPEC Fund | - | 13.2 | 108.6 | 57.1 | 93.5 | 110.8 | 175.0 | 165.6 | 62.3 | 74.7 | Fonds de l'OPEP |
| OAPEC Special Account | - | 33.5 | - | - | - | - | - | - | - | - | Compte spécial de l'OPAEP |
| SAAFA | 33.0 | 30.5 | - | - | - | - | - | - | - | - | FSAAA |
| Total | 98.9 | 223.4 | 264.0 | 93.0 | 134.4 | 211.1 | 272.6 | 302.9 | 236.2 | 272.1 | Total |
| GRAND TOTAL | 974.0 | 1126 | 1535 | 1220 | 1009.8 | 1405.2 | 1106.2 | 1538.9 | 1489.5 | 938.5 | TOTAL GENERAL |

Source: UNCTAD secretariat estimates.
For 1975-1976 : OECD secretariat estimates.

For abbreviations, see pages x and xi.

Source: Estimations du secrétariat de la CNUCED.
Pour 1975-1976 : estimations du secrétariat de l'OCDE.

Se reporter, pour les abréviations, aux pages xvii et xviii.

Table 48
ODA commitments from OPEC member countries
and multilateral agencies mainly financed by them
to individual LDCs, 1975-1984

$ million

Tableau 48
Engagements de l'APD à chacun des PMA, en provenance des pays
membres de l'OPEP et des institutions multilatérales
essentiellement financées par ceux-ci, 1975-1984

Millions de dollars

| Country | 1975 | 1976 | 1977 | 1978 | 1979 | 1980 | 1981 | 1982 | 1983 | 1984 | Pays |
|---|---|---|---|---|---|---|---|---|---|---|---|
| Afghanistan | 68.6 | 23.6 | 42.3 | 20.0 | 3.6 | - | 1.0 | - | - | 0.1 | Afghanistan |
| Bangladesh | 102.0 | 13.6 | 85.4 | 75.0 | 50.0 | 78.4 | 227.5 | 311.2 | 334.2 | 38.4 | Bangladesh |
| Benin | - | 9.1 | 2.5 | 9.7 | 4.5 | 4.5 | 6.0 | - | 9.4 | 14.2 | Bénin |
| Bhutan | - | - | - | - | - | - | - | - | 10.3 | 7.1 | Bhoutan |
| Botswana | 5.4 | 5.5 | 1.0 | 8.1 | 4.2 | 26.6 | 3.9 | 24.1 | 16.1 | 2.0 | Botswana |
| Burkina Faso | 2.9 | 2.2 | 23.3 | 6.0 | 14.4 | 7.0 | 12.0 | 20.3 | 14.6 | 26.2 | Burkina Faso |
| Burundi | - | 10.5 | 11.8 | 1.9 | 4.5 | 9.5 | 33.3 | 9.0 | 14.5 | 14.0 | Burundi |
| Cape Verde | 0.9 | 1.8 | 1.5 | - | 3.6 | 17.7 | 1.0 | 2.5 | 5.8 | 0.2 | Cap-Vert |
| Central African Rep. | 0.2 | 10.0 | - | - | 1.6 | 1.6 | 2.5 | 10.1 | 0.0 | - | Rép. centrafricaine |
| Chad | 11.0 | 10.0 | 2.8 | 22.4 | 1.6 | 2.1 | - | - | 0.0 | 8.1 | Tchad |
| Comoros | - | 20.5 | 20.1 | 1.9 | 34.5 | 4.5 | 11.9 | 34.3 | 5.9 | 1.5 | Comores |
| Democratic Yemen | 72.8 | 184.9 | 114.8 | 21.9 | 63.6 | 100.8 | 66.4 | 77.6 | 40.8 | 52.9 | Yémen démocratique |
| Djibouti | - | - | 19.7 | 64.0 | 0.5 | 62.6 | 29.8 | 52.6 | 52.2 | 59.9 | Djibouti |
| Equatorial Guinea | - | - | 0.5 | - | 1.0 | - | 1.0 | - | 4.7 | 1.6 | Guinée équatoriale |
| Ethiopia | 15.4 | - | 5.7 | 0.7 | 0.9 | 0.1 | 11.2 | - | - | 5.0 | Ethiopie |
| Gambia | - | 6.4 | 26.2 | 2.6 | 0.9 | 28.0 | 6.6 | 2.4 | 1.0 | 2.1 | Gambie |
| Guinea | 5.9 | 21.8 | 12.0 | 7.5 | 14.8 | 180.0 | - | 24.1 | 11.2 | 71.9 | Guinée |
| Guinea-Bissau | 6.2 | 1.6 | 2.1 | 14.0 | 1.0 | 5.2 | 2.5 | 1.5 | 24.6 | 1.0 | Guinée-Bissau |
| Haiti | - | - | 3.2 | - | 4.0 | 3.5 | - | - | 2.8 | 1.2 | Haïti |
| Lao People's Dem.Rep. | - | - | 2.2 | 5.0 | - | 1.5 | 4.0 | - | - | 3.1 | Rép. dém. pop. lao |
| Lesotho | - | - | 1.9 | 5.1 | 3.0 | 17.0 | 3.5 | - | 3.0 | 1.5 | Lesotho |
| Malawi | - | - | - | - | - | - | 1.0 | 0.0 | - | - | Malawi |
| Maldives | 1.3 | 6.8 | 1.5 | 12.2 | 2.1 | 33.7 | 8.2 | 3.3 | 1.4 | 4.6 | Maldives |
| Mali | 25.5 | 49.1 | 28.6 | 20.0 | 26.3 | 46.7 | 25.6 | 141.1 | 7.8 | 23.8 | Mali |
| Nepal | 0.3 | 17.1 | 37.1 | 3.0 | 12.2 | 1.3 | 11.0 | - | 30.6 | 25.4 | Népal |
| Niger | 17.8 | 15.8 | 11.5 | 17.7 | 5.2 | 42.3 | 100.6 | 47.0 | 5.0 | 37.8 | Niger |
| Rwanda | 11.6 | 5.0 | 15.6 | - | 4.8 | 3.0 | 9.3 | 10.0 | 18.8 | 5.0 | Rwanda |
| Samoa | - | 1.6 | - | 1.0 | - | 0.8 | 1.0 | 2.0 | 0.5 | 5.0 | Samoa |
| Sao Tome and Principe | 0.6 | 10.0 | 0.4 | - | - | - | 1.0 | - | 1.2 | 1.3 | Sao Tomé-et-Principe |
| Sierra Leone | 0.2 | 7.1 | 7.1 | 0.0 | 5.6 | 13.9 | 7.0 | 7.5 | 0.9 | 19.0 | Sierra Leone |
| Somalia | 96.8 | 67.1 | 430.7 | 68.3 | 80.8 | 105.3 | 90.0 | 205.8 | 22.5 | 76.3 | Somalie |
| Sudan | 258.2 | 286.3 | 215.9 | 401.9 | 169.6 | 269.4 | 130.9 | 118.9 | 585.1 | 69.6 | Soudan |
| Togo | 2.0 | 2.5 | 0.1 | - | 8.4 | 10.5 | 7.4 | - | 21.1 | 11.4 | Togo |
| Uganda | 79.8 | 2.1 | 14.7 | 27.2 | - | 5.0 | 10.5 | 16.3 | 0.1 | 14.4 | Ouganda |
| Un. Rep. of Tanzania | 15.7 | 5.0 | 11.6 | 5.1 | - | 36.6 | 85.0 | 22.0 | 5.0 | 15.0 | Rép.-Un. de Tanzanie |
| Vanuatu | - | - | - | - | - | - | - | - | - | - | Vanuatu |
| Yemen | 172.6 | 346.4 | 379.3 | 397.5 | 482.2 | 284.6 | 193.0 | 394.9 | 237.2 | 317.0 | Yémen |
| All LDCs | 974.0 | 1126.2 | 1536.0 | 1220.8 | 1010.1 | 1405.5 | 1106.4 | 1539.2 | 1489.5 | 938.7 | Ensemble des PMA |

Source: UNCTAD secretariat estimates.
For 1975-1976 : OECD secretariat estimates.

Source: Estimations du secrétariat de la CNUCED.
Pour 1975-1976 : estimations du secrétariat de l'OCDE.

Table 49
Grant element of ODA commitments from individual OPEC member
countries and multilateral agencies mainly financed by them,
to LDCs as a group, 1977-1984

Tableau 49
Elément de libéralité des engagements de l'APD de chaque pays
membre de l'OPEP et de chaque institution multilatérale essentiellement financée par ceux-ci, à l'ensemble des PMA, 1977-1984

| | 1977 | 1978 | 1979 | 1980 | 1981 | 1982 | 1983 | 1984 | |
|---|---|---|---|---|---|---|---|---|---|
| **Bilateral donors** | | | | | | | | | **Donneurs bilatéraux** |
| Algeria | 100.0 | 100.0 | 94.2 | - | 54.8 | 100.0 | - | - | Algérie |
| Iran (Islamic Rep.) | - | - | - | - | - | - | - | - | Iran (Rép. islamique) |
| Iraq | 50.0 | 66.6 | 52.5 | 56.1 | 42.4 | 42.1 | - | - | Iraq |
| Kuwait | 68.2 | 74.7 | 71.9 | 70.7 | 70.3 | 66.7 | 68.5 | 62.4 | Koweit |
| Libyan Arab Jamahiriya | 100.0 | 70.5 | 100.0 | 58.7 | 78.1 | - | - | - | Jamahiriya arabe libyenne |
| Nigeria | 50.0 | 100.0 | 100.0 | 98.0 | - | - | - | - | Nigéria |
| Qatar | 100.0 | 74.2 | 100.0 | 100.0 | 100.0 | 100.0 | 100.0 | 100.0 | Qatar |
| Saudi Arabia | 83.9 | 63.4 | 71.6 | 76.8 | 64.7 | 82.7 | 93.1 | 78.4 | Arabie saoudite |
| United Arab Emirates | 71.8 | 83.6 | 99.1 | 61.8 | 51.1 | 61.4 | 100.0 | 100.0 | Emirats arabes unis |
| Total | 79.6 | 67.5 | 67.4 | 67.8 | 65.6 | 76.8 | 90.0 | 78.8 | Total |
| **Multilateral donors** | | | | | | | | | **Donneurs multilatéraux** |
| BADEA | 47.4 | 60.1 | 39.5 | 35.7 | 31.3 | 32.3 | 33.3 | 100.0 | BADEA |
| AFESD | 42.2 | 100.0 | 41.1 | 37.4 | 40.1 | 38.6 | 37.2 | 38.1 | FADES |
| Islamic Dev. Bank | 56.3 | 49.0 | 53.0 | 56.3 | 53.2 | 60.6 | 59.5 | 69.6 | Banque islamique de dév. |
| OPEC Fund | 67.8 | 57.1 | 60.4 | 56.0 | 56.6 | 61.1 | 54.4 | 55.4 | Fonds de l'OPEP |
| Total | 55.0 | 57.0 | 56.0 | 47.8 | 51.3 | 53.1 | 42.0 | 52.9 | Total |
| GRAND TOTAL | 75.3 | 66.7 | 65.9 | 64.8 | 62.1 | 72.1 | 82.4 | 71.3 | TOTAL GENERAL |

Source : UNCTAD secretariat estimates.

For abbreviations see pages x and xi.

Source : Estimations du secrétariat de la CNUCED.

Se reporter, pour les abréviations, aux pages xvii et xviii.

Table 50

Tableau 50

Balance of payments summary for all LDCs, 1970, 1973, 1975 and 1978-1984

Situation récapitulative de la balance des paiements de l'ensemble des PMA, 1970, 1973, 1975 et 1978-1984

$ million

Millions de dollars

| | 1970 | 1973 | 1975 | 1978 | 1979 | 1980 | 1981 | 1982 | 1983 | 1984 | | |
|---|---|---|---|---|---|---|---|---|---|---|---|---|
| 1. Exports of goods and services | 2331 | 3907 | 4755 | 6922 | 8661 | 10534 | 10361 | 9499 | 9547 | 9991 | 1. | Exportations de biens et services |
| 1a. Goods f.o.b. | 1848 | 3060 | 3590 | 5386 | 6675 | 7863 | 7445 | 6543 | 6765 | 7347 | | 1a. Marchandises f.o.b. |
| 1b. Non-factor services | 483 | 847 | 1165 | 1536 | 1986 | 2671 | 2916 | 2956 | 2782 | 2644 | | 1b. Services non facteurs |
| 2. Imports of goods and services | 2979 | 5671 | 8714 | 13278 | 15940 | 20167 | 20361 | 19165 | 17817 | 18068 | 2. | Importations de biens et services |
| 2a. Goods f.o.b. | 2209 | 4258 | 6664 | 10079 | 12129 | 15625 | 16020 | 15277 | 13924 | 14195 | | 2a. Marchandises f.o.b. |
| 2b. Non-factor services | 770 | 1413 | 2050 | 3199 | 3811 | 4542 | 4341 | 3888 | 3893 | 3873 | | 2b. Services non facteurs |
| 3. Merchandise balance (1a-2a) | -361 | -1198 | -3075 | -4693 | -5454 | -7762 | -8574 | -8733 | -7159 | -6848 | 3. | Balance "marchandises" (1a-2a) |
| 4. Balance of goods and services (1-2) | -648 | -1764 | -3959 | -6356 | -7279 | -9633 | -10000 | -9666 | -8270 | -8077 | 4. | Balance des biens et services (1-2) |
| 5. Investment income receipts | 53 | 87 | 127 | 277 | 397 | 550 | 482 | 457 | 326 | 305 | 5. | Revenu des investissements, recettes |
| 6. Investment income payments | 164 | 234 | 281 | 539 | 603 | 829 | 911 | 1046 | 1134 | 1139 | 6. | Revenu des investissements, paiements |
| 7. Private transfers (net) | 111 | 333 | 515 | 1717 | 1860 | 2313 | 2340 | 2144 | 2792 | 2843 | 7. | Transferts privés (nets) |
| 8. Current account balance (4+5-6+7) | -647 | -1578 | -3598 | -4901 | -5624 | -7599 | -8089 | -8110 | -6286 | -6068 | 8. | Balance "compte courant" (4+5-6+7) |
| 9. Government transfers (net) | 352 | 1065 | 1561 | 2168 | 3144 | 2993 | 3037 | 3348 | 2980 | 2945 | 9. | Transferts publics (nets) |
| 10. Long term loans (net) | 328 | 879 | 1510 | 1828 | 2220 | 2731 | 2404 | 2163 | 2201 | 2194 | 10. | Prêts a long terme (nets) |
| 10a. Government | 308 | 730 | 1365 | 1670 | 1966 | 2461 | 2213 | 2035 | 2108 | 1979 | | 10a. Publics |
| 10b. Others | 20 | 149 | 145 | 158 | 254 | 270 | 191 | 128 | 93 | 215 | | 10b. Autres |
| 11. Direct investment and other long-term capital (net) | 35 | 8 | 85 | 256 | 361 | 348 | 354 | 433 | 264 | 139 | 11. | Investissements directs et autres capitaux à long terme (nets) |
| 12. Short-term capital (net) | 67 | -37 | 505 | 520 | 174 | 680 | 1288 | 483 | 19 | 202 | 12. | Capitaux à court terme (nets) |
| 13. Errors and ommissions (net) | -133 | -139 | -84 | 393 | -69 | 289 | 35 | 409 | 349 | -57 | 13. | Erreurs et omissions (nets) |
| 14. Overall balance (8+9+10+11+12+13) | 1 | 198 | -20 | 263 | 205 | -558 | -971 | -1274 | -473 | -645 | 14. | Balance générale (8+9+10+11+12+13) |

Source: UNCTAD secretariat estimates based on information from IMF.

Source: Estimations du secrétariat de la CNUCED d'après des renseignements du FMI.

a/ The "overall balance" equals change in reserves (including SDR allocations and gold monetization). A balance with a positive sign corresponds to an increase in reserve holdings and a negative sign indicates a decrease in such holdings. For a description of the balance of payments categories used in this table, see the general notes to table 5.1A of the UNCTAD Handbook of International Trade and Development Statistics, Supplement 1986.

a/ La "balance générale" est égale à la variation des réserves (y compris les allocations de DTS et la monétisation de l'or). Une balance comportant un signe positif correspond à une augmentation des disponibilités en réserves et un signe négatif indique une diminution de ces disponibilités. Pour la description des catégories utilisées dans ce tableau, se référer aux notes générales du tableau 5.1A du Manuel de statistiques du commerce international et du développement, supplément 1986 de la CNUCED.

Table 51

External debt outstanding, 1975, a/ and 1979-1984

Tableau 51

Encours de la dette extérieure, 1975, a/ et 1979-1984

A. $ million
A. millions de dollars

| Country | 1975 | 1979 | 1980 | 1981 | 1982 | 1982b/ | 1983b/ | 1984b/ | Pays |
|---|---|---|---|---|---|---|---|---|---|
| Afghanistan | 819 | 1285 | 1195 | 1242 | 1324 | 1382 | 1360 | 1350 | Afghanistan |
| Bangladesh | 1601 | 3348 | 3614 | 3938 | 4359 | 4479 | 4948 | 5264 | Bangladesh |
| Benin | 90 | 237 | 484 | 574 | 566 | 567 | 618 | 582 | Bénin |
| Bhutan | - | - | - | - | - | 2 | 2 | 3 | Bhoutan |
| Botswana | 278 | 295 | 283 | 286 | 389 | 303 | 324 | 371 | Botswana |
| Burkina Paso | 62 | 260 | 295 | 312 | 367 | 358 | 411 | 425 | Burkina Paso |
| Burundi | 17 | 112 | 151 | 175 | 223 | 228 | 305 | 346 | Burundi |
| Cape Verde | 1 | 18 | 20 | 40 | 60 | 66 | 82 | 73 | Cap-Vert |
| Central African Rep. | 82 | 132 | 164 | 188 | 211 | 155 | 152 | 131 | République centrafricaine |
| Chad | 67 | 172 | 156 | 126 | 129 | 136 | 127 | 121 | Tchad |
| Comoros | 5 | 39 | 50 | 53 | 67 | 70 | 85 | 106 | Comores |
| Democratic Yemen | 120 | 427 | 549 | 798 | 941 | 992 | 1181 | 1222 | Yémen démocratique |
| Djibouti | 27 | 51 | 28 | 22 | 43 | 29 | 55 | 123 | Djibouti |
| Equatorial Guinea | 27 | 36 | 57 | 67 | 81 | 92 | 107 | 103 | Guinée équatoriale |
| Ethiopia | 386 | 616 | 704 | 963 | 1057 | 1099 | 1307 | 1529 | Ethiopie |
| Gambia | 14 | 81 | 118 | 145 | 154 | 164 | 168 | 181 | Gambie |
| Guinea | 848 | 1064 | 1111 | 1301 | 1283 | 1343 | 1252 | 1197 | Guinée |
| Guinea-Bissau | 7 | 66 | 104 | 111 | 127 | 140 | 148 | 152 | Guinée-Bissau |
| Haiti | 57 | 227 | 269 | 356 | 394 | 454 | 522 | 593 | Haïti |
| Lao People's Dem.Rep. | 25 | 77 | 75 | 65 | 60 | 317 | 366 | 415 | République dém. pop. lao |
| Lesotho | 13 | 54 | 76 | 91 | 131 | 118 | 134 | 139 | Lesotho |
| Malawi | 279 | 567 | 746 | 767 | 786 | 748 | 744 | 761 | Malawi |
| Maldives | 1 | 10 | 28 | 39 | 44 | 44 | 49 | 52 | Maldives |
| Mali | 337 | 533 | 692 | 739 | 811 | 823 | 916 | 1039 | Mali |
| Nepal | 38 | 155 | 185 | 243 | 305 | 306 | 362 | 442 | Népal |
| Niger | 117 | 406 | 608 | 703 | 690 | 794 | 783 | 805 | Niger |
| Rwanda | 25 | 127 | 161 | 180 | 195 | 200 | 231 | 253 | Rwanda |
| Samoa | 16 | 49 | 57 | 56 | 60 | 61 | 63 | 61 | Samoa |
| Sao Tome and Principe | - | - | - | - | - | 19 | 28 | 29 | Sao Tomé-et-Principe |
| Sierra Leone | 169 | 360 | 389 | 392 | 394 | 446 | 407 | 463 | Sierra Leone |
| Somalia | 236 | 679 | 749 | 906 | 978 | 1189 | 1323 | 1462 | Somalie |
| Sudan | 1481 | 3396 | 3953 | 4731 | 5450 | 5129 | 5725 | 5484 | Soudan |
| Togo | 138 | 858 | 916 | 871 | 816 | 894 | 953 | 781 | Togo |
| Uganda | 213 | 492 | 609 | 593 | 654 | 617 | 685 | 710 | Ouganda |
| United Rep.of Tanzania | 836 | 1592 | 1734 | 1951 | 1988 | 2516 | 2698 | 2713 | Rép.-Unie de Tanzanie |
| Vanuatu | 6 | 12 | 10 | 7 | 6 | 11 | 46 | 65 | Vanuatu |
| Yemen | 248 | 627 | 984 | 1223 | 1406 | 1420 | 1746 | 1825 | Yémen |
| All LDCs c/ | 8685 | 18460 | 21323 | 24254 | 26550 | 27718 | 30413 | 31371 | Ensemble des PMAc/ |

For sources and notes see table 51 page 75.

Pour les sources et les notes, se référer au tableau 51, page 75.

Table 51 (continued)

External debt outstanding, 1975, and 1979-1984

Tableau 51 (suite)

Encours de la dette extérieure, 1975, et 1979-1984

B. As ratio to exports d/
B. Rapport dette/exportations d/

| Country | 1975 | 1979 | 1980 | 1981 | 1982 | 1982b/ | 1983b/ | 1984b/ | Pays |
|---|---|---|---|---|---|---|---|---|---|
| Afghanistan | 3.7 | 2.6 | 1.7 | 1.8 | 1.9 | 2.0 | 1.9 | 1.8 | Afghanistan |
| Bangladesh | 5.3 | 5.2 | 4.9 | 5.9 | 6.5 | 6.7 | 7.2 | 5.6 | Bangladesh |
| Benin | 2.8 | 5.2 | 7.7 | 16.9 | 23.6 | 23.6 | 19.3 | 17.6 | Bénin |
| Bhutan | - | - | - | - | - | .. | .. | .. | Bhoutan |
| Botswana | 2.0 | 0.7 | 0.6 | 0.8 | 0.9 | 0.7 | 0.5 | 0.6 | Botswana |
| Burkina Faso | 1.4 | 3.4 | 3.3 | 4.2 | 6.6 | 6.4 | 7.2 | 5.3 | Burkina Faso |
| Burundi | 0.5 | 1.1 | 2.3 | 2.5 | 2.5 | 2.6 | 3.8 | 3.5 | Burundi |
| Cape Verde | 0.5 | 9.0 | 5.0 | 13.3 | 15.0 | 16.5 | 16.4 | 14.6 | Cap-Vert |
| Central African Rep. | 1.7 | 1.7 | 1.4 | 2.4 | 1.9 | 1.4 | 2.0 | 1.5 | République centrafricaine |
| Chad | 1.4 | 2.0 | 2.2 | 1.5 | 2.2 | 2.3 | 1.7 | 1.1 | Tchad |
| Comoros | 0.5 | 2.3 | 2.5 | 3.3 | 3.4 | 3.5 | 4.2 | 5.0 | Comores |
| Democratic Yemen | 0.7 | 0.9 | 0.7 | 1.8 | 1.2 | 1.2 | 1.8 | 1.9 | Yémen démocratique |
| Djibouti | 0.8 | 4.6 | 1.5 | 1.0 | 2.2 | 1.4 | 2.2 | 4.7 | Djibouti |
| Equatorial Guinea | 1.0 | 1.2 | 4.1 | 4.2 | 4.8 | 5.4 | 5.4 | 5.2 | Guinée équatoriale |
| Ethiopia | 1.6 | 1.5 | 1.7 | 2.5 | 2.6 | 2.7 | 3.2 | 3.7 | Ethiopie |
| Gambia | 0.3 | 1.4 | 3.8 | 5.4 | 3.5 | 3.7 | 3.5 | 3.8 | Gambie |
| Guinea | 5.9 | 3.4 | 2.8 | 2.6 | 3.1 | 3.3 | 3.1 | 2.8 | Guinée |
| Guinea-Bissau | 1.0 | 4.7 | 9.5 | 7.9 | 10.6 | 11.7 | 6.4 | 8.4 | Guinée-Bissau |
| Haiti | 0.7 | 1.5 | 1.2 | 2.4 | 2.4 | 2.8 | 3.4 | 3.3 | Haïti |
| Lao People's Dem.Rep. | 2.3 | 2.2 | 2.4 | 2.0 | 1.5 | 7.9 | 9.2 | 20.8 | République dém. pop. lao |
| Lesotho | 1.0 | 1.2 | 1.3 | 1.8 | 3.7 | 3.4 | 7.0 | 6.6 | Lesotho |
| Malawi | 2.0 | 2.5 | 2.6 | 2.8 | 3.2 | 3.0 | 3.2 | 2.4 | Malawi |
| Maldives | 0.2 | 1.7 | 2.8 | 3.5 | 3.1 | 3.1 | 2.6 | 2.1 | Maldives |
| Mali | 6.2 | 3.6 | 3.4 | 4.8 | 5.6 | 5.6 | 5.6 | 5.7 | Mali |
| Nepal | 0.4 | 1.4 | 2.3 | 1.7 | 3.5 | 3.5 | 3.8 | 3.4 | Népal |
| Niger | 1.3 | 0.9 | 1.1 | 1.5 | 2.1 | 2.4 | 2.7 | 3.5 | Niger |
| Rwanda | 0.6 | 1.1 | 1.4 | 1.6 | 1.9 | 1.9 | 1.9 | 1.7 | Rwanda |
| Samoa | 2.3 | 2.7 | 3.4 | 5.1 | 4.6 | 4.7 | 3.3 | 3.2 | Samoa |
| Sao Tome and Principe | - | - | - | - | - | 2.1 | 4.7 | 4.1 | Sao Tomé-et-Principe |
| Sierra Leone | 1.4 | 1.7 | 1.9 | 2.6 | 4.4 | 5.0 | 4.4 | 3.1 | Sierra Leone |
| Somalia | 2.7 | 6.1 | 5.6 | 6.0 | 4.9 | 6.0 | 13.2 | 32.5 | Somalie |
| Sudan | 3.4 | 6.3 | 7.3 | 7.2 | 10.9 | 10.3 | 9.2 | 8.7 | Soudan |
| Togo | 1.1 | 3.9 | 2.7 | 4.1 | 4.6 | 5.0 | 5.9 | 4.1 | Togo |
| Uganda | 0.8 | 1.1 | 1.8 | 2.4 | 1.9 | 1.8 | 1.8 | 1.8 | Ouganda |
| United Rep.of Tanzania | 2.2 | 3.1 | 3.4 | 3.2 | 4.4 | 5.5 | 7.4 | 7.2 | Rép.-Unie de Tanzanie |
| Vanuatu | 0.6 | 0.2 | 0.3 | 0.2 | 0.3 | 0.5 | 1.6 | 1.5 | Vanuatu |
| Yemen | 22.5 | 44.8 | 42.8 | 26.0 | 36.0 | 36.4 | 64.7 | 28.1 | Yémen |
| All LDCs c/ | 2.4 | 2.8 | 2.7 | 3.5 | 3.8 | 4.0 | 4.4 | 4.2 | Ensemble des PMA c/ |

Source : UNCTAD secretariat based on information from the OECD secretariat.

Source : Secrétariat de la CNUCED d'après des renseignements du secrétariat de l'OCDE.

a/ Disbursed at year end.
b/ Data not comparable with those for previous years.
c/ Total of LDCs for which data are shown
d/ Goods only.

a/ Dette à la fin de l'année (montants versés).
b/ Les données ne sont pas comparables à celles des années précédentes.
c/ Total des PMA pour lesquels les données sont montrées.
d/ Marchandises seulement.

Table 52

Tableau 52

Debt service payments, 1975 and 1979-1984

Paiements effectués au titre du service de la dette, 1975 et 1979-1984

A. $ million
A. Millions de dollars

| Country | 1975 | 1979 | 1980 | 1981 | 1982 | 1982a/ | 1983a/ | 1984a/ | Pays |
|---|---|---|---|---|---|---|---|---|---|
| Afghanistan | 27 | 13 | 180 | 140 | 112 | 39 | 40 | 41 | Afghanistan |
| Bangladesh | 61 | 99 | 109 | 151 | 138 | 155 | 159 | 200 | Bangladesh |
| Benin | 9 | 16 | 24 | 55 | 52 | 18 | 23 | 39 | Bénin |
| Bhutan | - | - | - | - | - | 1 | 2 | 0 | Bhoutan |
| Botswana | 22 | 46 | 40 | 36 | 31 | 60 | 33 | 48 | Botswana |
| Burkina Faso | 8 | 10 | 17 | 15 | 19 | 26 | 20 | 26 | Burkina Faso |
| Burundi | 2 | 4 | 7 | 6 | 6 | 16 | 17 | 18 | Burundi |
| Cape Verde | 0 | 0 | 0 | 4 | 1 | 2 | 3 | 6 | Cap-Vert |
| Central African Rep. | 7 | 3 | 2 | 5 | 4 | 7 | 14 | 24 | République centrafricaine |
| Chad | 6 | 15 | 12 | 8 | 1 | 1 | 1 | 6 | Tchad |
| Comoros | 1 | 2 | 2 | 1 | 1 | 2 | 2 | 3 | Comores |
| Democratic Yemen | 4 | 13 | 23 | 68 | 46 | 34 | 42 | 56 | Yémen démocratique |
| Djibouti | 4 | 11 | 6 | 5 | 3 | 4 | 5 | 18 | Djibouti |
| Equatorial Guinea | 2 | 1 | 2 | 4 | 3 | 4 | 3 | 1 | Guinée équatoriale |
| Ethiopia | 31 | 28 | 35 | 55 | 61 | 67 | 89 | 124 | Ethiopie |
| Gambia | 0 | 1 | 2 | 7 | 6 | 12 | 7 | 8 | Gambie |
| Guinea | 54 | 117 | 128 | 118 | 78 | 95 | 83 | 107 | Guinée |
| Guinea-Bissau | - | 4 | 4 | 4 | 4 | 2 | 2 | 4 | Guinée-Bissau |
| Haiti | 8 | 12 | 22 | 16 | 16 | 18 | 18 | 24 | Haïti |
| Lao People's Dem.Rep. | 2 | 3 | 2 | 2 | 2 | 2 | 4 | 5 | République dém. pop. lao |
| Lesotho | 0 | 2 | 6 | 7 | 14 | 12 | 11 | 15 | Lesotho |
| Malawi | 20 | 46 | 70 | 91 | 76 | 68 | 60 | 84 | Malawi |
| Maldives | - | 0 | 0 | 1 | 3 | 2 | 4 | 11 | Maldives |
| Mali | 6 | 21 | 17 | 13 | 12 | 8 | 13 | 18 | Mali |
| Nepal | 5 | 5 | 13 | 8 | 10 | 10 | 9 | 11 | Népal |
| Niger | 9 | 46 | 87 | 116 | 151 | 163 | 115 | 112 | Niger |
| Rwanda | 1 | 2 | 3 | 4 | 6 | 7 | 6 | 8 | Rwanda |
| Samoa | 1 | 4 | 5 | 4 | 2 | 3 | 4 | 4 | Samoa |
| Sao Tome and Principe | - | - | - | - | - | 0 | 0 | 1 | Sao Tomé-et-Principe |
| Sierra Leone | 22 | 54 | 43 | 55 | 38 | 21 | 37 | 23 | Sierra Leone |
| Somalia | 5 | 9 | 20 | 31 | 33 | 22 | 31 | 46 | Somalie |
| Sudan | 166 | 96 | 100 | 135 | 180 | 160 | 139 | 155 | Soudan |
| Togo | 22 | 52 | 78 | 58 | 38 | 52 | 56 | 95 | Togo |
| Uganda | 20 | 17 | 15 | 61 | 70 | 63 | 73 | 108 | Ouganda |
| United Rep.of Tanzania | 40 | 108 | 115 | 93 | 88 | 71 | 69 | 85 | Rép.-Unie de Tanzanie |
| Vanuatu | 1 | 3 | 3 | 1 | 1 | 2 | 2 | 12 | Vanuatu |
| Yemen | 5 | 23 | 47 | 110 | 89 | 74 | 56 | 117 | Yémen |
| All LDCs c/ | 571 | 889 | 1241 | 1483 | 1393 | 1304 | 1252 | 1663 | Ensemble des PMA c/ |

For sources and notes, see table 52, page 77.

Pour les sources et les notes, se référer au tableau 52, page 77.

Table 52 (continued)

Debt service payments, 1975, and 1979-1984

Tableau 52 (suite)

Paiements effectués au titre du service de la dette, 1975, et 1979-1984

B. Per cent of exports c/

B. En pourcentage des exportations c/

| Country | 1975 | 1979 | 1980 | 1981 | 1982 | 1982a/ | 1983a/ | 1984a/ | Pays |
|---|---|---|---|---|---|---|---|---|---|
| Afghanistan | 12.1 | 2.6 | 25.5 | 20.2 | 15.8 | 5.5 | 5.5 | 5.6 | Afghanistan |
| Bangladesh | 20.1 | 15.4 | 14.8 | 22.8 | 20.7 | 23.2 | 23.0 | 21.4 | Bangladesh |
| Benin | 28.1 | 34.8 | 38.1 | 161.8 | 216.7 | 75.0 | 71.9 | 118.2 | Bénin |
| Bhutan | - | - | - | - | - | .. | .. | .. | Bhoutan |
| Botswana | 15.5 | 10.6 | 8.0 | 9.5 | 6.8 | 13.1 | 5.2 | 7.1 | Botswana |
| Burkina Faso | 18.2 | 13.0 | 18.9 | 20.0 | 33.9 | 46.4 | 35.1 | 32.5 | Burkina Faso |
| Burundi | 6.2 | 3.8 | 10.8 | 8.4 | 6.8 | 18.2 | 21.2 | 18.4 | Burundi |
| Cape Verde | 10.0 | 10.0 | 5.0 | 10.0 | 25.0 | 50.0 | 60.0 | 120.0 | Cap-Vert |
| Central African Rep. | 14.6 | 3.8 | 1.7 | 5.1 | 3.7 | 6.4 | 18.7 | 27.9 | République centrafricaine |
| Chad | 12.5 | 17.0 | 16.9 | 9.6 | 1.7 | 1.7 | 1.4 | 5.4 | Tchad |
| Comoros | 10.0 | 11.8 | 10.0 | 6.2 | 5.0 | 10.0 | 10.0 | 14.3 | Comores |
| Democratic Yemen | 2.3 | 2.8 | 3.0 | 15.8 | 5.8 | 4.3 | 6.2 | 8.7 | Yémen démocratique |
| Djibouti | 11.1 | 100.0 | 31.6 | 23.8 | 15.0 | 20.0 | 20.0 | 69.2 | Djibouti |
| Equatorial Guinea | 7.7 | 3.4 | 14.3 | 25.0 | 17.6 | 23.5 | 15.0 | 5.0 | Guinée équatoriale |
| Ethiopia | 12.9 | 6.7 | 8.2 | 14.1 | 15.1 | 16.6 | 22.1 | 29.7 | Éthiopie |
| Gambia | 0.8 | 1.7 | 6.4 | 25.9 | 13.6 | 27.3 | 14.6 | 17.0 | Gambie |
| Guinea | 37.8 | 36.9 | 32.8 | 24.1 | 19.0 | 23.2 | 20.8 | 24.9 | Guinée |
| Guinea-Bissau | - | 28.6 | 36.4 | 28.6 | 33.3 | 25.0 | 8.7 | 22.2 | Guinée-Bissau |
| Haiti | 9.9 | 8.1 | 9.7 | 10.6 | 9.8 | 11.0 | 11.7 | 13.4 | Haïti |
| Lao People's Dem.Rep. | 18.2 | 8.6 | 6.4 | 6.1 | 5.0 | 5.0 | 10.0 | 25.0 | République dém. pop. lao |
| Lesotho | 3.1 | 4.4 | 10.3 | 14.0 | 40.0 | 34.3 | 57.9 | 71.4 | Lesotho |
| Malawi | 14.4 | 20.6 | 24.6 | 33.7 | 30.9 | 27.6 | 26.2 | 26.8 | Malawi |
| Maldives | - | 3.3 | 4.0 | 9.1 | 21.4 | 14.3 | 21.0 | 44.0 | Maldives |
| Mali | 11.1 | 14.3 | 8.3 | 8.4 | 8.2 | 5.5 | 7.9 | 9.9 | Mali |
| Nepal | 5.0 | 4.6 | 16.2 | 5.7 | 11.4 | 11.4 | 9.6 | 8.6 | Népal |
| Niger | 9.9 | 10.3 | 15.4 | 25.5 | 45.3 | 48.9 | 39.9 | 49.1 | Niger |
| Rwanda | 2.4 | 1.7 | 2.7 | 3.6 | 5.8 | 6.8 | 5.0 | 5.5 | Rwanda |
| Samoa | 14.3 | 22.2 | 29.4 | 36.4 | 15.4 | 23.1 | 21.0 | 21.0 | Samoa |
| Sao Tome and Principe | - | - | - | - | - | .. | .. | 14.3 | Sao Tomé-et-Principe |
| Sierra Leone | 18.2 | 26.2 | 21.1 | 35.9 | 42.7 | 23.6 | 40.2 | 15.5 | Sierra Leone |
| Somalia | 5.6 | 8.0 | 15.0 | 20.4 | 16.6 | 11.0 | 31.0 | 102.2 | Somalie |
| Sudan | 37.9 | 17.9 | 18.4 | 20.5 | 36.1 | 32.1 | 22.3 | 24.6 | Soudan |
| Togo | 17.5 | 23.9 | 23.3 | 27.4 | 21.5 | 29.4 | 34.6 | 49.7 | Togo |
| Uganda | 7.5 | 3.9 | 4.3 | 25.2 | 20.2 | 18.2 | 19.6 | 27.1 | Ouganda |
| United Rep.of Tanzania | 10.8 | 21.1 | 22.6 | 15.2 | 19.3 | 15.6 | 18.8 | 22.5 | Rép.-Unie de Tanzanie |
| Vanuatu | 10.0 | 6.4 | 8.6 | 3.1 | 4.3 | 8.7 | 6.9 | 27.3 | Vanuatu |
| Yemen | 45.4 | 164.3 | 204.3 | 234.0 | 228.2 | 189.7 | 207.4 | 180.0 | Yémen |
| All LDCs b/ | 16.1 | 13.3 | 16.0 | 21.2 | 20.2 | 18.9 | 18.1 | 22.0 | Ensemble des PMA b/ |

Source : UNCTAD secretariat, based on information from the OECD secretariat.

a/ Data not comparable with those for previous years.

b/ Total of LDCs for which data are shown.

c/ Goods only.

Source : Secrétariat de la CNUCED, d'après des renseignements du secrétariat de l'OCDE.

a/ Les données ne sont pas comparables à celles des années précédentes.

b/ Total des PMA pour lesquels des données sont montrées.

c/ Marchandises seulement.

Table 53A                                                                    Tableau 53A

Area and population distribution                          Superficie du pays et distribution de la population

| Country | Area Superficie | | Population | | | Labour force participation rate[b/] Taux d'activité[b/] | | | Pays |
| | Total Totale (000 km²) | % of arable land and land under permanent crops % de terres arables et sous cultures permanentes | Density Densité Pop./ km² | Total Totale (mill.) | Urban Urbaine % | M | F | T | |
| | | 1983 | 1985 | 1985 | 1985 | 1981-1983 | | | |
| Afghanistan | 647.5 | 12.4 | 28 | 18.1 | 19 | 53 | 13 | 33 | Afghanistan |
| Bangladesh | 144.0 | 63.4 | 687 | 98.9 | 12 | 56 | 13 | 35 | Bangladesh |
| Benin | 112.6 | 16.0 | 36 | 4.0 | 35 | 50 | 39 | 44 | Bénin |
| Bhutan | 47.0 | 2.1 | 30 | 1.4 | 5 | .. | .. | 56 | Bhoutan |
| Botswana | 581.7 | 2.3 | 2 | 1.1 | 19 | 47 | 42 | 44 | Botswana |
| Burkina Faso | 274.2 | 9.6 | 25 | 6.9 | 8 | 56 | 49 | 52 | Burkina Faso |
| Burundi | 27.8 | 46.9 | 170 | 4.7 | 8 | 53 | 41 | 47 | Burundi |
| Cape Verde | 4.0 | 9.9 | 81 | 0.3 | 5 | 43 | 5 | 23 | Cap-Vert |
| Central African Rep. | 623.0 | 3.2 | 4 | 2.6 | 42 | 56 | 51 | 53 | Rép. Centrafricaine |
| Chad | 1284.0 | 2.5 | 4 | 5.0 | 27 | 59 | 18 | 38 | Tchad |
| Comoros | 2.2 | 42.4 | 205 | 0.4 | 25 | 45 | 23 | 34 | Comores |
| Democratic Yemen | 333.0 | 0.6 | 6 | 2.1 | 40 | 46 | 3 | 24 | Yémen démocratique |
| Djibouti | 22.0 | 0.0 | 17 | 0.4 | 77 | .. | .. | 24 | Djibouti |
| Equatorial Guinea | 28.1 | 8.2 | 14 | 0.4 | 60 | 58 | 3 | 30 | Guinée équatoriale |
| Ethiopia | 1221.9 | 11.4 | 35 | 43.2 | 12 | 51 | 25 | 37 | Ethiopie |
| Gambia | 11.3 | 14.2 | 64 | 0.7 | 20 | 54[a/] | 42[a/] | 48 | Gambie |
| Guinea | 245.9 | 6.4 | 25 | 6.1 | 22 | 52 | 35 | 43 | Guinée |
| Guinea Bissau | 36.1 | 7.9 | 25 | 0.9 | 27 | 52 | 2 | 26 | Guinée-Bissau |
| Haiti | 27.8 | 32.4 | 190 | 5.3 | 27 | 51 | 42 | 45 | Haïti |
| Lao P.D.R. | 236.8 | 3.8 | 16 | 3.8 | 16 | 50 | 40 | 45 | Rép. dém. pop. lao |
| Lesotho | 30.4 | 9.8 | 50 | 1.5 | 17 | 57 | 44 | 50 | Lesotho |
| Malawi | 118.5 | 19.8 | 59 | 6.9 | 12 | 53 | 31 | 41 | Malawi |
| Maldives | 0.3 | 10.0 | 611 | 0.2 | 20 | 55[a/] | 36[a/] | 46[a/] | Maldives |
| Mali | 1240.0 | 1.7 | 7 | 8.1 | 18 | '54 | 49 | 51 | Mali |
| Nepal | 140.8 | 16.6 | 117 | 16.5 | 8 | 57 | 37 | 47 | Népal |
| Niger | 1267.0 | 2.8 | 5 | 6.1 | 16 | 57 | 6 | 31 | Niger |
| Rwanda | 26.3 | 38.3 | 230 | 6.1 | 6 | 54 | 49 | 51 | Rwanda |
| Samoa | 2.8 | 42.7 | 56 | 0.2 | 22 | 41[a/] | 9[a/] | 25[a/] | Samoa |
| Sao Tome & Principe | 1.0 | 37.5 | 101 | 0.1 | 38 | .. | .. | 30 | Sao Tomé-et-Principe |
| Sierra Leone | 71.7 | 24.7 | 50 | 3.6 | 28 | 49 | 25 | 36 | Sierra Leone |
| Somalia | 637.7 | 1.7 | 8 | 5.4 | 34 | 52 | 21 | 36 | Somalie |
| Sudan | 2505.8 | 5.0 | 9 | 21.6 | 21 | 54 | 7 | 31 | Soudan |
| Togo | 56.8 | 25.1 | 52 | 3.0 | 22 | 49 | 32 | 40 | Togo |
| Uganda | 236.0 | 26.7 | 66 | 15.5 | 10 | 52 | 26 | 39 | Ouganda |
| U. R. of Tanzania | 945.1 | 5.5 | 24 | 22.2 | 22 | 52 | 28 | 40 | R.-U. de Tanzanie |
| Vanuatu | 14.8 | 6.4 | 9 | 0.1 | 25 | .. | .. | 45[a/] | Vanuatu |
| Yemen | 195.0 | 14.3 | 41 | 8.0 | 20 | 49 | 3 | 24 | Yémen |
| ALL LDCs | 13400.8 | 6.8 | 25 | 331.4 | 16 | 54 | 22 | 38 | Ensemble des PMA |
| All developing countries | 68223.7 | 10.4 | 37 | 2527.0 | 35 | 51 | 22 | 36 | Ensemble des pays en développement |

Source:  United Nations, Demographic Yearbook, 1984: United         Source:  Nations Unies, Annuaire démographique 1984; Nations
         Nations, World Population Chart 1985: FAO, Production                 Unies, World Population Chart 1985; FAO, Annuaire
         Yearbook 1984; World Bank, Social Indicators Data                     de la production 1984; Banque Mondiale, Social
         Sheets, June 1985.                                                    Indicators Data Sheets, juin 1985.

a/  Year other than 1981-1983.                                      a/  Année autre que 1981-1983.

b/  Economically active population as a percentage of               b/  Population active en pourcentage de la population
    total population of sex(es) specified of all ages.                  totale de tous âges du sexe ou des sexes précisés.

Table 53B

Tableau 53B

Birth and death rates, life expectancy

Taux de natalité et de mortalité, espérance de vie

| Country | Infant mortality rate (per 1000 live births) Taux de mortalité infantile (pour 1000 naissance vivantes) | | Average life expectancy at birth (Years) Espérance de vie moyenne à la naissance (années) | | | | | | Crude birth rate (per 1000) Taux brut de natalité (pour 1000) | | Crude death rate (per 1000) Taux brut de mortalité (pour 1000) | | Pays |
|---|---|---|---|---|---|---|---|---|---|---|---|---|---|
| | 1975-80 | 1980-85 | 1975-80 | | | 1980-85 | | | 1975-80 | 1980-85 | 1975-80 | 1980-85 | |
| | | | M | F | T | M | F | T | | | | | |
| Afghanistan | 194 | 194 | 37 | 37 | 37 | 37 | 37 | 37 | 48.6 | 48.9 | 27.2 | 27.3 | Afghanistan |
| Bangladesh | 137 | 128 | 47 | 46 | 47 | 48 | 47 | 48 | 47.2 | 44.8 | 19.0 | 17.5 | Bangladesh |
| Benin | 130 | 120 | 40 | 44 | 42 | 42 | 46 | 44 | 51.1 | 50.7 | 24.6 | 21.2 | Bénin |
| Bhutan | 147 | 139 | 45 | 43 | 44 | 47 | 45 | 46 | 40.0 | 38.4 | 19.8 | 18.1 | Bhoutan |
| Botswana | 82 | 76 | 51 | 54 | 53 | 53 | 56 | 55 | 50.6 | 49.9 | 14.0 | 12.6 | Botswana |
| Burkina Faso | 157 | 150 | 42 | 45 | 43 | 44 | 47 | 45 | 48.1 | 47.8 | 24.0 | 20.1 | Burkina Faso |
| Burundi | 130 | 124 | 43 | 47 | 45 | 45 | 48 | 47 | 48.2 | 47.2 | 20.5 | 19.0 | Burundi |
| Cape Verde | 87 | 75 | 55 | 58 | 57 | 57 | 61 | 59 | 32.9 | 30.9 | 9.7 | 11.4 | Cap-Vert |
| Central African Rep. | 145 | 142 | 40 | 44 | 42 | 41 | 45 | 43 | 44.9 | 44.6 | 23.5 | 21.8 | Rép. centrafricaine |
| Chad | 154 | 143 | 39 | 43 | 41 | 41 | 45 | 43 | 44.1 | 44.2 | 23.1 | 21.4 | Tchad |
| Comoros | 97 | 88 | 46 | 50 | 48 | 48 | 52 | 50 | 46.6 | 46.4 | 17.2 | 15.9 | Comores |
| Democratic Yemen | 150 | 135 | 45 | 47 | 46 | 47 | 50 | 48 | 47.6 | 47.0 | 20.9 | 17.4 | Yémen démocratique |
| Djibouti | 30a/ | .. | .. | .. | .. | .. | .. | 50d/ | .. | 49.2d/ | .. | 18.3d/ | Djibouti |
| Equatorial Guinea | 149 | 137 | 40 | 44 | 42 | 42 | 46 | 44 | 42.5 | 42.5 | 22.7 | 21.0 | Guinée équatoriale |
| Ethiopia | 155 | 155 | 39 | 43 | 41 | 39 | 43 | 41 | 48.3 | 49.7 | 23.0 | 23.2 | Ethiopie |
| Gambia | 185 | 174 | 32 | 35 | 34 | 34 | 37 | 35 | 48.3 | 48.4 | 30.4 | 29.0 | Gambie |
| Guinea | 171 | 159 | 37 | 40 | 38 | 39 | 42 | 40 | 46.9 | 46.8 | 25.3 | 23.5 | Guinée |
| Guinea-Bissau | 154 | 143 | 39 | 43 | 41 | 41 | 45 | 43 | 40.9 | 40.7 | 21.9 | 21.7 | Guinée-Bissau |
| Haiti | 139 | 128 | 49 | 52 | 51 | 51 | 54 | 53 | 41.8 | 41.3 | 15.7 | 14.2 | Haïti |
| Lao P.D.R. | 135 | 123 | 46 | 49 | 48 | 48 | 51 | 50 | 43.1 | 40.8 | 17.3 | 15.7 | Rép. dém. pop. lao |
| Lesotho | 123 | 111 | 44 | 50 | 47 | 46 | 52 | 49 | 41.9 | 41.8 | 17.9 | 16.5 | Lesotho |
| Malawi | 177 | 163 | 42 | 44 | 43 | 44 | 46 | 45 | 53.0 | 53.2 | 23.1 | 21.5 | Malawi |
| Maldives | 94b/ | 82 | .. | .. | 47b/ | 53 | 50 | 53 | 46.0b/ | 44.0 | 12.0b/ | 12.0 | Maldives |
| Mali | 191 | 180 | 39 | 42 | 40 | 40 | 44 | 42 | 50.9 | 50.6 | 24.5 | 22.5 | Mali |
| Nepal | 147 | 139 | 45 | 43 | 44 | 47 | 45 | 46 | 44.6 | 41.7 | 20.5 | 18.4 | Népal |
| Niger | 157 | 146 | 39 | 42 | 41 | 41 | 44 | 43 | 50.9 | 51.0 | 25.0 | 22.9 | Niger |
| Rwanda | 140 | 132 | 43 | 47 | 45 | 45 | 48 | 47 | 51.1 | 51.9 | 18.1 | 18.9 | Rwanda |
| Samoa | 13b/ | 33 | .. | .. | .. | .. | .. | 65d/ | 17.3b/ | 31.0 | 3.1b/ | 7.0 | Samoa |
| Sao Tome & Principe | 72c/ | 70 | .. | .. | .. | .. | .. | 65d/ | 38.5c/ | 38.7 | 10.2c/ | 10.2 | Sao Tomé-et-Principe |
| Sierra Leone | 191 | 180 | 31 | 33 | 32 | 33 | 36 | 34 | 47.8 | 47.4 | 31.9 | 29.7 | Sierra Leone |
| Somalia | 155 | 155 | 39 | 43 | 41 | 39 | 43 | 41 | 48.5 | 47.9 | 22.8 | 23.3 | Somalie |
| Sudan | 131 | 118 | 44 | 46 | 45 | 47 | 49 | 48 | 47.1 | 45.9 | 19.4 | 17.4 | Soudan |
| Togo | 111 | 102 | 46 | 50 | 48 | 49 | 52 | 51 | 45.5 | 45.2 | 18.6 | 15.7 | Togo |
| Uganda | 114 | 112 | 46 | 50 | 48 | 47 | 51 | 49 | 50.3 | 50.3 | 17.6 | 16.8 | Ouganda |
| U. R. of Tanzania | 125 | 115 | 47 | 51 | 49 | 49 | 53 | 51 | 50.9 | 50.4 | 16.8 | 15.3 | Rép.-Unie de Tanzanie |
| Vanuatu | .. | 94 | .. | .. | .. | .. | .. | 55 | .. | 45.0 | .. | 12.0 | Vanuatu |
| Yemen | 150 | 135 | 45 | 47 | 46 | 47 | 50 | 48 | 48.6 | 48.6 | 24.1 | 18.4 | Yémen |
| ALL LDCs | 145 | 138 | 44 | 45 | 44 | 45 | 46 | 46 | 47.8 | 47.0 | 20.9 | 19.5 | Ensemble des PMA |
| All developing countries | 107 | 96 | 53 | 55 | 54 | 55 | 57 | 56 | 37.7 | 35.5 | 14.1 | 12.8 | Ensemble des pays en développement |

Source: United Nations, Demographic Indicators By Countries as assessed in 1984; United Nations Demographic Yearbook 1981 and 1984; World Bank, Social Indicators Data Sheets, (various issues); ESCAP, Statistical Yearbook for Asia and the Pacific 1984.

Source: Nations Unies, Indicateurs démographiques par pays estimés en 1984; Nations Unies, Annuaire démographique 1981 et 1984; Banque mondiale, Social Indicators Data Sheets, (divers numéros); CESAP, Annuaire statistique pour l'Asie et le Pacifique 1984.

a/ 1978.
b/ 1980.
c/ 1979.
d/ Most recent estimates available between 1981 and 1983.

a/ 1978.
b/ 1980.
c/ 1979.
d/ Année la plus récente disponible entre 1981 et 1983.

Table 53C  |  Tableau 53C

Health at birth  |  Santé à la naissance

| Country | Low-birth-weight infants (percentage) / Enfants de poids insuffisant à la naissance (pour cent) 1979 | 1982 | % of women attending during childbirth by trained personnel / % de femmes ayant reçu des soins prodigués par du personnel qualifié pendant l'accouchement — Year b/ année b/ | Trained personnel c/ Personnel qualifié c/ | institutional delivery d/ accouchement dans une institution d/ | Pays |
|---|---|---|---|---|---|---|
| Afghanistan | .. | 20.0 | (1978) | 5 | .. | Afghanistan |
| Bangladesh | 50.0 | 50.0 | 1984 | .. | 1 | Bangladesh |
| Benin | .. | 9.6 | (1982) | .. | 19 | Bénin |
| Bhutan | .. | .. | (1982) | .. | 1 | Bhoutan |
| Botswana | .. | 12.0 | (1984) | 52 | .. | Botswana |
| Burkina Faso | 21.0 | .. | 1979 | 5 | .. | Burkina Faso |
| Burundi | 13.5 | .. | 1978 | .. | 15 | Burundi |
| Cape Verde | .. | .. | 1979 | 53 e/ | 51 e/ | Cap-Vert |
| Central African Rep. | 23.0 | .. | .. | .. | .. | République centrafricaine |
| Chad | 10.5 | 10.5 | 1978 | 45 | .. | Tchad |
| Comoros | .. | .. | (1982) | .. | 35 | Comores |
| Democratic Yemen | .. | .. | .. | .. | .. | Yémen démocratique |
| Djibouti | .. | .. | .. | .. | .. | Djibouti |
| Equatorial Guinea | .. | .. | .. | .. | .. | Guinée équatoriale |
| Ethiopia | 13.1 | 13.1 | (1980) | 10-15 | .. | Ethiopie |
| Gambia | 14.0 | 14.0 | 1978 | .. | 25 | Gambie |
| Guinea | 18.0 | .. | (1980) | .. | 90 | Guinée |
| Guinea Bissau | 9.0 | 13.0 | .. | .. | .. | Guinée-Bissau |
| Haiti | .. | .. | (1984) | .. | 15 | Haiti |
| Lao People's Dem. Rep. | 18.0 | .. | .. | .. | .. | Rép. dém. pop. lao |
| Lesotho | 14.5 | 7.6 | (1983) | 75 | .. | Lesotho |
| Malawi | .. | 12.0 | (1983) | .. | 45 | Malawi |
| Maldives | .. | .. | .. | .. | .. | Maldives |
| Mali | 12.7 | .. | (1981) | 14 | .. | Mali |
| Nepal | .. | .. | (1982) | .. | 4 | Népal |
| Niger | .. | 15.0 | (1983) | 25 | .. | Niger |
| Rwanda | 17.0 | 19.9 | (1981) | 20 | .. | Rwanda |
| Samoa | .. | .. | .. | .. | .. | Samoa |
| Sao Tome and Principe | .. | .. | (1983) | 88 | .. | Sao Tomé-et-Principe |
| Sierra Leone | .. | 17.0 | (1979) | 30 | .. | Sierra Leone |
| Somalia | .. | .. | (1983) | 2 | .. | Somalie |
| Sudan | 16.7 | 16.7 | (1982) | .. | 5 | Soudan |
| Togo | .. | 16.9 | 1978 | .. | 50 | Togo |
| Uganda | 10.0 | .. | .. | .. | .. | Ouganda |
| United Rep. of Tanzania | 13.0 | 14.4 | (1983) | 50 | .. | R.-U de Tanzanie |
| Vanuatu | .. | .. | .. | .. | .. | Vanuatu |
| Yemen | .. | .. | 1981 | 7 f/ | 4 f/ | Yémen |
| All LDCs a/ | 29.3 | 27.1 | | 16 | 9 | Ensemble des PMA a/ |
| All developing countries a/ | 21.4 | 20.6 | | 37 | 34 | Ensemble des pays en développement a/ |

Source: WHO, World Health Statistics Quarterly 33(3) (1980) and 38(3), 1985; Weekly Epidemiological Record No. 27, 6 July 1984.

a/ Average of countries for which data are available.
b/ The year to which the information refers, or if this is not known, the year of publication of the information, in brackets. c/ Trained personnel includes physicians, nurses, midwives, trained primary health care and other workers and trained traditional birth attendants. d/ "Institution" includes public and private hospitals, clinics, health centres. e/ Survey or sample, Sao Vicente only.
f/ Survey or sample.

Source: OMS, Rapport Trimestriel de statistiques sanitaires mondiales 33(3) 1980 et 38(3) 1985; OMS, Relevé épidémiologique hebdomadaire No. 27, 6 juillet 1984.

a/ Moyenne des pays pour lesquels les données sont disponibles. b/ Année à laquelle se rapporte les données, ou si cette année n'est pas connue, année de publication des données, entre parenthèses. c/ Sont englobés dans l'appellation "Personnel qualifié" les médecins, sages-femmes, agents de santé communautaires et autres personnels qualifiés ainsi que les accoucheurs traditionnels ayant reçu une formation. d/ Institution: comprenant les hopitaux publics et privés, les cliniques et les centres de soins. e/ Sondage ou échantillon, Sao Vicente uniquement. f/ Sondage ou échantillon.

Table 53D

Food and Water

Tableau 53D

Alimentation et eau

| Country | Average daily calorie intake per capita — Average (Moyenne) 1983 | As % of requirements 1983 | Urban/urbain Water (Eau) 1980 | Urban/urbain Water (Eau) 1983 | Urban/urbain Sanitation 1980 | Urban/urbain Sanitation 1983 | Rural Water (Eau) 1980 | Rural Water (Eau) 1983 | Rural Sanitation 1980 | Rural Sanitation 1983 | Pays |
|---|---|---|---|---|---|---|---|---|---|---|---|
| Afghanistan | 2285a/ | 94a/ | 28 | .. | .. | .. | 8 | .. | .. | .. | Afghanistan |
| Bangladesh | 1864 | 81 | 26 | 29 | 21 | 21 | 40 | 43 | 1 | 2 | Bangladesh |
| Benin | 1907 | 83 | 26 | .. | 48 | .. | 15 | .. | 4 | .. | Bénin |
| Bhutan | .. | .. | 50 | 40b/ | .. | .. | 5 | 14 | .. | .. | Bhoutan |
| Botswana | 2152 | 93 | .. | 98 | .. | 90 | .. | 47 | .. | 23 | Botswana |
| Burkina Faso | 2014 | 85 | 27 | 90 | 38 | 50 | 31 | 22 | 5 | .. | Burkina Faso |
| Burundi | 2378 | 102 | 90 | 90 | 40 | 50 | 20 | 22 | 35 | 52 | Burundi |
| Cape Verde | 2176a/ | 129a/ | 100 | 99 | 34 | 49 | 21 | 27 | 10 | 8 | Cap-Vert |
| Central African Rep. | 2048 | 91 | .. | .. | .. | .. | .. | .. | .. | .. | République centrafricaine |
| Chad | 1620a/ | 68a/ | .. | .. | .. | .. | .. | .. | .. | .. | Tchad |
| Comoros | 2291a/ | 111a/ | .. | .. | .. | .. | .. | .. | .. | .. | Comores |
| Democratic Yemen | 2254 | 94 | 85 | 73 | 70 | 69 | 25 | 39 | 15 | 33 | Yémen démocratique |
| Djibouti | .. | .. | 50 | 80 | 43 | 75 | 20 | 40 | 20 | 18 | Djibouti |
| Equatorial Guinea | 2169a/ | 93a/ | .. | 47 | .. | 99 | .. | .. | .. | .. | Guinée équatoriale |
| Ethiopia | 2223a/ | 86a/ | .. | .. | .. | .. | .. | .. | .. | .. | Éthiopie |
| Gambia | .. | .. | 85 | 100 | .. | .. | .. | 36 | .. | .. | Gambie |
| Guinea | 1939 | 84 | 69 | .. | 54 | .. | 2 | .. | 1 | .. | Guinée |
| Guinea-Bissau | 2230a/ | 68a/ | 18 | 21 | 21 | 22 | 8 | 37 | 13 | 18 | Guinée-Bissau |
| Haiti | 1887 | 83 | 48 | 58 | 39 | 41 | 8 | 25 | 10 | 12 | Haïti |
| Lao People's Dem.Rep. | 1992a/ | 90a/ | 21 | 28 | 13 | 13 | 12 | 20 | .. | 4 | République dém. pop. lao |
| Lesotho | 2376 | 104 | 37 | 66 | 13 | 75 | 11 | 49 | 14 | .. | Lesotho |
| Malawi | 2200 | 95 | 77 | 66 | 100 | 71 | 37 | 7 | 81 | 1 | Malawi |
| Maldives | 1983a/ | 91a/ | 11 | 54 | 60 | 60 | 3 | 7 | 0 | 1 | Maldives |
| Mali | 1597 | 68 | 37 | 46 | 79 | 91 | 0 | 8 | 1 | 3 | Mali |
| Nepal | 2047 | 93 | 83 | 71 | 16 | 16 | 7 | 11 | 1 | 1 | Népal |
| Niger | 2271 | 97 | 41 | 41 | 36 | 36 | 32 | 33 | 3 | 3 | Niger |
| Rwanda | 2276 | 98 | 48 | 55 | 60 | 60 | 55 | 60 | 50 | 60 | Rwanda |
| Samoa | 2527a/ | 94a/ | 97 | 95 | 86 | 82 | 94 | 94 | 83 | 86 | Samoa |
| Sao Tome & Principe | 2351a/ | 88a/ | .. | .. | .. | .. | .. | .. | .. | .. | Sao Tomé-et-Principe |
| Sierra Leone | 2082 | 91 | 50 | 61 | 31 | 52 | 2 | 6 | 6 | 10 | Sierra Leone |
| Somalia | 2063 | 89 | 60 | 65 | 45 | 48 | 20 | 21 | 5 | 5 | Somalie |
| Sudan | 2122 | 90 | 100 | 100 | 63 | 73 | 31 | 31 | 0 | .. | Soudan |
| Togo | 2156 | 94 | 70 | 68 | 24 | 24 | 31 | 26 | 10 | 8 | Togo |
| Uganda | 2351 | 101 | 45 | 45 | 40 | 34c/ | 8 | 12 | 10 | 10 | Ouganda |
| U. R. of Tanzania | 2271 | 98 | .. | 88 | .. | 83 | 53 | 39 | .. | 47 | République-Unie de Tanzanie |
| Vanuatu | 2122a/ | 80a/ | 65 | 100 | 95 | 86 | 68 | 50 | 68 | 64 | Vanuatu |
| Yemen | 2226 | 92 | 100 | 100 | 60 | 75 | 18 | 21 | .. | .. | Yémen |
| ALL LDCs d/ | 2056 | 89 | 49 | 58 | 40 | 47 | 27 | 33 | 8 | 12 | Ensemble des PMA d/ |
| All developing countries d/ | 2335 | 102 | 72 | 74 | 50 | 52 | 32 | 40 | 11 | 11 | Ensemble des pays en développement d/ |

Percentage of population with access to safe water or adequate sanitation

Pourcentage de la population disposant d'eau saine ou de mesures suffisantes d'hygiène du milieu

Source: FAO, Production Yearbook 1984 (Vol.38); WHO, The International Drinking Water Supply and Sanitation Decade: Review of National Progress (as at December 1983); World Bank, World Development Report 1986; World Bank, Social Indicators Data Sheets, June 1985.

Source: FAO, Annuaire de la production 1984 (vol.38); OMS, The International Drinking Water Supply and Sanitation Decade: Review of National Progress (as at December 1983); Banque Mondiale, Rapport sur le développement dans le monde 1986; Banque Mondiale, Social Indicators Data Sheets, juin 1985.

a/ Year other than 1983. b/ House connection. c/ Sewer connection.
d/ Average of countries for which data are available.

a/ Année autre que 1983. b/ Raccordement à domicile. c/ Raccordement à l'égout.
d/ Moyenne des pays pour lesquels les données sont disponibles.

Table 53E  
Education and literacy

Tableau 53E  
Enseignement et alphabétisme

| Country / Pays | Adult literacy rate / Taux d'alphabétisme (adultes) (%) around/vers 1985 | | | Number of illiterates / nombre d'illettrés (000) around/vers 1985 | | | School enrolment ratio (% of relevant age group) / Taux d'inscription scolaire (en % du groupe d'âge pertinent) | | | | | | | | | | | |
|---|---|---|---|---|---|---|---|---|---|---|---|---|---|---|---|---|---|---|
| | | | | | | | Primary / Primaire | | | | | | Secondary / Secondaire | | | | | |
| | | | | | | | 1980 | | | 1984 | | | 1980 | | | 1984 | | |
| | M | F | T | M | F | T | M | F | T | M | F | T | M | F | T | M | F | T |
| Afghanistan | 39 | 8 | 24 | 3114 | 4491 | 7605 | 54 | 12 | 34 | 22 | 10 | 16 | 16 | 4 | 10 | 10 | 5 | 8 |
| Bangladesh | 43 | 22 | 33 | 16313 | 20961 | 37274 | 76 | 46 | 62 | 70i/ | 50i/ | 60i/ | 26 | 9 | 18 | 26i/ | 10i/ | 18i/ |
| Benin | 37 | 16 | 26 | 679 | 951 | 1630 | 88 | 40 | 64 | 86 | 42 | 64 | 24 | 9 | 16 | 28 | 11 | 19 |
| Bhutan | .. | .. | .. | .. | .. | .. | 15f/ | 7f/ | 11f/ | 32 | 17 | 25 | 2f/ | 1f/ | 1f/ | 6 | 1 | 4 |
| Botswana | 73 | 69 | 71 | 56 | 83 | 139 | 82 | 100 | 91 | 94i/ | 104i/ | 99i/ | 18 | 21 | 19 | 26i/ | 30i/ | 28i/ |
| Burkina Faso | 21 | 6 | 13 | 1697 | 2079 | 3776 | 26 | 15 | 21 | 37 | 22 | 29 | 4 | 2 | 3 | 6 | 3 | 4 |
| Burundi | 43a/b/ | 26a/b/ | 34a/b/ | .. | .. | .. | 35 | 22 | 29 | 58 | 40 | 49 | 5 | 2 | 3 | 5d/ | 3d/ | 4d/ |
| Cape Verde | 61 | 39 | 47 | .. | .. | .. | 117 | 108 | 112 | 113d/ | 107d/ | 110d/ | 9 | 7 | 8 | 13d/ | 10d/ | 11d/ |
| Central African Rep. | 53 | 29 | 40 | 327 | 560 | 887 | 93 | 51 | 71 | 98a/ | 51a/ | 74a/ | 21 | 7 | 14 | 24a/ | 16a/ | .. |
| Chad | .. | .. | .. | .. | .. | .. | .. | .. | .. | 55 | 21 | 38 | 11 | 2 | 6 | .. | .. | .. |
| Comoros | .. | .. | .. | .. | .. | .. | .. | .. | .. | .. | .. | .. | 31 | 16 | 24 | .. | .. | .. |
| Democratic Yemen | 59 | 25 | 41 | 233 | 451 | 684 | 93 | 36 | 65 | 96d/ | 35d/ | 66d/ | 25 | 11 | 18 | 26d/ | 11d/ | 19d/ |
| Djibouti | .. | .. | .. | .. | .. | .. | .. | .. | .. | .. | .. | 32k/ | .. | .. | .. | .. | .. | 8k/ |
| Equatorial Guinea | .. | .. | 37c/ | .. | .. | 105c/ | .. | .. | 84 | .. | .. | 108a/ | .. | .. | .. | 10a/ | .. | 10a/ |
| Ethiopia | .. | .. | 55b/d/ | .. | .. | .. | 46 | 25 | 35 | 48d/ | 29d/ | 39d/ | 11 | 6 | .. | 14d/ | 8d/ | 11d/ |
| Gambia | .. | .. | .. | .. | .. | .. | 68 | 36 | 52 | 91 | 55 | 73 | 19 | 8 | 13 | 29 | 13 | 21 |
| Guinea | .. | .. | .. | .. | .. | .. | 42 | 20 | 31 | 44 | 20 | 32 | 20 | 8 | 14 | 20 | 7 | 13 |
| Guinea-Bissau | 46 | 17 | 31 | 101 | 160 | 261 | 95 | 41 | 67 | 84d/ | 40d/ | 62d/ | 10 | 12 | 6 | 19d/ | 4d/ | 11d/ |
| Haiti | 40 | 35 | 38 | 1080 | 1238 | 2318 | 72 | 62 | 67 | 81d/ | 72d/ | 76d/ | 13 | 12 | 13 | 16d/ | 16d/ | 16d/ |
| Lao People's Dem. Rep. | 92e/ | 76e/ | 84e/ | .. | .. | .. | 102 | 86 | 94 | 103d/ | 77d/ | 90d/ | 22 | 20 | 18 | 22d/ | 15d/ | 19d/ |
| Lesotho | .. | .. | .. | .. | .. | .. | 85 | 120 | 102 | 97d/ | 126d/ | 111d/ | 14 | 20 | 17 | 17d/ | 26d/ | 21d/ |
| Malawi | .. | .. | .. | .. | .. | .. | 74 | 49 | 61 | 71 | 53 | 62 | 5 | 2 | 4 | 6 | 2 | 4 |
| Maldives | .. | .. | .. | .. | .. | .. | .. | .. | .. | .. | .. | .. | 20h/ | 19h/ | 19h/ | .. | .. | .. |
| Mali | 23 | 11 | 17 | 1625 | 1979 | 3604 | 32 | 18 | 25 | 30a/ | 17a/ | 24a/ | 12 | 9 | 8 | 10a/ | 4a/ | 7a/ |
| Nepal | 39 | 12 | 26 | 2892 | 4001 | 6893 | 115 | 48 | 83 | 104 | 47 | 77 | 33 | 9 | 21 | 35 | 11 | 23 |
| Niger | .. | .. | .. | .. | .. | .. | 35 | 19 | 27 | .. | .. | 28d/ | 7 | 3 | 5 | .. | .. | 7d/ |
| Rwanda | 61 | 33 | 47 | 562 | 1025 | 1587 | 66 | 60 | 63 | 64d/ | 60d/ | 62d/ | 2 | 1 | 2 | 3d/ | 1d/ | 2d/ |
| Samoa | .. | .. | .. | .. | .. | .. | .. | .. | .. | .. | .. | .. | .. | .. | .. | .. | .. | .. |
| Sao Tome & Principe | .. | .. | .. | .. | .. | .. | .. | .. | .. | .. | .. | .. | .. | .. | .. | .. | .. | .. |
| Sierra Leone | .. | .. | .. | .. | .. | .. | 64 | 45 | 54 | 68a/ | 48a/ | 58a/ | 20 | 8 | 14 | 23d/ | 11a/ | 17a/ |
| Somalia | .. | .. | .. | .. | .. | .. | 43 | 24 | 34 | 32d/ | 18d/ | 25d/ | 19 | 9 | 13 | 23d/ | 12d/ | 17d/ |
| Sudan | .. | .. | .. | .. | .. | .. | 59 | 41 | 50 | 57d/ | 41d/ | 49d/ | 20 | 12 | 16 | 23d/ | 16d/ | 19d/ |
| Togo | 54 | 28 | 41 | 376 | 606 | 982 | 150 | 93 | 122 | 118 | 75 | 97 | 48g/ | 16g/ | 32g/ | 32 | 10 | 21 |
| Uganda | .. | .. | .. | .. | .. | .. | 56 | 43 | 50 | 66a/ | 50a/ | 58a/ | 7 | 3 | 5 | 11a/ | 5a/ | 8a/ |
| U. R. of Tanzania | .. | .. | .. | .. | .. | .. | 100 | 86 | 93 | 91d/ | 84d/ | 87d/ | 4 | 2 | 3 | 4d/ | 2d/ | 3d/ |
| Vanuatu | .. | .. | .. | .. | .. | .. | .. | .. | .. | .. | .. | .. | .. | .. | .. | .. | .. | .. |
| Yemen | .. | .. | .. | .. | .. | .. | 80 | 12 | 46 | 112d/ | 22d/ | 67d/ | 8 | 1 | 5 | 17d/ | 3d/ | 10d/ |
| All LDCs j/ / Ensemble des PMA j/ | 43 | 21 | 32 | .. | .. | .. | 69 | 41 | 55 | 65 | 43 | 54 | 18 | 7 | 13 | 18 | 8 | 13 |
| All developing countries j/ / Ensemble des pays en développement j/ | 67 | 49 | 58 | .. | .. | .. | 96d/ | 76d/ | 86d/ | 98d/ | 79d/ | 89d/ | 38d/ | 27d/ | 33d/ | 42d/ | 30d/ | 36d/ |

Source: UNESCO, Office of Statistics, World Bank, Social Data Sheets, June 1985.

a/ 1982. b/ Age group 10+. c/ 1980. d/ 1983. e/ Age group 15-45. f/ 1979. g/ 1981. h/ 1977. i/ 1985.
j/ Average of countries for which data are available. k/ Most recent estimates available between 1981 and 1983.

Source: UNESCO, Office des Statistiques; Banque Mondiale, Social Indicators Data Sheets, juin 1985.

a/ 1982. b/ Groupe d'âge 10+. c/ 1980. d/ 1983. e/ Groupe d'âge 15-45. f/ 1979. g/ 1981. h/ 1977. i/ 1985. j/ Moyenne des pays pour lesquels les données sont disponibles. k/ Année la plus récente disponible entre 1981 et 1983.

Table 53F      Tableau 53F

Communications and media      Communications et médias

| Country / Pays | Newsprint consumption (Kg. per 1000 inhabitants) / Consommation de papier journal (Kg. pour 1000 habitants) | | Mail traffic (number of items per 100 inhabitants) / Courrier postal (nombre d'envois pour 100 habitants) | | | Circulation of daily news-papers per 1000 inhabitants / Tirage de journaux quotidiens pour 1000 habitants | Telephones per 1000 inhabitants / Téléphones pour 1000 habitants | Radio receivers per 1000 inhabitants / Postes récepteurs de radio pour 1000 habitants | |
|---|---|---|---|---|---|---|---|---|---|
| | | | Domestic / Intérieur | Foreign / Étranger | | | | | |
| | 1980 | 1983 | 1984 | Received / Reçu 1984 | sent / Envoyé 1984 | 1982 | 1984 | 1980 | 1983 |
| Afghanistan | 6 | 6 | .. | .. | .. | 4 | 2.0b/ | 75 | 78 |
| Bangladesh | 214 | 486 | 321 | 75 | 68 | 6 | 1.4 | 8c/ | 8c/ |
| Benin | 29 | 26 | .. | .. | .. | 0.3 | 4.4 | 72 | 76 |
| Bhutan | .. | .. | .. | .. | .. | .. | 1.5d/ | 5c/ | 9c/ |
| Botswana | .. | .. | .. | .. | .. | 19 | 17.4e/ | 94 | 117 |
| Burkina Faso | .. | .. | 47f/ | 175f/ | 119f/ | 0.2 | 2.1 | 18 | 18 |
| Burundi | .. | .. | 7 | 22g/ | 6 | .. | 1.3e/ | 37 | 40 |
| Cape Verde | .. | .. | .. | .. | .. | .. | 7.5 | 139 | 150 |
| Central African Rep. | .. | .. | .. | .. | .. | .. | 2.6 | 52 | 57 |
| Chad | .. | .. | 11 | 0 | 0 | 0.3 | 1.7h/ | 168 | 219 |
| Comoros | .. | .. | .. | .. | .. | .. | 7.9h/ | 110 | 129 |
| Democratic Yemen | 269 | 247 | 29 | 90 | 44 | 6 | 11.9h/ | 63 | 65 |
| Djibouti | .. | .. | 63 | 232 | 192 | .. | 21.6 | 68 | 67 |
| Equatorial Guinea | .. | .. | 5e/f/ | 6e/f/ | 3e/f/ | 3 | 3.1d/ | 284 | 306 |
| Ethiopia | 53 | 37 | 47 | 10 | 9 | 1 | 2.8 | 80 | 81 |
| Gambia | .. | .. | .. | .. | .. | .. | 7.8h/ | 121 | 129 |
| Guinea | 18 | 17 | 172f/ | .. | 244f/ | 4b/ | 2.4h/ | 25 | 28 |
| Guinea-Bissau | 124 | 119h/ | .. | .. | .. | 7 | 2.7d/ | 31 | 33 |
| Haiti | 61 | 117 | 10e/ | 45e/ | 14e/ | 4 | 4.2d/ | 21 | 23 |
| Lao People's Dem. Rep. | 58 | 78h/ | 319f/ | 919f/ | 883f/ | .. | 2.5d/ | 102 | 109 |
| Lesotho | .. | .. | 614i/ | 622i/ | 212i/ | 33 | 7.4 | 22c/ | 28c/ |
| Malawi | 84 | 92 | 16b/ | 308b/ | 423b/ | 5 | 6.0 | 46 | 47 |
| Maldives | .. | .. | .. | .. | .. | 6 | 11.9d/ | 45 | 88 |
| Mali | .. | .. | 11 | 33 | 16 | 0.5 | 1.5h/ | 15 | 16 |
| Nepal | 19 | 17 | .. | .. | .. | 7 | 1.1 | 20 | 25 |
| Niger | .. | .. | 39 | 51 | 14 | 1 | 1.7h/ | 47 | 48 |
| Rwanda | 116 | .. | 116 | 42 | 33 | 0.1 | 1.2h/ | 29 | 53 |
| Samoa | .. | .. | 10e/f/ | 52e/f/ | 39e/f/ | .. | 37.8h/ | 205 | 443 |
| Sao Tome and Principe | .. | .. | 141 | 541 | 191 | 3 | 26.7 | 271 | 272 |
| Sierra Leone | 61 | 57 | .. | .. | .. | .. | 5.5h/ | 137 | 201 |
| Somalia | 43 | 39 | .. | 74 | 58 | .. | 1.6d/ | 24 | 26 |
| Sudan | 80 | 108 | 221 | 593b/ | 236b/ | 5 | 3.4h/ | 187 | 245 |
| Togo | .. | .. | 67b/ | .. | .. | 6 | 4.3e/ | 215 | 211 |
| Uganda | 15 | 14 | .. | 248f/ | 62f/ | 2 | 3.8e/ | 23 | 22 |
| United Rep. of Tanzania | 187 | 169 | 401f/ | .. | .. | 10 | 5.0e/ | 30 | 28 |
| Vanuatu | .. | .. | .. | 128 | 39 | .. | 19.2e/ | 228 | 242 |
| Yemen | .. | .. | 28 | .. | .. | .. | 5.7d/ | 16 | 16 |
| All LDCs / Ensemble des PMA | 123a/ | 224a/ | 222a/ | 110a/ | 67a/ | 5a/ | 2.7 | 49 | 56 |
| All developing countries / Ensemble des pays en développement | 1370 | 1280 | 1210 | 133 | 115 | 39 | 25.1 | 114 | 137 |

Source: FAO; UNESCO; Universal Postal Union, Statistiques des services postaux 1980, 1983 and 1984; ITU, Yearbook of Common Carrier Telecommunication Statistics (13th edition) and ITU, "Telecommunications for all" Nov. 1983.

a/ Total of LDCs for which data are shown.   b/ 1980.   c/ The number of licences issued or sets declared.   d/ 1981.
e/ 1983.   f/ Letters only.   g/ Excluding "small packets".
h/ 1982.   i/ Excluding "Printed Matter".

Source: FAO; UNESCO; Union Postale Universelle, Statistique des services postaux 1980, 1983 et 1984; UIT, Annuaire statistique des télécommunications du secteur public (13e édition) et UIT, "Telecommunications for all" nov.1983.

a/ Total des PMA pour lesquels les données sont indiquées.   b/ 1980.
c/ Nombre de licences délivrées ou de postes déclarés.   d/ 1981.   e/ 1983.
f/ Lettres seulement.   g/ Non compris "petits paquets".   h/ 1982.   i/ Non compris "Imprimés".

Table 53G
Energy

Tableau 53G
Energie

| Country / Pays | Coal, oil, gas and electricity — Charbon, pétrole, gaz et électricité (Consumption per capita in kg. of coal equivalent — Consommation par habitant en kg. équivalant en charbon) | | | | Fuelwood, charcoal and bagasse — Bois de chauffage, charbon de bois et bagasse (kg. of coal equivalent — kg. équivalant en charbon) | | | | Installed electricity capacity (kw./1000 inhabitants) — Puissance électrique installée (kw./1000 habitants) | | | |
|---|---|---|---|---|---|---|---|---|---|---|---|---|
| | 1981 | 1982 | 1983 | 1984 | 1981 | 1982 | 1983 | 1984 | 1981 | 1982 | 1983 | 1984 |
| Afghanistan | 49 | 51 | 56 | 56 | 88 | 85 | 82 | 80 | 23 | 25 | 25 | 25 |
| Bangladesh | 45 | 49 | 46 | 54 | 93 | 94 | 95 | 95 | 11 | 11 | 11 | 13 |
| Benin | 50 | 49 | 45 | 43 | 343 | 342 | 342 | 342 | 4 | 4 | 4 | 4 |
| Bhutan | 11 | 13 | 12 | 11 | 751 | 736 | 721 | 707 | 12 | 12 | 12 | 12 |
| Botswana | .. | .. | .. | 595 | 255 | 245 | 236 | 227 | .. | .. | .. | .. |
| Burkina Faso | 31 | 30 | 31 | 29 | 313 | 312 | 311 | 312 | 6 | 6 | 6 | 6 |
| Burundi | 18 | 16 | 16 | 16 | 249 | 248 | 248 | 248 | 2 | 2 | 2 | 2 |
| Cape Verde | 139 | 159 | 146 | 169 | .. | .. | .. | .. | 10 | 10 | 13 | 13 |
| Central African Rep. | 37 | 39 | 40 | 38 | 360 | 361 | 362 | 354 | 13 | 12 | 12 | 12 |
| Chad | 22 | 21 | 20 | 21 | 207 | 208 | 207 | 205 | 8 | 8 | 8 | 8 |
| Comoros | 46 | 44 | 43 | 42 | .. | .. | .. | .. | 10 | 10 | 10 | 9 |
| Democratic Yemen | 606 | 808 | 843 | 851 | 45 | 45 | 44 | 44 | 68 | 66 | 74 | 72 |
| Djibouti | 284 | 293 | 275 | 263 | .. | .. | .. | .. | 108 | 113 | 110 | 107 |
| Equatorial Guinea | 83 | 92 | 88 | 91 | 397 | 397 | 396 | 388 | 19 | 19 | 19 | 18 |
| Ethiopia | 18 | 22 | 20 | 17 | 237 | 236 | 236 | 237 | 9 | 8 | 8 | 8 |
| Gambia | 111 | 113 | 108 | 114 | 447 | 322 | 358 | 354 | 16 | 16 | 16 | 15 |
| Guinea | 75 | 75 | 74 | 72 | 189 | 184 | 180 | 174 | 32 | 31 | 30 | 29 |
| Guinea-Bissau | 42 | 42 | 41 | 42 | 171 | 167 | 164 | 162 | 8 | 8 | 8 | 8 |
| Haiti | 67 | 64 | 65 | 65 | 351 | 355 | 357 | 361 | 25 | 25 | 25 | 24 |
| Lao People's Dem. Rep. | 36 | 35 | 33 | 29 | 352 | 353 | 354 | 355 | 50 | 49 | 62 | 60 |
| Lesotho | .. | .. | .. | .. | 71 | 69 | 68 | 66 | .. | .. | .. | .. |
| Malawi | 52 | 49 | 46 | 43 | 323 | 323 | 322 | 320 | 24 | 23 | 23 | 24 |
| Maldives | 43 | 54 | 58 | 68 | .. | .. | .. | .. | 12 | 12 | 12 | 11 |
| Mali | 28 | 28 | 31 | 30 | 189 | 188 | 189 | 189 | 6 | 8 | 7 | 7 |
| Nepal | 17 | 15 | 16 | 17 | 308 | 308 | 308 | 308 | 5 | 9 | 10 | 11 |
| Niger | 54 | 58 | 58 | 56 | 200 | 200 | 200 | 200 | 7 | 9 | 11 | 11 |
| Rwanda | 33 | 32 | 35 | 34 | 294 | 295 | 297 | 298 | 8 | 8 | 8 | 8 |
| Samoa | 327 | 357 | 354 | 352 | 167 | 165 | 165 | 164 | 63 | 108 | 108 | 107 |
| Sao Tome & Principe | 195 | 191 | 185 | 181 | 705 | 705 | 704 | 706 | 57 | 56 | 65 | 64 |
| Sierra Leone | 95 | 69 | 77 | 67 | .. | .. | .. | .. | 32 | 31 | 30 | 30 |
| Somali | 109 | 105 | 104 | 102 | 326 | 331 | 334 | 332 | 6 | 6 | 6 | 6 |
| Sudan | 86 | 85 | 78 | 77 | 283 | 284 | 289 | 288 | 16 | 16 | 15 | 15 |
| Togo | 64 | 58 | 64 | 71 | 67 | 67 | 67 | 67 | 14 | 13 | 13 | 21 |
| Uganda | 24 | 24 | 25 | 24 | 236 | 237 | 237 | 239 | 12 | 12 | 11 | 11 |
| U. R. of Tanzania | 46 | 45 | 43 | 43 | 327 | 326 | 327 | 328 | 22 | 21 | 21 | 20 |
| Vanuatu | 212 | 207 | 210 | 203 | 68 | 66 | 64 | 63 | 85 | 83 | 81 | 86 |
| Yemen | 87 | 157 | 161 | 162 | .. | .. | .. | .. | 14 | 14 | 15 | 15 |
| All LDCs | 48 | 53 | 52 | 53 | 204 | 204 | 204 | 205 | 14 | 14 | 14 | 15 |
| All developing countries | 493 | 495 | 505 | 513 | 178 | 180 | 180 | 182 | 119 | 126 | 132 | 138 |

Pays:
Afghanistan, Bangladesh, Bénin, Bhoutan, Botswana, Burkina Faso, Burundi, Cap-Vert, Rép. centrafricaine, Tchad, Comores, Yémen démocratique, Djibouti, Guinée équatoriale, Ethiopie, Gambie, Guinée, Guinée-Bissau, Haïti, Rép. dém. pop. lao, Lesotho, Malawi, Maldives, Mali, Népal, Niger, Rwanda, Samoa, Sao Tomé-et-Principe, Sierra Leone, Somalie, Soudan, Togo, Ouganda, R.-U. de Tanzanie, Vanuatu, Yémen, Ensemble des PMA, Ensemble des pays en développement

Source: United Nations, Energy Statistics Yearbook 1984; FAO, Yearbook of Forest Products 1973-1984, and World Bank, World Development Report 1986.

Source: Nations Unies, Annuaire des statistiques de l'énergie 1984; FAO, Annuaire des produits forestiers 1973-1984 et Banque Mondiale, Rapport sur le développement dans le monde 1986.